THE DISCIPLE'S CROSS

MasterLife

BOOK 1

Avery T. Willis, Jr.
Kay Moore

LIFEWAY PRESS
Nashville, Tennessee

ISBN 0-7673-2579-6
Dewey Decimal Classification: 248.4
Subject Heading: DISCIPLESHIP

This book is text for course CG-0168 in the subject area Personal Life in the Christian Growth Study Plan.

Unless otherwise noted, Scripture quotations are from the Holy Bible,
New International Version,
copyright © 1973, 1978, 1984 by International Bible Society.

Scripture quotations marked AMP are from *The Amplified Bible* © The Lockman Foundation 1954, 1958, 1987.
Used by permission.

Scripture quotations marked GNB are from the *Good News Bible,* the Bible in Today's English Version.
Copyright © American Bible Society 1976. Used by permission.

Design: Edward Crawford
Cover illustration: Mick Wiggins

LifeWay Press
127 Ninth Avenue, North
Nashville, Tennessee 37234

Contents

10-5
10-12

1 ½
1 ½ x.
1
4
6 mls

The Authors

AVERY T. WILLIS, JR., the author and developer of *MasterLife,* is the senior vice-president of overseas operations at the International Mission Board of the Southern Baptist Convention. The original *MasterLife: Discipleship Training for Leaders,* published in 1980, has been used by more than 250,000 people in the United States and has been translated into more than 50 different languages for use by untold thousands. Willis is also the author of *Indonesian Revival: Why Two Million Came to Christ, The Biblical Basis of Missions, MasterBuilder: Multiplying Leaders, BibleGuide to Discipleship and Doctrine,* and several books in Indonesian.

Willis served for 10 years as a pastor in Oklahoma and Texas and for 14 years as a missionary to Indonesia, during which he served for 6 years as the president of the Indonesian Baptist Theological Seminary. Before assuming his present position, he served as the director of the Adult Department of the Discipleship and Family Development Division, the Sunday School Board of the Southern Baptist Convention, where he introduced the Lay Institute for Equipping (LIFE), a series of in-depth discipleship courses.

KAY MOORE served as the coauthor of this updated edition of *MasterLife.* Formerly a design editor in the Adult Department of the Discipleship and Family Development Division, the Sunday School Board of the Southern Baptist Convention, she led the editorial team that produced the LIFE Support Series, biblically based courses that help people deal with critical issues in their lives. A writer, editor, and conference leader, Moore has authored or coauthored numerous books on family life, relationships, and inspirational topics. She is the author of *Gathering the Missing Pieces in an Adopted Life* and is a frequent contributor to religious magazines and devotional guides.

D. Echols
1508 Forsyth Rd
Savannah, GA 31406
912-352-8048

Introduction

MasterLife is a developmental, small-group discipleship process that will help you develop a lifelong, obedient relationship with Christ. *MasterLife 1: The Disciple's Cross,* is the first of four books in that discipleship process. Through this study you will experience a deeper relationship with Jesus Christ as He leads you to develop six biblical disciplines of a disciple. The other three books in the *MasterLife* process are *MasterLife 2: The Disciple's Personality, MasterLife 3: The Disciple's Victory,* and *MasterLife 4: The Disciple's Mission.* These studies will enable you to acknowledge Christ as your Master and to master life in Him.

WHAT'S IN IT FOR YOU

The goal of *MasterLife* is your discipleship—for you to become like Christ. To do that, you must follow Jesus, learn to do the things He instructed His followers to do, and help others become His disciples. *MasterLife* was designed to help you make the following definition of *discipleship* a way of life:

> Christian discipleship is developing a personal, lifelong, obedient relationship with Jesus Christ in which He transforms your character into Christlikeness; changes your values into Kingdom values; and involves you in His mission in the home, the church, and the world.

As you progress through the *MasterLife* process and learn to follow Christ as His disciple, you will experience the thrill of growing spiritually. Here are several ways you will grow:

- You will discover that denying yourself, taking up your cross, and following Christ is such an exciting and challenging adventure that it will become the top priority of your life.
- You will understand what it means to abide, or live, in Christ, and you will experience the peace, security, and purpose that abiding in Christ brings.
- You will experience the assurance and confidence that come from living in the Word. You will

develop new skills for studying and interpreting the Bible. The Holy Spirit will use those skills to give you fresh insights into the Scriptures and into God's will for your life.

- You will experience new power in prayer as you learn to pray in faith.
- You will experience deeper fellowship with other believers.
- You will discover the joy of sharing Christ with others—both by the way you live and by what you say.
- You will experience the fulfillment of investing yourself in others by ministering to their needs.
- You will observe that Christlike attitudes develop naturally and spontaneously in your life. These include—
  —humility and servanthood;
  —dependence on God;
  —love for people, especially fellow Christians;
  —confidence in yourself and in God;
  —a sense of God's presence through His direct guidance;
  —a desire to serve God and people;
  —concern for unsaved people;
  —deepening faith;
  —overflowing joy;
  —perseverance in faithfulness;
  —appreciation of God's work through the church;
  —companionship with family members;
  —a prayerful spirit.

SIX KEY DISCIPLINES

As you develop a deeper relationship with Jesus Christ, you will experience His leading you to develop six biblical disciplines of a disciple. These disciplines are—

- spend time with the Master;
- live in the Word;
- pray in faith;
- fellowship with believers;
- witness to the world;
- minister to others.

THE *MASTERLIFE* PROCESS

MasterLife 1: The Disciple's Cross is part of a 24-week discipleship process. Completing all four courses in *MasterLife* will provide you information and experiences you need to be Christ's disciple. Each book builds on the other and is recommended as a prerequisite for the one that follows.

The *MasterLife* process involves six elements. Each element is essential to your study of *MasterLife,* as illustrated in the chair diagram shown.

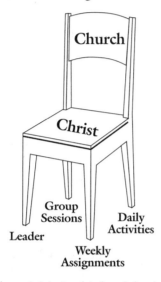

1. The *daily activities* in this book lead you into a closer walk with Christ. Doing these exercises daily is important.
2. The *weekly assignments* in "My Walk with the Master This Week" are real-life experiences that will change your life.
3. The *leader* is a major element. Discipleship is a relationship. It is not something you do by yourself. You need human models, instruction, and accountability to become what Christ intends for you to be. That is why Jesus commanded His disciples to make disciples (see Matt. 28:19-20). We all need someone who has followed Christ long enough to challenge us. To become a better disciple, you need a leader to whom you can relate personally and regularly—someone who can teach you, model behaviors, and hold you accountable.
4. The weekly *group sessions* help you reflect on the concepts and experiences in *MasterLife* and help you apply the ideas to your life. The group sessions allow you to experience in your inmost being the profound changes Christ is making in your life.

Each group session also provides training for the next stage of spiritual growth.

5. *Christ* is the Discipler, and you become His disciple. As you fully depend on Him, He works through each of the previous elements and uses them to support you.
6. The body of Christ—the *church*—is vital for complete discipling to take place. You depend on Christian friends for fellowship, strength, and ministry opportunities. Without the church, you lack the support you need to grow in Christ.

HOW TO STUDY THIS BOOK

Each day for five days a week you will be expected to study a segment of the material in this workbook and to complete the related activities. You may need from 20 to 30 minutes of study time each day. Even if you find that you can study the material in less time, spreading the study over five days will give you time to apply the truths to your life.

You will notice that discipline logos appear before various assignments:

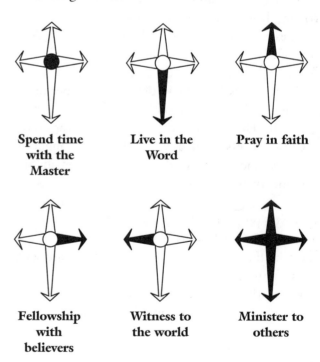

These logos link certain activities to the six disciplines you are learning to incorporate into your life as a disciple. These activities are part of your weekly assignments, which are outlined in "My Walk with the Master This Week" at the beginning of each week's material. The discipline logos differentiate your weekly assignments from the activities related to your study for that particular day.

✗ Set a definite time and select a quiet place to study with little or no interruption. Keep a Bible handy to find Scriptures as directed in the material. Memorizing Scripture is an important part of your work. You will be asked to memorize one Scripture each week. Set aside a portion of your study period for memory work. Unless I have deliberately chosen another version for a specific emphasis, all Scriptures in *MasterLife* are quoted from the *New International Version* of the Bible. However, feel free to memorize Scripture from any version of the Bible you prefer. I suggest that you write each memory verse on a card that you can review often during the week.

After completing each day's assignments, turn to the beginning of the week's material. If you completed an activity that corresponds to one listed under "My Walk with the Master This Week," place a vertical line in the diamond beside the activity. During the following group session a member of the group will verify your work and will add a horizontal line in the diamond, forming a cross in each diamond. This process will confirm that you have completed each weekly assignment before you continue. You may do the assignments at your own pace, but be sure to complete all of them before the next group session.

THE DISCIPLE'S CROSS
On page 136 you will find a diagram of the Disciple's Cross. The Disciple's Cross, which illustrates the six Christian disciplines, will be the focal point for all you learn in this book. Each week you will study an additional portion of the Disciple's Cross and will learn the Scripture that accompanies it. By the end of the study you will be able to explain the cross in your own words and to say all of the verses that go with it. You can learn to live the Disciple's Cross so that it embodies the way you show that you are Christ's follower.

Autobiography Worksheet

Session 1 provides an opportunity for you and other *MasterLife* participants to get to know one another. You will be asked to share your responses to the questions below. Jot down brief thoughts you want to share. Your response to each question should be no longer than one minute.

1. How have I become the person I am? What person(s) or event(s) have most influenced my values?

Through prayer, cheah Parents + family

2. What motivated me to take *MasterLife*? Why do I want to be in this *MasterLife* group?

Grow closer to Christ + be more christ Life

3. What may be my greatest weakness or difficulty in completing the course?

Not Listen to people that has Neg. idea if you Listen will be my weakness

Abiding in Christ

This Bible study will help you understand what it means to abide in Christ and will allow you to commit to abide in Christ. Read John 15:1-17. Then complete the following questionnaire. Later, you will share phase 1 with another person, phase 2 with three other persons, and phase 3 with your entire group.

PHASE 1

I find John 15:1-17 (check one)—
- ❑ challenging;
- ❑ confusing;
- ☑ comforting;
- ☑ scary;
- ❑ refreshing;
- ❑ restrictive;
- ❑ other: _____

Imagine that Jesus is speaking directly to you as you read John 15:1-17. He says (check the statements that apply)—
- ☑ "I love you" (v. 9);
- ☑ "You are My friend" (v. 15);
- ☑ "I have chosen you" (v. 16);
- ☑ "I have ordained you to bring forth fruit" (v. 16);
- ☑ "I am speaking to you so that you may have fullness of joy" (v. 11).

How do you feel when Jesus makes the previous statements about you? Check one:
- ❑ Praise the Lord!
- ❑ Surely You don't mean me, Lord.
- ☑ I am so unworthy.
- ❑ Wonderful; let's get on with it.
- ❑ What's the catch?

PHASE 2

Christ says that if I am to abide in His love, I must keep His commandments. That makes me feel that (check one)—
- ❑ He is trying to bribe me into being obedient;
- ❑ He is sharing His secret for the way He abides in the Father's love;
- ❑ He is asking too much;
- ❑ He does not love me;
- ☑ He really wants me as a friend;
- ☑ Keeping His commandments is a great way to show my love for Him.

As I read that Christ has ordained me to bear fruit and that my fruit will last, I feel (check two)—
- ☑ thankful;
- ❑ inadequate;
- ☑ overjoyed;
- ❑ strengthened;
- ❑ defeated;
- ❑ confident;
- ❑ enthusiastic;
- ❑ indifferent.

PHASE 3

To abide in Christ, I need to—

Keep his Commands
Love one another

Love on

Ask what your will &
will recur

In response to Jesus' speaking to me through John 15:1-17, for the next week I will concentrate on abiding in Christ by—

Love one
Another, study his
word, Prayar daily

Discipleship Covenant

To participate in *MasterLife,* you are asked to dedicate yourself to God and to your *MasterLife* group by making the following commitments. You may not currently be able to do everything listed, but by signing this covenant, you pledge to adopt these practices as you progress through the study.

As a disciple of Jesus Christ, I commit myself to—

- acknowledge Jesus Christ as Lord of my life each day;
- attend all group sessions unless providentially hindered;
- spend from 20 to 30 minutes a day as needed to complete all assignments;
- have a daily quiet time;
- keep a Daily Master Communication Guide about the way God speaks to me and I speak to Him;
- be faithful to my church in attendance and stewardship;
- love and encourage each group member;
- share my faith with others;
- keep in confidence anything that others share in the group sessions;
- submit myself to others willingly in accountability;
- become a discipler of others as God gives opportunities;
- support my church financially by practicing biblical giving;
- pray daily for group members.

_____   _____

_____   _____

_____   _____

_____   _____

Signed *Dorothy Echols* Date 10-11-99

WEEK 1

Spend Time with the Master

This Week's Goal

You will evaluate your discipleship and will focus on Christ as the center of your life.

My Walk with the Master This Week

You will complete the following activities to develop the six biblical disciplines. When you have completed each activity, draw a vertical line in the diamond beside it.

 SPEND TIME WITH THE MASTER
◇ Tell how to have a daily quiet time and begin to have one regularly.

 LIVE IN THE WORD
◇ Read your Bible every day. Write what God says to you and what you say to God.
◇ Memorize John 15:5.
◇ Review Luke 9:23, which you memorized in the introductory group session.

 PRAY IN FAITH
◇ Pray for each member of your *MasterLife* group by name at least twice this week.
◇ Find a prayer partner with whom you will pray each week.
◇ Use the World-Awareness Map to pray for people throughout the world.

 FELLOWSHIP WITH BELIEVERS
◇ Get better acquainted with a group member.

 WITNESS TO THE WORLD
◇ Demonstrate how others know that you are a Christian.

 MINISTER TO OTHERS
◇ Explain the center of the Disciple's Cross.

This Week's Scripture-Memory Verse

"'I am the vine; you are the branches. If a man remains in me and I in him, he will bear much fruit; apart from me you can do nothing'" (John 15:5).

DAY 1

The First Priority

When I went away to college, I had been a Christian for several years. I had done almost everything my church had asked me to do. I had tithed, attended church five times a week, occasionally visited prospects, and read my Bible daily. But when the influences of home and church were removed, I came face to face with who I really was. I realized that I possessed Christ as my Savior but that He did not possess me. I faced the decision, Am I going to be a disciple who gives everything to Christ? I spent many nights walking through the fields near the college, talking to God, and pondering whether I really meant business about being a Christian.

Then I started looking at the Scriptures to see what being a disciple involves. The Bible told me that a disciple of Christ is someone who makes Christ the Lord of his or her life. As you learned during your introductory group session, Luke 9:23 says, " 'If anyone would come after me, he must deny himself and take up his cross daily and follow me.' "

I realized that I would be either a real disciple of Christ or a mediocre Christian for the rest of my life. As people often do when they arrive at a crossroads in their walk with Christ, I began to make excuses. I began to tell God that I was not capable of doing all He wanted me to do, that I had failed many times, and that I was not even sure He would want me to be His disciple.

In answer to my excuses, God showed me 2 Chronicles 16:9: " 'The eyes of the Lord range throughout the earth to strengthen those whose hearts are fully committed to him.' " I remembered that evangelist D. L. Moody had heard his friend Henry Varley say, "It remains to be seen what God will do with a man who gives himself up wholly to Him." In response Moody said, "I will be that man."[1] If anyone gave himself up wholly to God, it was D. L. Moody. With only a third-grade education he led hundreds of thousands of people in England and America to God. My response was "Lord, I want to be like that. I want to have a heart committed to You. Then if You do anything with my life, everyone will know it was because You did it and not because of my abilities."

My heart has not always been right toward God since that time. However, because of the commitment I made, the Holy Spirit reveals whenever my heart is not right. I immediately confess and ask God to forgive me and to restore my heart.

That is how I decided to be a true disciple of Christ and to commit to a lifelong, obedient relationship with Him. At the outset I said, "I will obey and do whatever God tells me to do, and I will depend on

Am I going to be a disciple who gives everything to Christ?

I'm try to do my best Always

Fam chest fellowship will was

"Lord, I want to have a heart committed to You."

Always

Him to accomplish whatever He wants to accomplish through my life." The commitments I made during the following year set the course for my entire life. From that day forward God began to reveal Himself to me and to teach me how to walk with Him. Looking back, I can say that everything that has been accomplished in my life has been because God did it.

This study provides an opportunity for you to reassess your standing in your relationship with Christ. It will help you evaluate yourself as a disciple and take steps to follow Him. Throughout your study of *MasterLife* I will share with you how Christ continued to reveal to me what it means to be His disciple. As I share with you how Christ helped me through my pilgrimage as a student, a pastor, and a missionary and as I share other believers' testimonies, I hope that you will learn the concepts of truly mastering life as Christ lives through you—that you will learn what life in Christ is all about.

This study provides an opportunity for you to reassess your standing in your relationship with Christ.

WHAT IS A DISCIPLE?

We begin this study by looking at who a disciple is and what a disciple does. The New Testament uses the term *disciple* three ways. First, it is a general term used to describe a committed follower of a teacher or a group.

"John's disciples and the Pharisees were fasting. Some people came and asked Jesus, 'How is it that John's disciples and the disciples of the Pharisees are fasting, but yours are not?' " (Mark 2:18).

Read Mark 2:18 in the margin. The verse mentions three groups or individuals who have disciples. Who are they?

1. ~~Pharisees~~
2. ~~John~~
3. ~~Jesus~~ Apostles

The persons or groups who had disciples are John, the Pharisees, and Jesus. These disciples were committed followers of these teachers or groups.

Second, the New Testament uses the term *disciple* to refer to the twelve apostles Jesus called. Mark 3:14, in the margin, is very specific about why Jesus called these apostles.

"He appointed twelve—designating them apostles—that they might be with him and that he might send them out to preach and to have authority to drive out demons" (Mark 3:14).

In Mark 3:14 underline the phrases that show two reasons Jesus chose the twelve.

You probably underlined the words "that they might be with him" and "that he might send them out to preach."

Jesus also used disciple to describe a follower who meets His requirements. For example, He said that His disciples must forsake families, possessions, or anything else that might keep them from following Him.

Read these verses: "Large crowds were traveling with Jesus, and turning to them he said: 'If anyone comes to me and does not hate his father and mother, his wife and children, his brothers and sisters—yes, even his own life—he cannot be my disciple. And anyone who does not carry his cross and follow me cannot be my disciple' " (Luke 14:26-27). Write in your own words what Jesus did when people began to follow Him.

Put him first in all walk of Life.

You likely wrote something like this: He discouraged those who did not commit themselves fully to Him by first stating the requirements for being a disciple. Luke 9:23, the verse I hope you memorized in your introductory group session, also states those requirements.

In the margin write Luke 9:23 from one to three times.

You have seen that the term *disciple* is a general term for a committed follower of a teacher or a group, one of Jesus' twelve apostles, and a follower who meets Jesus' requirements.

LEARNING THE DISCIPLE'S CROSS

One way you can learn more about what Jesus had in mind for His disciples is to learn the Disciple's Cross, which is the cornerstone of this study. You can see the complete cross on page 136 and can read the presentation of the Disciple's Cross on pages 134–36. When you learn the cross thoroughly, you can use it in a variety of ways. It can help you reflect on where you stand in your discipleship. You can use it to witness. You can use it to evaluate your church. Many churches use the Disciple's Cross to organize their church ministries.

As you proceed through this book, you will study the various elements of the Disciple's Cross. Each week you will learn additional information. By the end of your study you will be able to explain the cross in your own words and to quote all of the Scriptures that go with it.

Begin learning the Disciple's Cross by drawing a circle, representing you, in the margin. Write *Christ* in the center of the circle. This circle will help you focus on ways Christ is to be at the center of your life.

The empty circle you drew represents your life. It pictures denying all of self for Christ. This means that you lose not your identity but your self-centeredness. No one can become a disciple who is not willing to

Jesus said that His disciples must forsake families, possessions, or anything else that might keep them from following Him.

9-23 If any man come after me let him deny himself and take up his cross daily and follow me

9.23 And he said to them All I If any man will come after me Let him deny himself And take up his cross daily And follow me

9.23 And he

One way you can learn more about what Jesus had in mind for His disciples is to learn the Disciple's Cross.

chRist

DAILY MASTER COMMUNICATION GUIDE

MATTHEW 6:25-34

What God said to me:

Don't worry about [illegible]

What I said to God:

[illegible]

deny himself or herself. Christ must be the number one priority in your life.

PUTTING CHRIST FIRST

When Kay Moore, who wrote this book with me, and her husband, Louis, married, they asked their pastor to make their wedding ceremony very personal. The pastor, knowing that their jobs were highly important to both the bride and the groom, wanted them to keep their priorities straight. In their wedding ceremony he wisely cautioned them, "In your marriage your first commitment is to Christ, your second is to each other, your third is to any children who are conceived, and your fourth is to your work."

If someone gave you a similar caution about your priorities, what would be on your list? Do you have a priority above Christ? For some that top priority might be a commitment to a sport. For others that priority might be acquiring material possessions. For still others that priority might be participating in religious activities. Religious activities? you may ask. Doesn't that mean I'm putting Christ first? Not always. Some people can be so involved in "doing church" that they forget the real reason for the activity. Their relationship with Christ may take a back seat to their desire to be recognized for their good works or to meet an inner drive to achieve.

List the three highest priorities in your life.

1. Christ
2. children & others
3. ~~Self~~ Church

You cannot become a disciple of Christ if you are not willing to make Him number one on your priority list. Stop and pray, asking God to help you remove any obstacles that keep Him from having first place in your life. What do you need to do to give Him first place? List one action you will take to remove an obstacle to placing Him first in your life.

Begin the practice of reading your Bible daily. Today read Matthew 6:25-34, a passage about priorities. After you have read this passage, complete the Daily Master Communication Guide in the margin.

DAY 2

Under Christ's Control

You may believe that you are unusual if you struggle with the issue of priorities. Your family, your job, and other responsibilities demand a great deal of your time. Maybe you think that because previous generations had simpler lives, it was easier for them to focus on Christ and to meet the requirements for discipleship.

If that was true, then why was it necessary for Jesus to remind His disciples, who lived two thousand years ago, that they must give Him supreme loyalty? Luke 14:26-33, in the margin, states that His followers must love Him more than any other person, possession, or purpose.

Read the Scripture passage in the margin. Circle the parts teaching that Christ must have priority over the following areas of life. Draw a line from the part of the passage to its corresponding area. I have drawn the first line for you.

Person

Possession

Purpose

Clearly, these areas were concerns in Jesus' day just as they are in ours. In the previous exercise the correct answers are: Possession: "Any of you who does not give up everything he has cannot be my disciple." Purpose: "And anyone who does not carry his cross and follow me cannot be my disciple." The highest purpose is to bear one's cross, which glorifies God. One of the best ways to express cross bearing is by voluntary commitment to Kingdom work that you know is costly.

A DISCIPLE'S PRIORITIES

Christ's disciples had to learn gradually, just as we do. His followers sometimes put their own selfish needs and concerns above Him. Two of them chose sleep over honoring His request to stay awake and pray with Him in the garden of Gethsemane. They argued about who would be chief in His kingdom. When Jesus was arrested, His followers fled, and one of the closest to Him denied Him. Who was the disciples' first priority on such occasions?

But Jesus never gave up on the disciples, and after His death and resurrection their lives changed dramatically. Acts 4:18-37 shows that His disciples loved Him more than any other person, possession, or purpose in their lives. Jesus never stopped working with them to transform them into His own character. Like them, you can begin to grow now, no matter in what stage of discipleship you find yourself.

Jesus' followers must love Him more than any other person, possession, or purpose.

" 'If anyone comes to me and does not hate his father and mother, his wife and children, his brothers and sisters—yes, even his own life—he cannot be my disciple. And anyone who does not carry his cross and follow me cannot be my disciple. … In the same way, any of you who does not give up everything he has cannot be my disciple' " (Luke 14:26-33).

Put christ first in your life,

DAILY MASTER COMMUNICATION GUIDE

ACTS 4:18-37

What God said to me:

When I talk
To God he work
... be his

What I said to God:

I Thank God
for accepting
Me as a Spoke
Person And will
Try to do God
will. I will Try
And not be Like
Randy why we do
only to be will
God him + PRASE
him Always

Continue the practice of reading your Bible daily. Read Acts 4:18-37 today and ask God to speak to you. Then complete the Daily Master Communication Guide in the margin. Pray about how you will respond to Him. Under "What I said to God" write a summary of your prayer.

The passage you just read indicates that the disciples loved Christ more than any other person, possession, or purpose. Can you say this about your relationship with Christ? Apply this passage to your life. List anyone or anything that presently takes priority over Christ in your life.

Person: _____

Possession: _____

Purpose: _____

As you began to draw the Disciple's Cross in day 1, you learned that Christ should have the main priority in your life, filling up the entire circle of your life as you focus on Him. This priority is necessary for a lifelong, obedient relationship with Him.

CHRIST AT THE CENTER

Randy prided himself on the work he did at church. Each Saturday he set up chairs for the Sunday worship service. He served as the chairman of a church committee, taught a weekly Bible study, and helped at all youth events. At least four nights a week he was involved in a project at church. Randy thought that if he did enough at church, people would appreciate and compliment him. When people told Randy that they admired him for his diligent church efforts, he beamed with pride. Soon Randy depended so much on others' praise of him that he forgot the real reason for his service. Randy thought that he was being obedient to Christ by his faithful church service, but his priorities had become misplaced, making his relationship with Christ secondary.

If Randy drew a circle representing his life, whose name would likely be in the center of the circle?

_____

What seems to be the motivation behind Randy's acts of service?

_____

In the case study about Randy, what looked like service from obedience to Christ was actually service for self. Instead of doing good deeds in Christ's name to serve others, Randy served to gain the approval of others. It could be said that Randy, instead of Christ, was at the center of his circle. Realizing that the focus of our lives is on self instead of on Christ can be a startling revelation, but it is very important to be honest with yourself and with God about this matter.

Stop and pray, asking God to show you ways other persons, possessions, or purposes motivate you instead of your love for Him.

Who or what motivates you?

Some of us has, home car, children Job,

Realizing that the focus of our lives is on self instead of on Christ can be a startling revelation.

If you listed anything or anyone besides your love for Jesus Christ, confess in prayer that your life is controlled by impure desires. Then list the steps you will take to give Christ control of your life.

First pray, study,

To be Christ's disciple, you need to surrender control to Him in every area of life. *MasterLife* will help you with this process.

To be Christ's disciple, you need to surrender control to Him in every area of life.

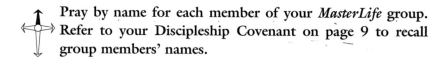 Pray by name for each member of your *MasterLife* group. Refer to your Discipleship Covenant on page 9 to recall group members' names.

DAY 3

Connected to the Vine

So far, so good, *you may think. I want to have Jesus at the center of my life. I want to adjust my relationship with anyone, anything, or any purpose that takes priority over Him. But I get distracted. I get busy. I forget about Him. I sometimes wait to call on Him until I'm at the end of my rope. How can I allow Him to be the first priority in my life so that I turn to Him first? How can I have a personal, lifelong, obedient relationship with Him?*

" 'I am the vine; you are the branches. If a man remains in me and I in him, he will bear much fruit; apart from me you can do nothing' " (John 15:5).

REMAINING IN CHRIST

The secret of discipleship is lordship. When you truly acknowledge Christ as Lord in all areas of your life, He lives in you in the fullness of His Spirit. He provides what you need to be like Him and to do His will.

 Read in the margin John 15:5, your Scripture-memory verse for this week, and complete this sentence:

Without Jesus' living in you and your living in Him, you can do ___Nothing___ **to bear fruit.**

You may try to make it on your own. You may try your own remedies and the world's remedies. You may do good deeds to satisfy your ego or to please others. But ultimately, the victory is His. You can do nothing to bear fruit without Him.

Jesus said that three things will characterize your life when He lives in you and you live in Him. Read the Scriptures in the margin. Match those three things with the appropriate verses.

A 1. Luke 6:46   a. obedience
C 2. John 15:8   b. love
B 3. John 13:34-35   c. fruit

" 'Why do you call me, "Lord, Lord," and do not do what I say?' " (Luke 6:46).

" 'This is to my Father's glory, that you bear much fruit, showing yourselves to be my disciples' " (John 15:8).

" 'A new command I give you: Love one another. As I have loved you, so you must love one another. By this all men will know that you are my disciples, if you love one another' " (John 13:34-35).

When He lives in you and you live in Him, obedience, love, and fruit are apparent to persons around you. The correct answers are 1. a, 2. c, 3. b. Remember these three things by putting them in sequence: love produces obedience, and obedience produces fruit.

In the diagram in the margin write the words *obedience, love,* and *fruit* in the correct sequence.

3. ___fRuit___

2. ___LoVE___

1. ___obebisnce___

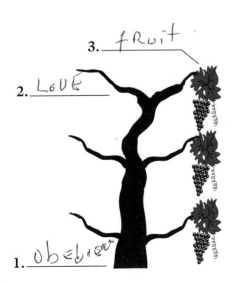

LIFE IN CHRIST

How do you abide in the Vine, as your Scripture-memory verse emphasizes? How do you make Christ the center of your Christian life? Consistently devote part of each day to a quiet time so that you can spend time with the Father and can stay attached to the Vine. Shut out all distractions and totally turn over that portion of your day to Him. If you do not already do so, begin having a daily quiet time to stay in touch with God on a regular, consistent basis.

The two things that will help you grow most as a Christian are a quiet time and Scripture memory. Part of discipleship is setting aside from 15 to 20 minutes every day to spend with Jesus Christ, who is at the center of your life.

 Here are guidelines for having a consistent quiet time. As you read, write decisions about your personal quiet time. Plan to explain to someone the importance of a quiet time.

HOW TO HAVE A QUIET TIME

1. Make a personal quiet time the top priority of your day.
   - Select a time to spend with God that fits your schedule. Usually, morning is preferable, but you may want or need to choose another time.

My quiet time is/will be ___6 AM Every___ every day.

2. Prepare the night before.
   - If your quiet time is in the morning, set your alarm. If it is difficult for you to wake up, plan to exercise, bathe, dress, and eat before your quiet time.
   - Select a place where you can be alone. Gather materials, such as your Bible, notebook, and a pen or a pencil, and put them in the place selected so that you will not waste time in the morning.

The place for my quiet time is/will be ___bed Room___.

3. Develop a balanced plan of Bible reading and prayer.
   - Pray for guidance during your quiet time.
   - Follow a systematic plan to read your Bible. This course suggests passages of Scripture for you to read each day. Later, I hope that you will develop your own plan. You may want to follow the one provided in *Day by Day in God's Kingdom: A Discipleship Journal.*[2]
   - Make notes of what God says to you through His Word (use Daily Master Communication Guide).

   For today's Bible passage read Luke 10:38-42. Write your responses in the Daily Master Communication Guide in the margin.

   - Pray in response to the Scriptures you have read.
   - As you pray, use various components of prayer. For example, using the acronym ACTS—adoration, confession, thanksgiving, supplication—helps you remember the components.

Write the components of prayer:

A ___Thanking___

C ___Ask for forgiven___

T ___for his blessing___

S _____

DAILY MASTER COMMUNICATION GUIDE

LUKE 10:38-42

What God said to me:

God is Saying Sometime we worry about food for the body. while we shald be worry about food for the Soul. Mary was Listen to Jesus Teach, while Martha was worry about food to EAT

What I said to God:

I will Put you + Your Words first which Study, PRay daily because to morrow Not PRomes So I'll PRayd Mary was Listen To the Master So she can know what best for her to study Gods Word

Be persistent until you are consistent.

4. Be persistent until you are consistent.
- Strive for consistency rather than for length of time spent. Try to have a few minutes of quiet time every day rather than long devotional periods every other day.
- Expect interruptions. Satan tries to prevent you from spending time with God. He fears even the weakest Christians who are on their knees. Plan around interruptions rather than being frustrated by them.

Check the days this week you have a quiet time.
☑ Monday ☑ Tuesday ☑ Wednesday ☑ Thursday
☐ Friday ☑ Saturday ☐ Sunday

Focus on the Person you are meeting.

5. Focus on the Person you are meeting rather than on the habit of having the quiet time. If you scheduled a meeting with the person you admire most, you would not allow anything to stand in your way. Meeting God is even more important. He created you with a capacity for fellowship with Him, and He saved you to bring about that fellowship.

LEARNING THE DISCIPLE'S CROSS
Now focus on the Disciple's Cross. Life in Christ is Christ living in you. John 15:5 says: " 'I am the vine; you are the branches. If a man remains in me and I in him, he will bear much fruit; apart from me you can do nothing.' " What can you do without abiding in Christ? Nothing!

Again, draw a circle in the margin. Write *Christ* in the center, and under *Christ* write *John 15:5*, your memory verse for the week, so that you will remember this central premise of discipleship.

Christ said that He is the Vine and that we are the branches. The branches are part of the Vine. We are part of Christ. He wants to live His life through us.

Is this the kind of life you would like to have? ☐ Yes ☐ No
Describe actions you need to take for Christ to live in you like that.

PRay, Study, miditate, stay of the Pher

You may have answered something like this: I would need to stop watching TV late at night so that I could have a quiet time at bedtime or could get up earlier and have a quiet time in the morning. Or I would need to give up certain bad habits so that I would be a better example of Christ living in me. No matter how you answered, remember Christ's admonition in John 15:5: " 'Apart from me, you can do nothing.' " It does not say that you can do some things on your own. Ultimately, you can do nothing without Him.

Stop and pray, asking God to help you remove stumbling blocks from your life that keep you from staying connected to Him.

 Continue memorizing John 15:5, this week's Scripture-memory verse. Say the verse aloud from one to three times from memory.

Learning your memory verse is an important part of *MasterLife* because memorizing Scripture is vital to mastering life in Christ. You can recall memorized verses when you need them to strengthen you and to fight temptation.

Memorizing Scripture is vital to mastering life in Christ.

You also abide in Christ by praying. Find a prayer partner if you have not already found one—someone who is not in your *MasterLife* group. Pray with your partner each week. You can meet to pray, or you can pray on the telephone. In the margin write the initials of someone you are considering to be your prayer partner. Tomorrow you will write the name of the person you selected.

Pray by name for each member of your *MasterLife* group. Refer to your Discipleship Covenant to recall members' names.

DAY 4

Learning Obedience

Once when I was a pastor, a couple in the church disagreed with me and vocally expressed their dislike for me. I unsuccessfully tried to seek reconciliation with them. I finally had to say: "I really want to be your pastor. I value my relationship with God more than anything in the world. To stay in a right relationship with Him, I cannot afford to hold anything against you. I am going to love you regardless of what you think of me."

"I value my relationship with God more than anything in the world."

List other responses I could have chosen that would not have honored or obeyed Christ.

_____

I could have made several choices that would not have honored Christ. I could have confronted the couple angrily. I could have said unkind things about them to others. I could have pressured them to leave the church.

I could have been tempted to make any of those choices. In the end, however, I was glad that I stayed connected to the Vine and held to my relationship with Christ as the guiding force in my life. The couple that had been angry with me stayed in the church, and later their daughter was converted and baptized. Because I was obedient to Christ and stayed in a right relationship with Him, the way I responded to the couple bore fruit later.

When you have life in Christ, having completely turned over your life to Him, a lifelong, obedient relationship with Him is a natural result. And when you obey Christ, you want to stay connected to Him and to follow His teachings. As a result of obeying His commands, you bear fruit.

When you have life in Christ, a lifelong, obedient relationship with Him is a natural result.

Stop and review what you just studied about obedience.

The key to discipleship is obedience to Christ's _____.

Find the following verses and match the benefits of obeying Christ's commands.

_D_ 1. John 15:10   a. You show that you are His disciple.
_C_ 2. John 14:21   b. You are blessed.
_A_ 3. John 13:34-35   c. The Father loves you and reveals
_b_ 4. John 13:17   Himself to you.
                   d. You remain in His love.

Obeying Christ's commands is the key to discipleship. When you obey these commands, you benefit because you remain in His love (1. d), the Father loves you and reveals Himself to you (2. c), you show that you are His disciple (3. a), and you are blessed (4. b). Christ does not want you to obey Him just to be good; He wants you to be obedient so that He can involve you in His mission.

OBEYING CHRIST'S COMMANDS

OK, you think, *that sounds good. I want to obey Christ's commands. I want to have those benefits I just read about. I want to be involved in His mission. But how do I take the first step? How do I start the process of obeying Him?* To obey Christ's commands requires two things: knowing them and doing them. Do you know them? Are you doing what Christ commanded?

To obey Christ's commands requires two things: knowing them and doing them.

Read the following verses and write in your own words what Christ wants you to emphasize.

1. Matthew 5:19-20: _telling what will happen if we break these commads but if you keep the command + teck_

2. Matthew 7:21,24-27: _Even if you can lead others_

3. Matthew 28:19-20: _When we are Disciple of christ me and to bring others to Chst_

4. James 1:22: _____

The Bible is very clear about what area Jesus wants you to emphasize. You may have answered something like this: 1. Doing and teaching His commands. 2. Doing His will and practicing His teachings. 3. Observing any or all of His commands. 4. Doing the Word.

Describe one step you can take to know and do His commands so that you can be obedient.

Study his word, Pray daily, bring other to Christ by tell the Thus said the Lond After you has heard +

You may have answered something like this: I need to set aside time each day to read the Bible consistently so that I will know what the Scriptures tell me to do. I need to develop a quiet time so that I can hear what God is saying to me through His Word. I need to respond immediately when I read Christ's commands or feel His Spirit urging me to obey a command or a Scripture in response to a situation.

Continue memorizing John 15:5. Say this verse aloud to someone in your group. Become better acquainted with the group member to whom you recited your memory verse. In the process of getting to know this person, describe in your own words how obedience relates to discipleship.

Have you chosen a prayer partner? Write the name of the person you chose: _Hutchingson + Washngton_

TAKING ACTION

Have you heard someone say, "Actions speak louder than words"? That admonition also applies to your Christian life. You may know the right thing to do, but what good is knowledge without action? If you are grounded in God's Word but it makes no difference in your life, your knowledge is fruitless. To show that you love Christ, you also need to obey, keep, and do His commandments.

To show that you love Christ, you need to obey, keep, and do His commandments.

Stop and pray, asking God to help you begin the practice you listed that will help you become more obedient.

DAILY MASTER COMMUNICATION GUIDE

MATTHEW 26:47-56

What God said to me:

_____

_____

_____

_____

_____

_____

_____

What I said to God:

_____

_____

_____

_____

_____

_____

_____

_____

Check one or more of the following that you are ready and willing to do.
☑ Give Christ first priority in your life
☑ Follow Christ by obeying His commands
❑ Abide in Christ so that He can produce His life and fruit in you

Suppose you lived in a country that wanted to put you in jail for being a Christian. Would members of a court of law be able to prove that you are a Christian? What evidence would they see in your life, based on the three choices above?

_____

_____

_____

_____

One way you demonstrate that you are a Christian is to follow Christ's command in Matthew 28:19-20, the ultimate demonstration of fruit bearing: " 'Go and make disciples of all nations, baptizing them in the name of the Father and of the Son and of the Holy Spirit, and teaching them to obey everything I have commanded you. And surely I am with you always, to the very end of the age.' " If you follow His commands, you will be aware of the world's needs and will pray daily for those needs.

Study a world map (one is provided on p. 137) or a globe and use it to pray for the world as you listen to news broadcasts, read newspapers and newsmagazines, and read Christian publications like *The Commission* magazine.[3] When you become aware of people who are in crisis and need the Lord, immediately pray for them as an ongoing conversation with Christ.

Continue having your daily quiet time. For your Bible reading use Matthew 26:47-56, a passage about an act of supreme obedience. After you have read this passage, complete the Daily Master Communication Guide in the margin.

DAY 5

Challenges to Obedience

When we were in the United States on furlough from Indonesia in 1977, I attended many churches that appeared apathetic, showing little vitality in their worship and ministry. This was at a time when our denomination had made a commitment to enlist 50,000 volunteers for short-term mission trips overseas. Having seen little evidence of Christ's lordship in these churches, I could not imagine exporting such apathy to other countries.

God spoke to me in a special way, directing me to return to the United States and make disciples so that our denomination could reach its commitment to share the gospel with everyone in the world. Deeply committed to my work as a missionary and to the work I had begun as the president of the Indonesian Baptist Theological Seminary, I struggled to understand why God would call a missionary from the fifth-largest nation in the world to the United States indefinitely. Week after week in my journal I wrote, "Lord, what are You trying to tell me?" For the next eight months I struggled with God about this matter.

As I preached about Peter's being commanded to eat unclean animals on a large sheet (see Acts 10), I began to see in that sheet the dead churches in which I had been preaching. Although I sensed that God was saying to me, "Rise and eat," I told God that I did not want to get involved with already dead churches and that I wanted to return to Indonesia. I retorted, "Peter had three men at the gate telling him what to do, and I don't have anyone!"

Immediately, three men asked me to do things that applied to my struggle. Our pastor, Tom Elliff, asked me to translate *MasterLife* into English to train his staff. Roy Edgemon, the leader of discipleship training with our denomination's publishing house, asked if I would adapt *MasterLife* for an English-speaking audience. A third, Bill Hogue, the director of our denomination's evangelism program, asked me to help design a plan to train people to witness. I continued to struggle for several months, but finally, God spoke very clearly to me about this matter, as well as about other plans, such as bringing revival and equipping His people to go on mission. Even though leaving Indonesia broke my heart, I knew that I must obey if I was going to teach others to be obedient disciples.

I knew that I must obey if I was going to teach others to be obedient disciples.

COMMITTED TO OBEY

Maybe you are like me. You are not as obedient as you could be or should be. Perhaps you make excuses for not being obedient, as I did. However, read Philippians 2:13 in the margin. Christ created in His disciples a desire and an increasing ability to obey Him. They were ordi-

"It is God who works in you to will and to act according to his good purpose" (Phil. 2:13).

nary people, but they had an extraordinary commitment to follow Christ. Again, He did not want them to obey just to be good; He wanted to involve them in His work here on earth.

Examine the following accounts of the process by which Jesus taught His disciples:
1. He commanded, and they obeyed.
2. They learned what Christ was trying to teach them by doing what He commanded them to do.
3. Afterward, Christ discussed with them the meaning of the experience.

Respond to the following accounts as directed.

Jesus called His disciples to leave what they were doing and to follow Him. Andrew, Peter, James, and John left their fishing businesses and followed Him (see Matt. 4:18-22). Matthew left his job as a tax collector (see Matt. 9:9). Describe something that would be difficult for you to leave behind or do if God asked you to.

Jesus told Peter to catch a fish, take a coin from its mouth, and pay their taxes (see Matt. 17:27). What would you do if God asked you to do something that seemed unreasonable or that did not make sense to you?

Jesus told His disciples to get a colt for Him and, if the owners asked what they were doing, to say: " ' "The Lord needs it" ' " (Mark 11:3). If Jesus told you to get a pickup truck parked at Main and Broad Streets, what would you do, especially if you had to answer the owner's questions with the statement "The Lord needs it"?

When Jesus told Philip to feed the five thousand, Philip said it was impossible. Andrew offered a boy's lunch even though he did not think it was enough (see John 6:5-11). Which disciple would you be most like?
❏ Philip   ❏ Andrew

Have you ever declined to be obedient because you believed that what God asked you to do was unreasonable or did not make sense? ❏ Yes ❏ No

The disciples' primary commitment was to be faithful to Jesus. Like the disciples, we are to obey Jesus' commands. Jesus provided resources to help His disciples obey: He prayed for them, sent the Holy Spirit, and provided His written Word. You and I have the same resources available to us. He will provide for us! If you obey His commands, you will experience His love and will bear His fruit. You can have a lifelong, obedient relationship with Him. He will lead your life if you allow Him to do so!

To review this week's theme, complete this sentence: If your life is characterized by _____, you will experience Christ's _____ and will bear _____.

If you had difficulty completing the sentence, review the illustration on page 18. As you have studied, you can let Christ lead you and help you so that your life is characterized by obedience, love, and fruit.

LEARNING THE DISCIPLE'S CROSS

Your primary task is to abide in Christ, the Vine. If you do this, He will be at the center of your life. Below I have drawn for you all of the elements of the Disciple's Cross but have not placed *Christ* at the center of the circle. Fill in the circle and under it write *John 15:5* as a reminder of the Vine and the branches. In the following weeks you will learn more about the components of the Disciple's Cross.

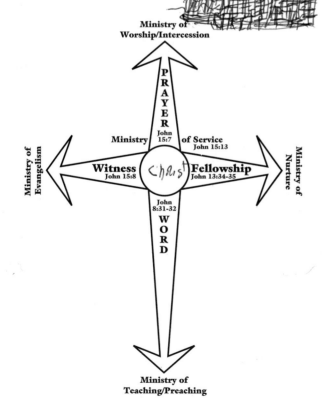

Ministry of Worship/Intercession

P R A Y E R John 15:7

Ministry of Service John 15:13

Ministry of Evangelism

Witness John 15:8

Christ

Fellowship John 13:34-35

Ministry of Nurture

John 8:31-32 W O R D

Ministry of Teaching/Preaching

DAILY MASTER COMMUNICATION GUIDE

JOHN 15

What God said to me:

JESUS is the
viNE his Fathu God
is the hosbnd
if we plant a tree
his the head, christ
is next we are
last

What I said to God:

we Must

Continue having your daily quiet time. Today read John 15, the chapter from which many of your memory verses in this book will be taken. As you read, look for ways this passage addresses your need to have Christ at the center of your life. Each week I will ask you to read this passage and to look for ways God uses it to speak to that week's discipline. After you have read this passage, complete the Daily Master Communication Guide in the margin.

HAS THIS WEEK MADE A DIFFERENCE?
Review "My Walk with the Master This Week" at the beginning of this week's material. Mark the activities you have finished by drawing vertical lines in the diamonds beside them. Finish any incomplete activities. Think about what you will say during your group session about your work on these activities.

Think about your experiences in completing week 1, "Spend Time with the Master."
• Has this week's study made a difference in your life?
• Is Christ more the center of your life now than He was last week?
Pray: "Lord, show me the areas of my life in which You want me to be more disciplined as a Christian" or "Lord, I am weak and need Your strength. Show me how to be disciplined in my walk with You as Master." When you have made the activities of today's lesson regular practices, the Holy Spirit will make a difference in the way you live your life in Christ from day to day.

The inventory beginning on the following page will help you evaluate your Christian life. It was designed for your private use, not for comparing yourself with anyone else. It is not a test, and no one is expected to make a perfect score. Your score reflects how you feel about your life of discipleship as much as it reflects what you do. Although most items are observable acts, one person may interpret his or her actions positively or negatively. You can know a person only by deeds or fruit, but God sees much deeper. Ask God to help you see where you are now and where He wants you to be in your lifelong, obedient relationship with Jesus Christ.

Read each item and fill in the circle in the column that most nearly represents an accurate evaluation.

	ALWAYS	USUALLY	SOMETIMES	SELDOM	NEVER

Spending Time with the Master

	ALWAYS	USUALLY	SOMETIMES	SELDOM	NEVER
• I have a daily quiet time.	●	○	○	○	○
• I try to make Christ Lord of my life.	○	●	○	○	○
• I feel close to the Lord throughout the day.	✗	○	●	○	○
• I try to discipline myself.	○	○	●	○	○
• I am aware that the Lord disciplines me.	●	○	○	○	○

Living in the Word

	ALWAYS	USUALLY	SOMETIMES	SELDOM	NEVER
• I read my Bible daily.	*lately* ●	○	○	○	○
• I study my Bible each week.	●	○	○	○	○
• I memorize a verse of Scripture each week.	*lately* ○	●	○	○	○
• I take notes at least once a week as I hear, read, or study the Bible in order to apply it to my life.	●	○	○	○	○

Praying in Faith

	ALWAYS	USUALLY	SOMETIMES	SELDOM	NEVER
• I keep a prayer list and pray for the persons and concerns on the list.	*not yet* ○	●	○	○	○
• I have experienced a specific answer to prayer during the past month.	●	○	○	○	○
• Each day my prayers include thanksgiving, praise, confession, petition, and intercession.	●	○	○	○	○

Fellowshipping with Believers

	ALWAYS	USUALLY	SOMETIMES	SELDOM	NEVER
• I seek to live in peace with my fellow Christians.	●	○	○	○	○
• I seek reconciliation with those who have a problem with me or with whom I have a problem.	*lately* ●	○	○	○	○
• Others know I am a Christian by the way I love God's people.	*I hope* ○	●	○	○	○
• I live in harmony with other members of my family.	●	○	○	○	○

Witnessing to the World

	ALWAYS	USUALLY	SOMETIMES	SELDOM	NEVER
• I regularly pray for lost persons by name.	●	○	○	○	○

$3 \times 8 = 24$

14
4
56
24
80

- I share my testimony with others when an appropriate opportunity arises. *yes* ⊙ ○ ○ ○ ○
- I share the plan of salvation with those who are open to hear it. *yes* ○ ⊙ ○ ○ ○
- I witness for Christ each week. *pray* ○ ⊙ ○ ○ ○
- I follow up on and encourage persons I have won to Christ. ○ ⊙ ○ ○ ○

Ministering to Others *Not a good way to serve people*
- I serve Christ by serving in my church. ○ ⊙ ○ ○ ○
- I give at least a tithe through my church. ⊙ ○ ○ ○ ○
- At least once a month I do kind deeds for persons less fortunate than I. ⊙ ○ ○ ○ ○
- I have goals for my life that I keep clearly in mind. ○ ○ ⊙ ○ ○

Subtotals 16 30 2 __ __
            x4 x3 x2 x1

Totals 3 __ 2 __

Score __

When you have finished checking each item, add each column except the "Never" column. Each check in the "Always" column is worth four points; the "Usually" column, three points; the "Sometimes" column, two points; the "Seldom" column, one point. Add these four totals together to get your overall score out of a possible one hundred.

Complete the following statements.

I feel that my score (does/does not) adequately reflect my life of discipleship because __they are not fully__.

Other factors that should be taken into account but are not reflected in the inventory and my feelings about them are

_____.

My personal, overall evaluation of my discipleship is

_____.

____

[1] R. A. Torrey, *Why God Used D. L. Moody* (Chicago: Moody Press, 1923), 10.
[2] *Day by Day in God's Kingdom: A Discipleship Journal* provides Scriptures, memory verses, and room to record what you experience in your quiet time. Order item 0-7673-2577-X by writing to the Customer Service Center; 127 Ninth Avenue, North; Nashville, TN 37234-0113; calling 1-800-458-2772; faxing (615) 251-5933; e-mailing customerservice@bssb.com; or visiting a Baptist Book Store or a Lifeway Christian Store.
[3] *The Commission* is a publication of the International Mission Board of the Southern Baptist Convention; P.O. Box 6767; Richmond, VA 23230.

WEEK 2

Live in the Word

This Week's Goal

You will grow closer to Christ as you learn to live in the Word by having a daily quiet time and by memorizing Scripture.

My Walk with the Master This Week

You will complete the following activities to develop the six biblical disciplines. When you have completed each activity, draw a vertical line in the diamond beside it.

SPEND TIME WITH THE MASTER
◇ During your daily quiet time use the Daily Master Communication Guides in the margins of this week's material.

LIVE IN THE WORD
◇ Read your Bible every day. Write what God says to you and what you say to God.
◇ Memorize John 8:31-32.
◇ Review Luke 9:23 and John 15:5, which you have already memorized.

PRAY IN FAITH
◇ Pray for each member of your *MasterLife* group by name.
◇ Pray with your prayer partner once this week. If you do not have a prayer partner yet, find one this week.

FELLOWSHIP WITH BELIEVERS
◇ Get better acquainted with a member of your group. Visit or call that person. Tell the person that you are praying for him or her. Talk about any blessings or challenges you are having in *MasterLife*.

WITNESS TO THE WORLD
◇ List the names of at least five lost persons on your Prayer-Covenant List. Begin praying regularly for them. Make any contacts the Spirit leads you to make.

MINISTER TO OTHERS
◇ Continue learning the Disciple's Cross. Learn the meaning of the bottom part of the cross to add to the information about the circle that you learned last week.

This Week's Scripture-Memory Verses

"'If you hold to my teaching, you are really my disciples. Then you will know the truth, and the truth will set you free'" (John 8:31-32).

DAY 1

A Close Relationship

A quiet time is more than merely a habit. It is an appointment with Jesus Christ.

When I was a young adult, I began trying to have a quiet time. I had read about Christians who got up at 4:00 a.m. to read the Bible for an hour and to pray for an hour before breakfast. I tried to do that, but I could not be consistent. I followed that schedule for a day or two, but then I would be so tired that I could not get up on time. I promised myself that I would try again the next day.

I felt guilty because I could not be consistent. In fact, I almost endangered my health before I realized that the Christians I was reading about were going to bed at 8:00 or 9:00 p.m. I was going to bed at 1:00 or 2:00 a.m.

Soon I read a tract that emphasized spending a short period with God every morning. It stressed the importance of consistency and suggested a simple plan to achieve that goal. I decided that no matter what the circumstances, I would spend seven minutes with God every morning. Of course, I soon realized that was not enough. I continually set the alarm earlier to have enough time with the Lord.

I learned that a quiet time is more than merely a habit. It is an appointment at the beginning of the day with Jesus Christ, who is at the center of my life. I suggest that you begin by setting aside a few minutes every morning with Jesus Christ, for He is also at the center of your life.

Your daily time with Christ is the first of six disciplines that are basic to a disciple's walk. Last week you studied denying yourself and putting Christ at the center of your life as part of becoming a disciple and developing a lifelong, obedient relationship with Him. This week you will begin learning what it means for Christ to be at the center of your life.

LEARNING THE DISCIPLE'S CROSS

Last week you began drawing the Disciple's Cross to understand what Christ expects of you. You drew the center part to represent the role Christ is to have in your life. As you continue in *MasterLife*, you will draw the cross around the center, one bar at a time, as you incorporate in your life the disciplines that keep you abiding in Christ. You can visualize the cross as representing the six disciplines a disciple needs to practice. Each week your assignments are related to those six disciplines:

You can visualize the cross as representing the six disciplines a disciple needs to practice.

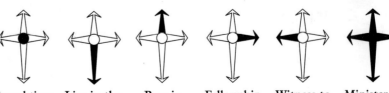

Spend time with the Master | Live in the Word | Pray in faith | Fellowship with believers | Witness to the world | Minister to others

✝ **List each discipline according to its position on the Disciple's Cross. Refer to page 32 if you need help.**

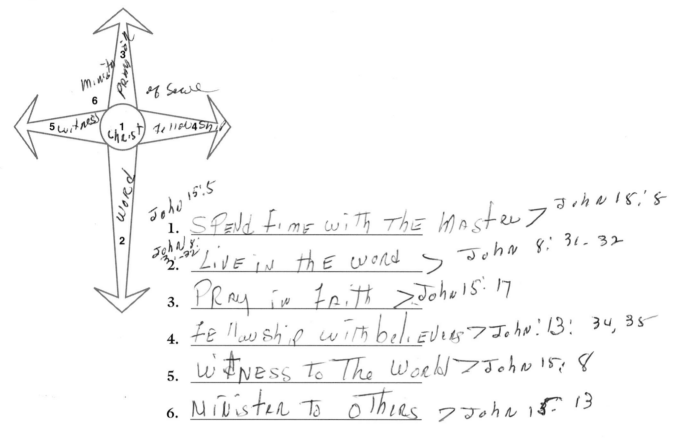

1. Spend time with the Master > John 15:5
2. Live in the Word > John 8: 31-32
3. Pray in faith > John 15: 17
4. Fellowship with believers > John 13: 34, 35
5. Witness to the World > John 15: 8
6. Minister to others > John 15: 13

Each week you will add new information about the Disciple's Cross. By the end of your study you will be able to explain the cross and to quote all of the Scriptures that go with it.

Each bar of the cross represents one part of the Christian life. The bottom part represents the Word, and the upper part, which you will add next week, represents prayer. Together these form the vertical crossbar, which represents your relationship with God. In two weeks you will begin drawing the horizontal crossbar, which represents your relationships with others. In your life in Christ you have one Lord, represented by the circle with Christ as the center, and two relationships—with God and other persons.

REMAINING IN THE WORD

The way to have Christ living in you is to have His Word in you. The first discipline in which you will become proficient is spending time with the Master by having a quiet time. The second and third disciplines, living in the Word and praying in faith, will support your quiet time. Jesus said in John 8:31-32: " 'If you hold to my teaching, you are really my disciples. Then you will know the truth, and the truth will set you free.' " The Word is food for you. You cannot grow unless you regularly partake of the Word.

The way to have Christ living in you is to have His Word in you.

Reread John 8:31-32, this week's Scripture-memory verses. Underline what the verses say about becoming Christ's disciple. Then begin memorizing John 8:31-32 by saying the verses aloud from one to three times.

You likely underlined the phrase "If you hold to my teaching." Christ's teaching is found in the Word. The absence of regular involvement with His Word keeps you from being the kind of follower Christ wants you to be.

You may wonder: *What difference does it make if I remain in His Word? Won't I still have the same problems as anyone else? Even though I hold to the teachings found in His Word, I will still have sorrows in my life. Will it really matter if I live as a disciple of Christ?* As a Christian, you are not exempt from difficulties. But remaining in His Word cultivates a relationship in which you can successfully weather those storms. When you have a relationship with Christ, He shows you how the Scriptures point to Him as the source of guidance and strength.

A DAILY APPOINTMENT

One way you can know Christ's teaching is through the habit of daily Bible reading, meditation, and prayer. No substitute exists for a quiet time. Persons God has used mightily are those who have discerned God's truth and power in private worship. Joshua 1:8 says of the Word, " 'Meditate on it day and night, so that you may be careful to do everything written in it.' " Memorizing puts God's Word in your head. Meditating puts it in your heart. Meditate on the Word until it is in your heart. With God's Word in your heart you can face any circumstance.

I had a significant experience in a quiet time several years ago. Getting ready for a second prostate surgery, I anticipated that this operation would be similar to the first one I had—although uncomfortable, without any lasting effects. In my quiet time I read Psalm 116:1-9. In verse 3 I read:

> *The cords of death entangled me,*
> *the anguish of the grave came upon me;*
> *I was overcome by trouble and sorrow.*

Becoming apprehensive, I wrote in my prayer journal, "This operation is going to be more dangerous than I thought." I prepared for the worst and then put my confidence in what God said in verses 7-9:

> *Be at rest once more, O my soul,*
> *for the Lord has been good to you.*
> *For you, O Lord, have delivered my soul from death,*
> *my eyes from tears,*
> *my feet from stumbling,*
> *that I may walk before the Lord*
> *in the land of the living.*

Memorizing puts God's Word in your head. Meditating puts it in your heart.

After the surgery the pathology report showed one cancer cell. At first I was startled by the word *cancer,* but the Scripture the Lord had given me came to mind and quieted my soul. The doctor said that the cancer cell might be the only one that existed and that he would monitor the situation every three months. I thanked God for His assurance. More than five years have passed since that surgery, and I have had no recurrence of cancer. However, the incident alerted the doctor to discontinue medicine that could have made the cancer cells grow faster.

I thanked God for His gracious warning about the cancer through His Word, which prepared me for the outcome of the surgery. Striving to live a life of obedience did not make me immune to cancer, but my habit of a regular quiet time made me open to a promise from God's Word that helped me get through a trying time with strength and comfort.

Have you had an experience that led you to closer fellowship with Christ so that you could be more receptive to His direction? ☑ Yes ❑ No If so, describe your experience.

My youngest son was very ill, Stranled At Age 10ms Just As he began to walk, he find his fever would go very high, I give him to Christ E in my faith to say he is grown + will have his 1st chil 12-5-99

FELLOWSHIP WITH GOD

The first reason for a quiet time is that it helps you get to know God through fellowship with Him. This week you will study this and three more reasons.

> **REASONS FOR A QUIET TIME**
> 1. **To know God through fellowship with Him**
> 2. To receive direction and guidance for daily decisions
> 3. To bring needs before God
> 4. To bear spiritual fruit

Why do you desire close fellowship with God? To begin with, wanting to communicate with someone you love is natural. Think about the way you feel when you go for a while without seeing or talking to someone you love, such as a parent, a child, a spouse, or a friend. You long to connect with that person once again. You cannot wait for a letter to arrive or to hear the voice on the phone. You hunger for that sweet time of fellowship. When you are a child of God, you have a deep desire for fellowship with your Heavenly Father.

Read in the margin the verses from 1 John. Then answer in your own words the following questions.

Why do you love God (see 1 John 4:19)?

because he did for me what no man could do, Altho I did not deserve it but his only Son die for my sin Christ was holy, He did not have to do it but his love for me so he give his life and keep on forgiving me

Margin notes

A quiet time helps you get to know God through fellowship with Him.

"We love because he first loved us" (1 John 4:19).

"This is how God showed his love among us: He sent his one and only Son into the world that we might live through him. This is love: not that we loved God, but that he loved us and sent his Son as an atoning sacrifice for our sins" (1 John 4:9-10).

A believer and the Father can enjoy the close relationship made possible by Jesus' sacrifice.

"[My determined purpose is] that I may know Him—that I may progressively become more deeply and intimately acquainted with Him, perceiving and recognizing and understanding [the wonders of His Person] more strongly and more clearly. And that I may in that same way come to know the power outflowing from His resurrection [which it exerts over believers]; and that I may so share His sufferings as to be continually transformed [in spirit into His likeness even] to His death" (Phil. 3:10, AMP).

How do you know that God loves you (see 1 John 4:9-10)?

WE had Sin Aganist God, he Ris Love US his Son Can And die for Us

You love God as a response to Him: He first loved you. You know that He loves you because He sent His Son to die for you. Failing to return God's love does not influence the way He feels about you. But your love for Him diminishes and grows stale if you do not have the nourishment of daily fellowship with Him. A daily quiet time is important so that a believer and the Father can enjoy the close relationship made possible by Jesus' sacrifice.

Read Philippians 3:10 in the margin. It is quoted from *The Amplified Bible*, which gives all possible meanings in the Greek language, in which the New Testament was written. Check the benefits Paul received from communion with Christ.
- ☐ 1. Knowledge of Christ
- ☑ 2. Freedom from problems
- ☑ 3. Resurrection power
- ☑ 4. Fellowship in suffering
- ☐ 5. Freedom from death

Christ does not promise that you will be free from death if you commune with Him. He does not promise that your struggles will be fewer. But He promises that you will have knowledge of Him, the power of the resurrection, and fellowship during times of suffering. The correct answers are 1, 3, and 4.

To summarize what you have learned so far, fill in the blank:

Closer to him when we fellowship with God we Cou

The first reason for a daily quiet time is

plan Find Strngh with him when we

When you love someone—and as a Christian, you are to love Christ above all else—you do not want to be separated from that person. You cannot really know someone unless you spend time with him or her. To answer the question in the previous activity, you likely wrote something like "so that I can know Him through fellowship with Him."

Your habit of a daily quiet time strengthens your relationship with the Vine, without whom you can do nothing. Last week's Scripture-memory verse, John 15:5, underscores your helplessness if you are not consistently connected to Christ. He wants to transform your character into Christlikeness as you stay connected to Him.

 Continue memorizing John 8:31-32 and review Luke 9:23, which you memorized earlier. Say them aloud to a family member or a friend.

 Continue reading your Bible daily. Today read Matthew 26:36-46, a passage describing a time when Jesus sought solitude for prayer. After you have read this passage, complete the Daily Master Communication Guide in the margin.

DAY 2

Guidance for Daily Decisions

As you consider living in the Word, the persistent problem of time may surface again. You may think: *Sure, it's good to read my Bible daily. I can try to establish that habit. But living in the Word sounds like something I do around the clock. Does anyone really have enough hours in the day to live in the Word continuously? I have my job, my family, and my other responsibilities. I can't walk around with a Bible in my hand all day.*

Certainly, reading your Bible regularly is a primary way to live in the Word. You need that daily discipline. However, you can receive the Word in many ways besides reading it. These include listening to someone preach it, studying it, memorizing it, meditating on it, recalling it, and applying it. Making Christ Lord and having a personal, lifelong, obedient relationship with Him mean that you want to study and meditate on the Word regularly. Then you live what it says.

In the previous paragraph underline ways to receive the Word.

God's Word can permeate your daily life in all kinds of situations. As you memorize Scripture, the verses you learn will surface in your thoughts when you are in various situations. In the same way, you find yourself in countless incidents that require you to apply scriptural truths. Even when you cannot have an open Bible in front of you, you can meditate on verses you have memorized. Hearing someone preach the Word teaches you what God has in mind for you. Developing daily habits of reading and studying the Scriptures helps you live in the Word. In the previous activity you likely underlined all of these ways.

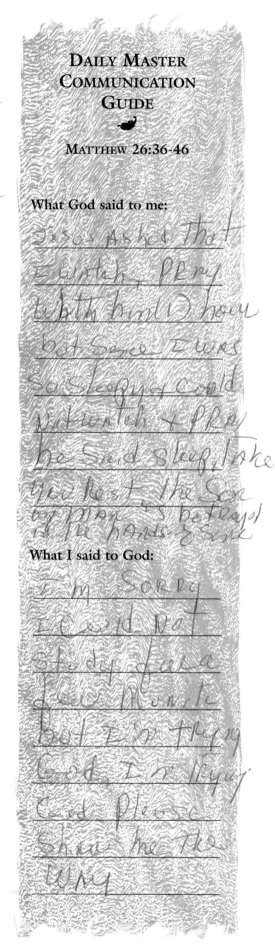

DAILY MASTER COMMUNICATION GUIDE

MATTHEW 26:36-46

What God said to me:

Jesus Asked that [illegible] watch, Pray with him 0 hour but Saw I was so sleepy could not watch + Pray he said sleep, take your rest, the son of man is betrayed in the hands of sin

What I said to God:

I'm Sorry I could not study luke too much but I'm Trying God. I'm trying God Please show me the way

Take time to work on this week's Scripture-memory verses, John 8:31-32. Say the verses aloud from one to three times. As you go about your activities this week, be aware of times you apply these verses to your life.

LEARNING THE DISCIPLE'S CROSS

To help reinforce what you are learning about living in the Word, draw the portions of the Disciple's Cross you have studied. Draw a circle with *Christ* and *John 15:5* in the center and draw the lower crossbar with *Word* written on it. Now write *John 8:31-32* on the lower crossbar. As you draw, say aloud what you have learned about the Disciple's Cross so far.

One way to get the Word into your mind and heart is through a daily quiet time. Today you will study the second reason for a quiet time.

A daily quiet time provides direction and guidance for your daily decisions.

> **REASONS FOR A QUIET TIME**
> 1. To know God through fellowship with Him
> 2. **To receive direction and guidance for daily decisions**
> 3. To bring needs before God
> 4. To bear spiritual fruit

ASKING GOD TO SHOW YOU THE WAY

A daily quiet time provides direction and guidance for your daily decisions. You discern God's will as you meditate on His Word and commune with His Spirit. Psalm 143:8 can be your prayer:

Show me the way I should go,
for to you I lift up my soul.

In Psalm 143:8 what did the psalmist ask God to do for him?

Asked God To Show him the way he Can walk close to Christ we to most ask God to Show use th wm

First John 5:14 says, "This is the confidence we have in approaching God: that if we ask anything according to his will, he hears us." What does this verse say about God's response if you pray according to His will?

16 You PRny according to his will You have the Assurance That he hears yo

If you pray according to His will, you have the assurance that He hears you.

Like the psalmist, you can ask God to show you the way you should walk in your life in Christ. If you pray according to His will, you have the assurance that He hears you. I know of no greater reason for taking time to strengthen your relationship with the Vine daily!

FINDING DIRECTION IN THE WORD

God has used His Word to reveal His direction for me over and over again. Once my wife and I were in South Africa leading *MasterLife* training for nine countries. Word arrived that because of a political boycott, no passengers from South Africa would be allowed to disembark in Nairobi, Kenya, where we were to conduct training for another nine countries. We tried to get around this ruling but could find no solution. If we would not be allowed to enter Kenya, we would be forced to proceed to Europe without leading the training.

The day before we were to leave, we decided to go to Harare, Zimbabwe, to get new passports, visas, and tickets in an attempt to travel to Nairobi. On the morning we were to leave, I read in my quiet time Psalm 118. Verses 5-8 say:

In my anguish I cried to the Lord,
and he answered by setting me free.
The Lord is with me; I will not be afraid.
What can man do to me?
The Lord is with me; he is my helper.
I will look in triumph on my enemies.
It is better to take refuge in the Lord
than to trust in man.

I felt that these verses were God's promise that we would be able to

DAILY MASTER COMMUNICATION GUIDE

PSALM 118

What God said to me:

_____

_____

_____

_____

_____

_____

_____

What I said to God:

_____

_____

_____

_____

_____

_____

_____

_____

enter Nairobi. Verses 14-16 seemed to offer further affirmation:

> _The Lord is my strength and my song;_
>   _he has become my salvation._
> _Shouts of joy and victory_
>   _resound in the tents of the righteous:_
> _"The Lord's right hand has done mighty things!_
>   _The Lord's right hand is lifted high;_
>   _the Lord's right hand has done mighty things!"_

We arrived in Harare, Zimbabwe, with only one hour to obtain the new passports, visas, and tickets, but God did it! If you have tried to get any one of those in your own country, you know that what occurred was a miracle. When we reached Nairobi, the officials turned back the three persons in front of us, but they examined our new passports and visas and let us walk through! Shouts of joy and victory resounded from us and from the participants who had prayed that we would be able to enter the country. God had performed a miracle, and I was thankful that I had sought answers from His Word. Without God's assurance, I would not have been bold enough to start on the journey.

Has God ever helped you make a decision as you sought answers from His Word? ☑ Yes ❑ No **If so, describe your experience.**

Having A problem I cou'd No So
I went To God to hetaken CAre of I

To summarize what you have learned today, fill in the blanks below. Check your work by reviewing the list on page 38.

The first two reasons for a daily quiet time are:

Tuknow God Through follow Ship
To Recieve Direction guidnce daily

 Read Psalm 118 as your Bible passage today and see how God uses it to speak to you. After you have read this passage, complete the Daily Master Communication Guide in the margin.

Pray for each member of your _MasterLife_ group. Refer to your Discipleship Covenant to recall their names.

DAY 3

Petitioning for Needs

By now you probably realize that remaining in Christ's Word, or holding to His teaching, is not a one-time action. Have you ever read your Bible, closed it, and had a self-satisfied feeling like "Whew! Now that's done"? This is not a task that can be accomplished and then set aside indefinitely. Remaining in His Word, or holding to His teaching, means His Word is so much a part of your life that it is like the air you breathe. Your memory verses for the week are John 8:31-32: " 'If you hold to my teaching, you are really my disciples. Then you will know the truth, and the truth will set you free.' " Today you will spend more time studying the concept of holding to Christ's teaching.

BRINGING YOUR NEEDS TO GOD

If you hold to Christ's teaching, you will not wait to ask for His help as a last resort. He will be your first source of help. You will seek the Scriptures first when you have needs. This is the third good reason to have a quiet time of reading and meditating on God's Word and fellowshipping with Him. Needs and problems in your life can make you realize your dependence on God. He wants to meet your needs. In a quiet time you can bring your needs before God.

Today you will study the third reason for a quiet time. In the list below, the first two reasons are blank. See if you can remember them from days 1 and 2.

REASONS FOR A QUIET TIME

1. To Know God Through fellowship

2. To Receive Direction + Guidance daily

3. To bring needs before God

4. To bear spiritual fruit

Read the verses in the margin. Match the references in the left column with the prayer promises from the Bible in the right column.

_D_ 1. Philippians 4:6-7   a. God renews our strength as we wait on Him.

_C_ 2. Psalm 34:17   b. In prayer we find grace in our need.

_B_ 3. Hebrews 4:16

_A_ 4. Isaiah 40:31   c. God delivers the righteous from trouble.

                  d. As we make our requests known to God, He gives us peace.

"Rejoice in the Lord always. I will say it again: Rejoice! Let your gentleness be evident to all. The Lord is near. Do not be anxious about anything, but in everything, by prayer and petition, with thanksgiving, present your requests to God. And the peace of God, which transcends all understanding, will guard your hearts and your minds in Christ Jesus" (Phil. 4:6-7).

The righteous cry out, and the Lord hears them;
*   he delivers them from all their troubles (Ps. 34:17).*

"Let us then approach the throne of grace with confidence, so that we may receive mercy and find grace to help us in our time of need" (Heb. 4:16).

Those who hope in the Lord will renew their strength.
They will soar on wings like eagles;
*   they will run and not grow weary,*
*   they will walk and not be faint (Isa. 40:31).*

These are wonderful promises about what happens when you pray! God provides grace, peace, strength, and deliverance from trouble. The correct answers are 1. d, 2. c, 3. b, and 4. a. Beautiful promises await you if you remain in the Word, as your memory verses, John 8:31-32, remind you.

Take a few minutes to review your memory verses, John 8:31-32. Without looking back at page 31, write the verses in the margin to see how well you can recall them.

By this point in *MasterLife* you may be saying to yourself: *This memory work is tough. I've never been very good at memorizing things.* You may think that you are too busy or too old to begin memorizing Scripture. But Scripture memorization is a major part of remaining in the Word. Being able to recall verses as you need them is important in a Christian's daily walk. Read this story about an amazing woman who overcame challenges to Scripture memorization.

Pearl Collinsgrove of Polo, Missouri, became a Christian at age 79 and began asking to study *MasterLife* after hearing participants in her church talk about experiencing life in Christ. Because Pearl had only a third-grade education and was blind, some church members thought that she would not be able to participate. But one member recorded all of the materials on tape for Pearl, who quickly memorized all of the Scripture-memory verses and many more.

Pearl, a former entertainer, began singing her memorized Scripture verses as she played the guitar. Civic clubs around town invited her to speak and sing. A member of her *MasterLife* group made a cross the same size as Pearl. When she spoke, she showed the cross and sang a song that related to each point and the center. She said, "My feet are planted in God's Word, my hands are lifted up to heaven in worship and prayer, one hand reaches out to my Christian brothers and sisters in fellowship, and the other hand reaches out to the lost world that we need to tell about Jesus."

Word spread about Pearl's testimony, and to rousing applause she sang John 15:5 at the 1985 Southern Baptist Convention in Dallas before 45,000 people. Neither age, blindness, nor a lack of education could deter this fervent woman's learning the *MasterLife* concepts and Scripture verses.

The same God who gives you strength to follow Him at all costs can also give you, like Pearl, the ability to memorize His Word.

Get better acquainted with a member of your *MasterLife* group by visiting or calling that person. Talk about any blessings or challenges you are having with Scripture memorization or with any other part of *MasterLife*. Tell the person that you are praying for his or her ability to memorize Scripture and for other needs the person expresses. Together review the verses you have memorized in *MasterLife*.

Being able to recall verses as you need them is important in a Christian's daily walk.

If you hold to my teaching you ARE my disciples. Then you will know the truth And the truth will Set you FREE

John 8: 31, 32

TRACING ANSWERS TO PRAYER

Another way to stay connected with God is to keep track of the way He meets your needs. Too often we approach His throne with a request but forget to thank Him for the way He answers our prayers. One way to keep track of your requests and answers is by keeping a Prayer-Covenant List. Many Christians have used this system to remind them of what God has done in their lives. Here are some tips on how to use the list.

HOW TO USE THE PRAYER-COVENANT LIST

1. Use the list on page 138. You may want to photocopy the list and make individual lists for various categories of prayer or for different days of the week. Make at least one list of requests for which you pray daily. Pray for other requests weekly or monthly.

2. List each request in specific terms so that you will know when it is answered. For example, do not write, "Bless Aunt Dolly." Instead, ask that Aunt Dolly might be able to use her arm again. Record the date you make the request. If the Holy Spirit at any time impresses on you a Bible verse related to that request, write that verse in the appropriate column. Be alert to verses in your Bible reading that might apply to your request. (Later, you will study more about the different ways God answers prayer.)

3. Leave two or three lines on which to write entries in the answer column. Your prayer may be answered in stages. Write the date when each prayer is answered.

Begin keeping your Prayer-Covenant List, using the one on page 138. Make copies of the list provided if you wish. You may want to make a prayer notebook to use as you complete *MasterLife*. At first you may not have enough prayer requests to fill all of the lines. Record only the requests that represent genuine concerns at the time.

Your prayer list with dated answers may become the best evidence you have to convince yourself or someone else of God's concern and power. This was the case for a young construction worker named Dyke Dyer, a member of a *MasterLife* group Shirley and I led at our church in Goodlettsville, Tennessee. Dyke consistently listed his boss on his Prayer-Covenant List as someone who needed salvation. As Dyke reported about his witnessing efforts to the group week after week, we prayed with him, but still no answer came.

Finally, Dyke found a way to take his boss to church and to win him to the Lord. Dyke excitedly told the group, "This is the best thing that has happened to me since I was saved!" It was a joy to see this young man use his Prayer-Covenant List as a means to pray consistently for someone's salvation and to witness this result.

You can not only approach God with your needs during your quiet time but also keep track of how He meets those needs. A quiet time is

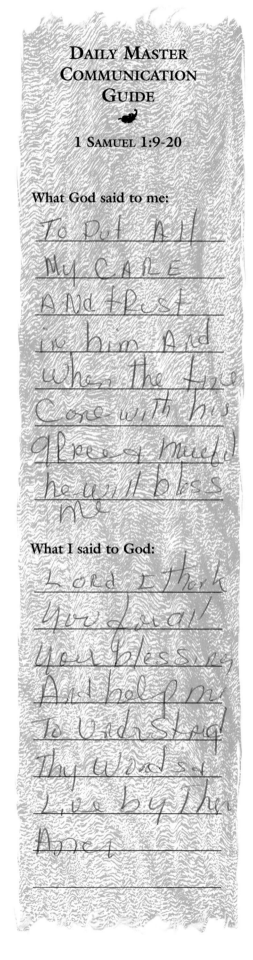

DAILY MASTER COMMUNICATION GUIDE

1 SAMUEL 1:9-20

What God said to me:

To Put All My CARE ANd trust in him And when the time Come with his glecey muefil he will bless me

What I said to God:

Lord I thank you Lual you blessing And help me To Undrstad Thy Words t Live by Then Amen

an important habit to develop in your lifelong, obedient relationship with Him.

Recap today's study by listing the first three reasons for having a quiet time. You will study the fourth reason tomorrow.

1. _To know God Through Fellowship_

2. _to Recieve direction + guidence daily_

3. _To Bring Need before God_

4. To bear spiritual fruit

Pray with your prayer partner once this week. If you do not have a prayer partner yet, find one this week.

Read 1 Samuel 1:9-20, about a person who prayed fervently, during your quiet time today. When you have read the passage, complete the Daily Master Communication Guide on page 43.

DAY 4

Abide and Obey

The disciples followed Jesus because they recognized Him as their Master.

A t our family devotional time one day I asked my children why they believed the disciples James and John dropped their nets at Jesus' command and followed Him—no questions asked. My 11-year-old son replied, "They were tired of mending those nets." I do not think that was the real reason the disciples followed Jesus on command. They followed Jesus because they recognized Him as their Master. If you want to sum up discipleship, it is obedience to the lordship of Christ. To remain in the Word, or hold to His teaching, then, means to obey it. You can read the Word, meditate on it, pray about it, hear it preached and taught, and see it demonstrated, but if you do not obey the Word, you have wasted your time.

" 'If you obey my commands, you will remain in my love, just as I have obeyed my Father's commands and remain in his love' " (John 15:10).

Read the verse in the margin and answer the following questions.

What happens when you keep Christ's commands?

If Christ Commands as kept we will Remain in his Love becase christ Obey God + he Remian' in God Love

Whose example do you follow when you keep Christ's commands?

God Crist Example

To abide in Christ means to _obey_ **Him.**

Obeying Christ's commands is the key to discipleship. When you obey them, you remain in a lifelong, obedient relationship with Him. You abide in His love. You obey because of the example Christ set in obeying His Father's commands. When you abide in Him, you obey Him.

How are you doing with your Scripture memorization? I hope that by now you are beginning to experience the benefits of having memorized verses to use instantly when you need them. When I give my testimony, I do not always have a Bible handy. I have found that the Holy Spirit brings to memory exactly the verses that fit each situation. Once when I talked with a woman who visited our church, she made numerous excuses for not coming to Christ. Because I had memorized many verses, the Holy Spirit led me to choose the right verse for each excuse. To each excuse I did not answer a word but asked her to read a verse I had memorized. After she read between 10 and 15 verses, she put her faith in Christ.

> You obey because of the example Christ set in obeying His Father's commands.

Describe a time when a memorized Scripture proved helpful.

when I was in school + taking a test using 23 Psalm or going on a Long Trip

Continue memorizing John 8:31-32. Say these verses aloud to someone in your family or to a friend.

Having a quiet time helps you obey Christ's teaching. When you have a daily reminder of what the Bible says, Christ's teaching is fresh on your mind. You do not have to wonder how Christ would have acted in a certain situation; those truths are hidden in your heart. And when you are obedient, you bear spiritual fruit—the fourth reason for a quiet time.

> You do not have to wonder how Christ would have acted in a certain situation; those truths are hidden in your heart.

Write the first three reasons for a quiet time.

REASONS FOR A QUIET TIME

1. _To Know God Through fellowship_
2. _To Recieve direction and guidance daily_
3. _To Bring Need before God_
4. **To bear spiritual fruit**

BEARING FRUIT

In John 15:4 Jesus said: " 'Remain in me, and I will remain in you. No branch can bear fruit by itself; it must remain in the vine. Neither can you bear fruit unless you remain in me.' "

What did Jesus say you must do to bear fruit?

No breech can ber frut by it self. at most Ramain in The Vine / Crist)

God does not want you to work *for* Him. He wants to work *through* you.

God will work through me if I obey And listen to him

God does not want you to work *for* Him. He wants to work *through* you. His work is accomplished only as you yield your will to Him daily through Bible study, prayer, and meditation. In your lifelong, obedient relationship with Him, He will repeatedly show you how the Scripture points to Him. You can bear fruit only if you remain faithful to the Vine and remain in Him. That is what life in Christ is all about.

Connie Baldwin, a schoolteacher in Virginia, gets up at 5:30 each morning to have her quiet time before she gets ready to teach school. She says this practice helps her bear fruit throughout the day as she works with children and helps her prepare for her job. "Getting up at 5:30 for me is quite a feat because I'm not a morning person," Connie relates. "But I know that God has given me the strength and determination to get up early to spend that time with Him. I know when I get to heaven, I'll never say, 'I wish I had slept more.' I'll say, 'I'm so glad I got up and spent time with my Master!' "

Jesus was prepared to bear spiritual fruit because His relationship with the Father was always up to date.

Jesus was prepared to bear spiritual fruit because His relationship with the Father was always up to date. Even when He was tired, He led the Samaritan woman to Christ (see John 4). When He met the funeral procession for the widow's son, He had no time to get prepared. He immediately raised the young man from the dead (see Luke 7:11-12). When He was asleep during the storm and His disciples woke Him crying: "Lord, save us! We're going to drown!" He was ready to act (see Luke 8:22-25).

KEEPING YOUR RELATIONSHIP FRESH

When opportunities arise, you often have no time to prepare to meet them. But if your relationship has been established during your quiet time and has been kept fresh through prayer and remembering the Word through the day, you will be ready. I am often surprised by what God says to me in my quiet time and by the way it applies to problems and opportunities I face during the day. The next morning, when I review what God revealed to me the day before, I often realize that He had prepared me for the situations that arose.

Check the opportunities you have had in the past week to bear spiritual fruit.
☑ Comforting a friend *n e b. jon*
❏ Witnessing

❑ Giving advice
☑ Sharing a memory verse or an insight from your quiet time
☑ Praying with someone
❑ Helping a needy person
❑ Encouraging someone
❑ Bearing a wrong action
☑ Controlling your emotions
❑ Loving the unlovely

Review what you have learned this week. Without looking back, list the four reasons for having a quiet time. Draw a star beside the area in which you feel the greatest need for growth.

1. _To know God through fellowship_
2. _To Receive dRirection and guidence/knowledge_
3. _To bRing Need before God_
4. _To bear SPiritful fRuit_

Continue to develop your Prayer-Covenant List by including the names of lost persons. Add the names of lost persons to your list until you have at least five. Begin praying regularly for them. Make any contact the Spirit leads you to make.

Your Prayer-Covenant List can become a living testimony of your living Lord. Once when I was witnessing to an atheist, I showed him my prayer list. I pointed out the date I had asked for seemingly impossible things and the date God had answered those prayers. I said, "If there's not a God, a lot of coincidences happen when I pray." Praise the Lord that He answers our prayers in ways that move even the most resistant person!

In your quiet time today, use Genesis 22:1-19, which focuses on an Old Testament figure who was obedient. After you have read this passage, complete the Daily Master Communication Guide in the margin.

DAILY MASTER COMMUNICATION GUIDE

GENESIS 22:1-19

What God said to me:

God is Telling us to tRust him And he will PRovide All of our Need oh what great faith Abraham had in God

What I said to God:

I too will TRust God with All of my might, he is worthy to know he will PRovide All of our Need Thank you God

DAY 5

A Daily Discipline

"Very early in the morning, while it was still dark, Jesus got up, left the house and went off to a solitary place, where he prayed" (Mark 1:35).

"One of those days Jesus went out to a mountainside to pray, and spent the night praying to God" (Luke 6:12).

"After he had dismissed them, he went up on a mountainside by himself to pray. When evening came, he was there alone" (Matt. 14:23).

"After leaving them, he went up on a mountainside to pray" (Mark 6:46).

Jesus modeled for us an obedient relationship with the Father.

In day 4 you studied about following Jesus' example for maintaining your growing relationship with the Father. You might wonder, *Why was it necessary for Him to pray, since He was God's Son?* The reason is that Jesus emptied Himself and became a human being (see Phil. 2:6). He placed Himself in the same relationship with God that we have: that of a learner (see Luke 2:52; Heb. 5:7-9). Jesus enjoyed a unique relationship with God the Father. Although He was God's Son and was filled with God's Spirit, He felt the need to maintain a practice of regular, private worship. He modeled for us an obedient relationship with the Father.

As you can see from the Scriptures in the margin, Jesus established patterns that enabled Him to maintain a special love relationship with God the Father. He prayed in the early morning, during the night without sleep, alone, and when He was away from others.

If Jesus felt a need for regular communion with the Father, we should feel an even greater need. Here is how you can have an effective quiet time.

HOW TO HAVE AN EFFECTIVE QUIET TIME
1. Schedule a regular time for it.
2. Find a place to be alone with God.
3. Follow a procedure.

A REGULAR TIME
Finding a regular time is the first key to an effective quiet time. Having your quiet time in the morning begins the day with a recognition of your dependence on God and His all-sufficiency. It gives you an opportunity to yield your will to Him and consciously dedicate the day to His glory.

What time do you usually get up in the morning? 6 x 7 AM
What adjustments would you need to make to get up 15 minutes earlier tomorrow morning?

get up app 15 - 30 Minutes
Early ea. Day

I believe it is important to meet with God in the morning so that you consciously seek His guidance and hear His word for the day. However, some Christians find that a quiet time at bedtime eases the tensions of the day, provides a peaceful prelude to rest, and prepares them for the next day. The important factor is that the time be daily and regular so that it becomes a habit.

Do you have a time of day when you habitually pray? ☑ Yes ☐ No
If not, make a commitment to schedule a quiet time at _6/15/a_
☑ **a.m.** ☐ **p.m. each day.**

A QUIET PLACE

A second requirement for an effective quiet time is a place where you can be alone with God. Matthew 6:6, in the margin, describes how Jesus encouraged His followers to pray. Most people find that they can concentrate best when they have an established place away from noise, distractions, and other people—a place like a bedroom, study, den, or garage—where they can focus on the One to whom they are praying.

Name the best place for you to have a quiet time: _Bed Room or backyard_

A PROCEDURE TO FOLLOW

A third requirement for an effective quiet time is to follow a procedure. Unless you consciously follow a pattern that keeps your mind focused on spiritual matters, you will probably find that your mind tends to wander.

The following elements may be included in your quiet time. Check the ones you are currently using.
☑ **Fellowshipping with God in prayer**
☑ **Bible reading or study**
☐ **Praying through the day's schedule**
☐ **Memorizing and/or reviewing memory verses**
☑ **Praying through your prayer list(s)**
☐ **Studying the day's *MasterLife* assignment**

☐ **Other:** _____

The following is my personal procedure. You may want to adapt it to determine your procedure.

1. I kneel in prayer and renew my relationship with God after the night's rest. During this time I often use the ACTS model on page 19.
2. After fellowshipping with God, I sit or kneel and read Scripture. I usually read a chapter a day as I read consecutively through a book of the Bible. During *MasterLife* I suggest that you read Scriptures related to the day's lesson. Later, you will determine which book of the Bible to read and how much to read each day.
3. While I read or after I have finished reading, I summarize in my journal what God said to me and what I said to God.

" 'When you pray, go into your room, close the door and pray to your Father, who is unseen. Then your Father, who sees what is done in secret, will reward you' " (Matt. 6:6).

your Room c The door close, And PRay PRiv to God.

Unless you consciously follow a pattern that keeps your mind focused on spiritual matters, you will probably find that your mind tends to wander.

_1 A christian mind is to be teachable
2 obey
do what thus said The Lord_

Use your Prayer-Covenant List to pray for the requests listed.

4. I use my Prayer-Covenant List to pray for the requests listed. I add other subjects God leads me to pray about.

You may use my procedure or may develop another. Perhaps you could try several different ways to organize your quiet time in the next several days to see which one you are most comfortable with and which helps you best relate to God.

Write the procedure you want to use in tomorrow's quiet time.

Up Early, Pray And thank God for his blessing - Lifting Me See A New day In my Right mind & God still do things for my Self

To recap what you have studied today, explain the significance of the three requirements for a quiet time. Check your answers by reviewing what you have read.

A regular time: 7 Am

A quiet place: Bid Room

A procedure to follow: B P dov

LEARNING THE DISCIPLE'S CROSS

In this week's Scripture-memory verses, John 8:31-32, Jesus said that His disciples are characterized by holding to His teaching.

✝ **To demonstrate that you understand the importance of remaining in His Word, or holding to His teaching, as a characteristic of a disciple, draw the portions of the Disciple's Cross you have studied so far. Draw the circle, the lower crossbar, and the words and verses that go in them. Explain mentally or aloud what you have learned about the Disciple's Cross this week.**

First Peter 2:5 refers to believers as priests who may "offer up spiritual sacrifices, acceptable to God by Jesus Christ." As priests, we have the privilege and responsibility to worship the Lord daily.

As priests, we have the privilege and responsibility to worship the Lord daily.

DAILY MASTER COMMUNICATION GUIDE

JOHN 15

What God said to me:

As Long As I pray faithful & Study his word loving one another As he Showed his Son To Love me to Love one another mean to go That EXTRA MilE for our bRo or SiS Then God will Reward us open we must be umble At All Tm

What I said to God:

I will TRy daily. to do Some good deed for Some one Else, I'll PRAy Study & mediate daily All that I do I know is not Enough only God's gRace will Save m

Evaluate the degree to which you do the following by filling in the circles in the appropriate columns.

	ALWAYS	USUALLY	SOMETIMES	SELDOM	NEVER
Have a regular time	◉	○	○	○	○
Have an established place to meet God	◉	○	○	○	○
Have a procedure to follow	◉	○	○	○	○

Enabling sinful people to commune with God cost Him His only Son. Yet God was willing to pay that price to have relationships with us. Part of your life in Christ is daily communication with the Father. What is it costing you to have fellowship with Him?

Will you give God at least 15 minutes daily, starting tomorrow?
☑ Yes ☐ No If this is your desire, tell Him so now in a prayer.

Again read John 15 in your quiet time today. This time look for ways God uses this passage to speak to you about remaining in His Word, or holding to His teaching. After you have read this passage, complete the Daily Master Communication Guide in the margin.

HAS THIS WEEK MADE A DIFFERENCE?
Review "My Walk with the Master This Week" at the beginning of this week's material. Mark the activities you have finished by drawing vertical lines in the diamonds beside them. Finish any incomplete activities. Think about what you will say during your group session about your work on these activities.

As you complete your study of "Live in the Word," think about the experiences you have had this week.
- Are you truly becoming a disciple, as John 8:31-32 describes?
- Have you observed growth in your life this week as a result of what you learned?
- Are you abiding in Christ more this week than you were last week?
- Have you progressed in developing a personal, lifelong, obedient relationship with Him?

MasterLife encourages you not to stand still in your life in Christ but to move forward. You would not be participating in this study if you wanted only to stand still. I pray that God is working through your experiences to help you grow as a disciple.

WEEK 3

Pray in Faith

This Week's Goal
You will grow in your relationship with Christ by praying in faith.

My Walk with the Master This Week
You will complete the following activities to develop the six biblical disciplines.
When you have completed each activity, draw a vertical line in the diamond beside it.

 SPEND TIME WITH THE MASTER
◇ Have a quiet time every day, using the Daily Master Communication Guides
in the margins of this week's material.

 LIVE IN THE WORD
◇ Read your Bible every day. Write what God says to you and what you say
to God.
◇ Memorize John 15:7.
◇ Review Luke 9:23, John 15:5, and John 8:31-32.

 PRAY IN FAITH
◇ Pray for each member of your *MasterLife* group by name.
◇ Pray with your prayer partner in person or by telephone.
◇ Pray for the needs on your Prayer-Covenant List.

 FELLOWSHIP WITH BELIEVERS
◇ Share with someone your testimony of having a quiet time.

 WITNESS TO THE WORLD
◇ Show God's love to a person who is not a Christian.

 MINISTER TO OTHERS
◇ Continue learning the Disciple's Cross. Learn the meaning of the top part of
the cross and memorize the Scripture that goes with it. Be ready to explain
the top and bottom parts of the cross to someone in your group at the next
session.

This Week's Scripture-Memory Verse
*" 'If you remain in me and my words remain in you, ask whatever you wish, and it
will be given you' " (John 15:7).*

DAY 1

Praying for What God Wants

God began to teach me to pray in faith.

When I was in college, God began to teach me to pray in faith. I read a sermon by evangelist Gypsy Smith based on John 15:7, your memory verse for this week: " 'If you remain in me and my words remain in you, ask whatever you wish, and it will be given you.' " It impressed me so much that I said to God: "Lord, I'm trying my best to abide in you. I ought to be able to ask anything and have my prayer answered because You promised it." I then felt impressed to pray that someone would trust Christ as Savior as I witnessed on the street that night. I wrote in my diary, "I believe that someone will be saved tonight (John 15:7)."

I went out on the street and began inviting people to attend services at the rescue mission. When two men accompanied me, I thought: *That's great. Maybe two are going to be saved tonight.* But when the sermon was over, I turned to them and asked, "Are you Christians?" They both said, "Yes." I could not understand that, because I had prayed that God would save someone. After the service I looked for someone else to whom I could witness but did not find anyone. On the way home my mind was bombarded by questions. I said: "Lord, as far as I know, I am abiding in You as John 15:7 says. Why haven't You answered as You promised? Isn't Your Word true?"

When I got back to campus, I remembered that I had forgotten to bring home a friend's coat for which I was responsible. When I went back for the coat, I decided once more to try to find someone to whom I could witness. I met an 18-year-old man standing on the street corner. After I explained how to be saved, he gave his life to Christ. I praised God for the man's salvation, and I rejoiced that His Word was true and that He did what He promised. Even before the man was baptized, he led someone else to Christ.

I rejoiced that His Word was true and that He did what He promised.

Eager to press on with my new understanding of prayer and faith, I remembered that I would preach the next Sunday night at the church in Tulsa where my father was the pastor. I seldom pray for exact numbers of persons to be saved, but I felt the Holy Spirit impressing me to ask that five persons be converted as I preached. At that time five persons had never made decisions when I preached unless they were decisions to leave! I said, "God, I believe your Word that you will save five persons." When I arrived in Tulsa, I asked my dad to give me prospect cards so that I could make visits, knowing that only if unsaved persons were at church could they be saved in the service. When the night arrived and I gave the invitation, five persons walked down the aisles to accept Christ, and another rededicated his life. I began to realize that God really wanted to do something if I prayed in accordance with His will.

The next week I went even a step farther. I asked God, "What about 10 persons this weekend?" But this time nothing happened, because God wanted me to learn an even more important lesson about prayer. This time people were not saved because I had begun trying to tell God what I wanted rather than praying on the basis of what He revealed. I learned that prayer is intended to involve me in God's purpose rather than my involving Him in my plans.

Think of a time when you prayed on the basis of what you wanted rather than seeking God's will first. Describe this experience below.

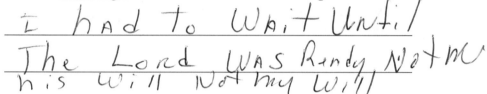

I had to Wait Until The Lord Was Ready, Not me his Will Not my Will

ASKING ACCORDING TO HIS WILL

God delights in answering prayer that is asked according to His will, but He refuses to answer prayer that is not consistent with what He wants. We need to hear God's voice so that we will know what to pray.

We need to hear God's voice so that we will know what to pray.

Most people are not asked to make the sacrifices Alex and Shelby Credle made, although all need to deny self to follow Him. Alex was a business executive who earned a large income and had job security. His wife, Shelby, was a college instructor who found meaning in her work teaching communications. They lived in a prosperous subdivision in North Carolina, and their grandchildren lived nearby. Yet Alex and Shelby quit their jobs, sold their home, gave away most of their possessions, and departed for Asia, where they began working for a humanitarian organization to share their faith. The Credles said they took this drastic step joyfully because they wanted to follow God's will for their lives.

Book James

The Credles had relocated many times during the course of Alex's employment, but one thing made this move different. "It's the first time we've ever prayed about a move and sought God's Word to guide us," said Shelby. "We've always gone it alone before." The Credles stayed close to the Vine and prayed in faith during their decision. This gave them the courage and confidence to make a major lifestyle change.

You may ask, *If I pray on the basis of what God wants rather than what I want, will I have to do what the Credles did?* Their case is rare. The important question to ask is, *Am I willing to pray as the Credles did?*

Do you read God's Word for direction and pray in faith when you need to make a major decision?
- ❏ Yes, I always do this.
- ❏ I try to do this most of the time.
- ☑ I know I should, but I don't as often as I'd like.
- ❏ I usually consult God after I've made the decision.

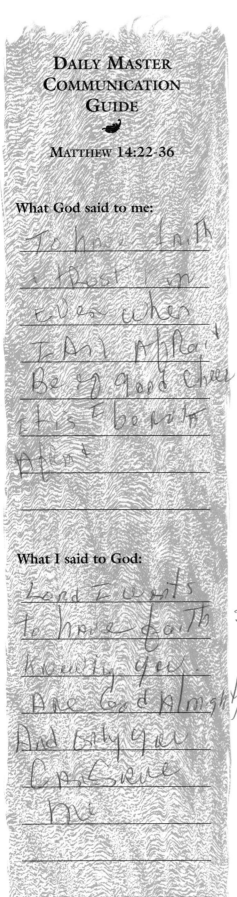

DAILY MASTER COMMUNICATION GUIDE

MATTHEW 14:22-36

What God said to me:

John 15:7
Rest in
Even when
I AM Afraid
Be of good cheer
it is I be not
afraid

What I said to God:

Lord I wants
to have faith
knowing you.
Are God Almighty
And only you
Can Save
me

Turn back to page 53 and read aloud John 15:7, your memory verse for the week. Write what you think this verse says about consulting God first when making a decision. Meditate on the verse. Ask God to show you what He wants and to give you faith to believe that He will do it.

LEARNING THE DISCIPLE'S CROSS
In *MasterLife* you are learning the disciplines around the Disciple's Cross. The first discipline you studied was spending time with the Master and keeping Him at the center of your life. Last week you studied the second discipline: living in the Word. A third discipline a disciple must practice is praying in faith. This week you will learn the role of prayer in keeping Christ at the center of your life.

To preview what you will learn this week about praying in faith, draw the portions of the Disciple's Cross you have studied. Draw a circle with *Christ* in the center and draw the lower crossbar with *Word* written on it. Add the verses that apply. Then draw the upper crossbar with *prayer* written on it. Refer to the completed Disciple's Cross on page 136 if you need help with your drawing.

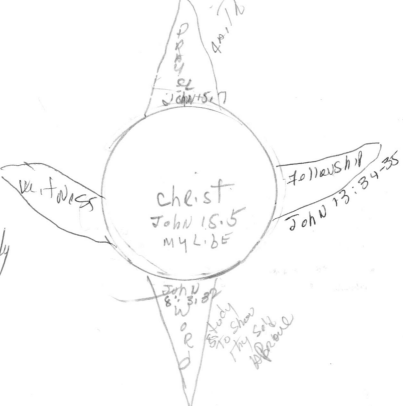

The center of the cross represents one Lord, since He is the first priority in your life. The bars of the cross represent two relationships. *Word* on the bottom and *prayer* on the top, forming the vertical crossbar, represent your relationship with Christ. The horizontal crossbar represents your relationships with others.

↕ Continue reading your Bible daily during your quiet time. Today read Matthew 14:22-36, a passage describing a time when Jesus went away to pray. After you have read this passage, complete the Daily Master Communication Guide on page 56.

DAY 2

Enter His Gates with Thanksgiving

As you studied day 1, you may have said to yourself: I'd really like to learn to pray like that. But how do I begin? How do I know the right way to talk to the Father? Maybe in the past you have prayed by reciting words you have memorized. Or maybe your prayers have merely been lists of requests rather than meaningful conversations with God. If you want to go deeper in your prayer life, you can learn to pray in faith as you develop your personal, lifelong, obedient relationship with Him.

ENTERING GOD'S PRESENCE

The Old Testament teaches that prayer is an act of actually coming into God's presence. If you think about prayer as a way to enter God's presence, you can understand why amazing things can happen when you pray.

Biblical comparisons of heaven and the temple can help you focus on entering God's presence. In Isaiah 6:1-3, in the margin, the prophet Isaiah depicted heaven as the temple. As Isaiah came into God's presence, he saw the train of God's robe filling the temple. Witnessing God's majesty, Isaiah experienced the holiness of His presence:

In Isaiah 6:1-3 underline words or phrases that describe how Isaiah viewed God during this experience.

Isaiah obviously became aware of God's awesome holiness. You may have underlined the words high, exalted, holy, and the whole earth is full of his glory.

When you pray, you too can imagine entering the temple as you approach God and experience His awesome holiness. The drawing in the margin gives you a general idea of what the temple in Jerusalem looked like. The temple provided various levels of access, beginning with the gates and culminating with the holy of holies. Each level suc-

"In the year that King Uzziah died, I saw the Lord seated on a throne, high and exalted, and the train of his robe filled the temple. Above him were seraphs, each with six wings: With two wings they covered their faces, with two they covered their feet, and with two they were flying. And they were calling to one another:
'Holy, holy, holy is the Lord Almighty;
the whole earth is full of his glory' " (Isa. 6:1-3).

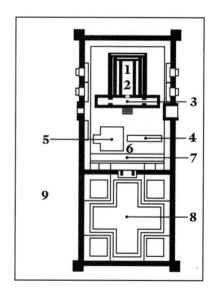

1. **Holy of holies**
2. **Holy place**
3. **Porch**
4. **Slaughterhouse**
5. **Altar**
6. **Court of priests**
7. **Court of Israel**
8. **Court of women**
9. **Court of Gentiles**

"Since we have a great high priest who has gone through the heavens, Jesus the Son of God, let us hold firmly to the faith we profess. For we do not have a high priest who is unable to sympathize with our weaknesses, but we have one who has been tempted in every way, just as we are—yet was without sin. Let us then approach the throne of grace with confidence, so that we may receive mercy and find grace to help us in our time of need" (Heb. 4:14-16).

Enter his gates with thanksgiving
and his courts with praise;
give thanks to him and praise his name (Ps. 100:4).

These things I remember
as I pour out my soul:
how I used to go with the multitude,
leading the procession to the house of God,
with shouts of joy and thanksgiving
among the festive throng (Ps. 42:4).

I will praise God's name in song
and glorify him with thanksgiving.
This will please the Lord more than an ox,
more than a bull with its horns and hoofs (Ps. 69:30-31).

cessively limited access to groups of people. In Bible times a layperson could enter only certain areas of the temple.

Only the high priest was permitted to enter the area that contained the holy of holies—the most sacred place and the innermost part of the temple. But Christ provided a way for all people to enter the holy of holies and to have an intimate relationship with God through prayer. His death on the cross broke through the limitations of earthly life, making it possible for you to enjoy direct access to God. Because Christ came to earth as a human being, His atoning death brought an end to the priests' role. He now represents you as your Great High Priest before God.

Read Hebrews 4:14-16 in the margin.

APPROACHING GOD
Although the holy of holies had limited access, the large, open courtyard at the edge of the temple was open to everyone. As people entered through those beautiful temple gates, they gave thanks. The verses from Psalms in the margin help you picture how the people approached the temple with thanksgiving. When you approach God, it is not proper to rush into His presence and bombard Him with your needs. First, thank Him for all He has done for you. Thanksgiving is the way to approach God.

T. W. Hunt, the author of *Disciple's Prayer Life*, described how he became aware of his need for an expanded attitude of thanksgiving. One morning as he brushed his teeth, T. W. asked himself, *What if tomorrow I had only the things for which I thanked God today?* He began to name things like his teeth, his eyes, the sense of touch, air, home, people— items he realized he sometimes took for granted. He changed his approach to prayer so that he began with thanksgiving to God.

What are things you take for granted for which you want to begin thanking God? Start now by writing a prayer thanking God for some of these items.

Thank You, God, for—

for Life, health food, clothing
Shelter and all of your blessing
I Praise you for your blessing

In thanksgiving you express gratitude toward God, generally in response to His concrete acts. Psalm 69:30-31, in the margin, shows the value God places on your prayers of thankfulness. He values prayers of thanksgiving more than acts of sacrifice.

What kinds of things do you thank God for? The psalms, in which an attitude of thankfulness is especially prominent, give examples of areas in which you can give thanks.

• **Deliverance from trouble:**

> *The angel of the Lord encamps around those who fear him,*
> *and he delivers them.*
> *Taste and see that the Lord is good;*
> *blessed is the man who takes refuge in him (Ps. 34:7).*

• **God's faithfulness:**

> *The Lord is good and his love endures forever;*
> *his faithfulness continues through all generations*
> *(Ps. 100:5).*

• **Forgiveness of sin:**

> *Sing to the Lord, you saints of his;*
> *praise his holy name.*
> *For his anger lasts only a moment,*
> *but his favor lasts a lifetime (Ps. 30:4-5).*

• **Creation:**

> *You make me glad by your deeds, O Lord;*
> *I sing for joy at the works of your hands (Ps. 92:4).*

Does that list prompt you to remember things for which you need to be thankful? Go back and draw a star beside one area in which you need to express gratitude. Then stop and pray, thanking God for what He brought to mind.

You can get so busy presenting your requests to God that you neglect a time of thankfulness. What about earlier requests He answered? True, not everything you have asked for is granted. You may be waiting for an answer. Sometimes the answer you wanted was not part of His plan, and He gave you an answer that was better for you than the one you desired. But He certainly answers many of your requests just as you asked. How many of them have you thanked Him for? Your Prayer-Covenant List is an obvious record of answered prayer. In the brief time you have kept a Prayer-Covenant List, what answers to prayer have you recorded?

Stop and review your Prayer-Covenant List or a list you kept previously. List two prayer requests for which you have already seen answers. Then enter God's presence and thank Him for them.

DAILY MASTER COMMUNICATION GUIDE

JOHN 15

What God said to me:

He + his Son is one, if I'm not a good brand + don't work for him Then I'm done, he will cast me aside

What I said to God:

Lord I will Try And Abide in Thy Word daily

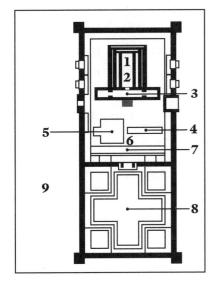

1. Holy of holies
2. Holy place
3. Porch
4. Slaughterhouse
5. Altar
6. Court of priests
7. Court of Israel
8. Court of women
9. Court of Gentiles

Enter his gates with thanksgiving and his courts with praise; give thanks to him and praise his name (Ps. 100:4).

My Son made healthy Thank you God
I still have a Pool of good health Thank you God

Prayer is the discipline you are studying this week. A part of life in Christ is praying in faith. Jesus said in John 15:7, " 'If you remain in me and my words remain in you, ask whatever you wish, and it will be given you.' "

Stop and review John 15:7, your memory verse you just read. Say it to your prayer partner in person or by phone during your prayer time this week. Also say the verses you memorized previously.

Again read John 15 as your Bible passage today. As you read the passage this time, look for ways God uses it to speak to you about praying in faith. After you have read this passage, complete the Daily Master Communication Guide on page 59.

DAY 3

Enter His Courts with Praise

The next step in learning to pray in faith involves focusing on who the Father is and what He means in your life. Jesus did not just teach His disciples how to pray. He taught them how to know the Father through prayer. Focusing on Him will continue to set the pace for your quiet time. It will help you overcome distractions or demands to acknowledge the One whose throne you are approaching. It will help you communicate with Him. Set other thoughts aside as you continue to make a deliberate effort to concentrate on the Father.

Again, think about the way people approached the temple in Jerusalem in Bible times as you consider how to approach God's throne in prayer. As the people entered the courts of the temple, they came with praise, as Psalm 100:4, in the margin, indicates. Praise is based on adoration of God. Adoration is what you do in worship.

PROCLAIMING HIS WORTH

The word *praise* originates from a Latin word meaning *value* or *price*. Thus, to give praise to God is to proclaim His merit or worth. How you do this—whether you are kneeling, standing, sitting, or reclining—does not matter. John 11:41 implies that Jesus prayed with His eyes open. Regardless of how you praise Him and under what circumstances, praise is an important element of prayer. It is to be constant, as Psalm 34:1, in the margin, indicates. Praise raises your prayer life above yourself.

Praise focuses on the person of God. Some of God's names that appear in the Bible reveal His character—ways He works in your life. You can praise God as you recognize the aspects of His character that are revealed in His names. To discover various aspects of God's character, study Psalm 91, which mentions several of His names.

 During your quiet time read Psalm 91. After you have read this passage, complete the Daily Master Communication Guide on page 62.

Here are the names of God that are used in Psalm 91:

El Elyon:

> *He who dwells in the shelter of the Most High*
> *will rest in the shadow of the Almighty (Ps. 91:1).*

The term *Most High* reveals the name *El Elyon*, the strongest of all gods and the possessor of heaven and earth—the strongest of the strong. Do you believe that you win the daily battles of life in your own strength? The true victory originates with *El Elyon*. He is capable of arranging even the most tedious details of your life.

Think about a time when you experienced the characteristic of God revealed by the name *El Elyon*. Has He worked out a circumstance in your life beyond anything you could have imagined? ☑ Yes ❑ No If so, describe this experience below. Stop and praise God as *El Elyon*, the Most High God.

_____

El Shaddai:

> *He who dwells in the shelter of the Most High*
> *will rest in the shadow of the Almighty (Ps. 91:1).*

The term *Almighty* reveals the name *El Shaddai*, the all-sufficient God. The name is first used in Genesis 17:1, when God appeared to Abraham and made great promises to Him. God promised to make of him a great nation and to give him a son at his advanced age. God keeps His promises. Read Romans 4:20-21 in the margin.

Think about a time when you experienced the characteristic of God revealed by the name *El Shaddai*. Can you think of an occasion

I will extol the Lord at all times;
   his praise will always be on my lips (Ps. 34:1)

"He did not waver through unbelief regarding the promise of God, but was strengthened in his faith and gave glory to God, being fully persuaded that God had power to do what he had promised" (Rom. 4:20-21).

DAILY MASTER COMMUNICATION GUIDE

PSALM 91

What God said to me:

If i come to him in thanksgiving ＋ pray he will protect me from all harm ＋ dagu All trop ＋ deseases he will protect me under his wing

What I said to God:

I will praise your Holy Name I ask forgiveness of my sin in Jesus Name I Pra

---

when He kept His promises to you? ❏ Yes ❏ No If so, describe it below and praise Him for being a promise-keeping God.

Lord you been so good to me I just praise your name for it

Yahweh:

> I will say of the Lord, "He is my refuge and my fortress,
> my God in whom I trust" (Ps. 91:2).

The term *LORD*, written in capital letters, reveals the personal name of God—*Yahweh* or *Jehovah*. (The word *Lord* in lowercase letters signifies *Adonai*—the master, the person with authority.) *Yahweh* signifies the God who is with you all the time. God used this name to reveal Himself to Moses in Exodus 3. When God said to Moses, " 'I AM WHO I AM,' " He was probably saying, in effect, "Go and do what you are told, for I am with you" (see Ex. 3:14).

Think about a time when you experienced the characteristic of God revealed by the name *Yahweh*. Have you been aware of His presence when you believed that He was asking you to do something difficult? ☑ Yes ❏ No If so, describe your experience below. Stop and pray, praising God for being *Yahweh* in your life.

When I was getting ready to move back here to help my brother illness I had to make this move all along, husband had died children had grew up had family I was alone, but had friends family

Elohim:

"My God in whom I trust" (Ps. 91:2) reveals the name *Elohim*. It first appears in Genesis 1:1 in the creation story, referring to the strong, covenant-keeping God who is the Creator. Do you regularly approach God as the Creator and worship Him?

Think about a time when you experienced the characteristic of God revealed by the name *Elohim*. When have you been aware of Him as the One who gave you life and created everything around you? Describe your experience below. Then stop and worship God as the Creator.

Other names of God also help you focus on who He is and enable you to praise Him. Consider these:
- *Jehovah Jireh*—the God who provides
- *Jehovah Shalom*—the God who brings peace
- *Jehovah Sabaoth*—the God who brings spiritual help
- *Jehovah Rapha*—the God who heals

You may want to use a Bible dictionary to examine some of the names of God. Understanding the characteristics of God will help you know how to praise Him. God's names are revealed in your experiences with Him. Let Him reveal Himself to you as you worship Him.

REASONS TO PRAISE GOD

As you practice praying in faith, consider these other reasons God is worthy of praise. You can praise Him because—

- *He is the living God.* Matthew 16:16 states Simon Peter's answer when Jesus asked who He is: " 'You are the Christ, the Son of the living God.' "
- *He is holy.* As people entered the temple area, they were aware of God's holiness. Psalm 29:2 says, "Worship the Lord in the splendor of his holiness."
- *He is spirit.* He is not material form but the highest form of existence. God's spirit form allows Him to be with people everywhere:

> *Where can I go from your Spirit?*
> *Where can I flee from your presence? (Ps. 139:7)*

- *He is love.* The primary purpose behind His revelation is love (see John 3:16).
- *He is Father.* He is the Father of our Lord Jesus Christ, whose death allows us to enter the Father's presence: " 'No one comes to the Father except through me' " (John 14:6).
- *He is glory.* The word glory refers to His influence and importance in the universe. Hebrews 1:3 says, "The Son is the radiance of God's glory and the exact representation of his being, sustaining all things by his powerful word."

Praise God because of who He is, not because of what He does. Praise is pure worship and adoration. In praise you affirm God and express your love for Him.

Stop and pray. Review the list of reasons God is worthy of your praise. Use each one to praise Him as you continue to develop the discipline of praying in faith.

I hope that by now you have seen growth in your life because of prayer—both praying alone during your quiet time and praying with your prayer partner. In your prayer time I hope that God has begun to reveal to you persons who are not Christians for whom you need to pray. One way to begin building a witnessing relationship is to show God's love to someone who is not a Christian. In the process of befriending that person, pave the way for sharing the gospel.

My family once lived across the street from a nice couple, who often asked our children to work for them. Although we became friends, this

Understanding the characteristics of God will help you know how to praise Him.

Praise God because of who He is, not because of what He does.

couple did not respond positively to a gospel witness. During the Christmas season I took a poinsettia to them. Soon the woman came over and asked if I would pray for her. She had obviously been drinking. Later, I was able to lead her to receive Christ. The act of giving the plant paved the way for me to witness. I was thankful that God had led me to prepare the way for the woman to receive the gospel.

 This week show God's love to a non-Christian by doing something kind for that person. Afterward, describe here what you did and the person's response.

_____

_____

 In the margin write this week's memory verse, John 15:7. Below the verse describe how you feel about beginning or developing the practice of praying in faith.

DAY 4

The Altar of Confession

After you have thanked God for what He has done and have praised Him for who He is, confess your sins to Him. In addition to glorifying and honoring God, you must also ask God to examine your heart.

THE NEED TO CONFESS SIN
Earlier this week you read about the prophet Isaiah's experience when he saw God and witnessed His glory. As this occurred, Isaiah also became aware of the contrast between God's holiness and his own sinfulness.

"At the sound of their voices the doorposts and thresholds shook and the temple was filled with smoke. 'Woe to me!' I cried. 'I am ruined! For I am a man of unclean lips, and I live among a people of unclean lips, and my eyes have seen the King, the Lord Almighty' " (Isa. 6:4-6).

Read Isaiah 6:4-6 in the margin and complete this sentence:

When Isaiah experienced the Lord's glory, he ___CONFESSED___ **his sin.**

When you approach God's throne and become aware of His presence, your personal sin confronts you and weighs heavy on your mind. After such a divine confrontation it is appropriate to confess your sin, just as Isaiah did when he experienced God's glory.

Before the death of Christ, people offered sacrifices in an effort to atone for their sins. They sacrificed blood offerings on an altar. Today no animal offering is required for you to atone for your sins. Christ offered Himself as a sacrifice for you so that your sins may be forgiven. First John 1:8-10, in the margin, says that when you confess your sins to the Father, He is faithful to forgive you.

In confession you let God examine your heart, and He shows you what separates you from Him—the barriers that keep you from experiencing Him to the fullest. Full fellowship with the Father is blocked if your life contains unconfessed sin. The beautiful words of Psalm 139 illustrate the proper attitude about confession. Read verses 23-24 in the margin. The psalmist displays an attitude of openness by asking God to make him aware of his unrighteousness so that he can grow. The Holy Spirit's job is to convict us of things that offend our holy God. You do not have to guess what might be sin in your life. If you open yourself to His leading, the Holy Spirit will show you things that offend God.

Reread 1 John 1:8-10 in the margin. According to this passage, why do you need to confess the sin in your life?
☑ The Father will forgive you and cleanse you.
☑ You deceive yourself and do not live in the truth if you claim to be above sin.
☑ The Father can show that He is faithful to His promise to forgive you when you confess sin.
☑ ~~So~~ that you will feel better.

The Father wants you to confess sin so that He can do what He has promised to do: forgive you and cleanse you. You fool only yourself when you claim to be sinless. The Father to whom you pray knows the sin in your heart. Confessing sin makes you feel better, but that is not the purpose. The purpose is to restore your fellowship with God. All of the answers except the last one are reasons for confessing sin.

Furthermore, as Psalm 66:18 reveals, God does not listen to your prayers if you continue to cling to your unrighteous ways, refusing to acknowledge and confess them. Confessing sin in your life is a crucial next step in your fellowship with the Father through prayer.

 In your quiet time today read Psalm 51, David's confession. After you have read this passage, complete the Daily Master Communication Guide on page 66. Do this before you read further.

WHAT DO YOU NEED TO CONFESS?

As you study about confession and ask the Lord to search your heart, a good passage to read is Ephesians 4:22-32. In this passage Paul addressed the church, but his admonitions apply in all relationships and to all behavior.

"If we claim to be without sin, we deceive ourselves and the truth is not in us. If we confess our sins, he is faithful and just and will forgive us our sins and purify us from all unrighteousness. If we claim we have not sinned, we make him out to be a liar and his word has no place in our lives" (1 John 1:8-10).

Search me, O God, and know my heart;
*   test me and know my anxious thoughts.*
See if there is any offensive way in me,
*   and lead me in the way everlasting (Ps. 139:23-24).*

If I had cherished sin in my heart,
*   the Lord would not have listened (Ps. 66:18).*

DAILY MASTER COMMUNICATION GUIDE

PSALM 51

What God said to me:

God is Mercifl
Loving, Father
Will Wash me
Clean, All
I has to ask
for forgive
Wesl

What I said to God:

God I Am
In A Sinfil
World Plas
help Me

Read Ephesians 4:22-32 and ask yourself, *What do I need to confess?* As you open yourself to the Lord, ask Him to point out what is not right in your life and to help you confess it.

You were taught, with regard to your former way of life, to put off your old self, which is being corrupted by its deceitful desires; to be made new in the attitude of your minds; and to put on the new self, created to be like God in true righteousness and holiness. Therefore each of you must put off falsehood and speak truthfully to his neighbor, for we are all members of one body. In your anger do not sin: Do not let the sun go down while you are still angry, and do not give the devil a foothold. He who has been stealing must steal no longer, but must work, doing something useful with his own hands, that he may have something to share with those in need. Do not let any unwholesome talk come out of your mouths, but only what is helpful for building others up according to their needs, that it may benefit those who listen. And do not grieve the Holy Spirit of God, with whom you were sealed for the day of redemption. Get rid of all bitterness, rage and anger, brawling and slander, along with every form of malice. Be kind and compassionate to one another, forgiving each other, just as in Christ God forgave you (Eph. 4:22-32).

Check anything of which the Lord convicted you:

- ☒ deceitful desires
- ☐ falsehood
- ☐ anger
- ☐ bitterness
- ☒ rage
- ☐ stealing
- ☒ brawling
- ☒ laziness
- ☒ slander
- ☐ unwholesome talk
- ☐ malice

Now write a confession in which you ask God to forgive you of the matter or matters you checked.

I Asked The Lord To forgive
me for all of The Above, bcause
doan Through Life I Shone I've didesoe
of any Then, when we say ontRue Abal
People they we steal Their Norl

Confession is an important part of maintaining a right relationship with God. Maturity in discipleship can be thought of as the degree to which you experience harmony, or wholeness, in relating to God and others. You experience this harmony when you have regular fellowship with Christ, that is, a daily pattern of praying in faith. That is why praying in faith is a major component of your lifelong, obedient relationship with Him.

LEARNING THE DISCIPLE'S CROSS

To summarize what you are learning about praying in faith, draw the portions of the Disciple's Cross you have studied. Draw a circle with Christ, the lower crossbar with Word written on it, and the accompanying Scriptures. Then draw the upper crossbar with prayer written on it. Under prayer write John 15:7, the verse that accompanies this discipline. Explain the cross aloud as you draw these parts. Be prepared to explain it at your next group session.

Maturity in discipleship can be thought of as the degree to which you experience harmony, or wholeness, in relating to God and others.

Continue memorizing John 15:7. Say this verse aloud to a family member or a friend. You may want to call one of your *MasterLife* group members for whom you are praying and to practice saying the verse to him or her as you remind the person of your prayers.

How are you progressing with your Prayer-Covenant List? Are you making notes of prayers as you see them answered? You may find it helpful to set aside a period of time every few weeks to study your Prayer-Covenant List and to praise God for answered prayers. You could do this as you travel by yourself on a lengthy trip. You could take it to a nearby park for time with the Lord. You could get up early one morning to examine it. I try to do this at least once a week. Then every month I go back over all of the requests to observe what God has done. I am constantly amazed that God answers so many of my prayers. As I read my prayer journal and prayer requests, God shows me how faithful He has been. Usually, not every request has been answered, but He teaches me to walk in faith by answering many of them.

Spend time on your Prayer-Covenant List. Pray for the prayer needs on it. Then decide on a time during the next week when you will study what God is doing in your life. Write the day and time here: _____.

DAY 5

In God's Presence

"Nothing in all creation is hidden from God's sight. Everything is uncovered and laid bare before the eyes of him to whom we must give account" (Heb. 4:13).

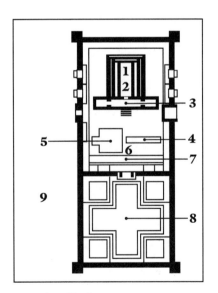

1. Holy of holies
2. Holy place
3. Porch
4. Slaughterhouse
5. Altar
6. Court of priests
7. Court of Israel
8. Court of women
9. Court of Gentiles

Now you find yourself in the presence of God. This is a holy place. The Father wants you to approach Him with your needs. He waits to grant what you ask that is in His will. He delights in doing so. Now that you have thanked Him for your blessings, have given Him the praise He is due, and have confessed your sins, you are ready to talk with Him about needs, both yours and others'.

BRINGING YOUR NEEDS TO GOD
When you think about praying for needs, you can think of the place in the temple called the holy of holies, the temple's most sacred area. In Bible times only the high priest had access to this innermost chamber. Because of Jesus Christ, however, you have access to God and can approach Him in all His holiness with the deepest needs of your heart. You can approach the innermost part of the very sanctuary of God. In that holy of holies everything is laid bare before Him, as the verse in the margin reveals.

In your quiet time today read Hebrews 4, which states that Jesus Christ is the only high priest you need. After you have read this passage, complete the Daily Master Communication Guide on page 71.

In the chapter you read, Hebrews 4:14-16, in the margin on the next page, states that Jesus, as our Great High Priest, understands our needs.

How does Hebrews 4:14-16 tell you that you are to approach God's throne of grace?
With CONfiDENCE

You can approach God's throne of grace with confidence because, as the Scripture says, He is ready to grant you mercy and grace to help you in your time of need. He is pleased to hear your personal requests. How do you know that Jesus wants you to pray freely about your needs? Your memory verse for this week ensures it.

As you think about the marvelous promise in your Scripture-memory verse, John 15:7, say the verse aloud again. As you say it, think about a loving God who finds your requests pleasing to His ears.

PRAYING FOR YOURSELF

Today you will study two types of requests: petition and intercession. Petition is asking for yourself. You know that God encourages people to pray for their personal concerns, because His Word is filled with answered requests. For example, Luke 1:13 contains God's response to Zechariah's petition for a son. His request was answered with the birth of John the Baptist.

God's answers to your prayers help mold you into the person He wants you to become. He does not grant petitions that you pray for the wrong reason or that He knows would bring the wrong outcome in your life. Read 1 John 5:14-15 in the margin.

List personal needs for which you desire to pray. Use the following categories to prompt your thinking, but do not limit your list to these or feel that you must write a request for each one. You may need to use extra paper to expand your list.

Christ-honoring relationships with others: _Lord I have family, Friends, Nab, Jon Also Eknow that Need Ya 2 PRaisE ya better than Amen_

The ability to manage my time wisely: _PRaisE you God And Thank you for helping me to do the Right Thing with my time on_

Concerns on my job: _Lord you Know my Need I thank you for the Job I did had And the one that will care me_

My ministry at church: _Lord I Thank you on PRaise your Name that I'll be able to do thy will on me_

Guidance in my vocation: _Lord help me to be worthy I know you has chose me I Thank you_

"Since we have a great high priest who has gone through the heavens, Jesus the Son of God, let us hold firmly to the faith we profess. For we do not have a high priest who is unable to sympathize with our weaknesses, but we have one who has been tempted in every way, just as we are—yet was without sin. Let us then approach the throne of grace with confidence, so that we may receive mercy and find grace to help us in our time of need" (Heb. 4:14-16).

"This is the confidence we have in approaching God: that if we ask anything according to his will, he hears us" (1 John 5: 14-15).

Physical and emotional health: *Thank you for my health I'll be able to do thy w/*

Ability to resist temptation: *Saten stay on my tail help me to tell him to git behind*

Material needs: *You knew my need z thank you for them*

"Confess your sins to each other and pray for each other so that you may be healed. The prayer of a righteous man is powerful and effective" (Jas. 5:16).

" 'Holy Father, protect them by the power of your name—the name you gave me—so that they may be one as we are one. My prayer is not that you take them out of the world but that you protect them from the evil one. Sanctify them by the truth; your word is truth' " (John 17:11,15,17).

God uses you as His vehicle to accomplish His will when you pray for others.

Now stop and pray about some of these requests. Pray for God's will in the outcomes of these situations and concerns.

PRAYING FOR OTHERS
The second type of prayer for needs is intercession—prayer for others. The Bible instructs us to pray for one another, as James 5:16, in the margin, indicates. Jesus prayed for His disciples many times. One of the best examples is found in John 17, in which Jesus prayed for His disciples before He went to the cross. A portion of that prayer appears in the margin. You pray for others for the same reason you pray for yourself: so that God can mold them into the persons He wants them to become. God uses you as His vehicle to accomplish His will when you pray for others.

How important to you is intercession for others? Check the answer that describes you.
❑ I am too busy taking care of my own needs to pray for others.
❑ I intercede for others after I handle other areas of ministry.
❑ I intercede for others only in extreme crises, such as when someone is critically ill.
❑ Interceding for others is highly important to me because God can use my intercession to accomplish His will.

Stop and pray, asking the Father to make you a more fervent intercessor for others.

As you have kept your Prayer-Covenant List for the past several weeks, you have been interceding for others. By lifting your concerns to Him, you have been an instrument God has used to accomplish His will in the lives of others. Now is a good time to review some of those prayers of intercession.

List two persons on your Prayer-Covenant List and their needs. Describe ways God has answered your prayers for these individu-

als. Even if you have seen only partial or incremental answers, list those below. Then pray, thanking God for hearing your prayers. Ask Him to continue to work His will in the lives of those individuals.

Name	Request	Answer
Cheglon Smily	healed brot stroke + nesbe	
Jackie + Anthoy	hns a Normul Heolthy baby in 206	

To review, list the two types of prayers for needs you have studied today. Look back if you need to refresh your memory.

Praying for yourself: _Lord Send Your Angel To Prot me And Luke 1:13_

Praying for others: _Lord I thank you for Reoting + Taking Cane of Thea John 17:11_

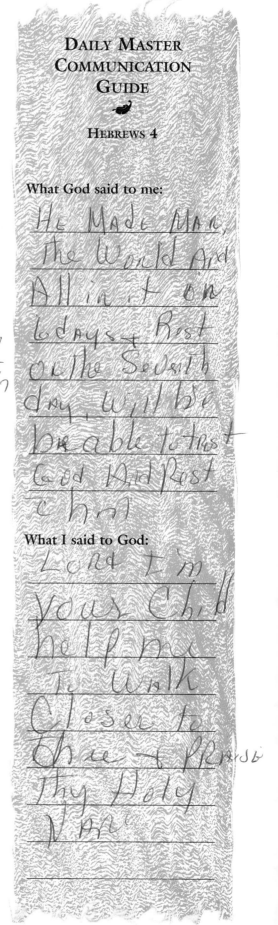

DAILY MASTER COMMUNICATION GUIDE

HEBREWS 4

What God said to me:

He Made Man, the World And All in it on 6days + Rest on the Sevnth day, will be be able to trust God And Rest c hm

What I said to God:

Lord I'm Your Child help me To Walk Closer to thee + Praise Thy Holy Nan

For several weeks you have practiced a daily quiet time. Even if you have struggled with it, find someone with whom you can share your testimony about having a daily quiet time. Share with someone who needs to develop this practice or with a friend. This will strengthen your resolve for having a quiet time.

HAS THIS WEEK MADE A DIFFERENCE?

Review "My Walk with the Master This Week" at the beginning of this week's material. Mark the activities you have finished by drawing vertical lines in the diamonds beside them. Finish any incomplete activities. Think about what you will say during your group session about your work on these activities.

As you complete your study of "Pray in Faith," reflect on the experiences you have had this week.
- Have you been praying in faith this week?
- Is having a quiet time becoming a regular part of your life?
- Are you keeping a Prayer-Covenant List and making notes of answers to prayer?

Through this week's work I hope that you have become more aware of how praying in faith helps you develop the disciplines of a disciple and contributes to your lifelong, obedient relationship with Christ. Jesus' purpose in teaching His disciples how to pray was to teach them how to know the Father through prayer. Have you come to know more about the Father through this week's study? Where do you stand now in terms of your lifelong, obedient relationship with Him? Congratulations on taking these important steps. Learning to pray the way Christ wants you to is not easy. It requires that you set aside a self-centered way of life and

Starting your prayers with thanksgiving, praise, and confession before making requests means that you have Someone besides yourself at the center of your life.

look for His will for you instead of your will for yourself. Starting your prayers with thanksgiving, praise, and confession before making requests means that you have Someone besides yourself at the center of your life.

Throughout *MasterLife* you will continue to learn how to pray in faith. When you study book 3, you will see the fullness of all God wants to do in your life through prayer. Following Jesus means that you seek to know and do His will, not just coast through life. By now in *Master-Life* you have seen the sacrifices you need to make in order to walk with the Master and to live in Him. I affirm your willingness to make these sacrifices in order to grow as a disciple of Christ.

WEEK 4

Fellowship with Believers

This Week's Goal
You will experience growth in Christ through relationships in His body.

My Walk with the Master This Week
You will complete the following activities to develop the six biblical disciplines. When you have completed each activity, draw a vertical line in the diamond beside it.

SPEND TIME WITH THE MASTER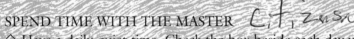
◇ Have a daily quiet time. Check the box beside each day you have a quiet time this week: ❑ Sunday ❑ Monday ❑ Tuesday ❑ Wednesday
❑ Thursday ❑ Friday ❑ Saturday

LIVE IN THE WORD
◇ Read your Bible every day. Write what God says to you and what you say to God.
◇ Memorize John 13:34-35.
◇ Review Luke 9:23, John 15:5, John 8:31-32, and John 15:7.

PRAY IN FAITH
◇ Pray with your prayer partner.
◇ Pray about your priorities and your use of time.
◇ Add requests to your Prayer-Covenant List.

FELLOWSHIP WITH BELIEVERS
◇ Befriend someone in the church who is not a close friend or is not in your *MasterLife* group.

WITNESS TO THE WORLD
◇ Plan your time, using "How to Use MasterTime" and the MasterTime form.
◇ Read "Redeeming the Time" and underline portions that apply to you.

MINISTER TO OTHERS
◇ Continue learning the Disciple's Cross. Explain the meaning of the right crossbar to add to the information about the circle and the vertical crossbar that you learned in previous weeks. Learn the Scriptures that go with each part of the cross.

This Week's Scripture-Memory Verses
" 'A new command I give you: Love one another. As I have loved you, so you must love one another. By this all men will know that you are my disciples, if you love one another' " (John 13:34-35).

DAY 1

❧

The Mark of a Disciple

When missionary Bruce Schmidt was negotiating to buy three acres of land in a Ugandan valley to begin a new work among unreached people, he found himself face to face with a leader of the Karamojong, one of the most feared tribes in East Africa. "Why are you here, and what do you want?" the chief demanded.

Bruce replied that he was in the valley because of two great things: the Great Commission, which he explained, and the Great Commandment. "In the Great Commandment Jesus said that we are to love God first and to love our neighbor as ourselves. I want to be your neighbor."

To Bruce's surprise, the Karamojong leader voiced no objection. Instead, he appeared to be moved by Bruce's remarks. "Nobody wants to be the neighbor of the Karamojong. We are the most despised tribe in Uganda. All of our neighboring tribes have had their cattle stolen, their women raped, and their men murdered. We can't believe you want to be our neighbor!" the man exclaimed.

By the time the meeting ended, God had melted hearts of stone. This feared Karamojong tribe ultimately gave Bruce and his coworkers 30 acres of land for their new mission work—all because of neighborly love that Bruce extended in Jesus Christ. Although most of us are not placed in a foreign land with hostile tribes as neighbors, we often face hostility as Christians in an evil world. Like Bruce, we are to love our neighbors.

LOVING ONE ANOTHER

Jesus never intended for you to operate in a vacuum. You cannot be a balanced Christian if you neglect loving relationships with others. If you try to live apart from the fellowship of other believers—the church, which is Christ's body—you will not experience fullness of life in Christ. The Lord put us in a body of believers because sustaining life outside the body is difficult. As we stay connected to people in fellowship and as we love one another, we gain strength from one another.

As we stay connected to people in fellowship and as we love one another, we gain strength from one another.

> "'A new command I give you: Love one another. As I have loved you, so you must love one another. By this all men will know that you are my disciples, if you love one another'" (John 13:34-35).

✞ **Read this week's Scripture-memory verses, John 13:34-35, in the margin. What did Jesus say identifies His disciples?**

by Loving one another all will Know ~~this name~~ *by C isa p18*

Now go back and read John 13:34-35 aloud from one to three times to begin memorizing these verses.

Jesus said that one identifying mark of a disciple is your love for others. Love shows the world that you are His disciple. Loving others and being involved in harmonious fellowship with them show that Christ is at the center of your life. Loving relationships are at the very heart of life in Christ. He shows you Himself through fellowship with others. Jesus did not tell His followers to go it alone but to demonstrate the love He modeled for them. You do this in fellowship with other believers.

Read the following case studies.

Martha loved the outdoors and enjoyed long walks in the woods. Although Martha was a Christian, she did not attend church, reciting an excuse many people use: "I can worship God better when I'm enjoying His creation." Members of a Bible-study group invited her to attend, but Martha chose to pursue her outdoor interests instead.

Joe had given his life to Christ several years ago but had never become involved in a church. Even though members of a church in his neighborhood visited him, Joe declined to attend. A shy person, Joe could not imagine himself conversing with strangers.

Underline the excuses Martha and Joe used for declining to fellowship with believers. What kinds of activities do you choose to do instead of fellowship with believers? List them.

Martha   outdoor interests
Joe   could not have Talk To strangers

Exploring God's creation is a wonderful way to be aware of His blessings and glory, but it does not take the place of the fellowship Christ intended for you to have with other believers. Shyness around others is a painful matter for some people, but the Father can give you strength to overcome weaknesses so that you can be part of the body. When you have life in Christ and abide in Him, you follow His commands. John 15:12 says, " 'My command is this: Love each other as I have loved you.' "

Why does John 15:12 say that you are to love other persons?

Christ Commanded it

John 15:12 says that you are to love other persons because Christ commanded it. Love flows from God through Christ to humankind. Having modeled love for you, Christ commands you to exhibit it to others. Shutting yourself off from the fellowship of others impairs your ability to show love to others and prevents their exhibiting love to you. Your local church represents the body of Christ, in which you can fellowship with other believers. Hebrews 10:24-25, in the margin, clearly teaches that we are to meet together with other believers.

Love shows the world that you are His disciple.

"Let us consider how we may spur one another on toward love and good deeds. Let us not give up meeting together, as some are in the habit of doing, but let us encourage one another—and all the more as you see the Day approaching" (Heb. 10:24-25).

"Each one should use whatever gift he has received to serve others, faithfully administering God's grace in its various forms" (1 Pet. 4:10).

" 'As the Father has loved me, so have I loved you. Now remain in my love' " (John 15:9).

Isolation and individualism are not Christ's ways. Christ brings believers together as a family. We should encourage our fellow Christians to express love for one another. Worshiping together is one way we gain strength and motivation from other disciples. As the verse from 1 Peter in the margin indicates, Christians are to be part of a body of believers, using their gifts to serve others and receiving instruction from God's Word. Anyone who professes to be a Christian but does not attend church is disregarding God's Word and is living outside His will.

The abundant love God the Father has for His Son, Jesus Christ, is the source of the love the Son has for His followers. It is also the model for the love you are to have for others. The depths of Jesus' love, which led Him to the cross, should not surprise you, because it is modeled in the love the Father has for the Son. Read John 15:9 in the margin.

LEARNING THE DISCIPLE'S CROSS

The fourth discipline of a disciple's life, then, is fellowshipping with believers. You will study this discipline this week as you continue to learn and add to the Disciple's Cross. While the vertical crossbar you have studied for the past two weeks emphasizes your relationship with Christ through the Word and prayer, the horizontal crossbar you will study this week and in week 5 stresses the importance of your relationship with others through fellowship and witness.

Draw the portions of the Disciple's Cross you have studied. Draw a circle with *Christ* in the center and draw the lower crossbar with *Word* written on it. Then draw the upper crossbar with *prayer* written on it. Add the verses that apply. Now draw the right crossbar and write *fellowship* on it. Under *fellowship* write *John 13:34-35,* the verses that accompany it. Refer to the completed cross on page 136 if you need help.

↕ Continue reading your Bible daily during your quiet time. Today read 1 Corinthians 12:12-31, which depicts the special relationship between you and other Christians. After you have read this passage, complete the Daily Master Communication Guide in the margin.

DAY 2

The Gift of Accountability

God has shown me many times that I can do nothing without the fellowship of believers in the body of Christ. When I was in college, my friends and I decided to conduct a huge youth revival in my friend's hometown of Borger, Texas. We secured the high-school auditorium, put up huge billboards, announced the event on the radio, and delivered posters to stores. But at the last minute high-school officials told us that church leaders in the community—members of our own denomination—had pressured the school not to let us use the facility. Because we had not sought the local churches' involvement in advance, our plan was backfiring.

I prayed, "Lord, You cannot let us down after we have done so much to prepare," but He taught us another lesson: that we could do nothing without Him. We had undertaken this task on our own for God rather than asking what He wanted. We had talked and prayed about the revival but had then gone ahead with our plans.

This experience was a crushing defeat but a lesson well learned. We left town, convinced that we would not again try to do anything without God's direct leadership and without working within the framework of the local church.

Have you ever had a disappointing experience in Christian service because you were working outside the fellowship of believers? ☑ Yes ❑ No If so, describe your experience.

_____

_____

My friends and I had not first prayed in faith for God's direction before we proceeded. We had not asked God to search our hearts to determine whether selfish motives and desires for success were driving our plans. We had not sought the local churches' support. We had failed to live as part of the body of Christ.

DAILY MASTER COMMUNICATION GUIDE

1 CORINTHIANS 12:12-31

What God said to me:

we
I Cant do nothing with out Christ And We Must Fellowship with Other becpse God Made All of US + Love all of us

What I said to God:

I will tay to do thy Will Fellow Ship with Other

↑ Say aloud your memory verses for the week. Write what these verses say about the importance of fellowshipping with Christ's people.

christ Give us a NEW Comand thrt we Lene EAch othr because he Caper did for that's his Command

You may have answered something like this: I may be obedient to Christ in a number of ways, but unless I demonstrate love for His people, I do not show that I am His disciple.

GOD WORKS THROUGH OTHERS

Many times God reveals Himself through the individuals He places in your path. Life in Christ includes trying to live in fellowship with your brothers and sisters. Often through that fellowship others speak a God-anointed word to you that helps you see a problem more clearly or make the right decision. Christian friends can help hold you accountable for times when you get off course. They can remind you of what the Word says. They can lovingly help you recognize your misplaced priorities. The Father works through others in the church to accomplish His will in your life.

Many times God reveals Himself through the individuals He places in your path.

Read these case studies and answer the questions that follow.

Anita and her grown daughter had not spoken in years. Anita longed to make relations right between them. She invited her daughter home for a special weekend to attempt to repair their relationship. Anita spent every spare moment of the weekend cooking food for her daughter and buying her presents, hoping these actions would make her daughter want to be close to her. She also asked her friends at church to pray for them.

How could Anita's friends at church show love for her?

PRay At her hone with her Asked her To Listen to what her daughter had to say

Charles worked two jobs to provide income for his family. He was away from home so much that he was seldom available to his wife and children. His children wanted him to attend their sports games and school events, but Charles had to miss most of them. He managed to take his family to church about twice a month.

How could fellowship with other believers help Charles?

work in some of chunk place so he can spent more time in family

In Anita's story you may have noted that Christian friends could have visited with Anita and prayed with her about her daughter. Without necessarily giving her advice, they could have helped Anita examine her choices. What had she done to make things right? Had Anita apologized to her daughter for any wrong on her part? Had she discussed the situation with her pastor or with a Christian counselor? Christian friends could invite Anita to church activities to give her other focuses in her life. They could lovingly model ways she could connect with the Vine as the source of help.

For Charles's situation you may have replied that Christian friends could help with his employment situation. They could help him network among church members to find a job with better pay, which would eliminate the need for two jobs. They could invite him to family activities planned by the church to provide opportunities for him to be with his children in a church setting. Men could include him in their accountability-and-support group. They could lovingly help Charles see his children's need for him and could help him connect with the Vine as the source of power.

AN INSTRUMENT OF CHRIST'S LOVE
If you want to be Jesus' true disciple and to have a personal, lifelong, obedient relationship with Him, you will show love for others by fellowshipping with them and by being Christ's instrument in their lives. Christ's love can flow through you to them. You can help them be all Christ wants them to be. The right crossbar of fellowship on the Disciple's Cross reminds you of the importance of your relationships with others.

 Say aloud your Scripture-memory verses for this week, John 13:34-35. Say them to your prayer partner in your prayer time this week.

Read 1 Corinthians 12:31—13:13 during your quiet time. Let God speak to you through this passage about loving one another. After reading this passage, complete the Daily Master Communication Guide in the margin.

DAILY MASTER COMMUNICATION GUIDE

1 CORINTHIANS 12:31—13:13

What God said to me:

_____

_____

_____

_____

_____

_____

What I said to God:

_____

_____

_____

_____

_____

_____

_____

_____

DAY 3

Help for Withered Christians

Fellowship with other Christians is also crucial to avoid withering in your Christian life.

Fellowship with other Christians is also crucial to avoid withering in your Christian life. Roy Edgemon, my longtime colleague and one of the "three men at the gate" who encouraged me to bring *MasterLife* to the United States, recalls a time when the fellowship of other Christians—the aspect of the Disciple's Cross you are studying this week— helped revive him in the midst of spiritual withering.

As a busy pastor in Texas, Roy was almost burned out from church building programs and heavy involvement in state denominational leadership. One night a missionary from Africa named Bud Frey conducted a rally at Roy's church in Odessa, Texas. As Frey described a recent period of spiritual withering and exhaustion, "I could tell he had been in the same shape I was in," Roy said. Frey said a Christian friend admonished him, "You're a Bud Frey cause, not a Jesus cause." The friend urged him to "find out how the Lord needs to have His way with you." Frey said he began learning how to be a Jesus cause, changing his lifestyle to ensure a daily quiet time and a more personal relationship with Christ.

Roy took out a slip of paper, wrote a note, and passed it down the aisle to Frey. The note said, "If you know how I can stop this world long enough to get off, I want to talk to you." But to Roy's embarrassment, before the note could make its way down the aisle to Frey, a friend, Bill Hogue, read the message and wrote under Roy's comment, "Me too."

"I didn't want anyone to know I was in that kind of shape," said Roy. But Roy, Bill Hogue, and their wives spent most of the remainder of the night talking and praying with Bud Frey. The meeting resulted in life change for Roy, he said.

"I started getting up in the morning and praying regularly," Roy recalls. "Before, if we didn't have decisions in every service, I had taken it as a personal defeat. I was doing the Lord's work but wasn't letting the Lord work through me." Fellowship with other Christians who shared their own brokenness helped encourage and restore this pastor to a life of usefulness in God's kingdom.

Has fellowship with a Christian friend ever helped you when you were withering spiritually and were not experiencing a victorious life in Christ? ❏ Yes ❏ No If so, describe this experience.

_____

_____

Read 2 Timothy 1:1-14, which depicts the special relationship between Paul and Timothy, during your quiet time today. After you have read this passage, complete the Daily Master Communication Guide in the margin.

A NETWORK OF SUPPORT

You can also encourage others as you become an instrument of Christ. What happens to your fellow church members is important to you. First Corinthians 12:27 says, "You are the body of Christ, and each one of you is a part of it." If one member of the body withers—experiences illness, loss, or a diminished spiritual life—the entire body suffers, including you. The body cares for each member of the body so that together all of the members become more complete in Christ's love.

Fellowship among Christians can span the globe, thanks to modern technological methods such as electronic mail. One of my colleagues at work regularly uses electronic mail to encourage a pastor in another state who is experiencing interpersonal challenges in his congregation. This fellowship across the miles and computer networks can help remedy the isolation and loneliness of pastors who sometimes feel that they have few confidantes in their communities. Christians urgently need fellowship with other believers.

SHARING WHAT GOD IS DOING

God may want you to help build up the body by sharing what He is doing in your life. Have you shared with other believers ways you are growing in Christ as you learn what being His disciple means? You can tell others about your experiences of praying in faith, memorizing Scripture, or a daily quiet time. Sharing your experiences may lead another person to seek a closer relationship with the Lord.

As you work today on this week's Scripture-memory verses, John 13:34-35, tell someone how you have grown in Christ from the practice of memorizing Scripture.

Stop and pray, asking God to show you how He wants you to work within the body of Christ to encourage others.

DAILY MASTER COMMUNICATION GUIDE

2 TIMOTHY 1:1-14

What God said to me:

3 _____
4 _____
5 _____
6 _____

_____
_____
_____
_____

What I said to God:

Thank you
God

DAY 4

What Christ Expects

" 'As the Father has loved me, so have I loved you. My command is this: Love each other as I have loved you. Greater love has no one than this, that he lay down his life for his friends' " (John 15:9,12-13).

When disciples fellowship with other believers, they take care to develop Christ-honoring relationships with others. Relationships do not just happen. They require careful cultivation and nurture. Because all of us have sinful natures, we can fall into patterns of thoughtlessness in the way we treat others. Hatred, snobbery, jealousy, and backbiting have no place in the life of a follower of Christ. The Scriptures instruct us about how Christ expects us to treat others with whom we fellowship.

FRIENDSHIP: A HIGH PRIORITY
Read John 15:9,12-13 in the margin.

Why are you to love other persons?

Because Christ FRist Love us

A friend loves at all times, and a brother is born for adversity (Prov. 17:17).

At the heart of friendship is the willingness to _give up our life_ **if necessary.**

" 'If your brother sins against you, go and show him his fault, just between the two of you. If he listens to you, you have won your brother over. But if he will not listen, take one or two others along, so that every matter may be established by the testimony of two or three witnesses' " (Matt. 18:15).

You should love other persons because of the love that flows from God through Christ to you. Jesus put so much value on friendship and fellowship that He said friends should be willing even to give their lives for one another if necessary. Jesus made friendship a high priority! Jesus laid down His life for others, and later, some of His disciples did, too. Fellowshipping with other believers and loving those believers with the kind of sacrificial love that Jesus demonstrated are important parts of life in Christ and of a lifelong, obedient relationship with Him.

"Brothers, do not slander one another. Anyone who speaks against his brother or judges him speaks against the law and judges it" (Jas. 4:11).

Examine what the Bible says about the way friends are to act toward one another. Read the verses in the margin. Then match each reference in the left column with the correct statement in the right column.

"We proclaim to you what we have seen and heard, so that you also may have fellowship with us. And our fellowship is with the Father and with his Son, Jesus Christ" (1 John 1:3).

__D__ 1. Proverbs 17:17   a. **Friends care enough to confront one another in love if necessary.**

__A__ 2. Matthew 18:15   b. **Friends do not gossip or make hurtful remarks about one another.**

__B__ 3. James 4:11   c. **Friends want the best for one another and therefore present the gospel to friends who do not know Christ.**

__C__ 4. 1 John 1:3   d. **Friends love one another regardless of the situations they face.**

Now review the statements in the right column that describe characteristics of friendship. Draw a star beside the trait or traits that represent the biggest challenges in your friendships. Stop and pray that God will change you in these areas through Christ's love.

Was one of the statements you checked item a—caring enough to confront? People sometimes struggle with this issue, believing that confronting a friend is not Christlike because it seems to call for hostility. Actually, confronting a friend in love is a very caring act. Sometimes people tell others that they have a problem with a friend yet never go directly to that person. That type of indirect communication can hurt the relationship. It can also hurt the body of Christ. Disagreements between individuals in a church can escalate, widening their circle to include others. Eventually, small disputes can develop into major rifts that prevent the body of Christ from doing its work.

Jesus was very clear about how Christians are to resolve difficulties face to face. These Bible verses tell you how a follower of Christ relates to others. You can learn loving, diplomatic ways to communicate how you feel so that such communication strengthens and does not harm the relationship. The correct answers to the previous exercise are 1. d, 2. a, 3. b, 4. c. Book 4 discusses more about how to reconcile broken relationships.

THE COST OF NEGLECTING RELATIONSHIPS
Sometimes you may find that you have closed yourself off from persons who care about you. Do you shut out persons rather than get involved in their lives? Do you avoid persons rather than risk cultivating relationships? Because you have been hurt in past friendships perhaps you withdraw rather than make yourself vulnerable again. Even if you attend church, you may not allow friendships to form there. You may think you can attend, listen to the sermon, and then spend the rest of the week avoiding fellow believers who might want to get involved in your life.

In the previous paragraph underline statements or questions with which you can identify.

If you avoid fellowshipping with believers because you do not want to risk relationships, you miss opportunities to serve your family in Christ. When difficulties come your way, relationships with other believers can provide resources to meet your needs. The most serious result of neglecting fellowship with believers is that it inevitably creates distance between you and God.

Read 1 Thessalonians 2:1-13 today during your quiet time. After you have read about Paul's love for and ministry with the Christians at Thessalonica, complete the Daily Master Communication Guide in the margin.

DAILY MASTER COMMUNICATION GUIDE

1 THESSALONIANS 2:1-13

What God said to me:

What I said to God:

Paul's example with the Thessalonians can guide you in relating to your *MasterLife* group members. Likely by now, after four group sessions together, you are forming a special bond with your group members. Although you may not have known some of these persons well before you began studying *MasterLife*, long, enduring friendships can form as a result of this fellowship. You may begin to see in these persons some of the traits of friendship you studied on page 82. Be thankful for the trust, support, and fellowship that have begun to develop.

Take to heart John 15:12-13, the verses you have read several times this week, and lovingly lift your group members to the Father in prayer. Stop now and pray for each of your *MasterLife* group members by name. Ask God to bless each person through this study. Ask Him to help you be available as a friend to your fellow members.

USING YOUR TIME EFFECTIVELY

A lack of time is an excuse you may use when you assess why you do not take advantage of—or create—opportunities to fellowship with believers. Perhaps you have already had difficulty finding time to do your daily assignments. For the rest of today and in day 5 you will learn ways to be a better steward of your time.

 The following suggestions can help you use your time more effectively. As you read them, underline statements that seem relevant to you.

> **REDEEMING THE TIME**
> We search for time and yearn for more. Time has become our most cherished possession. Our world focuses on the race against time, and the clock dictates the tempo of our lives.
>
> **Ask God's Purpose for Our Time**
> Time is God's gift to us. The art of having time occurs when we live according to God's purposes. We are responsible to Him for every minute He gives us. If we listen to Him more carefully, our lives are more harmonious. When we treat time as a gift from God, we spend our time in ways that are more consistent with His purposes. We become good stewards of our time. We find that the events of our lives flow together more smoothly and that we have more time to do the things that need to be done.
>
> **Ask God's Direction for the Day**
> Time is an opportunity God gives us to discover and carry out His purposes. If we believe that Christ is the Lord of our time, we can believe that He has a design for this day, as well as for our entire lives. Knowing and doing God's will for our lives involves knowing and doing God's will for this day in our lives.

When we treat time as a gift from God, we spend our time in ways that are more consistent with His purposes.

Prioritize What You Do Before You Do It

The apostle Paul said that wisdom is related to the use of time: "Be very careful, then, how you live—not as unwise but as wise, making the most of every opportunity, because the days are evil" (Eph. 5:15-16). The word translated "making the most of every opportunity" literally means "buying up every chance" or snapping up bargains at a sale. God's time is a priceless commodity. He calls us to invest our opportunities in worthwhile pursuits. The wise use of time means being alert to every opportunity for Christian ministry and witness. Seize the critical moment when it arrives: the chance encounter, the turn in conversation, the unplanned incident. Be prepared, expect such opportunities, and grasp them. Do not miss a chance to do Christ's work at the wise moment!

Do It in Priority Order, but Leave Yourself Open for God to Redirect You

We experience freedom when we obey God's purposes. Jesus was a truly free but purposeful person living an unhurried life. Jesus had plenty of time to speak to a foreign woman he met at a well, to spend holidays with His disciples, to admire the lilies of the field, to wash His disciples' feet, to answer their naive questions patiently. Most important, He had time to spend a whole night in prayer before an important decision.

A time of quiet meditation is good for our spiritual lives. We rediscover how to take things easily, how to rest as God commanded, how to meditate and pray. In quietness we rediscover the inner peace the world needs. We make a clear distinction between what is really important and what is secondary.

The wise use of time means being alert to every opportunity for Christian ministry and witness.

Check the benefits you are receiving from your daily quiet time.
- ☒ Learning how to take things easily
- ❏ Learning how to rest as God commanded
- ☒ Learning how to meditate and pray
- ❏ Rediscovering inner peace
- ❏ Learning to distinguish between what is really important and what is secondary

Draw a star beside the above area or areas you still need to work on.

 Continue to memorize this week's Scripture-memory verses, John 13:34-35. Write them in the margin from one to three times. Review the verses you memorized earlier.

True fellowship
is honesty

DAY 5

The Model of Friendship

"You are my friends if you do what I command. I no longer call you servants, because a servant does not know his master's business. Instead, I have called you friends, for everything that I learned from my Father I have made known to you'" (John 15:14-15).

"You did not choose me, but I chose you and appointed you to go and bear fruit—fruit that will last. Then the Father will give you whatever you ask in my name. This is my command: Love each other'" (John 15: 16-17).

"My prayer is ... that all of them may be one, Father, just as you are in me and I am in you. May they also be in us so that the world may believe that you have sent me. I have given them the glory that you gave me, that they may be one as we are one. May they be brought to complete unity to let the world know that you sent me and have loved them even as you have loved me'" (John 17:20-22).

Fellowship was the centerpiece of one of Jesus' last messages to His disciples as He was on the way to the cross. He wanted to tell His most beloved followers all they would need to know to carry on His work after He was no longer on earth physically.

Read John 15:14-15 in the margin. Underline two things Jesus considered important to communicate to His disciples.

Jesus wanted the disciples to know that He considered them friends, not servants. Their relationship was that of friends who loved one another in fellowship. He also wanted them to know that He had taught them everything He learned from His Father. Unlike the guarded way someone would treat servants, the Master openly discussed His business with the disciples. Jesus was reminding His disciples that they would have all the knowledge they needed to do His work after He was gone.

Like the disciples, you have all the knowledge you need to do the Father's work. The marching orders for discipleship that Jesus gave His followers are the same orders today for your lifelong, obedient relationship with Christ. Jesus is your friend. He set the model for fellowship, and you as His disciple can act on that model.

In John 15:16-17, in the margin, underline the three things Jesus wanted to happen in the lives of His disciples.

This passage emphasizes the high priority Jesus placed on fellowship with believers. He emphasized three reasons He chose the disciples: He appointed them to (1) bear fruit, (2) ask the Father in His name, and (3) love one another. In week 3 you learned about the second of those reasons as you studied praying in faith. You will study more in week 5 about bearing fruit. The third priority, loving one another, is the emphasis of this week's study. Christian love is not the identifying mark of extraordinary disciples—those who go beyond the call of duty. It is the identifying mark of all disciples. Those who obey His commands love one another.

A STRONG BODY

The encouragement that springs from fellowship with believers also gives you strength to witness. John 17:20-22, in the margin, describes the complete unity that Christ wants in the body. People who are united in Christ can be effective witnesses for Him. Jesus wanted unity, not division, in the church so that others would believe in Him. A church with members who argue and fail to demonstrate love to one another does not appear to a lost world as if it has something to offer.

Furthermore, believers need one another's encouragement when they try to win others to Christ. Fellow church members can pray for you, encourage you, and help ground you in Scripture as you prepare to share your faith. The church can make you feel useful and supported when you witness to persons who need the Lord.

If you have friends, coworkers, family members, or other acquaintances who do not know Jesus, perhaps you have listed them on your Prayer-Covenant List. Continue to pray in faith that you will seek strength from the body of Christ for witnessing opportunities that the Father puts in your path. Pray that God will give you an opportunity and will help you plan a time to share about your relationship with Christ.

 Stop now and review your Prayer-Covenant List. Perhaps this day's study has brought other persons or requests to mind. Add them to the list now.

 Say aloud your Scripture-memory verses, John 13:34-35, to someone you consider to be a caring friend. Use this as an opportunity to thank this person for his or her friendship.

 Again read John 15 in your quiet time today. This time look for teachings about the discipline a Christian needs to fellowship with believers. When you have read this passage, complete the Daily Master Communication Guide in the margin.

MOVING BEYOND YOUR COMFORT ZONE

Perhaps fellowshipping with believers is easy for you as long as you are within your comfort zone. You likely have a comfortable circle of friends in your Bible-study group, in your *MasterLife* group, or in another area of your church. But when Christ commands you to love others, He does not put restrictions on those you are to love. Sometimes you may need to reach outside your close circle of friends to extend fellowship.

Befriend someone in your church or at work who is not in your close circle of friends or in your *MasterLife* group.

When you think about extending yourself outside your familiar circle, the old protest about time may arise again. You may counter: I barely have time for myself and my family's needs. How can you ask me to take time to get to know someone else? Yesterday you read about redeeming the time to become a better steward of your time. Today you will learn to use a MasterTime form to set your priorities. You will find the MasterTime form on page 138.

Although I like to do things spontaneously, I have learned that in

DAILY MASTER COMMUNICATION GUIDE

JOHN 15

What God said to me:

_____

_____

_____

_____

_____

_____

_____

What I said to God:

_____

_____

_____

_____

_____

_____

_____

order to get the priority things done, I must plan my schedule every day, using the MasterTime process. I never get everything I planned to do finished, but at least I know that I have done the priority things. If I do not prioritize my time, others will prioritize it for me.

 Here are directions for using MasterTime. As you read, underline portions that seem important to you.

HOW TO USE MASTERTIME

1. Trust the Lord to direct you in all you do: "Trust in the Lord with all your heart. Never rely on what you think you know. Remember the Lord in everything you do, and he will show you the right way" (Prov. 3:5-6, GNB).
   - Ask God to show you His purposes for you in His kingdom: " 'Seek first his kingdom and his righteousness, and all these things will be given to you as well' " (Matt. 6:33).
   - Make annual, monthly, and weekly lists of the major goals you believe God has given you.

2. Plan your daily work under the Master's leadership: "You may make your plans, but God directs your actions" (Prov. 16:9, GNB).
   - List on the MasterTime form the things you need to do by basic categories. Plan one day or each day for a week, including all areas of your life: God, family, church, and recreation.
   - Write under the "Time" column on the form the amount of time you estimate you need to complete each task. You may prefer to write the time of day you plan to do it, for example, "See Mr. Jones, 9:00–9:30 a.m."
   - Rank the tasks according to your priorities and write that number in the "Priority" column on the form. You may choose to rank only within categories, since you can save time by doing similar tasks in order, such as telephoning. You may also rank them without any regard to category. Minutes spent in planning save hours. Set aside time for planning at the beginning of each day. Ten or 15 minutes will save hours later.

3. "Ask the Lord to bless your plans, and you will be successful in carrying them out" (Prov. 16:3, GNB).

4. Depend on the Lord to direct your actions: "You may make your plans, but God directs your actions" (Prov. 16:9, GNB).
   - Do the tasks in the order planned to save time and to receive immediate direction about the next task to do.
   - When God directs you otherwise, follow His immediate leading. Interruptions and unplanned events are sometimes God's ways to get you to do His will. However, ask His leadership, because Satan can also stop you from doing God's will. Ask yourself:

Plan your daily work under the Master's leadership.

Depend on the Lord to direct your actions.

—Is this one of God's priorities I might not have anticipated?

—Is God trying to teach me something?

—Does He want me to help someone I had not considered?

—Does it contribute to one of my long-range goals? If so, is it a high enough priority to interrupt my list of priorities for today?

—Is it important or merely urgent?

—Is this the best time to do it? Could I do it some other time?

—Can it be delegated to someone else?

—How much do someone else's responsibilities depend on my doing this task at this time?

5. Discipline yourself to carry out your plans: "It is better to win control over yourself than whole cities" (Prov. 16:32, GNB).

   • The key to self-control is Master control.

   • When you fail, do not waste time blaming yourself and feeling guilty. Ask forgiveness and submit yourself to the Master's will.

6. Leave the results to God. "Men cast lots to learn God's will, but God himself determines the answer" (Prov. 16:33, GNB).

At the end of the day, after you have used your MasterTime form, reevaluate unfinished tasks. Do not worry about being unable to do everything you planned, since you did the most important things in priority under God's direction. Leave them to the Lord tonight and add them to tomorrow's list with the priority each deserves that day.

Do not worry about being unable to do everything you planned, since you did the most important things in priority under God's direction.

Evaluate how often you feel that you accomplish the goals in "How to Use MasterTime." Circle the appropriate number: 4 = always, 3 = usually, 2 = often, 1 = sometimes. Then pray about areas in which you need to improve.

I trust the Lord to direct me in all I do.

4   3   2   1

I plan my daily work under the Master's leadership.

4   3   2   1

I ask the Lord to bless my plans.

4   3   2   1

I depend on the Lord to direct my actions.

4   3   2   1

Now begin to plan your time, using "How to Use Master-Time" and the MasterTime form on page 138. Use the MasterTime principles for at least the next six weeks. Feel free to make copies of the form as needed. If you already use another system for time management, apply these same principles to that process.

Stop and pray, asking God to help you establish Christ-honoring priorities and to help you use your time wisely.

If you manage your life so that you keep a proper balance, you can keep ministering to others without depleting your spiritual resources.

LEARNING THE DISCIPLE'S CROSS
You can use the Disciple's Cross to keep your time priorities balanced and to work toward the goals in "How to Use MasterTime." The cross shows two means of intake for a Christian: prayer and God's Word. It shows two means of output: fellowship and witness. You will study about witness in week 5. If you manage your life so that you keep a proper balance between intake and output, spiritual and physical growth, mental and social stimulation, and time for your needs and those of others, you can keep ministering to others without depleting your spiritual resources.

To summarize what you have learned this week, draw the portions of the Disciple's Cross you have studied, with the verses that accompany each discipline. At the next group session be ready to explain what you have learned about the cross.

HAS THIS WEEK MADE A DIFFERENCE?
Review "My Walk with the Master This Week" at the beginning of this week's material. Mark the activities you have finished by drawing vertical lines in the diamonds beside them. Finish any incomplete activities. Think about what you will say during your group session about your work on these activities.

As you complete your study of "Fellowship with Believers," I hope that you asked Christ to examine areas in which you are not loving others as He commanded. Sometimes this kind of examination is uncomfortable. Your best intentions will not make you a disciple of Christ until you follow His command about fellowship and loving others.

WEEK 5

Witness to the World

This Week's Goal
You will bear witness of Christ and your relationship with Him.

My Walk with the Master This Week
You will complete the following activities to develop the six biblical disciplines. When you have completed each activity, draw a vertical line in the diamond beside it.

SPEND TIME WITH THE MASTER
◇ Have a daily quiet time. Check the box beside each day you have a quiet time this week: ❑ Sunday ❑ Monday ❑ Tuesday ❑ Wednesday
❑ Thursday ❑ Friday ❑ Saturday

LIVE IN THE WORD
◇ Read your Bible every day. Write what God says to you and what you say to God.
◇ Memorize John 15:8.
◇ Review Luke 9:23, John 15:5, John 8:31-32, John 15:7, and John 13:34-35.
◇ Study the reasons for memorizing Scripture in "How to Memorize Scripture."

PRAY IN FAITH
◇ Pray about your priorities and use of time.
◇ Pray for the members of your *MasterLife* group.

FELLOWSHIP WITH BELIEVERS
◇ Share with your prayer partner some of your problems and pray about your and your partner's needs.

WITNESS TO THE WORLD
◇ Review "How to Use MasterTime." Use it to plan your days and week.
◇ Make a new friend who is not a Christian. Learn all you can about your new friend and be ready to tell your *MasterLife* group about him or her.

MINISTER TO OTHERS
◇ Continue learning the Disciple's Cross. Explain the meaning of the left cross-bar to add to the information you have already learned.

This Week's Scripture-Memory Verse
" 'This is to my Father's glory, that you bear much fruit, showing yourselves to be my disciples' " (John 15:8).

DAY 1

Bearing Fruit for Christ

The Holy Spirit empowers us to witness.

Every christian has the Holy spirit

" 'This is to my Father's glory, that you bear much fruit, showing yourselves to be my disciples' " (John 15:8).

When God's love flows through the Son to you and others, you want to share the good news of Christ with those around you.

After I made my initial commitment as a college student to be Christ's disciple, I felt a strong need to begin to witness. About four nights a week I began going to a rescue mission operated by college students. I thought I would witness there, but no one came to Christ. I would memorize Scriptures to counter the excuses I would hear when people rejected the gospel. Armed with about 50 Scriptures, I could answer almost any objection, but I had not discovered the real secret: the Holy Spirit is the one who empowers us to witness. He bears witness through us. When I allowed Him to fill me, the persons to whom I witnessed began to trust Christ. Book 2 discusses being filled with the Spirit.

A NATURAL DESIRE TO SHARE

Christ intends for His disciples to bear fruit. Your memory verse this week, John 15:8, says the way to show that you are His disciple is to bear much fruit. If you have an obedient relationship with Christ, you will want to share with friends about that relationship. Just as a woman who is getting married wants to talk about her fiancé, you will want to talk about Christ. The branch that lives in the Vine bears fruit. If you practice the disciplines around the Disciple's Cross, you have a desire to share with non-Christians. If you fellowship with God's people as you live daily in the Word and pray in faith, you naturally and normally share with others the Christ who lives in you. When God's love flows through the Son to you and others, you want to share the good news of Christ with those around you. The Holy Spirit will empower you to do so.

 What does John 15:8 say you will do to show that you are Christ's disciple?

_____

How does John 15:8 say that you bring glory to God?

_____

If you are Christ's disciple, you show it by bearing fruit for Him. You do this as a natural result of following Him. You do not do it in your own strength, as I tried to do at first. You allow the Holy Spirit to empower you for the task. When you bear fruit for Him, you bring glory to the Father. The Lord uses you to teach others about Himself.

THE FRUIT OF A LIFE IN CHRIST

What exactly does Christ mean when He talks about bearing fruit? Galatians 5:22-23, in the margin, describes the fruit of the Spirit—the traits of Christ that the Holy Spirit produces when you abide in Christ. How does fruit bearing relate to your life in Christ?

"The fruit of the Spirit is love, joy, peace, patience, kindness, goodness, faithfulness, gentleness and self-control. Against such things there is no law" (Gal. 5:22-23).

 Read aloud John 15:8, this week's Scripture-memory verse, in the margin. What is the fruit you are expected to produce?
☒ **The fruit of the Spirit, as listed in Galatians 5:22-23**
☒ **Producing other Christians**

" 'This is to my Father's glory, that you bear much fruit, showing yourselves to be my disciples' " (John 15:8).

Actually, both answers are correct. To understand more clearly the purpose of fruit bearing, consider what occurs when a vine produces grapes. A vine does not produce fruit just so that a person can eat; it also enables the seed from that plant to be scattered. You are a Christian not merely to produce the sweet fruit of good deeds and good actions. As a Christian, you live a life that reflects those Christlike traits. The fruit of the Spirit mentioned in Galatians 5:22-23 naturally flows from your life if you abide in Christ. The result of your fruit bearing is to produce other Christians.

To illustrate, let's identify some of the things the world, with all its troubles and difficulties, needs.

Check the qualities from Galatians 5:22-23 that the world needs.
1 ☑ love   ↑ ☑ patience   7 ☑ faithfulness
2 ☑ joy   5 ☑ kindness   ☑ gentleness
3 ☑ peace   ☑ goodness   9 ☑ self-control

Is love one of the things you checked that the world needs? Certainly, the world needs love, but most people look for it in the wrong places. One way you can exhibit Christ's character is to demonstrate love, for example, in loving your enemy. When others see you do that, they may be puzzled. They may ask: "How can you love like that? How can you love persons who mistreat you?" That is your opportunity for the seed to sprout. You can say, "The truth is, I can't love like that, but Christ can love that person through me." Your life is a witness, but a verbal witness is also necessary to glorify God instead of yourself. To accept credit for your good deeds would be wrong, because that is your chance to give credit to Christ. Only through Christ can you love your enemy. Demonstrating this fruit of the Spirit enables you to plant a seed that bears fruit.

The result of your fruit bearing is to produce other Christians.

What would happen if you demonstrated love without telling others why?

A follower of Christ confesses Christ as the reason for his or her love.

If you planted the seed without telling others why, they would think you are just different than they are. Along with demonstrating the fruit of the Spirit, a follower of Christ confesses Christ as the reason for his or her love. You have an opportunity to witness when you plant the seed of love and it bears fruit in your life. The Lord uses you to teach others about Himself.

You may have also answered that the world needs peace—which people also look for in the wrong places. When they see peace in your life that is different from the world's chaos, they wonder what makes you different. But if you do not tell them that you are peaceful and serene in the face of chaos because of Christ's peace that lives in you, they will not understand the source. If a person comments on your calmness when you confront difficulty, you can respond, "Can I tell you an experience I had with Christ that helps me respond this way?" This is a good way to introduce Christ as the source of your peace.

The world genuinely needs joy. You can be a joyful person and can radiate that joy. Instead of being disheartened when you encounter difficulties, you may look on the positive side. If people notice that you look for the good in a bad situation or that you refuse to give up when you are sick, they take notice. If you confess Christ as the source of joy in your life, you produce the fruit Christ desires for His disciples.

We have looked at three fruit of the Spirit mentioned in Galatians 5:22-23—love, joy, and peace—and ways they could lead to a witness. Now choose one of the remaining fruit and describe how it could become the seed of a verbal witness.

- ☒ patience
- ☐ faithfulness
- ☐ kindness
- ☐ gentleness
- ☐ goodness
- ☐ self-control

when you are patience, And wait on the Lord, People will see you patience with the little one → Thn they will kn al Christ give you the + patue

By the Power of the Holy Spirit

THE FRUIT OF NEW BELIEVERS

As you have learned, bearing fruit can mean having the fruit of the Spirit in your life. Bearing fruit also includes the result: producing another follower of Christ. Jesus said in Matthew 4:19, " 'Follow me, and I will make you fishers of men.' " Fruit bearing is the normal, natural result of a life that has Christ at the center.

Bearing fruit also includes producing another follower of Christ.

You might wonder: *How do I learn to witness, since all of my friends are Christians? I'm willing to be obedient and bear fruit, but how can I find someone with whom I can share the gospel?* One way is to broaden your horizons, to reach beyond your comfortable circle of friends. You have persons all around you with whom you can become acquainted. Perhaps the following assignment will help.

Make a new friend this week who is not a Christian. Learn all you can about your new friend. Make notes and be ready to tell your *MasterLife* group about him or her.

_____

_____

LEARNING THE DISCIPLE'S CROSS

This week introduces you to the fourth bar of the Disciple's Cross, witness to the world. Just as the vertical crossbar represents the two ways a disciple relates to God—through the Word and prayer—the horizontal crossbar represents the two ways a disciple relates to others—through fellowship and witness. The cross illustrates a disciple's balanced life in Christ.

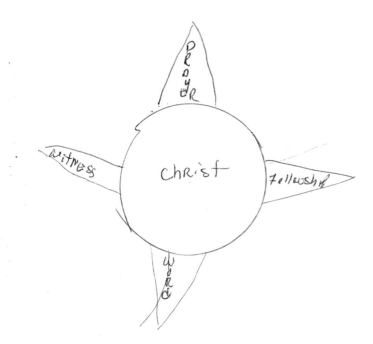 Draw the portions of the Disciple's Cross you have already studied. Now draw the left crossbar and write the discipline witness on it. Refer to the completed cross on page 136 if you need help with your drawing.

In your quiet time today read **Galatians 5**, the chapter containing the verses you studied about the fruit of the Spirit. When you have read it, complete the Daily Master Communication Guide in the margin.

DAILY MASTER COMMUNICATION GUIDE

GALATIANS 5

What God said to me:

_____

_____

_____

_____

_____

_____

_____

What I said to God:

_____

_____

_____

_____

_____

_____

_____

DAY 2

Relying on Christ

I kept Christ as my source of power instead of relying on my own strength, and the man was saved.

As the Holy Spirit worked through me and as I began to witness more effectively, I often witnessed on the streets and in bars. One night when I witnessed in a bar, I talked with a man who seemed to be under deep conviction about his need for salvation. As we talked, he wept, but he would not receive Christ as Savior.

At that time the barkeeper told me that I was not welcome in his bar and made me leave. I was crushed, because the man with whom I had conversed was so burdened. When I left the bar, I went across the street to my car, knelt in the back seat, and pleaded with the Lord to lead the man to give his life to Christ. At that time I heard a tapping noise and looked up. Standing beside my car was the man to whom I had witnessed. We talked for a few minutes, and he trusted Christ. This was an answer to prayer, illustrating how God uses all six disciplines of the Disciple's Cross to accomplish His purposes. I kept Christ as my source of power instead of relying on my own strength, and the man was saved.

Has Christ been your power source when you have witnessed? Describe an occasion when, as you witnessed, Christ was giving you the words to say and the strength to say them.

_____

_____

" 'I am the true vine, and my Father is the gardener. He cuts off every branch in me that bears no fruit, while every branch that does bear fruit he prunes so that it will be even more fruitful. You are already clean because of the word I have spoken to you. Remain in me, and I will remain in you' " (John 15:1-4).

Read John 15:1-4 in the margin. Then mark the statements that are true.
☒ Fruit bearing is not a choice for a Christian.
❑ Some Christians are expected to bear fruit, while others are not.
☒ Christ cleanses you so that you can bear more fruit.
☒ Fruit bearing depends on remaining in Christ.

You may have the idea that witnessing is only for persons with outgoing personalities. You may think that you are excused from witnessing if you are not particularly talkative or do not have time. You may think that witnessing is not your major strength. But John 15:1-4 says that persons who are in Christ bear fruit. It does not say that only a few believers are fruit bearers. All Christians are expected to bear fruit. Christ made you clean through His Word so that you can bear more fruit. You cannot bear fruit apart from Him, as I learned during my futile attempts to witness in my own strength. When Christ became my source and I shared from my lifelong, obedient relationship with Him,

I became more effective in witnessing. In the previous exercise all of the statements are true except the second one.

Have you ever made excuses for not witnessing? ❑ Yes ❑ No

 Try to say John 15:8, this week's Scripture-memory verse, several times from memory. Write what it says about making excuses for not witnessing.

God ARE glorifidy when we widrese to Sone owt

You may have answered something like this: The verse indicates that Christ's disciples bear fruit. If I want to be His disciple, no excuse is really valid for not witnessing.

How are you doing with the discipline of memorizing Scripture? By now you have likely memorized several verses you can use in various situations. I have found Scripture memorization helpful in times of temptation, trial, and testimony. When I am tempted, I remember 1 Corinthians 10:13, one of the earliest Scriptures I memorized. The Holy Spirit uses that verse to assure me that He will not allow me to be tempted more than I can bear but will offer an escape every time. Many times I have faced trials I could not understand. Each time the Holy Spirit reminded me of James 1:2-3: "Consider it pure joy, my brothers, whenever you face trials of many kinds, because you know that the testing of your faith develops perseverance. Perseverance must finish its work so that you may be mature and complete, not lacking anything."

By now, the fifth week of your study, you have likely memorized five verses and are beginning to learn a sixth. Describe situations when having memorized these verses helped you. Be ready to share what you have written at your next group session.

Luke 9:23: *To D allerd Christ we must deny our Sets + Pinecp en cresr daily + follow him*

John 15:5: *if we stay close to him + do God's will we will Christ is The VINE, we are The branchs bernf we must hold to the teching of Christ*

John 8:31-32: *we are his true disciples*

John 15:7: *As long as we Are true to Christ And Ask God in Jesus None he will help us*

John 13:34-35: *Christ said we must keep This New Command Love one another*

 Read Acts 8:26-40, about Philip's witness to the Ethiopian, during your quiet time today. Then complete the Daily Master Communication Guide in the margin.

DAILY MASTER COMMUNICATION GUIDE

ACTS 8:26-40

What God said to me:

To Go And

What I said to God:

DAY 3

Every Disciple's Orders

Witnessing is part of every disciple's marching orders.

" 'You did not choose me, but I chose you and appointed you to go and bear fruit—fruit that will last. Then the Father will give you whatever you ask in my name' " (John 15:16).

Maybe you think that witnessing is something Jesus expects only of preachers, evangelists, or missionaries. You may think that Jesus does not expect ordinary Christians to bear fruit for Him in this way. But John 15, the passage you have been reading, makes clear that witnessing is part of every disciple's marching orders.

Read John 15:16 in the margin and answer the questions below.

What did Jesus say His purpose was in choosing the disciples?

To go And witness to some one Bre who will come to Christ & do th Sin

What did Jesus promise fruitful disciples they could do?

Can PRay in Christ's None & the PRay will be Answer

Fruit bearing was not optional for the disciples. It was expected of them as part of their lifelong, obedient relationships with Him. Jesus told the disciples that to bear fruit that would last was the reason He chose them. Along with this expectation Jesus gave a promise: that the disciples could pray in Christ's name and have their prayers answered. Obedient disciples seek to live in keeping with the Father's will and to pray accordingly.

WITNESSING IS NOT OPTIONAL

In John 15:27 Jesus once again told the disciples that witnessing is not optional; it is a discipline He expects. The verse says, " 'You also must testify, for you have been with me from the beginning.' "

Why did Jesus tell the disciples that they must testify?

They Know who Jesus was

Jesus commanded the disciples to testify about Him because they had been with Him from the beginning and knew firsthand of His saving truth.

Again read John 15 in your quiet time today. Let God speak to you about the importance of bearing fruit and of testifying about Christ. After you have read this passage, complete the Daily Master Communication Guide on page 100.

Although you did not physically live alongside Jesus, as the disciples did, you know firsthand of His saving truth, and you experience a growing relationship with Him. You can tell others what Christ has done in your life just as the disciples did. You can tell others about Him, based on your experience.

As you study about witnessing to others, you may find yourself thinking: *I want to do that! I know that Christ wants me to be His witness. But how will I know the words to say? How do I know I won't freeze up or embarrass myself?*

Read John 15:4 in the margin and complete this sentence:

I am unable to bear fruit unless I _have christ in me_.

" 'Remain in me, and I will remain in you. No branch can bear fruit by itself; it must remain in the vine. Neither can you bear fruit unless you remain in me' " (John 15:4).

No branch can bear fruit by itself. The branch is part of the vine; it is not just attached to the vine. As the the sap and the life-giving power that produces the fruit flow through the branch, they originate in the vine. The end of the branch that bears the fruit is the part you see, but the vine is always the life-giving source.

THE PROMISE OF CHRIST'S POWER

When you were saved, you became part of the Vine. You cannot bear fruit if you do not remain in the Vine, that is, stay in fellowship with Christ. If you stay in fellowship with Christ, you will be empowered to witness. In my early attempts at witnessing I learned that I could not succeed just because I willed myself to succeed. Only when I allowed the Holy Spirit to take control of my thoughts, my words, and my actions could I witness effectively.

If you stay in fellowship with Christ, you will be empowered to witness.

See if you can recall John 15:5, one of your previous Scripture-memory verses. What does it promise will happen if you remain in Christ?

be able to witness To other

The verse does not say that perhaps you will bear fruit or that only exceptional disciples will bear fruit. It says that if you remain in Christ, you will bear fruit. This is a precious promise from God's Word to you about what happens to a person who abides in Christ and witnesses to others. He will enable you to bear fruit if you remain in Him and seek His will.

What are some ways you can remain in Christ so that you can bear fruit for Him?
☒ **Live in the Word by studying it and memorizing it.**
☒ **Pray that the Father will direct you to witness according to His will.**

DAILY MASTER COMMUNICATION GUIDE

JOHN 15

What God said to me:

_____

_____

_____

_____

_____

_____

What I said to God:

_____

_____

_____

_____

_____

_____

□ Fellowship with other believers to hear instruction from God's Word and to draw encouragement from the body of Christ.
☑ Have a daily quiet time to hear God speak to you.

Which discipline do you most need to work on? Draw a star beside it. Then ask God to help you be more diligent in that practice.

As you reviewed the above suggestions, how did you evaluate yourself on your practice of having a personal quiet time with God? I have found that nothing takes the place of a personal quiet time with God every day. Like manna, it does not last long enough to provide for tomorrow. If I write in my Daily Master Communication Guide each day, God says more and more to me. Then when times are difficult, I can go back and read what God said to me in the previous days, weeks, or months. Many times this perspective gives me new insights about my relationship with God and restores my spirit.

Complete this statement: The time that works best for my daily quiet time is _EARly Morning or Late Ng̱t_

If finding time for your daily, personal time with Christ is still a challenge for you, review what you learned in week 4 about ways to set priorities using MasterTime. Use MasterTime to plan your days and weeks.

Stop and pray, asking God to help you with your priorities and your use of time so that you will be able to find a consistent time every day to remain connected to the Vine.

You can also abide in Christ by fellowshipping with other believers and by expressing your care and concern for them. For example, the time you spend with your prayer partner can be a time of fellowship.

Share with your prayer partner some of your problems. Pray about your and your partner's needs. Before you finish your conversation, say John 15:8, this week's Scripture-memory verse, to your prayer partner.

As you studied in week 4, your fellowship with others naturally leads you to share Christ with them. The Lord will use you to teach others about Him. You will have fellowship as you demonstrate your love for fellow believers, as you did with your prayer partner. You also need to relate to persons who do not know Christ, attempting to bring them to a saving knowledge of Him. Continue to cultivate the friendship with your new non-Christian friend.

LEARNING THE DISCIPLE'S CROSS

To reinforce what you are learning, draw the portions of the Disciple's Cross you have studied. Now draw the left cross-bar and write *witness* on it. Write *John 15:8,* the Scripture reference that accompanies the left crossbar, under *witness.*

DAY 4

Compelled to Tell

When I was six years old, I made my profession of faith in Christ while my father was attending Southwestern Baptist Theological Seminary in Fort Worth. As he was preaching a revival service in a local rescue mission, I recognized that I was a sinner and that if a trap door were under me, I would go straight to hell. Realizing that I needed to repent of my sins, I almost ran down the aisle. I felt that a burden had been lifted from me. With the enthusiasm of a new convert I told my neighbor, my barber, and even the president of the seminary that I had trusted Christ. I could not help telling what I had seen and heard.

I could not help telling what I had seen and heard.

WHAT HAS CHRIST DONE FOR YOU?

The Bible says, " 'We cannot help speaking about what we have seen and heard' " (Acts 4:20). Has Christ ever been so real to you that you could not help testifying about what you saw and heard? Perhaps He answered a prayer in such a direct, specific, or meaningful way that you responded, "Only the Lord could have done that!" Perhaps you experienced physical or emotional healing. Perhaps He provided you special encouragement or counsel from a friend just when you needed it. You did not live at the time of Christ to observe His miracles firsthand, but perhaps you have experienced modern-day miracles. If so, how can you refrain from telling persons you encounter how awesome Christ is?

How ready are you to testify about what Christ has done in your life? Evaluate yourself by circling the appropriate number: 1 = sometimes, 2 = often, 3 = usually, 4 = always. Then pray about areas in which you need to improve.

I build relationships with non-Christian friends or acquaintances so that I can eventually have opportunities to witness to them.
1 (2) 3 4

I pray with persons or offer to pray for persons who have needs, and I remind them that God cares about them. (1) 2 (3) 4

I visit or contact persons who visit my church and express concern for them. (1) (2) 3 4

I tell lost persons about Christ even though it means risking that they will reject me. 1 (2) (3) 4

I do not hesitate to tell others when God answers my prayers.
1 2 3 (4)

Do not feel embarrassed or awkward if you answered with a 1 on several or most of the statements in the exercise. Learning to share your faith boldly can be a building process. Book 2 provides techniques and skills for sharing your personal testimony.

THE ROMAN ROAD

1. **God's power can make you secure.**
2. **God's power results in change.**
3. **Sin makes change necessary.**
4. **God still loves you.**
5. **Sin earns death, but God offers life.**
6. **Confessing Jesus as Lord means that you recognize His rightful authority over you.**
7. **Repentance means changing the direction of your life and living a God-oriented life.**
8. **Believing means trusting Jesus with your life.**
9. **Calling on the name of the Lord means asking Him for forgiveness of sin and for salvation.**
10. **You now have hope.**
11. **Faith = life for God.**

MAKE SURE OF YOUR RELATIONSHIP

As you think about witnessing to the world, first be sure of your own salvation so that you can bear fruit. Be sure that you are connected to the Vine so that you have Christ's love flowing through you in a life-long, obedient relationship with Him. The following gospel presentation is called the Roman Road.[1] You will read eight passages from the Book of Romans that clearly explain the gospel message. Study the presentation to determine how you measure up in your relationship with Christ. You may want to memorize the verses or to mark them in sequence in your Bible so that you can also share the good news with others. *MasterLife 4: The Disciple's Mission* teaches you another gospel presentation you can use to witness.

THE ROMAN ROAD

1. *God's power can make you secure.* Read Romans 1:16 in the margin. Many people today live without hope. They have no resources to strengthen them and guide them through their struggles in life. According to Romans 1:16, the focus of the Christian faith is the gospel, which is the good news that God's power is available to help you in whatever problems you face. Through Jesus Christ a power great enough to bring salvation and deliverance is available to any person who believes.

God's __POWER WORDS__ can make you secure.

"I am not ashamed of the gospel, because it is the power of God for the salvation of everyone who believes: first for the Jew, then for the Gentile" (Rom. 1:16).

2. *God's power results in change.* Read Romans 2:4 in the margin. Through God's power, people can change. The biblical word for *change* is *repentance.* This means allowing God to change the direction of your life.

God's power results in __Change__.

"God's kindness leads you toward repentance" (Rom. 2:4).

3. *Sin makes change necessary.* Read Romans 3:23 in the margin. Why do people need to change? From what does Jesus offer deliverance? According to the Bible, every man and woman has a problem. The problem can be described in many ways, but the most common biblical word is *sin.* One meaning of *sin* is *to fall short of the mark God has set.* The Bible teaches that God's standard for us is Jesus Christ. If Jesus were standing in front of you in the flesh, could you say that you are as good as He is? The failure to meet God's standard is sin, which means that all people have a sin problem. You may do much that is good, and you may not want to do anything bad, but none of us can measure up to God's standard of always doing right.

__Sin__ makes change necessary.

"All have sinned and fall short of the glory of God" (Rom. 3:23).

4. *God still loves you.* Read Romans 5:8 in the margin. Some people think that their failure to meet God's standard means that God is their enemy. Because they do not live up to His expectations, God must be against them. But the message of Jesus is that in spite of our sin, God still loves us.

God's love for you is not based on ignorance and an unawareness of sin. Nor is it based on a tolerance that overlooks your sin. Knowing your sin, God chose to love you, even though it meant His Son's death for you. In doing what was necessary to overcome your problem with sin, God demonstrated the depth and reality of His love for you (also see John 3:16).

God still __LOVE__ you.

"God demonstrates his own love for us in this: While we were still sinners, Christ died for us" (Rom. 5:8).

"The wages of sin is death, but the gift of God is eternal life in Christ Jesus our Lord" (Rom. 6:23).

5. *Sin earns death, but God offers life.* Read Romans 6:23 in the margin. According to the Bible, the consequences of sin are too serious to overlook. Although God is not your enemy, He is your judge. As judge He cannot ignore your failure to meet His standard of perfection. Romans 6:23 says that "the wages of sin is death." Whenever you sin, you earn the wages of death. Since every person is guilty of sin, every person is subject to the consequences of eternal death and separation from God (see John 3:36; Rev. 20:11-15).

An alternative exists. Through your works you earn death, but "the gift of God is eternal life in Christ Jesus our Lord" (Rom. 6:23). Jesus died on the cross in your place (see 1 Pet. 3:18). He took your guilt for sin upon Himself so that His death would fulfill the judgment of God against your sin (see 2 Cor. 5:21; Col. 2:13-14). Your sin is judged in the death of Jesus on the cross as our substitute. By your works you earn death, but by His grace you can receive eternal life. God offers eternal life and the forgiveness of sin through Jesus Christ as His gift.

Sin earns _death_, but God offers _life_.

6. *Confessing Jesus as Lord means that you recognize His rightful authority over you.*

Underline the words in Romans 10:9-10,13, in the margin, that indicate what you need to do to accept Christ as Savior and Lord.

Read Romans 10:9-10,13 in the margin. The words *confess, believe,* and *call* summarize what someone must do to receive God's free gift and be saved.

The biblical word translated *confess* means *to say the same thing. Lord* may be translated *ruler, boss,* or *sovereign authority.* When we confess Jesus as Lord, we are saying the same thing about God that He says about Himself (see Isa. 45:5-7,22-24; Phil. 2:10-11). We recognize His rightful authority over us. In acknowledging Jesus as Lord, we admit our sin in failing to meet His standard of perfect obedience and righteousness.

"If you confess with your mouth, 'Jesus is Lord,' and believe in your heart that God raised him from the dead, you will be saved. For it is with your heart that you believe and are justified, and it is with your mouth that you confess and are saved. For, 'Everyone who calls on the name of the Lord will be saved' " (Rom. 10:9-10,13).

Confessing Jesus as Lord means that you recognize His rightful _authority_ over you.

7. *Repentance means changing the direction of your life and living a God-oriented life.* To confess Jesus as Lord also means to repent of your sins. In accepting His rightful authority over you, you turn away from life on your terms in order to obey and serve

Him. This turning away from sin in order to follow Jesus is called repentance. More than feeling sorry, it is changing the direction of your life and living a God-oriented rather than a self-oriented life (see Luke 3:7-14).

Repentance means changing the _direction_ of your life and living a _God-ORIENTED_ life.

8. *Believing means trusting Jesus with your life. Believe means to trust.* When you "believe in your heart that God raised him from the dead" (Rom. 10:9), you have confidence that the death and resurrection of Jesus are enough to secure your salvation. You trust in the work of Christ rather than in the work of your life for your salvation. When you look at a bridge, you might know that it would hold you up if you crossed it. The bridge never actually holds you up, however, until you get on it and cross. Similarly, you may know a lot about Jesus, but until you trust Him with your life, putting your life into His hands, you are not believing in Him. To believe in Jesus is to put your life, both physically and spiritually, into His hands.

Believing means _trusting_ Jesus with your life.

When you acknowledge that Jesus is the rightful Lord or boss of your life and when you are willing to believe in Him, trusting in His work alone for your salvation, you need only call on Him to be saved. In Romans 10:13 Paul wrote, " 'Everyone who calls on the name of the Lord will be saved.' " Note how broad the invitation is. *Anyone* who is willing to call on the name of the Lord will be saved. No other qualifications are needed. If you are willing to call on Him, you can be saved.

Anyone who is willing to call on the name of the Lord will be saved.

9. *Calling on the name of the Lord means asking Him for forgiveness of sin and for salvation.* When you ask Him for salvation, you are acknowledging Him as your Lord and expressing your intention to live a life of obedience and service. Persons who call on Him will be saved.

Calling on the name of the Lord means asking Him for _forgiveness_ of sin and for _Salvation_.

The three words that summarize what someone must do to be saved are: _Call_, _on_, _him_.

As you have proceeded through *MasterLife 1: The Disciple's Cross*, you may have experienced some questions about where you stand in your commitment to Christ. As you have read about being totally committed to Christ, you may not be able to state firmly that you have taken that initial step of following Him that occurs when you receive Christ in salvation. *Master-Life* was designed for persons who have accepted Jesus as their Savior and Lord and who want to learn what it means to be His true followers. If you find that you cannot say with 100-percent surety that you have made that commitment, you can accept Him now by inviting Him into your life. If you wish, use this sample prayer to express your commitment:

> *Lord Jesus, I need You. I want You to be my Savior and my Lord. I accept Your death on the cross as the payment for my sins, and I now entrust my life to Your care. Thank You for forgiving me and for giving me new life. Please help me grow as a Christian so that my life will bring glory and honor to You. Amen.*

_____   _____
Signed   Date

Receiving Christ does not guarantee that you will not struggle with issues like self-denial, cross bearing, and following Jesus. It does not mean that you will not be tempted to give your devotion to someone or something else. It does not mean that you will not shy away from the costs of discipleship. It means that He forgives you; that He has a lasting relationship with you that extends into eternity; and that He will grant you strength, power, and wisdom as you seek to be His disciple. I suggest that you talk with your *MasterLife* leader, your pastor, a church-staff member, or a trusted Christian friend about any new commitment you have made.

10. *You now have hope.* Read Romans 8:16-17,38-39 in the margin. When you are saved, God adopts you as His child, and His Holy Spirit assures you that you are part of His family. According to Roman law at the time of Paul's writing, someone's adopted son also became his heir. While Christ is God's heir by nature, Christians have become God's heirs by adoption. Therefore, you are a joint-heir with Christ.

Verses 38-39 say that you are eternally secure in God. Because Christ has defeated the principalities and powers of this earth, you need not fear human and superhuman enemies. Nothing can separate you from God's love in Christ Jesus.

"The Spirit himself testifies with our spirit that we are God's children. Now if we are children, then we are heirs—heirs of God and co-heirs with Christ, if indeed we share in his sufferings in order that we may also share in his glory. For I am convinced that neither death nor life, neither angels nor demons, neither the present nor the future, nor any powers, neither height nor depth, nor anything else in all creation, will be able to separate us from the love of God that is in Christ Jesus our Lord" (Rom. 8:16-17,38-39).

"I urge you, brothers, in view of God's mercy, to offer your bodies as living sacrifices, holy and pleasing to God—this is your spiritual act of worship. Do not conform any longer to the pattern of this world, but be transformed by the renewing of your mind. Then you will be able to test and approve what God's will is—his good, pleasing and perfect will" (Rom. 12:1-2).

As a believer, you can live with hope because you are a child of God and are secure in His love.

You now have _____hoPE_____.

11. *Faith = life for God.* Read Romans 12:1-2 in the margin on the previous page. When you become a Christian, you begin to live your life for God. You can expect your life to be different. God wants your life to change as you follow Jesus, even if it means sacrifice. The goal for believers is to look and live less like the unsaved people of the world and more like Jesus. That kind of change happens because God brings it about. He will transform your life, making it more like the life of Jesus (see Phil. 1:6; 2:13). Jesus will make you look and live like one of His children as you follow Him.

Faith = life for _____God_____.

YOU ARE HIS WITNESS

Whether you just received Christ or have been His disciple for many years, you are His witness. You may want to learn the previous presentation so that you can explain to a lost person how to receive eternal life. You may first want to accompany your *MasterLife* leader when he or she uses it to witness to an unsaved person.

Do not be afraid to share your salvation experience with non-Christians. In *MasterLife 2: The Disciple's Personality* you will learn how to share your personal salvation experience. In *MasterLife 3: The Disciple's Victory* you will learn how to use a booklet to share the way someone can become a Christian. In *MasterLife 4: The Disciple's Mission* you will learn how to use another presentation to lead lost persons to receive Christ as Savior and Lord.

 Read Acts 16:11-15, describing Paul's witness to Lydia, during your quiet time today. Then complete the Daily Master Communication Guide in the margin.

Pray for each of your *MasterLife* group members by name. Ask God to help each person receive a blessing from *MasterLife* and especially from the gospel presentation you have studied. Ask Him to help you be available as a friend to your fellow members.

Continue to memorize John 15:8, this week's Scripture-memory verse, which goes with the left crossbar of the Disciple's Cross. On a sheet of paper, write the verse from one to three times.

DAILY MASTER COMMUNICATION GUIDE

ACTS 16:11-15

What God said to me:

_____

_____

_____

_____

_____

_____

_____

_____

What I said to God:

_____

_____

_____

_____

_____

_____

_____

_____

" 'Remember the words I spoke to you: "No servant is greater than his master." If they persecuted me, they will persecute you also. If they obeyed my teaching, they will obey yours also. They will treat you this way because of my name, for they do not know the One who sent me' " (John 15:20-21).

"While he was still speaking a crowd came up, and the man who was called Judas, one of the Twelve, was leading them. He approached Jesus to kiss him, but Jesus asked him, 'Judas, are you betraying the Son of Man with a kiss?' " (Luke 22:47-48).

"Jesus left there and went to his hometown, accompanied by his disciples. When the Sabbath came, he began to teach in the synagogue, and many who heard him were amazed. 'Where did this man get these things?' they asked. 'What's this wisdom that has been given him, that he even does miracles! Isn't this the carpenter? Isn't this Mary's son and the brother of James, Joseph, Judas and Simon? Aren't his sisters here with us?' And they took offense at him" (Mark 6:1-3).

"He then began to teach them that the Son of Man must suffer many things and be rejected by the elders, chief priests and teachers of the law, and that he must be killed and after three days must rise again" (Mark 8:31).

DAY 5

The Price of Bearing Fruit

High-school principal John Eluru was rehearsing to play the role of Jesus in the Ugandan translation of the *Jesus* film, a riveting movie about the life of Christ. The film has brought countless people to Christ in every corner of the globe. As crews carried John and other film personnel from their Ugandan village to the production site, guerrilla fighters burst onto the road and fired. John was shot in the heart.

That night as John lay dying, he urged the film technician: "Don't stop the dubbing. Uganda needs this film. I have done my part, but don't stop the work, and don't ever be afraid." The next morning John died, but today every time the completed film is shown in Uganda, John's voice as Jesus tells hundreds of people how to know Christ.[2]

Being Christ's disciple does not occur without sacrifice. Witnessing to the world as you bear fruit for Christ has its price. As John 15:20-21, in the margin, reveals, when you have a relationship with Him, you will be persecuted, just as He suffered. Everything you endure for Christ, He endured also. He knew rejection and suffering, and so will you.

In John 15:20-21 what do Jesus' words "No servant is greater than his master" mean to you?

You ARE Not greater then God
You will suffer also + be rejected

YOUR COMPANION IN SUFFERING
You are subject to the same rejection Jesus encountered. The same type of hard-hearted, closed-minded people who rejected the Master will also reject you. In contrast, the same type of people who were open to His teachings while He was on earth will be open to your words and deeds today.

What did Christ suffer for you? Read the three verses in the margin. Then match the statements in the right column with the correct references on the left.

  B 1. Luke 22:47-48   a. **Respected persons in authority**
  C 2. Mark 6:1-3   **rejected Him.**
  A 3. Mark 8:31   b. **A friend betrayed Him.**
                            c. **The people in His hometown took offense at Him.**

Go back and draw a star beside any type of persecution you have experienced.

Have you had an experience in which you felt persecuted because you witnessed for Christ? ☑ Yes ❑ No **If so, describe it below.**

_____

_____

How does it make you feel to realize that Christ has already endured any type of heartache you have suffered?

StRong good Thot God Love me So mcch

    Christ's suffering for you was so great that listing all of the trials He endured on earth would be impossible in this book. The Scriptures in the margin on page 108 represent only a few. Likewise, because of Christ-honoring stands you take, you sometimes experience the rejection of friends, family, neighbors, your community, and people you respect. I hope as you thought about the fact that Christ is your companion in suffering, you described feeling strengthened and encouraged by considering the depths of His love for you. The correct answers to the previous matching exercise are 1. b, 2. c, 3.a.

Because of Christ-honoring stands you take, you sometimes experience the rejection.

LEARNING THE DISCIPLE'S CROSS

After studying the Disciple's Cross for five weeks, you know that the left crossbar represents bearing fruit by witnessing. The Disciple's Cross itself embodies fruit bearing. If you learn and practice the six disciplines, you will live an obedient life and thus will bear fruit.

 Again draw the Disciple's Cross, writing *witness* on the left crossbar. Also include *John 15:8*, the Scripture that accompanies the left crossbar.

DAILY MASTER COMMUNICATION GUIDE

MATTHEW 4:1-11

What God said to me:

Satan tempt
Jesus 3 times
but each time
Jesus was strong
Enough to turn
The other chick
Satan misuses the
word of God
sow

What I said to God:

I will hold on
to God's
unchanging hand
for faith strought
by Living According
To

 To reinforce what you are learning about fruit bearing as a characteristic of a disciple, say aloud John 15:8, this week's Scripture-memory verse. Recite it to a family member or to someone you regularly see in the course of your day.

SCRIPTURE MEMORIZATION: A KEY TO BEARING FRUIT
Each day you have been asked to memorize Scripture. I hope you will not look at this merely as busy work or as course requirements. Memorizing Scripture enables you to claim victory over Satan, to claim victory over sin, to win others to Christ, to meditate on the Word, and to direct your daily life. Most important of all, you memorize Scripture because God commands it.

Try to memorize in your own words the six reasons listed in the following chart.

REASONS TO MEMORIZE SCRIPTURE
1. To claim victory over Satan.

Read Matthew 4:1-11, the account of Christ's temptation in the wilderness, during your quiet time today. When you finish, complete the Daily Master Communication Guide in the margin.

a. Jesus set the example. Read Matthew 4:7,10.
b. Satan sometimes misuses the Scriptures. Compare Matthew 4:6 with Psalm 91:11-12:

*He will command his angels concerning you
        to guard you in all your ways;
they will lift you up in their hands,
        so that you will not strike your foot against a stone.*

c. The Word is the sword of the Spirit:

*How can a young man keep his way pure?
        By living according to your word.
I have hidden your word in my heart
        that I might not sin against you (Ps. 119:9,11).*

2. To claim victory over sin. See Psalm 119:9,11.
3. To win others to Christ.
a. You will always be ready to give an answer about your faith: "Always be prepared to give an answer to everyone who asks you to give the reason for the hope that you have" (1 Pet. 3:15).

b. The Holy Spirit can bring to mind the word that is needed for any situation: " 'When he, the Spirit of truth, comes, he will guide you into all truth. He will not speak on his own; he will speak only what he hears, and he will tell you what is yet to come' " (John 16:13).

c. Understanding the Word will make you bold in your witness: "After they prayed, the place where they were meeting was shaken. And they were all filled with the Holy Spirit and spoke the word of God boldly" (Acts 4:31).

Understanding the Word will make you bold in your witness.

4. To meditate on the Word.

> *His delight is in the law of the Lord,*
> *and on his law he meditates day and night.*
> *He is like a tree planted by streams of water,*
> *which yields its fruit in season*
> *and whose leaf does not wither (Ps. 1:2-3).*

5. To direct your daily life.

> *Your word is a lamp to my feet*
> *and a light for my path (Ps. 119:105).*

6. Because God commands it. " 'These commandments that I give you today are to be upon your hearts' " (Deut. 6:6). "Let the word of Christ dwell in you richly as you teach and admonish one another with all wisdom, and as you sing psalms, hymns, and spiritual songs with gratitude in your hearts to God" (Col. 3:16).

Memorize Scripture because God commands it.

Give an example of how memorizing Scripture has helped you in one of the above ways.

_____

_____

_____

Read on the following page the suggestions for memorizing Scripture. Check any suggestion you have tried. Draw a star beside any you pledge to try.

Review is the most important secret of Scripture memorization.

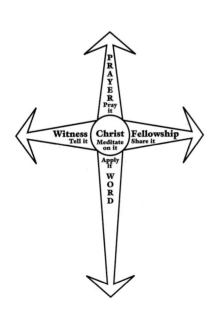

HOW TO MEMORIZE SCRIPTURE

1. Choose a verse that speaks to your need or, if the verse is assigned, discover how it meets a particular need in your life.

2. Understand the verse. Read the verse in relation to its context. Read the verse in various translations.

3. Record memory verses on a cassette tape so that you can listen to them. Leave a space after each verse so that you can practice quoting it. Then record the verse a second time so that you can hear it again after you have quoted it.

4. Locate and underline the verse in your Bible so that you can see where it is on the page.

5. Write the verse on a card, including the Scripture reference and the topic it addresses. This allows you to relate the verse to a particular subject so that you can find it when a need arises.

6. Place the written verse in prominent places so that you can review it while you do other tasks. Put it over the kitchen sink, on the bathroom mirror, on the dashboard for reviewing at stop lights, and on the refrigerator.

7. Commit the verse to memory. Divide it into natural, meaningful phrases and learn it word by word. If you learn it word-perfect in the beginning, it will be set in your memory, will be easier to review, will give you boldness when you are tempted, and will convince the person with whom you are sharing that he or she can trust your word.

8. Review, review, review. This is the most important secret of Scripture memorization. Review a new verse at least once a day for six weeks. Review the verse weekly for the next six weeks and then monthly for the rest of your life.

9. Use these activities to set a verse in your mind: see it in pictorial form; sing it, making up your own tune; pray it back to God; do it by making it a part of your life; and use it as often as possible.

10. Use the version of the Disciple's Cross in the margin to master the verse. Note that you can make the Scriptures a part of every facet of your life (see John 8:31-32).

11. Have someone check your memorization. Or write the verse from memory and then check it yourself, using your Bible.

12. Make Scripture memorization fun. Make a game of remembering verses with your family and friends. A game I have used is to cite a reference to a *MasterLife* group member before the person can cite it to me. For instance, if you cite John 15:5, the other person must quote it. If the other person says the reference first, you must quote it.

13. Set a goal for the number of verses you will memorize each week. State your goal: _____ per week. Do not try to learn too many verses so fast that you do not have time for daily review, which is essential to memorizing Scripture.

Since review helps you memorize, go back and work on this week's Scripture-memory verse. Choose one of the suggestions you read and practice it to reinforce your memorization of John 15:8.

If you have not already done so, write the verses you are memorizing in *MasterLife 1: The Disciple's Cross* on cards that you can carry with you. Review them often.

HAS THIS WEEK MADE A DIFFERENCE?
Review "My Walk with the Master This Week" at the beginning of this week's material. Mark the activities you have finished by drawing vertical lines in the diamonds beside them. Finish any incomplete activities. Think about what you will say during your group session about your work on these activities.

Think about your study of "Witness to the World" this week.
- Have you resolved to work on developing new relationships with persons who do not know Christ?
- Have your relationships with non-Christian friends taken on new meaning because of this week's study?
- Have you identified opportunities to witness that you had not thought about previously?
- Have you committed to bear fruit in a new way?

I hope that this week's study has prompted you to make new commitments in your continuing effort to abide in Christ and to develop your lifelong, obedient relationship with Him. Making new commitments requires honesty, because you may realize that you need to make improvements in your life. Look on these as opportunities to grow rather than judging your old ways of doing things.

------

[1]Adapted from Chuck Kelley, *Learning to Share My Faith* (Nashville: LifeWay Press, 1994), 27–34.
[2]Paul Eshleman, *The Touch of Jesus* (Orlando: NewLife, 1995), 157–58.

Making new commitments requires honesty, because you may realize that you need to make improvements in your life.

WEEK 6

Minister to Others

This Week's Goal

You will minister to others as you take up your cross and follow Jesus.

My Walk with the Master This Week

You will complete the following activities to develop the six biblical disciplines. When you have completed each activity, draw a vertical line in the diamond beside it.

SPEND TIME WITH THE MASTER
◇ Have a daily quiet time. Check the box beside each day you have a quiet time this week: ❏ Sunday ❏ Monday ❏ Tuesday ❏ Wednesday ❏ Thursday ❏ Friday ❏ Saturday

LIVE IN THE WORD
◇ Read your Bible every day. Write what God says to you and what you say to God.
◇ Memorize John 15:13.
◇ Review Luke 9:23, John 15:5, John 8:31-32, John 15:7, John 13:34-35, and John 15:8.

PRAY IN FAITH
◇ Pray for your pastor and your church.
◇ Pray for the lost persons the group members talked about at the previous session.
◇ Ask God to lead you as you plan your time with Him, using the MasterTime form.

FELLOWSHIP WITH BELIEVERS
◇ Share with someone what the Lord has done for you since you have been involved in *MasterLife*.

WITNESS TO THE WORLD
◇ Use MasterTime to plan your days.
◇ Do a kind act for your new non-Christian friend this week. Learn all you can about your new friend. Be ready to tell your *MasterLife* group what happened.

MINISTER TO OTHERS
◇ Finish learning the Disciple's Cross. Be ready to share it with a member of your *MasterLife* group before the Growing Disciples Workshop. Say all of the verses that go with the Disciple's Cross.

This Week's Scripture-Memory Verse

" 'Greater love has no one than this, that he lay down his life for his friends' " (John 15:13).

DAY 1

~

Take Up Your Cross

A group of people rushed into the room where my friend, a Christian relief worker in central Asia, was ministering. They pleaded, "Please come help this old man, or he will die!" In the war-torn area of the country where my friend served, mine fields were plentiful. The concerned individuals who pressed him to help had found a shepherd injured by a mine. My friend knew that he must quickly decide what to do. "I knew it was not wise to enter a mine field, but I felt that the Lord wanted me to help this person in need," my friend recalled. "As I crossed the field, I noticed that everyone following me was walking single file in my footsteps."

My friend at last located the man, carried him to the road, and hailed a truck. He begged the truck driver to carry the injured shepherd to a hospital, but no occupant of the crowded vehicle would give up his place. To a worker who spoke English my friend said, "Tell the truck driver that I will pay twice what any rider paid if you will take this man to the hospital." The worker, in translating to the truck driver, commented, "This Christian is going to pay the man's way when we Muslims won't do anything." At that point the truck driver refused the money and made a place for the injured man.

In this central-Asian country where Christianity is not accepted, this modern-day Good Samaritan story spread all over the countryside with the message "This is what a Christian does. This is the kind of service a Christian does in Jesus' name."

WHAT A CHRISTIAN DOES
When Christ is at the center of your life, how do you serve others? What does being a disciple of Christ lead you to do? Although you may not serve as a relief worker in a war-torn country as my friend does, your opportunities for sacrificial service for others are endless.

Describe an occasion when you served someone sacrificially.

_____

_____

What opportunities for service do you have that you are not taking advantage of?

_____

where we met

Your opportunities for sacrificial service for others are endless.

Every Christian is a minister if he or she follows Jesus and serves others as He did.

You probably identified someone in need or opportunities for sacrificial service in Jesus' name. The type of ministry we are examining does not mean being a pastor or another church minister. Every Christian is a minister if he or she follows Jesus and serves others as He did.

BEARING YOUR CROSS

To learn how a disciple ministers to others, start by reviewing one of your first memory verses, Luke 9:23, in which Jesus outlined the three basic commitments of a disciple.

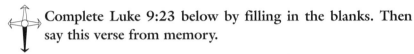 **Complete Luke 9:23 below by filling in the blanks. Then say this verse from memory.**

" 'If anyone would come after me, he must _at Ny_ himself and take up his ___CRoss___ daily and ___follow___ me.' "

The three basic commitments a disciple makes are to deny self, take up his or her cross, and follow Christ. In week 1 when you learned about putting Christ at the center of your life, you focused on self-denial. In week 5 when you learned about witnessing to the world and reproducing believers, you focused on Christ's command to follow Him. This week you will focus on the commitment to cross bearing.

For Jesus, the cross meant that He gave Himself to redeem the world. For believers, cross bearing is voluntary, redemptive, sacrificial service for others. You enter His ministry by taking up your cross.

" 'I tell you the truth, unless a kernel of wheat falls to the ground and dies, it remains only a single seed. But if it dies, it produces many seeds' " (John 12:24).

Read John 12:24 in the margin. Check the statement that best explains Jesus' comparison.
☑ 1. Death to the old way of life brings forth new life.
❑ 2. Dying to self means that you will probably live your life alone.

You must die to your old way of life before you can commit yourself to Christ. Self-denial emphasizes turning from commitment to self to commitment to Him. Taking up your cross involves turning with Christ to the world in need. The first result is a new vision of self; the second result is a new vision of the world's need. The correct answer is 1.

" 'Anyone who does not carry his cross and follow me cannot be my disciple' " (Luke 14:27).

Read Luke 14:27 in the margin. What happens to a person who refuses to be a cross bearer?

_____

If you refuse to be a cross bearer, you cannot be Jesus' disciple. To follow Christ, you must bear your cross.

In Philippians 2:8, in the margin, Paul explained why Jesus was willing to take up His cross. Jesus was obedient to God's will for His life even when it meant dying on a cross. We learn from Jesus' example in

Being found in appearance as a man,
  he humbled himself
  and became obedient to death—
  even death on a cross!
  (Phil. 2:8).

cross bearing that a Christian's cross has two characteristics: (1) it is a voluntary commitment, and (2) it is an act of obedience.

If you fail to take up your cross, which of the following sins have you committed? ❑ **disobedience** ❑ **disloyalty** ❑ **disbelief**

Disloyalty and disbelief may be involved, but you are disobedient to Christ if you fail to take up your cross, because cross bearing is a direct command of Christ. Obeying Jesus' commands is the primary motive for taking up your cross. This week's Scripture-memory verse, John 15:13, states the value Jesus placed on sacrificial service to others.

 Begin to memorize this week's Scripture-memory verse, John 15:13. Read it aloud. What did Jesus say that a disciple would be willing to do to demonstrate love for others?

_____

Jesus said that a disciple ministers to others, even if you have to experience hardship or give your life.

LEARNING THE DISCIPLE'S CROSS

The final addition to the cross will indicate how you relate to the world if you are Christ's disciple. If Christ is at the center of your life, you grow as His disciple through the discipline of ministering to others. As you grow in Christ, you reach out to others through service of all kinds. You bear Christ's cross even if it means experiencing difficulty.

 Draw the Disciple's Cross over this picture of the world to show how a disciple reaches out to the world in witness and ministry. Label each part of the cross.

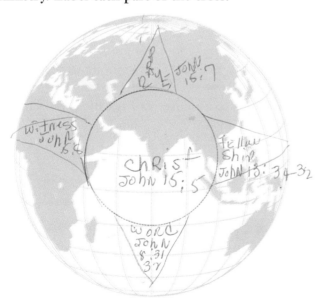

A disciple ministers to others, even if you have to experience hardship or give your life.

DAILY MASTER COMMUNICATION GUIDE

LUKE 10:26-35

What God said to me:

_____
_____
_____
_____
_____
_____
_____
_____

What I said to God:

_____
_____
_____
_____
_____
_____
_____
_____
_____
_____

 Read Luke 10:26-35, a passage about someone who took up his cross for others, during your quiet time today. After you have read this passage, complete the Daily Master Communication Guide in the margin.

DAY 2

Ministry in Christ's Name

When I was the president of the Indonesian Baptist Theological Seminary, I hired a former lieutenant colonel in the Indonesian Army to manage the seminary property and the employees who took care of it. Although he had been a Christian for only about six months, he was very committed to the Lord. The problem was that he tried to manage the seminary property and employees as he would manage an army. Time after time I had to intervene to keep war from breaking out between the employees and this supervisor.

Praying for God's guidance, I decided to bear the cross and take on the difficulties required to disciple this man and to teach him to be an effective manager. Using the Scriptures, I taught him how to relate to his employees with patience, kindness, and self-control. This man effectively served at the seminary for more than 10 years.

Throughout your study of *MasterLife* you have learned six biblical disciplines of a follower of Christ. In these disciplines four resources can be identified that are available to every disciple:
- the Word
- prayer
- fellowship
- witness

A growing disciple uses these four resources to help others in Christ's name. Your service expresses itself in various ministries:

> **1. The Word leads to a ministry of teaching/preaching.**
> 2. Prayer leads to a ministry of worship/intercession.
> 3. Fellowship leads to a ministry of nurture.
> 4. Witness leads to a ministry of evangelism.
> 5. Fellowship and witness lead to a ministry of service.

A MINISTRY OF TEACHING/PREACHING

Look at the first ministry you will learn about, which appears in bold type in the box above. You may instantly think: *That lets me out. I'm not called to be a pastor. How can I minister this way?*

Preaching a sermon is certainly one way to minister by using the discipline of living in the Word. God definitely calls some people to be preachers or evangelists. If you live in the Word, you may learn that this role is His will for you. But you can be involved in the ministry of teaching or preaching even if you never proclaim the gospel in front of a congregation. Most people who stay in the Word long enough have the opportunity to share in a variety of contexts what God has said to them.

Recall my story about the lieutenant colonel at the seminary. How did I use the resource of the Word in the ministry of teaching or preaching?

_____

_____

I used the resource of the Word to teach this man how the Lord wanted him to relate to his employees. By sharing with him what the Word says about patience, kindness, and self-control as fruit of the Spirit, I helped him manage in a more Christ-honoring manner.

To understand how to use the resource of the Word in a ministry of teaching/preaching, you can look at ways teaching occurs in the Bible. Match the Scriptures in the margin with the following examples.

___ 1. Job 36:22	a.	God is a teaching God. Many prophets such as Samuel also functioned as teachers.
___ 2. Matthew 28:19	b.	Parents are urged to tell their children about God's mighty acts and to instruct them in God's commandments.
___ 3. Ephesians 6:4	c.	In Jesus' ministry, teaching was His primary identity. In the Great Commission Jesus commanded His followers to make disciples and to instruct them in His teachings.
___ 4. 1 Timothy 5:17	d.	Whenever new churches were founded, Christian teachers were present.

Today teaching is part of sharing your faith. To witness to the world, believers must first understand the gospel and then teach others. A person can be involved in a teaching ministry whether from the pulpit, in a classroom, in a small-group study, or one-to-one. The correct answers are 1. a, 2. c, 3. b, 4. d.

You can be involved in the ministry of teaching or preaching even if you never proclaim the gospel in front of a congregation.

"God is exalted in his power. Who is a teacher like him?" (Job 36:22).

" 'Go and make disciples of all nations, baptizing them in the name of the Father and of the Son and of the Holy Spirit, and teaching them to obey everything I have commanded you' " (Matt. 28:19).

"Fathers, do not exasperate your children; instead, bring them up in the training and instruction of the Lord" (Eph. 6:4).

"The elders who direct the affairs of the church well are worthy of double honor, especially those whose work is preaching and teaching" (1 Tim. 5:17).

DAILY MASTER COMMUNICATION GUIDE

JOHN 17:6-19

What God said to me:

_____

_____

_____

_____

_____

_____

_____

What I said to God:

_____

_____

_____

_____

_____

_____

_____

_____

_____

Name ways you might be able to use the resource of the Word in a ministry of teaching or preaching.

_____

_____

Do not feel concerned if ideas for ministry do not immediately occur to you. The goal is to open new possibilities for you as you begin considering your ministry as a follower of Christ.

Memorizing Scripture is one way you can begin to use the resource of the Word. When you hide God's Word in your heart, you have it at instant recall when you want to share about Christ or to give scriptural guidance or encouragement.

 By now you have likely memorized six verses and are working on a seventh one. On a sheet of paper, see how accurately you can write each of the six by memory.

If you had difficulty writing any of the six verses, you may want to review "How to Memorize Scripture" in week 5.

Continue your work on this week's Scripture-memory verse, John 15:13. Say it aloud from one to three times. Ask a family member or someone you see each day if you can practice saying it aloud to him or her.

A MINISTRY OF WORSHIP/INTERCESSION
The ministry in bold type below is the next one you will study.

1. The Word leads to a ministry of teaching/preaching.
2. **Prayer leads to a ministry of worship/intercession.**
3. Fellowship leads to a ministry of nurture.
4. Witness leads to a ministry of evangelism.
5. Fellowship and witness lead to a ministry of service.

The more you get involved in prayer, the more you worship. Prayer is ministering before the Lord (see 1 Chron. 23:13). It is bowing before God and worshiping Him through praise, adoration, and devotion. Prayer enables you to develop a closer relationship with the Father. Intercession is a way you can minister to others by bringing their needs before God.

The ministry of worship can take the form of individual worship during your quiet time. But it goes beyond private prayer. You also worship as you fellowship with the body of Christ, gathered as His church. Worship as a church family has occurred since the time of the first Christians. Read the verses from Acts in the margin on the next page.

Again, you may think: *I'm not a minister or a church-staff member. How can I perform a ministry of worship?* The focus of true worship is on God and your personal relationship with Him. If you never lead others in worship, you can serve the Lord through worship. He waits for your worship. Worship is the primary way you glorify the Lord and is God's primary reason for creating and redeeming you (see 1 Pet. 2:9). The early church did not limit leadership in worship to professional ministers. Everyone has a responsibility for worship, whether God provides opportunities to lead groups in worship experiences or to participate in worship by following others' directions. We can also worship in our families as we minister to the persons closest to us. Read Deuteronomy 6:6-9 in the margin.

As you learned in week 4, intercession is a disciple's ministry to bring to God the needs of the church and the world. Intercession can result in changed lives and changed churches. Staying alert to persons' needs and jotting down their concerns allow you to intercede for them as you pray individually or with others.

How do you think God wants you to use the resource of prayer in a ministry of worship and intercession?

_____

_____

You can start by interceding for believers who serve the Lord by spreading the gospel throughout the world. Pray for them as they witness to the world and as they lead others to witness. Become a prayer partner with them. Let them know that you are praying for them and that they can depend on your prayers. You may want to add the names of your pastor and other church-staff members to your Prayer-Covenant List and to pray for their specific needs.

Before I became a missionary, I heard many missionaries say that their greatest need was prayer, even more than finances. I made a commitment to God that before I began to serve as a missionary, I would enlist as many prayer partners as possible so that He could do more than I could do as a missionary. I enlisted about two thousand people to pray daily. Over the years that list grew to six thousand. I wrote to them every month to give them prayer requests and to report answers to prayer. I believe that God's work through us in Indonesia was a direct answer to those prayer partners' prayers. Think about what God could do through your pastor and church-staff members if you and others regularly prayed for them!

Stop now and pray for your pastor and church-staff members by name. Pray for the other members of your church who serve in the areas of teaching, prayer, outreach, benev-

"They devoted themselves to the apostles' teaching and to the fellowship, to the breaking of bread and to prayer. Every day they continued to meet together in the temple courts. They broke bread in their homes and ate together with glad and sincere hearts" (Acts 2:42,46).

" 'These commandments that I give to you today are to be upon your hearts. Impress them on your children. Talk about them when you sit at home and when you walk along the road, when you lie down and when you get up. Tie them as symbols on your hands and bind them on your foreheads. Write them on the doorframes of your houses and on your gates' " (Deut. 6:6-9).

olence, missions, music, and others. Ask God to bless each person as he or she ministers to others. Ask Him to help you think of ways you can support and demonstrate love for your church leaders.

Read John 17:6-19 during your quiet time today. Let God speak to you through this passage about Jesus' intercession for His disciples. After you have read this passage, complete the Daily Master Communication Guide on page 120.

DAY 3

More Ways to Minister

You have already studied two ministries and the resources that lead to their expression in the life of a disciple. Now you will learn a third, listed in bold type with its corresponding resource.

> 1. The Word leads to a ministry of teaching/preaching.
> 2. Prayer leads to a ministry of worship/intercession.
> **3. Fellowship leads to a ministry of nurture.**
> 4. Witness leads to a ministry of evangelism.
> 5. Fellowship and witness lead to a ministry of service.

A MINISTRY OF NURTURE

Fellowshipping with believers eventually leads you to disciple new Christians. A normal outgrowth of being part of the body of Christ is taking care of spiritual infants and helping them grow into mature Christians. God gives some persons special gifts to counsel and train others in the various stages of spiritual growth. In the Bible this happens several times, as when Jesus saw Simon's potential and helped him grow into the rock called Peter (see John 21:15-17 in the margin). Barnabas encouraged the reluctant John Mark, who grew and later wrote one of the Gospels. Christ will show you Himself as you fellowship with other believers.

A ministry of nurture could involve—

❑ counseling new Christians at the time of decision;
❑ helping spiritual infants understand what it means to have life in Christ;
❑ leading a small group of disciples to know what following Christ means;
❑ serving on committees that see potential in members and recommending them for church offices;
❑ training leaders;

"When they had finished eating, Jesus said to Simon Peter, 'Simon, son of John, do you truly love me more than these?' 'Yes, Lord,' he said, 'you know that I love you.' Jesus said, 'Feed my lambs.' Again Jesus said, 'Simon, son of John, do you truly love me?' He answered, 'Yes, Lord, you know that I love you.' Jesus said, 'Take care of my sheep.' The third time he said to him, 'Simon, son of John, do you love me?' Peter was hurt because Jesus asked him the third time, 'Do you love me?' He said, 'Lord, you know all things; you know that I love you.' Jesus said, 'Feed my sheep' " (John 21:15-17).

❏ teaching persons how to witness;
❏ counseling persons about their interpersonal needs.

In all situations nurture can involve role modeling, as Christ did with those He trained as His disciples. Others need examples of the Christian life that point them to Christ.

In the previous list, check the ways you already serve and draw a star beside the one(s) you think God might want you to do in a ministry of nurture.

Remember the definition of *discipleship* you learned earlier? Now read this definition of *discipling*, or *making disciples*.

> Discipling is leading others to develop personal, lifelong, obedient relationships with Christ in which He transforms their character into Christlikeness, changes their values to Kingdom values, and involves them in His mission.

To carry out the Great Commission, you need to lead others into lifelong, obedient relationships with Jesus Christ. That is your responsibility. Then help them grow in their relationships with Him until He transforms them into His likeness and involves them in His mission. Every disciple is to help other disciples in the fellowship of believers grow.

Do you think you have been a role model for others during your study of *MasterLife*? Has anyone made a comment to you like "You seem to have changed since you began this study"? If so, perhaps this has occurred because of an increased understanding of what it means to live the Christian life. Maybe someone has observed you reaching out to nurture others as you have had fellowship with believers. Perhaps your family members have observed you having a quiet time. I hope that your lifestyle has changed to the point that new ways of thinking and behaving are obvious.

Every disciple is to help other disciples in the fellowship of believers grow.

 Tell someone how you have benefited from your study of *MasterLife*. Do this regardless of whether someone has commented about having observed changes in your life.

A MINISTRY OF EVANGELISM
The fourth ministry of a disciple appears in bold type below.

> 1. The Word leads to a ministry of teaching/preaching.
> 2. Prayer leads to a ministry of worship/intercession.
> 3. Fellowship leads to a ministry of nurture.
> **4. Witness leads to a ministry of evangelism.**
> 5. Fellowship and witness lead to a ministry of service.

The well-known evangelist D. L. Moody had a personal commitment

All evangelism starts with personal witness.

" 'Go and make disciples of all nations, baptizing them in the name of the Father and of the Son and of the Holy Spirit, and teaching them to obey everything I have commanded you' " (Matt. 28:19).

that he would witness to someone every day of his life. Even if he had already gone to bed when he remembered that he had not witnessed that day, he would get up and tell someone about Christ.[1] The final resource you have for living the Christian life is the resource of witness. Many believers do not think of witness as a resource. However, nothing encourages Christians more than bearing witness, especially when they see someone accept Christ. From the resource of witness grows a ministry of evangelism. Various types of evangelism exist—film evangelism, relational evangelism, tracts, crusades—but all start with personal witness.

Evangelism is the proclamation of the good news of salvation in Christ. Our evangelism is a means the Holy Spirit uses to convert the lost. It is the way the Lord uses us to teach others about Himself. As a Christian, you do not persuade persons simply to make decisions. Rather, you tell them about Christ, call them to repentance, and give God the glory for what occurs.

Read the Great Commission, Matthew 28:19, in the margin. What does Christ say about your responsibility for evangelism?

_____

_____

The Great Commission calls you to use the resource of witness. Through the Great Commission Christ gave you the responsibility to share with others your knowledge of His love.

You may think: *How do I do this? I'm not a D. L. Moody. I'm not a Billy Graham. I don't have the abilities of a TV evangelist or someone who draws large crowds to tell about Christ.* Remember that D. L. Moody used the resource of witness to deal with one person at a time long before he became a preaching evangelist. Personal witness is a significant way to express the ministry of evangelism.

 Write your memory verse, John 15:13, in the margin. Describe here what you think a person who is willing to give his or her life for a friend would do about witnessing.

_____

_____

You may have said that a person who would give everything for a friend would make sure that person has the gift of eternal life by witnessing to friends.

You can express this ministry of evangelism in a variety of ways:
❑ Lifestyle—living a Christian life that attracts a lost person's attention

and provides an opportunity for witness
- ❏ Small-group evangelism—participating in small groups of persons with similar interests to share the gospel of Christ
- ❏ Church evangelism—visiting homes, taking a religious census, or using other actions to ensure that every person in your church's range of influence hears the gospel message
- ❏ Mass evangelism—helping your church gather people for a community-wide revival in a church building or a stadium
- ❏ Missions ministry—entering other cultures to tell others about Jesus as a career, short-term, or bivocational missionary or through giving and praying for missions causes
- ❏ Other: _____

In the previous list, check the ways you have already served and draw a star beside the one(s) you think God might want you to do in a ministry of evangelism.

At this point you may not know exactly how God intends for you to minister in this area. The purpose of these exercises is to encourage you to begin thinking of ways you can use the valuable resources that are yours as a disciple of Christ.

LEARNING THE DISCIPLE'S CROSS

Again draw the Disciple's Cross over the picture of the world. Then add pointed arrows to the ends of the cross-bars. At the ends of the pointed arrows write the ministry areas that go with each part of the cross: *ministry of teaching/preaching* below the cross, *ministry of worship/intercession* above the cross, *ministry of nurture* to the right of the cross, and *ministry of evangelism* to the left of the cross.

Read 1 Timothy 6:11-21 in your quiet time today. Let God speak to you through this passage about the way Paul nurtured Timothy. After you have read this passage, complete the Daily Master Communication Guide in the margin on page 125.

DAY 4

The Demands of Christ

Jesus did not always paint a rosy picture for the disciples as He talked about what was ahead for them. During His last days on earth Jesus outlined for His disciples what they could expect if they followed Him. Any suffering they would encounter for taking up His cross would be sorrow He had already known. In the verse in the margin He told them that the world would hate them because they were associated with Him and because they would witness in His name. Sometimes you may be inclined to skip over verses like John 15:18 because they indicate that life in Christ will be difficult. Read what an Argentine pastor says about this subject:

" 'If the world hates you, keep in mind that it hated me first' "
(John 15:18).

> *The gospel which we have in the Bible is the gospel of the Kingdom of God. It presents Jesus as King, as Lord, as the maximum authority. Jesus is at the very center. The gospel of the Kingdom is a Christ-centered gospel.*
>
> *But in recent centuries we have been hearing another gospel—a man-centered, human gospel. It is the gospel of the big offer. The gospel of the hot sale. The gospel of the irresistible special deal. ... We have told people, "If you accept Jesus, you will have joy, you will have peace, health, prosperity. ... If you give Jesus ten dollars, you will get twenty dollars back." ... We are always appealing to man's interests. Jesus is the Savior, the Healer, and the King coming for me. Me is the center of our gospel.*
>
> *We take all the verses we like, all the verses that offer something or promise something—John 3:16, John 5:24, and so forth—and we make a systematic theology from these verses, while we forget the other verses that present the demands of Jesus Christ. ... Who said we were allowed to present only one side of Jesus? ... He is our Savior and our Healer, true. But we cannot cut Jesus Christ into pieces and take only the piece we like best.[2]*

We cannot accept the part of Jesus' message that we like and reject what we do not like. We must accept it all.

We cannot accept the part of Jesus' message that we like and reject what we do not like. We must accept it all.

List commands Christ gave for disciples that you have ignored.

_____

_____

_____

EXPECT TO BE REJECTED

The reality is, when you meet the demands of Christ as you minister to others, you may experience rejection. For example, did you feel rejection or sense a lack of openness to you as you began reaching out to your new non-Christian friend? Sometimes you may feel subtle rejection at first. Or you may initially sense that your friend would not be open to eventually learning about Christ.

One of my neighbors who was not a Christian began to play on the church softball team I played on. I tried to share my faith tactfully with him as we became better acquainted, but I never felt that he was ready to respond. I could not help feeling somewhat rejected when I continually sensed that he was not open to my witness.

One day as I was preparing to go overseas to lead *MasterLife* training, I sensed God leading me to talk to my neighbor before I left. That night my wife and I visited him and led him to Christ. Befriending him and regularly expressing concern for him eventually provided a witnessing opportunity. I was glad I had not become discouraged when at first I felt somewhat rejected.

This week do something kind for the non-Christian friend you made last week. Learn all you can about your new friend. Be ready to tell your *MasterLife* group what happened.

THE PROMISE OF HIS PRESENCE

After warning His disciples about the possibility of rejection, however, Jesus painted another picture designed to compel them to spread the good news fervently regardless of what they encountered. Read the verses in the margin.

Jesus reassured the disciples that they would have the Holy Spirit to assist them as they testified about Christ. He would not leave them without help or resources. The Holy Spirit would guide them as they moved out to serve others.

Two thousand years later, Jesus makes the same promise to you and gives you the same commands. As He sends you out to serve the world that He warns will hate you, He does not leave you without resources. He gives you the Holy Spirit to empower you and to make you bold.

> **When you meet the demands of Christ, you may experience rejection.**

> *" 'When the Counselor comes, whom I will send to you from the Father, the Spirit of truth who goes out from the Father, he will testify about me. And you also must testify, for you have been with me from the beginning' " (John 15:26-27).*

✝ Pray for the lost persons the group members mentioned at the previous session. You may have written their names on your Prayer-Covenant List or elsewhere. If you did not, you may want to add their names at the next group session. Meanwhile, continue praying that your fellow *MasterLife* group members will live Christlike lives that will model Christ to others.

Your witness and your fellowship involve Christian service to other persons.

A MINISTRY OF SERVICE

Could a ministry of service be the ministry to which Christ calls you? Your witness and your fellowship involve Christian service to other persons. These compose the fifth ministry area to add to the four you have already studied.

1. The Word leads to a ministry of teaching/preaching.
2. Prayer leads to a ministry of worship/intercession.
3. Fellowship leads to a ministry of nurture.
4. Witness leads to a ministry of evangelism.
5. **Fellowship and witness lead to a ministry of service.**

John 15:13 says, " 'Greater love has no one than this, that he lay down his life for his friends.' " You are to be involved in a ministry of service as Christ was.

LEARNING THE DISCIPLE'S CROSS

✝ Draw the Disciple's Cross as you learned to do in day 3, with the cross over the world and with the pointed arrows on the crossbars. Label the ministry areas. Then write *ministry of service, John 15:13* above the horizontal crossbar. As you label it with the disciplines, ministries, and Scriptures that accompany it, explain it aloud. Be sure to say aloud all of the memory verses you recorded on it.

A Growing Disciples Workshop will conclude this study. At this workshop you will review what you have learned and will prepare to begin *MasterLife 2: The Disciple's Personality.* Before the workshop share the Disciple's Cross with a member of your group.

WHAT IT MEANS TO BE A DISCIPLE
You can learn an easy way to remember what you have studied in book 1 of *MasterLife.* Summarizing what it means to be a disciple is as simple as 1-2-3-4-5-6:

1 Lord as the first priority of your life
- The center of the cross emphasizes spending time with the Master.

2 relationships
- The vertical crossbar represents your relationship with God.
- The horizontal crossbar represents your relationship with others.

3 commitments
- Deny yourself
- Take up your cross
- Follow Christ

4 resources to center your life in Christ
- The Word
- Prayer
- Fellowship
- Witness

5 ministries that grow from the four resources
- Teaching/preaching
- Worship/intercession
- Nurture
- Evangelism
- Service

6 disciplines of a disciple
- Spend time with the Master
- Live in the Word
- Pray in faith
- Fellowship with believers
- Witness to the world
- Minister to others

1 Lord
2 relationships
3 commitments
4 resources
5 ministries
6 disciplines

To reinforce this 1-2-3-4-5-6 plan for discipleship, fill in the blanks that follow.

A disciple of Christ has—

1 _____ .

DAILY MASTER COMMUNICATION GUIDE

JOHN 15

What God said to me:

_____

_____

_____

_____

_____

_____

_____

What I said to God:

_____

_____

_____

_____

_____

_____

_____

2 relationships: _____ .

3 commitments: _____

_____ .

4 resources: _____

_____ .

5 ministries: _____

_____

_____ .

6 disciplines: _____

_____

_____

_____ .

Again read John 15 in your quiet time today. This time look for ways God speaks to you through this passage about ministering to others. After you have read this passage, complete the Daily Master Communication Guide in the margin.

Are your daily quiet times making a difference in your life? Are you interceding for others? Are you gaining strength? Has your quiet time raised your entire walk with the Lord to a different level? If so, draw a star in the blank here: _____.

Everything you have done in your study of _MasterLife 1: The Disciple's Cross_, including memorizing seven Scriptures and learning the Disciple's Cross, has required quite a time commitment. I pray that you have found this commitment worthwhile. I hope that by improving the use of your time through the MasterTime concept, you have found time to commit to tasks the Lord has in mind for you. I hope that the MasterTime form is becoming a regular part of your life.

Stop and pray, asking God to continue to lead you as you plan your time, using the MasterTime form. Be ready to share with your group how your planning has benefited from using MasterTime.

HAS THIS WEEK MADE A DIFFERENCE?

Review "My Walk with the Master This Week." Mark the activities you have finished and finish the ones you have not completed. Then look back through all of book 1. Finish any activities from previous weeks that you may not have completed. Consider what you will report during the Growing Disciples Workshop about what these activities have meant to you.

DAY 5

A Disciple Indeed

In 1983 I led *MasterLife* training in Kenya after almost being denied access to the country. Four years earlier when Communists had taken control of Ethiopia, they had banned worship in churches by ordering that no more than five persons could meet at any time without a permit. Naturally, the Communists did not grant permission for worship services. An Ethiopian Christian I met at the training said that many members of his eight-hundred-member church became backsliders in their faith because circumstances were so difficult.

"Seven other men and I decided that we must do something to carry on the work," he told me. They approached missionary veterinarian Jerry Bedsole, who was allowed to stay in Ethiopia because he took care of the animals at the palace. Jerry began to disciple these Ethiopian Christians secretly at his house, using *MasterLife*. Later, each man discipled four persons. "We could not meet at the same place or time each week; we could not take Bibles to a meeting; and we had to pray with our eyes open, using conversational prayer, so that we would not be discovered," the man said.

Because the Ethiopian Christians feared that the Communists would soon confiscate their Bibles, they devised a plan for each person to memorize a part of the Bible so that they could reproduce it. "I'm memorizing one of the Gospels," he told me.

"Oh, yes, we know we will be put in jail. Some of us already have been, but the government doesn't know what to do with us once we are behind bars. We witness and win the other prisoners, so they soon kick us out," he said. Eventually, my friend began underground discipleship groups in 170 places around the country.

Several years later, after the Communists were overthrown, my Ethiopian friend was visiting Kenya when I returned there. This irrepressible man was still on fire for Christ—this time without an oppressive government to restrain him. He reported that the churches of Ethiopia had just purchased one hundred thousand sets of *MasterLife* to train Ethiopians to be disciples.

When the door seems to be closed, God can make a way for us to serve Him. Often, we must adjust our lives to follow Him in obedience.

What if you did not have a church in which to worship? What would you do if you could not sing praises to God? What if a government took away your Bible to prohibit your witness? Describe how you would stay connected to the Vine.

"We must do something to carry on the work."

When the door seems to be closed, God can make a way for us to serve Him.

The Disciple's Cross represents your relationship with Christ as His disciple.

I hope that as you have studied *MasterLife 1: The Disciple's Cross,* your relationship with Christ has become so important to you that you would bear your cross in any way possible to obey Christ.

LEARNING THE DISCIPLE'S CROSS

The Disciple's Cross has been the basis for impromptu sermons, conversations, and witnessing opportunities by persons who learned it and mastered its concepts. I hope that for you, however, the cross represents something even greater. It represents your relationship with Christ as His disciple. I hope that by this point in your study, the Disciple's Cross is at the very core of your being—that it is a way of life for you. I hope that spending time with the Master, praying in faith, living in the Word, fellowshipping with believers, witnessing to the world, and ministering to others are becoming disciplines you use every day to live in Christ.

If the Disciple's Cross is a part of your life—

❑ you will know six biblical disciplines of a disciple;
❑ you will experience a closer relationship with Christ as you practice the disciplines each day;
❑ you will use the Disciple's Cross as the standard to remind yourself and other Christians of the commitments required for being Christ's disciple;
❑ you will use the six disciplines to follow the Holy Spirit's direction as you confront problems;
❑ you will help other disciples live in Christ and bear fruit for His glory.

"If a man cleanses himself from the latter, he will be an instrument for noble purposes, made holy, useful to the Master and prepared to do any good work" (2 Tim. 2:21).

Your goal in discipleship is expressed in 2 Timothy 2:21, in the margin. Grow in all of the disciplines to master life and be prepared for the Master's use. If you develop all of these disciplines, your life will be balanced and fruitful.

Review the above list of ways that knowing the Disciple's Cross can help you as a disciple. Check the ways you are already benefiting from knowing the Disciple's Cross. Then draw a star beside ways you hope to continue growing in your use of the Disciple's Cross.

You learned the six disciplines by using a diagram of a cross. One way to reinforce the fact that you have learned these disciplines is to illustrate them in another form. Think about another item—a car, a tree, a mountain, a building, an ice-cream cone, or another object—you can draw to illustrate the elements of the Disciple's Cross. Perhaps you feel that you do not have artistic ability. Do not worry about how the final product looks; the most important point is to include all of the concepts.

✝ Draw the alternative item you have chosen to illustrate the disciplines. Include the memory verses that go with them. If you need more room, use a blank sheet of paper. When you finish, insert the sheet in your book at this place. Be prepared to explain your illustration at the Growing Disciples Workshop.

 Read 2 Timothy 2 during your quiet time and complete the Daily Master Communication Guide in the margin.

WHERE ARE YOU IN YOUR RELATIONSHIP WITH CHRIST? How equipped are you to be Christ's disciple? The Growing Disciples Workshop that follows this study will help you determine the answer. Before you attend the workshop, complete the Discipleship Inventory on pages 139–43 to evaluate your growth in discipleship. The inventory, based on the characteristics of a disciple, can help you determine where you are in your growth as a disciple. Even though the inventory will help you look at yourself in terms of behavior and attitudes, the most important questions you can ask yourself are: *Where am I in my relationship with Christ? How far am I from the lifelong, obedient relationship with Him that I desire? If He desires to transform my values into Kingdom values, have I arrived?*

When you attend the Growing Disciples Workshop, you will learn how to interpret your answers. At this point you may decide that you need to do additional work in certain areas of your relationship with Christ. You will take this inventory again at the end of book 4 to identify the areas in which you have grown.

Congratulations on completing *MasterLife 1: The Disciple's Cross.* I hope that you are beginning to learn what being a follower of Christ means. But the pilgrimage has just begun. I encourage you to study *MasterLife 2: The Disciple's Personality* to continue the journey of your lifelong, obedient relationship with your Savior and Lord, Jesus Christ.

---

[1] R. A. Torrey, *Why God Used D. L. Moody* (Chicago: Moody Press, 1923), 42.
[2] Juan Carlos Ortiz, *Disciple* (Carol Stream, Ill.: Creation House, 1975), 12–16.

DAILY MASTER COMMUNICATION GUIDE

2 TIMOTHY 2

What God said to me:

_____

_____

_____

_____

_____

_____

What I said to God:

_____

_____

_____

_____

_____

_____

_____

The Disciple's Cross

The Disciple's Cross is the focal point for all you learn in *MasterLife 1: The Disciple's Cross*. The cross provides an instrument for visualizing and understanding your opportunities and responsibilities as a disciple of Christ.

Following are step-by-step instructions for presenting the Disciple's Cross to another person. Each week of this study you learn a portion of the Disciple's Cross and the Scripture that accompanies it. As you learn the cross and review it in the future, you may find it helpful to refer to this step-by-step explanation and to the completed drawing on page 136. Do not attempt to memorize this presentation. You will learn how to present it in your own words. Do not feel overwhelmed by the amount of material involved. You will learn it in weekly segments. By the end of the study you will be able to explain the entire cross and to say all of the verses that accompany it.

To explain the cross to someone, use a blank, unlined sheet of paper to draw the illustration developed here in stages. Instructions to you are in parentheses. The following material is the presentation you make to the other person.

A disciple of Christ is a person who makes Christ the Lord of his or her life. (Quote Luke 9:23 and write the reference and the three commitments in the upper right corner of the page: *deny, cross, follow.*) A disciple's first commitment is to deny yourself. That does not mean to reject your identity but to renounce the self-centered life. To do that, a disciple of Christ learns the following six disciplines of the Christian life.

SPEND TIME WITH THE MASTER
(In the center of the page draw a circle.) The empty circle represents your life. It pictures denying all of self for Christ. You cannot be a disciple of Christ if you are not willing to deny self. If this circle represents your life, Christ should fill the entire circle as you focus on Him. (Write the word *Christ* in the circle.) Christ is to have priority in everything. Life in Christ is Christ living in you.

(Write *John 15:5* under the word *Christ* in the circle and quote the verse from memory.) What can you do without remaining in Christ? Nothing! Christ said that He is the Vine and that we are the branches. The branches are part of the Vine. You are part of Christ. He wants to live His life through you. Is this the kind of life you would like to have?

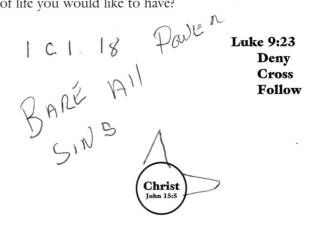

In addition to denying yourself, you need to take up your cross. The Disciple's Cross pictures the resources Christ gives us to help us live in Him. (Draw the cross around the circle.)

LIVE IN THE WORD
The way to have life in Christ is to have His Word in you. (Write *Word* and *John 8:31-32* on the lower crossbar and quote these verses from memory.) The Word is your food. You cannot grow closer to Christ unless you regularly partake of the Word. You receive the Word in many ways: by listening to someone preach it, by reading it, by studying it, by memorizing it, by meditating on it, and by applying it. Making Christ Lord means that you want to study, meditate on, and apply the Word regularly.

PRAY IN FAITH
Part of life in Christ and of having a relationship with Him is praying in faith. (Write *prayer* and *John 15:7* on the upper crossbar and quote the verse from memory. Point to the words *Christ, Word,* and *prayer* as you quote the corresponding parts of the verse.) If you

abide in Christ and His Word abides in you, you can ask what you want, and God will do it. Notice that the vertical bar of the cross, representing the Word and prayer, highlights your relationship with God, the basic ways you communicate with God, and the basic ways He communicates with you.

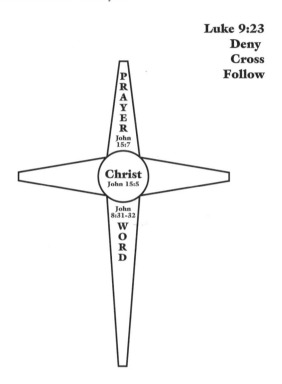

FELLOWSHIP WITH BELIEVERS
Life in Christ means that you live in fellowship with your brothers and sisters in Christ. (Write *fellowship* and *John 13:34-35* on the right crossbar and quote these verses from memory.) Jesus said the way to show that you are His disciple is to love one another. God provided the ideal place for you to grow—His church. A church is not a building or an organization, although it uses both of these. A church is a body of baptized believers who have agreed to carry out Christ's ministry in the world. A committed Christian stays in fellowship with a local body of believers in order to grow in Christ. The church is the body of Christ! If you have life in Christ, you realize how important living in His body, the church, is.

WITNESS TO THE WORLD
Life in Christ includes witnessing to others. It involves following Him, another commitment of a disciple. Witnessing is sharing with others about Christ and

your relationship with Him. (Write *witness* and *John 15:8* on the left crossbar and quote the verse from memory.) If you abide in Christ, you eventually bear fruit. Fruit can be the fruit of the Spirit or a new Christian. Galatians 5:22-23 lists the fruit of the Spirit as love, joy, peace, patience, kindness, goodness, faithfulness, gentleness, and self-control. Fruit does not always grow quickly, but it grows continually and bears in season. Fruit bearing is the normal, natural result when you have Christ at the center of your life.

Jesus said the way to show that you are His disciple is to bear much fruit. This includes witnessing. Witnessing is the natural outgrowth of living in Christ. If you are spending time with the Master, living daily in the Word, praying in faith, and fellowshipping with God's people, you naturally share with others the Christ who lives in your heart.

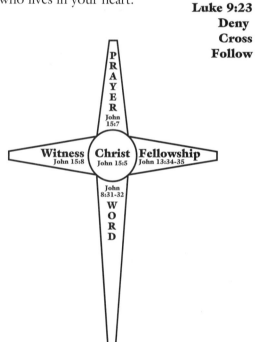

MINISTER TO OTHERS
As the fruit of the Spirit grows in your life in Christ, you also reach out to others through ministry. You take up your cross in service to others, which is another commitment of a disciple. Cross bearing is voluntary, redemptive service for others.

Look again at the circle in the center of the cross. Your life in Christ should continue to grow and expand. (Make circular broken lines that move out from the center of the circle.)

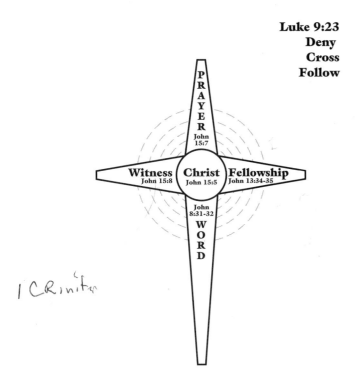

1 CRinite

As you grow in Christ, you reach out to others through all kinds of ministry and service. (Add pointed arrows to the ends of the crossbars.) The arrows indicate that your growth in Christ should express itself in ministries. Living in the Word leads to a ministry of teaching or preaching. (Write *ministry of teaching/preaching* below the cross.)

Praying in faith leads to a ministry of worship or intercession. (Write *ministry of worship/intercession* above the cross.)

Fellowshipping with believers leads to a ministry of nurture to other believers. (Write *ministry of nurture* to the right of the cross.)

Witnessing to the world leads to a ministry of evangelism. (Write *ministry of evangelism* to the left of the cross.)

Your witness and your fellowship lead to Christian service to other persons. (Write *ministry of service: John 15:13* above the horizontal bar and quote the verse.) Notice that the horizontal bar of the cross, representing witness and ministry, highlights your relationships with others.

These five ministry areas compose the ministry of a disciple and of Christ's church. The goal of discipleship is expressed in 2 Timothy 2:21: "If a man cleanses himself from the latter, he will be an instrument for noble purposes, made holy, useful to the Master and prepared

to do any good work." You need to grow in all spiritual disciplines and ministries to master life and to be prepared for the Master's use. If you develop all of these disciplines, your life will be balanced and fruitful.

(As you present the following, write the number and the first word following the number in the upper left corner of the page.) To remember this illustration, notice that you have—

1 Lord as the first priority of your life;
2 relationships: a vertical relationship with God and horizontal relationships with others;
3 commitments: deny self, take up your cross daily, and follow Christ;
4 resources to center your life in Christ: the Word, prayer, fellowship, and witness;
5 ministries that grow from the four resources: teaching/preaching, worship/intercession, nurture, evangelism, and service;
6 disciplines of a disciple: spend time with the Master, live in the Word, pray in faith, fellowship with believers, witness to the world, and minister to others.

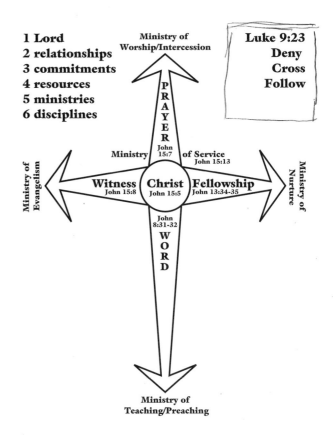

By practicing these biblical principles, you can abide in Christ and can be useful in the Master's service.

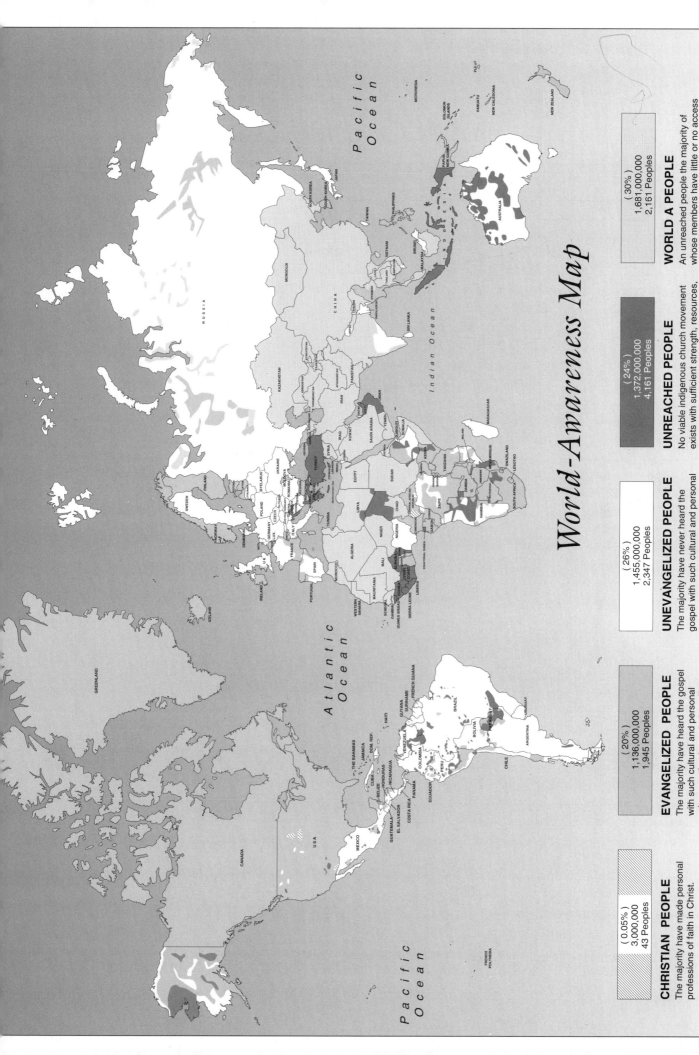

World-Awareness Map

CHRISTIAN PEOPLE
(0.05%)
3,000,000
43 Peoples

The majority have made personal professions of faith in Christ.

EVANGELIZED PEOPLE
(20%)
1,136,000,000
1,945 Peoples

The majority have heard the gospel with such cultural and personal relevance that it results in sufficient understanding to accept Christ by faith or to reject Him.

UNEVANGELIZED PEOPLE
(26%)
1,455,000,000
2,347 Peoples

The majority have never heard the gospel with such cultural and personal relevance that it results in sufficient understanding to accept Christ by faith or to reject Him.

UNREACHED PEOPLE
(24%)
1,372,000,000
4,161 Peoples

No viable indigenous church movement exists with sufficient strength, resources, and commitment to sustain and ensure the continuous multiplication of churches.

WORLD A PEOPLE
(30%)
1,681,000,000
2,161 Peoples

An unreached people the majority of whose members have little or no access to the gospel of Jesus Christ.

Prayer-Covenant List

Request	Date	Bible Promise	Answer	Date
Neb jor healing	10/15/99	MAlAchi 4:2		
SON All the Time		Psolm 103:1-22 Psolm 23	Alwoy Answer when ever I Proy + thonk him Luvl You Jascs	
for Art, Jackie New baby be Normol + Holly 4.99				
Work on my home Ready for christmas				

Liony/M *Alum* *9/99*

MasterTime

Day _____ Date _____

Priority

My Walk with the Master This Week Commitments

Minutes

Planning Ahead

Work to Do

Telephone (Person, Subject, Number)

Discipleship Inventory

This Discipleship Inventory[1] measures the functional discipleship level of individuals, groups, and churches. By using the inventory, believers can assess their development by considering 30 characteristics of a New Testament disciple in the categories of attitudes, behavior, relationships, ministry, and doctrine.

Follow these directions to complete the inventory:

- Respond to each statement as honestly as possible. Select an answer that most clearly reflects your life as it is, not as you would like it to be.
- Choose one answer for each statement.
- Note changes in the types of answers from section to section.
- Do not spend too much time on any one question.

You will receive instructions for scoring your inventory at the Growing Disciples Workshop that follows this study.

How true is each of the following statements of you? Choose from these responses:

> 1 = never true   4 = often true
> 2 = rarely true   5 = almost always true
> 3 = sometimes true

1. I strive to live by the Bible's moral and ethical teachings. 1 2 3 ④ 5
2. Reading and studying the Bible has made significant changes in the way I live my life. 1 2 3 4 ⑤
3. My faith shapes how I think and act each day. 1 2 3 ④ 5
4. I talk with other persons about my beliefs in Christ as Savior and Lord. 1 2 3 4 ⑤
5. I take time for periods of prayer or meditation. 1 2 3 4 ⑤
6. Because God has forgiven me, I respond with a forgiving attitude when others wrong me. 1 2 3 ④ 5
7. While interacting with others in everyday contacts, I seek opportunities to speak out about Jesus Christ. 1 2 ③ 4 5
8. My neighbors and the persons I work with know that I am a Christian. 1 2 3 ④ 5

9. I go out of my way to show love to persons I meet. 1 2 3 ④ 5
10. When I realize that I have disobeyed a specific teaching of the Bible, I correct the wrongdoing. 1 2 3 4 5
11. I pray for God's help when I have needs or problems. 1 2 3 4 ⑤
12. I share personal feelings and needs with Christian friends. 1 2 3 ④ 5
13. I hold a grudge when treated unfairly. 1 2 ③ 4 5
14. I devote time to reading and studying the Bible. 1 2 3 ④ 5
15. I like to worship and pray with others. 1 2 3 ④ 5
16. I use my gifts and talents to serve others. 1 2 3 ④ 5
17. When I become aware that I have offended someone, I go to him or her to admit and correct my wrongdoing. 1 2 ③ 4 5
18. I pray for the salvation of friends and acquaintances who are not professing Christians. 1 2 3 ④ 5
19. I work to remove barriers or problems that develop between me and my friends. 1 2 3 ④ 5
20. I feel too inadequate to help others. 1 2 ③ 4 5

How often, if ever, do you do each of the following? Choose from these responses:

1 = seldom or never   4 = several times a week
2 = about once a month   5 = once a day or more
3 = about once a week

21. Pray with other Christians, other than during church 1 2 3 ④ 5
22. Participate in a small-group Bible study, other than Sunday School 1 2 3 ④ 5
23. Pray or meditate, other than at church or before meals 1 2 3 4 ⑤
24. Memorize verses or passages of the Bible 1 2 ③ 4 5
25. Study the Bible on my own 1 2 3 ④ 5
26. Pray specifically for missions and missionaries 1 2 3 ④ 5

Indicate how much you agree or disagree with each of the following statements. Choose from these responses:

1 = definitely disagree   4 = tend to agree
2 = tend to disagree   5 = definitely agree
3 = not sure

27. It is my personal responsibility to share the gospel message with non-Christians in my life. 1 2 3 4 ⑤

28. Once a person is saved, he cannot lose his salvation. 1 2 3 4 5

29. I often accept other Christians' constructive criticism and correction. 1 2 3 4 5

30. I believe that the Holy Spirit is active in my life. 1 2 3 ④ 5

31. If a person sincerely seeks God, she can obtain eternal life through religions other than Christianity. 1 2 3 4 5

32. I know how to explain the gospel clearly to another person without relying on an evangelistic tract. 1 2 ③ 4 5

33. A Christian should consider himself accountable to other Christians. 1 2 3 4 ⑤

34. A Christian should regularly find ways to tell others about Jesus. 1 2 3 4 ⑤

35. Salvation is available only through receiving Jesus Christ. 1 2 3 4 ⑤

36. The way I live my Christian life is not others' business. ① 2 3 4 5

37. The Holy Spirit comes into a person the moment she accepts Jesus as Savior. 1 2 3 ④ 5

38. A literal place called hell exists. 1 2 3 4 ⑤

39. I believe that I have a personal responsibility to help the poor and hungry. 1 2 3 4 ⑤

40. The complete indwelling of the Holy Spirit occurs through an experience that is usually separate and distinct from the conversion experience. 1 2 3 4 ⑤

How many hours during the past month have you done each of the following through church, other organizations, or on your own? Do not count time spent in a paid job. Choose from these responses:

1 = 0 hours   3 = 3–5 hours
2 = 1–2 hours   4 = 6–9 hours
                    5 = 10 hours or more

41. Donated time helping persons who are poor, hungry, sick, or unable to care for themselves

(don't count family members) 1 2 ③ 4 5

42. Visited those who have visited my church ① 2 3 4 5

43. Helped friends or neighbors with problems 1 2 ③ 4 5

44. Been involved in a missions-related ministry or cause (for example, teaching about missions, raising money for missions, missions volunteer work) 1 ② 3 4 5

45. Visited persons in the hospital 1 2 ③ 4 5

46. Given volunteer time at my church to teach, lead, serve on a committee, or help with a program or event 1 2 3 4 5

47. Visited in the homes of Christian friends 1 2 3 ④ 5

48. Visited the elderly or the homebound 1 2 ③ 4 5

How true is each of the following statements for you? Choose from these responses:

1 = absolutely false   4 = mostly true
2 = somewhat false   5 = absolutely true
3 = not sure

49. I am open and responsive to Bible teachers in my church. 1 2 3 4 ⑤

50. I readily receive and forgive those who offend me. 1 2 3 4 5

51. I see myself as loved and valued by God. 1 2 3 ④ 5

52. I express genuine praise and gratitude to God even in the midst of difficult circumstances. 1 2 3 ④ 5

53. I avoid close relationships with others who hinder the expression of my Christian values and principles. 1 2 3 ④ 5   Witness

54. I am consciously aware that God placed me on earth to contribute to the fulfillment of His plans and purposes. 1 2 3 4 ⑤

55. I recognize that everything I have belongs to God. 1 2 3 4 ⑤

56. My life is filled with stress and anxiety. 1 2 3 ④ 5

57. I believe that God will always provide my basic needs in life. 1 2 3 4 ⑤

58. I am somewhat hesitant to let others know that I am a Christian. 1 2 3 4 5

59. I avoid situations in which I might be tempted by sexual immorality. 1 2 3 4 ⑤

60. I am presently struggling with an unforgiving atti-

tude toward another person. **1 2 3 4 5**

61. I feel very inferior to others in my church.
1 2 3 4 5
62. I seek God first in expressing my values and setting my priorities. **1 2 3 4 5**
63. I am able to remain confident of God's love and provision even during very difficult circumstances.
1 2 3 4 5
64. I forgive those who offend me even if they do not apologize. **1 2 3 4 5**
65. Being a Christian is a private matter and does not need to be discussed with others. **1 2 3 4 5**

Last year what percentage of your income did you contribute to each of the following? Choose from these responses:

1 = 0%	4 = 6–9%
2 = 1–2%	5 = 10% and above
3 = 3–5%	

66. To my church **1 2 3 4 5**
67. To other religious groups or religious organizations **1 2 3 4 5**
68. To charities or social-service organizations
1 2 3 4 5
69. To international missions (through my church and denomination) **1 2 3 4 5**

For the following question choose from these responses:

1 = none	4 = the majority
2 = a few	5 = all
3 = several	

70. How many of your closest friends do you consider to be unbelievers? **1 2 3 4 5**

How often have you done each of the following during the past year? Choose from these responses:

1 = never	4 = 6–9 times
2 = once	5 = 10 times or more
3 = 2–5 times	

71. Clearly felt God's presence in my life **1 2 3 4 5**
72. Shared with someone how to become a Christian
1 2 3 4 5
73. Invited an unchurched person to attend church, Bible study, or another evangelistic event
1 2 3 4 5

74. Experienced the Holy Spirit's providing understanding, guidance, or conviction of sin
1 2 3 4 5
75. Met with a new Christian to help him grow spiritually **1 2 3 4 5**
76. Told others about God's work in my life
1 2 3 4 5
77. Helped someone pray to receive Christ
1 2 3 4 5
78. Gave a gospel tract or similar literature to an unbeliever **1 2 3 4 5**

Indicate how much you agree or disagree with each of the following. Choose from these responses:

1 = strongly disagree	4 = agree
2 = disagree	5 = strongly agree
3 = not sure	

79. It is very important for every Christian to serve others. **1 2 3 4 5**
80. One day God will hold me accountable for how I used my time, money, and talents. **1 2 3 4 5**
81. All Christians are to follow Bible teachings.
1 2 3 4 5
82. The Bible is the authoritative source of wisdom for daily living. **1 2 3 4 5**
83. A Christian must learn to deny herself to serve Christ effectively. **1 2 3 4 5**
84. I have a hard time accepting myself. **1 2 3 4 5**
85. I have identified my primary spiritual gift.
1 2 3 4 5
86. Following death, an unbeliever goes to a place called hell. **1 2 3 4 5**
87. Jesus' teachings are binding for the modern Christian. **1 2 3 4 5**
88. Giving time to a specific ministry in the church is necessary for a Christian's spiritual welfare.
1 2 3 4 5
89. Regardless of my circumstances, I believe God always keeps His promises. **1 2 3 4 5**
90. Without the death of Jesus, salvation would not be possible. **1 2 3 4 5**
91. The Bible is a completely reliable revelation from God. **1 2 3 4 5**

Indicate how well-trained and prepared you believe you are in the following areas. Choose

from these responses:

1 = not trained at all   4 = adequately
2 = somewhat trained   trained
3 = average   5 = well-trained

92. Presenting the plan of salvation   1 2 3 4 5
93. Individually following up or helping a new Christian grow and develop spiritually   1 2 3 4 5
94. Leading someone to pray to receive Christ   1 2 3 4 5
95. Visiting a prospect for my church   1 2 3 4 5
96. Leading a small-group Bible study   1 2 3 4 5
97. Sharing my personal testimony about how I became a Christian   1 2 3 4 5

How often during the past two or three years have you done each of the following? Choose from these responses:

1 = never   4 = weekly
2 = a few times   5 = daily
3 = monthly

98. Read the Bible by myself   1 2 3 4 5
99. Consciously put into practice the teachings of the Bible   1 2 3 4 5
100. Prayed by myself   1 2 3 4 5
101. Provided help to needy persons in my town or city   1 2 3 4 5
102. Read and studied about the Christian faith   1 2 3 4 5
103. Participated in Bible studies, religious programs, or groups outside my church   1 2 3 4 5
104. Made the necessary changes when I realized, as a result of exposure to the Bible, that an aspect of my life was not right   1 2 3 4 5
105. Shared an insight, idea, principle, or guideline from the Bible with others   1 2 3 4 5
106. Experienced the care, love, and support of other persons in a church   1 2 3 4 5
107. Directly tried to encourage someone to believe in Jesus Christ   1 2 3 4 5
108. Intentionally spent time building friendships with non-Christians   1 2 3 4 5

How true is each of these statements for you? Choose from these responses:

1 = never true   4 = often true
2 = rarely true   5 = almost always true
3 = sometimes true

109. I feel God's presence in my relationships with other persons.   1 2 3 4 5
110. I treat persons of the other gender in a pure and holy manner.   1 2 3 4 5
111. When convicted of sin in my life, I readily confess it to God as sin.   1 2 3 4 5
112. Through prayer I seek to discern God's will for my life.   1 2 3 4 5
113. I readily forgive others because of my understanding that God has forgiven me.   1 2 3 4 5
114. I help others with their religious questions and struggles.   1 2 3 4 5
115. I have learned through my faith and the Scriptures how to sacrifice for the good of others.   1 2 3 4 5
116. I share my faults and weaknesses with others whom I consider to be close to me.   1 2 3 4 5
117. I am generally the same person in private that I am in public.   1 2 3 4 5
118. When God makes me aware of His specific will for me in an area of my life, I follow His leading.   1 2 3 4 5
119. I regularly find myself choosing God's way over my way in specific instances.   1 2 3 4 5
120. I am honest in my dealings with others.   1 2 3 4 5
121. I regularly pray for my church's ministry.   1 2 3 4 5

How often do you attend the following activities? Choose from these responses:

1 = never   4 = weekly
2 = a few times   5 = more than once a week
3 = monthly

122. Worship services at my church   1 2 3 4 5
123. Sunday School class   1 2 3 4 5
124. Bible studies other than Sunday School   1 2 3 4 5
125. Prayer groups or prayer meetings   1 2 3 4 5

Indicate how much you agree or disagree with each of the following statements. Choose from these responses: 3 = not sure

1 = definitely disagree   4 = tend to agree
2 = tend to disagree   5 = definitely agree

126. God fulfills His plan primarily through believers within a local-church context.   1 2 3 4 5

127. Christ designated local churches as His means and environment for nurturing believers in the faith. 1 2 3 4 5

128. A new believer should experience believer's baptism by immersion prior to acceptance by a local church as a member. 1 2 3 4 5

129. Baptism and the Lord's Supper are local church ordinances and should not be practiced outside the gathered church. 1 2 3 4 5

130. Each person born into the world inherited a sinful nature as a result of Adam's fall and is thereby separated from God and is in need of a Savior. 1 2 3 4 5

131. Each local church is autonomous, with Jesus Christ as the Head, and should work together with other churches to spread the gospel to all people. 1 2 3 4 5

132. There is only one true and personal God, who reveals Himself to humanity as God the Father, God the Son, and God the Holy Spirit. 1 2 3 4 5

133. Christ will return a second time to receive His believers, living and dead, unto Himself and to bring the world to an appropriate end. 1 2 3 4 5

134. Jesus Christ is God's Son, who died on the cross for the sins of the world and was resurrected from the dead. 1 2 3 4 5

135. Jesus Christ, during His incarnate life on earth, was fully God and fully man. 1 2 3 4 5

136. How religious or spiritual would you say your 3 or 4 best friends are? 1 2 3
   1 = not very religious
   2 = somewhat religious
   3 = very religious

137. How many of your closest friends are professing Christians? 1 2 3 4 5
   1 = none   4 = the majority
   2 = a few   5 = all
   3 = several

138. Are you male or female? Male (Female)

139. Indicate your age group: 1 2 3 4 5 6
   1 = 18–22   4 = 41–50
   2 = 23–30   5 = 51–60
   3 = 31–40   6 = 61 and over

140. I have been an active member of a local church. 1 2 3 4 5

1 = never   4 = a large part of my life
2 = a short time   5 = most of my life
   in my life
3 = about half of
   my life

141. How long have you been a Christian? 1 2 3 4 5 6
   1 = less than 1 year   4 = 6–10 years
   2 = 1–3 years   5 = 11–20 years
   3 = 4–5 years   6 = More than 20 years

142. Identifying as a member of a local church wherever I live is— 1 2 3 4 5
   1 = unnecessary   4 = of great value
   2 = of little value 5 = imperative
   3 = of some value

143. Have you ever been involved in discipleship training (an organized, weekly discipleship group)? Yes   No
   If so, which discipleship-training program were you involved in?

144. *MasterLife*   Yes   No
145. Navigators   Yes   No
146. *Survival Kit*   Yes   No
147. Evangelism Explosion   Yes   No
148. *Continuing Witness Training*   Yes   No
   If other, please provide the name:

_____

149. How many weeks were you involved in this discipleship training? 1 2 3 4 5
   1 = 0–5 weeks   4 = 16–25 weeks
   2 = 6–10 weeks   5 = More than 25 weeks
   3 = 11–15 weeks

150. When were you involved in this training? From 10-5-99 to _____

151. Was this discipleship training sponsored by your local church? Yes   No
   If not, what group or organization sponsored the training?_____

152. Have you ever been discipled one-to-one by another Christian? Yes   No

[1]James Slack and Brad Waggoner, "The Discipleship Inventory" (Richmond: The International Mission Board of the Southern Baptist Convention). Used by permission.

CHRISTIAN GROWTH STUDY PLAN

Preparing Christians to Serve

In the **Christian Growth Study Plan (formerly the Church Study Course)** *MasterLife 1: The Disciple's Cross* is a resource for course credit in the subject area Personal Life in the Christian Growth category of diploma plans. To receive credit, read the book; complete the learning activities; attend group sessions; show your work to your pastor, a staff member, or a church leader; and complete the following information. This page may be duplicated. Send the completed page to:

**Christian Growth Study Plan
127 Ninth Avenue, North, MSN 117
Nashville, TN 37234-0117
FAX: (615) 251-5067**

For information about the Christian Growth Study Plan, refer to the current *Christian Growth Study Plan Catalog*. Your church office may have a copy. If not, request a free copy from the Christian Growth Study Plan office, (615) 251-2525.

MasterLife 1: The Disciple's Cross
COURSE NUMBER: CG-0168
PARTICIPANT INFORMATION

Social Security Number | Personal CGSP Number* | Date of Birth

Name (First, MI, Last)
❑Mr.   ❑Miss
❑Mrs.   ❑

Home Phone

Address (Street, Route, or P.O. Box) | City, State | ZIP

CHURCH INFORMATION

Church Name

Address (Street, Route, or P.O. Box) | City, State | ZIP

CHANGE REQUEST ONLY

❑Former Name

❑Former Address | City, State | ZIP

❑Former Church | City, State | ZIP

Signature of Pastor, Conference Leader, or Other Church Leader | Date

*New participants are requested but not required to give SS# and date of birth. Existing participants, please give CGSP# when using SS# for the first time.
Thereafter, only one ID# is required. *Mail to:* Christian Growth Study Plan, 127 Ninth Ave., North, MSN 117, Nashville, TN 37234-0117. Fax: (615) 251-5067.

THE DISCIPLE'S PERSONALITY

MasterLife

BOOK 2

Avery T. Willis, Jr.
Kay Moore

Dorothy Echols
1508 Forsyth Rd
Savannah, GA 31406
912 52-8048

Thankyou
God

LifeWay Press
Nashville, Tennessee

✚

© Copyright 1996 • LifeWay Press
All rights reserved
3rd reprint 1998

ISBN 0-7673-2580-X
Dewey Decimal Classification: 248.4
Subject Heading: DISCIPLESHIP

This book is text for course CG-0169 in the subject area Personal Life in the Christian Growth Study Plan.

Unless otherwise noted, Scripture quotations are from the Holy Bible,
New International Version,
copyright © 1973, 1978, 1984 by International Bible Society.

Scripture quotations marked RSV are from the *Revised Standard Version of the Bible,*
copyrighted © 1946, 1952, 1971, 1973.

Printed in the United States of America

Design: Edward Crawford
Cover illustration: Mick Wiggins

LifeWay Press
127 Ninth Avenue, North
Nashville, Tennessee 37234

Contents

The Authors

AVERY T. WILLIS, JR., the author and developer of *MasterLife,* is the senior vice-president of overseas operations at the International Mission Board of the Southern Baptist Convention. The original *MasterLife: Discipleship Training for Leaders,* published in 1980, has been used by more than 250,000 people in the United States and has been translated into more than 50 different languages for use by untold thousands. Willis is also the author of *Indonesian Revival: Why Two Million Came to Christ, The Biblical Basis of Missions, MasterBuilder: Multiplying Leaders, BibleGuide to Discipleship and Doctrine,* and several books in Indonesian.

Willis served for 10 years as a pastor in Oklahoma and Texas and for 14 years as a missionary to Indonesia, during which he served for 6 years as the president of the Indonesian Baptist Theological Seminary. Before assuming his present position, he served as the director of the Adult Department of the Discipleship and Family Development Division, the Sunday School Board of the Southern Baptist Convention, where he introduced the Lay Institute for Equipping (LIFE), a series of in-depth discipleship courses.

KAY MOORE served as the coauthor of this updated edition of *MasterLife.* Formerly a design editor in the Adult Department of the Discipleship and Family Development Division, the Sunday School Board of the Southern Baptist Convention, she led the editorial team that produced the LIFE Support Series, biblically based courses that help people deal with critical issues in their lives. A writer, editor, and conference leader, Moore has authored or coauthored numerous books on family life, relationships, and inspirational topics. She is the author of *Gathering the Missing Pieces in an Adopted Life* and is a frequent contributor to religious magazines and devotional guides.

Introduction

MasterLife is a developmental, small-group disciple-ship process that will help you develop a lifelong, obedient relationship with Christ. This book, *MasterLife 2: The Disciple's Personality,* is the second of four books in that discipleship process. The other three books are *MasterLife 1: The Disciple's Cross, MasterLife 3: The Disciple's Victory,* and *MasterLife 4: The Disciple's Mission.* These studies will enable you to acknowledge Christ as your Master and to master life in Him.

WHAT'S IN IT FOR YOU
The goal of *MasterLife* is your discipleship—for you to become like Christ. To do that, you must follow Jesus, learn to do the things He instructed His fol-lowers to do, and help others become His disciples. In these ways *MasterLife* will enable you to discover the satisfaction of following Christ as His disciple and the joy of that relationship with Him. *MasterLife* was designed to help you make the following definition of *discipleship* a way of life:

> Christian discipleship is developing a personal, lifelong, obedient relationship with Jesus Christ in which He transforms your character into Christlikeness; changes your values into Kingdom values; and involves you in His mission in the home, the church, and the world.

In *MasterLife 1: The Disciple's Cross* you explored your personal relationship with Jesus Christ. You learned how to draw the Disciple's Cross to illustrate the balanced life Christ wants His disciples to have. You learned that Christ wants to be at the center of your life so that everything you do is an outgrowth of your relationship with Him.

You will continue to focus on your relationship with Christ in *MasterLife 2: The Disciple's Personality.* However, in this study you will focus on Christ's transforming your character into Christlikeness through the work of the Holy Spirit. Although you are a Christian, you may wonder why you continue to

sin despite your best intentions, as if two selves are at war inside you—one controlled by the Spirit and one controlled by the flesh. Jesus' disciples were not Christlike when they were born again, and neither were you. In this study you will learn how the Holy Spirit can change your character and behavior into Christlikeness so that He can work through your will and your life. If you deny yourself and open yourself to the leading of the Holy Spirit, who lives in you, your character can grow more like that of Christ. The outgrowth of having Christ at the center of your per-sonality is life in the Spirit. He will build Christlike character in you as you practice the six disciplines you learned in *MasterLife 1: The Disciple's Cross:*
- Spend time with the Master
- Live in the Word
- Pray in faith
- Fellowship with believers
- Witness to the world
- Minister to others

THE *MASTERLIFE* PROCESS
MasterLife 2: The Disciple's Personality is part of a 24-week discipleship process. Completing all four cours-es in *MasterLife* will provide you information and experiences you need to be Christ's disciple. Each book builds on the other and is recommended as a prerequisite for the one that follows.

The *MasterLife* process involves six elements. Each element is essential to your study of *MasterLife.*
1. The *daily activities* in this book lead you into a clos-er walk with Christ. Doing these exercises daily is important.
2. The *weekly assignments* in "My Walk with the Mas-ter This Week" are real-life experiences that will change your life.
3. The *leader* is a major element. Discipleship is a rela-tionship. It is not something you do by yourself. You need human models, instruction, and account-ability to become what Christ intends for you to be. To become a better disciple, you need a leader to whom you can relate personally and regularly—

someone who can teach you, model behaviors, and hold you accountable.

4. The weekly *group sessions* help you reflect on the concepts and experiences in *MasterLife* and help you apply the ideas to your life. The group sessions allow you to experience the profound changes Christ is making in your life. Each group session also provides training for the next stage of spiritual growth.

5. *Christ* is the Discipler, and you become His disciple. As you fully depend on Him, He works through each of the previous elements and uses them to support you.

6. The body of Christ—the *church*—is vital for complete discipling to take place. You depend on Christian friends for fellowship, strength, and ministry opportunities. Without the church, you lack the support you need to grow in Christ.

HOW TO STUDY THIS BOOK

Each day for five days a week you will be expected to study a segment of the material in this workbook and to complete the related activities. You may need from 20 to 30 minutes of study time each day. Even if you find that you can study the material in less time, spreading the study over five days will give you time to apply the truths to your life.

You will notice that discipline logos appear before various assignments:

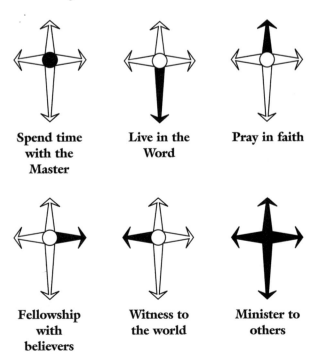

Spend time
with the
Master

Live in the
Word

Pray in faith

Fellowship
with
believers

Witness to
the world

Minister to
others

These logos link certain activities to the six disciplines you are learning to incorporate into your life as a disciple. These activities are part of your weekly assignments, which are outlined in "My Walk with the Master This Week" at the beginning of each week's material. The discipline logos differentiate your weekly assignments from the activities related to your study for that particular day.

Set a definite time and select a quiet place to study with little or no interruption. Keep a Bible handy to find Scriptures as directed in the material. Memorizing Scripture is an important part of your work. Set aside a portion of your study period for memory work. Unless I have deliberately chosen another version for a specific emphasis, all Scriptures in *MasterLife* are quoted from the *New International Version* of the Bible. However, feel free to memorize Scripture from any version of the Bible you prefer. I suggest that you write each memory verse on a card that you can review often during the week.

After completing each day's assignments, turn to the beginning of the week's material. If you completed an activity that corresponds to one listed under "My Walk with the Master This Week," place a vertical line in the diamond beside the activity. During the following group session a member of the group will verify your work and will add a horizontal line in the diamond, forming a cross in each diamond. This process will confirm that you have completed each weekly assignment before you continue. You may do the assignments at your own pace, but be sure to complete all of them before the next group session.

THE DISCIPLE'S PERSONALITY

On pages 133–39 you will find the Disciple's Personality presentation. The Disciple's Personality, which explains how to become more Christlike in character and behavior, will be the focal point for all you learn in this book. Each week you will study an additional portion of the Disciple's Personality and will learn the Scripture that accompanies it. By the end of the study you will be able to explain the Disciple's Personality in your own words and to say all of the verses that go with it.

Discipleship Covenant

To participate in *MasterLife*, you are asked to dedicate yourself to God and to your *MasterLife* group by making the following commitments. You may not currently be able to do everything listed, but by signing this covenant, you pledge to adopt these practices as you progress through the study.

As a disciple of Jesus Christ, I commit myself to—
- acknowledge Jesus Christ as Lord of my life each day;
- attend all group sessions unless providentially hindered;
- spend from 20 to 30 minutes a day as needed to complete all assignments;
- have a daily quiet time;
- keep a Daily Master Communication Guide about the way God speaks to me and I speak to Him;
- be faithful to my church in attendance and stewardship;
- love and encourage each group member;
- share my faith with others;
- keep in confidence anything that others share in the group sessions;
- submit myself to others willingly in accountability;
- become a discipler of others as God gives opportunities;
- support my church financially by practicing biblical giving;
- pray daily for group members.

_____   _____

_____   _____

_____   _____

_____   _____

Signed _____ Date _____

Do God's Will

This Week's Goal

You will be able to understand and do God's will as the Holy Spirit works in you.

My Walk with the Master This Week

You will complete the following activities to develop the six biblical disciplines. When you have completed each activity, draw a vertical line in the diamond beside it.

SPEND TIME WITH THE MASTER
◇ Have a quiet time each day, working toward the goal of having quiet times 21 consecutive days. Check the box beside each day you have a quiet time this week: ❑ Sunday ❑ Monday ❑ Tuesday ❑ Wednesday ❑ Thursday ❑ Friday ❑ Saturday

LIVE IN THE WORD
◇ Read your Bible every day. Write what God says to you and what you say to God.
◇ Memorize Philippians 2:13.

PRAY IN FAITH
◇ Pray for non-Christian friends of group members.
◇ Confess your sins to God and accept that God has forgiven you.

FELLOWSHIP WITH BELIEVERS
◇ Spend time with a member of your family.

WITNESS TO THE WORLD
◇ Think of five persons to whom you need to witness and write their names on the Prayer-Covenant List. Or make friends with five persons to whom you can witness in the future.

MINISTER TO OTHERS
◇ Learn the Unified Personality and Natural Person parts of the Disciple's Personality.

This Week's Scripture-Memory Verse

"It is God who works in you to will and to act according to his good purpose" (Phil. 2:13).

Cit Rotoy

DAY 1

Who's in Charge?

DAILY MASTER COMMUNICATION GUIDE

LUKE 2:41-52

What God said to me:

_____

_____

_____

_____

_____

_____

_____

One day a 16-year-old girl asked me about God's will. I told her that God has a purpose for every person. To make my point, I used several illustrations: "Do you know how many sections are in an orange? An orange usually has 10 sections. A watermelon usually has an even number of stripes. Grains like wheat, barley, millet, and rye have an even number of grains on a stalk. In a fully developed ear of corn an even number of rows are on each ear, an even number of grains are in each row, and an even number of silks are in the tassel." I asked her, "Do you think it's just an accident that so many things God has made have such symmetry?"

She asked, "Does that mean I have to do whatever God wills me to do?" I answered: "No, although God has a perfect will for your life that He wants you to follow, He does not force you to. He leads you to do His will, but He gives you the freedom to make your own choice."

I went on to explain: "It's as if God has a blueprint for your life. Although He may want to build a beautiful mansion from your life, you can still choose to build a shack. But God's intent is that you build according to His will. Make sure that Christ is the foundation of your life. Let the Holy Spirit be the Builder. He can build far better than you can."

Holy Spirit

I watched to see how God worked in the girl's life. Later she became a pastor's wife, and eventually she and her husband served God as missionaries in a foreign country. She made Christ the foundation and let the Holy Spirit guide her and build her life.

In the account you read, what was the key to this young woman's finding God's will in her life?

The Key To finding God's will was making Christ the foundation, and allowing the Holy Spirit to guide her instead of acting on her own will.

The key to finding God's will was making Christ the foundation and allowing the Holy Spirit to guide her instead of acting on her own will. When she gave up her own desires and allowed the Holy Spirit to lead her, He directed her to the center of God's will.

You may wonder: *How do I do that? How do I know that I'm living in the center of His will instead of acting on my own desires?* Jesus chose you and called you to do His will. Because you have chosen to deny yourself, take up your cross, and follow Him, He is now your Savior and Master. This week you will examine guidelines for doing God's will.

What I said to God:

_____

_____

_____

_____

_____

_____

_____

" 'This day I call heaven and earth as witnesses against you that I have set before you life and death, blessings and curses. Now choose life, so that you and your children may live and that you may love the Lord your God, listen to his voice, and hold fast to him. For the Lord is your life, and he will give you many years in the land he swore to give to your fathers, Abraham, Isaac and Jacob' " (Deut. 30:19-20).

"I know that nothing good lives in me, that is, in my sinful nature. For I have the desire to do what is good, but I cannot carry it out" (Rom. 7:18).

"Be very careful, then, how you live—not as unwise but as wise, making the most of every opportunity, because the days are evil. Therefore do not be foolish, but understand what the Lord's will is" (Eph. 5:15-17).

[handwritten margin notes:] Listen / Make a choice / between Like a / death

When you have completed this week's study, you should be able to—
- distinguish between God's will and your will;
- state God's purpose in your doing His will;
- explain the process and the provision by which God accomplishes His will;
- apply to your life the teachings about God's will.

YOU CAN CHOOSE

The Bible teaches that God has given you the capacity to purpose and to choose. This capacity is called your will. The Bible refers to will as a desire, intent, or purpose to do something.

Read the verses in the margin, which refer to a person's will. Indicate whether you agree with each statement:
1. A person's will can be used for good or evil. ☒ Yes ☐ No
2. God is always in control of a person's will. ☐ Yes ☒ No
3. A person can always do what he or she wills to do. ☐ Yes ☒ No

You may think that you are in control of your will, but your sinful nature may prevent your doing good. God wants you to do right, but He leaves that ultimate choice to you. In making your choice, you can choose good or evil. God wants you to choose His way, and His heart breaks when you choose ways that turn you away from Him. This week's Scripture-memory verse reminds you: "It is God who works in you to will and to act according to his good purpose" (Phil. 2:13). The correct answers are 1. yes, 2. no, 3. no.

God does not omit anyone in accomplishing His will. Every person is included in the scope of God's will. Second Peter 3:9 says, "The Lord is not slow in keeping his promise, as some understand slowness. He is patient with you, not wanting anyone to perish, but everyone to come to repentance." When a person becomes a Christian, the Holy Spirit begins revealing to that person God's will for his or her life. If you have life in the Spirit, you will experience this type of activity in your life.

Describe ways the Holy Spirit began revealing God's will in your life after you became a Christian.

[handwritten:] he clean up my Life hove me that I Learn how to Love other

Your answer may be similar to one of these statements: After I became a Christian, the Lord revealed that He wanted me to stop using profane language. He showed me that He wanted me to start attending church regularly. He pointed out that He wanted me to enter a church-related vocation.

The first four Scriptures in the margin mention God's will. Read them and mark the statements *T* (true) or *F* (false).

T 1. Jesus claimed a special relationship with those who follow God's will.

T 2. Jesus said that His purpose was to do God's will.

F 3. Finding God's will is impossible.

T 4. You can discover God's will.

Jesus said that those who do His will have a special relationship with Him. For Jesus, doing God's will was like food—a constant part of His obedient life and purpose. You can find God's will when you are willing to be transformed and to have a renewed mind. All of the statements are true except 3.

CHARACTERISTICS OF GOD'S WILL

God's will and the human will are vastly different. They differ in capacity and purpose. Your capacity to carry out your own will is limited. Even good purposes can be ill motivated and corrupted. For example, you could desire to win persons to the Lord so that others think you are a great Christian. You could also waver in your desire to reach persons for Christ. When the task becomes difficult, you could decide that it is not worth the effort.

Unlike your frail, human capacity, however, God's capacity to carry out His will is unlimited. His purpose is always holy, upright, and constant. He does not change His mind on a whim or when the way is difficult. He always wants His will to be done, and He sends His Holy Spirit to help accomplish it.

 This week's Scripture-memory verse describes the way God works in you to help you find His will. To begin your memory work, read aloud Philippians 2:13 from one to three times. Check this box when you have done so: ❏

FULFILLING GOD'S PURPOSE

When you think about finding God's will for your life, you may wonder where to begin. You may feel that you cannot think God's thoughts or learn what He has in store for you. God wants to teach you how He reveals His will and how you can do His will. Doing God's will begins when you have a vision of God and His purpose for your life and are open to letting the Holy Spirit teach you.

Read Ephesians 1:5-6,12-14 in the margin. Check what these verses emphasize as God's primary purpose for your life.

❏ 1. To make me happy

❏ 2. To win the lost

☒ 3. To bring glory to God

" 'Whoever does the will of my Father in heaven is my brother and sister and mother' " (Matt. 12:50).

" 'My food,' said Jesus, 'is to do the will of him who sent me and to finish his work' " (John 4:34).

"Do not conform any longer to the pattern of this world, but be transformed by the renewing of your mind. Then you will be able to test and approve what God's will is—his good, pleasing and perfect will" (Rom. 12:2).

"For this reason, since the day we heard about you, we have not stopped praying for you and asking God to fill you with the knowledge of his will through all spiritual wisdom and understanding" (Col. 1:9).

"He predestined us to be adopted as his sons through Jesus Christ, in accordance with his pleasure and will—to the praise of his glorious grace, which he has freely given us in the One he loves.

"In order that we, who were the first to hope in Christ, might be for the praise of his glory. And you also were included in Christ when you heard the word of truth, the gospel of your salvation. Having believed, you were marked in him with a seal, the promised Holy Spirit, who is a deposit guaranteeing our inheritance until the redemption of those who are God's possession—to the praise of his glory" (Eph. 1:5-6,12-14).

" 'Father, if you are willing, take this cup from me; yet not my will, but yours be done' " (Luke 22:42).

" 'By myself I can do nothing; I judge only as I hear, and my judgment is just, for I seek not to please myself but him who sent me' " (John 5:30).

" 'I have come down from heaven not to do my will but to do the will of him who sent me' " (John 6:38).

" 'I have brought you glory on earth by completing the work you gave me to do' " (John 17:4).

Your purpose for living is to bring glory to God so that His name will be praised. The correct answer is 3.

Jesus' life depicts someone whose purpose for living was to bring glory to God so that His name would be praised. Jesus lived to do God's will. The Scriptures in the margin express how Jesus felt about doing God's will.

Read the Scriptures in the margin. Then match each Scripture reference with its summary statement.

C 1. Luke 22:42   a. **Jesus glorified God while He was on earth.**

B 2. John 5:30   b. **Jesus did not seek His own will.**

D 3. John 6:38   c. **Jesus prayed for God's will, not His, to be done.**

A 4. John 17:4   d. **Jesus came from heaven to do God's will.**

Jesus sought God's will while He was on earth and did not seek to do His own will. Would a person deliberately wish humiliation, anguish, and death for himself? If Jesus could have had His way, would He have chosen for friends and family to reject Him and for crowds to mock and scorn Him? Jesus experienced these things because they were part of His Father's perfect will, not because He wanted them. The correct answers are 1. c, 2. b, 3. d, 4. a.

Jesus' commitment to God's purpose made His ministry on this earth effective. Your development in every part of your Christian life and ministry depends on your commitment to God's purpose. Can you let Jesus be your example and guide in doing God's will?

Can you honestly state that the purpose of your life is to glorify God? ☑ **Yes** ☐ **No If you could not answer yes, what takes priority over glorifying God?** _____

What changes would you need to make for your life purpose to be glorifying God?

You can find God's will by Regularly feeding on his word by spending time with him in prayer

You can find God's will by regularly feeding on His Word and by spending time with Him in prayer. In *MasterLife 1: The Disciple's Cross* you learned the disciplines of living in the Word and praying in faith. I hope that having a daily quiet time, which incorporates these two disciplines, is a regular part of your life now. Each day during this study you will be asked to have a quiet time.

Read Luke 2:41-52, an early example of Jesus' doing His Father's will, during your quiet time today. Then complete the Daily Master Communication Guide on page 9.

DAY 2
About Your Personality

As you studied about doing God's will in day 1, did you wonder why you often try to carry out your own will instead of first seeking God's will? Do you ever wonder why you have thoughts, feelings, and behaviors that do not honor Christ? Today you will begin learning the Disciple's Personality, a simple illustration that is a major part of our study of life in the Spirit. The drawing will illustrate biblical teachings about your personality. It will show you how to make Christ the Master of your life and how to master life as you strive to do God's will instead of your own.

Do you ever wonder why you have thoughts, feelings, and behaviors that do not honor Christ?

LEARNING THE DISCIPLE'S PERSONALITY
God created you as a physical and spiritual being. The physical part came from the earth. The spiritual part originated in God's Spirit. The illustration you will draw over the next few days will help you understand how you are made.

✝ The first part of the Disciple's Personality is called "A Unified Personality." Read that section on page 133. Begin by drawing a circle below, leaving openings at the top and the bottom of the circle. Write *God* above the circle. Refer to the Disciple's Personality presentation (pp. 133–39) if you need help.

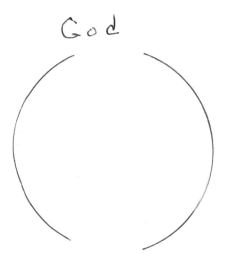

The Bible describes you as a unity, a whole. That is why you drew one circle to represent your total personality. When you learned the Disciple's Cross, you drew a circle representing your life, with Christ at the center. In the Disciple's Personality presentation the circle also represents you. As you develop your understanding of your personality and behavior, you will add to your drawing. When you understand each element of your personality and how it functions, you will discover how to integrate your personality under the lordship of Christ. The Disciple's Personality also encourages you to continue practicing the six disciplines you learned in *MasterLife 1: The Disciple's Cross.* By the end of this study you will be able to draw the complete Disciple's Personality.

GROWING IN CHRISTLIKENESS

The Bible emphasizes building Christlike character, which is a part of the following definition of *discipleship.*

> Discipleship is developing a personal, lifelong, obedient relationship with Jesus Christ in which **He transforms your character into Christlikeness; changes your values into Kingdom values;** and involves you in His mission in the home, the church, and the world.

As you complete this study, you will work on aspects of your character that Christ desires to mold into His likeness. When you read this definition, you may have asked yourself: *What exactly is Christlikeness? How will I know whether my character is Christlike?*

"We know that in all things God works for the good of those who love him, who have been called according to his purpose. For those God foreknew he also predestined to be conformed to the likeness of his Son, that he might be the firstborn among many brothers" (Rom. 8:28-29).

Read the verses in the margin. What is God's will for you?

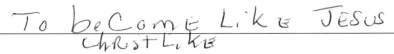
To beCome Like Jesus
ChRistLike

God's purpose and will for you are that you become like Jesus. Transforming your character into Christlikeness means that the Holy Spirit helps you increasingly become like Christ in every character trait.

In day 1 you read that Jesus did God's will. He came from heaven to do God's will. Doing God's will was a constant part of Jesus' obedient life and purpose. He glorified God while He was on earth. He prayed for God's will, not His own, to be done.

Do you desire to do what Jesus did? Check the statements that apply to you.

❑ I want to be like Jesus and to do God's will, but I'm afraid that it may require me to give up something.

❑ I want to be like Jesus and to do God's will, but I'm afraid that I don't have the ability to do as He directs me.

❑ Being like Jesus is impossible for me. I can never do God's will if this is required of me.

☑ Yes, I want to do God's will, as Jesus did. Lord, please show me how.

In this study you will learn more about how to be like Jesus, how increasingly to develop Christlike character, and how developing His character traits helps you do His will.

↑↓ **Say aloud this week's Scripture-memory verse, Philippians 2:13. Write what God says to you through this verse about doing God's will and about building Christlike character.**

It is God who works in you to will And to Act According To his good PURPOSE

You may have answered something like this: I need to allow the Holy Spirit to work in me to remove harmful character traits and build new ones that honor Christ.

How are you doing in your practice of having a daily quiet time? Your goal is to have quiet times 21 straight days to establish it as part of your daily life. I hope that having a quiet time is a meaningful experience for you.

↑↓ **Read John 5:16-30 during your quiet time today. See what God reveals to you through this passage about another time Jesus mentioned pleasing the Father. Then complete the Daily Master Communication Guide in the margin.**

DAY 3

Committing Your Personality

Doing God's will depends on committing your whole personality to God. Even when you commit yourself to God, you soon discover that doing His will is not easy. Many factors influence you.

Schoolteacher Connie Baldwin described this type of struggle when she and her husband, Mark, a church-staff member, were searching to know God's will several years ago. "Mark felt that God was leading him to another church, but he didn't know where," Connie said. "He received a few offers but turned them down, saying he didn't feel that these offers were part of God's will. Unfortunately, I didn't have as much faith. I felt that Mark was crazy for turning down those churches."

The Holy Spirit then led Connie to Ephesians 3:20-21, which says that God is able to do immeasurably more than all we ask or imagine. "I realized that I was wrong to limit God's will and to mistrust my hus-

DAILY MASTER COMMUNICATION GUIDE

JOHN 5:16-30

What God said to me:

_____

_____

_____

_____

_____

_____

_____

What I said to God:

_____

_____

_____

_____

_____

_____

_____

_____

"It is God who works in you to will and to act according to his good purpose" (Phil. 2:13).

"Do not conform any longer to the pattern of this world, but be transformed by the renewing of your mind. Then you will be able to test and approve what God's will is—his good, pleasing and perfect will" (Rom. 12:2).

"Offer your bodies as living sacrifices, holy and pleasing to God—this is your spiritual act of worship" (Rom. 12:1).

"The acts of the sinful nature are obvious: sexual immorality, impurity and debauchery; idolatry and witchcraft; hatred, discord, jealousy, fits of rage, selfish ambition, dissensions, factions and envy; drunkenness, orgies, and the like. I warn you, as I did before, that those who live like this will not inherit the kingdom of God. But the fruit of the Spirit is love, joy, peace, patience, kindness, goodness, faithfulness, gentleness and self-control. Against such things there is no law. Those who belong to Christ Jesus have crucified the sinful nature with its passions and desires" (Gal. 5:19-24).

"I have been crucified with Christ and I no longer live, but Christ lives in me. The life I lived in the body, I live by faith in the Son of God, who loved me and gave himself for me" (Gal. 2:20).

band's faith. Then God called us to the church where we now serve. I never expected God's call to be to a church so loving, so God-centered, so caring—yet God knew all along!" Connie said that her lack of faith could have caused the couple to miss truly knowing and doing God's will and the Holy Spirit's leading.

GOD PROVIDES THE WAY
Read 1 John 2:15-17 below.

"Do not love the world or anything in the world. If anyone loves the world, the love of the Father is not in him. For everything in the world—the cravings of sinful man, the lust of his eyes and the boasting of what he has and does—comes not from the Father but from the world. The world and its desires pass away, but the man who does the will of God lives forever" (1 John 2:15-17).

Check the factor(s) that most hinder you from doing God's will.
☑ **sinful nature** ❑ **environment** ❑ **heredity**

Although you may have checked more than one answer, the verses from 1 John clearly indicate that your sinful nature keeps you from doing God's will. Other factors may predispose you to it. You may live in an environment in which sin is rampant. You may come from a family that did not honor Christ. But you have a choice about whether to do God's will. Your sinful nature is the primary culprit that causes you to refuse to listen to the Holy Spirit and decline to do God's will.

How do you commit your whole personality to God? Does that mean losing your identity? Does that mean becoming passive and simply letting life roll over you? Does that mean never again struggling with what God wants you to do? Even Jesus struggled when He was tempted. But even though you struggle, God provides a way to accomplish His will in you when you commit your entire personality to Him.

Read the Scriptures in the margin. Describe how God enables you to commit each part of your personality to His will. The first reference is this week's Scripture-memory verse. See if you can recite it from memory.

Will (Phil. 2:13): God's Work in me Prove the will

Mind (Rom. 12:2): God Renew my mind

Body (Rom. 12:1): Make my body A Sacrifice living

Emotions (Gal. 5:19-24): The Fruit of the Spirit

Life (Gal. 2:20): The Holy Spirit Christ Live in You

Here are some ways you could have answered: *Will:* God works in you to provide the will and the ability to do His good pleasure. *Mind:* God renews your mind so that you can prove that His will is good, pleasing, and complete. *Body:* God tells you to present your body as a living sacrifice to Him as your reasonable service; Jesus encourages you to pray because your body is weak (see Matt. 26:41). *Emotions:* The Holy Spirit produces the fruit of the Spirit in you to replace evil emotions and actions. *Life:* Christ lives in you when you are crucified with Him, and He provides the power to do His will.

Here is a summary of what you have learned about God's will:

The process of doing God's will is accomplished through—
- a vision of God's purpose for your life;
- a commitment of your whole personality to God;
- actions based on God's provision for doing His will.

LEARNING THE DISCIPLE'S PERSONALITY

The Bible depicts you as a body and a soul. Read the sections "Body" and "Soul" (pp. 133–34) in the Disciple's Personality presentation.

✝ Draw a circle with *God* above it and *body* beneath it. Write the five senses—*sight, sound, smell, taste,* and *touch*—on each side of the circle. Now write *soul* on the inner top rim of the circle and *mind, will,* and *emotions* in the exact center of the circle. Refer to the Disciple's Personality presentation (pp. 133–39) if you need help. By the end of this study you will be able to draw the complete Disciple's Personality and to explain it in your own words.

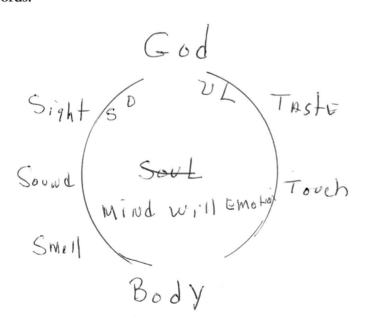

"Live by the Spirit, and you will not gratify the desires of the sinful nature. For the sinful nature desires what is contrary to the Spirit, and the Spirit what is contrary to the sinful nature. They are in conflict with each other, so that you do not do what you want. But if you are led by the Spirit, you are not under law.

"The acts of the sinful nature are obvious: sexual immorality, impurity and debauchery; idolatry and witchcraft; hatred, discord, jealousy, fits of rage, selfish ambition, dissensions, factions and envy; drunkenness, orgies, and the like. I warn you, as I did before, that those who live like this will not inherit the kingdom of God. But the fruit of the Spirit is love, joy, peace, patience, kindness, goodness, faithfulness, gentleness and self-control. Against such things there is no law. Those who belong to Christ Jesus have crucified the sinful nature with its passions and desires. Since we live by the Spirit, let us keep in step with the Spirit" (Gal. 5:16-25).

What happens when you shift from the image of self to the image of Christ? What happens when you set aside the inclinations of the natural person and increasingly become more Christlike? In day 2 you learned that God expects you to be like Jesus, becoming more Christlike day by day. Today you will learn more about what that means.

IN THE CARPENTER'S SHOP
When you think about setting aside old traits and becoming more Chistlike, you can picture tearing down an old house and building a new one. What will you tear down and replace to become more Christlike? Ask the Holy Spirit to show you as you read Galatians 5:16-25 in the margin.

Galatians 5:16-25 is one of three similar Bible passages that illustrate what it means to leave the old life behind, or tear it down, and to take up, or build, the new life. You will study the other two passages in days 4 and 5 this week.

Below are statements from the passage you just read from Galatians 5. Write *O* beside the statements that apply to the old person in Christ and *N* beside those that describe a new person in Christ.

N 1. **"Keep in step with the Spirit."**
O 2. **"Gratify the desires of the sinful nature."**
O 3. **"[Desire] what is contrary to the Spirit."**
N 4. **"[Crucify] the sinful nature."**
N 5. **"Live by the Spirit."**
N 6. **"[Be] led by the Spirit."**
N 7. **"[Have] the fruit of the Spirit."**

As you know Christ more intimately, your life will change. You want to do God's will, to be like Christ, and to have Christ's character. The answers are 1. N, 2. O, 3. O, 4. N, 5. N, 6. N, 7. N.

 Stop and pray for the salvation of the non-Christian friends group members mentioned during group session 1.

In this study you are using your Daily Master Communication Guide to record what God says to you and what you say to God. You may want to begin keeping a journal so that you will have more room to write. I suggest that you use *Day by Day in God's Kingdom: A Discipleship Journal.* This journal not only suggests Scriptures and memory verses but also provides room for you to record what you experience in your quiet time.[1]

 Read Exodus 4:1-17 during your quiet time today. See how God speaks to you through this passage about Moses' struggle with doing God's will. Then complete the Daily Master Communication Guide on page 17.

DAY 4

Supplying Your Need

When you think about doing God's will, you may feel helpless. You may believe that you need to be a scholar with vast theological knowledge. You may feel that only a pastor, an evangelist, or someone who studies the Bible and prays around the clock can be enough in tune with God to detect His will under the Holy Spirit's leading.

But the Scriptures say that God provides you exactly what you need to achieve His will. Both Philippians 4:19 and Romans 8:28, in the margin, illustrate how well He equips you to know His will.

Read the verses in the margin. Describe what God has promised to do.

Philippians 4:19: _All that I Need God will Supply_

Romans 8:28: _when God Calleds us, he will Supply our Need with faith_

These passages provide marvelous reassurance that extraordinary knowledge or intellect is not required to know God's will. He will supply your needs and will work all things together for good.

Describe a time when God supplied your needs so that you could know His will.

Any time I Asked And trust hy

You might read these verses and think, *If all of my needs are supplied, I can make it without God.* But doing God's will on your own is impossible. Only God has the capacity to do exactly what He intends. Doing God's will involves a process in which God uses the provisions He has given you to accomplish His work. The two verses in the margin describe this process.

 In the margin write from memory this week's Scripture-memory verse, Philippians 2:13. Describe in your own words how God accomplishes His will in you.

"My God will meet all your needs according to his glorious riches in Christ Jesus" (Phil. 4:19).

"We know that in all things God works for the good of those who love him, who have been called according to his purpose" (Rom. 8:28).

"Being confident of this, that he who began a good work in you will carry it on to completion until the day of Christ Jesus" (Phil. 1:6).

"The one who calls you is faithful and he will do it" (1 Thess. 5:24).

You may have answered something like this: God works in me to will and to do what pleases Him. He also gives me the ability to do His will.

Reread Philippians 1:6 in the margin on page 19. What good work do you think Christ has begun in you?

_____

How can you see that He is being faithful to complete this good work in you?

_____

Perhaps you believe that one of the good works Christ has begun in you is a new willingness to witness to the world. Perhaps you have begun to see new opportunities to witness that you never thought about before. Perhaps you have begun to build relationships with persons that will provide entry points for you to witness. Christ promises that He will be faithful to complete work He has begun in you. He has given you the task of witnessing, and He will strengthen you for it.

Think of five persons who need you to witness to them. Write their names on your Prayer-Covenant List. (You learned in _MasterLife 1: The Disciple's Cross_ how to keep such a list. Use the form on p. 143 to start a list if you are not already keeping one.) If you cannot think of five unsaved persons, begin making friends with others so that you can witness to them in the future.

You may desire to do God's will, but internal conflicts and barriers may arise. That is why it is important to continue learning to integrate your personality under the lordship of Christ. As you study the Disciple's Personality today, you will learn how the Bible pictures you as spirit and will understand how His will can truly be done in you as you live in the Holy Spirit.

LEARNING THE DISCIPLE'S PERSONALITY
Read the section "Spirit" (p. 134) in the Disciple's Personality presentation. Read the two verses in the margin to learn how the Bible pictures you as spirit.

On the next page draw a circle, leaving openings at the top and bottom. Write _God_ above it and _body_ beneath it. Write the five senses—_sight, sound, smell, taste,_ and _touch_—on each side of the circle. Write _soul_ inside the top rim of the circle and _mind, will,_ and _emotions_ in the exact center. Write _spirit_ vertically down the center of the circle, stopping at the word _will_. Refer to

Christ promises that He will be faithful to complete work He has begun in you.

"Who among men knows the thoughts of a man except the man's spirit within him? In the same way no one knows the thoughts of God except the Spirit of God" (1 Cor. 2:11).

"The Spirit himself testifies with our spirit that we are God's children" (Rom. 8:16).

the Disciple's Personality presentation (pp. 133–39) if you need help. By the end of this study you will be able to draw the complete Disciple's Personality and to explain it in your own words.

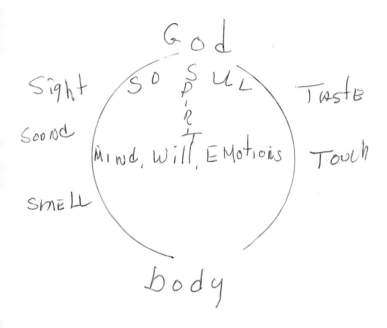

IN THE CARPENTER'S SHOP

As you become more like Christ, with the Holy Spirit's help you will continue to put aside, or tear down, traits of the old person and to substitute traits of the new person. The verses from Colossians 3, in the margin, illustrate what leaving the old life behind and taking up the new one mean.

Read in the margin the passage from Colossians 3. Underline statements that describe the tendencies of the old life before Christ. Circle statements describing the tendencies of the new life after Christ.

I hope that this exercise continued to emphasize what must happen for you to become like Christ. For the old life, you may have underlined such phrases as "rid yourselves of all such things," "Put to death, therefore, whatever belongs to your earthly nature," and "you have taken off your old self with its practices." For the new life, you may have circled "set your hearts on things above," "Set your minds on things above," "clothe yourselves with compassion, kindness, humility, gentleness and patience," and "over all these virtues put on love, which binds them all together in perfect unity."

"Since, then, you have been raised with Christ, set your hearts on things above, where Christ is seated at the right hand of God. Set your minds on things above, not on earthly things. For you died, and your life is now hidden with Christ in God. When Christ, who is your life, appears, then you also will appear with him in glory.

"Put to death, therefore, whatever belongs to your earthly nature: sexual immorality, impurity, lust, evil desires and greed, which is idolatry. Because of these, the wrath of God is coming. You used to walk in these ways, in the life you once lived. But now you must rid yourselves of all such things as these: anger, rage, malice, slander, and filthy language from your lips. Do not lie to each other, since you have taken off your old self with its practices and have put on the new self, which is being renewed in knowledge in the image of its Creator. Here there is no Greek or Jew, circumcised or uncircumcised, barbarian, Scythian, slave or free, but Christ is all, and is in all.

"Therefore, as God's chosen people, holy and dearly loved, clothe yourselves with compassion, kindness, humility, gentleness and patience. Bear with each other and forgive whatever grievances you may have against one another. Forgive as the Lord forgave you. And over all these virtues put on love, which binds them all together in perfect unity" (Col. 3:1-14).

**DAILY MASTER
COMMUNICATION
GUIDE**

JOB 42

What God said to me:

_____

_____

_____

_____

_____

_____

What I said to God:

_____

_____

_____

_____

_____

_____

_____

 Read Job 42 during your quiet time today, describing the way God supplied the needs of someone who did His will. Then complete the Daily Master Communication Guide in the margin.

Sometimes people ask me: "Do I need to be alone when I have my quiet time? Can I have a quiet time with my spouse or family?" Certainly, having couple or family devotions and praying and studying the Bible with a friend are excellent ways to spend time with the Master. (You will learn more about conversational prayer during this study.) But these cannot take the place of individual time you spend with Christ. Kay Moore, who wrote this book with me, prays and reads the Bible with her husband when they awake every morning. During this time they place before God their family's needs and seek His direction for their lives that day. Later in the day, before she begins working at her desk, Kay has her own private devotional time with God. Her husband, Louis, has his personal quiet time during his lunch hour after eating at his desk.

Make sure that your day includes a personal quiet time.

Ask God to help you continue to find the right time and setting each day to devote to a quiet time with Him.

DAY 5

Shutting the Door of the Flesh

You may think that you are the only person who struggles with knowing God's will. Perhaps you think that people in Bible times whom God used to accomplish His purposes automatically knew exactly what God wanted them to do and never considered their own preferences. You may think that their lives were easy because they chose God's way.

Your daily Bible passages this week have focused on Bible figures and their struggles to do God's will. In today's study you will examine three more. Read about Moses, Jesus, and Paul in the Scriptures in the margin on the next page.

Moses, Jesus, and Paul willingly suffered in order to follow God's will. Each displayed these three components of doing God's will:

> Doing God's will is accomplished through—
> ❑ a vision of God's purpose for your life;
> ❑ a commitment of your entire personality to God;
> ❑ actions based on God's provision for doing His will.

In the previous box check the component you believe is the most difficult for you in your effort to do God's will.

CONFORMED TO HIS LIKENESS

Read Romans 8:29: "Those God foreknew he also predestined to be conformed to the likeness of his Son, that he might be the firstborn among many brothers." This verse says that if God's will is accomplished in your life, you will be conformed to the likeness of Christ, God's Son. You will act like Him, will think like Him, and will have the kind of relationships with God and others that Christ did. You will have Him at the center of your life, and you will yield to the Holy Spirit's leading in your life.

Say aloud this week's Scripture-memory verse, Philippians 2:13, to someone in your family or to a close friend. Tell that person how this verse has made you more aware of doing God's will.

Apply this verse to your life by writing your personal response to each of the following statements.

The vision I have of God's purpose for my life is—

_____.

If I said, "I commit my whole personality to God," that would mean that I—

_____.

Because I know that God will provide for me when I do His will, I will take the following action(s):

_____

_____

What hinders you from keeping these commitments? A look at the Natural Person, another part of the Disciple's Personality, provides an answer.

LEARNING THE DISCIPLE'S PERSONALITY

Today you will begin learning the Natural Person part of the Disciple's Personality. Read the section "The Flesh" (p. 134) in the Disciple's Personality presentation.

The Bible uses the word *flesh* in two ways.

"By faith Moses, when he had grown up, refused to be known as the son of Pharaoh's daughter. He chose to be mistreated along with the people of God rather than to enjoy the pleasures of sin for a short time. He regarded disgrace for the sake of Christ as of greater value than the treasures of Egypt, because he was looking ahead to his reward. By faith he left Egypt, not fearing the king's anger; he persevered because he saw him who is invisible" (Heb. 11:24-27).

"[Jesus] withdrew about a stone's throw beyond them, knelt down and prayed, 'Father, if you are willing, take this cup from me; yet not my will, but yours be done' " (Luke 22: 41-42).

"If anyone else thinks he has reasons to put confidence in the flesh, I [Paul] have more: circumcised on the eighth day, of the people of Israel, of the tribe of Benjamin, a Hebrew of Hebrews; in regard to the law, a Pharisee; as for zeal, persecuting the church; as for legalistic righteousness, faultless.

"But whatever was to my profit I now consider loss for the sake of Christ. What is more, I consider everything a loss compared to the surpassing greatness of Christ Jesus my Lord, for whose sake I have lost all things. I consider them rubbish, that I may gain Christ" (Phil. 3:4-8).

"Do not let sin reign in your mortal body so that you obey its evil desires" (Rom. 6:12).

"Live by the Spirit, and you will not gratify the desires of the sinful nature. For the sinful nature desires what is contrary to the Spirit, and the Spirit what is contrary to the sinful nature. They are in conflict with each other, so that you do not do what you want. But if you are led by the Spirit, you are not under law" (Gal. 5:16-18).

Read the two verses in the margin and describe the two ways these verses refer to flesh.

Romans 6:12: _Flesh_

Galatians 5:16-18: _Sinful Nature_

The general meaning of *flesh* is body, referring to the physical body (see Rom. 6:12). The other meaning is symbolic, referring to the lower nature (see Gal. 5:16-18). The *King James Version* uses *flesh* to mean *sinful nature*. It refers to the human capacity to sin and to follow Satan instead of God.

✝ **Draw the portions of the Disciple's Personality you learned this week. Close the door of the spirit by completing the circle at the top. Leave the door of the flesh open at the bottom of the circle. Now draw an *I* in the center of the circle that surrounds the words *spirit* and *will*. Write *flesh* vertically under *will*. Draw a line through *spirit*. Write *Satan* outside the circle beneath *body*. Then write *1 Corinthians 2:14* above *God* and label your drawing *The Natural Person*. Refer to the Disciple's Personality presentation (pp. 133–39) if you need help. By the end of this study you will be able to draw the entire Disciple's Personality and to explain it in your own words.**

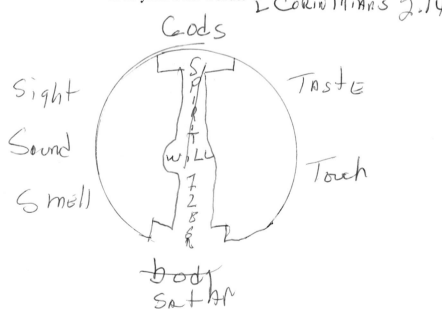

Now read the section "The Condition of the Natural Person Today" (p. 135) in the Disciple's Personality presentation. These teachings help you understand why even a natural person's best intentions sometimes fail when he or she wants to do right but cannot seem to. During the coming weeks, learning the Disciple's Personality will help you compare the way you live to God's plan for you.

 How have you kept the door of the flesh open in your life? On a separate sheet of paper write the things you do that displease God. Confess your sins to God. Read 1 John 1:9: "If we confess our sins, he is faithful and just and will forgive us our sins and purify us from all unrighteousness." Accept that God has forgiven you. Tear up or burn the list to signify that your sins are forgiven.

Pray that as God works through the Holy Spirit, He will help you keep the commitments you wrote on page 23 and will shut the door of the flesh, which would prevent your carrying them out.

IN THE CARPENTER'S SHOP
Read in the margin the verses from Ephesians to continue learning how to build Christlike character. In the left column write statements that refer to actions of the old person. In the right column write statements that describe what a new person does after coming to know Christ.

Old Person	New Person
Put of The old Solf or don't grieve the Holy Spirt	BE NEW Attitode of your mind be christLike, Like Love put on a New Person

For actions of the old person, you may have listed "no longer live as the Gentiles do," "put off your old self," or "do not grieve the Holy Spirit." For steps that the new person would take, you may have listed "be made new in the attitude of your minds; and to put on the new self," "be like God in true righteousness and holiness," or "live a life of love." As you learn to live like Jesus, you will learn that the ways of the world present a stark contrast to the Christian lifestyle.

Putting on the new person may involve new attitudes toward your family members.

Spend time with a member of your family, maybe one with whom you have not talked in a long time. Write or call the person if he or she does not live in your locale.

"I tell you this, and insist on it in the Lord, that you must no longer live as the Gentiles do, in the futility of their thinking. They are darkened in their understanding and separated from the life of God because of the ignorance that is in them due to the hardening of their hearts. Having lost all sensitivity, they have given themselves over to sensuality so as to indulge in every kind of impurity, with a continual lust for more.

"You, however, did not come to know Christ that way. Surely you heard of him and were taught in him in accordance with the truth that is in Jesus. You were taught, with regard to your former way of life, to put off your old self, which is being corrupted by its deceitful desires; to be made new in the attitude of your minds; and to put on the new self, created to be like God in true righteousness and holiness.

"And do not grieve the Holy Spirit of God, with whom you were sealed for the day of redemption. Get rid of all bitterness, rage and anger, brawling and slander, along with every form of malice. Be kind and compassionate to one another, forgiving each other, just as in Christ God forgave you.

"Be imitators of God, therefore, as dearly loved children and live a life of love, just as Christ loved us and gave himself up for us as a fragrant offering and sacrifice to God" (Eph. 4:17-24,30—5:2).

DAILY MASTER COMMUNICATION GUIDE

*

GENESIS 3:1-7

What God said to me:

_____

_____

_____

_____

_____

_____

_____

What I said to God:

_____

_____

_____

_____

_____

_____

_____

_____

_____

Read Genesis 3:1-7, about something that introduced problems into God's creation, during your quiet time today. Then complete the Daily Master Communication Guide in the margin.

HAS THIS WEEK MADE A DIFFERENCE?

Review "My Walk with the Master This Week" at the beginning of this week's material. Mark the activities you have finished by drawing vertical lines in the diamonds beside them. Finish any incomplete activities. Think about what you will say during your group session about your work on these activities.

To assess your progress this week, check the appropriate boxes.
❑ I understand the roles played by body, soul, and spirit in forming my total personality.
❑ I understand the role the flesh plays in my personality to undermine my good intentions.
❑ Instead of seeking what I want, I strive to do God's will and to have Christ's character.
❑ Seeking God's will in decisions is a major part of my life in the Spirit.
❑ I truly desire to be like Jesus.

From this week's study of "Do God's Will" you can see that keeping the door of the flesh closed and refusing to allow Satan to get a foothold in your life are challenges that require constant vigilance. Developing a daily quiet time and spending regular time with the Master allow the Holy Spirit to work in your life when it would be easier to keep the door of the flesh open.

---

[1]*Day by Day in God's Kingdom: A Discipleship Journal* (item 0-7673-2577-X) is available from the Customer Service Center; 127 Ninth Avenue, North; Nashville, TN 37234; 1-800-458-2772; and from Baptist Book Stores and Lifeway Christian Stores.

WEEK 2

Renew Your Mind

This Week's Goal
You will be able to renew your mind through the transforming power of the Word and Holy Spirit.

My Walk with the Master This Week
You will complete the following activities to develop the six biblical disciplines. When you have completed each activity, draw a vertical line in the diamond beside it.

 SPEND TIME WITH THE MASTER
◇ Have a quiet time each day, working toward the goal of having quiet times 21 consecutive days. Check the box beside each day you have a quiet time this week: ☑Sunday ☑Monday ❑ Tuesday ❑ Wednesday ❑ Thursday ❑ Friday ❑ Saturday

 LIVE IN THE WORD
◇ Read your Bible every day. Write what God says to you and what you say to God.
◇ Memorize Romans 12:1-2.
◇ Review Philippians 2:13.

 PRAY IN FAITH
◇ Pray with a friend, a family member, or your prayer partner.
◇ Teach someone "Principles of Conversational Prayer."

 FELLOWSHIP WITH BELIEVERS
◇ Go out to dinner or plan a private time with your spouse or, if you are not married, a close friend. Talk about matters that are most important to you.

 WITNESS TO THE WORLD
◇ Do something kind for a member of your immediate or extended family who does not know Christ.

MINISTER TO OTHERS
◇ Learn the Worldly Christian part of the Disciple's Personality.

This Week's Scripture-Memory Verses
"I urge you, brothers, in view of God's mercy, to offer your bodies as living sacrifices, holy and pleasing to God—this is your spiritual act of worship. Do not conform any longer to the pattern of this world, but be transformed by the renewing of your mind. Then you will be able to test and approve what God's will is—his good, pleasing and perfect will" (Rom. 12:1-2).

DAY 1

~

Making the Wrong Decisions

Your mind is much like a tape recorder or a video recorder. You record events and thoughts and continue to listen to them even when other options are open to you. These tapes from the past often lead you repeatedly to make the same wrong choices.

Paul described his situation in these words: "I do not understand what I do. For what I want to do I do not do, but what I hate I do. I know that nothing good lives in me, that is, in my sinful nature. For I have the desire to do what is good, but I cannot carry it out. For what I do is not the good I want to do; no, the evil I do not want to do—this I keep on doing. Now if I do what I do not want to do, it is no longer I who do it, but it is sin living in me that does it" (Rom. 7:15,18-20).

Like me, you sometimes feel as Paul did—that you are trapped with a sinful nature that does not want to do God's will. Even though you want to do what is right, your mind thinks about doing wrong. I believe that the devil plays tapes of wrong actions. As a result, you keep making wrong decisions.

In Romans 7:25 Paul provided an answer to his dilemma: "Thanks be to God—through Jesus Christ our Lord!" He added in Romans 8:1-2, "There is now no condemnation for those who are in Christ Jesus, because through Christ Jesus the law of the Spirit of life set me free from the law of sin and death."

The Holy Spirit takes God's Word and the words spoken by Christ, makes them real, and applies them to your life.

Read John 14:16-20 in the margin and answer the following questions.

Why did Jesus say that He was sending the Holy Spirit?

To PRoVide the same Kind of help +
Conford Jesus did. the holy spiet will
Live in US

How did Jesus say that the disciples would recognize the Holy Spirit?

beCAse Holy spiet Lve
iN US

Jesus told the disciples that He was sending the Holy Spirit to pro-

> " 'I will ask the Father, and he will give you another Counselor to be with you forever—the Spirit of truth. The world cannot accept him, because it neither sees him nor knows him. But you know him, for he lives with you and will be in you. I will not leave you as orphans; I will come to you. Before long, the world will not see me anymore, but you will see me. Because I live, you also will live. On that day you will realize that I am in my Father, and you are in me, and I am in you' " (John 14:16-20).

vide the same kind of help, comfort, and teaching He had provided them while on earth. He said that they would know the Holy Spirit because He would live within them. The Holy Spirit does not merely walk alongside you but actually lives in your heart and life.

John 14:26, in the margin, also depicts the Holy Spirit as a counselor, or personal teacher. In this week's study you will discover how to let the Holy Spirit renew your mind. When you have completed this week's study, you should be able to—

- describe the difference between the natural mind and the renewed mind;
- explain what it means to have the mind of Christ in you;
- describe the process of renewal of the mind;
- identify at least three ways to be more spiritually minded.

FOLLOWING THE NATURAL MIND

When I talk about the natural mind, I am referring to the thinking process that is limited to human reason and resources (see 1 Cor. 2:14 in the margin). Human history shows that the natural mind becomes progressively self-destructive if left to its own desires.

Read Ephesians 4:17-18 in the margin. What do these verses say about people who live according to their natural minds? Fill in the blanks.

Their thinking is ____futility____ .

They walk in the ____darkened____ of their understanding.

They are separated from God because of ____ignorance____ .

They are ignorant because of their ____hearts hardly____ .

People who follow their natural minds and live as these natural minds direct walk in darkness and have futile thinking. Ignorance, which results because their hearts are hardened, separates them from God. They live hopeless lives.

The natural mind inevitably becomes enslaved to other masters. Romans 1:28-31 says: "Since they did not think it worthwhile to retain the knowledge of God, he gave them over to a depraved mind, to do what ought not to be done. They have become filled with every kind of wickedness, evil, greed and depravity. They are full of envy, murder, strife, deceit and malice. They are gossips, slanderers, God-haters, insolent, arrogant and boastful; they invent ways of doing evil; they disobey their parents; they are senseless, faithless, heartless, ruthless." The natural mind in turn enslaves a personality by reducing it primarily to the world of the senses and evil.

" 'The Counselor, the Holy Spirit, whom the Father will send in my name, will teach you all things and will remind you of everything I have said to you' " (John 14:26).

"The man without the Spirit does not accept the things that come from the Spirit of God, for they are foolishness to him, and he cannot understand them, because they are spiritually discerned" (1 Cor. 2:14).

"I tell you this, and insist on it in the Lord, that you must no longer live as the Gentiles do, in the futility of their thinking. They are darkened in their understanding and separated from the life of God because of the ignorance that is in them due to the hardening of their hearts" (Eph. 4:17-18).

"The god of this age has <u>blinded</u> the minds of unbelievers, so that they cannot see the light of the gospel of the glory of Christ, who is the image of God" (2 Cor. 4:4).

"Since they did not think it worthwhile to retain the knowledge of God, he gave them over to a <u>depraved</u> mind, to do what ought not to be done" (Rom. 1:28).

" … constant friction between men of <u>corrupt</u> mind, who have been robbed of the truth and who think that godliness is a means to financial gain" (1 Tim. 6:5).

"Do not let anyone who delights in false humility and the worship of angels disqualify you for the prize. Such a person goes into great detail about what he has seen, and his <u>unspiritual</u> mind puffs him up with idle notions" (Col. 2:18).

To what masters are you enslaved? Meditate on the words in Romans 1:28-31 in the previous paragraph. Can you identify with some of these masters? If you can, underline the types of wrongdoing with which you struggle.

Read the Scriptures in the margin. Then draw a line between each word in the left column that describes the natural mind and the Scripture reference in the right column in which the word is found.

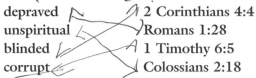

depraved   2 Corinthians 4:4
unspiritual   Romans 1:28
blinded   1 Timothy 6:5
corrupt   Colossians 2:18

These Scriptures clearly teach what happens to a person whose mind is not focused as the Spirit directs. The words used to describe such an existence are horrifying. The correct answers are: *depraved*, Romans 1:28; *unspiritual*, Colossians 2:18; *blinded*, 2 Corinthians 4:4; *corrupt*, 1 Timothy 6:5.

THE RENEWED MIND
The Holy Spirit uses God's Word to renew a person's mind. The natural mind and the renewed mind have the same basic functions: thinking, judging, reasoning, and evaluating. The difference is who controls these processes.

Turn to page 27 and read this week's Scripture-memory verses, Romans 12:1-2. Begin to memorize them as you reflect on what they say about the renewed mind. Review page 112 in *MasterLife 1: The Disciple's Cross* if you need to to recall memorization methods.

The renewed mind is obedient to Christ. The natural mind thinks from a humanistic, sin-debased viewpoint. The renewed mind frees the personality by enlarging it to encompass the world of the Spirit in addition to the senses.

Write *N* beside the statements that describe the natural mind and *R* beside the ones that describe the renewed mind.
____ 1. Becomes progressively self-destructive
____ 2. Is limited to purely human reason and resources
____ 3. Thinks from Christ's viewpoint as the Holy Spirit directs
____ 4. Frees the personality by including the Spirit
____ 5. Thinks from the viewpoint of the flesh

The natural mind leads to a path of self-destruction. It does not rely on the mind of Christ but is limited to the resources of the human mind. The viewpoint of the flesh directs its thoughts. On the other hand, the renewed mind thinks from Christ's viewpoint as guided by the Holy Spirit. The correct answers are 1. N, 2. N, 3. R, 4. R, 5. N.

When the Holy Spirit rules your mind, you obey Christ. You think, *What would Christ have me do in this situation?* You try to understand what the Holy Spirit, who lives in you as your personal teacher, is leading you to do.

In contrast, fleshly, worldly thoughts rule the worldly, sinful mind.

> Read Romans 8:1-14 in your Bible and mark the following statements *T* (true) or *F* (false).
>
> __F__ 1. The worldly mind concentrates on spiritual things.
> __T__ 2. To set your mind on things of the flesh brings death.
> __T__ 3. The worldly mind does not submit to the Holy Spirit's control.
> __F__ 4. A worldly mind sometimes pleases God.
> __F__ 5. No hope exists for changing a worldly mind.

The worldly mind is in the control of Satan, not of the Holy Spirit. Setting your mind on things of the flesh without turning to Christ brings death. Yet persons who set aside worldly ways and turn over their lives and thoughts to Christ can know forgiveness and joy. You can have a spiritual mind even if a worldly mind has ruled you in the past. The correct answers are 1. F, 2. T, 3. T, 4. F, 5. F.

> Again read Romans 8:1-14, which contrasts the worldly mind and the spiritual mind, during your quiet time today. Then complete the Daily Master Communication Guide in the margin.

> In week 1 you were asked to spend time with a family member. This week go out to dinner or plan a private time with your spouse or, if you are not married, a close friend. Talk about the things that are most important. Satan would like nothing better than to gain control of your relationships, especially your home. Spending time with your spouse or someone close to you can help keep you from a path of self-destruction in your personal life. I pray that the Holy Spirit will direct you to give this relationship more emphasis.

DAILY MASTER COMMUNICATION GUIDE

ROMANS 8:1-14

What God said to me:

_____

_____

_____

_____

_____

_____

What I said to God:

_____

_____

_____

_____

_____

_____

DAY 2

Ruled by the Flesh

"As for you, you were dead in your transgressions and sins, in which you used to live when you followed the ways of this world and of the ruler of the kingdom of the air, the spirit who is now at work in those who are disobedient. All of us also lived among them at one time, gratifying the cravings of our sinful nature and following its desires and thoughts. Like the rest, we were by nature objects of wrath" (Eph. 2:1-3).

"Because of his great love for us, God, who is rich in mercy, made us alive with Christ even when we were dead in transgressions—it is by grace you have been saved. And God raised us up with Christ and seated us with him in the heavenly realms in Christ Jesus, in order that in the coming ages he might show the incomparable riches of his grace, expressed in his kindness to us in Christ Jesus. For it is by grace you have been saved, through faith—and this not from yourselves, it is the gift of God—not by works, so that no one can boast. For we are God's workmanship, created in Christ Jesus to do good works, which God prepared in advance for us to do" (Eph. 2:4-10).

When you studied about the natural person in week 1, you probably realized that this person does not know Christ. He or she lives a natural, unregenerate life without Christ.

Read Ephesians 2:1-3 in the margin and underline the phrases that describe your former way of life.

Now read Ephesians 2:4-10 in the margin and underline what God did for you.

Before you knew Christ, you were dead in your transgressions and sins. When you repented of your sins and your sinful way of life and asked Christ to be your Savior and Lord, God made you alive with Christ. By His grace He saved you and raised you up with Christ. You are now God's workmanship, created in Christ Jesus to do good works.

However, many persons who have received Christ and have the Holy Spirit living in their hearts still do not live as God intended. That is why Paul told the Ephesians in Ephesians 4:17-24 that they had not learned the ways of the world from Christ and that they should move away from that way of living.

A WORLDLY CHRISTIAN

If a Christian lives like the unbelieving world, this person is a worldly Christian. The *King James Version* calls this person *carnal*, which means *fleshly*. It refers to a person who is governed by human nature more than by the Spirit of God. Paul contrasts spiritual people—those who are under the control of the Holy Spirit—with those who are carnal—those who are under the control of the flesh. First Corinthians 3:1 describes worldly Christians: "Brothers, I could not address you as spiritual but as worldly—mere infants in Christ."

Second Peter 1:3 makes clear that God has provided you His power: "His divine power has given us everything we need for life and godliness through our knowledge of him who called us by his own glory and goodness." He has given you the rich promise of eternal life. He has given you the resources you need for life and righteous living. However, a few verses later, in 2 Peter 1:5, you are told to add certain things to your faith that God has provided for you.

In 2 Peter 1:5-9, in the margin on the next page, underline the things you are told to add to your faith.

You likely underlined that you are to add to your faith goodness, knowledge, self-control, perseverance, godliness, brotherly kindness, and love. If you continue to manifest the traits of a worldly Christian—

- you are ineffective and unproductive. A worldly Christian is sluggish and does not grow in his or her faith. A worldly Christian does not have a productive life for Christ.
- you are nearsighted and blind. This person is blind to the Holy Spirit's truth and listens to Satan's lies.
- you have forgotten that you have been cleansed. This person has forgotten his cleansing from sin and does not appreciate God and Christ for his or her forgiveness.

Reread the results if persons do not grow and add to their faith. Check any results you see in your life.

MASTERING THE MIND

God never intends for a Christian to be worldly. Yet some Christians are. Probably because they have not been guided in how to grow, they are still guided more by fleshly desires than by spiritual desires. Christ secures your salvation, but you are still responsible for how you live. You are responsible for using His resources and for following Him.

The Holy Spirit wants to be to your mind what a rudder is to a ship. A rudder keeps the ship on course so that it arrives at its destination. In 2 Corinthians 10:3-5, in the margin, Paul described a two-step plan for mastering the human mind. Paul described an offensive-defensive game plan that worked for his life, as it will for yours. In the defensive game plan you are to defeat worldly ideas that obstruct the knowledge of God. In the offensive game plan you are to keep Christ in control.

This week you will learn specific ways to renew your mind by defeating worldly ideas and making every thought obedient to Christ.

 This week's Scripture-memory verses address renewing your mind. Write them from memory in the margin. Then describe one way you need to renew your mind.

Learning the Worldly Christian part of the Disciple's Personality will help you visualize what you have learned about the worldly mind.

LEARNING THE DISCIPLE'S PERSONALITY

Read the section "The Worldly Christian" (p. 136) in the Disciple's Personality presentation.

On the next page begin drawing the Worldly Christian. Leave open the doors of the spirit and the flesh. Draw a big *I* in the circle. Above the circle write *The Worldly Christian.*

"For this very reason, make every effort to add to your faith goodness; and to goodness, knowledge; and to knowledge, self-control; and to self-control, perseverance; and to perseverance, godliness; and to godliness, brotherly kindness; and to brotherly kindness, love. For if you possess these qualities in increasing measure, they will keep you from being ineffective and unproductive in your knowledge of our Lord Jesus Christ. But if anyone does not have them, he is nearsighted and blind, and has forgotten that he has been cleansed from his past sins" (2 Pet. 1:5-9).

"Though we live in the world, we do not wage war as the world does. The weapons we fight with are not the weapons of the world. On the contrary, they have divine power to demolish strongholds. We demolish arguments and every pretension that sets itself up against the knowledge of God, and we take captive every thought to make it obedient to Christ" (2 Cor. 10:3-5).

The World's Way

"The acts of the sinful nature are obvious: sexual immorality, impurity and debauchery" (Gal. 5:19-21).

"Put to death, therefore, whatever belongs to your earthly nature: sexual immorality, impurity, lust, evil desires and greed, which is idolatry." (Col. 3:5-7).

"Among you there must not be even a hint of sexual immorality, or of any kind of impurity, or of greed, because these are improper for God's holy people. Nor should there be obscenity, foolish talk or coarse joking" (Eph. 5:3-5).

The Spirit's Way

"The fruit of the Spirit is love, joy, peace, patience, kindness, goodness, faithfulness, gentleness and self-control. Against such things there is no law" (Gal. 5:22-23).

"Since, then, you have been raised with Christ, set your hearts on things above, where Christ is seated at the right hand of God. Set your minds on things above, not on earthly things. For you died, and your life is now hidden with Christ in God" (Col. 3:1-3).

"Be imitators of God, therefore, as dearly loved children and live a life of love, just as Christ loved us and gave himself up for us as a fragrant offering and sacrifice to God" (Eph. 5: 1-2).

Trace over the letter *s* in *spirit* with a capital *S*. Refer to the Disciple's Personality presentation (pp. 133–39) if you need help. By the end of this study you will be able to draw the complete Disciple's Personality and to explain it in your own words.

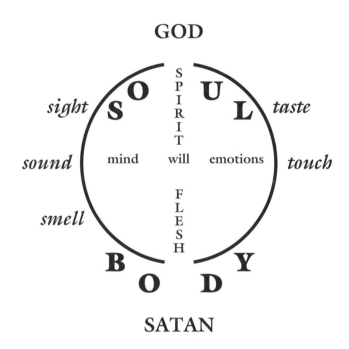

IN THE CARPENTER'S SHOP

In week 1 you learned the difference between the old person and the new person. This week you are focusing on specific ways your character can change with the help of the Holy Spirit.

Read the Scriptures in the margin that relate to immorality or impure thinking. From the verses under "The World's Way" identify a specific behavior you want to get rid of. From the verses under "The Spirit's Way" identify an action you will take to replace it. Each day this week you will record your progress in working on this trait. If you feel that this matter is too personal to write about here, you may write about it elsewhere, but please address this critical change.

Here is an example.

Behavior I want to work on: sexually impure thoughts or actions

An action I will take to put off the old self: stop looking at sexually explicit material

An action I will take to let the Holy Spirit make me more like Christ: memorize Scripture to have a pure heart and mind

Now you try it.

Behavior I want to work on: _____

An action I will take to put off the old self:

_____

An action I will take to let the Holy Spirit make me more like Christ:

Memorize Scripture to Make my heart pure

THE DESIRE TO CHANGE

A word about putting off old behaviors: *in some cases you cannot change these practices overnight.* Do not be discouraged if you do not see instant results. But by asking the Lord to renew your mind and by committing this process to Him, you will eventually change. If you need a quick reference on how to renew your mind, see the chart in the margin on page 44. Feel free to copy it to keep in a convenient place.

Find a way to do something kind for a member of your family who does not know Christ. Be ready to share your experience at your next group session.

Read Ephesians 2:1-10, a passage explaining how we are made alive in Christ, in your quiet time today. Then complete the Daily Master Communication Guide in the margin.

DAY 3

Replacing Your Thoughts

Jimmie and Edna Harrison were long-time church members in West Columbia, Texas, but they found that committing every aspect of their lives to the Lord was difficult for them. Putting church ahead of work schedules was especially challenging. But when Jimmie heard about the *MasterLife* group beginning at their church, he became interested and urged Edna to study it with him. Edna went along with much reluctance.

When the group began to study about the worldly Christian and the need to renew their minds, however, the Holy Spirit began working in Edna's life, the minister reported. "She began to see herself as a worldly Christian who thought only of herself, and God began to work.

DAILY MASTER COMMUNICATION GUIDE

EPHESIANS 2:1-10

What God said to me:

_____
_____
_____
_____
_____
_____
_____

What I said to God:

_____
_____
_____
_____
_____
_____
_____

MasterLife became a joy, and she could not wait until the next week to learn more. She was a changed person."

THE MIND OF CHRIST

As a Christian, you have the goal of thinking and acting from the mind of Christ. In Philippians 2:5 Paul said, "Let this mind be in you, which was also in Christ Jesus" (KJV). He also referred to the mind of Christ in 1 Corinthians 2:16: " 'Who has known the mind of the Lord that he may instruct him?' But we have the mind of Christ" (1 Cor. 2:16).

In 1 Corinthians 2:16 what did Paul claim that Christians have?

A mind Like Christ

Paul said that Christians have the mind of Christ. Can you sincerely say that you desire to think Christ's thoughts?
☑ Yes ❑ No

Ideally, you were able to answer yes to that question. You may sincerely desire to be Christlike and to think Christ's thoughts. But how do you do that? Renewing your mind is accomplished by filling your mind with Christ's thoughts.

Check the phrases that explain what having the mind of Christ means.
☑ 1. Making thoughts obedient to Christ
☑ 2. Exercising the ability to think spiritually
❑ 3. Having a high IQ
☑ 4. Seeing things from Christ's viewpoint
❑ 5. Meditating to empty your mind

If you think Christ's thoughts, you try to see things as Christ would, and you let Him, not Satan, be the master of your mind. You make your thoughts obedient to Christ, and you think spiritually. Having a high IQ and emptying your mind by meditation have nothing to do with having the mind of Christ. Every Christian has the mind of Christ, but he or she does not always choose to engage it. The correct answers are 1, 2, and 4.

Based on what you have learned so far, fill in each blank with one of the following words to describe a way Christ can be the master of your mind.

renewing   thought   mind   knowledge

By removing all obstacles to your Knowledge **of God**

> **Renewing your mind is accomplished by filling your mind with Christ's thoughts.**

> **Every Christian has the mind of Christ, but he or she does not always choose to engage it.**

By making every ___*Thought*___ obedient to Christ

By possessing the ___*Mind*___ of Christ

By ___*Renewing*___ your mind

You can make Christ the master of your mind by removing all obstacles to your knowledge of God, by making every thought obedient to Christ, by possessing the mind of Christ, and by renewing your mind.

✝ **What do this week's Scripture-memory verses say about renewing your mind? Say them aloud from one to three times to continue your memory work on them. Review your memorization of Philippians 2:13 from last week.**

THE RENEWAL PROCESS
To renew your mind, you begin filling your mind with Scriptures to replace bad thoughts with good thoughts. The more you live in the Word, the more your mind will be renewed.

The Scriptures in the margin give you further instruction on how Christ renews your mind. Read the verses and match the references in the left column with the summary statements in the right column.

___D___ 1. Colossians 3:2   a. **Think on praiseworthy things.**
___B___ 2. Romans 8:5-6   b. **Give attention to things of the Spirit.**
___C___ 3. John 16:13   c. **Let the Holy Spirit guide you into truth.**
___E___ 4. Psalm 1:2   d. **Set your heart's desire on heavenly things.**
___A___ 5. Philippians 4:8   e. **Meditate on God's Word.**

Do not let your mind linger on evil thoughts; instead, think about wholesome things, such as God's Word. Remember the computer axiom: "Garbage in, garbage out." When you realize that you are having worldly thoughts, think of them as red, flashing emergency lights that warn you to turn your thoughts to spiritual things. The correct answers are 1. d, 2. b, 3. c, 4. e, 5. a.

Here are simple, practical steps for activating the mind of Christ when you are tempted to act in harmful ways.

> **ACTIVATING THE MIND OF CHRIST**
> 1. Remember that Christ was tempted in every way you are tempted yet overcame the temptation (see Heb. 4:15).
> 2. Pray for grace in time of need (see Heb. 4:16).
> 3. Express humility by getting on your knees (see Phil. 2:5-11).

"Set your minds on things above, not on earthly things" (Col. 3:2).

"Those who live according to the sinful nature have their minds set on what that nature desires; but those who live in accordance with the Spirit have their minds set on what the Spirit desires. The mind of sinful man is death, but the mind controlled by the Spirit is life and peace" (Rom. 8:5-6).

" 'When he, the Spirit of truth, comes, he will guide you into all truth. He will not speak on his own; he will speak only what he hears, and he will tell you what is yet to come' " (John 16:13).

His delight is in the law of the Lord,
*   and on his law he meditates day and night (Ps. 1:2).*

"Finally, brothers, whatever is true, whatever is noble, whatever is right, whatever is pure, whatever is lovely, whatever is admirable—if anything is excellent or praiseworthy—think about such things" (Phil. 4:8).

DAILY MASTER COMMUNICATION GUIDE

PHILIPPIANS 2:5-11

What God said to me:

_____

_____

_____

_____

_____

_____

What I said to God:

_____

_____

_____

_____

_____

_____

4. Adopt God's attitude and choose His response toward the temptation.
5. Ask the Holy Spirit to impress you with a way to deal with the temptation (see Prov. 3:5-6).
6. Ask for God to walk with you past the temptation.
7. Look for a Scripture to claim during the temptation.
8. Ask God to help you focus on His will (see Phil. 2:13).
9. Acknowledge and ask forgiveness for thinking about the temptation (see 1 John 1:9).
10. Obey God's commands, knowing that you are in spiritual warfare (see Rom. 8:26-27).

IN THE CARPENTER'S SHOP

What progress are you making in putting off the old self and replacing it with the new?

Yesterday you listed a behavior you wanted to reject in order to build Christlike character. Describe an instance in which you have already put aside that behavior.

_____

_____

_____

_____

As you continue to put off the old self and put on new, Christlike traits, I hope that you are spending time with the Master daily. Keeping a journal, using the Daily Master Communication Guide in the margins of this book, or expanding that method in a notebook can help you examine daily what God says to you and what you say to God. In addition to my daily Bible reading, I reflect for an hour or two each week on what God has said to me that week. Each month I take a half day or a day to evaluate what God has said to me that month. Often, I realize that God has been saying something to me for a month that I became conscious of only a day or so earlier. By keeping me in touch with what God is saying to me, this practice has helped me obey Him.

Read Philippians 2:5-11 during your quiet time today. See how God speaks to you through this passage on having the mind of Christ. I hope that you are continuing to meet your goal of having quiet times 21 consecutive days. Then complete the Daily Master Communication Guide in the margin.

DAY 4

Thinking Christ's Thoughts

You may think: *Is it really possible for me—a sinful human being—to have the mind of Christ? I can imagine a well-known evangelist's being able to think Christ's thoughts, but someone like me? Isn't it presumptuous to believe that I can think as Christ does?*

YOU HAVE THE MIND OF CHRIST

Believing that you can have the mind of Christ is not presumptuous. The mind of Christ came to you when you were saved (see 1 Cor. 2:16 in the margin). God created you to be like Jesus. Romans 8:29 says, "Those God foreknew he also predestined to be conformed to the likeness of his Son, that he might be the firstborn among many brothers." Hebrews 2:10 says that God is the process of "bringing many sons to glory." The glory you are to have is the glory of being like God's perfect Son, Jesus Christ. Philippians 2:5, which you read yesterday as part of your daily Bible reading and quiet time, reminds you that you have Christ's mind. Would the Bible remind you that you have Christ's mind if engaging it and putting it to work for you were impossible? How, then, do you know how to think the thoughts of Christ? By knowing Christ, hearing Him, and learning His truth.

From what book can you know Christ, hear Him, and learn His truth?

The Bible

Read John 8:31-32 in the margin or quote it from memory, having learned it in your study of *MasterLife 1: The Disciple's Cross*. What does living in God's truth do for the enslaved mind?

Set You Free

Living in God's Word, the Bible, is the primary source of your knowledge about Christ. The Word reveals His truth. As you hold to, or remain in, the Word, He speaks to you through the Holy Spirit. One of the Holy Spirit's roles is to show you the truth. His truth sets the enslaved mind free.

Live in His Word now by working on this week's Scripture-memory verses, Romans 12:1-2. Write them in the margin.

" 'Who has known the mind of the Lord
    that he may instruct him?'
But we have the mind of Christ" (1 Cor. 2:16).

" 'If you hold to my teaching, you are really my disciples. Then you will know the truth, and the truth will set you free' " (John 8:31-32).

DAILY MASTER COMMUNICATION GUIDE

LUKE 4:14-21

What God said to me:

_____

_____

_____

_____

_____

_____

_____

What I said to God:

_____

_____

_____

_____

_____

_____

_____

What term did Jesus use in John 8:31-32 to describe a person who holds to, or remains in, His Word?

follower   disciple   convert   sinner

A person who holds to His Word is His disciple. These verses say that you will be His disciple indeed if you hold to, or remain in, His Word.

Having your daily quiet time is a way you continue in His Word. One goal in shaping your personality to be like Christ is to have quiet times 21 consecutive days. If you miss a day, start over. During your quiet time today read Luke 4:14-21, about a time when Jesus read from the Scriptures about His Father's will for Him. Then complete the Daily Master Communication Guide in the margin.

Use the following questions to evaluate the degree to which your mind is being renewed daily.

Are you really Jesus' disciple? ☑ Yes ❑ No If so, how do you know? Review 1 Corinthians 2:16 and John 8:31 in the margin on page 39 and state how you know that you are Christ's disciple.

_____

If you are Jesus' disciple, what source of power renews your mind daily?

_____

Are you willing to commit to make God's Word a part of your daily life? ☑ Yes ❑ No If so, write a specific goal you have set for yourself.

I will _____.

IN THE CARPENTER'S SHOP
Does your character reveal that you have a renewed mind? What progress are you making in putting off the old self and developing a new character, with the Holy Spirit's help?

Yesterday you described a step you have taken to get rid of the old self. Today describe a new quality Christ is adding to your life.

_____

PRAYING FOR CHRISTLIKE CHARACTER

One way to seek insight into building Christlike character is to ask others to pray with you about it. One of the most rewarding and effective ways to pray with others is conversational prayer. Used correctly, conversational prayer has brought genuine revival in numerous groups around the world.

Conversational prayer is a group's talking together with God. In any group conversation each person says a few sentences, and then someone else adds something to the subject. When that subject comes to a natural conclusion, someone brings up another subject. The same process takes place in conversational prayer. The following guidelines can help you experience prayer in a new, exciting way.

Read the principles of conversational prayer that follow. Draw a star beside the aspect of conversational prayer you think you will find most challenging. Ask God to help you with that aspect.

PRINCIPLES OF CONVERSATIONAL PRAYER

1. Recognize that God is in the group and that you, as a group, are conversing with Him about matters of mutual interest. Some groups even place an empty chair in their midst to remind them that He is present.
2. Pray about one subject at a time. No one should begin praying about a new subject until everyone who wants to pray about the present subject has had an opportunity. Do not be afraid of silence. You can discern when it is time to move to another subject. Do not talk about the subject; do not make lists; just pray.
3. Pray brief prayers. One or two sentences by each person on one subject are usually sufficient. This allows everyone to be involved in the conversation.
4. Speak normally. Do not use formal terms of address or a closing such as *Amen* at the end of each short prayer. Though prayed by a group, it is still one continuous prayer.
5. Use the first-person singular pronoun whenever possible: *I* and *me* instead of *we* and *us*. New Christians often do this more easily than long-term Christians do.
6. Be specific in requests and in confessions of sins. If you are specific, God helps other persons pray about the same need. One person in a group might say, "Help me with pride." Another says, "Lord, I have that problem, too." People do not recognize many answered prayers because they did not pray specifically.
7. Continue the conversation as long as the group desires or the time limit allows. Someone may have to slip out for a few minutes. Bodily position is not important. Pray with your eyes open if that is comfortable. John 11:41 implies that Jesus did. You may need to close your eyes in order to concentrate on the Lord. Let God talk to you as you talk to God.

Recognize that God is in the group.

Be specific in requests and in confessions of sins.

Pray with a friend, a family member, or your prayer partner and teach that person the principles of conversational prayer. Write a day and a time when you plan to do this:

_____

Stop and ask God to help you with the challenging area beside which you drew a star in "Principles of Conversational Prayer." Ask Him to make conversational prayer a rewarding part of your life in the Spirit.

DAY 5

A Reminder of Who You Are

You truly have the mind of Christ and can think His thoughts.

This week you have learned what the Bible says about the need to renew your mind. You have learned that you truly have the mind of Christ and can think His thoughts. But how does this ability apply to you on the job, in your family life, in your church relationships, and in daily challenges?

Read the following case studies and explain how each person could renew his or her mind.

Linda and her husband, Frank, were burdened with debt. Credit-card bills and loans kept them financially strapped. Linda and Frank both had to work two jobs to make ends meet. At the end of the day both were so tired that they had little energy to devote to their two children. Linda's weakness was catalog shopping. Anytime an appealing catalog arrived in the mail, Linda felt an overwhelming temptation to order something. When she charged the order on her credit card, she increased her family's debt even more. What could Linda do to renew her mind?

Throw Away The Catalog when They Come

Tony had been without work for three months. Being unemployed made him feel embarrassed. His wife tried to maintain a supportive environment at home, but sometimes she lapsed into criticizing Tony, which made him feel even worse. During his daily run in the park, Tony encountered an attractive woman who ran at the same time he did. They started talking at the water fountain. When he told her about his unemployment, she sympathized. Soon Tony found himself thinking more and more about this new female acquaintance and the way she encouraged him. What could Tony do to renew his mind?

Run another day or time of day

Linc was involved in his church's program of evangelistic outreach. Recently, his team had experienced much success in visiting non-Christian prospects and leading them to Christ. Each week for the past five weeks one or more persons had given their hearts to Christ during one of Linc's visits. Word of these conversions spread throughout Linc's church. One day during the sermon his pastor commended Linc for his witness. Linc began to think that his success in witnessing might help him be elected chairman of the deacons. Enjoying the attention the church gave him, Linc became proud. What could Linc do to renew his mind?

Read his bible asking the holy Spirit to help him

You may have answered something like this:

Linda could renew her mind by recognizing her temptation and by discarding catalogs as they arrive before looking through them. She could replace thoughts of acquiring more by learning biblical teachings about material possessions and by developing a specific plan for reducing the family's debt.

Tony could renew his mind by changing his running time or place so that he will not encounter a situation that could lead him to ruin his marriage. He could pray for the Holy Spirit to show him ways to strengthen his marriage, such as spending more time with his spouse, talking honestly about their issues, and consulting a minister or a Christian counselor to help him and his spouse through this stressful period.

Linc could renew his mind by asking the Holy Spirit to help him as he reads what the Bible says about the reason Christians witness: to obey Christ, not to gain others' favor. As he reads Philippians 2:5-8, he could let the mind of Christ teach him how to be humble.

REPLACING OLD THOUGHTS

Read in the margin what the Bible says about how your thoughts shape your desires and actions. When you replace harmful thoughts with ones you know will honor Christ, your entire concept of yourself can change. If you constantly tell yourself, *I'm no good*, you may begin to act out those thoughts as a self-fulfilling prophecy. If you remind yourself of

"As he thinketh in his heart, so is he" (Prov. 23:7, KJV).

Christ's great love for you and of your worthiness in His sight, you will begin to act like a person of worth. You can renew your mind by replacing negative thoughts about yourself with the reminder that Christ died for you. You can renew your mind by remembering who—and whose—you are.

Describe specific situations in which you need to renew your mind.

Pray more g Reas Gods Word dont Talk on The Phone So mcy

Identify actions you will take to renew your mind. See the list in the margin for possibilities. Also review your answers, as well as the suggested answers, to the case studies you read. Some of those may apply to you.

_____

_____

_____

Stop and pray, asking God to give you courage to take the action you described.

Say aloud this week's Scripture-memory verses, Romans 12:1-2, to someone you think could benefit from them. Explain to that person how these verses encourage you to renew your mind.

No doubt you sometimes feel conflict in your heart when you try to have the thoughts, attitudes, and actions of Jesus. Why does such conflict arise to interfere with your commitment to have the mind of Christ? Another look at the Worldly Christian portion of the Disciple's Personality provides an answer.

LEARNING THE DISCIPLE'S PERSONALITY
Read 1 Corinthians 3:1-3 in the margin. Why did Paul say that the Corinthian Christians were worldly instead of mature?

_____

Paul told the Christians at Corinth that they were not yet mature Christians because they had allowed jealousy and quarreling among them. If you do not allow Christ continually to be the Master of your life through His Spirit, you are a worldly Christian. Although you have

---

HOW TO RENEW YOUR MIND
Here is a quick reference for renewing your mind. Keep a copy in your Bible, wallet, or purse for ready access.
- **Sing songs of praise.**
- **Memorize applicable Scriptures.**
- **Pray.**
- **Bring every thought under Christ's control.**
- **Set your mind on things above.**
- **Demolish Satan's strongholds.**
- **Commit yourself to God as a living sacrifice.**
- **Talk to a friend.**
- **Help someone in need.**
- **Claim the mind of Christ.**

"Brothers, I could not address you as spiritual but as worldly—mere infants in Christ. I gave you milk, not solid food, for you were not yet ready for it. Indeed, you are still not ready. You are still worldly. For since there is jealousy and quarreling among you, are you not worldly? Are you not acting like mere men?" (1 Cor. 3:1-3).

allowed Christ to enter your life, you still struggle to control your own life. The big *I* of the old, natural person still dominates you. Worldly Christians, though children of God, continually open the door of the flesh, allowing the old nature to determine what they think, do, and feel, rather than follow the Spirit of God. You observed this situation when you read about Linda, Tony, and Linc in the case studies. You may see it in yourself, too.

✝ The part of the Disciple's Personality drawing you learned in day 2 appears below. Write *1 Corinthians 3:1-3* under the heading *The Worldly Christian*. By the end of this study you will be able to draw the complete Disciple's Personality and to explain it in your own words.

The Worldly Christian

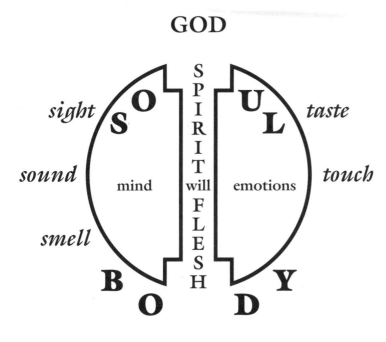

Setting aside old patterns can be challenging, but do not despair. Christ wants to be your Lord and to give you daily victory. The Holy Spirit will help you renew your mind. Week 3 will provide more positive steps to take.

Bob Dutton, a teacher and conference leader from Hendersonville, North Carolina, became aware of the worldly lives of many American Christians when he led *MasterLife* training in the village of Krasnoyarsk Krai in Russia, once under the control of an atheistic government. Bob wept when he led these inspired Russian Christians, who had sacrificed time and possessions to travel to the training. "I was ashamed," Bob said. "I was there to help dedicated Christians learn more about the

Christ wants to be your Lord and to give you daily victory.

DAILY MASTER COMMUNICATION GUIDE

GENESIS 50:15-21

What God said to me:

_____

_____

_____

_____

_____

_____

What I said to God:

_____

_____

_____

_____

_____

_____

_____

Bible, and I had to admit that most Christians in America are more concerned with themselves than with following Christ. It was hard to admit that our government leaves God out of its decisions while I sat in a classroom in Siberia teaching persons who have experienced persecution and oppression."

Read Genesis 50:15-21 during your quiet time today. See how God speaks to you through this passage, which focuses on someone who replaced evil thoughts with good thoughts. Then complete the Daily Master Communication Guide in the margin.

IN THE CARPENTER'S SHOP
How have you done this week getting rid of the old self and adopting new characteristics and behaviors?

Answer these questions about the area you identified on page 35.

A characteristic or behavior I have been getting rid of this week:

_____

Something Christ has added to my character this week:

_____

Stop and pray, thanking God for helping you in the areas you recorded. Ask Him to continue to give you the courage to make changes.

HAS THIS WEEK MADE A DIFFERENCE?
Review "My Walk with the Master This Week" at the beginning of this week's material. Mark the activities you have finished by drawing vertical lines in the diamonds beside them. Finish any incomplete activities. Think about what you will say during your group session about your work on these activities.

As a result of your study of "Renew Your Mind," I hope that you understand ways being a worldly Christian holds you back from being all God wants you to be. I hope that the Worldly Christian part of the Disciple's Personality will help you identify areas of weakness or compromise in your life in the Spirit. The ability to think Christ's thoughts is crucial to your life in the Spirit. Allowing Christ-honoring thoughts to replace worldly, fleshly thoughts is a challenge for most Christians. The Holy Spirit is with you to help you renew your mind. You do not have to be a victim of Satan's efforts to have you adopt his destructive attitudes. Satan is defeated when you push his thoughts out of your mind and replace them with those that please Christ.

WEEK 3

Master Your Emotions

This Week's Goal
You will be able to use an ACTION plan to master your emotions.

My Walk with the Master This Week
You will complete the following activities to develop the six biblical disciplines. When you have completed each activity, draw a vertical line in the diamond beside it.

 SPEND TIME WITH THE MASTER
◇ Have a quiet time each day, working toward the goal of having quiet times 21 consecutive days. Check the box beside each day you have a quiet time this week: ❑ Sunday ❑ Monday ❑ Tuesday ❑ Wednesday ❑ Thursday ❑ Friday ❑ Saturday
◇ During one day's quiet time, hold for five minutes the nail your leader gave you in your group session.

 LIVE IN THE WORD
◇ Read your Bible every day. Write what God says to you and what you say to God.
◇ Memorize Galatians 5:22-23.
◇ Review Philippians 2:13 and Romans 12:1-2.
◇ Read "How to Listen to God's Word."
◇ Write important points from a sermon on the Hearing the Word form.

 PRAY IN FAITH
◇ Pray for your family members and relatives.

FELLOWSHIP WITH BELIEVERS
◇ Have coffee or a soft drink with someone you do not like or with a person who does not like you.

 WITNESS TO THE WORLD
◇ Read "Testimony Outline" and write information to use in your testimony.

 MINISTER TO OTHERS
◇ Learn the Spiritual Christian part of the Disciple's Personality.

This Week's Scripture-Memory Verses
"The fruit of the Spirit is love, joy, peace, patience, kindness, goodness, faithfulness, gentleness and self-control. Against such things there is no law" (Gal. 5:22-23).

DAY 1

A Gift from God

My father often told about having a terrible temper when he was young. Even after becoming a Christian at age 19, he often still exploded in anger. He struggled over and over again to remain calm and to have an attitude that would honor Christ.

After much prayer and Bible study my father began to notice a change in his responses to situations. One night a man stuck his fist in my dad's face and threatened him. But Dad refused to fight. He later related, "I knew I had won the battle over my temper when I did not respond as I had in the past."

Describe a situation in which your emotions got the best of you.

when I was a child and I did not want to do what I was told, but did it anyway sometime had to do it over, late & approved what I was told to do to admit say help[?]

Almost everyone has had experiences in which controlling emotions has seemed like an overwhelming battle. In this week's study you will learn how the Holy Spirit can help you gain the victory and master your emotions.

"If it feels good, do it!" seems to be this generation's motto. This self-centered philosophy claims that your emotions are your master. Emotions make good servants but harmful masters. Christ is to be your Master, even of your emotions. He wants to help you use your emotions in a responsible way. The Bible has a plan to help you deal with your emotions. This week you will learn that plan and will understand how the Holy Spirit can help you take charge of your emotions. After this week's study you will be able to—

* relate your emotions to your values;
* list a six-step ACTION plan to deal with your emotions;
* apply the ACTION plan to an emotional experience.

Lesson 1 Youth Bible Study

WHAT ARE EMOTIONS?

Emotions are God-given feelings of pleasantness or unpleasantness. They are reactions to internal or external stimuli. Emotions are not good or bad; you make the choice of whether you use emotions to honor Christ or to harm yourself or others.

Emotions are an essential part of your personality. Life without emotions would be dull. If you did not have emotions, you would not experience anger or anxiety, but you also would not experience joy or love. God created you to experience a variety of emotions.

"He looked around at them in anger and, deeply distressed at their stubborn hearts, said to the man, 'Stretch out your hand.' He stretched it out, and his hand was completely restored" (Mark 3:5).

" 'A new command I give you: Love one another. As I have loved you, so you must love one another' " (John 13:34).

"Jesus wept" (John 11:35).

" 'I am coming to you now, but I say these things while I am still in the world, so that they may have the full measure of my joy within them' " (John 17:13).

Read the verses in the margin on the previous page and check the emotions Jesus experienced.

☑ anger ☑ love ☑ grief *Jesus wept* ☑ joy

Because Jesus was fully human, He experienced the whole range of human emotions. He experienced all of those listed. The difference between Jesus and you is that He did not sin when He experienced emotions.

THE SOURCE OF YOUR EMOTIONS

Emotions are spontaneous responses to your values and beliefs. Over the years your emotional responses have been either affirmed or challenged. Because your values and beliefs are not exactly the same as any other person's, you react to the same circumstances differently than someone else does.

During your quiet time today read Matthew 21:12-16, which describes ways Jesus used His emotions. Then complete the Daily Master Communication Guide in the margin.

Answer the following questions about Matthew 21:12-16.

The selling and buying in the temple caused different emotions in Jesus than in the chief priests and the teachers of the law. What were these emotions, and why did they experience them?

Jesus felt ___ANGER And GRief___ *but in control*.

Why? ___PEOPLE took Gods house to make money And not serve God___

The chief priests and the teachers of the law might have felt

___they Also felt Anger + grief___

Why? ___becAuse Jesus came to take Their place they wanted to be head + PRAISE___

The healing of the blind and lame man in the temple caused different emotions in the children than it did in the chief priests and the teachers of the law. What were these emotions, and why did they experience them?

The children felt ___LOVE + Joy___.

Why? ___JESus is Love + Was helping them___

The chief priests and the teachers of the law felt ___Anger___.

DAILY MASTER COMMUNICATION GUIDE

MATTHEW 21:12-16

What God said to me: *God head Father Son Holy Spirit*

What I said to God:

Why? _The children Called Jesus the Messiah_

One set of circumstances can affect different persons in different ways. You may have said that Jesus felt anger because He believed that the temple should be a house of prayer, while the chief priests and the teachers of the law might have felt indifference or perhaps joy because they believed that the temple was a place where people could buy sacrifices and keep the law. They were undoubtedly enraged after Jesus drove out the money changers. You may have said that the children felt joy because people were being healed and the Messiah had come, while the chief priests and the teachers of the law felt indignant because Jesus was proclaimed the Son of David (the Messiah).

Analyze another Bible passage, Luke 10:30-37, in the margin. How did circumstances affect different persons in different ways?

The Levite seems to have felt indifferent. What value judgments do you think he made that produced this feeling? _May have been Afraid for his Life Also Thought his work what he was doing more important then helping someone in need_

The Samaritan evidently felt compassion and concern. What value judgments do you think he made that produced those feelings? _The Samaritan did a good deed, he felt sure Like was in danger + he stop to help Also he went the Extra mile when telling the innkeeper he would pay for what Ever the man need on his way back_

You may have answered that the Levite did not value the injured man as important or that he was in a hurry because he valued his work more than he valued the man. You may have said that the Samaritan valued the injured man enough to disrupt his plans and to contribute his resources to his healing.

Your values help determine whether you make the correct emotional response in a given situation. Too many people are glad, sad, or mad about the wrong things for the wrong reasons. If you can discern what makes you glad, sad, or mad, you can know your true values. A worldly Christian places his or her values on a self-centered life.

Think about the most recent time you were angry. Describe that experience.

Getting Angery sometime you let Anger take over your emotion goes out board And you Loose self Control And it has to go back + correct That wrong, it take a midy big Person to say I'm sorry, we alway say Children should Respect other but what about as As Adult

" 'A man was going down from Jerusalem to Jericho, when he fell into the hands of robbers. They stripped him of his clothes, beat him and went away, leaving him half dead. A priest happened to be going down the same road, and when he saw the man, he passed by on the other side. So too, a Levite, when he came to the place and saw him, passed by on the other side. But a Samaritan, as he traveled, came where the man was; and when he saw him, he took pity on him. He went to him and bandaged his wounds, pouring on oil and wine. Then he put the man on his own donkey, took him to an inn and took care of him. The next day he took out two silver coins and gave them to the innkeeper. "Look after him," he said, "and when I return, I will reimburse you for any extra expense you may have."

" 'Which of these three do you think was a neighbor to the man who fell into the hands of robbers?' The expert in the law replied, 'The one who had mercy on him.' Jesus told him, 'Go and do likewise' " (Luke 10: 30-37).

What caused this anger? Check the items that were challenged.
- ❑ My position or reputation
- ☑ My plans
- ❑ My rights
- ☑ My possessions
- ❑ My identity
- ☑ My ideas
- ☑ My physical needs
- ☑ My desires

Look again at the list and mentally check which items relate to the most recent time you felt fear, grief, joy, loneliness, anxiety, and embarrassment. Why did you feel these emotions? If you felt affirmed about the matters in the previous list, you probably experienced an emotion like joy or delight. If you felt challenged about these matters, you probably experienced fear, anger, loneliness, or betrayal. Often, a person cannot control emotions because they are narrowly focused on himself and arise from his worldly nature.

Read 1 Corinthians 3:1-3 in the margin. What did Paul call these Christians who were controlled by the emotions of jealousy and strife?

You ARE woRldly Not SPiritual

In previous weeks you have studied the natural person and the worldly Christian, which is what Paul called the Christians in 1 Corinthians 3:1-3. This week you will learn about the spiritual Christian, another part of the Disciple's Personality. Spiritual Christians also have strong emotions, but they have learned to master their emotions by controlling their responses to their emotions instead of letting their emotions control their responses. A spiritual Christian learns more and more to rely on the Holy Spirit instead of the flesh.

"Brothers, I could not address you as spiritual but as worldly—mere infants in Christ. I gave you milk, not solid food, for you were not yet ready for it. Indeed, you are still not ready. You are still worldly. For since there is jealousy and quarreling among you, are you not worldly? Are you not acting like mere men?" (1 Cor. 3:1-3).

RELYING ON THE SPIRIT

Turn to page 47 and read your Scripture-memory verses, Galatians 5:22-23. What do these verses say about the Holy Spirit's role in self-control?

Holy Spirit in Control give you The Ability To Control your Emotion

When the Holy Spirit transforms you, He is present in your life to give you the ability to control your emotions. The Holy Spirit can even influence you as you relate to persons whom you do not particularly like or who do not like you. Sally Smith, a pastor's wife in Texas, reports that this occurred with a couple she met in *MasterLife* training in Lugansk, Ukraine. When the husband became a Christian, his wife told him that he must choose between her and God. Her father was a prominent leader in the Communist party, and she would not allow her husband to disgrace the family. As her husband struggled with his choice for about a year, great bitterness grew between the two. Finally, their

12-year-old son told his mother, "If you leave Daddy, I'm going with him." When she realized that she would lose her son, she began reading the Bible. The Holy Spirit began moving in her heart, prompting her to become a Christian and to restore the relationships with her husband and her son.

Have coffee or a soft drink with someone you do not like or with a person who does not like you. If you do not know such a person, do something for someone you do not know very well. Be prepared to share with the group what happened.

You may think: *I could never do something kind for or reach out to someone who dislikes me. If I tried, I would lose my temper.* You may not be able to, but the Holy Spirit can give you that ability by influencing you and renewing your mind. With His help, you can learn to control your emotions.

Ask the Holy Spirit to help you master your emotions and relate redemptively to others in difficult situations.

DAY 2

Taking Positive Steps

Your emotions cause you to act, but you can also act your way into an emotion.

Sometimes you may believe that your emotions are so strong that you cannot master them. You may feel that when they sweep over you like a giant tide, you have no choice but to drift along with them. However, you are not helpless in learning to control your emotions. The Holy Spirit can help you when you are tempted to give in to your emotions.

A specific course of action can help you master your emotions. It is known by the simple acrostic ACTION. Emotions are closely tied to actions. Your emotions cause you to act, but you can also act your way into an emotion. Here is what ACTION means:

A cknowledge the emotion.
C onsider why you have it.
T hank God that He will help you master it.
I dentify the biblical response to it.
O bey the Holy Spirit's leading.
N urture the appropriate fruit of the Spirit.

Over the next few days you will examine each element of this ACTION plan to learn how to deal with your emotions.

1) ACKNOWLEDGE THE EMOTION

The first step is to **acknowledge the emotion**. Denying or suppressing your emotions does not help. Have you heard someone shout through clenched teeth, "I am not angry!"? The words are entirely different from the emotion communicated. You can deal with an emotion only if you recognize it.

Read Matthew 26:37-38 in the margin. What was the first thing Jesus did about His grief and distress as He faced the cross?

He talk about his feeling To
Sone one who Listen

"He took Peter and the two sons of Zebedee along with him, and he began to be sorrowful and troubled. Then he said to them, 'My soul is overwhelmed with sorrow to the point of death. Stay here and keep watch with me'" (Matt. 26:37-38).

Can you not Watch 1 ho_

Sleep or take your Rest,

Jesus did not try to deny or suppress His grief and distress as He faced the cross but admitted that He was sorrowful. Burying an emotion can cause it to emerge in an unhealthy way later. Suppressing emotions can make you physically ill as well as add to the emotional load you carry.

Learning to identify your exact emotion will help you acknowledge your feelings. For example, you may think you are feeling sad about a matter when a closer look reveals that you actually feel lonely, abandoned, helpless, or overwhelmed. Giving an exact name to an emotion helps with the later steps of this action plan. Try this activity to identify emotions more accurately.

Reflect on the most recent time you remember feeling a strong emotion about a matter. Check the feeling or feelings that most precisely described you at that time.

☑ disappointed	❑ hopeful	❑ abandoned	❑ validated
❑ satisfied	☑ lonely	❑ excited	❑ other:
☑ frightened	❑ victorious	☑ embarrassed	wont to
❑ jubilant	☑ helpless	❑ assured	have my
☑ betrayed my Sit	❑ calm	☑ confused	own way

Certainly, many more feeling words than these exist to describe emotions. You may want to add to this list.

2) CONSIDER WHY YOU HAVE THE EMOTION

A second action step toward mastering an emotion is to **consider why you have it**. After you have acknowledged a feeling, it is important to understand why you are experiencing it. Doing this may not be as simple as you think. Sometimes an event that occurred several hours or days before is still in your subconscious, causing an emotional reaction. Try this exercise.

Identify an emotion you had recently: _____

Why did you feel this way? Check all appropriate responses.

❑ My physical condition
❑ What someone said to me or about me
☑ What someone did to me or for me
❑ My thoughts
❑ My will
☑ My flesh (sinful desires)
❑ My relationship with God
❑ Other: _____

Identifying the underlying cause of an emotion is a big step toward mastering your reaction to that emotion.

You may have identified that you felt confused because of something someone said to you. For example, when your boss questioned whether you have the skills to do a project, you were confused because you completed training two months ago that you thought qualified you. Or maybe you identified feeling embarrassed about the physical condition of your body. Identifying the underlying cause of an emotion is a big step toward mastering your reaction to that emotion.

This week's Scripture-memory verses, Galatians 5:22-23, emphasize self-control. The verses also list characteristics you will have if the Spirit controls your life. To work on memorizing the verses, list the nine fruit of the Spirit. Check your work by referring to page 47.

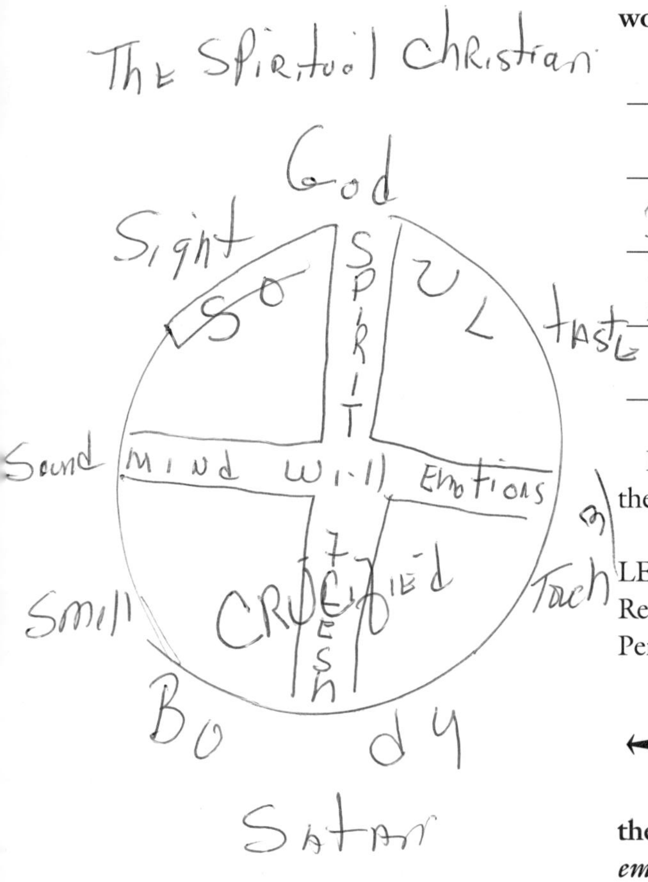

LOVE	GOODNESS
JOY	FAITHFULNESS
PEACE	GENTLENESS
PATIENCE	SELF-CONTROL
KINDNESS	

Learning the next portion of the Disciple's Personality will reinforce the first two steps you have studied for mastering your emotions.

LEARNING THE DISCIPLE'S PERSONALITY
Read the section "The Spiritual Christian" (p. 137) in the Disciple's Personality presentation.

Begin drawing the Spiritual Christian portion of the Disciple's Personality. The basic diagram is drawn for you on the next page. Close the door of the flesh as you draw a cross in the center of the circle to encompass *spirit, flesh, mind, will,* and *emotions.* Write *crucified* across *flesh.* Above the circle write *The Spiritual Christian.* Refer to the Disciple's Personality presentation (pp. 133–39) if you need help. By the end of this study you will be

[Handwritten diagram in left margin: a circle labeled "The Spiritual Christian" with "God" at top, "Satan" at bottom, cross inside containing "SPIRIT," "SOUL," "MIND," "WILL," "Emotions," "CRUCIFIED," "FLESH," "BODY," and the five senses "Sight," "Sound," "Smell," "taste," "Touch" around it.]

able to draw the complete Disciple's Personality and to explain it in your own words.

The spiritual christian

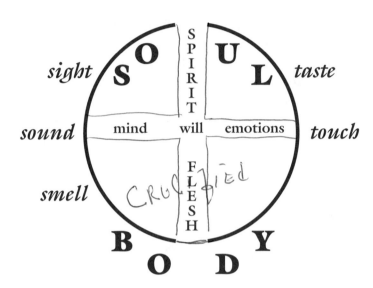

GOD

sight

sound

smell

taste

touch

mind will emotions

SPIRIT

FLESH

CRUCIFIED

SATAN

Read Galatians 2:20: "I have been crucified with Christ and I no longer live, but Christ lives in me. The life I live in the body, I live by faith in the Son of God, who loved me and gave himself for me" (Gal. 2:20). Can you make the statement Paul made? Write your name in the blanks in this adaptation of Galatians 2:20.

I, *Dorothy Echols*, am crucified with Christ and I no longer live, but Christ lives in me. The life I live in the body, I, *Dorothy Echols*, live by faith in the Son of God, who loved me and gave himself for me.

Write *S* beside the statements that describe the spiritual Christian.
S Puts the old self to death
S Is promised victory over the world, the flesh, and the devil
S Sets aside the lusts of the flesh
S Has the Holy Spirit dwelling in his or her personality
S Has God in control of both soul and body

A spiritual Christian sets aside old ways as though he or she has buried them. Some of those old ways may be fleshly lusts. A spiritual Christian can do this because God promises victory over Satan and over the world, the flesh, and the devil. The Holy Spirit, dwelling in this Christian's personality, gives God control of both soul and body. All five statements describe the spiritual Christian.

The World's Way

"The acts of the sinful nature are obvious: sexual immorality, impurity and debauchery. ... I warn you, as I did before, that those who live like this will not inherit the kingdom of God" (Gal. 5:19-21).

"Now you must rid yourselves of all such things as these: anger, rage, malice, slander, and filthy language from your lips" (Col. 3:8).

"Do not let any unwholesome talk come out of your mouths, but only what is helpful for building others up according to their needs, that it may benefit those who listen" (Eph. 4:29).

The Spirit's Way

"The fruit of the Spirit is love, joy, peace, patience, kindness, goodness, faithfulness, gentleness and self-control. Against such things there is no law" (Gal. 5:22-23).

"You have taken off your old self with its practices and have put on the new self, which is being renewed in knowledge in the image of its Creator" (Col. 3:9-10).

"Be imitators of God, therefore, as dearly loved children, and live a life of love, just as Christ loved us and gave himself up for us as a fragrant offering and sacrifice to God" (Eph. 5: 1-2).

IN THE CARPENTER'S SHOP

Are you continuing to set aside, or tear down, the old self and to add new, Christlike traits to your character? In week 2 you identified a specific behavior you wanted to get rid of and an action you would take to replace it. This week you will look at more ways the Holy Spirit can help you become a new person in Christ.

Read the Scriptures in the margin, which relate to the improper use of language. From the verses marked "The World's Way" identify a specific behavior of this nature that you want to get rid of. From the verses marked "The Spirit's Way" identify an action you will take to replace it. I have given you an example. Each day for the rest of this week you will record your progress in working on this behavior.

Here is an example.

Behavior I want to work on: saying hateful things about others
think before to speack
An action I will take to put off the old self: stop being critical of my friends

An action I will take to let the Holy Spirit make me more like Christ: consciously be loving in my conversations about and to others

Now you try it.

Behavior I want to work on: _____
be more friendly toward other
An action I will take to put off the old self:

_____

An action I will take to let the Holy Spirit make me more like Christ:

_____

In your quiet time today read Galatians 2:11-21, the passage in which Paul speaks of being crucified with Christ. Then complete the Daily Master Communication Guide on page 55.

Pray for your family members and relatives. Remember to keep a record of your prayers and answers to them on your Prayer-Covenant List (p. 143).

DAY 3

Giving Thanks in All Things

DAILY MASTER COMMUNICATION GUIDE

PSALM 42

Sometimes people are unable to identify the causes of their emotions. You may have been able to check one of the feelings listed on page 53 or to write another one in the blank, but when you tried to determine the cause of it, you were clueless. Or perhaps you sense that your emotion is out of proportion to the event that caused it.

For example, you may know that you feel a deep sense of anger because your boss overlooked you in your company's awards ceremony, but you are puzzled about why a simple slight like this should evoke such strong feelings. Or you may know that you feel lonely and abandoned when a friend forgets a luncheon engagement with you, but you do not understand why you have great difficulty accepting her apology for her absentmindedness. If this is your situation, you may want to talk to your pastor or to a professional Christian counselor or participate in a Christ-centered support group that helps people understand more about their emotions.[1]

The person who reacts strongly to a boss who forgets to announce an award may learn that he or she has difficulty relating to authority figures because of a painful childhood relationship with a parent. The person who feels lonely and abandoned after an appointment falls through may still be struggling unconsciously with childhood feelings of abandonment by a relative. A person can take big steps toward mastering his or her emotions by discovering the deeper issues behind the strong feelings.

THANK GOD THAT HE WILL HELP YOU
MASTER THE EMOTION
Whether or not you can identify the cause of your emotion, you can take the third action step: **thank God that He will help you master it**. Observe where this step fits into the ACTION acrostic.

Recall the key words in the first two steps in the ACTION acrostic.

A CKNOWLEDGE the emotion.
C ONSIDER why you have it.
T hank God that He will help you master it.
I dentify the biblical response to it.
O bey the Holy Spirit's leading.
N urture the appropriate fruit of the Spirit.

 Read Psalm 42 during your quiet time today. Then complete the Daily Master Communication Guide in the margin.

What God said to me:

_____

_____

_____

_____

_____

_____

_____

What I said to God:

_____

_____

_____

_____

_____

_____

_____

_____

In Psalm 42 what are the action steps David took when he felt strong emotion about his sin?

> He Called on The Living
> God

In grief about the death of his son and about his own spiritual condition, David took action steps that are good examples for us. David admitted that he was downcast, analyzed why he felt this strong emotion, and thanked God because he believed that God would help him.

You do not have to understand a situation to believe that God will work in it and to be grateful that He will do so.

"Give thanks in all circumstances, for this is God's will for you in Christ Jesus" (1 Thess. 5:18).

Read 1 Thessalonians 5:18 in the margin. In which situations are you to give thanks?

> All Circumstances

"We know that in all things God works for the good of those who love him, who have been called according to his purpose" (Rom. 8:28).

Read Romans 8:28 in the margin. Why can a person of faith give thanks in everything?

> All things God work the good those who love him

"About midnight Paul and Silas were praying and singing hymns to God, and the other prisoners were listening to them" (Acts 16:25).

Read Acts 16:25 in the margin. How did Paul and Silas prevent their situation from producing harmful emotions?

> Praying And Singing

You are to give thanks in all things, not just the ones you understand or the ones that please you. If you are a person of faith, you can do this because you believe that God will work all things together for good. Paul and Silas prayed and sang hymns to keep themselves from reacting harmfully to being jailed. When by faith you trust God to work in a situation and when you thank Him for doing so, your mind is open to consider the benefits that may result.

List benefits that might result because you have the following emotions.

Fear: _____ from taking Risk

Anger: Lead you To Right A wrong injustice

Loneliness: may help you to Lean on God

Joy: you Reach out by kindness

Jealousy: _NEED To work on your Relationship_

Even though you may not like to think about feeling fear, anger, loneliness, or jealousy, these emotions can have good results. Fear may keep you from taking unnecessary risks or may prompt you to take extra precautions in a situation. Anger might lead you to right a wrong or an injustice. A person who is lonely may learn to rely on God to fill the emptiness in his or her life. Jealousy can make you realize that you need to work more diligently in a relationship or to strive harder toward a goal. From joy you may reach out in kindness to others or may give praise to God for a development in your life.

⤡ **Continue working on your memory verses, Galatians 5:22-23. Say them aloud to a friend. Share the way you believe the Holy Spirit is helping you learn to have self-control, the final fruit of the Spirit mentioned.**

IN THE CARPENTER'S SHOP
What progress are you making in getting rid of the old self and adding new behaviors to your life?

Yesterday you identified a behavior you hoped to put away in order to build Christlike character in the way you use language. Today describe an instance in which you have acted to set aside the old behavior.

Smiling & Speaking Kindly

Spending time in the Word through study and prayer often helps you make progress toward putting off the old self and adding Christlike thoughts and actions to your life. Besides reading the Word, you can also receive insight by hearing the Word preached or taught. Many times insight from a preacher, speaker, or Bible-study leader is the exact tool the Holy Spirit uses to help you meet your goal.

⤡ **Read "How to Listen to God's Word" and answer the questions.**

You can receive insight by hearing the Word preached or taught.

HOW TO LISTEN TO GOD'S WORD
1. Evaluate what kind of hearer you are. Read Matthew 13:3-23 and classify yourself as one of the following.
   a. *Apathetic hearer:* hears the word but is not prepared to receive and understand it (see v. 19).

Do I let the message go in one ear and out the other?
❏ Yes ❏̌ No

    b. *Superficial hearer:* receives the word temporarily but does not let it take root in the heart (see vv. 20-21).

Do I simply accept what is said without making specific, personal application? ❏ Yes ❏ No *Not all the time*

    c. *Preoccupied hearer:* receives the word but lets the worries of this world and the desire for things choke it (see v. 22).

Do I remember to practice the message during the week, or do I let other priorities crowd it out? ❏ Yes ❏ No *sometime*

    d. *Reproducing hearer:* receives the word, understands it, bears fruit, and brings forth results (see v. 23).

Does the message yield maximal fruit in my life? ❏ Yes ❏ No

2. Be alert for a word from God: "Be quick to hear" (Jas. 1:19, RSV).
3. Clear away all sin and pride so that the word can be planted in your heart (see Jas. 1:21).
4. Pay attention to what the Bible says about you, just as you would to your reflection in a mirror (see Jas. 1:23).
   a. Takes notes on the Hearing the Word form (see p. 141). List the date, place, speaker, text, and title of the message if given.
   b. Write the points of the message as the speaker presents them.
   c. Under each point write explanation, illustrations, and application. If all of these elements are not mentioned, write those that are.
   d. Write any specific statements the Spirit impresses on you.
   e. Summarize as soon as possible the main point the speaker wants you to do, be, and/or feel as a result of this sermon. Use the following questions to write your summary.
   • What did God say to me through this message? Write the specific point that you feel God wanted you to hear in the message. It may not have been what the speaker intended, but the Lord applied it to your heart.
   • How does my life measure up to this word? Look in the mirror of the word and recognize ways you fall short of what God has said. Be specific.
   • What actions will I take to bring my life in line with this word? These actions need to be specific, immediate, measurable, and attainable within a reasonable length of time.
   • What truth do I need to study further? The Lord may impress you to search the Scriptures for more information on a particular subject mentioned in the message.

Pay attention to what the Bible says about you, just as you would to your reflection in a mirror.

5. Do the Word, and you will be blessed in what you do (see Jas. 1:25). Check yourself several times in the days that follow to determine whether you have incorporated the message into your life and have begun to bear fruit from it.

Do the Word, and you will be blessed in what you do.

 Write important points from a sermon on the Hearing the Word form on page 141. Copy the form to use with all sermons.

DAY 4

A Biblical Response

The fourth step in your ACTION plan to master an emotion is to identify the biblical response to it. Review the steps in the plan.

IDENTIFY THE BIBLICAL RESPONSE TO THE EMOTION
Supply the key words in the first three steps you have studied.

A cKNowledge _____ the emotion.

C onsiden _____ why you have it.

T hank _____ God that He will help you master it.

I dentify the biblical response to it.

O bey the Holy Spirit's leading.

N urture the appropriate fruit of the Spirit.

Although emotions are spontaneous, the actions they produce do not have to be. The Bible teaches that you are responsible for how you choose to let your emotions cause you to behave. You cannot escape responsibility by blaming your behavior on a negative feeling or on the person or circumstance stimulating that feeling.

You may believe that someone wronged you or that your family background programmed you or predisposed you to act a certain way. You may think: *I can't help that I act this way. He made me angry when he criticized me.* But can someone really *make* you angry and *make* you respond improperly? Regardless of what precipitates the event, the choice of how to respond is yours. You can sin in that response, or you can choose to honor Christ. One sin does not justify another.

Although emotions are spontaneous, the actions they produce do not have to be.

In the following case studies underline each person's blaming response.

Carlene worked in an office in which she felt that her coworkers constantly antagonized her and criticized her work. One day, reaching her saturation point, Carlene raged: "What about all of the wrong things you do? You're not perfect either, you know!"

Jed was reared in a home in which his father was an alcoholic and wrote bad checks. Jed did not have a role model for dependability. As an adult, Jed tried to manage his family's finances but occasionally forgot to pay the bills. When his wife expressed concern about late payments, Jed fired back: "It's all my father's fault! He never taught me how to do this! This is just the way I am!"

Wanda's father beat her, and her mother never acted lovingly toward her. As an adult, Wanda was unforgiving and refused to communicate with her parents. She told her pastor, "I hate them for the way they treated me."

In each case the individual blamed someone else for his or her wrong actions. Even though Carlene's coworkers, Jed's father, and Wanda's parents certainly sinned in their mistreatment or bad habits, Carlene, Jed, and Wanda had choices whether to sin or take responsibility for their actions.

The Bible gives principles for responding to emotions. The better you know the Bible, the more easily you can apply it to deal with all emotions.

Read the Scriptures in the margin. Write in your own words biblical responses to the following emotions.

Hate (Luke 6:27-28): _Love the person you think are you enemies, do good for sure one that hate you. Not easy but with Pod it can be due_

Anxiety (Phil. 4:6-7): _Prayer about every thing_

Joy (Phil. 4:4): _we must give thanks & rejoice in christ goodnes_

Anger (Eph. 4:25-26,31-32): _we must not sin if we are angry please do not let the sun ao down mad or angery with any or easy said then don avoic sinn_

" 'Love your enemies, do good to those who hate you, bless those who curse you, pray for those who mistreat you' " (Luke 6:27-28).

"Do not be anxious about anything, but in everything, by prayer and petition, with thanksgiving, present your requests to God. And the peace of God, which transcends all understanding, will guard your hearts and your minds in Christ Jesus" (Phil. 4:6-7).

"Rejoice in the Lord always" (Phil. 4:4).

"Each of you must put off falsehood and speak truthfully to his neighbor, for we are all members of one body. 'In your anger do not sin.' Do not let the sun go down while you are still angry. Get rid of all bitterness, rage and anger, brawling and slander, along with every form of malice. Be kind and compassionate to one another, forgiving each other, just as in Christ God forgave you" (Eph. 4:25-26,31-32).

Envy (1 Pet. 2:1; 1 Cor. 13:4): _Lay it Aside +_
Love one Another

"Rid yourselves of all malice and all deceit, hypocrisy, envy, and slander of every kind. Like newborn babies, crave pure spiritual milk, so that by it you may grow up in your salvation, now that you have tasted that the Lord is good" (1 Pet. 2:1).

"Love ... does not envy" (1 Cor. 13:4).

For *hate* you may have written that the biblical response is to do good to those who hate you; for *anxiety,* that you are to pray to God and not to be anxious; for *joy,* that you are to acknowledge the source of goodness; for *anger,* that you are to avoid sinning from anger and to settle matters quickly; for *envy,* that you are to lay envy aside and to love others.

Based on the Scriptures you read in the previous exercise, describe how the characters in the three case studies might have responded in a Christ-honoring way if they had sought biblical solutions for their emotions.

Carlene: _Should have asked her coworker do they mind showing her how this is done_

Jed: _instead upset i his wife Asked her to be patient with him + help him to Learn + to Remind him if he forgot_

Wanda: _Learn how to forgive herself then should realize her mistake Also All should Pray for God's guidance_

You might have answered something like this: Instead of turning on her coworkers in anger, Carlene could have set a Christian example by asking her coworkers to sit down with her, individually or as a group, and calmly listen to one another's concerns about work-related issues. Instead of blaming his family background and continuing the cycle of irresponsibility, Jed could have offered to take a money-management course or could have listened to audiotapes on the subject. Or he and his wife could have reached an equitable agreement about steps each would take to manage the finances. Instead of harboring bitterness toward her parents, Wanda could have prayed that the Holy Spirit would help her forgive. She might have sought the help of a professional Christian counselor or a Christ-centered support group to learn positive ways to relate to her parents despite her painful past.

Say aloud your Scripture-memory verses, Galatians 5:22-23. Choose one of the nine fruit of the Spirit and describe on the next page how you plan to use it to master your emotions. Each fruit of the Spirit is not only an emotion but also a tool for mastering your emotions.

DAILY MASTER COMMUNICATION GUIDE

JOHN 19:17-37

What God said to me:

_____

_____

_____

_____

_____

_____

_____

What I said to God:

_____

_____

_____

_____

_____

_____

_____

_____

_____

_____

_____

HOW WOULD CHRIST RESPOND?

As you think about ways Christ would have you master your emotions, you can remember His example on the cross—the ultimate example of a person's control of emotions. Think of the ways Christ could have responded to this event: He could have raged, threatened, blamed, or scolded. He could have called on angels to protect Him. Instead, He sought God's will in His responses, even to the end. Certainly, He expressed His sorrow, as you studied in day 2. He expressed His concern for His mother. He expressed His human physical need. But the ultimate mastery occurred when He surrendered everything to God's will, even when that meant suffering and dying on the cross.

Read John 19:17-37, the passage that describes Jesus' death on the cross, during your quiet time today. See how God speaks to you. Then complete the Daily Master Communication Guide in the margin.

Also during your quiet time today hold for five minutes the nail your leader gave you in your group session. Feel and smell the nail. Press the point of the nail against your palm. Think about Christ's suffering for you and let the Holy Spirit show you the importance of Jesus' pain for you. Read aloud Galatians 2:20 as you contemplate His suffering: "I have been crucified with Christ and I no longer live, but Christ lives in me. The life I live in the body, I live by faith in the Son of God, who loved me and gave himself for me."

IN THE CARPENTER'S SHOP

If Christ is the Master of your life, you will want to be like Him—even in your language. How is the Holy Spirit helping you tear down the old self and replace old behaviors with new ones?

List a new thought or action that replaced the one you tore down in the way you use language. How are you working to put this new thought or action in place of the old?

_____

_____

DAY 5

The Higher Calling

The fifth action step is to **obey the Holy Spirit's leading**.

OBEY THE HOLY SPIRIT'S LEADING
**Look at the way this step fits into the ACTION acrostic. This time
I will supply the key word and will let you finish the statement.**

A cKNowLedge THE EMotion.

C onsider why you hnre, +

T hank God That he will help you. + mAstie

I dENtify The biblicol Response to it

O bey the Holy Spirit's leading.

N urture the appropriate fruit of the Spirit.

Natural and worldly persons want to do what their emotions, mind, or will tells them. In contrast, spiritual persons obey the higher call to do what the Holy Spirit reveals. Doing what God says is right, rather than what you want to do, is a conscious act of the will. Christians understand their obligations to act rightly toward others even if they do not feel like doing so. If you wait until you feel like doing right, you may find yourself excusing your failure.

Read the following accounts. Write *E* beside those that describe someone who used feelings as an excuse for irresponsibility. Write *R* beside those in which the person acted responsibly.

_E__ Jim slammed on his brakes and bore down on the horn while an elderly man crept across the street. Then Jim sped away so that he would not miss the next light.

_E__ When Tommy accidentally spilled his milk, his mother grabbed him and spanked him, yelling at him to be more careful.

_E__ The woman tried on many pairs of shoes in the store before announcing that she really could not afford to buy any. Then she asked directions to another shoe store. The salesperson drew her a map and thanked her for stopping by. _R_

**DAILY MASTER
COMMUNICATION
GUIDE**

MATTHEW 26:57-68

What God said to me:

_____

_____

_____

_____

_____

_____

_____

_____

What I said to God:

_____

_____

_____

_____

_____

_____

_____

_____

_____

_____

" 'Leave your gift there in front of the altar. First go and be reconciled to your brother; then come and offer your gift' " (Matt. 5:24).

" 'Do not judge, or you too will be judged. For in the same way you judge others, you will be judged, and with the measure you use, it will be measured to you' " (Matt. 7:1-2).

"Love is patient, love is kind. It does not envy, it does not boast, it is not proud. It is not rude, it is not self-seeking, it is not easily angered, it keeps no record of wrongs. Love does not delight in evil but rejoices with the truth. It always protects, always trusts, always hopes, always perseveres" (1 Cor. 13:4-7).

"He that is slow to anger is better than the mighty; and he that ruleth his spirit than he that taketh a city" (Prov. 16:32, KJV).

You likely recognized that the person in the last illustration—the salesperson who went the extra mile—was the only one who dealt responsibly with emotions.

Not only do your feelings influence the way you act, but the way you act also determines how you feel. You can change your feelings by changing your actions, as the adage "Act your way into a new feeling" states. Jesus' solution for many emotional responses was to command an action rather than a feeling. Read Matthew 5:24 and Matthew 7:1-2 in the margin.

Read 1 Corinthians 13:4-7 in the margin. When the Bible tells you to love your fellow Christians, love is described as (check one)—
❏ **an emotional feeling;**
❏ **a way of behaving.**

Love is something you do. Love manifests itself in the way you act. Acting lovingly toward someone even if you do not feel like doing so is the essence of love. The Holy Spirit can help you do this.

Read Proverbs 16:32 in the margin. This verse says that a person who remains in control of self is stronger than the strong and mightier than the mighty. A person who declines to reply in anger, conquering his or her emotions, demonstrates more strength than does a person who conquers a city.

During your quiet time today read Matthew 26:57-68, about a time when Jesus maintained self-control in a difficult situation. Then complete the Daily Master Communication Guide in the margin on page 65.

NURTURE THE APPROPRIATE FRUIT OF THE SPIRIT
The sixth action step in mastering your emotions is to **nurture the appropriate fruit of the Spirit.**

In the ACTION acrostic below write the steps you have studied.

A cknowledge _____.

C onsider _____.

T hank _____.

I dentify _____.

O bey _____.

N urture the appropriate fruit of the Spirit.

Each fruit of the Spirit is more than an emotion. Each is a stable trait of character. You develop each by having a close relationship with Christ through the Holy Spirit and by growing in maturity through experience.

Say aloud your memory verses, Galatians 5:22-23, which mention all of the fruit of the Spirit. Then check which fruit of the Spirit you believe you most need to develop in mastering your emotions. You may check more than one.

☑ love ☑ patience ☑ faithfulness
☑ joy ☑ kindness ☑ gentleness
☐ peace ☐ goodness ☐ self-control

How do you plan to develop this trait or these traits of character?

_____

_____

Stop and ask God to help you develop the aspect of your character you identified. Ask Him to help you make this a meaningful part of your life in the Spirit.

Say again the verses you memorized in previous weeks, Philippians 2:13 and Romans 12:1-2.

Before your next group session apply the ACTION steps to an emotion. Write the results below. Be prepared to describe your experience to your fellow group members.

_____

_____

_____

IN THE CARPENTER'S SHOP
Review the progress you have made this week in building Christlike character. How is the Holy Spirit helping you become more like Jesus in your use of pure language?

Name the behavior you have put aside this week.

_____

You develop the fruit of the Spirit by having a close relationship with Christ.

List what Christ has been adding to your character this week.

_____

LEARNING THE DISCIPLE'S PERSONALITY

Review what you have learned about the Spiritual Christian portion of the Disciple's Personality. The basic diagram has been drawn for you below. Draw the elements of the spiritual Christian as you did in day 2. Label the drawing *The Spiritual Christian* and write *Galatians 2:20* under the label. Refer to the Disciple's Personality presentation (pp. 133–39) if you need help. By the end of this study you should be able to draw the complete Disciple's Personality and to explain it in your own words.

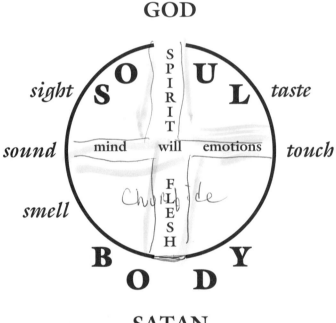

One of the most amazing stories of an individual who mastered the Disciple's Personality occurred in prison. A man named J. D., an inmate in a state penitentiary in Texas, told *MasterLife* leader Don Dennis that concepts of the Disciple's Personality now keep him from reacting violently when people make him angry.

"My old way was to react from my emotions," J. D. told Dennis, himself a former-convict-turned-preacher who pioneered using *Master-Life* in prisons. "When J. D. was in control, if someone got in my face, I would go off. I would shoot him, stab him, whatever was convenient. Part of the game I would play was to be a tough guy, a bad guy. It's one way you think you win respect, but people don't respect you. They fear you. Respect is something you get from people when you show love and kindness and consideration."

"Respect is something you get from people when you show love and kindness and consideration."

As you think about becoming a spiritual Christian and developing Christlike character, you want to share the good news. You want others to have the assurance of knowing that through Christ they can master their emotions. How do you share your joy in Christ and your assurance that the Holy Spirit will help you maintain self-control? In the next few weeks you will learn basic guidelines for writing your Christian testimony. You will develop a three-minute presentation you can share with others.

 Read the following guidelines for writing your testimony. Complete the activities as you read.

> **TESTIMONY OUTLINE**
> Do you remember what the word *witness* means? It means *someone who gives evidence.* You have evidence of a changed life through the indwelling Christ. You need to verbalize that witness—to tell others who Christ is, what He has done, and how much He means to you.
>
> These guidelines will help you prepare a basic testimony of your salvation experience. During the next weeks you will learn to enlarge or adapt this basic testimony to meet the needs of particular witnessing opportunities.
>
> The apostle Paul knew how to verbalize his witness. Furthermore, he did so at every opportunity to everyone who would listen. In the margin read the words Paul wrote in Romans 1:16.
>
> Even Christians who are skilled in giving their testimonies and in adapting their testimonies to specific situations begin with a basic testimony of conversion. And regardless of how they enlarge or adapt it, their testimonies follow a basic outline.
>
> The Scriptures provide at least two detailed records of occasions when Paul verbalized his witness, Acts 22:1-15 and Acts 26:9-20. In both cases Paul used his conversion experience as evidence for his witness. And in both cases he mentioned four facts about it in the same order as they appear in the chart in the following activity.
>
> **Read Acts 22:1-15 and Acts 26:9-20 in your Bible. Use the following chart to analyze Paul's testimony and to identify the four necessary components of a salvation testimony. In the proper column write the references of from two to four consecutive verses from Acts 22 in which Paul told about each of four parts of his conversion experience. Then follow the same instructions when Paul verbalized his witness in Acts 26. You should be able to find each of these four components in from two to four verses, and all of these should come in the order the chart lists them. Answers appear at the end of this section.**

A witness is someone who gives evidence.

"I am not ashamed of the gospel, because it is the power of God for the salvation of everyone who believes: first for the Jew, then for the Gentile" (Rom. 1:16).

	Acts 22	Acts 26
1. Paul had not always followed Christ.	✓	
2. God began to deal with Paul's rebellion.	✓	
3. Paul received Christ as his Lord.	✓	
4. Paul's new life was centered on Christ's purposes.	✓	

Your testimony of how you came to know Christ is personal and unique.

You may be amazed to discover that most unbelievers have never heard anyone share information of the type Paul shared in verbalizing his witness. Each conversion experience is different. Therefore, your testimony of how you came to know Christ is personal and unique. It is evidence that only you can give. No one else can duplicate it.

Although your conversion experience is unique, it can probably be outlined in much the same way Paul outlined his, especially if you became a Christian as an adult. In verbalizing your witness, share the same four types of information that Paul shared, even though the evidence itself will sound quite different.

Write four facts about your conversion that should be shared with unbelievers.

1. My life and attitudes before I followed Christ: _____

_____

2. How I realized that God was speaking to me: _____

_____

3. How I became a Christian: _____

_____

4. What being a Christian means to me: _____

_____

You do not need to prepare enough material for a sermon. Witnessing is not preaching; it is giving evidence. If you can develop even a one-minute testimony of your conversion experience, you will find many opportunities to share it. In week 4 you will take the next steps in writing your testimony.

Check to see if you identified these verses on the chart of the components of Paul's testimonies: Acts 22: verses 3-5,6-9,10-13,14-15. Acts 26: verses 9-12,13-18,19,19-20.

HAS THIS WEEK MADE A DIFFERENCE?
Review "My Walk with the Master This Week" at the beginning of this week's material. Mark the activities you have finished by drawing vertical lines in the diamonds beside them. Finish any incomplete activities. Think about what you will say during your group session about your work on these activities.

As a result of your study of "Master Your Emotions" this week, I hope that you feel more confident in your ability to act in Christ-honoring ways as the Holy Spirit helps you bring your emotions under control. You may not be able to achieve the ideal results instantly. Changing old patterns takes practice. Do not be discouraged if you occasionally revert to old, out-of-control behaviors. When you do, ask forgiveness and ask God to make you aware of the Holy Spirit's presence in your life to help you make better choices.

Do not be discouraged if you occasionally revert to old, out-of-control behaviors.

[1]The following Christ-centered support-group resources are recommended to help people understand more about their emotions:
McGee, Robert S. *Search for Significance*. Nashville: LifeWay Press, 1992.
McGee, Robert S., Pat Springle, Jim Craddock, and Dale W. McCleskey. *Breaking the Cycle of Hurtful Family Experiences*. Nashville: LifeWay Press, 1994.
Sledge, Tim. *Making Peace with Your Past*. Nashville: LifeWay Press, 1992.
Springle, Pat, and Susan Lanford. *Untangling Relationships*. Nashville: LifeWay Press, 1993.

Joshxoel

WEEK 4
Present Your Body

This Week's Goal
You will be able to submit your body to Christ's lordship in order to glorify God.

My Walk with the Master This Week
You will complete the following activities to develop the six biblical disciplines. When you have completed each activity, draw a vertical line in the diamond beside it.

SPEND TIME WITH THE MASTER
◇ Have a quiet time each day, working toward the goal of having quiet times 21 consecutive days. Check the box beside each day you have a quiet time this week: ❑ Sunday ❑ Monday ❑ Tuesday ❑ Wednesday ❑ Thursday ❑ Friday ❑ Saturday

LIVE IN THE WORD
◇ Read your Bible every day. Write what God says to you and what you say to God.
◇ Memorize 1 Corinthians 6:19-20.
◇ Review Philippians 2:13, Romans 12:1-2, and Galatians 5:22-23.
◇ Write important points from a sermon on the Hearing the Word form.

PRAY IN FAITH
◇ Pray that you will have victory every day with Christ.

FELLOWSHIP WITH BELIEVERS
◇ Tell a Christian friend how you began to prepare your testimony in week 3. Explain what you wrote in the outline and how you plan to expand it.

WITNESS TO THE WORLD
◇ Work on your written testimony, using the ideas in "Guidelines for Writing Your Testimony."

MINISTER TO OTHERS
◇ Learn the Steps to Victorious Living and Who Are You? parts of the Disciple's Personality.

This Week's Scripture-Memory Verses
"Do you not know that your body is a temple of the Holy Spirit, who is in you, whom you have received from God? You are not your own; you were bought at a price. Therefore honor God with your body" (1 Cor. 6:19-20).

Joshxoel

DAY 1

Surrendering Yourself to God

When I was a missionary in Indonesia, I heard Bill Tisdale, a missionary from the Philippines, speak on surrendering the body to the Lord. He said:

Sometimes we have a problem surrendering ourselves to God. We try to surrender our spirits to God, and we tell God that we want to dedicate ourselves to Him. Here is a simple way to present the members of your body one by one to Christ for His use. You can say: "Lord, here are my eyes. I want to give them to You. I want them to see only the things you want them to see. Help me always look at the things You want to look at and avoid the things You do not want to look at. Here are my hands. I present them to You. Work through my hands to do what You want to do. I do not want to use my hands just for me anymore. I want You to use my hands. Here are my feet. Guide them to go where You want them to go. I give You the lordship of my body." You can take every member of your body and present it to Christ for His use.

That illustration helped me with my difficulty in presenting my body to Christ as a living sacrifice through which He could work. Each time I was tempted to let a part of my body dominate me, I offered that part of my body to Christ so that He could master it and use it for His glory.

The stomach is a means He has provided for me to live but not indulge, so He can help me control my eating. James 3:6, in the margin, says that the tongue is a wildfire, but if I present it to God, I do not say anything He does not want me to say. I bite my tongue so that I do not say the wrong things. If I give my ears to God, I decide to listen to what honors Him.

Is your body or the way you feel about it mastering you?

When you look in the mirror, does what you see make you—

☒ glad?　☐ sad?　☐ mad?

Today you will consider the relationship of your physical body to your spiritual life. At the end of this week's study you may be able to answer the previous question differently. When you have completed this week's work, you will be able to—

- list three functions of the body in the human personality;
- write three facts about the nature of your body;
- distinguish between the body and the flesh;

You can take every member of your body and present it to Christ for His use.

"The tongue also is a fire, a world of evil among the parts of the body. It corrupts the whole person, sets the whole course of his life on fire, and is itself set on fire by hell" (Jas. 3:6).

- apply Christ's incarnation, crucifixion, and resurrection to your use of your body;
- explain how to use your body for God's glory.

GOD'S INTENTIONS FOR YOUR BODY

"The Lord God formed the man from the dust of the ground and breathed into his nostrils the breath of life, and the man became a living being" (Gen. 2:7).

God created Adam's body from the dust of the earth (see Gen. 2:7 in the margin). God intends for the body to perform three essential functions:
1. Identification as a unique person—the way you look
2. Participation in the world—the way you act
3. Communication with others—the way you relate to others
Without a body you would have no contact with the physical world.

Give an example of how your body enables you to be involved in the world through each of the three functions.

1. Identification as a unique person: We NONE Look Alike

2. Participation in the world: You CAN Experience the world and do God's will

3. Communication with others: talking to others About that thus Say the Lord

You may have answered something like this: 1. No one is exactly like me. The way I look makes it possible for others to identify me. 2. I can experience the world, and I can do God's business. 3. Talking and body language are important in spreading the gospel.

Your body allows you to influence the created order. Because you have mobility, you can move from place to place to perform God's tasks. Because you have strength in your body, you can accept assignments for Him.

After reading Genesis 1:27-28 in the margin, list three verbs that tell three *different* things God intended for human beings to do in the world.

"God created man in his own image, in the image of God he created him; male and female he created them. God blessed them and said to them, 'Be fruitful and increase in number; fill the earth and subdue it. Rule over the fish of the sea and the birds of the air and over every living creature that moves on the ground'" (Gen. 1:27-28).

_____

God expected you to be fruitful and multiply, to subdue the earth and make it useful, and to master or have dominion over living creatures. Your body makes you feel at home in the created order.

How do your body's three functions help you do what God asks you to do in relating to the world?

Identification—the way you look: _____

_____

Participation—the way you act: *Give Your dominion*

over other creature, you can be on
a mission per christ + you put christ for
Communication—the way you relate to others: *more it possible*

or impossible to lead other to christ you must
be umble

Here are possible answers: Because of identification—the way I look—someone may be attracted to my unique identity and may want to get acquainted. If we fall in love and God leads us to marry, we form a family to which children may be born. Participation—the way I act—gives me dominion over other creatures and the ability to be on mission with God in the world. Communication—the way I relate—makes it possible for me to lead, make decisions, and communicate them.

Turn to page 72 and read aloud this week's Scripture-memory verses, 1 Corinthians 6:19-20. How does God intend for you to regard your body?

_____

God intends for you to have a high regard for your body because it is the dwelling for His Spirit. You likely want to provide only the best dwelling for the Spirit of God.

Being disciplined is not in my nature. I have found that Spirit-control, not self-control, makes the difference. The Holy Spirit can control what I cannot control. I say again and again, "Lord, I can't control this; will You control it?" Then He takes over and controls the part of my life that my physical body might lead me to misuse or misapply.

Stop and ask the Holy Spirit to work in your life so that you have victory every day with God—in the control of your body and in other areas that come to mind.

IN THE CARPENTER'S SHOP
One way to gain control over your body is striving to change your character. The Holy Spirit can help change your character when you are in Christ. How are you working to put off the old person and to put on the new?

DAILY MASTER COMMUNICATION GUIDE

JAMES 3:1-12

What God said to me:

_____

_____

_____

_____

_____

_____

_____

What I said to God:

_____

_____

_____

_____

_____

_____

_____

The World's Way

"Do not be foolish, but understand what the Lord's will is. Do not get drunk on wine, which leads to debauchery" (Eph. 5:17-18).

"The acts of the sinful nature are obvious: sexual immorality, impurity, and debauchery. … I warn you, as I did before, that those who live like this will not inherit the kingdom of God" (Gal. 5:19-21).

"Put to death, therefore, whatever belongs to your earthly nature: sexual immorality, impurity, lust, evil desires and greed, which is idolatry" (Col. 3:5).

The Spirit's Way

"Instead, be filled with the Spirit" (Eph. 5:18).

"Live by the Spirit, and you will not gratify the desires of the sinful nature" (Gal. 5:16).

"Since, then, you have been raised with Christ, set your hearts on things above, where Christ is seated at the right hand of God. Set your minds on things above, not on earthly things. For you died, and your life is now hidden with Christ in God" (Col. 3:1-3).

Read the Scriptures in the margin that relate to abusing the body. From the verses marked "The World's Way" identify a specific behavior you want to get rid of. From the verses marked "The Spirit's Way" identify an action you will take to replace it. I have given you an example. Each day this week you will record your progress in working on this behavior. If this matter is too personal to write about here, you may write about it elsewhere, but please address this critical change.

Here is an example.

Behavior I want to work on: drinking substances that are harmful to me as a way of dealing with emotional pain

An action I will take to put off the old self: inquire about a support group that helps persons overcome alcohol dependency

An action I will take to let the Holy Spirit make me more like Christ: face my pain and rely on Christ's power to help me through difficult issues

Now you try it.

Behavior I want to work on: _Speaking before Thinking things clearly when I got upset_

An action I will take to put off the old self: _Think things through clearly, asking Christ into my life daily_

An action I will take to let the Holy Spirit make me more like Christ: _Let the Holy Spirit Lead me Each day in my life_

↑ Read James 3:1-12, which discusses the power of the tongue, in your quiet time today. Then complete the Daily Master Communication Guide in the margin on page 75.

↑ How are you progressing in writing your testimony? Preparing your testimony and the encouragement of your *MasterLife* group can help you become bolder in your efforts to witness. Tell a Christian friend how you began to prepare your testimony in week 3. Explain what you wrote in the outline and how you plan to expand it.

DAY 2

Doing Things Your Own Way

In day 1 you learned that God had a plan for humankind to follow in the use of the body. He intended for people to replenish the earth, subdue it, and rule it. But the first human beings failed to do what God asked. Instead of being partners with God in ruling the world, they selfishly decided to do things their own way. The result was chaos. The good bodies of those people were invaded by a sinful nature.

What is another word for *body* that also means *the sinful nature*?

FlESh

The words translated *flesh* in the Bible have two distinct meanings: *the physical body* and *the sinful nature*.

WHAT GOD EXPECTS

God created the physical body to be good, but when people sinned, the body was affected. Although the body itself is not evil in itself, it is weak and susceptible to the flesh (the sinful nature). God expects you to honor Him through your physical body and to decline to let the flesh, or the sinful nature, take over. The body has the capacity to do good if the flesh is not in control.

Read in the margin the Scriptures that show the possibility of using the body for good. Then match the references with the summary statements below.

B 1. Genesis 1:31   **a. Jesus compared His church to His body.**

D 2. John 1:14   **b. Human bodies were created as good and were pleasing to God.**

C 3. Romans 8:23   **c. Your body will be redeemed.**

A 4. Ephesians 1:22-23   **d. Jesus was incarnated in a human body.**

Your body can be used for good. The fact that Jesus was incarnated in a human body testifies to the fact that God looked with favor on the physical body. You will not always have this body but will someday redeem it for a form that Jesus wants you to have in heaven. The correct answers are 1. b, 2. d, 3. c, 4. a.

You have studied three facts about the nature of your body. Write what the following statements mean to you.

"God saw all that he had made, and it was very good. And there was evening, and there was morning—the sixth day" (Gen. 1:31).

"The Word became flesh and made his dwelling among us. We have seen his glory, the glory of the One and Only, who came from the Father, full of grace and truth" (John 1:14).

"Not only so, but we ourselves, who have the firstfruits of the Spirit, groan inwardly as we wait eagerly for our adoption as sons, the redemption of our bodies" (Rom. 8:23).

"God placed all things under his feet and appointed him to be head over everything for the church, which is his body, the fullness of him who fills everything in every way" (Eph. 1:22-23).

1. God created the body as good.

We must take care of it

2. Something happens to the body when flesh takes over.

Sin   flesh

3. God created the body for His use.

God can do Anything to my body

You may have responded in ways similar to this: 1. Because God created my body as good, He expects me to take care of it. 2. Because I have sinned, my body is susceptible to the ways of the flesh, and I must be on guard against the domination of worldly ways. 3. God can do anything, even use my weak body for His good.

To review what you learned earlier, list the three functions your body performs that involve you in the world.

I _dentification_

P _Articipation_

C _ommunication_

If you had difficulty recalling the three functions, refer to yesterday's lesson.

IN THE CARPENTER'S SHOP
What progress are you making in allowing the Holy Spirit to help you put off the old self and replace it with the new?

Yesterday you identified a behavior you hoped to put away in order to build Christlike character. Describe an instance in which you have set aside that behavior.

_____

_____

You grow in your faith when you learn to give your Christian testimony.

One way to keep your body from being susceptible to un-Christlike ways is to know who you are in Christ, to stand firm in that identity, and to share your convictions with others. You grow in your faith when you learn to give your Christian testimony. Last week you began to draft a basic testimony. Yesterday you were to discuss with a friend your basic testimony and your ideas for expanding it. Today you will receive specific help for writing your testimony.

 Read the following guidelines for writing your testimony.

GUIDELINES FOR WRITING YOUR TESTIMONY

As you become more skilled at witnessing, various situations will call for you to give your testimony differently. You will use a variety of sentences each time you give your testimony. Because each situation will be unique, your testimony will be unique to each situation.

Your testimony will probably always include the four points that you used to develop your basic testimony last week. But a particular situation may call for you to say more about one point than the others. Or you may discover that the person to whom you are witnessing identifies more closely with different illustrations and examples.

This material will prepare you to write an improved, expanded version of the basic testimony you have already developed. You will learn how to gather background material for each point in your testimony to use as needed in specific witnessing opportunities.

Find the basic testimony you have written and place it where you can see it. Write each heading on a separate sheet of paper. Make notes on each sheet as you study the following material. Your goals are to—

- be certain you said everything you needed to say about each part of your testimony;
- develop background information for adapting or emphasizing each part of your testimony when the occasion calls for it.

My Life and Attitudes Before I Followed Christ

When you tell what your life was like before you became a Christian, do not make all of it sound bad. Share the good things as well as the bad. This allows others to identify with what you say.

Share interesting details about yourself that will make you come across as an ordinary person. Be prepared to talk about—

- where you lived before you became a Christian;
- what you did before you became a Christian;
- your interests and hobbies before you became a Christian;
- your priorities before you became a Christian.

Share details about your life indicating that you truly needed greater meaning and purpose or the ability to overcome failings. Some examples are temper, habits, greed, and self-centeredness. Your purpose is not to confess your evil life but to tell your story.

Share details about your life indicating that you truly needed greater meaning and purpose or the ability to overcome failings.

DAILY MASTER COMMUNICATION GUIDE

ACTS 16:25-34

What God said to me:

_____

_____

_____

_____

_____

_____

_____

What I said to God:

_____

_____

_____

_____

_____

_____

_____

How I Realized That God Was Speaking to Me

Explain how God began to show you His love while you were still an unbeliever. Be general enough for a person to identify with your description. How, when, and where did God get through to you? What person(s) did He use? Did He use a book, a film, or a Scripture? Did He shape events to speak about His waiting presence?

How I Became a Christian

Share how you trusted your life to Christ. Let the Bible be your authority rather than what someone said to you: "Here is a Bible verse that made me realize what Jesus did for me: ..." Be sure to state that you prayed to receive Christ.

You might be inclined to use "church language" here. Be sensitive to those who will not understand the meanings of such words. Also be sensitive to the fact that the person may have been frightened away by high-pressure tactics or by a zealous but tactless witness.

Make short statements about four important facts:

- Sin is an I-controlled life. It is failing or refusing to be what God wants you to be.
- Sin's penalty is separation from God both in this life and in the life to come for eternity.
- Christ paid the penalty for sin when He took your sin to the cross, accepted the judgment for it, and made it possible for you to be accepted by the Father.
- Receiving Christ is acknowledging to Him that you are a sinner, accepting forgiveness from Him, inviting Him to enter your life as your Savior and Lord, and trusting Him to do for you the things you could never do for yourself.

Check your testimony to be certain you have at least one sentence about each of these facts.

What Being a Christian Means to Me

Be careful not to give the impression that becoming a Christian automatically solved all of your problems. Describe your lifestyle as a Christian. You may not realize how different your lifestyle is from that of an unbeliever. Many things you take for granted will be significant to a non-Christian. Describe the changes that have taken place in your life in the following areas.

- Relationships with family
- Use of money
- Purpose of life
- Attitude toward death
- Value of Christian friends
- How you deal with problems, frustration, and failure

Suggestions for Giving Your Testimony

1. Keep it short so that your listener will not become uncomfortable.
2. Tell what happened to you. It is your story that others want to hear. Do not say "you"; say "I" and "me."
3. Avoid negative remarks. Do not criticize religious groups or a specific church.
4. Ask yourself, *If I were an unbeliever, what would this mean to me?*
5. Eliminate religious words. Lost persons do not understand religious jargon like *repented, made a decision for Christ, invited Jesus into my heart, walked the aisle, joined the church, saved,* and *was baptized.*

If You Accepted Christ When You Were a Child
If you were reared in a Christian home and accepted Christ as a child, do not feel that your conversion is not dramatic enough to share. It is *always* significant for an unbeliever to learn the way God enters human lives.

 Read Acts 16:25-34, the passage in which Paul and Silas witnessed to the jailer, in your quiet time today. Then complete the Daily Master Communication Guide on page 80.

DAY 3

Who Is the Master of Your Body?

An award-winning athlete spent much of his spare time working with handicapped young people. A newscast showed this athlete helping physically challenged individuals. A few seconds later in the newscast another athlete was reported to have used his strong body in a harmful way. I feel sad when I hear that a successful athlete has been arrested on drug charges or has violated the law in another way.

THE STRUGGLE FOR CONTROL
The potential for your body to be used in positive, Christ-honoring ways is tremendous. However, in reality, your body is still subject to sin and death.

Read Romans 7:18-23 in the margin. Describe an experience in which you desired to do good yet did the opposite.

_____

_____

"I know that nothing good lives in me, that is, in my sinful nature. For I have the desire to do what is good, but I cannot carry it out. For what I do is not the good I want to do; no, the evil I do not want to do—this I keep on doing. Now if I do what I do not want to do, it is no longer I who do it, but it is sin living in me that does it. So I find this law at work: When I want to do good, evil is right there with me. For in my inner being I delight in God's law; but I see another law at work in the members of my body, waging war against the law of my mind and making me a prisoner of the law of sin at work within my members" (Rom. 7:18-23).

You may have answered something like this: I know that I hurt my children when I speak harshly to them, but I keep doing it. I know that overeating is not good for me, but I do it in spite of my good intentions.

As you became aware when you did the previous exercise, the flesh tends to use the senses and the normal desires of your body to master you. Check the pursuits that have become your masters at one time or another:

☑ food	❏ sex	☑ work
❏ money	❏ sports	☑ clothing
☑ religion	❏ others' approval	❏ beauty
❏ television	☑ education	☑ recreation
❏ other: _____		

_____

Were you surprised to see *religion* in the list? Did you think that pursuing religious matters is a way to honor Christ? Certainly, attending church and involving yourself in the fellowship of believers are what Christ intends as part of a disciple's disciplined life. Sometimes, however, your desire to be very active in your church can be motivated by harmful reasons. You may do so to obtain others' approval. You can become enslaved by this worldly desire, forgetting that God calls you to serve from obedience to Him.

Read the verses in the margin. Write three primary actions Christ took to free you from bondage to the flesh.

Christs' _INCARNATION_ _coming As human_ condemns sin in the flesh (Rom. 8:3).

Christ's _CRUCIFIXION_ frees you from the bondage of the body of sin (Rom. 6:6-7).

Christ's _RESURRECTION_ gives you life through the Spirit so that you can put to death the deeds of the body (Rom. 8:11-13).

Christ's coming to earth as a human being—His incarnation—condemns sin, His crucifixion frees you from sin's bondage, and His resurrection gives you life through the Spirit. The Holy Spirit takes these three actions of Christ and makes them real in your life. Life in the Spirit applies that work of Christ to your life.

"What the law was powerless to do in that it was weakened by the sinful nature, God did by sending his own Son in the likeness of sinful man to be a sin offering. And so he condemned sin in sinful man" (Rom. 8:3).

"We know that our old self was crucified with him so that the body of sin might be done away with, that we should no longer be slaves to sin—because anyone who has died has been freed from sin" (Rom. 6:6-7).

"If the Spirit of him who raised Jesus from the dead is living in you, he who raised Christ from the dead will also give life to your mortal bodies through his Spirit, who lives in you" (Rom. 8:11-13).

Continue working on this week's Scripture-memory verses, 1 Corinthians 6:19-20, by saying them aloud. Check commitments you will make to honor Christ with your physical body.

I will—
❑ watch my intake of empty calories that do not add to my nutrition;
❑ begin an exercise program;
❑ increase the amount of rest I get each day;
❑ examine my eating patterns and find an alternative approach when I realize that I am eating from anxiety or tension rather than from hunger;
❑ monitor my intake of substances like caffeine that do not nourish me and may make me irritable;
❑ stop using substances such as nicotine, alcohol, or other drugs that harm my body.

IN THE CARPENTER'S SHOP
In the previous exercise you checked commitments you will make. Was one of these commitments similar to the step you described yesterday to get rid of a behavior? Today describe what Christ is adding to your life to replace that part of your old self.

_____

_____

You may be interested in noting how many sermons you hear in the next few weeks focus on honoring Christ with your body instead of allowing fleshly, sinful concerns to take control. Begin paying particular attention to encouragement you receive from sermons about this matter.

 Continue to use the Hearing the Word form on page 141 to take notes on sermons. Especially note any sermon references that address the subjects you are studying this week.

 In your quiet time today read Judges 16:15-30, about an Old Testament character who used his body for both good and evil. Then complete the Daily Master Communication Guide in the margin.

DAILY MASTER COMMUNICATION GUIDE

JUDGES 16:15-30

What God said to me:

_____

_____

_____

_____

_____

_____

_____

_____

What I said to God:

_____

_____

_____

_____

_____

_____

_____

_____

DAY 4

Useful to the Master

What positive steps can you take when you find yourself doing things that are the opposite of what you know is right? How can Christ master your body so that it is useful to Him in the world? You can apply to your everyday life the three actions Christ took for your salvation.

To review, list the three actions you learned in day 3.

I _NCARNACTION_

C _RUCIFIXION_

R _ESURRECTION_

Christ's incarnation condemns sin, His crucifixion frees you from sin's bondage, and His resurrection gives you life through the Spirit.

Say aloud this week's Scripture-memory verses, 1 Corinthians 6:19-20. How does Christ's incarnation in you through the Holy Spirit apply to your body?

The Holy Spirit live in you I'm God's And my body Exists to God's Glory only

You may have written something like this: The Holy Spirit lives in me. I am God's, and my body exists to glorify God. I can use my body for His purposes.

Christ's incarnation—His coming to earth as a human being—led to His crucifixion. Christ was crucified for you.

Read the verses in the margins on this page and the next. Answer this question about each: How does your acceptance of Christ's crucifixion as the substitute for your crucifixion apply to your body?

1. Romans 6:6: _When Christ was Crucified I Also was Crucified_

"We know that our old self was crucified with him so that the body of sin might be done away with, that we should no longer be slaves to sin" (Rom. 6:6).

2. Colossians 3:3-4: _When Christ die my_
old self die with him

3. Galatians 5:24-25: _my Sinful Nature_
was put to death I new
walk in the Spirit

You may have responded this way: 1. Because my old self was crucified with Christ, I am no longer a slave to the body of sin. I am a new creature in Christ and can act accordingly. 2. Because I have died with Christ, I am to consider my bodily members dead to the deeds of the flesh (or I am to put to death the deeds of the flesh). 3. My sinful nature, with its lusts and desires, has been put to death; so I can walk in the Spirit as He directs my thoughts and actions.

Paul said, "If we died with Christ, we believe that we will also live with Him" (Rom. 6:8). Christ rose and gave you new birth.

INSTRUMENTS OF RIGHTEOUSNESS

Read Galatians 2:20 and Romans 6:11-14 in the margin. How does your participation in Christ's resurrection through the new birth and His living in you apply to your body?

1. Galatians 2:20: _I live for christ_
He rules my body like

2. Romans 6:11-14: _I'm alive because christ_
die for me So he live in me
He is the instrument of Righteousness

You may have responded something like this: 1. The life I now live is not my own but Christ's. He reigns in my body. 2. I am alive to God. I will let Him reign in my body by yielding members of my body to Him as instruments of righteousness instead of letting them be instruments of wrong living.

Your body will not be perfect until it is completely redeemed at Christ's return. In the meantime your identification with Christ's incarnation, crucifixion, and resurrection gives you potential for righteous living. You still have potential for unrighteous living. The Scriptures you have studied urge you to put to death the deeds of the flesh.

How often does Christ expect you to take up your cross? _daily_ How, then, can you live victoriously as you take up your cross daily? Through the Disciple's Personality presentation you have learned how to let God take control of your mind, your will, your emotions, and therefore your soul and body. Today you will learn another part of the Disciple's Personality presentation, Steps to Victorious Living.

"You died, and your life is now hidden with Christ in God. When Christ, who is your life, appears, then you also will appear with him in glory" (Col. 3:3-4).

"Those who belong to Christ Jesus have crucified the sinful nature with its passions and desires. Since we live by the Spirit, let us keep in step with the Spirit" (Gal. 5:24-25).

I have been crucified with Christ and I no longer live, but Christ lives in me. The life I live in the body, I live by faith in the Son of God, who loved me and gave himself for me" (Gal. 2:20).

"In the same way, count yourselves dead to sin but alive to God in Christ Jesus. Therefore do not let sin reign in your mortal body so that you obey its "evil desires. Do not offer the parts of your body to sin, as instruments of wickedness, but rather offer yourselves to God, as those who have been brought from death to life; and offer the parts of your body to him as instruments of righteousness. For sin shall not be your master, because you are not under law, but under grace" (Rom. 6:11-14).

LEARNING THE DISCIPLE'S PERSONALITY
Read the section "Steps to Victorious Living" (p. 137) in the Disciple's Personality presentation.

✝ On the Disciple's Personality illustration below write the components of the spiritual Christian as you learned to do in week 3. Then write *Philippians 2:13* under *will*, *Ephesians 5:18* above *Spirit*, *Romans 12:2* under *mind*, *Galatians 5:22-23* under *emotions*, *Romans 6:12-13* under *flesh*, *1 Corinthians 6:19-20* on one side of the circle, and *Romans 12:1* on the other side. All but two of these Bible verses have been memory verses in this study. Those two will be your memory verses in weeks 5 and 6. Refer to the Disciple's Personality presentation (pp. 133–39) if you need help. By the end of this study you should be able to draw the complete Disciple's Personality and to explain it in your own words.

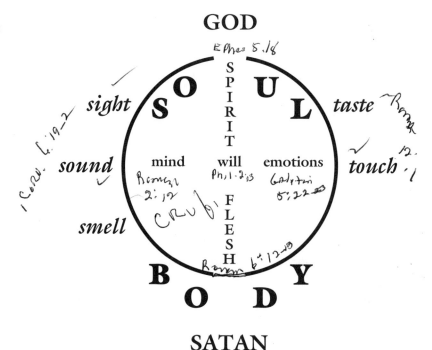

✝ Read John 20:1-18, the passage that describes Jesus' resurrection, during your quiet time today. See how God speaks to you through this passage. Then complete the Daily Master Communication Guide in the margin.

DAY 5

A Living Sacrifice

Romans 12:1 says that you are to present your body as a living sacrifice. What does that mean? Think about the days before Christ when people presented animal sacrifices. Christ came to change that practice when He died on the cross as the ultimate sacrifice. Christ wants you in His service not as a dead sacrifice but as a living one. He wants not material things sacrificed but lives sacrificed on the altar of service to Him. He does not want a life half lived. He wants a life fully invested in Him.

Christ wants a life fully invested in Him.

If you present your body as a living sacrifice, what does that mean you will do?

Old my People brought Animal To SACR. die befor God but not Chris Came as a Living Sacrifice that me God want live Tu Live fully for h n

You might have answered: If I present my body as a living sacrifice for the Master's use, it means that I will be more than a Christian in name only. It means that I will do more than give lip service to my faith. I will sacrifice every area of my life to Him and will commit my body to holy, righteous living.

COMMITTING TO CHRIST'S SERVICE

In day 1 I told you about missionary Bill Tisdale, who regularly prayed a prayer committing every part of His body to Christ's service. Will you do that, too?

Write how you will use each part of your body as you present it to God for His glory.

Hands: *C l A P ~~Sound~~ Touch*

Eyes: *Sight SEE*

Feet: *Walk, Pat*

Stomach: _Eat to much_
drink to mun

Sex organs: _____

Ears: _Sound Ear +_
Listing for God

⭐ Tongue: _talk for God   taste_

Draw a star beside the area in which you feel you need the most help in surrendering to God.

Stop and ask God to help you remove barriers to surrendering that member of your body to the Master's service. Ask Him to help you by making you aware of the Holy Spirit's presence when you are tempted to use that part of your body in wrong living.

In day 1 you learned that God intended for you to use your body for three functions:
• Identification as a distinct personality
• Participation in the world
• Communication with others

Write one way you will commit to use your body for each of these functions in God's service.

Identification as a distinct personality: _____

_____

Participation in the world: _____

_____

Communication with others: _____

_____

With the relationship of your body and your spiritual life in mind, answer this question: If you were to present your body as a living

sacrifice for God's glory, how would your body make you feel?
☑ glad ❑ sad ❑ mad

Presenting your body to God can be the most freeing, gratifying, and joyful feeling in the world. You have a choice about how your body responds to situations. Recall that in the illustration of the Disciple's Personality, your will is located in a position to decide between the spirit and the flesh. If you choose to close the door of the flesh, the door will close. The decision to present your body as a living sacrifice means that you close the door of the flesh. With the Holy Spirit's help, you can change harmful habits and yield all of your life, not just part of it, to the Master.

Will you present your body as a living sacrifice for God's glory?
☑ Yes ❑ No If so, tell Him so in a prayer right now.

LEARNING THE DISCIPLE'S PERSONALITY

✝ Read the section "Who Are You?" (p. 138) in the Disciple's Personality presentation.

Answer the following questions.
• Are you a natural person whose spirit is dead? Do your bodily senses and your natural desires control you?
  ❑ Yes ☑ No
• Are you a worldly Christian who has allowed Christ to enter your life but is still being mastered by the desires of the flesh? Is the big *I* still in control? ❑ Yes ☑ No
• Are you a spiritual Christian who has been crucified with Christ and is being controlled by the Holy Spirit?
  ☑ Yes ❑ No

Read 1 Thessalonians 5:23-24 in the margin. What do these verses tell you about the support you have for living blamelessly?
❑ Living a holy life is too difficult; it's all up to me, and I can't handle it.
☑ The Lord Jesus Christ who calls me will empower me to use my body, soul, and spirit in right living.

These verses assure you that the Lord who calls you to serve Him will be faithful to help you act in the right way. He has sent the Holy Spirit to help you in this daily challenge.

✝ On the next page is the spiritual-Christian illustration with blanks for you to add the Scripture references that go with it, as you learned yesterday. Many of these are memory verses you have learned in this study. Say them aloud as you write the references on the illustration. Refer to the Disciple's Personality

With the Holy Spirit's help, you can change harmful habits and yield all of your life, not just part of it, to the Master.

[handwritten] Lord my Heavy Father I Present my Life + World Soft as a Liveñ Sacrifice for you in Jesus Name I Pray 1-1-2000

"May God himself, the God of peace, sanctify you through and through. May your whole spirit, soul and body be kept blameless at the coming of our Lord Jesus Christ. The one who calls you is faithful and he will do it" (1 Thess. 5:23-24).

presentation (pp. 133–39) if you need help. By the end of this study you should be able to draw the complete Disciple's Personality and to explain it in your own words.

The Spiritual Christian
Gal. 2:20

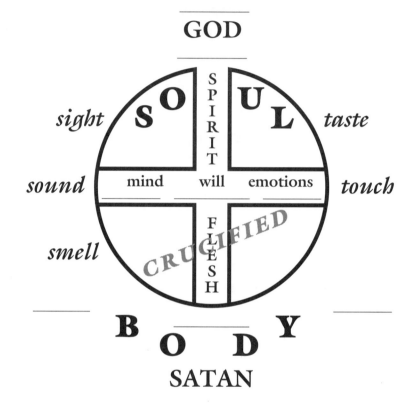

The Disciple's Personality presentation has been used many times to win someone to faith in Christ. David Carter, while serving as a Florida pastor, was visiting a couple he had visited several times before. The wife was a Christian, but the husband, an unbeliever, had always been unwilling to listen to a traditional gospel presentation. This time David decided to use the Disciple's Personality to confront the man with his spiritual condition. Drawing the natural-person and spiritual-Christian diagrams, he asked the man, "Which are you?" The husband pointed to the natural person. David asked, "Which would you like to be?" He pointed to the spiritual-Christian diagram and replied, "I've always wanted to be a Christian." David then led the man to pray to receive Christ as Savior and Lord.

"I've always wanted to be a Christian."

After the prayer the wife spoke up: "I am not either one." David replied, "I may have a diagram that represents you." When he drew the worldly-Christian diagram, she immediately said, "That's me!" David then led her to rededicate her life to Christ.

After learning the Disciple's Personality, you will be able to use it not only to lead persons to salvation but also to help others—

• deal with their emotions;

- close the door to Satan;
- renew their minds;
- find assurance that they can say no to temptation.

IN THE CARPENTER'S SHOP

Review your work this week and recall your efforts to get rid of the old self and to put on new actions and thoughts. How has the Holy Spirit helped you become more Christlike? Answer these questions about the area of change you identified on page 76:

Something I have been getting rid of this week:

_____

Something Christ has been adding to my character this week:

_____

Stop and pray. Thank God for helping you in the ways you listed. Ask Him to continue giving you the courage to make changes.

In your quiet time today read Philippians 1:19-26, which describes the priority Paul placed on exalting Christ in his body. Then complete the Daily Master Communication Guide in the margin.

HAS THIS WEEK MADE A DIFFERENCE?

Review "My Walk with the Master This Week" at the beginning of this week's material. Mark the activities you have finished by drawing vertical lines in the diamonds beside them. Finish any incomplete activities. Think about what you will say during your group session about your work on these activities.

As you complete your study of "Present Your Body," I hope that you have gained new insights about why you sometimes take actions that contradict your good intentions. I hope that you have committed each part of your body to the Lord's service and that you will let the Holy Spirit help you when you are tempted to make wrong choices.

DAILY MASTER COMMUNICATION GUIDE

PHILIPPIANS 1:19-26

What God said to me:

_____

_____

_____

_____

_____

_____

_____

What I said to God:

_____

_____

_____

_____

_____

_____

_____

_____

WEEK 5

Be Filled with the Spirit

This Week's Goal
You will be able to allow the Holy Spirit to fill you.

My Walk with the Master This Week
You will complete the following activities to develop the six biblical disciplines. When you have completed each activity, draw a vertical line in the diamond beside it.

SPEND TIME WITH THE MASTER
◇ Have a quiet time each day, working toward the goal of having quiet times 21 consecutive days. Write the number of minutes you spend in your quiet time each day: Sunday:___ Monday:___ Tuesday:___ Wednesday:___ Thursday:___ Friday:___ Saturday:___

LIVE IN THE WORD
◇ Read your Bible every day. Write what God says to you and what you say to God.
◇ Memorize Ephesians 5:18.
◇ Review Philippians 2:13, Romans 12:1-2, Galatians 5:22-23, and 1 Corinthians 6:19-20.
◇ Using the Hearing the Word form, write notes from a sermon or a Bible study to apply in your life this week.

PRAY IN FAITH
◇ Pray for persons in your circles of influence.

FELLOWSHIP WITH BELIEVERS
◇ Share with another church member what God is doing in your life—struggles as well as victories.

WITNESS TO THE WORLD
◇ Write your testimony, using the ideas in "How to Write Your Testimony." Be ready to share it at the next group session.

MINISTER TO OTHERS
◇ Explain how to apply the Disciple's Personality, using James 4:1-8.

This Week's Scripture-Memory Verse
"Do not get drunk on wine, which leads to debauchery. Instead, be filled with the Spirit" (Eph. 5:18).

1-11-900

DAY 1

A Changed Life

When I was a freshman in college, the Holy Spirit created in my heart an overwhelming desire to bear witness to Christ. In the months that followed, His presence overcame my natural shyness and thrust me several times each week into the streets and bars to witness. However, I was not successful in leading persons to Christ. I memorized Scriptures, studied soul-winning books, and prayed. But something was missing.

One day I received a booklet that told about the experiences of D. L. Moody, R. A. Torrey, Billy Sunday, Billy Graham, and others whose ministries had been transformed when they experienced the filling of the Holy Spirit. I had a burning desire to be used by God, but no one could tell me how. Finally, a friend lent me the book *The Holy Spirit: Who He Is and What He Does* by R. A. Torrey. For the first time I realized that the Holy Spirit is a person who possesses us instead of a power, an influence, or an attitude we possess. I learned that the Holy Spirit, who lives in me, wants to fill me for service. By the next evening I had finished the book and was ready to follow its instructions to be filled with the Spirit. I confessed all of my sins, presented myself fully to God, and asked in faith for the Holy Spirit to fill me. As I confessed my sins, I realized how much the Holy Spirit loved me and had been grieved by my ignoring Him. Then I presented my body, will, emotions, mind, and spirit to be used by God in any way. I accepted by faith the filling of the Holy Spirit without an outward sign or manifestation. I told God, "I will accept the fact that I am filled with the Spirit on the basis of faith in the Word, no matter what happens afterward." I immediately sensed a deep awareness of the Spirit's love, which has grown stronger through the years as my relationship with God has deepened.

The next morning when I went to class, I was so aware of the Spirit's presence that I wanted to move over on the sidewalk to let Him walk beside me. That evening I witnessed to a boy on the street, and he accepted Christ as his Savior. Two nights later, two teenagers accepted Christ. The following night a man professed faith in Christ; the night after, another man did.

I remarked to a friend: "I don't see how this can continue. Every night I go out to witness, someone accepts Christ." That night no one did. I asked forgiveness for daring to think I had won those persons to Christ myself. God refilled me with His Spirit when I was willing to confess my sin, yield myself to Him, and ask in faith. Once again the persons to whom I witnessed accepted Christ.

In the years since that experience the Holy Spirit has taught me that the secret is to be filled for each task of service. Thousands of times

The Holy Spirit is a person who possesses us instead of a power, an influence, or an attitude we possess.

DAILY MASTER COMMUNICATION GUIDE

ACTS 2:1-21

What God said to me:

_____

_____

_____

_____

_____

_____

_____

What I said to God:

_____

_____

_____

_____

_____

_____

_____

when I have sinned, I have asked Him to refill me, and He has done so. The filling of the Spirit energizes and empowers different gifts in different persons, but in every case the result brings glory to Christ and attracts others to Him.

In the previous account what was the turning point at which God was able to do as He desired in my life?

_____

The turning point in my story was when I asked in faith for the Holy Spirit to fill me after I had confessed my sins and had yielded myself to God. Until that point I had not allowed Him to work through me in His fullness.

Every person who has been born of the Spirit has the Holy Spirit living in his or her heart. Romans 8:16 says, "The Spirit himself testifies with our spirit that we are God's children." However, not everyone is filled with the Spirit and equipped for service (see Rom. 8:9).

Look again at Romans 8:16. Do you have the Holy Spirit living in you? ☑ Yes ❑ No ❑ Not sure

If you have given your life to Christ, He lives in you through His Spirit. However, you may or may not be filled with the Spirit at the present time.

Read Ephesians 5:18: "Do not get drunk on wine, which leads to debauchery. Instead, be filled with the Spirit."

Are you filled with the Spirit right now? ☑ Yes ❑ No ❑ Not sure

God wants your personality to be filled and overflowing with His Spirit. As you yield yourself to God, He takes control of every facet of your personality. Your inner self is integrated, and you experience constant fellowship with Him.

The purpose of this week's study is to explain God's purpose in filling you with the Spirit and to show you how to be filled daily. As a result of this week's study, you should be able to—
- explain the relationship between God's Spirit and the human spirit;
- list four important facts about being filled with the Holy Spirit;
- identify two purposes of being filled and explain the way God accomplishes each purpose;
- list three steps to being filled with the Spirit.

WHAT IT MEANS TO BE FILLED

A distinct difference exists between having the Spirit of God in you and being filled with the Spirit. Peter is a good example of this difference.

Even before Pentecost Peter had the Spirit of Christ. John 20:22 says, "With that he [Christ] breathed on them and said, 'Receive the Holy Spirit.' " In this verse Jesus breathed the Spirit into the disciples. This allowed the disciples to take up His mission, which they could accomplish only under the Spirit's leadership. But even though Peter had the Spirit of Christ in him already, at Pentecost a major change occurred in his life. When the Holy Spirit came in His fullness on the church, Peter was filled with the Spirit.

Before Pentecost Peter was cowardly and denied Jesus. Hot-tempered, he cut off a soldier's ear with a sword. After Pentecost we see no evidence of instability or superficiality in Peter. He became a totally different person. He began to preach boldly, he allowed God to work miracles through him, he proclaimed Christ while he risked his life, and he spoke with certainty and faith.

EXPERIENCING THE SPIRIT'S POWER

Everyone who has accepted Christ has the Spirit of Christ living in him or her. Read 2 Corinthians 1:21-22 in the margin.

But a distinct difference exists between having a small amount of water in a cup and having the water fill or overflow the cup. That is why Jesus spoke of the Spirit's overflowing you. Read John 7:38-39 in the margin.

The Holy Spirit wants to flow through you like the living water Jesus mentioned. Whenever the disciples in the Book of Acts encountered persons who were not filled with the Spirit, they prayed for them to be filled. Then God would move in their lives.

> **Ephesians 5:18 is this week's Scripture-memory verse. Turn to page 92 and read it aloud to begin learning it.**

Today's Christians face the same problem the disciples faced—trying to fight spiritual battles with human resources. A majority of Christians live and serve as if Pentecost never happened. They try to obey Christ's commands in their own strength; yet they wonder how Satan so often outsmarts and overpowers them. They ignore the mission of the Holy Spirit, who came to continue Jesus' roles of inspiring, empowering, and guiding them. For them, the third member of the Trinity—the Holy Spirit—is almost "the unknown God." They think of Him as an influence, an attitude, or a way to express the fact that God is everywhere.

Is the Holy Spirit a personal, intimate friend who fills your life?
☑ Yes ❑ No ❑ Not sure

You may have tried to witness or teach a Bible study without relying on the Holy Spirit's power. You may have tried to solve a problem in your personal life, such as dealing with a rebellious child or improving an estranged relationship, without asking God to fill you with His Spirit.

"It is God who makes both us and you stand firm in Christ. He anointed us, set his seal of ownership on us, and put his Spirit in our hearts as a deposit, guaranteeing what is to come" (2 Cor. 1:21-22).

" 'Whoever believes in me, as the Scripture has said, streams of living water will flow from within him.' By this he meant the Spirit, whom those who believed in him were later to receive" (John 7:38-39).

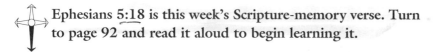

Getting Ready for Church ANR

The solution to your inadequacy lies in experiencing the Holy Spirit's presence and power as the disciples did at Pentecost. Pentecost cannot be repeated any more than Calvary can be repeated. However, Christians can lay hold of the power of Pentecost just as surely as they can experience the redemption of Calvary. This week you will learn more about how this occurs.

IN THE CARPENTER'S SHOP
One work of the Holy Spirit is to help you be like Jesus. Today you will choose another area of your life in which you want to be more Christlike.

Read the Scriptures in the margin that relate to anger and similar behaviors. From the verses marked "The World's Way" identify a specific behavior you want to get rid of. From the verses marked "The Spirit's Way" identify an action you will take to replace it. I have given you an example. Each day this week you will record your progress in working on this behavior.

Here is an example.

Behavior I want to work on: becoming angry and saying things I later regret

An action I will take to put off the old self: ask the Holy Spirit to teach me how to let Him control me and my tongue even when something angers me

An action I will take to let the Holy Spirit make me more like Christ: be more loving and kind in all of my relationships

Now you try it.

Behavior I want to work on: Speaking before Thinking

An action I will take to put off the old self: Pray and Think having more faith in God

An action I will take to let the Holy Spirit make me more like Christ: Stop & Pray faithfully

Stop and pray that you will constantly be filled with the Spirit and that He will work through you.

The World's Way

"Now you must rid yourselves of all such things as these: anger, rage, malice, slander, and filthy language from your lips" (Col. 3:8).

"The acts of the sinful nature are obvious: sexual immorality, impurity and debauchery. … I warn you, as I did before, that those who live like this will not inherit the kingdom of God" (Gal. 5:19-21).

"Get rid of all bitterness, rage and anger, brawling and slander, along with every form of malice" (Eph. 4:31).

The Spirit's Way

"As God's chosen people, holy and dearly loved, clothe yourselves with compassion, kindness, humility, gentleness and patience" (Col. 3:12).

"The fruit of the Spirit is love, joy, peace, patience, kindness, goodness, faithfulness, gentleness and self-control" (Gal. 5: 22-23).

"Be kind and compassionate to one another, forgiving each other, just as in Christ God forgave you" (Eph. 4:32).

Share with a fellow church member your struggles and victories. Share with that person the area of your life you selected for the Holy Spirit to help you change.

 Read Acts 2:1-21, the passage about the day of Pentecost, during your quiet time today. Then complete the Daily Master Communication Guide on page 94.

DAY 2

Your Spirit and God's Spirit

When you are born of the Spirit, your spirit is made alive, and you are able to respond spiritually. The Holy Spirit helps you—
• understand spiritual things;
• allow God to work through you.

SPIRITUAL UNDERSTANDING
Read 1 Corinthians 2:14 in the margin. What can people understand without the Spirit's help? Check the correct answer.
❑ The deep things of God
❑ The basic truths of God
☑ No spiritual truths

Without the Spirit a person can understand nothing about God.

Read John 16:8-11 in the margin. In the blanks write ways the Holy Spirit convicts the world.

The Holy Spirit convicts people of ___*Sin*___ because they do not believe in Jesus.

The Holy Spirit convicts the world of
___*UNRighteousNESS*___ by His sinless life.

The Holy Spirit convicts the world in ___*Judgement*___ by condemning and judging Satan. Anyone who follows Satan, therefore, is also condemned.

The answers are *sin, unrighteousness,* and *judgment*.
The Holy Spirit helps you understand the truths of God. Read 1 Corinthians 2:9-10 in the margin. I have heard this verse applied to what is in heaven, but it clearly says that God, through His Spirit, has already revealed truths that were not previously known by humankind.

"The man without the Spirit does not accept the things that come from the Spirit of God, for they are foolishness to him, and he cannot understand them, because they are spiritually discerned" (1 Cor. 2:14).

" 'When he comes, he will convict the world of guilt in regard to sin and righteousness and judgment: in regard to sin, because men do not believe in me; in regard to righteousness, because I am going to the Father, where you can see me no longer; and in regard to judgment, because the prince of this world now stands condemned' " (John 16:8-11).

*"It is written:
'No eye has seen,
   no ear has heard,
no mind has conceived
   what God has prepared for
those who love him'
but God has revealed it to us by
his Spirit" (1 Cor. 2:9-10).*

"We have not received the spirit of the world but the Spirit who is from God, that we may understand what God has freely given us" (1 Cor. 2:12).

" 'The counselor, the Holy Spirit, whom the Father will send in my name, will teach you all things and will remind you of everything I have said to you' " (John 14:26).

"You will receive power when the Holy Spirit comes on you; and you will be my witnesses in Jerusalem, and in all Judea and Samaria, and to the ends of the earth" (Acts 1:8).

"Peter, filled with the Holy Spirit, said to them: 'Rulers and elders of the people! If we are being called to account today for an act of kindness shown to a cripple and are asked how he was healed, then know this, you and all the people of Israel: It is by the name of Jesus Christ of Nazareth, whom you crucified but whom God raised from the dead, that this man stands before you healed' " (Acts 4:8).

"After they prayed, the place where they were meeting was shaken. And they were all filled with the Holy Spirit and spoke the word of God boldly" (Acts 4:31).

Read 1 Corinthians 2:12 and John 14:26 in the margin. What is the Spirit trying to teach you?

The Holy Spirit help You Recall Christ's teaching

The Holy Spirit helps you recall Christ's teachings. He will teach you all things (see John 16:15) and guide you into His truth.

THE SPIRIT WORKS THROUGH YOU
Not only does the Holy Spirit make you aware of the truth, but He also does God's work through you and other believers.

Read Acts 1:8 in the margin. What does the Spirit enable you to do?

Holy Spirit Enables you to be christ Witness

The Holy Spirit enables you to be Christ's witness. Zechariah 4:6 says, "Not by might nor by power, but my spirit, says the Lord Almighty."

Read Acts 4:8 and Acts 4:31 in the margin and underline the words showing that the filling of the Spirit was the key element in God's speaking or working through persons.

Perhaps you underlined such words as "Peter, filled with the Holy Spirit, said to them" in the first verse and "they were all filled with the Holy Spirit and spoke" in the second verse.

Review by listing the two things the Spirit enables you to do. Check your answers by looking at the list on page 97.

1. *Holy Spirit help you to understand spiritual Things*
2. *Allow God to work Through you*

LETTING THE SPIRIT ENTER
The Spirit of God and the human spirit are different. God is divine; you are human. God's Spirit enters your personality through your human spirit. You are responsible for letting the Spirit of God come in or for shutting Him out.

Read Revelation 3:20: " 'Here I am! I stand at the door and knock. If anyone hears my voice and opens the door, I will come in and eat with him, and he with me.' " How does this verse picture Jesus?

Jesus Standing at the door of our heart And gently Asking to Entrance

This verse depicts Jesus standing outside the door of your heart and gently asking for entrance. People who accept Christ open their lives to Him and invite Him to dwell in them. When you open the door to His marvelous invitation, God's Spirit enters your life and brings peace to your soul.

Pray for persons within your circles of influence—those with whom you associate occasionally or regularly. Pray that you will have opportunities to share God's love and His availability to them. Write their names on your Prayer-Covenant List (p. 143).

A CONTINUAL FILLING

A true disciple lets the Spirit of God continually fill and control his or her entire personality, as this week's Scripture-memory verse instructs.

Stop and say aloud your memory verse, Ephesians 5:18.

Read Acts 4:29: " 'Now, Lord, consider their threats and enable your servants to speak your word with great boldness.' " What did the apostles ask for when they were threatened?

Speak God's word boldNESS

When they were threatened, the apostles did not ask for release or safety. They asked to be able to speak the Word with great boldness, and God gave them boldness. As a result, many people came to Christ.

Ask the Holy Spirit to fill you this week and to give you boldness to speak for Christ.

IN THE CARPENTER'S SHOP

How is the Holy Spirit working to change you into the image of Christ? What progress are you making in developing Christlike character?

In day 1 you listed a behavior related to anger that you hoped to get rid of to be more like Jesus. Today describe an instance in which you have already worked to set aside that behavior.

_____

_____

_____

DAILY MASTER COMMUNICATION GUIDE

ACTS 4:13-31

What God said to me:

_____

What I said to God:

_____

↕ **Read Acts 4:13-31, the passage from which the verse you read about boldness is taken, during your quiet time today. Then complete the Daily Master Communication Guide on page 99.**

DAY 3

Filled Without Limit

In day 2 you learned that true disciples let the Spirit of God continually fill and control their entire personalities. However, not all Christians allow God to control their lives. Worldly Christians still struggle with the big *I* of the natural person.

Based on what you learned as you studied the Disciple's Personality, describe in your own words why the Spirit of God does not fill everyone's personality.

> Everyone has not opened The door of his or her heart To God we must 1st opened the door before Christ will come in

You may have answered something like this: Not everyone has opened the door of his or her spirit to God's Spirit. You must first open the door before the Spirit of God can fill your personality.

CONTROLLED BY THE SPIRIT

You have the Spirit of Christ dwelling in you if you belong to Jesus. You may treat Him as a guest, a servant, a tenant, or Lord and Master—the owner of the property. But the Spirit will not fill you completely until you acknowledge Christ's lordship and submit to His personal and divine authority. First Thessalonians 5:23, in the margin, describes what God does in your personality.

Sanctify means *to set apart* or *to cleanse*. **Write *T* beside the statement that best expresses the truth of 1 Thessalonians 5:23.**
T God sets apart or cleanses your entire personality.
___ God cleanses your spirit only.

Your entire personality is cleansed as God's Spirit controls your spirit. When God sanctifies your entire personality, He and you enjoy mutual fellowship.

Although you have the Holy Spirit living in you, you might not be

---

Handwritten margin note: Surrender all to him

Margin quote: "May God himself, the God of peace, sanctify you through and through. May your whole spirit, soul and body be kept blameless at the coming of our Lord Jesus Christ" (1 Thess. 5:23).

giving Him His rightful place. Check the box that best describes how the Holy Spirit would say that you treat Him.
❑ As a guest
❑ As a servant
❑ As a tenant
☑ As Master—the owner of the property

What relationship should exist between God's Spirit and your spirit? Check the correct answer.
❑ Your spirit should control God's Spirit.
❑ God's Spirit and your spirit should be on equal terms.
☑ God's Spirit should control your spirit.

God's will is that you be completely controlled by His Spirit. This week's Scripture-memory verse, Ephesians 5:18, tells how this occurs.

Say aloud this week's Scripture-memory verse, Ephesians 5:18, as you continue to memorize it.

OCCUPIED WITH CHRIST
John 3:34, in the margin, states that Jesus was filled with God's Spirit without limit. Jesus had the Spirit filling Him constantly and empowering Him in everything He did. I urge you to open your entire life to the Holy Spirit.

" 'The one whom God has sent speaks the words of God, for God gives the Spirit without limit' " (John 3:34).

What would be required for you to follow totally the Holy Spirit's guidance in everything you do? Check the following statements that apply.

I would have to—
☑ confess and forsake sin in my life;
☑ spend more time in Bible study to hear the Spirit speaking to me;
☑ spend more time in prayer asking for the Spirit to reveal God's will for me;
☑ ask the Spirit to fill me;
☑ turn to God first when a crisis occurs rather than as the last resort;
❑ be alert and open to opportunities to witness;
☑ seek the Christ-honoring solution to situations rather than my solutions;
❑ take this action: _____.

In his book *The Full Blessing of Pentecost* Andrew Murray lists seven main points about a Christian's being filled with the Holy Spirit.

As you read the following quotation by Andrew Murray, underline troublesome areas that limit your being filled with the Holy Spirit.

"Without being filled with the Spirit, it is utterly impossible that an individual Christian or a church can ever live or work as God desires."
—Andrew Murray

1. It is the will of God that every one of His children should live entirely and unceasingly under the control of the Holy Spirit.

2. Without being filled with the Spirit, it is utterly impossible that an individual Christian or a church can ever live or work as God desires.

3. Everywhere and in everything we see the proofs, in the life and experience of Christians, that this blessing is but little enjoyed in the Church, and alas! is but little sought for.

4. This blessing is prepared for us and God waits to bestow it. Our faith may expect it with the greatest confidence.

5. The great hindrance in the way is that the self-life, and the world, which it uses for its own service and pleasure, usurp the place that Christ ought to occupy.

6. We cannot be filled with the Spirit until we are prepared to yield ourselves to be led by the Lord Jesus to forsake and sacrifice every thing for this pearl of great price.[1]

Now read the following quotation by L. L. Letgers. As you read, think about ways your life resembles or does not resemble this description.

Your evidence that you are filled with the spirit is that Jesus becomes everything to you. You see Him. You are occupied with Him. You are fully satisfied with Jesus. He becomes real, and when you witness about Him, the Holy Spirit witnesses with you regarding the truth about Him. … Jesus is your Lord and Master and you rest in His Lordship. … The real evidence of a Spirit-filled life is … first, that others see the Holy Spirit working in your life the character of Christ, the fruit of the Spirit, and second, that you in your own private life see in the Book the things of Jesus, and that you are personally rejoicing in Him, and are occupied with Him.[2]

Which of the following best reflect your response to the quotations you read about being filled with the Spirit? Check all that apply.
❑ I have never known the kind of life described.
☑ Lord, I have wandered from You. I want to return.
☑ I have not yet arrived, but I'm working on living in this manner.
☑ Lord, please fill me so that I may experience this kind of life.
☑ Lord God, I praise You for the mighty work You have done in my life.
❑ Other: _____

One aid to being occupied with Jesus is to apply the word you hear preached. Genuinely looking forward to the times you hear God's word preached can help you discern its relevance for you and can make you receptive to the Holy Spirit as He speaks to you through it. The next activity will help you look for the Holy Spirit's work in your life.

✠ Write notes from a sermon or a Bible study—something you learned or want to learn more about—on the Hearing the Word form on page 141.

✠ Read Luke 24:13-53, the passage that describes Jesus' ascension into heaven, during your quiet time today. See how God speaks to you through this passage. Then complete the Daily Master Communication Guide in the margin.

DAY 4

How to Be Filled

If you still have questions about how to be filled with the Holy Spirit, this week's Scripture-memory verse contains several clues about how this occurs. It gives four important facts about the directive "Be filled with the Spirit."

✠ Before you read about these important facts, say aloud this week's Scripture-memory verse, Ephesians 5:18, three times from memory. Also take this opportunity to review the other verses you have memorized since you began this study.

We can learn a great deal by examining the meaning of this verse in its original language. The phrase *be filled* is— *the Spirit*

- passive voice. *Passive* means that you cannot do something yourself. Someone has to do it to you. Only God can fill you. You cannot do it to yourself or cause yourself to be filled.
- present tense. You are to be filled now. This refers to the state you are to be in.
- continuous action. Present tense in Greek indicates continuous action. It means *keep on being filled*. Although your conversion was a one-time experience, the filling of the Spirit is not. It needs to keep on happening. Envision a pipe through which water passes at all times. If the Spirit is filling you, He is always going through you as He works to minister to others.
- imperative mood. "Be filled" is an order, a command to all Christians. It is not just an option or something you can dismiss because you do not understand it. It is a teaching of God's Word. My understanding of being filled was greatly affected by my personal experience of being filled with the Holy Spirit, which I related in day 1. However, the Bible teaches that some Christians are filled when they are saved, like Cornelius in Acts 10.

DAILY MASTER COMMUNICATION GUIDE

LUKE 24:13-53

What God said to me:

_____
_____
_____
_____
_____
_____
_____
_____

What I said to God:

_____
_____
_____
_____
_____
_____
_____
_____

Go back and draw a star beside the fact you most need to be reminded of. Why do you need this reminder?

_____

THE SPIRIT FLOWS THROUGH YOU

How can someone personally experience the filling of the Holy Spirit? If you belong to Jesus, His Spirit already dwells in you. But His purpose is to fill you continually and to flow through you to others. You are not to be a container but a conduit or a channel for Him. The filling of the Spirit enables God to communicate His message to others through you.

A Christian must take three steps to be filled and controlled by the Holy Spirit:

1. Confess your sin, disobedience, emptiness, and need for God's cleansing. Read 1 John 1:9 in the margin.
2. Present every member of your body to be made a righteous instrument in God's hands. Recall Romans 12:1, one of your Scripture-memory verses.
3. Ask God to fill, control, and empower you, as Luke 11:13, in the margin, promises. Believe that God has answered your prayer.

"If we confess our sins, he is faithful and just and will forgive us our sins and purify us from all unrighteousness" (1 John 1:9).

" 'If you then, though you are evil, know how to give good gifts to your children, how much more will your Father in heaven give the Holy Spirit to those who ask him!' " (Luke 11:13).

What steps do you need to take to experience the filling of God's Spirit? Bow your head now and open your spirit to the Spirit of God. Follow the three steps listed above. Write what you experienced by faith.

_____

_____

Stop and pray. Say aloud Ephesians 5:18, this week's Scripture-memory verse. Thank God for the gift of His fullness.

In the verses in the margin find two results of being filled with the Spirit.

1. Ephesians 5:19: _____

2. Ephesians 5:20: _____

"Speak to one another with psalms, hymns and spiritual songs. Sing and make music in your heart to the Lord" (Eph. 5:19).

"Always giving thanks to God the Father for everything, in the name of our Lord Jesus Christ" (Eph. 5:20).

Christians today can be like those in the early church, in which Spirit-filled members learned to worship God with thanksgiving for everything. These early Christians often expressed thanksgiving through music. You may have responded like this: 1. speaking to one another and singing to the Lord, 2. giving thanks.

GOD'S PURPOSES IN FILLING YOU

God has a double purpose in filling you with His Spirit. First, God wants to develop Christlike character in you. In 1 Thessalonians 5:23 Paul prayed that your personality would be found blameless: "May God himself, the God of peace, sanctify you through and through. May your whole spirit, soul and body be kept blameless at the coming of our Lord Jesus Christ." Second, God wants to empower you to do His work.

Read Acts 1:8 and Acts 4:31 in the margin. Explain what the Holy Spirit enables you to do.

_____

The Holy Spirit provided power for witnessing with boldness. The disciples, timid and fearful earlier, now preached fearlessly. The Holy Spirit empowers ordinary people to testify boldly even under difficult circumstances. You need the power of the Spirit to enable you to witness. Being bold does not mean that you are never nervous or that you never fear an opportunity to witness. It means that you have the courage to do it even when you are afraid.

I hope that you also look forward to the time when you can share your prepared testimony with persons in your circles of influence.

APPLYING THE DISCIPLE'S PERSONALITY

Each week of this study you have learned a different component of the Disciple's Personality. Now that you have learned the entire presentation, you may wonder how you can use this knowledge in everyday situations.

The Disciple's Personality contains many Bible truths that apply to a variety of situations:
1. Use it to evaluate your spiritual growth.
2. Apply its teachings to gain victory in your personal life:
   a. Use it when you face temptation to overcome the flesh and Satan.
   b. Use it in prayer as you dedicate your total personality to the Master. Pray about each part of your personality.
   c. Use it to review the Scripture-memory verses related to the victorious life.
   d. Use it to review Bible teachings about each part of your personality.
3. Draw it to help others evaluate whether they are natural, worldly, or spiritual persons and to explain how they can apply it to their lives.
4. Use it with an unsaved person to explain how to become a disciple of Christ. First draw and explain the Natural Person. Next draw and explain the Spiritual Christian. If the person accepts Christ, draw the Worldly Christian to show how not to live. If he or she does not accept Christ, you may need to draw and explain the Worldly Chris-

" 'You will receive power when the Holy Spirit comes on you; and you will be my witnesses in Jerusalem, and in all Judea and Samaria, and to the ends of the earth' " (Acts 1:8).

"After they prayed, the place where they were meeting was shaken. And they were all filled with the Holy Spirit and spoke the word of God boldly" (Acts 4:31).

Being bold does not mean that you are never nervous or that you never fear an opportunity to witness. It means that you have the courage to do it even when you are afraid.

tian to explain why some Christians do not live victorious lives. Otherwise, do not present the Worldly Christian to this person.

Practice explaining in your own words how to apply the Disciple's Personality, using the basic drawing below. Your leader showed you in the previous group session how to apply the illustration, using James 4:1-8. Close the door of the flesh as you draw a cross in the center of the circle to encompass *spirit, flesh, mind, will,* and *emotions*. Write *crucified* across *flesh*. Now write *submit* above the circle. Write *Draw near to God* and draw an arrow toward God. Write *God will draw near to you* and draw an arrow from *God* toward the circle. Write *resist* below the circle and draw an arrow toward *Satan*. Write *will flee from you* below *Satan* and draw a downward arrow. See page 140 if you need help with your drawing.

GOD

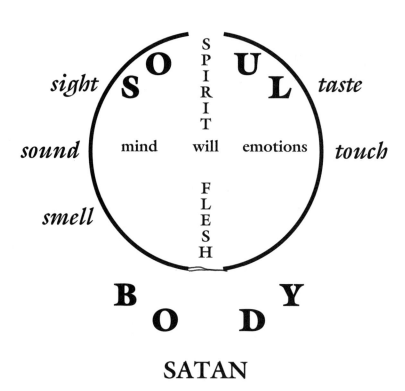

SATAN

Now use James 4:1-8 to explain the presentation in your own words.

_____

_____

_____

_____

Have you already used the Disciple's Personality? ❑ Yes ❑ No If so, describe your experience below. If not, be open to ways the Holy Spirit reveals to you.

_____

_____

IN THE CARPENTER'S SHOP
How is the Holy Spirit guiding your efforts to put off the old self and to replace it with the new?

In day 2 you recorded your progress in tearing down old habits related to anger. Today describe what you see Christ adding to your life to replace that old trait or behavior.

_____

_____

During your quiet time today read Acts 10, describing Cornelius's salvation and the filling of the Holy Spirit. Let God speak to you through this passage. Then complete the Daily Master Communication Guide in the margin.

DAY 5

Accomplishing God's Purposes

You learned in day 4 that God wants to accomplish two purposes in the life of a Spirit-filled Christian:
• To develop Christlike character
• To equip you for ministry

DAILY MASTER COMMUNICATION GUIDE

ACTS 10

What God said to me:

_____

_____

_____

_____

_____

_____

What I said to God:

_____

_____

_____

_____

_____

_____

_____

"For this very reason, make every effort to add to your faith goodness; and to goodness, knowledge; and to knowledge, self-control; and to self-control, perseverance; and to perseverance, godliness; and to godliness, brotherly kindness; and to brotherly kindness, love. For if you possess these qualities in increasing measure, they will keep you from being ineffective and unproductive in your knowledge of our Lord Jesus Christ" (2 Pet. 1:5-8).

DEVELOPING CHRISTLIKE CHARACTER

The first purpose, developing Christlike character, is achieved through the fruit of the Spirit and the second through the gifts of the Spirit.

Let's look at the way the fruit of the Spirit produces Christlike character.

Review the fruit of the Spirit in Galatians 5:22-23, your Scripture-memory verses in week 3. Then read 2 Peter 1:5-8 in the margin, in which Peter named the building blocks of Christian character. List these qualities.

_____ _____

_____ _____

_____ _____

_____ _____

Why did Peter say that you need these qualities?

_____

Peter said you need these qualities so that you will be effective and productive in the Christian life. A person who has life in the Spirit bears fruit for Christ.

IN THE CARPENTER'S SHOP

How has the Holy Spirit worked in you this week to build Christlike character? Are you getting rid of the old self and adding new behaviors to your life?

Answer the questions about the area related to anger that you identified on page 96.

Something I have been getting rid of this week:

_____

Something Christ has been adding to my character this week:

_____

Stop and thank God for the Holy Spirit, who molds you into Christlikeness.

EQUIPPING FOR MINISTRY

The Holy Spirit accomplishes the second purpose, equipping you for ministry, by bestowing gifts of the Spirit. He empowers you to minister to others through the gifts He has given you. When you see persons who are filled with the Spirit, you immediately see that they want to minister. They want to let God work through them and to join God on His mission. Only the continual filling and refilling of the Spirit can produce this desire. Fruit produces character, and gifts produce effectiveness in ministry.

Some gifts of the Holy Spirit are listed in 1 Corinthians 12:7-11 and Romans 12:6-8, which are in the margin. Read the verses and write any gift(s) you believe the Holy Spirit has given you.

_____

To what extent have you developed the gift(s) you have been given? Write the number(s) beside the gift(s) you listed above.
1. none   2. some   3. much

Stop and ask God to help you surrender your gifts to Him and to help you find ways to develop your gifts to their fullest.

Christlike character and effectiveness in ministry are possible only through the continual filling of the Spirit. Trying to achieve either by your own efforts is an exercise in futility. *MasterLife 4: The Disciple's Mission*, will define the ministry gifts and will help you discover the gifts the Spirit has given you. Develop your spiritual gifts so that you can minister as the Spirit desires.

To summarize what you have learned about God's purposes in filling you with the Spirit, fill in the blanks below.

God's first purpose: _____

How He accomplishes it: _____

God's second purpose: _____

How He accomplishes it: _____

> **HOW TO WRITE YOUR TESTIMONY**
> You can compile facts about your Christian life in a clear, concise testimony. Here are reasons to write your testimony.
> • To clarify experiences in your mind
> • To allow your leader to give feedback so that you can sharpen your testimony

"To each one the manifestation of the Spirit is given for the common good. To one there is given through the Spirit the message of wisdom, to another the message of knowledge by means of the same Spirit, to another faith by the same Spirit, to another gifts of healing by that one Spirit, to another miraculous powers, to another prophecy, to another distinguishing between spirits, to another speaking in different kinds of tongues, and to still another the interpretation of tongues. All these are the work of one and the same Spirit, and he gives them to each one, just as he determines" (1 Cor. 12: 7-11).

"We have different gifts, according to the grace given us. If a man's gift is prophesying, let him use it in proportion to his faith. If it is serving, let him serve; if it is teaching, let him teach; if it is encouraging, let him encourage; if it is contributing to the needs of others, let him give generously; if it is leadership, let him govern diligently; if it is showing mercy, let him do it cheerfully" (Rom. 12:6-8).

Write the way you talk.

- To develop a standard testimony to adapt to specific situations
- To master your testimony so that you are ready to use it anytime

Essential Preliminary Steps

1. Use the brief testimony you wrote in week 3 and the notes you made in week 4 as resources for your first draft. After the first draft has been evaluated, you may rewrite it in a more polished version. Write the way you talk. Use *I* and *me*. Do not worry about formal rules of grammar. You will communicate your testimony verbally by sharing, not preaching.

2. Choose one of the following approaches to write the testimony.
   a. *Chronological.* This approach is better when enough significant experiences happened before your conversion to distinguish clearly between your life before and after conversion.

CHRONOLOGICAL

1. **Before I met Christ**
2. **How I realized my need**
3. **How I became a Christian**
4. **What being a Christian means to me**

   b. *Thematic.* This approach is the better choice when you were saved as a child and/or do not remember enough significant events before your conversion that the other person can identify with. Begin by focusing on an experience, problem, issue, or feeling, such as a fear of death, a desire for success, a basic character flaw, a search for identity, or a crisis.

THEMATIC

1. **A theme, a need, or a problem**
2. **How I became a Christian**
3. **What being a Christian means to me**

Begin with a brief testimony about your current situation:
- I have discovered how not to worry.
- I have discovered a purpose for living.
- I have overcome loneliness.
- I have overcome my fear of death.
- I have learned how to integrate my life into a meaningful whole.
- I have found the secret to a happy life.

State the theme and tell how you solved your problem. This flashback technique can take the place of telling your experience before conversion. It is also effective if you cannot remember the exact sequence of events in your conversion experience. Many people have full assurance that they are saved, but they have trouble identifying the exact time of their conversion. If that is your case, be sure that you are saved now. If you have doubt, talk with your *MasterLife* leader or with another Christian who can help you find assurance of salvation. The date of your conversion is not as important as your personal relationship with Christ as Savior and Lord. The flashback technique allows you to give the facts without detailing when they happened. Even though you may not remember consciously thinking through each of the four facts of the gospel (sin, sin's penalty, Christ's payment, and receiving Christ) at conversion, you can mention them in the flashback approach, since you have become aware of them and believe them now.

Check the approach above that you intend to use.

Writing Your Testimony

1. Write an interesting introduction about your life and attitudes before following Christ. Help the person see you as an ordinary person. Give a few brief facts about your early life to set the scene. Use facts that the person can identify with or that help him or her see you as a normal person. Sound adult, not juvenile. For example, do not say, "My dad used to set me on his knee and talk to me." Say, "One day as my dad and I were talking, he said …" Do not reminisce too much about details that would be unimportant to a stranger. Use concrete words and word pictures to describe the situation. Be brief.

2. Highlight the events that led to your salvation (how you realized your need). Summarize the events that led you to realize your need for Christ. Avoid using the name of your church, your specific age, or the date of conversion unless the person hearing your testimony has the same background. Keep these facts general to make it easier for others to identify with you. Do not use religious jargon or church words that might not be understood by persons with limited or different religious backgrounds.

3. Summarize the facts of salvation (how you became a Christian).
   a. *Chronological.* Tell how you became aware that sin involves living an "I-controlled" life. State how you felt when you realized the penalty of sin. Explain how you knew that Christ paid the penalty for your sin. Summarize how you received Christ. Be sure to emphasize repentance and faith in Christ as the way to salvation.
   b. *Thematic.* Even if you cannot remember each of the previous stages clearly, you can state your realization without referring

Summarize the events that led you to realize your need for Christ.

to the time you realized each. However, state with confidence that you received Christ and are following Him as your Lord. Sometimes a personal testimony is a good way to begin a witnessing encounter. If you use your testimony to introduce a presentation of the gospel, you may omit the next point and tell how to receive Christ through the gospel presentation.

4. Share the results of knowing Christ as Lord and Savior (what being a Christian means to you). Quickly summarize the difference Christ has made in your life. Give concrete examples.

    a. Mention the struggles of your continuing pilgrimage so that you do not give the impression that you think you are perfect. For example, "Being a Christian doesn't mean that I don't have problems, but now Christ helps me through them."

    b. Do not spend too much time on this point. Many Christians tend to focus on what has happened since conversion. Mention it, but the non-Christian also needs to know how you reached this point. He should relate more to the beginning experience than to later experiences. Revise your testimony to focus on salvation.

Close your testimony in a way that leads to further conversation about salvation.

5. Close your testimony in a way that leads to further conversation about salvation. Use questions such as:

    a. Has anything like that ever happened to you?

    b. Does that make sense to you?

    c. Have you ever thought that you would like to have such peace (assurance, joy, experience, and so on)?

    d. Do you know for certain that you have eternal life and that you will go to heaven when you die?

Evaluating Your Testimony

1. Check your testimony by using the following criteria. Revise your rough draft as needed. You will rewrite your testimony after it has been evaluated during your next group session.

    a. Does it have a clear story line that ties everything together?

    b. Are all parts of the testimony developed proportionally?

    c. In explaining how you became a Christian, did you include the four doctrinal truths of the gospel (see p. 80)?

    d. Is the testimony too brief? Too long? Does it need details?

    e. Does the testimony conclude with a final sentence that will lead to further conversation?

    f. Does the testimony sound conversational, formal, or preachy?

2. Writing your testimony may be difficult. The time required to write it will depend on its complexity and on the number of times you have given it before. It does not relate to your intelligence or to your testimony's validity. Thinking about unpleasant events in your life may be upsetting. You may discover the need to be sure that you have been saved. Satan does not want you to prepare a testimony. Ask God to help you.

As you read this section, if you had any question about whether you are saved, you can receive Jesus Christ now by invitation. Romans 10:13 says, "Everyone who calls on the name of the Lord will be saved." You may use this prayer to express your commitment:

Lord Jesus, I am a sinner. I need You. I want You to be my Savior and Lord. I accept Your death on the cross as the payment for my sins, and I now entrust my life to Your care. Thank You for forgiving me and for giving me a new life. Please help me grow in my understanding of Your love and power so that my life will bring glory and honor to You. Amen.

Signed _____ Date _____

 Write your testimony, using the ideas in "How to Write Your Testimony." Be ready to share it at the next group session. It should be only three minutes long. That is equivalent to about one page, typed and double-spaced, or two pages handwritten.

During your quiet time today read Romans 12:1-8, which mentions spiritual gifts that build up the body of Christ. Then complete the Daily Master Communication Guide in the margin.

HAS THIS WEEK MADE A DIFFERENCE?
Review "My Walk with the Master This Week" at the beginning of this week's material. Mark the activities you have finished by drawing vertical lines in the diamonds beside them. Finish any incomplete activities. Think about what you will say during your group session about your work on these activities.

As you complete your study of "Be Filled with the Spirit," consider the following statements and check the boxes beside those that apply.
❑ I am more aware than ever of the gracious gift of the Holy Spirit, who lives in me.
❑ I desire to be filled with the Spirit and will take steps to be filled.
❑ The filling of the Holy Spirit in me is already motivating me to use my gifts to minister to others.
❑ The Holy Spirit has helped me build more Christlike character this week by tearing down old thoughts and actions and by replacing them with new ones.

[1]Andrew Murray, *The Full Blessing of Pentecost* (Port Washington, Pa.: Christian Literature Crusade, 1954), 7.
[2]L. L. Letgers, *The Simplicity of the Spirit-Filled Life* (Farmingdale, N.Y.: Christian Witness, 1968), 51–52.

DAILY MASTER COMMUNICATION GUIDE

ROMANS 12:1-8

What God said to me:

_____

_____

_____

_____

_____

_____

_____

What I said to God:

_____

_____

_____

_____

_____

_____

_____

WEEK 6

Live Victoriously

This Week's Goal

You will be able to explain how you became a Christian and how to live a life of victory in the Spirit.

My Walk with the Master This Week

You will complete the following activities to develop the six biblical disciplines. When you complete each activity, draw a vertical line in the diamond beside it.

SPEND TIME WITH THE MASTER

◇ Have a quiet time each day. Write the number of minutes you spend in your quiet time each day: Sunday: 30 Monday: 20 Tuesday: 25 Wednesday: 100 Thursday: 50 Friday: 35 Saturday: 15

LIVE IN THE WORD

◇ Read your Bible every day. Write what God says to you and what you say to God.

◇ Memorize Romans 6:12-13.

◇ Review Ephesians 5:18, Philippians 2:13, Romans 12:1-2, Galatians 5:22-23, and 1 Corinthians 6:19-20.

◇ Use the Hearing the Word form with a Sunday School lesson or a sermon.

PRAY IN FAITH

◇ Pray for two lost coworkers or neighbors.

FELLOWSHIP WITH BELIEVERS

◇ Share with your prayer partner ways the Holy Spirit helps you.

WITNESS TO THE WORLD

◇ Work on your testimony, using the ideas your leader gave you last week.

MINISTER TO OTHERS

◇ Practice giving your testimony.

◇ Draw and explain the Disciple's Personality.

◇ Explain how to apply the Disciple's Personality, using Galatians 5:16-25.

This Week's Scripture-Memory Verses

"Do not let sin reign in your mortal body so that you obey its evil desires. Do not offer the parts of your body to sin, as instruments of wickedness, but rather offer yourselves to God, as those who have been brought from death to life; and offer the parts of your body to him as instruments of righteousness" (Rom. 6:12-13).

DAY 1

Victory over Sin

As a group of Colorado pastors finished *MasterLife* training, one of them received a call to visit a young woman who had just attempted suicide. As the pastor spoke with the patient, her nurse remained in the hospital room. In counseling the young woman, the pastor related the basic elements of the Disciple's Personality he had just learned at the training. He explained how all aspects of our personality work together, why we make the choices we do, and how Satan influences us to sin.

When the pastor had finished the visit and left the room, the nurse followed him outside. "That was the most helpful thing I've ever heard," the nurse said. "Please tell me more." The pastor further explained how to be saved, and the nurse made a profession of faith.

"The fruit of that pastor's sharing the Disciple's Personality was immediate," recalled Jimmy Crowe, who was conducting the training. "It helped the patient, but it helped the nurse even more."

By learning how your personality works, you can understand how to live a victorious life. Just understanding these concepts does not stop sin in the world. Satan is always at work, seeking to devour anyone he can. Knowledge is power, but the real power is the Holy Spirit. By learning how easily you can falter and how easily you can leave open the door of the flesh, you can stay on guard against thoughts and actions that are part of the old self and can put Christlike traits in their place.

When Jesus died on the cross and rose from the grave, He won the victory over sin. He promised that His disciples would share in His victory (see 1 John 5:4-5 in the margin). A victorious Christian life is a Spirit-filled life.

You discovered in last week's work that being filled with God's Spirit is a daily process of crucifying the flesh and allowing the Spirit to have control. In this week's study you will learn how to participate in the victory over sin that Jesus has already won for you. As a result of this week's study, you should be able to—

- explain how the Disciple's Personality can be used to bring defeat or to achieve victory;
- express how Jesus has ensured victory for His disciples;
- evaluate the degree to which you are living in victory.

INTERNAL CONFLICT

In every person a civil war rages between the forces of Satan and the forces of God. Every person is made in God's image. He or she has God's moral law stamped into his or her being. Yet this person's fallen bodily senses and fleshly desires are in control. Read about this person's dilemma in Romans 7:19-24 in the margin.

"Everyone born of God overcomes the world. This is the victory that has overcome the world, even our faith. Who is it that overcomes the world? Only he who believes that Jesus is the Son of God" (1 John 5:4-5).

"What I do is not the good I want to do; no, the evil I do not want to do—this I keep on doing. Now if I do what I do not want to do, it is no longer I who do it, but it is sin living in me that does it. So I find this law at work: When I want to do good, evil is right there with me. For in my inner being I delight in God's law; but I see another law at work in the members of my body, waging war against the law of my mind and making me a prisoner of the law of sin at work within my members. What a wretched man I am! Who will rescue me from this body of death?" (Rom. 7:19-24).

Think about the passage you just read and write a brief summary of what Paul described.

When I want to do good but can't because of Sin I Relize The worldy Prnt in me is God's I wont So I Let the Holy Spirit Lead me thorg me to ovr ... it God ... ...

You may have written a response similar to this: I want to do good, but I cannot because of sin. I am captive to the law of sin.

The worldly Christian is in a constant state of tension. Because the door of the flesh is still open and because the big *I* is still in control, evil desires enter and work to crowd out the Holy Spirit.

Read what Paul said about the worldly mind in Romans 8:6-8: "The mind of sinful man is death, but the mind controlled by the Spirit is life and peace; the sinful mind is hostile to God. It does not submit to God's law, nor can it do so. Those controlled by the sinful nature cannot please God." Check the correct responses:
☑ **1. The worldly mind is God's enemy.**
☐ **2. The worldly mind is life and peace.**
☑ **3. The worldly mind does not submit to God's law.**
☑ **4. The worldly mind cannot please God.**

God is not pleased with a mind that yields itself to sin. He considers it an enemy. It operates outside God's law. It brings the exact opposite of life and peace. The correct answers to the above exercise are 1, 3, and 4.

CHOOSING CHRIST DAILY
The spiritual Christian is not perfect. But daily this Christian crucifies the flesh and consciously allows the Spirit to fill him or her. When this person is tempted, he or she closes the door to Satan and opens the door to Jesus.

Read Romans 6:17-18: "Thanks be to God that, though you used to be slaves to sin, you wholeheartedly obeyed the form of teaching to which you were entrusted. You have been set free from sin and have become slaves to righteousness." Check the way a person who is a servant of sin can be made free from sin.
☑ **1. By obeying God's Word** ☐ **2. By refusing to be tempted**

Obeying God's Word is the way you can refrain from being a slave to sin. The Word contains everything you need for life and peace. It contains every instruction you need for living. You can recall the Word when you need a reminder of how you are to think and act. The correct answer is 1.

⬆ Memorizing Scripture helps you resist temptation. This
week's Scripture-memory verses are Romans 6:12-13. Turn
⬇ to page 114 and read them aloud. Then write how you
think memorizing these verses will help you resist temptation.

USing yOUR body fOR
good And Not Evil

You may have said that these verses remind you to use your body for
good and not evil. Recalling them in a time of temptation can help you
bind Satan and can remind you to ask God to help you.

IN THE CARPENTER'S SHOP
What are practical ways you can replace evil with good? Today look at
another area of your life in which you want to be more Christlike.

**Read the Scriptures in the margin that relate to greed. Underline
the words or phrases related to greed. From the verses marked "The
World's Way" identify a specific behavior you want to get rid of.
From the verses marked "The Spirit's Way" identify an action you
will take to replace it. I have given you an example. Each day this
week you will record your progress in working on this behavior.**

Here is an example.

Behavior I want to work on: overspending

An action I will take to put off the old self: no longer incur credit-
card debt when I see an item I think I must purchase

**An action I will take to let the Holy Spirit make me more like
Christ:** be content with what I have and control my material desires;
memorize Hebrews 13:5 to help me do this

Now you try it.

Behavior I want to work on: _Short Patience_
getting UP Set
An action I will take to put off the old self:
thinK Things Through with A
PRAyER FRist
**An action I will take to let the Holy Spirit make me more like
Christ:** _tURN all thing + Thoughts_
Over to God in PRAyER
Asking Telling SAtAN to Step
ASide I'm God's Child

The World's Way

"Among you there must not be
even a hint of sexual
immorality, or of any kind of
impurity, or of greed, because
these are improper for God's
holy people" (Eph. 5:3).

"Put to death, therefore,
whatever belongs to your earthly
nature: sexual immorality,
impurity, lust, evil desires and
greed, which is idolatry"
(Col. 3:5).

"The acts of the sinful nature
are obvious: sexual immorality,
impurity and debauchery. ...
I warn you, as I did before, that
those who live like this will not
inherit the kingdom of God"
(Gal. 5:19-21).

The Spirit's Way

"Be imitators of God, therefore,
as dearly loved children and
live a life of love, just as Christ
loved us and gave himself up
for us as a fragrant offering
and sacrifice to God"
(Eph. 5:1-2).

"Set your minds on things
above, not on earthly things"
(Col. 3:2).

"The fruit of the Spirit is love,
joy, peace, patience, kindness,
goodness, faithfulness,
gentleness, and self-control.
Against such things there is no
law" (Gal. 5:22-23).

Share with your prayer partner how the Holy Spirit helps you. Tell that person about the area you wish to change and ask him or her to pray with you that the Holy Spirit will help you set aside this behavior.

During your quiet time today read Ephesians 5, one of the chapters you have been reading for instructions on Christ-like behaviors. Then complete the Daily Master Communication Guide on page 116.

DAY 2

Alert to the Enemy

Victorious living involves being aware of Satan's potential hold on you and keeping the enemy at a distance. Even though the human personality is God's highest creation, an individual's personality is damaged when he or she follows Satan and chooses to sin. Satan's weapons are powerful. Only a foolish Christian fails to take Satan seriously.

THE FORCES YOU FACE

Read the verses in the margin. Record the forces mentioned that are fighting against the Spirit of God within you.

Galatians 5:17: _____

1 John 2:15: _____

1 Peter 5:8: _____

These verses make clear that the enemy is alive and vigilant in seeking to destroy Christians. He constantly looks for a weak point in your personality so that he can cause you to stumble. Your sinful nature, the world, and the devil are the forces that fight against the Spirit of God within you.

In each of the following case studies, underline the point at which Satan is fighting against the Spirit of God within the person.

Julie badly needed a job because she was the sole provider for herself and her son. Although she had taken courses to update her skills and had sought the help of an employment agency, she was still unemployed after a six-month search. Her bank account was drained, and her financial picture looked bleak. Julie, a

"The sinful nature desires what is contrary to the Spirit, and the Spirit what is contrary to the sinful nature. They are in conflict with each other, so that you do not do what you want" (Gal. 5:17).

"Do not love the world or anything in the world. If anyone loves the world, the love of the Father is not in him" (1 John 2:15).

"Be self-controlled and alert. Your enemy the devil prowls around like a roaring lion looking for someone to devour" (1 Pet. 5:8).

Christian, had trusted God with her job search but was beginning to doubt that God was aware of her distress.

Ken, a middle-aged father of three, was diagnosed with a life-threatening illness. At first he vowed that fighting this disease would not get him down, but the treatments and his discomfort were taking an emotional and physical toll. The time away from work because of the illness was endangering his job. Having served God faithfully as a Sunday School teacher for years, Ken wondered why God did not intervene.

Ray had worked diligently in his business and was successful. As his income increased, he acquired a larger home, a finer car, and numerous material possessions. Ray had always been active in his church, but his increased travel schedule, as well as his heightened interest in leisure activities, began taking more of his time. Soon he began to tell himself that he did not have time for church because he was such a busy, important person.

Satan attacked each individual at a point of weakness. When Julie questioned whether God was aware of her distress and when Ken questioned why God did not intervene in his suffering, they gave Satan an entry point in their lives. When Ray thought that he could make it on his own without the fellowship of other believers, he became vulnerable to the enemy.

Satan looks for moments of distress, doubt, fear, and pain to gain a foothold in your life. He sees these as golden opportunities to destroy your trust in God. The Holy Spirit can help you rest in the Lord and exercise self-control while you wait for God's help.

As you read the case studies, could you identify with any of them? Has Satan attempted to destroy you in a weak or anxious moment? If so, draw a star beside the illustration that is similar to the way you have been challenged. Identify a weak area of your life now or in the recent past. Briefly describe your struggle.

_____

_____

_____

This week's Scripture-memory verses address the challenges you face when sin attempts to reign in your life. To continue your memory work, try to write Romans 6:12-13 in the blanks on the following page.

DAILY MASTER COMMUNICATION GUIDE

GALATIANS 5

What God said to me:

What I said to God:

_____

_____

_____

THE VICTORY HAS BEEN WON

What has Jesus done to secure victory for you over the forces that fight against the Spirit of God within you? The three verses in the margin answer this question.

"What the law was powerless to do in that it was weakened by the sinful nature, God did by sending his own Son in the likeness of sinful man to be a sin offering. And so he condemned sin in sinful man" (Rom. 8:3).

" 'I have told you these things, so that in me you may have peace. In this world you will have trouble. But take heart! I have overcome the world' " (John 16:33).

"He who does what is sinful is of the devil, because the devil has been sinning from the beginning. The reason the Son of God appeared was to destroy the devil's work" (1 John 3:8).

Read the verses in the margin and describe what Jesus has done to conquer the enemy.

Jesus die That I might be fou

Romans 8:3: _Are he Jesus Condomnad Sin in m Christ_

John 16:33: _the world, But take heart SRid I have over com_

1 John 3:8: _The Reason Gods Son Christ To distroy the devil wor_

What a victory! You are not alone when you sustain Satan's attacks. Christ has gone before you to provide victory for you. In Christ's death on the cross He condemned sin in the flesh, He overcame the world, and He destroyed the devil's work. He has also given you the Holy Spirit to strengthen you in times of temptation.

Doesn't this marvelous news make you long for everyone you know to have this kind of power? Can you think of persons in your circles of influence who yield to temptation because they have never accepted Jesus? Perhaps you see them sinning as the devil takes control of them, and you long for them to know the One who has crushed Satan and has overcome the world.

Pray for two persons with whom you work or for two neighbors who do not know Jesus.

IN THE CARPENTER'S SHOP

How well are you withstanding Satan's attacks in your life? The Holy Spirit will help you put off a harmful thought or action and put on more Christlike character.

In day 1 you listed a behavior you hope to tear down to become more Christlike. Today describe an instance in which you have already begun to set aside that behavior.

Reading The Bible + Pray daily & Claming Victory in Christ Jesus

✝ **During your quiet time today read Galatians 5, another chapter you have been reading for instructions on Christlike behavior. Then complete the Daily Master Communication Guide on page 119.**

DAY 3

A Victory You Can Claim

Yesterday you learned that Jesus has already provided the victory for you when Satan tries to catch you at a weak moment and to turn your trust away from God. Picture the scene of Jesus dying on the cross for you. Do you know why He was there? So that you can participate in His victory over sin. Under the law no forgiveness of sins could occur without the shedding of blood. Jesus' death and resurrection make possible your righteousness before God. His sinless perfection is the only acceptable offering for your atonement. Without the shedding of Jesus' blood, no remission (removal) of sins could happen. Read Hebrews 9:22 in the margin.

Read the verses in the margin that describe Jesus' victory over sin. Match each verse with the correct summary statement.

C 1. Hebrews 9:26

A 2. Romans 6:11

D 3. 1 Corinthians 15:56-57

B 4. 1 John 1:7

a. You are dead to sin through Jesus.

b. Jesus' blood cleanses you from sin.

c. Jesus purified us from sin by His sacrifice.

d. You have victory over sin through Jesus.

The blood of our sinless Savior is the source of your cleansing from sin. It is as though you are dead to the power of sin. Sin is no longer your master. Jesus has provided a way out. The correct answers are 1. c, 2. a, 3. d, 4. b.

A LIFE OF VICTORY

Jesus' victory can be yours. Galatians 2:20 states two inseparable dynamics of victory: "I have been crucified with Christ and I no longer live, but Christ lives in me. The life I live in the body, I live by faith in the Son of God, who loved me and gave himself for me." One of those dynamics is death. The other is new life. One is repudiation of self-seeking and self-will. The other is complete commitment to Christ's lordship and God's will.

"In fact, the law requires that nearly everything be cleansed with blood, and without the shedding of blood there is no forgiveness" (Heb. 9:22).

"Then Christ would have had to suffer many times since the creation of the world. But now he has appeared once for all at the end of the ages to do away with sin by the sacrifice of himself" (Heb. 9:26).

"Count yourselves dead to sin but alive to God in Christ Jesus" (Rom. 6:11).

"The sting of death is sin, and the power of sin is the law. But thanks be to God! He gives us the victory through our Lord Jesus Christ" (1 Cor. 15:56-57).

"If we walk in the light, as he is in the light, we have fellowship with one another, and the blood of Jesus, his Son, purifies us from all sin" (1 John 1:7).

DAILY MASTER COMMUNICATION GUIDE

COLOSSIANS 3

What God said to me:

_____

_____

_____

_____

_____

_____

_____

What I said to God:

_____

_____

_____

_____

_____

_____

_____

Complete this verse with the words that describe these two dynamics in action. Check your work by looking in the previous paragraph.

"I have been _CRuCified_ with Christ and I no longer _Live_."

Death to a life of defeat at the hands of the world, the flesh, and the devil produces a life that is victorious over these three familiar foes. This theme is repeated in Romans 6:11, which appears in the margin on the previous page.

Read Romans 6:11 in the margin on the previous page. Write in your own words what this verse means.

You Are dead to Sin through Jesus

Maybe you paraphrased the verse like this: I think of myself as dead to sin but alive through Jesus Christ.

The verse you paraphrased, Romans 6:11, appears in your Bible just before this week's Scripture-memory verses, Romans 6:12-13. Practice saying aloud your memory verses. Take this opportunity to review the other verses you have memorized in this study.

How do you feel about the fact that Jesus' victory over sin can be yours? Check the statement or statements that apply:
❑ I have a difficult time believing that this is possible. Sin and the devil are too powerful to be overcome.
❑ I want to believe that I have victory over sin, but I feel unworthy.
☒ I don't deserve this kind of love, but I believe God's Word when it says that this is a precious gift to me, and I accept it freely.
❑ Other: _____

_____

Christ's victory over sin is a popular theme in sermons and lessons in churches. Using the Hearing the Word form on page 141, write what you learn from a Sunday School lesson or a sermon this week or in the next few weeks, especially on the topic of victorious living.

IN THE CARPENTER'S SHOP
How are you claiming Christ's victory in your efforts to put off the old self and to replace it with the new?

Yesterday you wrote about progress you are making in tearing down old habits in areas related to greed. Today describe something new Christ is adding to your life to replace the old.

_____

_____

During your quiet time today read Colossians 3, the third passage from which you have been receiving instruction about living a Christlike life. Let God speak to you through this passage. Then complete the Daily Master Communication Guide on page 122.

DAY 4

Resisting Temptation

Victory in Jesus Christ may seem easy enough to claim when you are listening to a good sermon at church or when you are having a meaningful quiet time at home. But what about when you are on the job, in a family conflict, or in a personal struggle? How do you experience victory in the heat of daily circumstances?

STRENGTH TO WITHSTAND TEMPTATION
To understand how to experience this victory, first study how sin takes root in your life. Sin begins with temptation. The Bible says that Jesus was tempted in every way you are tempted; yet He did not sin (see Heb. 4:15 in the margin). How reassuring it is to realize that He knows and understands when you find yourself on the verge of falling into Satan's snares. Because Jesus understands, He can help you when you are tempted (see Heb. 2:18 in the margin).

Read 1 Corinthians 10:13 in the margin. Based on what you read, explain what is wrong with this statement: Some temptations are so strong that they cannot be resisted.

No Temptation is too strong to withstand

For Every temptation God Provide a way to Escape

"We do not have a high priest who is unable to sympathize with our weaknesses, but we have one who has been tempted in every way, just as we are—yet was without sin" (Heb. 4:15).

"Because he himself suffered when he was tempted, he is able to help those who are being tempted" (Heb. 2:18).

"No temptation has seized you except what is common to man. And God is faithful; he will not let you be tempted beyond what you can bear. But when you are tempted, he will also provide a way out so that you can stand up under it" (1 Cor. 10:13).

" 'Watch and pray so that you will not fall into temptation. The spirit is willing, but the body is weak' " (Matt. 26:41).

blish

"Flee the evil desires of youth, and pursue righteousness, faith, love and peace, along with those who call on the Lord out of a pure heart" (2 Tim. 2:22).

No temptation is too strong to withstand. For every temptation God provides a way of escape.

What impact does prayer have on temptation? Read Matthew 26:41 in the margin. Then check the correct answer.
❑ **If you pray, you will not be tempted.**
☑ **Through prayer you can resist temptation.**

The verse from Matthew that you read contains words spoken by Jesus when He was in the garden of Gethsemane with the disciples. He knew that they would need more than willing spirits to withstand the temptation ahead of them. He knew that they needed to be fortified with prayer. Prayer does not prevent temptation. Temptation will always occur. Prayer can give you the spiritual strength to resist temptation.

FLEEING TEMPTATION
Evil thoughts and desires may pass through a person's mind. That is temptation. Temptation itself is not sin. Dwelling on those thoughts—letting the mind entertain the idea—*is* sin. When a worldly Christian "window-shops" for sin, the devil comes to the door and invites the worldly Christian in. The worldly Christian responds, "Oh, no, just looking." Yet this person's openness to temptation often leads to sin.

What does the Bible warn a spiritual Christian to do about temptation? Read 2 Timothy 2:22 in the margin. A spiritual Christian is warned to—
☑ **run away from temptation;**
❑ **seek it.**

What does the same verse say that a spiritual Christian is to follow?

To Follow Righteousness, Faith, Love and Peace And Call ou The Name of The Lord

A spiritual Christian is to follow righteousness, faith, love, and peace. If right living; faith in God; and loving, peaceful relationships are the goals, a spiritual Christian has an arsenal of weapons to use in times of temptation.

Reread the case studies on page 118–19. Describe the steps each Christian could take to withstand temptation.

Julie: Need to Remember That her faith need to be Strong in time of trouble, Pray, Read the word talk c a friend

Ken: *Should called his christian*
friend, pastor, prayer partner
Read his bible daily in trouble
trouble, Called up, etc?

Ray: *Should, should, should take*
along his daily word or
bible + Read while
Praying

Julie is a prime candidate for Satan's attack because of her discouragement. She could resist Satan by admitting her frustration in her job hunt while remembering God's faithfulness to her in the past and seeking assurance from Scripture that He cares about His children. She could ask other Christians to give her other tips for finding a job. She could consider other sources of financial help if she feels that she is becoming destitute.

Resisting temptation during physical pain like Ken's takes strength of character that only the Holy Spirit makes possible. Ken could lay his physical condition and his future at the foot of the cross, believing that he can trust the days ahead to the God who created him and preserved him until this time. He could acknowledge his feelings of loneliness and helplessness. He could pray about his options, including other courses of treatment or other medical opinions. He could examine alternative ways of generating income for his family, such as working at home or working part-time, until his health improves.

Ray's arrogance and self-importance are ways Satan is gaining a foothold in his life. The Holy Spirit can convict Ray of sin in his life and can bring him to seek forgiveness. Ray could reexamine his use of time and resources. Besides returning to regular fellowship with believers, he could spend some of his leisuretime in ministry programs of the church. Instead of placing self-gratification at the center of his life, he could focus on Christ as his main priority.

Everyone, even a spiritual person, sins. What should you do when the Holy Spirit convicts you of sin in your life? Read 1 John 1:9-10 in the margin and write *true* beside the correct statement:

_____ 1. You should say that you have not sinned.

_____✓_____ 2. You should confess your sin.

_____ 3. You should punish yourself for your sin.

"If we confess our sins, he is faithful and just and will forgive us our sins and purify us from all unrighteousness. If we claim we have not sinned, we make him out to be a liar and his word has no place in our lives" (1 John 1:9-10).

DAILY MASTER COMMUNICATION GUIDE

JOB 1

What God said to me:

_____

_____

_____

_____

_____

_____

_____

What I said to God:

_____

_____

_____

_____

_____

_____

_____

_____

_____

No one is above sin. God wants you to confess sin. Confession enables God to keep His promise to forgive you. The correct statement is 2.

Whom do you know who needs to hear the healing message that God forgives sin? Many persons within your circles of influence live in the bondage of sin, not knowing that they can claim God's promise to wipe away their sins. Your testimony can help you share that good news.

 Continue to work on your testimony, using the ideas your leader gave you last week. Remember to limit it to three minutes. Be ready to give your testimony at the Testimony Workshop that follows this study.

What do this week's Scripture-memory verses say that you are to do about the sin in your life?

_____

_____

Say aloud this week's Scripture-memory verses. Then review the verses you memorized during the previous weeks of this study.

During your quiet time today read Job 1, which describes Job's refusal to sin in the face of discouragement. See how God speaks to you through this passage. Then complete the Daily Master Communication Guide in the margin.

APPLYING THE DISCIPLE'S PERSONALITY

Practice explaining in your own words how to apply the Disciple's Personality, using Galatians 5:16-25. Your leader should have explained how to do this in your previous group session. On the basic diagram on the following page, close the door of the flesh as you draw a cross in the center of the circle to encompass _spirit, flesh, mind, will,_ and _emotions._ Write _crucified_ across _flesh._ Now write _walk, led,_ and _live_ above the circle and draw an arrow above these words pointing up. Write _fruit of the Spirit_ above the arrow and draw above these words another upward arrow pointing to _God._ Then write _lusts_ and _desires_ below the circle with an arrow pointing down toward _works of the flesh._ Draw another arrow that points down toward _Satan._ See page 140 if you need help with your drawing.

GOD

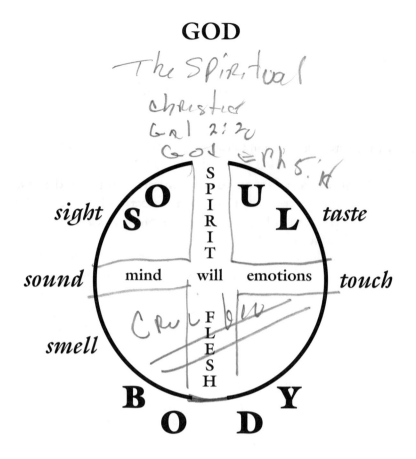

The Spiritual
Christia
Gal 2:20
God = Ph 5:k

(Diagram text:)
SOUL
sight — taste
sound — mind | will | emotions — touch
SPIRIT
Crucified
FLESH
smell
BODY

SATAN

Now write your explanation here.

_____

_____

_____

_____

_____

_____

DAY 5

Victory in Jesus

Once as I returned on a flight from a speaking engagement, a young woman who attended the conference sat down next to my wife and me and told one of the most amazing stories about victorious living that I have ever heard. She now lets her light shine in a country that allows little access to the gospel, but she described a life that began anything but victoriously.

The young woman was one of six children of an alcoholic father. By the age of 13 she was living on the street on her own. From there her life spiraled downward. Yet through determination she went to college, got a degree in elementary education, and started teaching. She noticed that one of her students, a nine-year-old girl, seemed different. After school she helped erase the chalkboard and clean the room, and the two became good friends. One day the student asked the woman if she went to church. The woman answered that she used to go to confession with her mother. The girl asked her teacher to help her learn Scripture verses she needed to learn before being baptized. The first Scripture was John 3:16. When the woman read it, she cried. "I couldn't imagine that God loved me after what I had done," the woman recalled.

The woman then attended a church service and cried all the way through it. "I talked to my live-in boyfriend and told him that we needed to change," she said. One day when he was away, she returned home to find a man ransacking her apartment in search of money. When she could give him no money, he raped her. The woman recounted what happened next: "After it was over, I opened the Bible to John 3:16, which was the only verse I knew. Then he said that he knew what he had done was wrong but that his mother was sick and needed money. He asked me to forgive him. I responded, 'If God is willing to forgive me for all I've done, how can I refuse to forgive you?' We knelt, and he asked for forgiveness. Asking forgiveness for my sinful lifestyle, I turned over my life to Christ. Two weeks later I went back to church and made my profession of faith. My boyfriend would not change, so I moved out."

The woman then began praying for her parents' salvation. Six years later, they gave their lives to Christ. She began serving at church, then went on mission trips to Mexico and Belize. Now she serves as a missionary. She concluded her story: "I praise God for His goodness and His love. I am thankful that I can show His love to people who don't know anything about Him."

As she returned to her seat on the plane, I said to myself: "O the depth of riches both of the wisdom and knowledge of God! How unsearchable are His ... ways" (Rom. 11:33, KJV). After I heard the

"If God is willing to forgive me for all I've done, how can I refuse to forgive you?"

way Christ had graciously forgiven her and had helped her become a fervent, bright witness for Him, I understood even more clearly the victory we have in Christ.

Because of the cross, God forgives and accepts you, just like the woman on the plane. Therefore, you have no need to try to make things right yourself or to give up in despair. From the cross Jesus gives you His righteousness as you are crucified and resurrected with Him.

Jesus assures His disciples that those who suffer with Him will someday reign with him (see 2 Tim. 2:11-13 in the margin). His victory points to the future, but it is also present tense.

IN THE CARPENTER'S SHOP

How has the Holy Spirit been working in you this week to build Christlike character? How are you progressing in getting rid of the old self and in letting the Spirit add new behaviors to your life?

Complete the following as you think about the changes related to greed that you identified earlier this week.

Something I have been getting rid of this week:

_____

Something Christ has been adding to my character this week:

_____

Stop and thank God for the gift of the Holy Spirit to help mold you into Christlikeness.

Meditate on the moral and spiritual victories Jesus has won for you during the past few weeks. Identify areas of your life in which you are still suffering defeat.

_____

_____

Review the seven steps to Christlike character listed at the end of the Disciple's Personality presentation (p. 139). What steps do you need to take to achieve victory in every area of your life?

_____

_____

_____

"If we died with him,
* we will also live with him;*
If we endure,
* we will also reign with him.*
if we disown him,
* he will also disown us;*
if we are faithless,
* he will remain faithful,*
* for he cannot disown himself"*
(2 Tim. 2:11-13).

APPLYING THE DISCIPLE'S PERSONALITY

Now that you are approaching the end of *MasterLife 2: The Disciple's Personality*, you are asked to demonstrate your knowledge of the Disciple's Personality, which you have been learning throughout this study. Draw and explain in your own words the Disciple's Personality to another group member. Say the verses that go with it. See pages 133–39 if you need help.

I hope that you have found worthwhile your Scripture memorization during this study. You have memorized six Scriptures that accompany various aspects of the Disciple's Personality. Nothing you have done in this study has been without an investment of time. I hope that this process has helped you hide God's Word in your heart so that you can use it, along with the concepts of the Disciple's Personality, in a variety of situations.

Write the verses you have memorized during this study. See how well you can remember them without looking back. Be prepared to say them to a partner at the Testimony Workshop at the end of this study.

Romans 6:12-13: _____

_____

Ephesians 5:18: _____

_____

Philippians 2:13: _____

_____

Romans 12:1-2: _____

_____

Galatians 5:22-23: _____

1 Corinthians 6:19-20: _____

_____

THE TESTIMONY WORKSHOP

As you have participated in this study, you have learned essential elements for writing your Christian testimony, which you should be ready to present at the Testimony Workshop that follows this study. I hope that this will be a meaningful experience for you.

✝ **Practice giving your testimony to others as you prepare to present it during the Testimony Workshop at the conclusion of this study. Remember to limit it to three minutes. Be prepared to present it in a variety of situations—to a skeptical person, to someone who is eager to hear, to someone who believes that he or she can earn salvation, and so on.**

✝ **During your quiet time today read 2 Timothy 2, in which Paul instructed Timothy about claiming victory in Christ. Then complete the Daily Master Communication Guide in the margin.**

HAS THIS WEEK MADE A DIFFERENCE?

Review "My Walk with the Master This Week" at the beginning of this week's material. Mark the activities you have finished by drawing vertical lines in the diamonds beside them. Finish any incomplete activities.

Congratulations on completing your study of *MasterLife 2: The Disciple's Personality*. I hope that the concept of life in the Spirit has new meaning for you after these six weeks of study. Examining the warring components of your personality is challenging, often requiring that you admit your weaknesses and temptations even though you like to think of yourself as someone who does not easily stumble. I pray that this process has made you more aware of the vulnerable areas of your life so that you can be more alert to times when you need to close the door of the flesh. May the Holy Spirit strengthen you as you claim victory in Christ.

What a great time of fellowship and growth you have to look forward to when you attend the Testimony Workshop! By now your leader has probably given you details about this workshop. I predict that you will be moved in ways you cannot imagine when you hear reports of ways the Holy Spirit has worked in group members' lives. Most importantly, you will be empowered and motivated as you refine and polish your own three-minute testimony and prepare to share it with persons who need to hear it. The workshop will give you strength and courage to bear witness that you never thought you could experience. Furthermore, you will receive an exciting preview of *MasterLife 3: The Disciple's Victory*, which I hope you are planning to study next. You have great days ahead as a disciple of Jesus Christ!

DAILY MASTER COMMUNICATION GUIDE

2 TIMOTHY 2

What God said to me:

_____

_____

_____

_____

_____

_____

What I said to God:

_____

_____

_____

_____

_____

_____

_____

_____

The Disciple's Cross

The Disciple's Cross provides an instrument for visualizing and understanding your opportunities and responsibilities as a disciple of Christ. It depicts the six biblical disciplines of a balanced Christian life. *MasterLife 1: The Disciple's Cross* interprets the biblical meanings of the disciplines and illustrates in detail how to draw and present the Disciple's Cross.

Because *MasterLife 2: The Disciple's Personality* refers to elements of the Disciple's Cross and your weekly work includes assignments related to the six disciplines, a brief overview of the Disciple's Cross is provided here.

As a disciple of Jesus Christ, you have—
1 Lord as the first priority of your life;
2 relationships: a vertical relationship with God and horizontal relationships with others;
3 commitments: deny self, take up your cross daily, and follow Christ;
4 resources to center your life in Christ: the Word, prayer, fellowship, and witness;
5 ministries that grow from the four resources: teaching/preaching, worship/intercession, nurture, evangelism, and service;
6 disciplines of a disciple: spend time with the Master, live in the Word, pray in faith, fellowship with believers, witness to the world, and minister to others. By practicing these biblical principles, you can abide in Christ and can be useful in the Master's service.

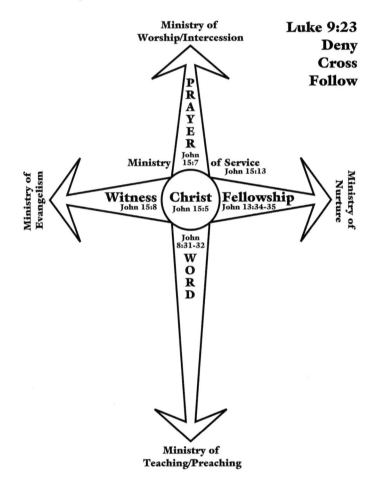

Ministry of Worship/Intercession

Luke 9:23
**Deny
Cross
Follow**

PRAYER
John 15:7

Ministry of Service
John 15:13

Ministry of Evangelism

Witness
John 15:8

Christ
John 15:5

Fellowship
John 13:34-35

Ministry of Nurture

John 8:31-32
WORD

Ministry of Teaching/Preaching

The Disciple's Personality

The Disciple's Personality is the focal point for all you learn in *MasterLife 2: The Disciple's Personality*. This presentation provides an instrument for understanding why you think, feel, and act as you do and explains how to become more Christlike in character and behavior.

Following are step-by-step instructions for presenting the Disciple's Personality to another person. Each week of this study you learn an additional portion of the presentation and the Scripture that accompanies it. As you learn the Disciple's Personality and review it in the future, you may find it helpful to refer to this step-by-step explanation and to the drawings. Do not attempt to memorize this presentation. You will learn how to present it in your own words. Do not feel overwhelmed by the amount of material involved. You will learn it in weekly segments. By the end of the study you will be able to explain the entire Disciple's Personality and to say all of the verses that accompany it.

To explain the Disciple's Personality to someone, use blank, unlined sheets of paper to draw the illustrations shown. Instructions to you are in parentheses. The material that follows is the presentation you make to the other person. The words in **bold type** indicate when to add to your drawings.

Perhaps you sometimes wonder why you think, feel, and act as you do. May I draw an illustration that helped me understand myself? This drawing illustrates biblical teachings about your personality. It shows you how to make Christ Master of your life and how to master life.

A UNIFIED PERSONALITY

(Draw an incomplete circle in the center of a blank sheet of paper, leaving spaces at the top and the bottom of the circle as shown below. Write the word *God* above the circle.) **God** created you as a physical and spiritual being. The physical part came from the earth.

The spiritual part originated in God's Spirit. The circle represents you—your total personality. The Bible describes you as a unity. That's why I drew one circle to represent your personality. I will add each element of your personality as I explain it. When you understand each element of your personality and how it functions, you will discover how to integrate your personality under the lordship of Christ.

Body

(Write *body* beneath the circle. Write the five senses on each side of the circle as illustrated below.) The Bible

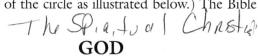

GOD

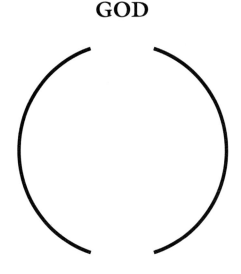

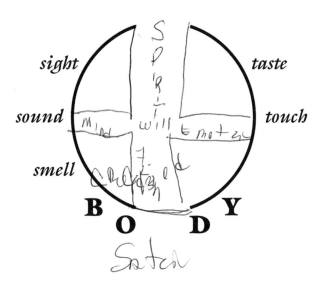

pictures you as a **body.** God made your body from the earth to serve several functions. Through your body you are able to participate in the physical world. Your **five senses** relate you to the rest of God's creation. Your body makes it possible to communicate with the world around you and with other living creatures. Your body gives you a physical identity that makes you a distinct, unique personality. God created your body good.

Soul

(Write the word *soul* inside the circle as illustrated. Write the words *mind, will,* and *emotions* as illustrated. Write the word *spirit* as illustrated below.) The Bible also pictures you as a **soul.** You do not just have a soul; you *are* a soul. Genesis 2:7 says that the first human being became a living soul when God breathed into his nostrils the breath of life. God imparted His life to the

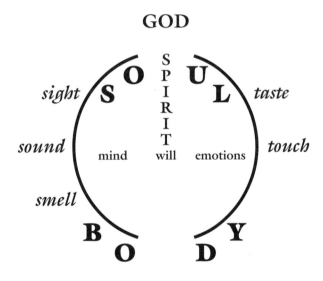

person He had made. The words for *soul* in the Bible generally mean *life* or *the total self.* When the Bible says that a person's soul is saved or lost, it refers to the total person. Sometimes the word for *soul* means *heart* or *the seat of the will, desires, and affection—the inner human being.* The word *psyche* originates from the Greek word for *soul.* The soul's ability to think, will, and feel provides additional evidence that human beings are created in the image of God. These three elements—**mind, will, and emotions**—help form your distinctive personality.

Spirit

The Bible also pictures you as **spirit.** Your spirit directly relates you to God's image. It gives you the capacity to be aware of yourself and to fellowship and work with God. People and God are able to communicate directly. When God finished creating the first person, Genesis 1:31 says, "It was very good."[1]

THE NATURAL PERSON

The Flesh

(Write *Satan* beneath the circle.) Soon after the creation another spiritual being entered God's good creation. Humanity succumbed to **Satan's** temptation and disobeyed God. A different aspect of the spiritual nature entered the personality of human beings. That aspect is called the flesh. The Bible uses the word *flesh* in two ways. The general meaning is *body,* referring to the physical body. The other meaning is symbolic, referring to the lower nature. It refers to the human capacity to sin and to follow Satan instead of God.

(Draw two open doors on the inside of the circle. Draw a handle inside each door.) Notice that the illustration has two doors. The top door, **the door of the spirit,** allows you to relate to God. The bottom door, **the door of the flesh,** allows you to relate to Satan. God created human beings with free will. Notice that the will stands between the door of the spirit and the door of the flesh and that the door handles are on the

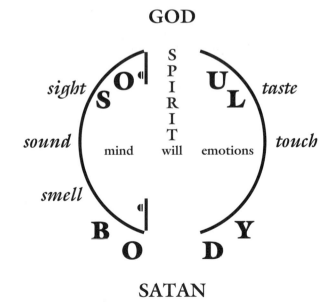

inside. Unfortunately, when Adam and Eve, the first human beings, were tempted by Satan, they chose to turn from God's leading to follow Satan's leading. At that moment the human being's ego, the big *I,* took over. (Draw lines between the two doors to form an *I* as illustrated below. Close the door of the spirit by completing the circle at the top. Draw a line through the word *spirit* as shown. Write *flesh* as illustrated. Leave the door of the flesh open.) The door of the **spirit** closed, and humanity died spiritually. The door of the **flesh** opened, and the sinful nature became the spiritual part of human personality. The results were terrible. The flesh came alive, causing the mind, will, and emotions to degenerate. The entire personality—body, soul, and spirit—was infiltrated by evil and death.

GOD

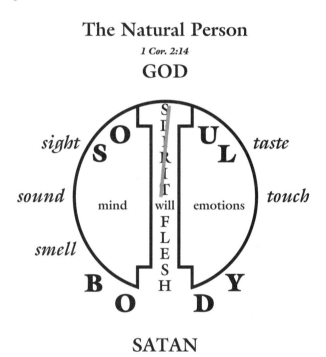

SATAN

Through Satan's temptation humanity transgressed God's command and fell from its original innocence. Consequently, the descendants of the first sinful human beings inherit a nature and an environment inclined toward sin. As soon as they are capable of moral action, they become transgressors and are responsible to God for closing the door of the spirit and for shutting Him out.

The Condition of the Natural Person Today
(Write *The Natural Person* and *1 Corinthians 2:14* above the drawing.) **The natural person** is centered in himself or herself and is open to Satan's temptation and power. This person is unable to relate to God proper-

ly. **First Corinthians 2:14** says, "The man without the Spirit does not accept the things that come from the Spirit of God, for they are foolishness to him, and he cannot understand them, because they are spiritually discerned."

Your thoughts are influenced by evil; your emotions control you; your will is weak. Even strong-willed and disciplined persons are not able to overcome the effects of the flesh. No matter how many good things you do, the Bible says that a natural person cannot please God. People can come to God only as the Holy Spirit draws them.

The Natural Person
1 Cor. 2:14
GOD

SATAN

God loves you even though you have sinned. He sent His only Son to pay for your sins so that you would not perish but have eternal life. Jesus died on the cross to save you from sin and death and to bring you to God. After His resurrection He sent the Holy Spirit to earth to draw you to God.

The Holy Spirit can speak to a natural person even though the door of the spirit is closed. When you open the door of the spirit, the Spirit of God enters your personality, and your spirit is born again.

(If you are using this illustration with a lost person, move directly to the section "The Spiritual Christian." If you are talking with a Christian, proceed with "The Worldly Christian.")

THE WORLDLY CHRISTIAN
(Draw the illustration shown below. It is the same as the previous one without the line through *spirit* and with both doors left open. Write *The Worldly Christian* and *1 Corinthians 3:1-3* above the diagram.) Now I will draw the same **circle** to illustrate the worldly Christian. This person has **opened the door of the spirit** but has also **left open the door of flesh**. This person still lives in the flesh even though he or she has

The Worldly Christian
1 Cor. 3:1-3
GOD

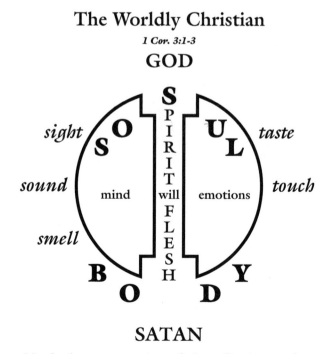

SATAN

been born again. At some point this person realized that Christ could give him or her eternal life. This person opened the door of the spirit and was born again by the power of the Holy Spirit. This Christian was made alive and became a partaker of the divine nature but failed to grow as he or she should.

Second Peter 1:3-4 says: "His divine power has given us everything we need for life and godliness through our knowledge of him who called us by his own glory and goodness. Through these he has given us his very great and precious promises, so that through them you may participate in the divine nature and escape the corruption in the world caused by evil desires." This passage then lists character traits a Christian needs to add as he or she grows: "Make every effort to add to your faith goodness; and to goodness, knowledge; and to knowledge, self-control; and to self-control, perseverance; and to perseverance, godliness; and to godliness,

brotherly kindness; and to brotherly kindness, love" (2 Pet. 1:5-7). If the person does not do this, he or she will be ineffective, unproductive, nearsighted, and blind. The person will have "forgotten that he has been cleansed from his past sins" (2 Pet. 1:9). These characteristics describe the worldly Christian. Christians who are not taught how to grow and live in the Spirit remain as they were when they were born again. They are still babies in the faith, although they may have been believers for many years. **First Corinthians 3:1-3** describes this person's immature spiritual life: "Brothers, I could not address you as spiritual but as worldly—mere infants in Christ. I gave you milk, not solid food, for you were not yet ready for it. Indeed, you are still not ready. You are still worldly."

(Trace over the letter *s* with a capital *S* as shown below.) I will trace over the letter *s* in *spirit* with a **capital *S*** to show that the Holy Spirit is eternally a part of your spirit when you are born again. The worldly Christian's big mistake is having left open the door of the flesh. Satan still has access to this person, because the flesh dominates his or her thoughts, will, and emotions. The word *worldly* means *fleshly* or *carnal*. This type of Christian is more likely to follow the physical senses and fallen nature than the spiritual nature he or she received at conversion.

The Worldly Christian
1 Cor. 3:1-3
GOD

SATAN

No doubt you sometimes feel conflict in your heart when you try to have the thoughts, attitudes, and actions of Jesus. Why does such conflict arise? If you do not allow Christ continually to be the Master of your life through His Spirit, you are a worldly Christian. Although you have allowed Christ to enter your life, you still struggle to control your own life. The big *I* of the old, natural person still dominates you. Worldly Christians continually open the door of the flesh, allowing the old nature to determine what they think, do, and feel, rather than follow the Spirit of God.

Competing influences cause this conflict in your personality. You hear Satan's voice through your flesh, and you hear God's voice as His Spirit speaks to your spirit. You hear the voice of self through your mind, will, and emotions. You become a battleground. How can you have victory in this kind of situation? Do not despair. Christ wants to be your Lord and to give you daily victory.

THE SPIRITUAL CHRISTIAN

(Draw another circle with the labels you used previously. Add the cross in the center as shown below. Leave the door of the spirit open and close the door of the flesh. Write *The Spiritual Christian* and *Galatians 2:20* above the circle as illustrated. Write *crucified* across *flesh.*) I will draw the **circle** once more to illustrate the spiritual Christian. As Christ's disciple, you are promised victory over the world, the flesh, and the devil. Here is how. Notice that your **will** is located

between **the door of the spirit** and **the door of the flesh.** The door of the spirit is open, while the door of the flesh is closed. When you are willing to let Christ master your life, His death on the cross and His resurrection give you a life of victory. You can say, as the apostle Paul did in **Galatians 2:20:** "I have been crucified with Christ and I no longer live, but Christ lives in me. The life I live in the body, I live by faith in the Son of God, who loved me and gave himself for me."

The way to have victory is to consider your flesh **crucified.** Because this is an ongoing act of your will, the indwelling Christ helps you keep the door of the spirit open and the door of the flesh closed. As you put your old self to death, the Spirit of God gives you life daily to live in victory. When you do this, you are filled with the Spirit of God. You are able to live in the Spirit. God takes control of your mind, your will, your emotions, and therefore your soul and body.

Now you can see the contrast between the natural person and the worldly Christian. You can also see that the **spiritual Christian** walks in the Spirit so that he or she will not yield to the desires of the flesh.

STEPS TO VICTORIOUS LIVING

(Write *Philippians 2:13* under *will.* Write *Ephesians 5:18* above *Spirit.* Write *Romans 12:2* under *mind.* Write *Galatians 5:22-23* under *emotions.* Write *Romans 6:12-13* under *flesh.* Read or quote these

The Spiritual Christian
Gal. 2:20
GOD

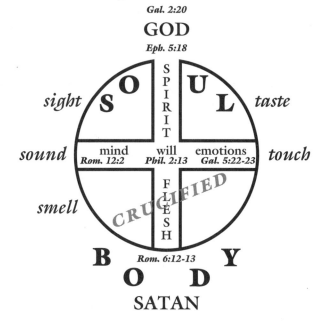

The Spiritual Christian
Gal. 2:20
GOD
Eph. 5:18

Scriptures as you write.) Your victory is not automatic. As long as you live in your body, you continually fight the good fight of faith. But God promises you victory. Let me explain in practical terms how to let Christ master your total personality and how to let Him enable you to live in the Spirit.

Philippians 2:13 says, "It is God who works in you to will and to act according to his good purpose." God helps you want to do His will and then gives you the ability to do it. By an act of your will, claim Galatians 2:20 as your own experience.

Ephesians 5:18 says, "Be filled with the Spirit." Ask the Holy Spirit to fill your personality and to keep filling you so that He can guide you, teach you, and give you the power to be a spiritual person.

Romans 12:2 says: "Do not conform any longer to the pattern of this world, but be transformed by the renewing of your mind. Then you will be able to test and approve what God's will is—his good, pleasing and perfect will."

Galatians 5:22-23 says: "The fruit of the Spirit is love, joy, peace, patience, kindness, goodness, faithfulness, gentleness and self-control. Against such things there is no law." As you allow the Spirit of God to fill you, He produces in you the fruit of the Spirit. The fruit of the Spirit helps produce the right emotions in you and helps you control your emotions.

Romans 6:12-13 says: "Do not let sin reign in your mortal body so that you obey its evil desires. Do not offer the parts of your body to sin, as instruments of wickedness, but rather offer yourselves to God, as those who have been brought from death to life; and offer the parts of your body to him as instruments of righteousness." Your body is God's gift to you so that you can have an identity, participate in this world, and communicate with others. It is not evil in itself; only the flesh or your sinful nature is evil. Jesus came to live in your body to make it an instrument of righteousness instead of an instrument of sin. Present your body and all of its members to God to do good.

(Write *1 Corinthians 6:19-20* on one side of the circle and *Romans 12:1* on the other side of the circle.) The idea of punishing the body because it is evil is not a Christian idea. **First Corinthians 6:19-20** says: "Do you not know that your body is a temple of the Holy Spirit, who is in you, whom you have received from God? You are not your own; you were bought at a

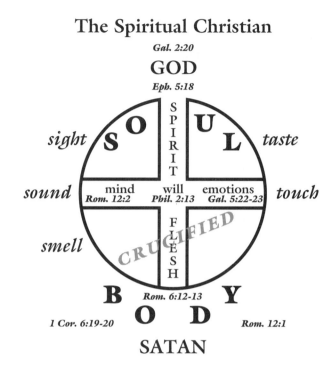

The Spiritual Christian

Gal. 2:20

GOD

Eph. 5:18

SOUL
SPIRIT
sight S U *taste*
sound mind will emotions *touch*
Rom. 12:2 Phil. 2:13 Gal. 5:22-23
smell CRUCIFIED
FLESH
B Rom. 6:12-13 **Y**
1 Cor. 6:19-20 **O D** *Rom. 12:1*
SATAN

price. Therefore honor God with your body." **Romans 12:1** says, "I urge you, brothers, in view of God's mercy, to offer your bodies as living sacrifices, holy and pleasing to God—this is your spiritual act of worship." Christ's incarnation in a human body shows its potential for being restored to its original condition when Christ returns again and gives you a spiritual body like His.

As you fully yield yourself to God, the Holy Spirit helps you master your mind, your will, your emotions, your body, and your soul through the power of Christ. The life you live now, you live "by faith in the Son of God," as Galatians 2:20 says. As you obey Christ and His commands, He lives in you and you in Him. Christ lives in the world through you. Your inner self is integrated, and you experience peace. You are continually being filled with the Holy Spirit, and you overflow with joy, love, peace, praise, and thanksgiving. Rivers of living water flow from you to other persons as a witness to Christ, who lives in you through the Spirit.

WHO ARE YOU?

Now evaluate your life.

- Are you a natural person whose spirit is dead? Do your bodily senses and your natural desires control you?
- Are you a worldly Christian who has allowed Christ to enter your life but is still being mastered

by the desires of the flesh? Is the big *I* still in control?

- Are you a spiritual Christian who has been crucified with Christ and is being controlled by the Holy Spirit?

(Write *1 Thessalonians 5:23-24* under *Galatians 2:20*.) **First Thessalonians 5:23-24** says: "May God himself, the God of peace, sanctify you through and through. May your whole spirit, soul and body be kept blameless at the coming of our Lord Jesus Christ. The one who calls you is faithful and he will do it."

Spiritual Christians are not perfect, but daily they crucify the flesh and consciously allow the Holy Spirit to fill them. When they are tempted, they invite Christ to fill their lives, and they close the door of the flesh. When they sin, they ask for God's forgiveness and strength to help them overcome the next temptation.

Remember these seven steps to Christlike character:

1. Ask God, through the Holy Spirit's guidance, to help you *will* to do the right thing.
2. Open the door of the *spirit* to the Spirit of God by asking Him to fill you.
3. Close the door of the *flesh* to Satan by confessing your sins and by claiming Christ's crucifixion of the flesh.
4. Renew your *mind* by saturating it with the Word of God.
5. Allow the Holy Spirit to master your *emotions* by producing the fruit of the Spirit in you.
6. Present your *body* to Christ as an instrument of righteousness.
7. Love the Lord your God with all your *heart,* with all your *soul,* with all your *mind,* and with all your *strength.*

———

[1]Some people believe that the soul and the spirit are the same rather than two distinct aspects of your personality. Their function is the same whether you think of your soul as having three parts (body, soul, and spirit) or two parts (body and soul, with the spirit being seen as the part of the soul). Although people who hold to each position believe they have a biblical basis for their position, your view of this matter does not affect the meaning of this presentation. It deals with the battle between the flesh and the spirit, not between the soul and the spirit.

The Spiritual Christian
Gal. 2:20
1 Thess. 5:23-24
GOD
Eph. 5:18

sight — SOUL — *taste*

SPIRIT

sound — mind / will / emotions — *touch*
Rom. 12:2 / Phil. 2:13 / Gal. 5:22-23

FLESH

smell — CRUCIFIED

BODY
Rom. 6:12-13
1 Cor. 6:19-20   *Rom. 12:1*
SATAN

Applying the Disciple's Personality

James 4:1-8

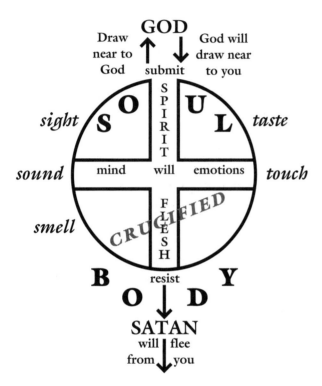

Galatians 5:16-25

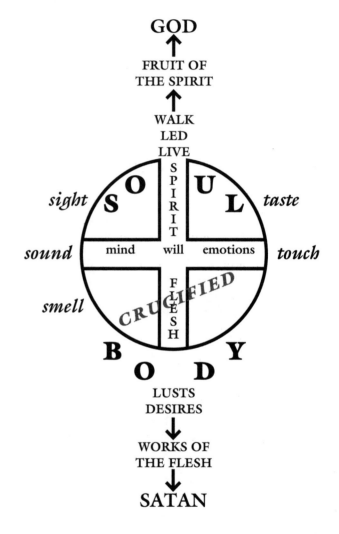

Hearing the Word

Date _____ **Place** _____

Speaker _____ **Text** _____

Title _____

Message
Points, explanation, illustrations, application:

_____

_____

_____

_____

_____

_____

_____

_____

_____

_____

_____

_____

_____

_____

_____

_____

Summary

The main thing the speaker wants me to do, be, and/or feel as a result of this message:

_____

_____

_____

_____

Application to My Life

What did God say to me through this message?

_____

_____

_____

How does my life measure up to this word?

_____

_____

_____

What action(s) will I take to bring my life in line with this word?

_____

_____

_____

_____

What truth do I need to study further?

_____

_____

Prayer-Covenant List

Request	Date	Bible Promise	Answer	Date

CHRISTIAN GROWTH STUDY PLAN
Preparing Christians to Serve

In the **Christian Growth Study Plan (formerly the Church Study Course)** *MasterLife 2: The Disciple's Personality* is a resource for course credit in the subject area Personal Life in the Christian Growth category of diploma plans. To receive credit, read the book; complete the learning activities; attend group sessions; show your work to your pastor, a staff member, or a church leader; and complete the following information. This page may be duplicated. Send the completed page to:

**Christian Growth Study Plan
127 Ninth Avenue, North, MSN 117
Nashville, TN 37234-0117
FAX: (615) 251-5067**

For information about the Christian Growth Study Plan, refer to the current *Christian Growth Study Plan Catalog*. Your church office may have a copy. If not, request a free copy from the Christian Growth Study Plan office, (615) 251-2525.

MasterLife 2: The Disciple's Personality
COURSE NUMBER: CG-0169
PARTICIPANT INFORMATION

Social Security Number	Personal CGSP Number*	Date of Birth

Name (First, MI, Last)
☐Mr. ☐Miss
☐Mrs. ☐

Home Phone

Address (Street, Route, or P.O. Box) | City, State | ZIP

CHURCH INFORMATION

Church Name

Address (Street, Route, or P.O. Box) | City, State | ZIP

CHANGE REQUEST ONLY

☐Former Name

☐Former Address | City, State | ZIP

☐Former Church | City, State | ZIP

Signature of Pastor, Conference Leader, or Other Church Leader | Date

*New participants are requested but not required to give SS# and date of birth. Existing participants, please give CGSP# when using SS# for the first time.
Thereafter, only one ID# is required. *Mail to:* Christian Growth Study Plan, 127 Ninth Ave., North, MSN 117, Nashville, TN 37234-0117. Fax: (615) 251-5067.

THE DISCIPLE'S VICTORY

MasterLife

BOOK 3

Avery T. Willis, Jr.
Kay Moore

Dorothy Echols
1508 Forsyth Rd
Savannah, Ga 31406
912- 352- 8048

LifeWay Press
Nashville, Tennessee

ISBN 0-7673-2581-8
Dewey Decimal Classification: 248.4
Subject Heading: DISCIPLESHIP

This book is text for course CG-0170 in the subject area Personal Life in the Christian Growth Study Plan.

Unless otherwise noted, Scripture quotations are from the Holy Bible,
New International Version,
copyright © 1973, 1978, 1984 by International Bible Society.

Scripture quotations marked AMP are from *The Amplified New Testament* © The Lockman Foundation
1954, 1958, 1987. Used by permission.

Scripture quotations marked Phillips are printed with permission of Macmillan Publishing Co., Inc.
from J. B. Phillips: *The New Testament in Modern English,* Revised Edition. © J. B. Phillips 1958, 1960, 1972.

Scripture quotations marked RSV are from the *Revised Standard Version of the Bible,*
copyrighted © 1946, 1952, 1971, 1973.

Printed in the United States of America

Design: Edward Crawford
Cover illustration: Mick Wiggins

LifeWay Press
127 Ninth Avenue, North
Nashville, Tennessee 37234

Contents

The Authors

AVERY T. WILLIS, JR., the author and developer of *MasterLife*, is the senior vice-president of overseas operations at the International Mission Board of the Southern Baptist Convention. The original *MasterLife: Discipleship Training for Leaders*, published in 1980, has been used by more than 250,000 people in the United States and has been translated into more than 50 different languages for use by untold thousands. Willis is also the author of *Indonesian Revival: Why Two Million Came to Christ*, *The Biblical Basis of Missions*, *MasterBuilder: Multiplying Leaders*, *BibleGuide to Discipleship and Doctrine*, and several books in Indonesian.

Willis served for 10 years as a pastor in Oklahoma and Texas and for 14 years as a missionary to Indonesia, during which he served for 6 years as the president of the Indonesian Baptist Theological Seminary. Before assuming his present position, he served as the director of the Adult Department of the Discipleship and Family Development Division, the Sunday School Board of the Southern Baptist Convention, where he introduced the Lay Institute for Equipping (LIFE), a series of in-depth discipleship courses.

KAY MOORE served as the coauthor of this updated edition of *MasterLife*. Formerly a design editor in the Adult Department of the Discipleship and Family Development Division, the Sunday School Board of the Southern Baptist Convention, she led the editorial team that produced the LIFE Support Series, biblically based courses that help people deal with critical issues in their lives. A writer, editor, and conference leader, Moore has authored or coauthored numerous books on family life, relationships, and inspirational topics. She is the author of *Gathering the Missing Pieces in an Adopted Life* and is a frequent contributor to religious magazines and devotional guides.

Introduction

MasterLife is a developmental, small-group discipleship process that will help you develop a lifelong, obedient relationship with Christ. This book, *MasterLife 3: The Disciple's Victory,* is the third of four books in that discipleship process. The other three books are *MasterLife 1: The Disciple's Cross, MasterLife 2: The Disciple's Personality,* and *MasterLife 4: The Disciple's Mission.* These studies will enable you to acknowledge Christ as your Master and to master life in Him.

WHAT'S IN IT FOR YOU

The goal of *MasterLife* is your discipleship—for you to become like Christ. To do that, you must follow Jesus, learn to do the things He instructed His followers to do, and help others become His disciples. In these ways *MasterLife* will enable you to discover the satisfaction of following Christ as His disciple and the joy of that relationship with Him. *MasterLife* was designed to help you make the following definition of *discipleship* a way of life:

> Christian discipleship is developing a personal, lifelong, obedient relationship with Jesus Christ in which He transforms your character into Christlikeness; changes your values into Kingdom values; and involves you in His mission in the home, the church, and the world.

In *MasterLife 1: The Disciple's Cross* you explored your personal relationship with Jesus Christ. You learned how to draw the Disciple's Cross to illustrate the balanced life Christ wants His disciples to have. You learned that Christ wants to be at the center of your life so that everything you do is an outgrowth of your relationship with Him.

In *MasterLife 2: The Disciple's Personality* you focused on Christ's transforming your character into Christlikeness through the work of the Holy Spirit. You learned how to live a life of victory by building Christlike character. You were introduced to your personal counselor, the Holy Spirit, who lives in you and teaches, guides, directs, prays for, and empowers you to do God's will and work.

This book, *MasterLife 3: The Disciple's Victory,* was designed to help you achieve victory in spiritual warfare. While in book 2 you focused on inner victory, in book 3 you will focus on outer victory as you learn how to advance against the enemy in spiritual warfare. This study also introduces you to the Spiritual Armor. You will learn the defensive weapons of the Spiritual Armor, which protect you, and the offensive weapons, which lead you to advance against the world, the flesh, and the devil. You will learn how to demolish your personal spiritual strongholds and to "take captive every thought to make it obedient to Christ" (2 Cor. 10:5). You will learn to believe God for all He wants to do through you as you practice the six disciplines you learned in *MasterLife 1: The Disciple's Cross:*

- Spend time with the Master
- Live in the Word
- Pray in faith
- Fellowship with believers
- Witness to the world
- Minister to others

THE *MASTERLIFE* PROCESS

MasterLife 3: The Disciple's Victory is part of a 24-week discipleship process. Completing all four courses in *MasterLife* will provide you information and experiences you need to be Christ's disciple. Each book builds on the other and is recommended as a prerequisite for the one that follows.

The *MasterLife* process involves six elements. Each element is essential to your study of *MasterLife.*

1. The *daily activities* in this book lead you into a closer walk with Christ. Doing these exercises daily is important.
2. The *weekly assignments* in "My Walk with the Master This Week" are real-life experiences that will change your life.
3. The *leader* is a major element. Discipleship is a relationship. It is not something you do by yourself. You need human models, instruction, and account-

ability to become what Christ intends for you to be. You need a leader to whom you can relate personally and regularly—someone who can teach you, model behaviors, and hold you accountable.

4. The weekly *group sessions* help you reflect on the concepts and experiences in *MasterLife* and help you apply the ideas to your life. The group sessions allow you to experience the profound changes Christ is making in your life. Each group session also provides training for the next stage of spiritual growth.

5. *Christ* is the Discipler, and you become His disciple. As you fully depend on Him, He works through each of the previous elements to support you.

6. The body of Christ—the *church*—is vital for complete discipling to take place. You depend on Christian friends for fellowship, strength, ministry opportunities, and support.

HOW TO STUDY THIS BOOK

Each day for five days a week you will be expected to study a segment of the material in this workbook and to complete the related activities. You may need from 20 to 30 minutes of study time each day. Even if you find that you can study the material in less time, spreading the study over five days will give you time to apply the truths to your life.

You will notice that discipline logos appear before various assignments. These logos look like this:

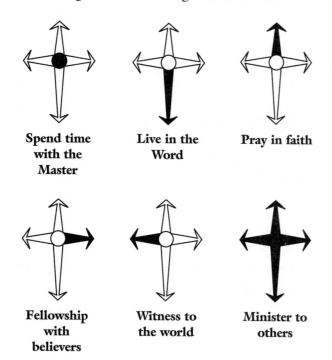

Spend time with the Master	Live in the Word	Pray in faith
Fellowship with believers	Witness to the world	Minister to others

These logos link certain activities to the six disciplines you are learning to incorporate into your life as a disciple. These activities are part of your weekly assignments, which are outlined in "My Walk with the Master This Week" at the beginning of each week's material. The discipline logos differentiate your weekly assignments from the activities related to your study for that particular day.

Set a definite time and select a quiet place to study with little or no interruption. Keep a Bible handy to find Scriptures as directed in the material. Memorizing Scripture is an important part of your work. Set aside a portion of your study period for memory work. Unless I have deliberately chosen another version for a specific emphasis, all Scriptures in *MasterLife* are quoted from the *New International Version* of the Bible. However, feel free to memorize Scripture from any version of the Bible you prefer. I suggest that you write each memory verse on a card that you can review often during the week.

After completing each day's assignments, turn to the beginning of the week's material. If you completed an activity that corresponds to one listed under "My Walk with the Master This Week," place a vertical line in the diamond beside the activity. During the following group session a member of the group will verify your work and will add a horizontal line in the diamond, forming a cross in each diamond. This process will confirm that you have completed each weekly assignment before you continue. You may do the assignments at your own pace, but be sure to complete all of them before the next group session.

THE SPIRITUAL ARMOR

On pages 129–31 you will find the Spiritual Armor presentation. The Spiritual Armor, which explains how to use spiritual resources to fight the forces of evil, will be the focal point for all you learn in this book. Each week you will study an additional portion of the Spiritual Armor. By the end of the study you will be able to explain the Spiritual Armor in your own words. As a follower of Christ, you can learn to live the Spiritual Armor so that it embodies how you live in the world.

Discipleship Covenant

To participate in *MasterLife,* you are asked to dedicate yourself to God and to your *MasterLife* group by making the following commitments. You may not currently be able to do everything listed, but by signing this covenant, you pledge to adopt these practices as you progress through the study.

As a disciple of Jesus Christ, I commit myself to—
- acknowledge Jesus Christ as Lord of my life each day;
- attend all group sessions unless providentially hindered;
- spend from 20 to 30 minutes a day as needed to complete all assignments;
- have a daily quiet time;
- keep a Daily Master Communication Guide about the way God speaks to me and I speak to Him;
- be faithful to my church in attendance and stewardship;
- love and encourage each group member;
- share my faith with others;
- keep in confidence anything that others share in the group sessions;
- submit myself to others willingly in accountability;
- become a discipler of others as God gives opportunities;
- support my church financially by practicing biblical giving;
- pray daily for group members.

Signed _Dorothy L. Echels_____ Date _____

WEEK 1

Overcoming the Enemy

This Week's Goal

You will be able to describe in your own words the spiritual warfare in which we are engaged and to explain how to apply the Spiritual Armor.

My Walk with the Master This Week

You will complete the following activities to develop the six biblical disciplines. When you have completed each activity, draw a vertical line in the diamond beside it.

SPEND TIME WITH THE MASTER
◇ Have a quiet time each day. Check each day you have a quiet time: ❑ Sunday ❑ Monday ❑ Tuesday ❑ Wednesday ❑ Thursday ❑ Friday ❑ Saturday

LIVE IN THE WORD
◇ Read your Bible every day. Write what God says to you and what you say to God.
◇ Memorize 1 John 4:4.
◇ Read "How to Read God's Word."

PRAY IN FAITH
◇ Use "Guide to Thanksgiving" during your prayer time.
◇ Use the Spiritual Armor during your prayer time.

FELLOWSHIP WITH BELIEVERS
◇ Share with someone the Helmet of Salvation part of the Spiritual Armor.

WITNESS TO THE WORLD
◇ List on the Relational-Witnessing Chart the names of persons who do not or may not know Christ. Finish listing your immediate family and relatives.

MINISTER TO OTHERS
◇ Learn the Helmet of Salvation part of the Spiritual Armor.

This Week's Scripture-Memory Verse

"You, dear children, are from God and have overcome them, because the one who is in you is greater than the one who is in the world" (1 John 4:4).

DAY 1

Under Attack

When our family visited Greece on our way home from our first term of missionary service in Indonesia, I began to understand what Paul had in mind when he wrote 2 Corinthians 10:3-5 (in the margin). I rented a Volkswagen "bug" and crowded our four children into it for a tour of the magnificent ruins of the temples, cities, and amphitheaters of the old Greek civilization.

When we reached Corinth, we did not have much time left before we had to return the rental car. Corinth was situated at the base of a huge mountain. We decided that we had enough time to drive to the top, where I had heard that an almost impregnable fortress stood. The little Volkswagen struggled up the mountain until we reached the top. Around the entire top of the mountain was a huge wall wide enough for chariots to drive on. We walked into the fortress to see what was there.

As we went through the first gate, we saw another wall, or fortress, one hundred yards up the mountain. When we reached that one, we saw that farther up the hill was another wall completely encircling the mountain. It was becoming evident why, by the time of Paul, no one had ever been able to defeat the occupants of the fortress. After Paul's death another 1,200 years passed before someone broke through the fortress, and only twice in history did that occur. By the time we reached the third wall, my wife, Shirley, and our two daughters decided to wait for our two boys and me to climb to the top of the mountain.

At the top of the mountain we looked back at Shirley and the girls, who looked about an inch tall. Then I turned around to catch a panoramic view of the Mediterranean Sea. To the left I saw the city of Athens, and if I could have seen far enough to the right, I would have seen the city of Rome. Obviously, whoever held this fortress would have had a very strong position in the ancient world. I realized that the Corinthians to whom Paul wrote would have easily identified with fortresses that needed to be demolished. In light of this description, read again 2 Corinthians 10:3-5 in the margin.

We are in a spiritual battle with the kingdom of darkness. We live behind enemy lines, and we face the forces of Satan. Many fortresses need to be demolished for the kingdom of light to be established.

> A stronghold is an idea, a thought process, a habit, or an addiction through which Satan has set up occupancy in your life—a place where he has the advantage.

This study provides insights into how these spiritual strongholds are established. You will learn how the enemy uses these strongholds to undermine you unless you are armed with the Word and prayer. At the

"Though we live in the world, we do not wage war as the world does. The weapons we fight with are not the weapons of the world. On the contrary, they have divine power to demolish strongholds. We demolish arguments and every pretension that sets itself up against the knowledge of God, and we take captive every thought to make it obedient to Christ" (2 Cor. 10:3-5).

Spiritual Warfare

The Corinthians would have easily identified with fortresses that needed to be demolished.

end of this week' study you will be able to—
• define *spiritual warfare*;
• identify the enemy in spiritual warfare;
• describe Jesus' victory over Satan;
• identify three types of spiritual strongholds of evil: personal, ideological, and cosmic;
• practice a plan for demolishing strongholds.

WHAT IS SPIRITUAL WARFARE?

Spiritual warfare is the conflict between the forces of God and the forces of Satan, with the goal being your victory in Christ.

Describe a time when you experienced a conflict like the one described in the definition above.

_____

_____

Learn what the Bible says about spiritual warfare. In the verses in the margin, underline all references to Satan or spiritual powers.

You probably underlined terms such as "all rule and authority," "rulers and authorities in the heavenly realms," "powers of this dark world," and "spiritual forces of evil in the heavenly realms." The Bible reveals everything God wanted us to know about spiritual warfare.

Check the boxes beside the statements that are true.
❑ **Spiritual warfare is no serious threat to me.**
❑ **If I read the Bible daily, I will never confront spiritual warfare.**
❑ **I try to live a peaceful life. The term *war* does not apply to my lifestyle.**
☒ **I live behind enemy lines. Satan's forces can and do attack me.**

Only the last statement is true. Spiritual warfare is a threat to everyone, even the most fervent Christian. Satan will attack anyone—especially those who believe that they are not vulnerable. Therefore, you need to be armed and ready. Strongholds begin in your life when Satan gets a foothold in you. Even if you love peace, Satan would like nothing better than to wage war with you. The moment you start thinking that you are incapable of such behaviors as coveting, raging, or entertaining lustful thoughts, Satan will launch a surprise attack, trying to trip you in the areas you feel most impenetrable. The greater threat you are to him and the kingdom of darkness, the more he attacks you.

THE CONFLICT

We will examine spiritual conflict as Scripture portrays it.

"That power is like the working of his mighty strength, which he exerted in Christ when he raised him from the dead and seated him at his right hand in the heavenly realms, far above all rule and authority, power and dominion, and every title that can be given, not only in the present age but also in the one to come" (Eph. 1:19-21).

"His intent was that now, through the church, the manifold wisdom of God should be made known to the rulers and authorities in the heavenly realms" (Eph. 3:10).

"Our struggle is not against flesh and blood, but against the rulers, against the authorities, against the powers of this dark world and against the spiritual forces of evil in the heavenly realms" (Eph. 6:12).

1 Peter 1:2

Eph 2:2

Check the following ways you think Scripture portrays Satan.

☑ The wicked one   ☑ The adversary

☑ The deceiver   ☑ The enemy of our souls

☑ The destroyer   ☑ The prince of the power of the air

All of the previous descriptions of Satan are from Scripture. *Satan* appears as a proper name in the Old Testament, referring to the superhuman enemy of God, humanity, and good (see 1 Chron. 21:1). This word also occurs frequently in the New Testament.

Below are titles the New Testament uses for Satan. Read the Scriptures in the margin and match the references with the titles used.

C 1. John 12:31   a. The tempter

D 2. 2 Corinthians 4:4   b. The evil one

A 3. 1 Thessalonians 3:5   c. The prince of this world

B 4. Matthew 13:19,38   d. The god of this age

E 5. Revelation 12:10   e. The accuser of our brothers

Go back and draw a star beside a title that describes an encounter you have had with Satan. Explain why you chose that title.

_____

You may have answered something like this: I realize that Satan has been working throughout history to control and destroy, and I am aware of how powerful his influence can be. The answers to the matching exercise are 1. c, 2. d, 3. a, 4. b, 5. e.

SATAN'S CHARACTERISTICS

Satan's power is so great that Michael the archangel viewed him as a foe too powerful to oppose (see Jude 9). The Bible also reveals Satan's influence in worldly events. First John 5:19 declares, "The whole world is under the control of the evil one."

Identify an occurrence in which you believe that Satan was active.

Mᴬᵗᵗ 13. _____

Satan is a highly intelligent being. Observe Satan's cunning in tricking Adam and Eve and in taking over their rule of the world:

"Now the serpent was more crafty than any of the wild animals the Lord God had made. He said to the woman, 'Did God really say, "You must not eat from any tree in the garden"?' The woman said to the serpent, 'We may eat fruit from the trees in the garden, but God did say, "You must not eat fruit from the tree that is in the middle of the garden, and you must not touch it, or you will die.'" 'You will not surely die,' the serpent said to the woman. 'For God knows that when

---

" 'Now is the time for judgment on this world; now the prince of this world will be driven out' " (John 12:31).

"The god of this age has blinded the minds of unbelievers, so that they cannot see the light of the gospel of the glory of Christ, who is the image of God" (2 Cor. 4:4).

"For this reason, when I could stand it no longer, I sent to find out about your faith. I was afraid that in some way the tempter might have tempted you and our efforts might have been useless" (1 Thess. 3:5).

" 'When anyone hears the message about the kingdom and does not understand it, the evil one comes and snatches away what was sown in his heart. This is the seed sown along the path. The field is the world, and the good seed stands for the sons of the kingdom. The weeds are the sons of the evil one' " (Matt. 13:19,38).

The accuser of our brothers, who accuses them before our God day and night, has been hurled down" (Rev. 12:10).

"The coming of the lawless one will be in accordance with the work of Satan displayed in all kinds of counterfeit miracles, signs and wonders" (2 Thess. 2:9).

" 'You belong to your father, the devil, and you want to carry out your father's desire. He was a murderer from the beginning, not holding to the truth, for there is no truth in him. When he lies, he speaks his native language, for he is a liar and the father of lies' " (John 8:44).

"Do not deprive each other except by mutual consent and for a time, so that you may devote yourselves to prayer. Then come together again so that Satan will not tempt you because of your lack of self-control" (1 Cor. 7:5).

"The evening meal was being served, and the devil had already prompted Judas Iscariot, son of Simon, to betray Jesus. As soon as Judas took the bread, Satan entered into him" (John 13:2,27).

"The reason I wrote you was to see if you would stand the test and be obedient in everything. If you forgive anyone, I also forgive him. And what I have forgiven—if there was anything to forgive—I have forgiven in the sight of Christ for your sake, in order that Satan might not outwit us. For we are not unaware of his schemes" (2 Cor. 2:9-11).

Ephesians 6:10

you eat of it your eyes will be opened, and you will be like God, knowing good and evil.' " (Gen. 3:1-5).

Satan also tempted Jesus by offering to give Him all of the kingdoms of the world if Jesus would worship him (see Matt. 4:8-9). He certainly tries to persuade us to sin.

When I think about Satan's power to trick me, I feel—
❑ **totally hopeless. How can I attempt to overcome such cunning?**
❑ **very wary. Satan lies in wait for me at every turn in my life.**
❑ **confident and sure. With God's power I can have victory over temptation when Satan sets a trap for me.**

Sometimes Satan overwhelms you to the point that you feel powerless. God expects you to be wary of the tempter, but He can help you be victorious in spiritual warfare. Look at more of Satan's methods.

Satan uses several means to lead people to sin. Read the verses in the margin and match the references with the means listed below.

C **1. 2 Thessalonians 2:9**   a. **Through unforgiveness**
E **2. John 8:44**   b. **Through prompting**
D **3. 1 Corinthians 7:5**   c. **Through counterfeit miracles, signs, and wonders**
B **4. John 13:2,27**   d. **Through your weaknesses**
A **5. 2 Corinthians 2:9-11**   e. **Through his lying nature**

Circle the means Satan uses most often to lead you to sin.

Satan's methods are designed to defeat God and humanity by limiting the gospel. He seeks to keep you from giving a verbal testimony and a testimony through example. You will not be able to spread God's Word by your word or by your actions if you give in to Satan, and that is exactly how he tries to silence you. The correct answers are 1. c, 2. e, 3. d, 4. b, 5. a.

Some people do not admit that the enemy exists. But the Bible makes it plain that Satan exists and that his main work is to oppose God's rule in events and in people's lives.

This week's Scripture-memory verse, 1 John 4:4, assures you that you have power over the enemy. To begin your memory work, turn to page 8 and read the verse aloud.

PUTTING ON THE SPIRITUAL ARMOR
Putting on the Spiritual Armor (see Eph. 6:10-20) is a key way you can stand against Satan and his schemes in spiritual warfare. Each week in this study you will learn one part of the Spiritual Armor presentation, which you can find on pages 129–31. By the end of this study you will be able to explain in your own words how to use the Spiritual Armor.

Begin learning the Spiritual Armor presentation today by studying the Helmet of Salvation. Turn to page 129 and read the entire presentation, with special emphasis on the Helmet of Salvation.

The Helmet of Salvation should remind you to—

1. thank God that you are His child;
2. praise God for your eternal life;
3. claim the mind of Christ.

 Focusing on the first instruction, stop and thank God that you are His child. Thank Him for your salvation.

 The guide that follows will help you give thanks to God. Read it and use it in your prayer time.

GUIDE TO THANKSGIVING

Thanksgiving lays the foundation for other forms of prayer. Use these guidelines to make thanksgiving a part of every prayer.

1. The source of thanksgiving is grace. Thanks is our reaction when we realize that all we have, receive, and are is a gift of God's grace. Thanksgiving is rejoicing at what God gave when we were undeserving. True gratitude registers surprise that God could be so good to us when we deserve nothing. (See Acts 27:35; 28:15; Rom. 6:17; 1 Cor. 1:4; Col. 1:12; Rev. 11:17.)
2. The condition of thanksgiving is agreement. Thanksgiving means that you agree with God. Thus, the Bible encourages you to give thanks in all circumstances (see 1 Thess. 5:18) and to pray about the things that concern you most by making your petitions with thanksgiving (see Phil. 4:6).
3. The response of thanksgiving is worship. Thanksgiving responds to God's specific acts. Praise and thanks are thus natural partners in worship (see Ps. 100:4; Heb. 13:15). Your prayers and your actions worship your Creator. When you thank God, you enter His presence, worship Him, and present an offering to Him.
4. The occasion for thanksgiving is everything. Nothing should escape your thanksgiving. God is active in every area of your life and can show you His direction even in the darkest hour. Thanking God frees Him to work in your life through those circumstances.
5. The reward of thanksgiving is the enjoyment of God's blessings: peace, joy, growth, worship, and life in Christ. If you have trouble giving thanks under any circumstance, ask the Spirit to fill you (see Eph. 5:18-20).

 Read Psalm 119:1-8 during your quiet time today. Let God speak to you through this passage. Then complete the Daily Master Communication Guide in the margin.

DAILY MASTER COMMUNICATION GUIDE

PSALM 119:1-8

What God said to me:

_____

_____

_____

_____

_____

_____

_____

What I said to God:

_____

_____

_____

_____

_____

_____

_____

_____

DAY 2

Defining the Battleground

"No temptation has seized you except what is common to man. And God is faithful; he will not let you be tempted beyond what you can bear. But when you are tempted, he will also provide a way out so that you can stand up under it" (1 Cor. 10:13).

"Having disarmed the powers and authorities, he made a public spectacle of them, triumphing over them by the cross" (Col. 2:15).

"Though we live in the world, we do not wage war as the world does. The weapons we fight with are not the weapons of the world. On the contrary, they have divine power to demolish strongholds. We demolish arguments and every pretension that sets itself up against the knowledge of God, and we take captive every thought to make it obedient to Christ" (2 Cor. 10:3-5).

As you learned in day 1, the devil is strong. However, through the Lord, Christians are stronger than the devil. They have the protection they need to withstand Satan's assaults. Satan tempts, but God provides a way of escape, as 1 Corinthians 10:13, in the margin, states.

Many times when I have been tempted, the Holy Spirit has brought to mind a verse I had memorized. Then I began to look for the way to escape the temptation.

SPIRITUAL BATTLE

We can triumph because Jesus triumphed over Satan and his forces in His death and resurrection. Read Colossians 2:15 in the margin.

How did Jesus triumph over Satan? Circle all that apply.

incarnation   crucifixion   resurrection

In His crucifixion and resurrection Christ triumphed over the devil. Of course, He had to come in the incarnation to fight the battle as a human being. This week's Scripture-memory verse assures you of that victory.

 Stop and begin hiding in your heart this week's Scripture-memory verse, 1 John 4:4. Write it in the margin from one to three times.

The battle is spiritual in nature, and your weapons are spiritual, not weapons of the world.

In the margin read the verses from 2 Corinthians that you read at the beginning of this week's work. Underline what kind of power is possessed by the weapons you use in spiritual battle.

The weapons we use in spiritual battle have the divine power to demolish strongholds. These verses promise you that you have the power to take all thoughts captive and to make them obedient to Christ.

This week you will study three types of spiritual strongholds that define the battleground for spiritual warfare:
- Personal strongholds
- Ideological strongholds
- Cosmic strongholds

Today you will study the first type of stronghold.

PERSONAL STRONGHOLDS

Christians struggle against the world, the flesh, and the devil. In *MasterLife 2: The Disciple's Personality* the term *flesh* was used to define the body and the sinful nature. In this study I will use a broader definition of it. Watchman Nee defines *flesh* as "any attitude or action done without total dependence on the Lord Jesus Christ."[1]

Personal strongholds are areas of our lives in which we are most vulnerable to Satan's attacks. They are areas in which Satan always seems to get advantage of you.

Satan first attacks the flesh, which is the inner tendency and capacity to sin. Through the flesh Satan influences the mind, the will, and the emotions. He wants us to depend on ourselves and on our own strength. Paul warns you "not to give the devil a foothold" (Eph. 4:27). Satan's footholds soon become his strongholds if not defeated by spiritual weapons.

Check all that apply:
❑ **I have no spiritual strongholds.**
☒ **I have one or more spiritual strongholds.**
❑ **Satan may have a foothold in one or more areas of my life.**

If part of your life is not fully committed to God, name that area and describe ways it is vulnerable to satanic attack.

_____

_____

In the Sermon on the Mount Jesus taught how to deal with several basic areas that can become personal strongholds of Satan:
☒ **bitterness**   ❑ **religious ritual**
❑ **lust**   ☒ **greed**
❑ **improper speech**   ☒ **pride**

In the previous list, check the strongholds in your life. In the margin add others you discovered through the "In the Carpenter's Shop" sections of *MasterLife 2: The Disciple's Personality.*

DEMOLISHING PERSONAL SPIRITUAL STRONGHOLDS

During this study you will identify ways the Holy Spirit is helping you build Christlike character as you select strongholds to be demolished and character traits to be built up in Christlikeness. This is the next step in the process of Christian character building you began in book 2.

Read the verses in the margin, which deal with the stronghold of bitterness. Then describe the area of bitterness in your life that needs to be demolished, what you need to do to demolish it, and

Satan's footholds soon become his strongholds if not defeated by spiritual weapons.

" 'You have heard that it was said, "Eye for eye, and tooth for tooth." But I tell you, Do not resist an evil person. If someone strikes you on the right cheek, turn to him the other also. And if someone wants to sue you and take your tunic, let him have your cloak as well. If someone forces you to go one mile, go with him two miles. Give to the one who asks you, and do not turn away from the one who wants to borrow from you. You have heard that it was said, "Love your neighbor and hate your enemy." But I tell you: Love your enemies and pray for those who persecute you, that you may be sons of your Father in heaven. He causes his sun to rise on the evil and the good, and sends rain on the righteous and the unrighteous' " (Matt. 5:38-45).

DAILY MASTER
COMMUNICATION
GUIDE

PSALM 119:9-16

What God said to me:

_____

_____

_____

_____

_____

_____

_____

What I said to God:

_____

_____

_____

_____

_____

_____

_____

the spiritual weapon(s) to be used in demolishing it. Later this week you will record your progress. Here is an example.

Stronghold to be demolished: bitterness toward my boss

What I need to do to demolish it: pray for my boss instead of harboring anger toward him

Spiritual weapons to be used: Helmet of Salvation—claim the mind of Christ; Sword of the Spirit—learn what God's Word says about bitterness and its results

Now you try it.

Stronghold to be demolished: _____

_____

What I need to do to demolish it: _Hold ARms_
faiTh All And ail to God
I'L PRay think God for his
or her.

Spiritual weapon(s) to be used: _PRay for The_
oTheR PERSON Ask God to help
him or her And give Then Their daily NEW

When you demolish a stronghold, this does not mean that you will never again be tempted in this area, but it does mean that Satan will not set up camp inside you to entrap you in his snares.

 Read Psalm 119:9-16 during your quiet time today. Then complete the Daily Master Communication Guide in the margin.

DAY 3

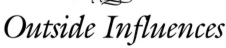

Outside Influences

This week you are studying three types of spiritual strongholds that define the battleground for spiritual warfare:
- Personal strongholds
- Ideological strongholds
- Cosmic strongholds

Today you will study the second type of spiritual stronghold.

IDEALOGICAL STRONGHOLDS

Idealogical strongholds are built around systems of thought and ideas that are embodied in cultures and that exert pressure on members of that culture. Through this influence, which the Bible calls the world, a whole society begins to hold certain values. What Satan does to individuals through the flesh, he does to society through the world. Over time personal strongholds become embodied in cultures as strongholds.

In the world you find "arguments and every pretension that sets itself up against the knowledge of God" (2 Cor. 10:5). The world includes the following.

❑ philosophical systems   ☑ educational systems
❑ value systems   ❑ religious systems
❑ economic systems   ☑ political systems

Joesoph

In the previous list check the systems you have seen or experienced Satan using as a stronghold.

Systems Satan has used could include Communism; capitalism, when it leads people to turn their backs on the poor; humanism; Darwinism; and dictatorships. They can also include claims of intolerance. If you say that you are a Christian, some people automatically respond that you are a bigot. Christians encounter claims that they are intolerant when they take stands against such issues as homosexuality, abortion, and pornography. These claims subtly destroy our society's sense of right and wrong.

Strongholds of Satan could also include—

Do Like Joesph did RuN for your Life

- the gambling industry;
- pornography in the name of freedom of speech;
- the sexual revolution;
- secularism;
- the religious revolution in America, which has embraced other world religions and has created new ones.

Were you surprised to see religious systems on the list? I am talking about the hollow, ritualistic religion the Pharisees exhibited in which the focus becomes an addictive effort to do the right thing rather than a dependent, personal relationship with God. Jesus said that the Pharisees and their religious system were from their father, the devil. Paul warned, "See to it that no one takes you captive through hollow and deceptive philosophy, which depends on human tradition and the basic principles of this world rather than on Christ" (Col. 2:8).

Read 1 Corinthians 10:13 in the margin. Underline the phrase that tells what God does when you are tempted.

Read 1 John 5:4 in the margin. On the next page write the word that identifies how you have victory to overcome the world.

"No temptation has seized you except what is common to man. And God is faithful; he will not let you be tempted beyond what you can bear. But when you are tempted, he will also provide a way out so that you can stand up under it" (1 Cor. 10:13).

"Everyone born of God overcomes the world. This is the victory that has overcome the world, even our faith" (1 John 5:4).

"I urge you, brothers, in view of God's mercy, to offer your bodies as living sacrifices, holy and pleasing to God—this is your spiritual act of worship. Do not conform any longer to the pattern of this world, but be transformed by the renewing of your mind. Then you will be able to test and approve what God's will is—his good, pleasing and perfect will" (Rom. 12: 1-2).

DAILY MASTER COMMUNICATION GUIDE

PSALM 119:17-24

What God said to me:

PRay

ASk for help Right choice to make will help you stay Seek only friend who

1st
2nd
3

What I said to God:

The flesh and the world are the devil's habitats, but that does not mean spirit possession. In the Bible, people possessed by evil spirits were not yet Christians. Because you are a Christian, God has given you the power to escape any temptation. Your faith is the victory that claims God's power over the world, the flesh, and the devil.

Based on this week's Scripture-memory verse, what do you have that is greater than the tempter in the world?

Christ Who Live in You

Christ, who lives in you, gives you the victory over the world and its tempter, Satan.

Romans 12:1-2, in the margin on page 17, gives Christians an antidote to the world's systems.

PUTTING ON THE SPIRITUAL ARMOR

As you think about fighting the evil systems of the world, recall the weapons you are learning in the Spiritual Armor presentation.

Stop and pray through each weapon below, as shown in the Spiritual Armor presentation on pages 129–31.

- **Helmet of Salvation**
- **Breastplate of Righteousness**
- **Belt of Truth**
- **Gospel Shoes**
- **Shield of Faith**
- **Sword of the Spirit**

REad EPhESIANs 6: 10 -20

In day 1 you learned three instructions to follow in putting on the Helmet of Salvation. Review them on page 13.

Take the second step in putting on the Helmet of Salvation by praising God for eternal life. Stop and praise God for the security of eternal life you have in Jesus Christ.

Read Psalm 119:17-24 during your quiet time today. Let God speak to you through this passage. Then complete the Daily Master Communication Guide in the margin.

DAY 4

To Steal, Kill, and Destroy

Satan rules a group of evil spirits that, with the aid of humanity, establishes a counterculture of sin defying God's righteous order. Its goal is to oppose God's work and to steal, kill, and destroy.

This week you are studying three types of spiritual strongholds that define the battleground for spiritual warfare:

- Personal strongholds
- Ideological strongholds
- Cosmic strongholds.

Today you will examine the third stronghold, which centers on the satanic counterculture.

COSMIC STRONGHOLDS

Read the verses from John 10 in the margin. Then answer the following.

What does Jesus, the Good Shepherd, offer? _A good shepherd_
Enter into by the gate

What is Satan's purpose? _To steal, kill +_
destroy

What is the way to life at its fullest? _____

_____

Jesus Christ is the only way to salvation. The world offers many alluring ways that appear to provide enjoyment and pleasure, but the world's promises are shallow. People who believe Satan's lies find themselves on a path of destruction that leads away from the abundant life in Jesus.

In the world around us—in the atmosphere—are evil beings under Satan's leadership. When I was in seminary, some scholars claimed that evil spirits were psychological states of mind. The devil was dismissed as a general force or thought that represented evil, natural forces in humankind. At the same time, I met missionaries who were encountering many manifestations of Satan and his evil spirits in other cultures. When I went abroad as a missionary, I did not claim that the evil spirits did not exist. Instead, I emphasized that the Holy Spirit of God, through the victory of Jesus Christ, is more powerful than any evil spirit or satanic representative (see Col. 2:13-15 in the margin).

" 'I tell you the truth, the man who does not enter the sheep pen by the gate, but climbs in by some other way, is a thief and a robber. The man who enters by the gate is the shepherd of his sheep. The thief comes only to steal and kill and destroy; I have come that they may have life, and have it to the full' " (John 10:1-2,10).

THE SPIRITUAL ARMOR
Eph 6:10-2○

"When you were dead in your sins and in the uncircumcision of your sinful nature, God made you alive with Christ. He forgave us all our sins, having canceled the written code, with its regulations, that was against us and that stood opposed to us; he took it away, nailing it to the cross. And having disarmed the powers and authorities, he made a public spectacle of them, triumphing over them by the cross" (Col. 2:13-15).

"The prince of the Persian kingdom resisted me twenty-one days. Then Michael, one of the chief princes, came to help me, because I was detained there with the king of Persia" (Dan. 10:13).

During the latter years of the 20th century Satan's forces have gained so many strongholds in the United States that Americans have begun to be aware of evil spirits, the occult, mediums, channeling, demon possession, and satanic worship. Obviously, all of these are not merely psychological interpretations: "Our struggle is not against flesh and blood, but against the rulers, against the authorities, against the powers of this dark world and against the spiritual forces of evil in the heavenly realms" (Eph. 6:12). Strongholds in the heavenlies, or the atmosphere around us, seem to be the abodes of various kinds of spiritual beings that fight against the cause of God and Christ. In the Old Testament the prince of Persia prevented the angel from coming to Daniel until the archangel Michael helped him. Read Daniel 10:13 in the margin.

Some people use the term *strategic spiritual warfare* to refer to the aggressive confrontation of Satan and his demons by intercessors. In the wilderness, in the garden of Gethsemane, and at other critical times in His ministry Jesus showed us how to confront Satan. A word of caution, however: many present-day teachings seem to be based more on experience than on biblical teaching. Bring your experiences in line with the Bible and avoid interpreting the Bible to fit your experiences.

The bottom line is that Christ has already won the victory over spiritual forces of evil. We need to claim it and exalt Christ. He will lead in victory.

ALERT TO THE ENEMY

Christians need to be alert to the reality of spiritual warfare. In the following list check any positive results you may have already experienced from being more attuned to spiritual warfare.

Bring your experiences in line with the Bible and avoid interpreting the Bible to fit your experiences.

An awareness of spiritual warfare—
- ❑ makes Christians more aware of Satan and his forces;
- ☑ helps Christians realize that they are in a cosmic spiritual battle;
- ❑ prompts Christians to study the Scriptures to understand Satan's deceptions, temptations, persecutions, and occult practices;
- ❑ helps identify major schemes of the devil, which include unforgiveness, accusations, distractions, deception, manipulation, division, confusion, discouragement, despair, and heresy;
- ☑ helps Christians learn to depend on God for victory.

Check any of the following consequences of dwelling unduly on spiritual warfare that you have experienced or seen.

An overemphasis on spiritual warfare—
- ❑ causes people to become preoccupied with Satan and his forces instead of with God. Undue attention to satanic forces may make people more vulnerable to them.
- ❑ causes people to attribute to Satan actions that result from the flesh and the world. We should take responsibility for our sins

instead of saying, "The devil made me do it."

❑ causes people to put undue emphasis on directly rebuking Satan. Not even Michael the archangel dared to do that (see Jude 9). Some practices of rebuking Satan sound as if the person is praying to the devil instead of to God.

❑ causes people to put undue emphasis on directly binding Satan. Jesus is the one who binds the strong man, as Matthew 12:28-29, in the margin, states.

 What does this week's Scripture-memory verse, 1 John 4:4, say about Satan's power in comparison to God's power? Practice your memory work by saying this verse aloud to someone today.

Stop and pray that you will keep a proper perspective on your attitude about spiritual warfare while always being aware of your need to claim Christ's victory over the enemy.

> " 'If I drive out demons by the Spirit of God, then the kingdom of God has come upon you. Or again, how can anyone enter a strong man's house and carry off his possessions unless he first ties up the strong man? Then he can rob his house' " (Matt. 12:28-29).

PUTTING ON THE SPIRITUAL ARMOR

As you are learning, the Spiritual Armor is a useful means of dealing with spiritual battles. Review on page 13 the three instructions for putting on the Helmet of Salvation.

Practice the third instruction by claiming the mind of Christ. First Corinthians 2:16 says,

> *"Who has known the mind of the Lord*
> *that he may instruct him?"*
> *But we have the mind of Christ.*

The mind of Christ was given to you with your salvation. Stop now and thank God that you have the mind of Christ as you experience spiritual struggles and victories.

The mind of Christ was given to you with your salvation.

Explain to your family, a Christian friend, or a group the Helmet of Salvation part of the Spiritual Armor. God will help you find a way to minister to the person(s).

Use the Spiritual Armor in your prayer life this week.

DEMOLISHING PERSONAL SPIRITUAL STRONGHOLDS

In day 2 you identified a stronghold you wanted to demolish in the area of bitterness or a wrong attitude or action. Give a progress report on how you are using the spiritual weapon(s) you listed to demolish this stronghold.

How I am using a spiritual weapon(s) to help demolish bitterness:

DAILY MASTER COMMUNICATION GUIDE

PSALM 119:25-32

What God said to me:

_____

_____

_____

_____

_____

_____

What I said to God:

_____

_____

_____

_____

_____

_____

_____

_____

RELATIONAL WITNESSING

No doubt your heightened awareness about Satan's attacks and humans' vulnerability to them has made you aware of persons who do not know Christ. Perhaps you realize their need to know Him so that they will have His power in their lives. If you have not already done so, begin consciously to let Christ flow through your personal relationships. Three basic types of personal witnessing can be used:

1. _Relational witnessing_—sharing Christ through kinship and friendship
2. _Lifestyle witnessing_—sharing Christ with persons you meet in the normal traffic pattern of your life
3. _Visitation witnessing_—intentionally visiting someone to share Christ

Begin where you are to reach persons for Christ in your circles of influence. This simple procedure can progress as slowly or as quickly as you desire:

1. List on the Relational-Witnessing Chart (p. 135) and on the Prayer-Covenant List (p. 143) family members and relatives who you think may not know Christ. In the following weeks you will list persons in each circle of influence in your life.
2. Evaluate your relationship with each person. We often hesitate to witness to our relatives because our lives have not been as they should be. Now that you have studied two _MasterLife_ books, the testimony of your life should be improving.
3. Regularly pray for these persons. Enlist others to pray for them. Prayer plows the soil of the heart for the seed of the gospel to be planted later.
4. Serve them by discovering and meeting their needs. When you serve others because of your love for them and because you are Christ's servant, the Holy Spirit will work in their hearts.
5. Relate Christ's provision to their needs. As you pray, open lines of communication, and serve them, the Holy Spirit will provide opportunities to witness.

Begin to list persons for each circle of influence on the Relational-Witnessing Chart (p. 135) who do not or may not know Christ. Also write their names on the Prayer-Covenant List on page 143. Finish the list for your immediate family and relatives.

Read Psalm 119:25-32 during your quiet time today. Let God speak to you through this passage. Then complete the Daily Master Communication Guide in the margin.

DAY 5

Winning the Victory

All Christians engage in spiritual warfare on personal, ideological, and cosmic levels as they confront the world, the flesh, and the devil. Christ has won the victory over all evil powers and gives victory to Christians who totally depend on Him and use the spiritual weapons He gives. We face an escalation of spiritual warfare and must use God's power to overcome Satan and his forces. First Peter 5:8-9, in the margin, confirms the fact that the devil is alive and well and is waiting to attack.

Those who wrestle with personal strongholds also need to fight the ideological systems of the world so that we can live holy lives and fulfill God's mission for us in the world. Let's look further at 2 Corinthians 10:3-5, which began our study and which addresses the matter of Satan's attack. Read those verses in the margin.

SPIRITUAL WEAPONS

The Greek word for *weapons* is *panoplia* (from which the English word *panoply* is derived). The *panoplia* was the complete equipment used by the 'Greeks' heavily armed infantry. Weapons, then, refers to the complete array of spiritual helps God supplies for overcoming the devil's temptations.

List weapons the world uses to fight.

_____

You may have listed tangible weapons like fists, guns, knives, and other objects that cause physical harm. You may have also listed intangible weapons like slander, gossip, and backbiting. Second Corinthians 10:3-5 clearly indicates that Christians are to choose other ways to fight besides these harmful choices.

Logic, physical efforts, positive thinking, and psychological tactics will not win over Satan. Only the spiritual weapons God gives you can win spiritual victories.

Read Ephesians 6:11-18 in the margin on the next page. Underline the six weapons God supplies for the battle against Satan.

Another significant word in 2 Corinthians 10:3-5 is *demolish*, which comes from a Greek word meaning *a taking down* or *a pulling down*. You are in the process of pulling down strongholds of the devil, like a demolition crew tearing down an old building by using a wrecking ball.

"Be self-controlled and alert. Your enemy the devil prowls around like a roaring lion looking for someone to devour. Resist him, standing firm in the faith, because you know that your brothers throughout the world are undergoing the same kind of sufferings" (1 Pet. 5: 8-9).

"Though we live in the world, we do not wage war as the world does. The weapons we fight with are not the weapons of the world. On the contrary, they have divine power to demolish strongholds. We demolish arguments and every pretension that sets itself up against the knowledge of God, and we take captive every thought to make it obedient to Christ" (2 Cor. 10:3-5).

"Put on the full armor of God so that you can take your stand against the devil's schemes. For our struggle is not against flesh and blood, but against the rulers, against the authorities, against the power of this dark world and against the spiritual forces of evil in the heavenly realms. Therefore put on the full armor of God, so that when the day of evil comes, you may be able to stand your ground, and after you have done everything, to stand. Stand firm then, with the belt of truth buckled around your waist, with the breastplate of righteousness in place, and with your feet fitted with the readiness that comes from the gospel of peace. In addition to all this, take up the shield of faith, with which you can extinguish all the flaming arrows of the evil one. Take the helmet of salvation and the sword of the Spirit, which is the word of God. And pray in the Spirit on all occasions with all kinds of prayers and requests. With this in mind, be alert and always keep on praying for all the saints" (Eph. 6:11-18).

DEMOLISHING PERSONAL SPIRITUAL STRONGHOLDS
In day 2 you identified a stronghold you wanted to demolish in the area of bitterness. Give a progress report on how well you have used the spiritual weapon(s) you listed to demolish this stronghold.

How I have used a spiritual weapon(s) to help demolish bitterness:

_____

_____

Demolishing strongholds is not easy. You will encounter claims that threaten to undermine your faith, and you will have thoughts that do not honor Christ.

As you have studied this week, you may have been frightened by teachings about the enemy. Do not let Satan frighten you. Christ has defeated this foe. Jesus said that He came to give you abundant life in opposition to the one who steals, kills, and destroys. Over the next weeks you will be equipped through the Spiritual Armor to stand victorious and, when the battle is over, to be left standing. Remember that you are studying the disciple's victory, not just spiritual warfare.

HOW TO DEMOLISH A STRONGHOLD
Here is a brief summary of how to demolish a stronghold. You may photocopy this summary and keep it in your Bible, wallet, or another convenient place for ready reference when you need it.
1. Identify the wrong argument or pretension that establishes itself against God. Identify what is wrong with it.
2. Identify the ways the stronghold has become established—through the flesh, desire, society, or the devil. Read 1 John 4: 1-6 about testing the spirits.
3. Identify the spiritual weapons for the warfare, in contrast to the worldly solutions.
4. Declare war on the thought or pretension that positions itself against the knowledge of Christ by—
   a. using thoughts or arguments from the Word;
   b. claiming the mind of Christ;
   c. using spiritual weapons (see Eph. 6:11-17), followed by asking for the power of the Spirit through prayer (see Eph. 6:18);
   d. boldly making the truth of the gospel clear (see Eph. 6:19);
   e. claiming the victory by faith.
      • Remember, "the one who is in you is greater than the one who is in the world" (1 John 4:4).
      • Christ has defeated Satan and has spoiled all of the principalities.

5. Win the victory promised in 1 John 5:2-3,18-20 (read these verses in the margin) by—
   a. loving God (see 1 John 5:3);
   b. keeping His commandments (see 1 John 5:3);
   c. being sure that you are born of God;
   d. believing that Jesus is God's Son;
   e. believing that because God keeps you safe, the evil one cannot harm you (see 1 John 5:18).

Read John 15:5 in the margin. What does this verse say about spiritual warfare?

_____

_____

You may have answered: All my thinking should reflect the fact that Christ is the center of my life. Without Him I can do nothing, including evaluating the thoughts and claims that come from the world.

While the world might use weapons like the ones you listed on page 23, a follower of Christ uses the Sword of the Spirit—God's Word—to wage war. You will use this weapon in the following three activities.

 By now you have likely memorized this week's Scripture-memory verse, 1 John 4:4. Say it to a family member or a friend.

 Read Psalm 119:33-40 during your quiet time today. Let God speak to you. Then complete the Daily Master Communication Guide in the margin on page 26.

 Learn to handle the Sword of the Spirit effectively. The following material will help you get more from your Bible reading and study.

HOW TO READ GOD'S WORD
Listen to God speak as you read His Word.
1. Read the Bible systematically. Read through an entire book of the Bible, more or less a chapter a day. Balance your choice of books by reading different types of writings in the Bible.
2. Listen to God speak in one of the four areas for which the Bible states it is to be used: teaching—teaching the faith, rebuking—correcting error, correcting—resetting the direction of a person's life, and training—training a person in right living (see 2 Tim. 3:16-17). As you read the Bible, review these four areas until you automatically recognize when God is speaking in these ways.

"This is how we know that we love the children of God: by loving God and carrying out his commands. This is love for God: to obey his commands. And his commands are not burdensome. We know that anyone born of God does not continue to sin; the one who was born of God keeps him safe, and the evil one cannot harm him. We know that we are children of God, and that the whole world is under the control of the evil one. We know also that the Son of God has come and has given us understanding, so that we may know him who is true. And we are in him who is true—even in his Son Jesus Christ. He is the true God and eternal life" (1 John 5:2-3, 18-20).

" 'I am the vine; you are the branches. If a man remains in me and I in him, he will bear much fruit; apart from me you can do nothing' " (John 15:5).

DAILY MASTER COMMUNICATION GUIDE

PSALM 119:33-40

What God said to me:

_____

_____

_____

_____

_____

_____

What I said to God:

_____

_____

_____

_____

_____

_____

_____

3. Mark words, phrases, and verses that appeal to you. In the margin you may want to place *M* beside verses you want to memorize, *T* beside verses with significant teachings for your life, *C* for correcting life's course, *R* for rebuke, or *I* for instruction in right living. Periodically review verses you have marked in a category.

4. Summarize what God has said to you through the Scripture. You may want to use *Day by Day in God's Kingdom: A Discipleship Journal.* This journal not only suggests Scriptures and memory verses but also provides room for you to record what you experience in your quiet time.[2] Review what you record. See whether a pattern emerges.

5. Pray about what God has said to you. Use the Daily Master Communication Guide format to write what God says to you and what you say to God. If you use this plan regularly, it will become second nature to you as you talk with God. Later, as you review your notes, you will see patterns in what God has communicated to you over a period of time.

6. Be persistent until you are consistent. Aim for consistency rather than for length of time spent.

HAS THIS WEEK MADE A DIFFERENCE?
Review "My Walk with the Master This Week" at the beginning of this week's material. Mark the activities you have finished by drawing vertical lines in the diamonds beside them. Finish any incomplete activities. Think about what you will say during your group session about your work on these activities.

As you complete your study of "Overcoming the Enemy," read the following statements and check all that apply.
❏ **I am more aware than ever of how Satan tries to overpower me.**
❏ **I am committed to using God's Word and prayer as weapons against Satan's attacks.**
❏ **I am trying to replace Satan's strongholds in my life with Christlike character traits.**
❏ **I truly desire to make Christ the center of my life by taking each thought captive and evaluating it against Christ's standard.**

Acknowledging that Satan has a grasp on an area of your life takes courage. Being aware that you are vulnerable is a healthy first step to loosening Satan's grip and to replacing his ways with Christlike ways. As you continue this study, you will be armed with more weapons to use in this spiritual battle.

---

[1]Edward Rommen, ed., *Spiritual Power and Missions: Raising the Issues* (Pasadena, Calif.: William Carey Library, 1995), 152.
[2]*Day by Day in God's Kingdom: A Discipleship Journal* (item 0-7673-2577-X) is available from the Customer Service Center; 127 Ninth Avenue, North; Nashville, TN 37234; 1-800-458-2772; and from Baptist Book Stores and Lifeway Christian Stores.

WEEK 2

Truth and Faith

This Week's Goal

You will be able to explain the relationship between truth and faith. You will be able to exercise your faith, based on God's Word, to pray about a need or a problem.

My Walk with the Master This Week

You will complete the following activities to develop the six biblical disciplines. When you have completed each activity, draw a vertical line in the diamond beside it.

SPEND TIME WITH THE MASTER
◇   Have a quiet time each day. Check each day you have a quiet time: ❑ Sunday ❑ Monday ❑ Tuesday ❑ Wednesday ❑ Thursday ❑ Friday ❑ Saturday

LIVE IN THE WORD
◇ Read your Bible every day. Write what God says to you and what you say to God.
◇ Memorize 2 Timothy 3:16-17.
◇ Review 1 John 4:4.
◇ Read "How to Listen to God's Word."
◇ Use the Hearing the Word form with a Sunday School lesson, sermon, or tape.

PRAY IN FAITH
◇ Use "Guide to Praise" during your prayer time.
◇ Write prayer promises that apply to the requests on your Prayer-Covenant List.

FELLOWSHIP WITH BELIEVERS
◇ Identify the sources of help you receive from your church for spiritual warfare.
◇ Share with someone the Breastplate of Righteousness part of the Spiritual Armor.

WITNESS TO THE WORLD
◇ List on the Relational-Witnessing Chart the names of lost persons.
◇ Make friends of non-Christians.

MINISTER TO OTHERS
◇ Learn the Breastplate of Righteousness part of the Spiritual Armor.

This Week's Scripture-Memory Verses

"All Scripture is God-breathed and is useful for teaching, rebuking, correcting and training in righteousness, so that the man of God may be thoroughly equipped for every good work" (2 Tim. 3:16-17).

DAILY MASTER COMMUNICATION GUIDE

❧

PSALM 119:41-48

What God said to me:

_____

_____

_____

_____

_____

_____

What I said to God:

_____

_____

_____

_____

_____

_____

_____

DAY 1

~

The Source of Truth

Don Dennis's problems began when he was a child. Both parents were alcoholics, and he repeatedly saw his father physically abuse his mother until they divorced. He was then sent to live with his grandparents. Don started drinking and taking drugs. When he was 16, he was sent to jail for the first of many times for writing bad checks and for armed robbery. At age 43 he received a life sentence as an incorrigible sociopath and was told that he would never get out of prison.

While Don was in prison, another prisoner sent him a note witnessing about his faith in God. He recalls: "I started reading in the New Testament that Jesus died for the downtrodden. I had thought that Jesus was only for righteous people, but I realized that Jesus was saying, 'I will forgive you.' I invited Jesus into my life and was baptized."

The truth from God's Word was crucial for the salvation experience of this inmate. This week's Scripture-memory verses speak of the importance of God's Word. Turn to page 27 and read this Scripture aloud to begin hiding it in your heart.

Three months after Don was baptized, the Washington state supreme court heard an appeal of his case, overturned his life sentence on a technicality, and released him on the basis of time served. A new set of problems began for Don when he tried to live the Christian life as a free man. He attended several churches, but his status as a former convict got in the way. Don explains: "People feared me. It made me resentful." Don said that misunderstandings between himself and church members frustrated his efforts to mature as a Christian. "I knew how to live for Jesus in a prison chapel, but I didn't know how to live for Him on the streets."

Don remembered a promise made by a man from Prison Fellowship that he would be glad to help him if Don were ever released. He moved Don into his home and helped him get a job, where Don met his future wife, Carol. They began to go to church and were invited to participate in a *MasterLife* group. Don said, "When I saw the Disciple's Cross, I finally understood how to internalize a structure that would help me deal with the world." Don grew fast as a Christian, and God called him to begin a prison ministry using *MasterLife* with prisoners during and after incarceration in the United States and overseas. The use of *MasterLife* in prisons has spread across the United States with an unusually high degree of success.

Just like Don Dennis, who struggled with Satan's ways and the Spirit's ways, every Christian must decide what is true. In spiritual warfare

you must determine whether truth is what the world says or what God's Word says. Satan tries to make you doubt God's Word and listen to His lies. You must take up the Sword of the Spirit, which is His Word, and the Shield of Faith to help you walk by faith even when you cannot see the outcome. At the end of this week's study you will be able to—
- define *truth*;
- define *faith* by paraphrasing Hebrews 11:1;
- develop a plan for showing faith in action;
- explain the relationship between truth and faith.

THE TRUTH OF JESUS CHRIST
Read John 8:31-32 in the margin. In verse 32 Jesus spoke of His mission on earth: to communicate truth, the reality of God, to all people. To love the truth is to love Christ.

Answer these questions based on what you read in John 8:31-32.

Who is the source of truth? _____

What is the source of truth? _____

How should you react to the truth? _____

What does spiritual truth do for you? _____

In the spiritual sense truth is God's revelation of Himself to you. That truth is most clearly revealed in Jesus, the incarnate Word (read John 14:6 and 1 John 1:1-4 in the margin). The Bible is the written record of God's revelation. You react to the truth by continuing in it, or by following Christ. Continuing in that truth will set you free from sin's captivity. Acknowledging that Christ is the Savior and trusting in Him set you free from the fear of death. You are then free to believe that you will live forever with the Father.

Based on Romans 6:17-18, in the margin, from what are you freed?

_____

Truth sets you free from the captivity of sin. The truth of Jesus Christ liberates people from sin and gives them eternal life.

The words "the truth will set you free" often appear over the entrances of universities and justice departments. They seem to signify that knowledge and understanding can make you free. Do you think this use of the phrase conveys the same meaning Jesus meant by it? ❏ Yes ❏ No Why? Answer on the next page.

" 'If you hold to my teaching, you are really my disciples. Then you will know the truth, and the truth will set you free' " (John 8:31-32).

"Jesus answered, 'I am the way and the truth and the life. No one comes to the Father except through me' " (John 14:6).

"That which was from the beginning, which we have heard, which we have seen with our eyes, which we have looked at and our hands have touched—this we proclaim concerning the Word of life. The life appeared; we have seen it and testify to it, and we proclaim to you the eternal life, which was with the Father and has appeared to us. We proclaim to you what we have seen and heard, so that you also may have fellowship with us. And our fellowship is with the Father and with his Son, Jesus Christ. We write this to make our joy complete" (1 John 1:1-4).

"Thanks be to God, that though you used to be slaves to sin, you wholeheartedly obeyed the form of teaching to which you were entrusted" (Rom. 6:17-18).

When Jesus made this statement in John 8:32, He referred to the truth that represented God's revelation. This is the only kind of truth that can set people free from the clutches of sin.

PUTTING ON THE SPIRITUAL ARMOR
As you learned in week 1, putting on the Spiritual Armor is a key way to keep Satan from exerting his influence in your life. Turn to page 129 and review the Spiritual Armor presentation, with special emphasis on the Breastplate of Righteousness. By the end of this study you will be able to explain the entire presentation in your own words.

The Breastplate of Righteousness reminds you to do three things:
1. Ask God to search your heart to reveal any wicked ways in it.
2. Confess any sin.
3. Claim Christ's righteousness to cover your sins and to give you right standing with Him.

Search me, O God, and know my heart;
    test me and know my anxious thoughts.
See if there is any offensive way in me,
    and lead me in the way everlasting (Ps. 139:23-24).

Focus on the first of the three reminders. Stop and ask God to search your heart to reveal any wicked ways in it. Read Psalm 139:23-24 in the margin.

Read Psalm 119:41-48 during your quiet time today. Let God speak to you through this passage. Then complete the Daily Master Communication Guide in the margin on page 28.

DAY 2

God's Truth Revealed

In day 1 you read about a major reversal in the direction of Don Dennis's life. This hardened criminal responded to the truth in God's Word, realized that he was lost in sin, was forgiven, and now has victory in Christ. Before that change, Don had listened to a different source, which had lied to him and had convinced him that thievery, alcohol, and other drugs were ways to meet his needs.

" 'You belong to your father, the devil, and you want to carry out your father's desire. He was a murderer from the beginning, not holding to the truth, for there is no truth in him. When he lies, he speaks his native language, for he is a liar and the father of lies' " (John 8:44).

Read John 8:44 in the margin. Who is the source of lies? _____

The opposite of truth is error, and Satan is its source. Satan's assault is aimed directly at God's truth. The ungodly boast of humanity's wisdom and self-sufficiency contradict that truth.

Read Romans 1:25 in the margin. What did Paul accuse the ungodly of doing?
❑ **Exchanging the truth of God for a lie**
❑ **Worshiping and serving the Creator**

People who follow the world's ways and worship what the world offers exchange what God created for falsehood. The first statement above is the correct one.

As stated in *MasterLife 2: The Disciple's Personality*, a natural person is someone who is closed to the Spirit of God but is open to Satan's temptation and power. The natural person makes decisions on the basis of physical information and whatever logic or emotion the person attaches to it. The natural person gathers information through the senses and interprets this information with the mind. Sometimes the natural person's will, emotions, and sinful nature cause him or her to draw erroneous conclusions. At best, the natural person's personality is tied to the world and is under the influence of evil and error. As a result, this person cannot understand spiritual truth.

Read 1 Corinthians 2:14 in the margin; then fill in the blanks:
The man without the _____ does not accept the things that come from the _____ ___ _____, for they are _____ to him.

DEMOLISHING PERSONAL SPIRITUAL STRONGHOLDS
Last week you focused on the stronghold of bitterness in your life. Today you will look at another stronghold mentioned in the Sermon on the Mount and will consider ways the Holy Spirit helps you build Christlike character as you work to demolish this stronghold.

Read the verses in the margin that deal with the stronghold of lust. Lust is a desire for what is forbidden—a desire for things that are contrary to God's will. Describe the area of lust in your life that needs to be demolished, what you need to do to demolish it, and the spiritual weapon(s) to be used in demolishing it. Later this week you will record your progress.

Here is an example.

Stronghold to be demolished: lust; difficulty resisting sexually explicit magazines that cause me to lust

What I need to do to demolish it: avoid looking at sexually explicit magazines on newsstands; destroy copies of pictures I have collected; review and obey John 8:31-32

Spiritual weapons to be used: Helmet of Salvation—claim the mind

"They exchanged the truth of God for a lie, and worshiped and served created things rather than the Creator—who is forever praised" (Rom. 1:25).

"The man without the Spirit does not accept the things that come from the Spirit of God, for they are foolishness to him, and he cannot understand them, because they are spiritually discerned" (1 Cor. 2:14).

" 'You have heard that it was said, "Do not commit adultery." But I tell you that anyone who looks at a woman lustfully has already committed adultery with her in his heart. If your right eye causes you to sin, gouge it out and throw it away. It is better for you to lose one part of your body than for your whole body to be thrown into hell. And if your right hand causes you to sin, cut it off and throw it away. It is better for you to lose one part of your body than for your whole body to go into hell' " (Matt. 5:27-30).

"Those who belong to Christ Jesus have crucified the sinful nature with its passions and desires. Since we live by the Spirit, let us keep in step with the Spirit" (Gal. 5:24-25).

of Christ; Breastplate of Righteousness—confront my sin; Sword of the Spirit—replace those thoughts with God's Word

Now you try it.

Stronghold to be demolished: _____

_____

What I need to do to demolish it: _____

_____

Spiritual weapon(s) to be used: _____

_____

Christians can resist lust through the Holy Spirit's power. The flesh, with its passions and lusts, is to be crucified, as Galatians 5:24 states. The Holy Spirit gives you the ability to overcome the personal stronghold of lust and to bring it captive to Christ.

To help you deal with spiritual strongholds, God has given you His truth. Truth is reality God has chosen to reveal to you. You can discern spiritual truth for two reasons:

- You are born again of the Spirit. John 3:6 says, " 'Flesh gives birth to flesh, but the Spirit gives birth to spirit.' " Because you are born again, the Holy Spirit enables you to discern truth.
- God has given you His revealed Word.

To help you deal with spiritual strongholds, God has given you His truth.

What do this week's Scripture-memory verses, 2 Timothy 3:16-17, say about God's revealed Word and its functions in your life?

_____

_____

You may have answered like this: God's Word is revealed to me to equip me completely for every challenge of the Christian life.

How does God's Spirit convey spiritual truth to you? Circle two:

Through my spirit	Through my flesh
Through my body	Through astrology
Through the Bible	Through direct revelation

God reveals His truth to you so that you can know His will and His way. He conveys this to you through your spirit and through the Bible.

How do you know what God is revealing to you through His Word? One way is knowing how to listen as His Word is preached. You may hear excellent sermons week after week, yet you fail to understand how God may be speaking to you through them because you do not know how to process what you are hearing. The following guide may help you. If you have studied *MasterLife 2: The Disciple's Personality,* you may recognize this material, but read it again as a review.

HOW TO LISTEN TO GOD'S WORD

1. Evaluate what kind of hearer you are. Read Matthew 13:3-23 and classify yourself as one of the following.

   a. *Apathetic* hearer: hears the Word but is not prepared to receive and understand it (see v. 19).

   b. *Superficial* hearer: receives the Word temporarily but does not let it take root in the heart (see vv. 20-21).

   c. *Preoccupied* hearer: receives the Word but lets the worries of this world and the desire for things choke it (see v. 22).

   d. *Reproducing* hearer: receives the Word, understands it, bears fruit, and brings forth results (v. 23).

2. Be alert for a Word from God: (see Jas. 1:19, RSV).

3. Clear away all sin and pride so that the Word can be planted in your heart (see Jas. 1:21).

4. Pay attention to what the Bible says about you, just as you would to your reflection in a mirror (see Jas. 1:23).

   a. Take notes on the Hearing the Word form (see p. 141).

   b. Write the points of the message as the speaker presents them.

   c. Under each point write explanation, illustrations, and application.

   d. Write any specific statements the Spirit impresses on you.

   e. Summarize as soon as possible the main point the speaker wants you to do, be, and/or feel. Ask:
   - What did God say to me through this message?
   - How does my life measure up to this Word?
   - What actions will I take to bring my life in line with this Word?
   - What truth do I need to study further?

5. Do the Word, and you will be blessed in what you do (see Jas. 1:25).

Be alert for a Word from God.

Hearing the Word and learning to apply it to your life are key ways to demolish personal spiritual strongholds. Be a diligent hearer of the Word by using the Hearing the Word form provided on page 141. Copy and use this form so that taking notes will be a regular part of your life.

Hearing the Word and learning to apply it to your life are key ways to demolish personal spiritual strongholds.

Record on the Hearing the Word form what you learn from a Sunday School lesson, a sermon, or a tape.

DAILY MASTER COMMUNICATION GUIDE

❧

PSALM 119:49-56

What God said to me:

_____

_____

_____

_____

_____

_____

_____

What I said to God:

_____

_____

_____

_____

_____

_____

_____

_____

STRENGTH FROM THE BODY OF CHRIST

The body of Christ is another source of help in spiritual warfare. In the body of Christ not only do you hear the Word preached and learn to apply it, but other Bible-believing Christians also hold you accountable for how you live in Christ and help strengthen you for the journey.

 Attend worship services in your church and check the sources of help you receive from the body for spiritual warfare.

❑ Hearing God's Word proclaimed and taught
❑ Fellowshipping with other Christians
❑ Having a group hold you accountable
❑ Being aware that other Christians have struggled as you do
❑ Having a group pray with you about a task, decision, or battle
❑ Ministering to and serving others
❑ Having Christian role models to emulate
❑ Other: _____

 Read Psalm 119:49-56 during your quiet time today. Then complete the Daily Master Communication Guide in the margin.

DAY 3

✑

Encountering Satan's Lies

When we lived in Jember in East Java on our second term as missionaries, every street except one in this city of 75,000 people had a three-way intersection. You see, the people of Jember believed that everything has a spirit and that spirits cannot turn corners. If the city did not have a four-way intersection, then the spirit was stymied at that point. At the one four-way intersection, the police department was on one corner and the Catholic church on another.

One day my secretary, a well-educated Muslim, told me that her mother had back problems because she had once moved a heavy rock at the spring. The secretary said the spirit in the rock, unhappy that the rock had been moved, came to reside in her mother's back to plague her. Animists believe that they must give offerings to keep these spirits from annoying them.

These people's lives were governed by errors originated by Satan. Our job as missionaries was to teach the truth and proclaim God's power over all. But you do not have to serve in a foreign country to encounter Satan's lies in every area of life. Only the Holy Spirit can enable you to discern God's truth from Satan's half-truths and lies.

KNOWING SPIRITUAL TRUTH

According to John 8:31, in the margin, what is the best way to know spiritual truth?

_____

In John 16:13, in the margin, who is the Spirit of truth, who guides you into all truth?

_____

The Holy Spirit guides you into all truth and helps you discern what is truth as opposed to Satan's lies. The best way to know spiritual truth is to hold to Christ's teachings. According to Scripture, this obedience indicates that you are Christ's disciple.

Read 2 Timothy 2:15 in the margin. Underline the term Paul used to describe God's Word.

    A workbook   A course of study   <u>The Word of truth</u>

Define _truth_, based on what you have read so far. Contrast it with error.

_____

_____

The Word of God is the <u>Word of truth</u>. Carriers of God's truth are to represent that truth and its author unapologetically. Your job is to be a worker or craftsperson who correctly handles the Word of truth.

✝ This week's Scripture-memory verses, 2 Timothy 3:16-17, underscore the way the Word of truth can equip you so that you never have to be ashamed of it. In the margin write your memory verses from one to three times.

PUTTING ON THE SPIRITUAL ARMOR

In day 1 you learned the the Breastplate of Righteousness in the Spiritual Armor presentation. You studied three steps in putting on the Breastplate of Righteousness. Review them on page 30.

✝ **Focus on the second step in putting on the Breastplate of Righteousness. Stop and confess any sin that separates you from full fellowship with Christ.**

Kerry Skinner, while serving as a church-staff member in Florida, used the Spiritual Armor to help a couple whose infant was seriously ill

---

Margin notes:

" 'If you hold to my teaching, you are really my disciples' " (John 8:31).

" 'When he, the Spirit of truth, comes, he will guide you into all truth. He will not speak on his own; he will speak only what he hears, and he will tell you what is yet to come' " (John 16:13).

"Do your best to present yourself to God as one approved, a workman who does not need to be ashamed and who correctly handles the word of truth" (2 Tim. 2:15).

Handwritten note: Asking God to to search your heart to reveal any wicked ways in it. Confess any sin. Claim Christ Righteousness

DAILY MASTER COMMUNICATION GUIDE

PSALM 119:57-64

What God said to me:

_____

_____

_____

_____

_____

What I said to God:

_____

_____

_____

_____

_____

_____

_____

with meningitis. The couple, understandably fearful for the child's life, grew doubtful that God was present in the situation. Kerry explained the Spiritual Armor to the parents and helped them pray through the armor for their crisis. A couple who had lost three children overheard his conversation about the Spiritual Armor. Afterward, they took Kerry aside and told him that the Spiritual Armor was helpful to them. I pray that you will continue to find ways the Spiritual Armor will strengthen your walk and that of others, giving you victory over Satan.

 What better way to arm yourself than through prayer? Read "Guide to Praise" and pray through it step by step in your prayer time.

GUIDE TO PRAISE

Praise and thanksgiving are two ways to glorify God, but each has a different focus. Praise is adoring God for who He is—His person, character, and attributes. Thanksgiving, which you studied last week, is expressing gratitude to God for what He has done—His actions. You may find it easier to give thanks than to praise, but a greater act of worship than thanking God for what He does is praising Him for who He is. Thanksgiving leads to praise. Thank God in everything and praise Him continually.

Why Should You Praise God?
1. God should be praised by His people (see Ps. 22:3; Rev. 19:5).
2. Praise is our gift (sacrifice) to God (see 1 Pet. 2:5; Heb. 13:15).
3. God saved us to glorify Him (see Isa. 43:21; Ps. 50:23).
4. Praise is commanded (see 1 Chron. 16:28-29; Ps. 147—150).
5. Praise prepares us for what we will do in heaven (see Rev. 5: 9-14; 7:9-17).

How Should You Praise God?
1. Bless, glorify, praise, and adore God, using your own words.
2. Use scriptural prayers to glorify God.
3. Use spiritual songs, hymns, and scriptural melodies (see Eph. 5: 18-19).
4. Use instruments to praise Him.
5. Recount God's glorious acts. This differs from thanksgiving in that it speaks of past acts as manifestations of God's glory.

What Should You Say When You Praise God?
1. Read aloud and pray the following prayers of praise and adoration.
   a. Glorify God's person, character, and attributes (see Ps. 8; 19; 24; 65; 92; 104; 139).
   b. Praise God's goodness (see Ps. 9; 30; 108; 138; Ex. 15:1-19; 1 Sam. 2:1-10; 1 Chron. 29:10-19; Luke 1:46-55).

c. Enjoin others to honor Him (see Luke 19:37-38; Eph. 3:
20-21; 1 Tim. 1:17; Jude 25; Rev. 5:9-14; 7:9-12; 15:3-4;
19:1-7).

2. Use words of praise such as *worship, adore, bless, exalt, magnify, laud, extol, glorify,* and *honor.*

Praise Exclamations
- Hallelujah!
- Hosanna!
- Praise God!

When Should You Praise the Lord?
Continually!

Where Should You Praise the Lord?
Everywhere!

Who Should Praise the Lord?
Everyone!

Read Psalm 119:57-64 during your quiet time today. Let God speak to you through this passage. Then complete the Daily Master Communication Guide in the margin on page 36.

DAY 4

Faith Grounded in Truth

When you have discerned the truth of God's Word, you have something in which to put your faith. The word *faith* is often misunderstood and misused. A child once defined *faith* as *believing something even when you know it isn't true.* That is not biblical faith. Faith is not blind allegiance that hopes against hope that something is true. Biblical faith is grounded in truth. God's Word is truth.

According to Romans 10:17, in the margin, from where does faith come?

_____

People cannot hear the message unless the Word of Christ is proclaimed. Faith is their response when God's Word is revealed to them.

When should you praise the Lord? Continually!

[handwritten notes in margin]
Remmber
Read
Revelation
12:1-9
in other bible
What I got here
Also 5: 13-14

CREATURE MEAN

"Faith comes from hearing the message, and the message is heard through the word of Christ" (Rom. 10:17).

"Faith is being sure of what we hope for and certain of what we do not see" (Heb. 11:1).

"When Jesus had entered Capernaum, a centurion came to him, asking for help. 'Lord,' he said, 'my servant lies at home paralyzed and in terrible suffering.' Jesus said to him, 'I will go and heal him.' The centurion replied, 'Lord, I do not deserve to have you come under my roof. But just say the word, and my servant will be healed. For I myself am a man under authority, with soldiers under me. I tell this one, "Go," and he goes; and that one, "Come," and he comes. I say to my servant, "Do this," and he does it.' When Jesus heard this, he was astonished and said to those following him, 'I tell you the truth, I have not found anyone in Israel with such great faith. I say to you that many will come from the east and the west, and will take their places at the feast with Abraham, Isaac and Jacob in the kingdom of heaven. But the subjects of the kingdom will be thrown outside, into the darkness, where there will be weeping and gnashing of teeth.' Then Jesus said to the centurion, 'Go! It will be done just as you believed it would.' And his servant was healed at that very hour" (Matt. 8:5-13).

SURE OF WHAT WE HOPE FOR

The words *being sure* in Hebrews 11:1, in the margin, can be translated *assurance*. This verse says that faith is *believing God's promises* as strongly as if they were already objective realities.

Which of these statements is a truer definition of *faith*?
❑ **Something God says is true but you cannot perceive with your senses**
❑ **Something you can perceive with your senses**

Faith involves having absolute confidence in something without physical evidence. We can know God only when we have faith in what He says, since God is invisible. Your assurance comes as God reveals His will through His Word. Often, Christians try to manufacture faith by desperately trying to believe that something will happen. Their "faith" is based not on God's revealed will but on the desires of their hearts.

The account of Jesus' healing of the centurion's servant in Matthew 8:5-13, in the margin, is an example of true faith. When Jesus offered to heal the servant, the centurion believed that Jesus would do it. For this man, Jesus' promise of healing was a reality waiting to be claimed. The servant was healed immediately.

In Matthew 8:5-13 what was the basis of this man's faith?
❑ **The word of the Lord**
❑ **The desire of his heart**
❑ **A difference in his situation**

The man's actions were based on Jesus' assurance to him. When Jesus commanded him to go, assuring him that his servant would be healed, this promise came to pass. The centurion had such faith that he believed that the servant would be healed by Jesus' saying the words without even traveling to his home. The man's assurance occurred at the moment he heard and believed what the Lord said.

CERTAIN OF WHAT WE DO NOT SEE

The second part of Hebrews 11:1 says that faith is being "certain of what we do not see." The words *being certain* refer to a conviction. It has been said that while a belief is something you hold, a conviction is something that holds you.

Write a definition of *faith* by paraphrasing Hebrews 11:1: "Faith is being sure of what we hope for and certain of what we do not see."

_____

_____

Faith pleases God because it shows that we trust His promises even when they seem to be impossible. You may have written something like, Faith is being sure that something God promises is a reality.

Say aloud this week's Scripture-memory verses, 2 Timothy 3:16-17. Based on these verses, describe how you think God's Word thoroughly equips you to have faith in things you cannot see.

_____

_____

As you have studied about faith and believing in things you cannot see, based on God's promises, maybe you have thought about requests on your Prayer-Covenant List. Has God revealed a promise from Scripture that you have claimed for some of those requests? As you learn about faith, you realize that God's Word is the basis for believing in things you cannot see.

Turn to your Prayer-Covenant List on page 143. Ask God to reveal a prayer promise about each item you have listed. When He does, write the prayer promise for each request on your list.

DEMOLISHING PERSONAL SPIRITUAL STRONGHOLDS
In day 2 you identified a stronghold you wanted to demolish in the area of lust. Today give a progress report on how you are using the spiritual weapon(s) you listed to demolish this stronghold.

How I am using a spiritual weapon(s) to demolish the stronghold of lust:

_____

_____

 Continue to use "Guide to Praise," which you learned in day 3, during your quiet time this week.

 Read Psalm 119:65-72 during your quiet time today. Let God speak to you through this passage. Then complete the Daily Master Communication Guide in the margin.

DAILY MASTER COMMUNICATION GUIDE

PSALM 119:65-72

What God said to me:

What I said to God:

**DAILY MASTER
COMMUNICATION
GUIDE**

PSALM 119:73-80

What God said to me:

_____

_____

_____

_____

_____

_____

_____

What I said to God:

_____

_____

_____

_____

_____

_____

DAY 5

Believing Without Seeing

Faith is being convinced that something is real because God said it, even though you cannot see it. Faith is possible even when your physical senses cannot prove the reality of something. In fact, *The Amplified Bible* says that faith is "the proof of things [we] do not see *and* the conviction of their reality—faith perceiving as real fact what is not revealed to the senses" (Heb. 11:1, AMP).

You do not have to see something to believe that it exists. You may not understand electricity; yet you still turn on the light when you enter a dark room. The reason you can believe without seeing is the evidence that the thing exists. You have never seen the Holy Spirit, but you can experience Him at work in your life and in the lives of others. You have not seen Jesus, but you know that He is present within you. Jesus told Thomas, " 'Blessed are those who have not seen, and yet have believed' " (John 20:29). You can believe because the Holy Spirit reveals truth to you through God's Word.

 This week's Scripture-memory verses, 2 Timothy 3:16-17, promise that God's Word can equip you for all things— including the steps of faith you take. Write these verses in the margin from one to three times. Also take this opportunity to review 1 John 4:4, the verse you memorized in week 1.

Write in your own words Hebrews 11:1: Faith is being "certain of what we do not see."

_____

_____

Faith is the conviction that something is real even though you cannot see it. Perhaps you wrote a similar statement.

FAITH IN ACTION
Hebrews 11:2 affirms that many persons in the Old Testament were noted for their faith. The remaining verses of Hebrews 11 records ways their lives demonstrated faith. This roll call of faith does not mention them merely because of what they thought. They are listed and praised because of their works of faith—their faith in *action*.

Faith is not just an intellectual belief or an emotional response. You show faith when you act on the revealed will of God. God's will is revealed in His Word. His Word says that your life should exercise faith.

In the margin read the Scriptures about faith. Then match the Scripture references with the summary statements.

___ 1. Matthew 21:22   a. Pray in faith.
___ 2. Hebrews 11:3   b. Understand by faith.
___ 3. Ephesians 2:8-9 c. Live by faith.
___ 4. 2 Corinthians 5:7 d. Be saved by faith.

Did you answer 1. a, 2., b, 3. d, 4.c? Faith in action uses God's Word to know and do God's will. To use God's Word effectively, become and remain familiar with it. Being familiar with the Word and hiding it in your heart will help you know the truth when Satan's lies confront you. What is your commitment to daily, personal Bible study?

Describe how you are doing in reading your Bible daily. How many of the past 11 days have you read your Bible since you began this study? _____

If you have not read your Bible for all of the past 11 days, describe what you will do to improve your consistency.

_____

After you have learned to use God's Word to discern His will, your lifestyle will be to walk in faith. Faith is acting on God's revealed will.

Describe something God has recently revealed to you through His Word on which you are acting by faith.

_____

Review by describing the relationship between truth and faith.

_____

God's Word is truth—the truth revealed by God and not the lies revealed by the devil. The devil would like for you to believe that if you cannot see something, you cannot believe it. By faith you believe in God's Word and act on its reality, even when what you believe cannot be physically seen. Faith gives you victory over the devil's snares.

PUTTING ON THE SPIRITUAL ARMOR
Focus again on the importance of wearing the Breastplate of Righteousness. Review on page 30 the three steps you learned for putting on the Breastplate of Righteousness.

" 'If you believe, you will receive whatever you ask for in prayer' " (Matt. 21:22).

"By faith we understand that the universe was formed at God's command, so that what is seen was not made out of what was visible" (Heb. 11:3).

"It is by grace you have been saved, through faith—and this not from yourselves, it is the gift of God—not by works, so that no one can boast" (Eph. 2:8-9).

"We live by faith, not by sight" (2 Cor. 5:7).

Faith gives you victory over the devil's snares.

"God made him who had no sin to be sin for us, so that in him we might become the righteousness of God" (2 Cor. 5:21).

Focus on the third step in putting on the Breastplate of Righteousness. Read 2 Corinthians 5:21 in the margin. Stop and claim Christ's righteousness to cover your sins and to give you right standing with Him. Ask Christ to forgive you and to help you live a righteous life. Taking this step illustrates that you believe what God says even though you cannot see it.

Share with your family, a Christian friend, or a group the Breastplate of Righteousness part of the Spiritual Armor.

Continue listing on the Relational-Witnessing Chart (p. 135) the names of persons who are not saved. Also write their names on the Prayer-Covenant List on page 143. Make friends with them and pray for them.

Over the next few days as you read the Word, be alert to Scriptures that relate to the requests on your Prayer-Covenant List. When you pray about that request, if you sense that God is impressing you to believe that scriptural promise, write it in the space provided on your list. Do not make this just a routine action. The Holy Spirit needs to give you the faith to believe that a Scripture is God's promise to be applied to the problem. I write a need and a date in the margin of my Bible beside the promise that I sense God has given me for that need. As I read my Bible later, those promises become faith builders.

Read Psalm 119:73-80 during your quiet time today. Let God speak to you through this passage. Then complete the Daily Master Communication Guide in the margin on page 40.

HAS THIS WEEK MADE A DIFFERENCE?
Review "My Walk with the Master This Week" at the beginning of this week's material. Mark the activities you have finished by drawing vertical lines in the diamonds beside them. Finish any incomplete activities. Think about what you will say during your group session about your work on these activities.

Growing in your faith to believe God's promises can help you continue to replace Satan's strongholds in your life with Christlike character traits.

I hope that this study of "Truth and Faith" has made you aware of ways Satan tries to entrap you by making you doubt God's Word and things you cannot see or physically experience. Satan is never more unhappy than when you act on faith, because in that act you state your belief in God's promises rather than in Satan's lies. Growing in your faith to believe God's promises can help you continue to replace Satan's strongholds in your life with Christlike character traits. The Spiritual Armor gives you weapons to help you forge ahead when you need to walk by faith and not by sight.

WEEK 3

Rely on God's Word

This Week's Goal
You will be able to depend on and use the Sword of the Spirit in spiritual warfare.

My Walk with the Master This Week
You will complete the following activities to develop the six biblical disciplines. When you have completed each activity, draw a vertical line in the diamond beside it.

SPEND TIME WITH THE MASTER
◇ Have a quiet time each day. Check each day you have a quiet time: ❑ Sunday ❑ Monday ❑ Tuesday ❑ Wednesday ❑ Thursday ❑ Friday ❑ Saturday

LIVE IN THE WORD
◇ Read your Bible every day. Write what God says to you and what you say to God.
◇ Read "How to Study God's Word."
◇ Memorize Psalm 1:2-3.
◇ Review 1 John 4:4 and 2 Timothy 3:16-17.
◇ Read the God's Word in Your Heart and Hand presentation.

PRAY IN FAITH
◇ Select an ideological stronghold and pray through the Spiritual Armor about it.
◇ Use "Guide to Confession and Forgiveness" during your prayer time.

FELLOWSHIP WITH BELIEVERS
◇ Share with someone the Sword of the Spirit part of the Spiritual Armor.

WITNESS TO THE WORLD
◇ List on the Relational-Witnessing Chart the names of lost persons.
◇ Begin using the witnessing booklet your leader gave you.

MINISTER TO OTHERS
◇ Learn the Sword of the Spirit part of the Spiritual Armor.

This Week's Scripture-Memory Verses
His delight is in the law of the Lord,
and on his law he meditates day and night.
He is like a tree planted by streams of water,
which yields its fruit in season
and whose leaf does not wither.
Whatever he does prospers (Ps. 1:2-3).

DAY 1

God's Reliable Word

God most often gives me guidance as I read through a book of the Bible one chapter at a time.

I have learned that God most often gives me guidance as I read through a book of the Bible one chapter at a time. I usually keep a list of questions or problems I am facing to refer to during my quiet time. At one time an agenda item was my need to find a successor to a retiring leader at the International Mission Board. I had been praying about this matter for several months when I went to Brazil to speak at a meeting of missionaries. Traveling with me were Ron Wilson, the area director for Brazil and the Caribbean, and John White, the treasurer of three missionary organizations represented at the meeting.

During the trip I read the next chapter in my Bible reading, Luke 19, in which Jesus told the parable of a nobleman who called his servants around him, gave them different amounts of money, and told them to put it to work. He was testing his servants to discover who could assume greater responsibility. That was what I was doing in seeking a replacement for the retiring leader. I knew that I needed to find a leader who could make long-range plans as well as build on past accomplishments.

Not knowing what I was thinking, Ron Wilson had remarked to me that John White was so industrious that Ron continually sought ways to challenge him. Ron commented that he believed one day John would have an even more responsible position. I began to see that my reading Luke 19 related to my enlisting the right person and that I needed to find out more about John White. John had been an assistant to Truett Cathy, the founder of the Chick-Fil-A restaurant chain, and had performed the same type of duties he would have in this position. With a doctor's degree in law and a master's degree in business administration, John possessed the skills that would be required for this position. In addition, John had been a missionary for 10 years and had pastored in Rio de Janeiro and Belo Horizonte.

Ron Wilson told me that John had been the treasurer for one mission and had been given the responsibility of three missions. With his financial and administrative gifts and his experience as a missionary, he was well qualified to help me direct mission work around the world. Through the right Scripture at the right time, God led me to choose the right person to fill a major position. John's performance since then has confirmed that he was God's choice for the job.

Through the right Scripture at the right time, God led me to choose the right person to fill a major position.

Describe a time when God led you through His Word to make a crucial decision.

_____

Your study this week will focus on various ways God's Word imparts truth so that you can overcome the enemy and can have victory in Christ. At the end of this week's study you will be able to—
- define the ways God's Word equips you to serve Him;
- study God's Word effectively.

THE STANDARD OF TRUTH

According to 2 Timothy 3:16-17, last week's Scripture-memory verses, what should be the basis of your standard for truth?

_____

Why do these verses say that you can rely on Scripture for teaching as well as correcting and training?

_____

Ministry that Christians perform needs to be based on the Bible. Scripture is God-breathed and therefore has authority for all correcting and training. It is the standard for truth and right.

Describe a time when you relied on sources other than God's Word to receive guidance for your life.

_____

_____

"All men are like grass, and all their glory is like the flowers of the field; the grass withers and the flowers fall, but the word of the Lord stands forever" (1 Pet. 1: 24-25).

Standards are based on truth only when they are in line with God's Word. The inspired (God-breathed) Word is the only standard that stands the test of time. Our opinions and cultural priorities change, but the Word of God always endures. Read 1 Peter 1:24-25 in the margin.

In 2 Timothy 3:16-17, in the margin, underline the four areas Scripture can be used for. Draw a star beside the area with which you feel you have the least experience.

Scripture is useful for teaching, rebuking, correcting, and training in righteousness. You may believe that areas involving doctrinal issues are the ones in which you have the most need for instruction. A Scripture may have rebuked you about an evil practice. You may need the Scripture to help you examine ways to live rightly and to hold you accountable for sinful behavior. You may have experienced Scripture correcting your direction back to the right path. You may have experienced scriptural training in right living. God's Word is authoritative in all areas of ministry because God is its source. This week you will study in depth these four ways Scripture can be used.

"All Scripture is God-breathed and is useful for teaching, rebuking, correcting and training in righteousness, so that the man of God may be thoroughly equipped for every good work" (2 Tim. 3:16-17).

DAILY MASTER COMMUNICATION GUIDE

PSALM 119:81-88

What God said to me:

_____

_____

_____

_____

_____

_____

What I said to God:

_____

_____

_____

_____

_____

_____

_____

 Begin working on this week's Scripture-memory verses, Psalm 1:2-3, which focus on the importance of God's Word. Turn to page 43 and read them aloud.

 Learning how to study the Bible will make it easier for you to obtain all God wants to provide for you in His Word. Examine the following guidelines for studying the Word.

HOW TO STUDY GOD'S WORD

Many methods of Bible study exist:
- Studying a theme of the Bible
- Studying a book of the Bible
- Studying a passage in the Bible
- Studying a Bible word

Detailed instructions for each of these methods is provided at the back of _Disciple's Study Bible_ and in the course _BibleGuide to Discipleship and Doctrine_.[1]

The Bible is about God more than about people. However, the Bible is filled with people's stories. Whether they interacted with Him positively or negatively, God included them to teach us through examples from real life. Bible characters show God's principles as expressed in human experience. Studying a Bible character encourages you to apply God's principles to your life.

Choose a Bible character and discover what God teaches you through this person's life.

1. Gather basic information about the character:
   - Genealogy: what shaped the person's formative years?
   - Geography: where was the person born?
   - Significant events in the person's life
   - How the person responded to events
   - What other characters were this person's contemporaries
   - Statements the character made and what others said about this person
   - What impact the person had on others
   - The person's strengths and weaknesses
   - Evidence of the person's devotion to the Lord
2. Establish a lifeline for the Bible character and document with Scripture.
3. Write biblical principles you learn from the character's life. Read in one sitting all the Bible has to say about the character and draw lessons from his or her life.
4. Apply the teaching to your life. What strengths or weaknesses do you share with the person? Can you identify with this person's temptations and victories? Ask God to help you incorporate the truths you have learned from this character to make you a better disciple.

Read Psalm 119:81-88 during your quiet time today. Let God speak to you through this passage. Then complete the Daily Master Communication Guide on page 46.

DAY 2

The Basis of All Teaching

Yesterday you learned that God's Word is profitable in four specific ways. Today you will focus on the first of these, shown below in bold type:

1. **teaching**
2. rebuking
3. correcting
4. training in righteousness

GOD'S WORD TEACHES

The Phillips translation of 2 Timothy 3:16-17, the verse you are studying, uses the term "teaching the faith." Sometimes false doctrines steal into our lives. Someone may say that Jesus did not really have a human nature. Another person may say that Jesus did not actually die on the cross but only fainted. Satan can use your ignorance and false beliefs to bring you under attack. In contrast to lies and false teachings, we can rely on God's Word, which is absolutely true and totally dependable.

Teaching is preventative. Biblical instruction and guidance are designed to prevent a problem or to help a person correct it. If you are grounded in truth, you have God's Word as a point of reference when Satan tempts you to stray, and you can have victory.

Describe a time when proper instruction in God's Word prevented you from making a harmful decision.

_____

_____

Teaching is the primary way Jesus communicated with His disciples.

Read 2 Timothy 1:5 and 2 Timothy 3:15-17 in the margin. How was Timothy taught God's Word?

_____

Evidently, Timothy's mother and grandmother taught him. Who

"I have been reminded of your sincere faith, which first lived in your grandmother Lois and in your mother Eunice and, I am persuaded, now lives in you also" (2 Tim. 1:5).

"From infancy you have known the holy Scriptures, which are able to make you wise for salvation through faith in Christ Jesus. All Scripture is God-breathed and is useful for teaching, rebuking, correcting, and training in righteousness, so that the man of God may be thoroughly equipped for every good work" (2 Tim. 3:15-17).

have been influential teachers in your life? List several.

_____

_____

What was the result of Timothy's being taught the Scriptures?

_____

They led him to salvation, and now, Paul says, they will equip Timothy for every good work. The Bible is the ultimate source of all teaching. Reading it and applying its precepts prepare people for salvation because they call people to believe in Jesus.

This week's Scripture-memory verses, Psalm 1:2-3, urge you to delight in God's Word, not just to read it. Read the verses aloud again and see how much you can already say from memory.

I hope that you are developing such a hunger and thirst for the Scriptures that you genuinely feel that your day is not complete until you have spent time in the Word.

DEMOLISHING PERSONAL SPIRITUAL STRONGHOLDS
In the past two weeks you focused on personal spiritual strongholds in your life. Today you will look at another stronghold mentioned in the Sermon on the Mount and will consider ways the Holy Spirit helps you build Christlike character as you demolish it.

Read the verses in the margin, which deal with the stronghold of harmful speech. People can use the tongue to bring glory to the Lord or to utter caustic, poisonous words. Satan can use the tongue to destroy you and others. Possible strongholds of improper speech are exaggeration, swearing for emphasis, lying, using big words to strengthen your argument, hurtful criticism, and profanity. Describe the area of improper speech in your life that needs to be demolished, what you need to do to demolish it, and the spiritual weapon(s) to be used in demolishing it. Later this week you will record your progress.

Here is an example.

Stronghold to be demolished: taking God's name in vain to strengthen the impact of what I am saying

What I need to do to demolish it: learn more effective ways to com-

---

" 'You have heard that it was said to the people long ago, "Do not break your oath, but keep the oaths you have made to the Lord." But I tell you, Do not swear at all: either by heaven, for it is God's throne; or by the earth, for it is his footstool; or by Jerusalem, for it is the city of the Great King. And do not swear by your head, for you cannot make even one hair white or black. Simply let your "Yes" be "Yes," and your "No," "No"; anything beyond this comes from the evil one' " (Matt. 5:33-37).

"The tongue also is a fire, a world of evil among the parts of the body. It corrupts the whole person, sets the whole course of his life on fire, and is itself set on fire by hell" (Jas. 3:6).

Reckless words pierce like a sword,
*   but the tongue of the wise brings healing (Prov. 12:18).*

" 'The things that come out of the mouth come from the heart, and these make a man unclean' " (Matt. 15:18).

municate so that I can reveal my true feelings without using words that hurt God and others

Spiritual weapons to be used: Sword of the Spirit—replace my desire to say more than I should by reading what the Scripture says about improper language; Breastplate of Righteousness—confess my sin and begin to live rightly

Now you try it.

Stronghold to be demolished: _____

_____

What I need to do to demolish it: _____

_____

Spiritual weapon(s) to be used: _____

_____

The tongue reflects a person's spirit; it reveals what is in the heart. Satan is pleased when you do not guard your tongue, because you demonstrate that he, not Christ, controls you.

Reread James 3:6, Proverbs 12:18, and Matthew 15:18 in the margin on page 48. Then match their references below with the statements that describe what the tongue is capable of doing.

___ 1. James 3:6   a. Reveals what is in the heart
___ 2. Proverbs 12:18   b. Destroys the course of one's life
___ 3. Matthew 15:18   c. Brings healing

The tongue is capable of both good and evil. It can bring healing, redirect the course of a person's life, or reveal the depravity of someone's heart. The correct answers are 1. b, 2. c, 3. a.

Read Psalm 119:89-96 during your quiet time today. Then complete the Daily Master Communication Guide in the margin.

DAILY MASTER COMMUNICATION GUIDE

PSALM 119:89-96

What God said to me:

_____

_____

_____

_____

_____

_____

What I said to God:

_____

_____

_____

_____

_____

_____

_____

DAY 3

Straying from the Way

How do you know when you are living outside God's standards? How do you know when you have drifted from right living? God's Word is the standard against which you measure yourself. God's Word can reach out and pull you back onto the path if you have strayed from the way.

Today you will study the second of the four specific ways God's Word is profitable for you, shown below in bold type.

1. teaching
2. **rebuking**
3. correcting
4. training in righteousness

GOD'S WORD REBUKES

A rebuke is a reproof that brings conviction, an awareness that you have done wrong. As you have read the Scriptures in the past, has a verse ever seemed to jump out to identify a way you have strayed? For example, you may be reading in Matthew 5 and reach the verse " 'Love your enemies and pray for those who persecute you' " (Matt. 5:44). Suddenly, you feel that this verse has flashing neon lights around it. You say to yourself: *He's talking to me! I haven't loved and prayed for my enemies. Instead, I've been wishing them ill.* When that happens, it is no coincidence. The Lord is identifying a weakness in you. This is a wake-up call from the Scriptures telling you to get back in line with God's will and ways.

Describe a time when a verse of Scripture seemed to convict you that you had strayed from the right way of living.

_____

_____

Scriptural rebuke gives you guidance. It makes you aware that you are traveling in the opposite direction you should be going—that Satan has misled you. Through a verse of Scripture the Lord seems to say, "Here is the way; turn around from the way you are going and walk in the truth."

The Bible speaks of rebuke in a variety of situations. Read the verses in the margin that contain rebukes. Then match the references on the next page with the statements describing situations in which a rebuke is to be used.

"If anyone does not obey our instructions in this letter, take special note of him. Do not associate with him, in order that he may feel ashamed. Yet do not regard him as an enemy, but warn him as a brother" (2 Thess. 3:14-15).

"Those who sin are to be rebuked publicly, so that the others may take warning. I charge you, in the sight of God and Christ Jesus and the elect angels, to keep these instructions without partiality, and to do nothing out of favoritism" (1 Tim. 5:20-21).

" 'If your brother sins against you, go and show him his fault, just between the two of you. If he listens to you, you have won your brother over' " (Matt. 18:15).

"He sent messengers on ahead, who went into a Samaritan village to get things ready for him; but the people there did not welcome him, because he was heading for Jerusalem. When the disciples James and John saw this, they asked, 'Lord, do you want us to call fire down from heaven to destroy them?' But Jesus turned and rebuked them, and they went to another village" (Luke 9:52-55).

___B___ 1. 2 Thessalonians 3:14-15

___A___ 2. 1 Timothy 5:20-21

___D___ 3. Matthew 18:15

___E___ 4. Luke 9:52-55

___C___ 5. John 14:9-10

a. When the person sinning is in a position of leadership that will cause others to stray

b. When the person will not respond to the teaching of sound doctrine

c. When a person needs to be shocked into realizing his or her spiritual dullness or lack of understanding

d. When a person does not realize or does not admit that he or she is living contrary to the truth

e. When a person has a wrong spirit

> "Jesus answered, 'Don't you know me, Philip, even after I have been among you such a long time? Anyone who has seen me has seen the Father. How can you say, 'Show us the Father'? Don't you believe that I am the Father, and that the Father is in me?' " (John 14:9-10).

God's Word contains all you need to show you the way when Satan influences you to sin. The statements you read indicate times when the teachings of Scripture were used for rebuke or reproof. The correct answers are 1. b, 2. a, 3. d, 4. e, 5. c. Scripture is used to rebuke a wrong behavior or a wrong belief.

PUTTING ON THE SPIRITUAL ARMOR
This week's study underscores the importance of taking up the Sword of the Spirit, which is God's Word, as part of the Spiritual Armor. Turn to page 129 and review the Spiritual Armor presentation, with special emphasis on the Sword of the Spirit. By the end of this study you will be able to explain the entire presentation in your own words.

The Sword of the Spirit reminds you to do three things:
1. Grasp the Word. Use it whether or not the enemy acknowledges that it is God's Word.
2. Let the Holy Spirit use the Word. It is His sword.
3. Pray on the basis of the Word. The Spirit will use the Word to reveal God's will to you and to help you know what to pray for and do.

Focus on the first of the three reminders. Be prepared to use God's Word when you face an attack by Satan. When you feel that the enemy is tempting you, search your heart for God's Word, which you have hidden there, to remind you how you are to respond. Read Hebrews 4:12 in the margin.

GOD'S WORD IN YOUR HEART AND HAND
The hand in which you grasp the Word can be used to show several levels of Bible awareness and Bible study and to illustrate the importance of dwelling on the truths of God's Word. To keep Christ at the center of your life, you need God's Word in your heart. As you pray through

> "The word of God is living and active. Sharper than any double-edged sword, it penetrates even to dividing soul and spirit, joints and marrow; it judges the thoughts and attitudes of the heart" (Heb. 4:12).

DAILY MASTER COMMUNICATION GUIDE

PSALM 119:97-104

What God said to me:

_____

_____

_____

_____

_____

_____

_____

What I said to God:

_____

_____

_____

_____

_____

_____

_____

_____

the Spiritual Armor, imagine grasping God's Word, the Sword of the Spirit, as you fight spiritual battles.

Read the God's Word in Your Heart and Hand presentation on pages 132–34.

Continue to hide the Word in your heart. In the margin on page 51 write from memory this week's Scripture-memory verses, Psalm 1:2-3. Then say aloud your memory verses from weeks 1 and 2.

Read Psalm 119:97-104 during your quiet time today. Let God speak to you through this passage. Then complete the Daily Master Communication Guide in the margin.

DAY 4

Resetting Your Direction

As you learned in day 3 about rebuke, God's Word is useful to remind you when the rudder of the ship is steering the ship in the wrong direction—when God intends for you to pursue one course of action, but you are doggedly pursuing another. But Scripture is also useful for those who are not going in the opposite direction but have strayed from the path. The longer they go off course, the farther they move from the right way. They need a slight change of direction to get back on course before they go so far that rebuke is necessary.

Isaiah 30:21 says, "Whether you turn to the right or to the left, your ears will hear a voice behind you, saying, 'This is the way; walk in it.'" In 2 Timothy 3:16-17 you learned four specific ways God's Word keeps you on course. The third way appears below in bold type.

1. teaching
2. rebuking
3. **correcting**
4. training in righteousness

GOD'S WORD CORRECTS

God's Word profits a person or a church that needs to be corrected. It corrects your sins and failures. The word _correct_ comes from a Greek word that means _to restore_. The Phillips translation of the Bible translates the term as "resetting the direction of a man's life." Correction is a Word from God that causes you to get back on the right track.

When do you need to reset your direction? Perhaps you read Matthew 6:19-34 and feel that this passage speaks a Word of correction to you, making you aware that you have spent your life amassing earthly goods instead of laying up treasures in heaven. In this case the direction of your life could be reset because of an encounter with God's Word.

Read the Scriptures in the margin about times when a Word from the Lord was used to correct. Then match their references with the reasons the correction was needed.

_c_ 1. Matthew 19:13-14   a. **For making someone aware that he or she is acting contrary to his or her best interests**

_a_ 2. Luke 9:49-50   b. **For getting someone back on the proper course**

_b_ 3. 2 Timothy 2:24-25   c. **When someone does not understand the Kingdom**

God's correction of you is motivated by love. When you have Christ at the center of your life, you need to have your direction properly set. It would be impossible to be an intimate disciple of Christ if you strayed from the path. The correct answers to the exercise are 1. c, 2. a, 3. b.

PUTTING ON THE SPIRITUAL ARMOR
In day 3 you reviewed the importance of the Sword of the Spirit in the Spiritual Armor presentation. You learned three guidelines for taking up the Sword of the Spirit. Review them on page 51.

Focus on the second guideline for taking up the Sword of the Spirit. Stop and ask the Holy Spirit to bring the Word to mind as you carry out your daily activities and need a reminder of how you should live, even if the Word brings correction to your life.

Say aloud this week's Scripture-memory verses, Psalm 1: 2-3. What occurs when a person delights in the Word and allows it to correct him or her when necessary?

When a person delights in the Word, then the correction that springs from the Word will be welcome. Such a person will not wither in the time of temptation and trial and will prosper.

Have you become more aware of your sins as you have just studied about correction from the Word? God offers forgiveness and fellowship with Him through confession. When you feel a barrier between you and God, use the following guide to discover and confess any sin that may be blocking the way.

"Little children were brought to Jesus for him to place his hands on them and pray for them. But the disciples rebuked those who brought them. Jesus said, 'Let the little children come to me, and do not hinder them, for the kingdom of heaven belongs to such as these'" (Matt. 19:13-14).

"'Master,' said John, 'we saw a man driving out demons in your name and we tried to stop him, because he is not one of us.' 'Do not stop him,' Jesus said, 'For whoever is not against you is for you'" (Luke 9:49-50).

"The Lord's servant must not quarrel; instead, he must be kind to everyone, able to teach, not resentful. Those who oppose him he must gently instruct, in the hope that God will grant them repentance leading them to a knowledge of the truth, and that they will come to their senses and escape from the trap of the devil, who has taken them captive to do his will" (2 Tim. 2:24-25).

✠ As you pray today, follow the instructions in "Guide to Confession and Forgiveness."

GUIDE TO CONFESSION AND FORGIVENESS

God wants you to walk in the light and to have fellowship with Him and with other Christians (see 1 John 1:5-10).

Ask the Holy Spirit to Convict You of Sins

See John 16:8-11.

1. Do not try to convict yourself or to become involved in morbid introspection.
2. Ask God to search your heart, thoughts, and ways (see Ps. 139:23-24).
3. Let the Holy Spirit use the Word to show you how God views your heart, thoughts, and ways (see Rom. 8:26-27; Heb. 4: 12-13).
   a. Read your Bible daily.
   b. Read special passages as you feel the need.

Agree with God About the Seriousness of Your Sins

1. To confess, agree with God. The word *confess* means *to agree with or admit*. Do not try to excuse your behavior but accept what God convicts you of (see 1 John 1:8-10).
2. To confess, walk in the light of His holiness (see 1 John 1:7). Do not compare yourself to someone else to try to walk in that person's light.
3. To confess, be honest with God (see 1 John 1:8-10). Do not hide anything from God or from yourself.

Acknowledge Christ as the Atoning Sacrifice for Your Sins

See 1 John 2:1-2.

1. Express your sorrow and repentance to God (see Ps. 51).
2. Ask for forgiveness based on the blood of Christ, which cleanses us from all sin (1 John 1:7; 2:2). Do not base your request on works of righteousness you have done in the past or plan to do in the future (see Titus 3:5).
3. Turn over your sins to your advocate, Christ (see Heb. 4:14,16; 7:25; 9:24-26; 10:19,22; 1 John 2:2). Do not consider your sins again. Because God has forgiven you, consider those sins to be history.

Walk in the Light with Other Christians

See 1 John 1:7.

1. Be honest with other Christians about your sins. To walk in the light is to be open and honest (see 1 John 1:7).
2. Confess your sins to other understanding Christians as needed (see Jas. 5:16).

Let the Holy Spirit use the Word to show you how God views your heart, thoughts, and ways.

Ask for forgiveness based on the blood of Christ.

a. Confess during prayer with other believers.

b. Confess only to those who can help bear your burden in the spirit of humility (see Gal. 6:1). They should be persons who can keep a confidence and can help you overcome temptation.

c. Tell others only what is necessary. On some occasions you need to confess only that you have sinned and that God has forgiven you. At other times you may confess the sin but not the details. (If your confession relates to sexual impurity, do not go into detail. If you need to discuss details, do so with your pastor or a trained counselor.) If your sin is known or affects the church, ask others to forgive you as God has.

d. Confess only your sin, not someone else's. Do not blame any-one for your sin. Accept your part of the responsibility and do not implicate others.

3. Renounce your sin and make restitution if possible (see Luke 19:8). Any restitution is not to be considered penance and in no way pays for your sin. It is not done to relieve any guilt feelings, because Christ has already forgiven you. Yet restitution helps restore anything you have taken from another person and may witness to that person.

Walk in the Light with Christ
See 1 John 1:7.

1. When you sin again, confess immediately and ask God to forgive you.

2. Do not give up your struggle to be free from a sin you repeat-edly commit. Satan will try to convince you that God will not forgive you for committing the same sin again. Of course, gen-uine repentance and turning from sin are necessary for you to receive forgiveness. However, sometimes you sin again in spite of your good intentions. If you seek forgiveness in genuine repentance, God will forgive you again. He will do for you as much as Jesus asked Peter to do: " 'If he sins against you seven times in a day, and seven times comes back to you and says, "I repent," forgive him' " (Luke 17:4).

a. Be careful that you do not sin because you know that you can ask to be forgiven. God does not play games. If you willfully sin, you treat lightly Christ's sacrifice for you.

b. If you continually commit the same sin, counsel with your pastor or a trained Christian counselor.

3. Sin in a Christian's life does not change the person's relationship as a child of God, but it creates a barrier to fellowship with Him.

Forgiveness is God's gift. Confession and repentance are the God-ordained ways to free you from sin's penalty, presence, and power. Although you never reach perfection in this world, through Christ you can continually walk in the light with our holy God.

Restitution helps restore anything you have taken from another person and may witness to that person.

Confession and repentance are the God-ordained ways to free you from sin's penalty, presence, and power.

**DAILY MASTER
COMMUNICATION
GUIDE**

PSALM 119:105-112

What God said to me:

_____

_____

_____

_____

_____

_____

_____

What I said to God:

_____

_____

_____

_____

_____

_____

_____

_____

As you read "Guide to Confession and Forgiveness," if you had a question about whether you have made that initial confession of your sins and experienced salvation, you can receive Jesus Christ now by inviting Him into your heart. Romans 10:13 says, "Everyone who calls on the name of the Lord will be saved." If you wish, use this prayer to express your commitment:

Lord Jesus, I need You. I am a sinner. I want You to be my Savior and my Lord. I accept Your death on the cross as the payment for my sins, and I now entrust my life to Your care. Thank You for forgiving me and for giving me a new life. Please help me grow in my understanding of Your love and power so that my life will bring glory and honor to You. Amen.

Signed _D. Echols_   Date _4/3/2000_

I hope that you do not feel awkward if you began this study thinking that you were a Christian, only to realize that you had never fully given your heart and life to Christ. Often, as people learn through _MasterLife_ what it means to commit their lives to Christ, they become aware that they have not taken this crucial first step.

 Read Psalm 119:105-112 during your quiet time today. Let God speak to you through this passage. Then complete the Daily Master Communication Guide in the margin.

DAY 5

Thoroughly Equipped

When you studied the Breastplate of Righteousness, you learned that you were to keep the breastplate firmly fastened in place with upright character and righteous living. But how do you know what is involved in righteous living? In learning the Spiritual Armor, you read Psalm 66:18:

_If I had cherished sin in my heart,
the Lord would not have listened._

You may yearn to live rightly and to remove yourself from a situation in which your heart cherishes sin. But how do you know what thoughts to avoid? How do you know how to separate yourself from wrong?

God's Word supplies ample instruction for how to live. Everything you need for guidance is contained in the Bible. You have been learning four ways the Scriptures benefit you. Today you will focus on the last way, shown below in bold type.

1. teaching
2. rebuking
3. correcting
4. training in righteousness

GOD'S WORD INSTRUCTS IN RIGHTEOUSNESS

Instruction in righteousness is more than just rearing a child or learning how to discipline. The Bible teaches moral character—how to live life rightly. The Phillips translation of 2 Timothy 3:16-17 says that the Bible is profitable for "training … in good living."

In Galatians 5:19-26, in the margin, underline with one line the things you are to put off. Underline with two lines the Spirit's ways a Christian is to add to his or her life.

As a Christian you are not left to guess which way is right. Again and again the Bible instructs you in the practical, day-to-day ways to live.

Describe a time when you found the Bible useful in instructing you how to act in a specific situation.

_____

_____

You are learning about this use of the Bible when you work on demolishing personal spiritual strongholds in your life.

DEMOLISHING PERSONAL SPIRITUAL STRONGHOLDS

In day 2 you identified a stronghold you wanted to demolish in the area of speech. Today give a progress report on how you have used the spiritual weapon(s) you listed to demolish this stronghold.

How I have used a spiritual weapon(s) to help demolish the stronghold of improper speech:

_____

_____

Select an ideological stronghold such as gambling, pornography, humanism, or secularism. Then pray through the Spiritual Armor about its influence in your personal life and in society.

"The acts of the sinful nature are obvious: sexual immorality, impurity and debauchery; idolatry and witchcraft; hatred, discord, jealousy, fits of rage, selfish ambition, dissensions, factions and envy; drunkenness, orgies, and the like. I warn you, as I did before, that those who live like this will not inherit the kingdom of God. But the fruit of the Spirit is love, joy, peace, patience, kindness, goodness, faithfulness, gentleness and self-control Against such things there is no law. Those who belong to Christ Jesus have crucified the sinful nature with its passions and desires. Since we live by the Spirit, let us keep in step with the Spirit. Let us not become conceited, provoking and envying each other" (Gal. 5:19-26).

"All Scripture is God-breathed and is useful for teaching, rebuking, correcting and training in righteousness, so that the man of God may be thoroughly equipped for every good work" (2 Tim. 3:16-17).

What happens when you use the Scriptures in the four ways you have studied—for teaching, rebuking, correcting, and training in righteousness? Read 2 Timothy 3:16-17 in the margin and check the correct response.

If I rely on the Scriptures in these four ways, I will—
❑ **never sin again;**
❑ **never have problems;**
☑ **be equipped for how God wants me to live;**
❑ **have plenty of money.**

Scripture equips you for all you do. Being well grounded in God's Word does not guarantee that you will never have problems and that you will have all the money you want. It does not mean that you will not sin, because all human beings are sinful and are bound to stray. But you can rely on Scripture to give you victory in troubled times; to help keep you from giving in to Satan's attacks; and to show you ways your needs, even monetary ones, can be supplied.

By now you should have memorized this week's Scripture-memory verses, Psalm 1:2-3. Say them aloud to a friend or a family member. Ask this person to check the verses for you.

PUTTING ON THE SPIRITUAL ARMOR
Continue to study the importance of using the Sword of the Spirit in spiritual warfare as part of the Spiritual Armor. Review on page 51 the three guidelines for taking up the Sword of the Spirit.

" 'When he, the Spirit of truth, comes, he will guide you into all truth. He will not speak on his own; he will speak only what he hears, and he will tell you what is yet to come. He will bring glory to me by taking from what is mine and making it known to you. All that belongs to the Father is mine. That is why I said the Spirit will take from what is mine and make it known to you' " (John 16: 13-15).

Focus on the third guideline. Stop and pray on the basis of the Word. The Holy Spirit will guide you into all truth and will help you know how to pray even if you do not have a particular agenda in mind (read John 16:13-15 in the margin). Allow the Spirit to bring God's Word to mind as you pray.

Share with your family, a Christian friend, or a group the Sword of the Spirit part of the Spiritual Armor.

As you delight in God's Word, you naturally think of persons who do not have this Guidebook as a daily part of their lives. Earlier this week you listed on your Relational-Witnessing Chart the names of lost family members and relatives. Today you will focus on other lost individuals in your circles of influence.

List the names of lost persons in each circle on the Relational-Witnessing Chart (p. 135) and on the Prayer-Covenant List (p. 143).

Begin using the witnessing booklet your leader gave you at the previous group session. Use one of the following suggestions to introduce the booklet to someone.
- I have a booklet that means a lot to me. May I share it with you?
- May I share a booklet with you that explains how you can know for certain that you have eternal life?
- This booklet has a wonderful message about how to have a full and meaningful life. May I share it with you?

 Read Psalm 119:113-120 during your quiet time today. Let God speak to you through this passage. Then complete the Daily Master Communication Guide in the margin.

HAS THIS WEEK MADE A DIFFERENCE?
Review "My Walk with the Master This Week" at the beginning of this week's material. Mark the activities you have finished by drawing vertical lines in the diamonds beside them. Finish any incomplete activities. Think about what you will say during your group session about your work on these activities.

As you complete your study of "Rely on God's Word," I hope that you realize the treasure you possess in God's Word. In the Scriptures you have everything you need to learn right doctrine and right living, to get back onto the right path, and even to reset your life course. Look to God's Word for spiritual instruction, guidance, and weapons to fight Satan. The Word will thoroughly equip you to be useful to the Master as you victoriously fend off the enemy's attacks.

---

[1]Available from the Customer Service Center; 127 Ninth Avenue, North; Nashville, TN 37234; 1-800-458-2772; from Baptist Book Stores; and from Lifeway Christian Stores.

DAILY MASTER COMMUNICATION GUIDE

PSALM 119:113-120

What God said to me:

_____

_____

_____

_____

_____

_____

_____

What I said to God:

_____

_____

_____

_____

_____

_____

_____

WEEK 4

Pray in Faith

This Week's Goal
You will be able to experience God's victory in spiritual battles by praying in faith.

My Walk with the Master This Week
You will complete the following activities to develop the six biblical disciplines. When you have completed each activity, draw a vertical line in the diamond beside it.

 SPEND TIME WITH THE MASTER
◇ Have a quiet time each day. Check each day you have a quiet time: ❑ Sunday ❑ Monday ❑ Tuesday ❑ Wednesday ❑ Thursday ❑ Friday ❑ Saturday

 LIVE IN THE WORD
◇ Read your Bible every day. Write what God says to you and what you say to God.
◇ Memorize 1 John 5:14-15.
◇ Review 1 John 4:4, 2 Timothy 3:16-17, and Psalm 1:2-3.
◇ Meditate on 1 John 5:14-15, following "How to Use the Guide to Meditation."
◇ Continue learning the God's Word in Your Heart and Hand presentation.

 PRAY IN FAITH
◇ Use the Praying in Faith form in your prayer time.

 FELLOWSHIP WITH BELIEVERS
◇ Share with someone the Shield of Faith part of the Spiritual Armor.

 WITNESS TO THE WORLD
◇ Add to the Relational-Witnessing Chart the names of lost persons.
◇ Look for opportunities to use a witnessing booklet or a gospel presentation to share the good news with someone.

 MINISTER TO OTHERS
◇ Learn the Shield of Faith part of the Spiritual Armor.

This Week's Scripture-Memory Verses
"This is the confidence we have approaching God: that if we ask anything according to his will, he hears us. And if we know that he hears us—whatever we ask—we know that we have what we asked of him" (1 John 5:14-15).

DAY 1

Claiming God's Promises

How do you let God tell you what He is doing so that you can join Him in His work? Several years ago our work group at our denominational publishing house went on a retreat to plan the products and services we would develop. The first day we shared what God had been saying to us through our daily quiet times. As we prayed, we asked the question "Lord, what are You doing or going to do that we need to be involved in?" God led us to Isaiah 61, which is quoted in Luke 4:18-19 in the margin.

We left the retreat believing that God wanted us to focus our work on the types of people Jesus came to serve: prisoners, the blind, and the oppressed. We planned products to help them. Based on this Word from the Father, we also began to look for where God was at work.

The first time I noticed God using this Scripture to lead us was when Don Dennis, a former convict, requested help in launching a program to use *MasterLife* in Texas prisons. We responded, and throughout the years thousands of prisoners have been spiritually released through *MasterLife* in the United States and in many other countries.

Then First Baptist Church of Houston offered to let us publish *First Place: A Christ-Centered Health Program*. It has helped thousands learn healthful eating and exercise habits in the context of Christian discipleship. Next Rapha, a nationally known Christian health-care organization, offered to let us publish biblical materials they had developed to help people with addictions and other emotional difficulties. We launched the LIFE Support series, which support-group ministries could use to help people with critical issues in their lives, such as painful pasts, sexual abuse, eating disorders, chemical dependency, divorce, loss, and harmful compulsions. Through these materials thousands of people have experienced healing that has brought them to Christ or has removed barriers to serving Him.[1]

Check the answer that best describes how we approached our search for God's will for our work. We—
❏ **told God what we wanted to do and asked Him to bless it;**
❏ **implemented our ideas without praying and relied on instinct;**
❏ **told God what we wanted to do and asked Him to show us a Scripture that would support our strategy;**
☑ **asked God to show us where He wanted us to work next, and He led us to a Scripture that guided us.**

We would have been operating outside God's will if we had asked Him to bless a set of plans we had developed without consulting Him

" 'The Spirit of the Lord is on me,
because he hath anointed me to preach good news to the poor.
He has sent me to proclaim freedom for the prisoners and recovery of sight for the blind,
to release the oppressed, to proclaim the year of the Lord's favor' " (Luke 4: 18-19).

first. We asked God to show us in His Word where He wanted us to work, and He led us to a Scripture. The last answer is the correct one.

A LAMP TO YOUR FEET

God provides daily guidance for you in making decisions, facing problems, and meeting needs. As He works through the indwelling presence of the Holy Spirit, God's Word becomes active, alive, and dynamic in directing your life. As you base your life on the Word by faith, it becomes a lamp to your feet and a light for your path. In the margin read Psalm 119:105.

"Your word is a lamp to my feet and a light for my path" (Ps. 119:105).

God reveals His will through His Word to spiritually sensitive, believing Christians who meet His conditions. This week you will learn steps for praying in faith. At the end of this week's study you will be able to—
- identify occasions when you have linked prayer and God's Word;
- list three stages in making a covenant with God;
- list six steps for praying in faith;
- give examples of persons who prayed in faith on the basis of a Word from God;
- select a problem or a need about which you want to pray in faith.

God reveals His will through His Word to spiritually sensitive, believing Christians who meet His conditions.

A COVENANT WITH GOD

The relationship between praying in faith and living in the Word may have come into clearer focus as you reflected on what you have already studied in *MasterLife*. When you used the Prayer-Covenant List, you may have wondered how to find a Bible promise on which to base your prayers. A covenant is a promise or a pledge between persons to do something together, based on a common agreement. God's covenant with His people is one of the basic ideas in the Bible. Biblical covenants between God and His people had three stages:
Stage 1: God revealed His will and made a promise.
Stage 2: The people met the conditions God established.
Stage 3: The people believed God and received the blessing.

Keeping the three stages of covenant making in mind, read the following Scriptures. Circle the parts that illustrate stage 1. Underline the parts that illustrate stage 2. Use brackets for the parts that illustrate stage 3.

" 'I am going to bring floodwaters on the earth to destroy all life under the heavens, every creature that has the breath of life in it. Everything on earth will perish. But I will establish my covenant with you, and you will enter the ark—you and your sons and your wife and your sons' wives with you. Noah did everything just as God commanded him. Noah was six hundred years old when the floodwaters came on the earth. And Noah and his sons and his wife and his sons' wives entered the ark to escape the waters of the flood' " (Gen. 6:17-18,22; 7:6-7).

"Having said this, he [Jesus] spit on the ground, made some mud with the saliva, and put it on the man's eyes. 'Go,' he told him, 'wash in the Pool of Siloam' (this word means Sent). So the man went and washed, and came home seeing" (John 9:6-7).

God made promises to His people; the people met God's conditions; they believed Him and were blessed.

Using the same stages in the process of making a covenant, beside the following accounts write the number of the first stage in which the process was not followed.

____ 1. Jim wanted to be wealthy, so he asked God to give him one million dollars.

✓ 2. As Nancy read James 1:27, the Spirit impressed her to visit a nearby orphanage, but she decided not to because she felt that it would remind her of her unhappy childhood.

✓ 3. As John heard a sermon on Matthew 28:18-20, he felt led to resign from his job and become a missionary. The next day he applied for missionary service. Soon he was offered a significant promotion at work, which he accepted.

____ 4. Steve decided that he needed a new house, so he secured a loan and bought one.

The answers are 1. stage 1, 2. stage 2, 3. stage 2, 4. none. This week you will learn how God reveals His will as you pray in faith.

As you learned in week 3, one way you live in the Word and the Word lives in you to help you experience victory is to think about it, or meditate on it. This week you will learn to meditate on God's Word.

Meditation has been called reflective thinking with a view to application. It involves musing, pondering, and thinking about God's Word in such a way that the message of the Scripture is applied to a specific need in your life. A great promise in God's Word, 1 John 5:14-15, deals with the relationship between God's blessings and meditation.

Meditation applies Scripture to a specific need in your life.

Turn to page 60 and read aloud 1 John 5:14-15 to begin memorizing this week's Scripture-memory verses.

"How to Use the Guide to Meditation," which follows, directs you through a process for meditating on a passage of Scripture. Use 1 John 5:14-15 and a copy of the Guide to Meditation form on page 136 in your quiet time every day this week. You do not need to finish your meditation of these verses today but may do so at your own pace between now and the end of day 5. These periods of meditation will replace your Daily Master Communication Guides this week. Copy the Guide to Meditation form for future periods of meditation.

Do a meditation study in sections a few minutes each day, concentrating on one verse a week.

HOW TO USE THE GUIDE TO MEDITATION[2]

You may do a meditation study in sections a few minutes each day, concentrating on one verse a week. Ordinarily, you may prefer to select a verse you have been memorizing or perhaps the key verse in a passage or a chapter you have read or studied during *MasterLife*. After you select a verse, pray, claiming James 1:5 for wisdom to apply God's Word.

Perimeter of the Verse

Read the verses before and after the verse to establish the theme and the setting, which will aid you in interpretation. Then write a summary of the passage.

Paraphrase the Verse

Write the verse in your own words. Say your paraphrase aloud.

Pulverize the Verse

Digest the verse by using three ways to assimilate its truths.
1. Emphasize a different word in the verse as you read or repeat it. Then state the opposite meaning to reveal what the verse says.
2. Write at least two important words from those you have emphasized in the verse.
3. Ask these questions about the two words to relate the Scripture to your needs: What? Why? When? Where? Who? How?

Let the Holy Spirit apply the verse to a need, a challenge, an opportunity, or a failure in your life.

Personalize the Verse

Let the Holy Spirit apply the verse to a need, a challenge, an opportunity, or a failure in your life. What will you *do* about this verse as it relates to your life? Be specific.

Pray the Verse Back to God

Pray the verse back to God, making it personal. Vocalize or write the verse as you pray it back to God.

Parallel Passages

Refer to other passages that emphasize the truth of the verse.

Problems in the Verse

List thoughts or ideas you might not understand or might have difficulty applying in your life. Discuss them with a Sunday School teacher or with a Christian friend.

Possibilities for Helping Others Through the Verse

Write a way you can use the verse to help another person.

Protracted Study

Record plans for further study of this verse.

DEMOLISHING PERSONAL SPIRITUAL STRONGHOLDS

By now you should be becoming more and more aware of personal spiritual strongholds in your life that need to be demolished. Based on your study in previous weeks, I hope that you are able to see changes in the areas of bitterness, speech, and lust through the work of the Holy Spirit in your life. Today you will look at another area to demolish: the stronghold of religious ritual. Four criteria in Matthew 23:1-8 tell us when religious ritual becomes a spiritual stronghold:

1. When you tell others to do what you are not practicing (vv. 2-3)
2. When you demand actions that Jesus has not commanded (v. 4)
3. When you do religious activities to be seen by others (vv. 5-7)
4. When you accept honor, position, or authority for religious service (vv. 8-12)

Read the verses in the margin, which deal with the stronghold of religious ritual. Then describe the area of religious ritual in your life that needs to be demolished, what you need to do to demolish it, and the spiritual weapon(s) to be used in demolishing it. Later this week you will record your progress.

Here is an example.

Stronghold to be demolished: teaching a Sunday School class so that others will think I am a good Christian, not from obedience to God

What I need to do to demolish it: ask God to change my heart and to help me respond to what He wants me to do

Spiritual weapons to be used: Breastplate of Righteousness—confess my sin and self-righteousness and claim the righteousness of Christ; Belt of Truth—remember that Satan tries to deceive me into believing that my worth is based on what others think. Hold to God's truth, which assures me that my worth originates in Him.

Now you try it.

Stronghold to be demolished: _____

What I need to do to demolish it: _____

Spiritual weapon(s) to be used: _____

" 'Be careful not to do your "acts of righteousness" before men, to be seen by them. If you do, you will have no reward from your Father in heaven. So when you give to the needy, do not announce it with trumpets, as the hypocrites do in the synagogues and on the streets, to be honored by men. I tell you the truth, they have received their reward in full. But when you give to the needy, do not let your left hand know what your right hand is doing, so that your giving may be in secret. Then your Father, who sees what is done in secret, will reward you. And when you pray, do not be like the hypocrites, for they love to pray standing in the synagogues and on the street corners to be seen by men. I tell you the truth, they have received their reward in full. But when you pray, go into your room, close the door and pray to your Father, who is unseen. Then your Father, who sees what is done in secret, will reward you. And when you pray, do not keep on babbling like pagans, for they think they will be heard because of their many words. Do not be like them, for your Father knows what you need before you ask him' " (Matt. 6:1-8).

DAY 2

God Communicates Truth

"Continue to tell of Me and My love for people."

My longtime colleague, Jimmy Crowe, tells about praying in faith as he prepared to undergo his third heart surgery. His two previous heart surgeries had been successful, but they occurred when Jimmy was younger. Now retired, Jimmy said he began to fear that his age—and his seeming lack of purpose as a retiree—would keep him from full recovery from another operation.

Jimmy prayed: "Lord, You know that I am much older now. My life's work is finished. Those other times You had work for me to do. Can I really endure this surgery? And should I even try now that I don't accomplish for You as much as I once did?" A friend alerted me about Jimmy's state of mind. I called him and encouraged him to help with this edition of *MasterLife* you are studying. He also received phone calls of support from friends as far away as Australia.

The night before his surgery Jimmy read from Psalms. In Psalm 118:17 the Lord revealed the answer:

> *I will not die but live,*
> *and will proclaim what the Lord has done.*

"It was a promise but also a correction," Jimmy recalled. "It was as if the Father were saying to me: 'You seem to have forgotten your primary task. You still have much to do because I have commanded that you continue to tell of Me and My love for people.' Afterward the doctor said that this surgery was easy, and my recovery was quick. The time since then has been one of the most fruitful periods of my ministry, with many opportunities to teach and minister."

Describe a crisis during which you found comfort and victory from Scripture.

_____

_____

When you act in faith on what God communicates to you as truth, you will have victory.

You may think: *I'd really like to pray in faith, based on a Word from the Lord, but how can I do that? How can I know that God is speaking to me through a specific part of His Word to apply to a specific situation? How can I use promises from His Word to help me claim victory in spiritual warfare?* When you act in faith on what God communicates to you as truth, you will have victory.

This week you will discover six steps for praying in faith. The first three relate to God's communicating truth to you. The second three relate to your communicating faith to God. Today you will explore the first step.

> **GOD COMMUNICATES TRUTH TO YOU**
> 1. **Abide in Christ.**
> 2. Abide in the Word.
> 3. Allow the Holy Spirit to lead you in truth.

Your greatest concern as a Christian disciple is to find and do God's will. How do you find God's will? Jesus no longer physically walks by and beckons you to follow Him. Yet He is just as concerned about your doing His will. He has given you the written Word of God, which He reveals to you through the Holy Spirit. He gives you light through His Word, and He expects you to follow it by faith. God "works in you to will and to act according to his good purpose" (Phil. 2:13).

Praying in faith is two-way communication: God reveals truth to you, and you exercise faith toward Him. The Praying in Faith form (p. 139) provides a practical checklist to help you apply this teaching.

"Guide to Praying in Faith," which follows, uses elements of the Praying in Faith form (p. 139) to help you work through a problem you currently face. Use copies of the Praying in Faith form to pray about future problems.

STEP 1: ABIDE IN CHRIST

> **GUIDE TO PRAYING IN FAITH**
>
> **What is the problem?** _____
>
> _____
>
> First recognize that God can and will work in your problem for your good and for His glory. Romans 8:28 reminds you, "We know that in all things God works for the good of those who love him, who have been called according to his purpose." That does not mean that all things *are* good but that ultimately, God will work together all things to produce good.
>
> Second, recognize that God is sovereign. He knew about your circumstances before they happened. Although God may not have caused the events to occur, He did not choose to alter their course.
>
> **How could God possibly use my problem?**
> ❑ **A platform for God to demonstrate His power**
> ❑ **A blessing from God for which I have not asked**
> ❑ **An opportunity for God to develop in me faith, love,**

Your greatest concern as a Christian disciple is to find and do God's will.

Recognize that God can and will work in your problem for your good and for His glory.

patience, or another Christlike character trait
❏ An opportunity to develop a more effective prayer life

Rewrite the problem in the form of a question to God.

_____

Am I abiding in Christ and committed to His will for my life?
☑ Yes ❏ No

The first way to learn God's will is to abide, or remain, in Christ, as John 15:7 reminds you. Read this verse in the margin.

What does _remaining in Christ_ mean to you?

_____

_____

Are you living in vital connection with Christ, the Vine? ❏ Yes ❏ No If not, what do you need to do to be in a right relationship with Him?

_____

Make sure that you are abiding in Christ. Lay aside your own will and desires, as much as possible, to seek God's will. Be sure that your fleshly desires are not standing in the way of your discovering God's will. These are the areas that can be affected:
❏ Your senses (body)   ❏ Your wishes (will)
❏ Your logic (mind)   ❏ Your desires (flesh)
❏ Your feelings (emotions)

In the list above, check any areas that might be keeping you from discovering God's will.

Stop and ask for the Holy Spirit to fill you and to lead you to know and do God's will as you abide in Him.

 This week's Scripture-memory verses, 1 John 5:14-15, remind you to accept God's Word in faith. Try to write these verses from memory in the margin.

 Meditate on 1 John 5:14-15 during your quiet time today, following the guidance on page 64.

Margin notes:

" 'If you remain in me and my words remain in you, ask whatever you wish, and it will be given you' " (John 15:7).

Be sure that your fleshly desires are not standing in the way of your discovering God's will.

DAY 3

Turning to God First

Today you will continue to examine six steps for praying in faith. The first three relate to discovering God's will about a matter. Yesterday you learned the first one. Today you will examine the second.

> **GOD COMMUNICATES TRUTH TO YOU**
> 1. Abide in Christ.
> **2. Abide in the Word.**
> 3. Allow the Holy Spirit to lead you in truth.

STEP 2: ABIDE IN THE WORD
In John 15:7 a second step to learning God's will about a matter is abiding in the Word. When you have a problem, first turn to God and seek His Word to find the solution to your problem. Read Psalm 27:13-14 in the margin.

I am still confident of this:
  I will see the goodness of the
Lord
  in the land of the living.
Wait for the Lord;
  be strong and take heart
  and wait for the Lord
(Ps. 27:13-14).

"**Guide to Praying in Faith**," which follows, uses elements of the Praying in Faith form (p. 139) to help you continue working through the problem you identified in day 2. Use copies of the Praying in Faith form to pray about future problems.

> **GUIDE TO PRAYING IN FAITH**
> **Ask yourself:**
> • **Have I brought my problem to God first?** ☑ **Yes** ❑ **No**
> • **Am I systematically abiding in His Word?** ☑ **Yes** ❑ **No**
> • **Am I willing to wait for His solution?** ☑ **Yes** ❑ **No**

To whom have you already gone to get help in solving your problem? Check all that apply.

❑ neighbor   ❑ counselor
☑ physician   ❑ relative
☒ lawyer   ☑ fellow church member
❑ accountant   ❑ other: ___Christ___

Sometimes you consult neighbors, doctors, lawyers, accountants, counselors, or others instead of God. God uses other sources to help you solve your problem, but He wants you to seek Him first.

Read the Scriptures in the margin on the following page and write in your own words what each teaches about how to abide, or remain, in the Word.

" 'If you hold to my teaching, you are really my disciples. Then you will know the truth, and the truth will set you free' " (John 8:31).

" 'Whoever has my commands and obeys them, he is the one who loves me. He who loves me will be loved by my Father, and I too will love him and show myself to him' " (John 14:21).

"He knows the way that I take;
   when he has tested me, I will come forth as gold.
My feet have closely followed his steps;
   I have kept to his way without turning aside.
I have not departed from the commands of his lips;
   I have treasured the words of his mouth more than my daily bread" (Job 23:10-12).

John 8:31: _____

_____

John 14:21: _____

_____

Job 23:10-12: _____

_____

Write *A* beside the accounts describing persons who are abiding properly in the Word.

___A___ Oscar is studying the Bible and doing God's will as best he knows how. Whenever he fails, he asks for forgiveness. He is committed to doing whatever God asks him to do.

_____ Reggie is active in his church but does not see how the Bible relates to what he does every day. He reads some of it every week. He has many goals for his life. He has asked God to help him achieve them and believes that God will.

_____ Stella has discovered several verses that apply to her life as she reads the Bible day by day. She has underlined the conditions in each verse and is doing as commanded.

_____ Richard believes that God gave him a promise through a verse he memorized. But it has been six months, and little has happened. He believes that God gives more light to those who follow the light they have. So he keeps obeying the Word and believes that he will receive more light in God's time.

As you meet the conditions for learning God's will about a matter, you can receive input on what God's will is for your life and prayers. In the exercise all of the individuals are abiding properly in the Word except Reggie, who was not discerning God's will through the Word.

What are ways to let God speak to you as you abide in His Word?

• Read the Bible systematically and let God speak through passages He brings to mind.
• Look for specific principles and truths that apply to your situation.
• Look for the meaning of the Scripture passage to the original readers.
• Look for a present-day application of a truth or a biblical situation.
• Be willing to look and wait for a Word from God.

You may be concerned when I suggest that you find a specific verse to communicate in a present-day situation. You might think, *Certainly you don't mean that I should open the Bible and put my finger on a verse at random.* Many abuses of Scripture occur when people use that approach. Clearly, this is not what is meant by praying in faith by claiming a verse from God's Word. It is not a verse you grab but a verse that grabs you as the Holy Spirit applies it to you in your context.

Read James 4:3 in the margin. Why was this prayer not answered?

_____

"When you ask, you do not receive, because you ask with wrong motives, that you may spend what you get on your pleasures" (Jas. 4:3).

Abuses of Scripture can also occur when you pray with wrong motives. The person to whom James 4:3 referred prayed according to the flesh rather than abiding in Christ.

Ask yourself these questions again about your problem:
• Have I brought my problem to God first? ❏ Yes ❏ No
• Am I systematically abiding in His Word? ❏ Yes ❏ No
• Am I willing to wait for His solution? ❏ Yes ❏ No
If you cannot answer yes to these questions, go back to step 1 and work through these matters before you continue.

Write the first two steps for praying in faith that you have studied before you study the third one tomorrow.
1. A _____
2. A _____
3. Allow the Holy Spirit to lead you in all truth.

PUTTING ON THE SPIRITUAL ARMOR
This week you will study the Shield of Faith as you continue to learn the Spiritual Armor. Turn to pages 129–31 and quickly review the entire Spiritual Armor presentation, with special emphasis on the Shield of Faith. By the end of this study you will be able to explain the entire presentation in your own words.

In one hand you hold the Sword of the Spirit. In the other hand picture yourself holding the Shield of Faith. The Roman shield was a long, oblong piece of wood. When the enemy's fiery arrows hit it, they buried themselves in the wood and were extinguished. So as the arrows of evil are aimed at you, advance with the Shield of Faith and quench the fiery darts of the wicked. Let the Shield of Faith remind you to do the following.

Advance with the Shield of Faith and quench the fiery darts of the wicked.

1. Claim the victory. Faith is the victory that overcomes the world (see 1 John 5:4).
2. Advance in faith. Faith without works is dead (see Jas. 2:20). Put feet to your prayers.
3. Quench all of the fiery darts of the wicked.

Focus on the first of the three reminders. Claim the fact that you already have the victory. As you pray, thank God in advance because you know that you will be victorious.

Practice saying this week's Scripture-memory verses, 1 John 5:14-15, to a friend or a family member. Explain what these verses are helping you learn about praying in faith.

 Meditate on 1 John 5:14-15 during your quiet time today, following the guidance on page 64.

DAY 4

Leading You in Truth

Today you will continue to examine six steps for praying in faith. The first three relate to discovering God's will about a matter. You have learned the first two. Today you will examine the third.

> **GOD COMMUNICATES TRUTH TO YOU**
> 1. Abide in Christ.
> 2. Abide in the Word.
> **3. Allow the Holy Spirit to lead you in truth.**

STEP 3: ALLOW THE HOLY SPIRIT TO LEAD YOU IN TRUTH

"Guide to Praying in Faith," which follows, uses elements of the Praying in Faith form (p. 139) to help you continue working through the problem you identified in day 2. Use copies of the Praying in Faith form to pray about future problems.

> **GUIDE TO PRAYING IN FAITH**
> Am I allowing the Holy Spirit to fill me, to lead me to a Scripture, and to apply it to my problem? ☑ Yes ❑ No
> What is the Scripture?
>
> _____
>
> How do I think this Scripture applies to my problem?
>
> _____
>
> _____

God reveals His will through His Word but only to those who allow the Holy Spirit to lead them in truth.

God reveals His will through His Word but only to those who allow the Holy Spirit to lead them in truth. The Holy Spirit needs to work both to reveal God's truth to you and to help you receive the truth.

Read the Scriptures in the margin. What is one of the basic jobs of the Holy Spirit?

_____

Notice that in John 16:13-15 Jesus promised in three different ways that the Spirit will reveal truth to you. Underline them.

The Holy Spirit is the teacher in Christians' lives. Under His guidance the words of the Bible become a Word from the Father for each of us. He is present as each Christian studies. You may have underlined that the Spirit "will guide you," "will speak," and "will tell you" to indicate how the Holy Spirit works.

A basic job of the Holy Spirit is to show truth to you. If you read the Bible with a logical, analytical approach and conclude, _This is what God is saying to me_, you are missing the vital element of letting the Spirit guide you and illuminate the Scripture. When you let the Spirit do so, you can then walk on the basis of that illumination. You might think, _That approach sounds a little mystical to me_. The essence of true Christianity _is_ a little mystical. It is your relationship with Jesus Christ. You cannot put it in a test tube. The Holy Spirit reveals God's presence in your life. The Holy Spirit inspired those who wrote the Word. Now the Holy Spirit works in you to interpret what is written and to help you apply it to your life.

Continue reading and studying until the Holy Spirit impresses you with a Scripture. As the Holy Spirit illuminates the Scripture and you apply it to your situation, ask these test questions about the conclusion you have drawn:
- Is it consistent with truth revealed in the rest of the Bible?
- Is it consistent with God's character?
- Is it consistent with the meaning of the Scripture in context?
- Does it violate the original meaning of the Scripture?
- Does the Holy Spirit continue to bear witness to its validity as you continue to pray about it?

Review by listing the three ways to get input from God on which to base your prayers of faith. Remember that these are the first three of the six steps for praying in faith.

God communicates truth to you when you—
1. A _____
2. A _____
3. A _____

A systematic study of God's Word and a systematic application of His Word in your life by the Holy Spirit help prevent abuses of praying in faith. Write yes beside the following situations in which

" 'When he, the Spirit of truth, comes he will guide you into all truth. He will not speak on his own; he will speak only what he hears, and he will tell you what is yet to come. He will bring glory to me by taking from what is mine and making it known to you. All that belongs to the Father is mine. That is why I said the Spirit will take from what is mine and make it known to you' " (John 16: 13-15).

" 'The Counselor, the Holy Spirit, whom the Father will send in my name, will teach you all things and will remind you of everything I have said to you' " (John 14:26).

you see a correct application of what you have studied. Write *no* when the principles are used improperly.

_____ 1. You open your Bible and put your finger on a verse.

_____ 2. The Holy Spirit illuminates a verse to you during your daily Bible-reading time. God seems to speak to you about a specific matter.

_____ 3. You read about someone in the Bible, and the Holy Spirit bears witness by saying: "That is just like you. God is saying the same thing to you now that He said to that person then."

_____ 4. You decide what you want to do about a problem and look for a verse that supports your decision.

_____ 5. You think that God may be speaking to you through a verse, but you realize that the interpretation you have made would contradict another clearly revealed truth in God's Word. You reconsider and seek further guidance through the Scriptures.

Although some cases certainly exist in which God has used the method of turning to a verse to which your Bible opens, God usually does not speak to you when you randomly select a passage or when you make a decision about a matter before you seek His counsel. He speaks to you when the Holy Spirit illuminates a verse for you during your regular Bible reading or when the Spirit tells you that your situation is like the one you are reading about. If you are in doubt or think that another Scripture contradicts the premise of your passage, seek further guidance in the Word. Situations 2, 3, and 5 are the ones in which the principles you have studied are applied properly.

What if you do not find a Scripture that gives you direct guidance for a problem or a need? Continue reading your Bible and praying until an answer comes (see Matt. 7:7-8). God may be letting you come to the end of yourself before He reveals His answer. Wait on the Lord. What if you must make a decision before you get an answer? Be sure that it must immediately be made before using your own reason (see Prov. 3: 5-6; 16:3). But if circumstances force you to make a decision before you get a specific Word from God, submit yourself to His will and make the decision in light of the total biblical revelation and the Spirit's leading.

The Holy Spirit illuminates the Word for those who seek to know and do God's will. You discover God's will through the systematic intake of the Word. It becomes God's personal Word to you as you obey it by faith.

PUTTING ON THE SPIRITUAL ARMOR

In day 3 you reviewed the importance of the Shield of Faith as you continued to learn the Spiritual Armor presentation. You learned three steps for putting on the Shield of Faith. Review them on page 71.

The Holy Spirit illuminates the Word for those who seek to know and do God's will.

Focus on the second step in putting on the Shield of Faith. If God has given you a Word, claim the victory and advance in faith. Ask Him to give you courage to move forward boldly as the Lord directs you and not just to give lip-service to your faith.

GOD'S WORD IN YOUR HEART AND HAND
Last week you began learning a simple illustration for grasping the Sword of the Spirit, God's Word, so that you can live in victory. This week you will learn scriptural support for the illustration.

Referring to the hand drawing on page 132, review the Scripture references in "Level 2: Explanation" (p. 133) in the God's Word in Your Heart and Hand presentation.

On the illustration below write the five ways to get God's Word into your heart and the way to get a firm grip on the Word. Then add the following Scripture references in the appropriate places on the drawing. Refer to pages 132–34 if you need to review.
- Mark 4:23; Romans 10:17
- Psalm 1:2-3; Joshua 1:8
- Revelation 1:3
- Acts 17:11; 2 Timothy 2:15
- Psalm 119:9,11; Deuteronomy 6:6
- Luke 6:46-49; James 1:22

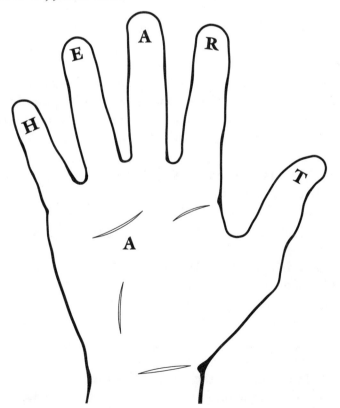

If God has given you a Word, claim the victory and advance in faith.

Meditate on 1 John 5:14-15 during your quiet time today, following the guidance on page 64. Then test your memorization by trying to say these verses aloud. Recall from memory your Scripture-memory verses from weeks 1, 2, and 3.

DAY 5

Communicating Your Faith

This week you are learning six steps for praying in faith. The first three relate to God's communicating truth to you. The last three relate to your communicating faith to God:

> **YOU COMMUNICATE FAITH TO GOD**
> **4. Ask according to God's will.**
> 5. Accept God's will in faith.
> 6. Act on the basis of God's Word to you.
> These last three steps can be accomplished only after God has led you to know His will through the Word.

" 'If you remain in me and my words remain in you, ask whatever you wish, and it will be given to you' " (John 15:7).

" 'Ask and it will be given to you; seek and you will find; knock and the door will be opened to you. For everyone who asks receives; he who seeks finds; and to him who knocks, the door will be opened' " (Matt. 7:7-8).

"You want something but don't get it. You kill and covet, but you cannot have what you want. You quarrel and fight. You do not have, because you do not ask God. When you ask, you do not receive, because you ask with wrong motives, that you may spend what you get on your pleasures" (Jas. 4:2-3).

STEP 4: ASK ACCORDING TO GOD'S WILL

 "Guide to Praying in Faith," which follows, uses elements of the Praying in Faith form (p. 139) to help you continue working through the problem you identified in day 2. If you do not have His leading yet about the problem you have been praying about this week, review the material you have studied and wait to complete the questions about your request until you have a Scripture on which to base your faith. Use copies of the Praying in Faith form to pray about future problems.

> **GUIDE TO PRAYING IN FAITH**
> What is my specific request?
>
> _____

Read John 15:7 and Matthew 7:7-8 in the margin. What is the additional step you must take after God has revealed His will about a particular matter through His Word?

_____

Read James 4:2-3 in the margin. On the next page write two reasons many people do not have all God wants to give them.

God is willing to give to us abundantly, but we often fail to ask for the things He wants us to have. He expects us to ask after we discern what His will is for us. When we do not ask or when we ask with improper motives, we do not receive the good gifts God has for us.

Many incidents in the Bible illustrate occasions when persons discerned God's will and then asked on the basis of it. When Nehemiah learned about his people in exile, he remembered the word of God to Moses (see Neh. 1:8-9). On the basis of that, Nehemiah prayed that God would allow him to go back to Jerusalem and build the walls. Read Nehemiah's words in the margin. The crippled man Jesus healed at the pool of Bethesda had lain there for 38 years, but then Jesus told him, " 'Pick up your mat and walk.' " Read John 5:5-9 in the margin. On the basis of that word from Jesus, he stood and walked.

Describe a time when God showed you His will through Scripture.

_____

_____

God will do as He has promised or will help you do as He has directed you. The first step in communicating your faith to God is to ask according to His will. God's greatest blessings and your greatest usefulness in His kingdom result when you completely fulfill His covenant.

Remain in the verse God reveals to you. As you read your Bible each day, God's Spirit has the power to make His will known to you. Ask God to answer, based on His Word, and be specific in your request.

STEP 5: ACCEPT GOD'S WILL IN FAITH
This week's Scripture-memory verses, 1 John 5:14-15, identify another step that communicates your faith to God.

 Say aloud this week's Scripture-memory verses, 1 John 5:14-15. Write the step the verses mention.

_____

The second way to communicate faith is to accept God's will in faith:

> **YOU COMMUNICATE FAITH TO GOD**
> 4. Ask according to God's will.
> **5. Accept God's will in faith.**
> 6. Act on the basis of God's Word to you.

" 'Remember the instruction you gave your servant Moses, saying, "If you are unfaithful, I will scatter you among the nations, but if you return to me and obey my commands, then even if your exiled people are at the farthest horizon, I will gather them from there and bring them to the place I have chosen as a dwelling for my Name' ' " (Neh. 1:8-9).

"One who was there had been an invalid for thirty-eight years. When Jesus saw him lying there and learned that he had been in this condition for a long time, he asked him, 'Do you want to get well?' 'Sir,' the invalid replied, 'I have no one to help me into the pool when the water is stirred. While I am trying to get in, someone else goes down ahead of me.' Then Jesus said to him, 'Get up! Pick up your mat and walk.' At once the man was cured; he picked up his mat and walked" (John 5:5-9).

"In the first year of his reign, I, Daniel, understood from the Scriptures, according to the word of the Lord given to Jeremiah the prophet, that the desolation of Jerusalem would last seventy years. So I turned to the Lord God and pleaded with him in prayer and petition, in fasting, and in sackcloth and ashes. 'O Lord, in keeping with all your righteous acts, turn away your anger and your wrath from Jerusalem, your city, your holy hill. Our sins and the iniquities of our fathers have made Jerusalem and your people an object of scorn to all those around us. Now, our God, hear the prayers and petitions of your servant. For your sake, O Lord, look with favor on your desolate sanctuary' " (Dan. 9:2-3,16-17).

"Then he said to them, 'My soul is overwhelmed with sorrow to the point of death. Stay here and keep watch with me.' Going a little farther, he fell with his face to the ground and prayed, 'My Father, if it is possible, may this cup be taken from me. Yet not as I will, but as you will' " (Matt. 26:38-39).

" 'Do you think I cannot call on my Father, and he will at once put at my disposal more than twelve legions of angels? But how then would the Scriptures be fulfilled that say it must happen this way?' " (Matt. 26:53-54).

If God has said it, believe it and practice it. I do not always know how He will solve my problem, but I begin to accept as certainty the fact that He will provide an answer, and I praise Him for it.

"Guide to Praying in Faith," which follows, uses elements of the Praying in Faith form (p. 139) to help you continue working through the problem you identified in day 2. Use copies of the Praying in Faith form to pray about future problems.

GUIDE TO PRAYING IN FAITH

What do I believe that God will do about my problem?

_____

Do I accept God's promise as a God-revealed certainty?
❑ Yes ❑ No

First John 5:14-15 says that we can feel assured that if we ask according to His will, He hears us. We can depend on God's Word in this matter and can accept it not by signs but by faith. God will answer when Christians ask according to His will. When the Holy Spirit puts together truth and faith in your life, the request you make will be answered.

Praying in faith based on God's Word is not a new concept. Individuals of faith have been taking these steps since Bible times. Read the Scriptures in the margin. Daniel prayed that God's anger would be turned away from Jerusalem and the desolate sanctuary restored. He prayed because he read that Jeremiah had written that God would bring his people back from exile after 70 years. After 68 years there was no sign that God was accomplishing this. Jesus prayed that God's will would be done about the crucifixion. He knew that the Scriptures, as recorded in Isaiah, needed to be fulfilled.

Make your request specific so that you will know whether it is answered. Begin to visualize the request being granted. Live in the joy of His assurance through the Word. Memorize and repeat His Word to you. Affirm it whenever doubts arise. Trust what God has told you in His Word rather than your feelings or hopes.

Stop and pray the following prayer or one similar to it: "Father, I accept Your Word in faith. I believe that You will provide an answer for my problem, and I praise You already, even though I don't know the specific details of how You will answer. I claim this verse, _____, as Your Word to me, and I thank You for revealing Your Word to me. Amen."

STEP 6: ACT ON THE BASIS OF GOD'S WORD TO YOU
One step remains in communicating your faith to God:

> YOU COMMUNICATE FAITH TO GOD
> 4. Ask according to God's will.
> 5. Accept God's will in faith.
> **6. Act on the basis of God's Word to you.**

The third step to take in communicating your faith to God is to act on the basis of the Word from God. After you have prayed in faith, you act even when you cannot see the answer to your request. Too many of us want to depend on our physical senses and our intellect for truth.

Jesus often instructed persons to do something as evidence of their faith before He answered their requests. Read John 9:7 and Luke 17:14 in the margin. The essence of walking by faith is that we believe God and what He communicates through the objective Word of God with the subjective application of the Spirit of God. Then we act because we know that it is true, even when our physical senses do not say so. When you pray in faith, you begin to act as if you already know what will happen.

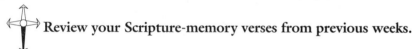 Following the guidance on page 64, meditate on this week's Scripture-memory verses, 1 John 5:14-15, as quoted in the margin from *The Amplified Bible*. This translation gives several possible meanings of selected Greek words in which the New Testament was written. Underline the words that give reasons for you to act in faith on the basis of God's Word for your need.

Review your Scripture-memory verses from previous weeks.

Now you will respond to the final questions on the Praying in Faith form. As you respond, consider these suggestions.
- If the answer is obvious, write it down.
- If the answer is long in coming, be faithful in believing prayer (see Rom. 4:18-21).
- If the answer is not given in the way you asked, use the Praying in Faith form (p. 139) to repeat the process for further guidance.
- When you are convinced that God has answered the prayer differently from your request, accept it.
- Keep a record of God's answers to prayers. Watch your faith grow.

For example, God sometimes allows problems to enter our lives to increase our dependence on and faith in Him. When something like this occurs, pray, "Teach me through this so that I'll know better how to walk in the Spirit by faith."

"Guide to Praying in Faith," which follows, uses elements of the Praying in Faith form (p. 139) to help you continue working through the problem you identified in day 2. Use copies of the Praying in Faith form to pray about future problems.

" 'Go,' he told him, 'Wash in the Pool of Siloam' (this word means Sent). So the man went and washed, and came home seeing" (John 9:7).

"When he saw them, he said, 'Go, show yourselves to the priests.' And as they went, they were cleansed" (Luke 17:14).

"This is the confidence—the assurance, the [privilege of] boldness—which we have in Him: [we are sure] that if we ask anything (make any request) according to His will (in agreement with His own plan) He listens to and hears us. And if (since) we [positively] know that He listens to us in whatever we ask, we also know [with settled and absolute knowledge] that we have [granted us as our present possessions] the request made of Him" (1 John 5:14-15, AMP).

GUIDE TO PRAYING IN FAITH

What actions(s) will I take, based on this Word from God?

_____

_____

What action(s) did God take in answer to my prayer of faith?

_____

_____

What else do I need to do?

_____

_____

You show a full faith when you act on the basis of what you believe.

Now carry out those actions. You show a full faith when you act on the basis of what you believe. God delights in answering the prayers of His faithful, believing servants. Use the same six steps with your major problems and decisions.

To review, write the six steps for praying in faith.

God communicates truth to me:

1. _____

2. _____

3. _____

I communicate faith to God:

4. _____

5. _____

6. _____

DEMOLISHING PERSONAL SPIRITUAL STRONGHOLDS

In day 1 you identified a stronghold you wanted to demolish in the area of religious ritual. Today give a progress report on how you have used the spiritual weapon(s) you listed to demolish this stronghold.

How I have used a spiritual weapon(s) to help demolish religious ritual:

_____

_____

PUTTING ON THE SPIRITUAL ARMOR

Continue to study the importance of taking up the Shield of Faith. Review on page 71 the three steps for putting on the shield.

 Focus on the third step in taking up the Shield of Faith. Stop and pray, asking God to help you hold up the Shield of Faith when Satan hurls darts at you that would cause you to doubt. Act on faith and not from fear.

 Share with your family, a Christian friend, or a group the Shield of Faith part of the Spiritual Armor.

Many persons do not know the Source of faith.

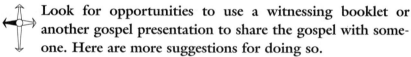 Add to the Relational-Witnessing Chart (p. 135) and to the Prayer-Covenant List (p. 143) the names of persons who do not know Christ.

Look for opportunities to use a witnessing booklet or another gospel presentation to share the gospel with someone. Here are more suggestions for doing so.

Look for opportunities to share the gospel with someone.

- Ask, Would you follow along with me while I read something that has made a difference in my life?
- As you read, stop periodically and involve the person in what you are reading. Ask nonthreatening questions like, Have you ever had an experience like the one the book describes? or, Have you ever had questions like the ones the book describes?
- To hold the person's attention, ask him or her to read some verses the book mentions rather than your reading all of them.

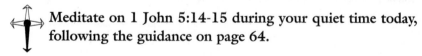 Meditate on 1 John 5:14-15 during your quiet time today, following the guidance on page 64.

List problems or requests for which you are seeking God's direction through His Word.

_____

_____

↑
↔ Make copies of the Praying in Faith form on page 139.
↓ Record the problems you listed and begin to pray for them
as you answer the questions on the form during the next
two weeks.

HAS THIS WEEK MADE A DIFFERENCE?
Review "My Walk with the Master This Week" at the beginning of
this week's material. Mark the activities you have finished by drawing vertical lines in the diamonds beside them. Finish any incomplete activities. Think about what you will say during your group
session about your work on these activities.

Check the following statements that describe you.
❑ God wants me to discern His will by staying connected to His
Word.
❑ God truly desires to answer my prayers that are prayed accord-
ing to His will.
❑ Through the Holy Spirit, God's Word becomes active and
dynamic in directing my life.
❑ God is interested in revealing His desires about everyday matters
in my life.
❑ God will show me answers to my problems when I pray in faith.
❑ God will give me victory over Satan's attacks when I pray in
faith.

God is eager to give good gifts to His children who pray in faith based on His Word.

As you conclude your study of "Pray in Faith," I hope that you are
digging deep into God's Word to find the precious promises that await
you. I hope that now you are more aware of God's eagerness to give
good gifts to His children who pray in faith based on His Word. I hope
that this week's study has begun to revolutionize your prayer life and
has given you encouragement about prayer so that you can live victoriously when Satan attacks.

---

[1]*First Place: A Christ-Centered Health Program* and LIFE Support courses are available
from the Customer Service Center; 127 Ninth Avenue, North; Nashville, TN 37234;
1-800-458-2772; from Baptist Book Stores; and from Lifeway Christian Stores.
[2]Guide to Meditation steps © copyright Waylon Moore.

WEEK 5

Look to Jesus

This Week's Goal

You will be able to write your life purpose and life goals.

My Walk with the Master This Week

You will complete the following activities to develop the six biblical disciplines. When you have completed each activity, draw a vertical line in the diamond beside it.

SPEND TIME WITH THE MASTER
◇ Have a quiet time each day. Check each day you have a quiet time: ❑ Sunday ❑ Monday ❑ Tuesday ❑ Wednesday ❑ Thursday ❑ Friday ❑ Saturday

LIVE IN THE WORD
◇ Read your Bible every day. Write what God says to you and what you say to God.
◇ Memorize Ephesians 6:18.
◇ Review 1 John 4:4, 2 Timothy 3:16-17, Psalm 1:2-3, and 1 John 5:14-15.
◇ Continue learning the God's Word in Your Heart and Hand presentation.

PRAY IN FAITH
◇ Use "Guide to Intercession" during your prayer time.
◇ Begin making a personal prayer journal.

FELLOWSHIP WITH BELIEVERS
◇ Show God's love to someone every day this week.
◇ Share with someone the Gospel Shoes part of the Spiritual Armor.
◇ Select one level of the God's Word in Your Heart and Hand presentation and share it with your family or a Christian friend.

WITNESS TO THE WORLD
◇ Read "Expanding Your Witness Circle."
◇ Add to the Relational-Witnessing Chart the names of lost persons.

MINISTER TO OTHERS
◇ Learn the Gospel Shoes part of the Spiritual Armor.

This Week's Scripture-Memory Verse

"Pray in the Spirit on all occasions with all kinds of prayers and requests. With this in mind, be alert and always keep on praying for all the saints" (Eph. 6:18).

DAY 1

Your Overarching Vision

Define your life purpose and life goals so that Satan cannot distract you.

When you are at war, you need an overarching vision to stay focused on what you need to accomplish. We are in a huge battle with Satan. You must know clearly what your life purpose is if you are to be a part of God's purpose. You must define your life purpose and life goals so that in the midst of warfare Satan cannot distract you from what God wants you to do.

THE IMPORTANCE OF STAYING FOCUSED
Jesus' experience in the wilderness clarified His life purpose. He had just been baptized and had heard John pronounce Him " 'the Lamb of God who takes away the sin of the world' " (John 1:29). His Father had said, " 'This is my Son, whom I love' " (Matt. 3:17). In the wilderness Jesus came to grips with the fact that He had the power to do everything Satan tempted Him to do. Yet He chose to do things the Father's way instead.

You must know your life purpose when you are in the midst of battle. God uses His Word to teach you your life purpose and goals. God gave me a Scripture passage, Psalm 71:17-18, when I was in my 20s. Although I did not fully understand it, I felt that it was a goal for my life that He had given to me. The passage says:

> *O God, thou hast taught me from my youth: and hitherto have I declared thy wondrous works. Now also when I am old and greyheaded, O God, forsake me not; until I have shewed thy strength unto this generation, and thy power to every one that is to come (KJV).*

I claimed those verses for the rest of my life, asking the Lord not to forsake me until I had shown His strength to this generation and His power to future generations. I did not know what that meant then as the pastor of a small church while in seminary, and I still do not understand all it means. But those verses have focused my life on glorifying God so that people now and in future generations may know Him. From the day after I was saved as a child, I have told people what God did to save me. This has been a mark in my ministry—to tell others about the wonderful things God does.

A Christian's purpose and goals must be Christ-centered.

Someone who aims at nothing usually hits it. As the Bible says, "Where there is no vision, the people perish" (Prov. 29:18, KJV). Great accomplishments can be traced to people with a vision, or a life purpose. A Christian's purpose and goals must be Christ-centered.

Your study this week will help you determine your life purpose and

set life goals consistent with the plan God wishes to accomplish in spite of spiritual warfare. At the end of this week's study you will be able to—
- define *life purpose* and *life goals* and explain the difference;
- identify Christ's life purpose and life goals;
- write your life purpose and life goals;
- prioritize your life goals;
- commit yourself to accomplishing your life goals in spite of Satan's opposition.

DISCOVERING YOUR LIFE PURPOSE

One blessing of being a Christian is having a purpose for living. Without Christ, life resembles a jigsaw puzzle. The pieces do not fit together when we have no vision of the finished product. A believer's completed life vision should come from God and should resemble Christ Himself. In Him we discover the meaning of our lives.

Read John 4:31-34 in the margin. What did Jesus say was His purpose for living?

_____

Jesus did the Father's work in complete obedience. Nothing was as important to Him as doing God's will and finishing the work He was sent to do.

> A life purpose is an overarching goal for you to accomplish in your lifetime. It provides direction for everyday activities and determines your priorities.

Some people spend their lives trying to be successful. Others desire wealth or fame. Others vainly attempt to find happiness, love, and security through human relationships. The Westminster Confession states that humans' chief end is to glorify God and to enjoy Him forever.

A scribe asked Jesus to summarize humanity's duty. In His reply Jesus called attention to two life purposes.

Read Mark 12:29-31 in the margin and underline the two life purposes Jesus identified.

Does your life purpose relate to the first commandment of loving God with all your heart, soul, mind, and strength? ❏ Yes ❏ No

Write a statement of your life purpose in relation to God.

_____

_____

"His disciples urged him, 'Rabbi, eat something.' But he said to them, 'I have food to eat that you know nothing about.' Then his disciples said to each other, 'Could someone have brought him food?' 'My food,' said Jesus, 'is to do the will of him who sent me and to finish his work' " (John 4:31-34).

" 'The most important one,' answered Jesus, 'is this: "Hear, O Israel, the Lord our God, the Lord is one. Love the Lord your God with all your heart and with all your soul and with all your mind and with all your strength." The second is this: "Love your neighbor as yourself." There is no commandment greater than these' " (Mark 12:29-31).

Jesus' second command gives you another clue to a life purpose—loving others as you love yourself. Loving your fellow human beings is second only to loving God. Your life purpose should relate to these two commands regardless of your job or profession. Everything you do should glorify God (see 1 Cor. 10:31; Col. 3:17; 1 Pet. 4:11).

Write a life purpose related to your fellow human beings.

_____

_____

This week's Scripture-memory verse, Ephesians 6:18, speaks to the issue of determining your life purpose. Turn to page 83 and read this verse aloud. What is one way to know the purpose God has for you?

_____

God desires to reveal His goal for you. Through prayer for all kinds of requests, He will hear you and answer you.

DEMOLISHING PERSONAL SPIRITUAL STRONGHOLDS

God wants your life to be free of personal strongholds, and He gives you the strength and the means to demolish them. You have examined the strongholds of bitterness, speech, lust, and religious ritual. Today look at the stronghold of greed in your life and prayerfully consider how the Lord might be directing you to demolish this stronghold.

Read the verses in the margin, which deal with the stronghold of greed. Greed, or covetousness, is an intense desire to possess something or someone that belongs to another person or to acquire more than you need. This desire springs from greedy self-centeredness and an arrogant disregard of God's law.

After you have read the Scripture verses, describe the area of greed in your life that needs to be demolished, what you need to do to demolish it, and the spiritual weapon(s) to be used in demolishing it. Later this week you will record your progress. Here is an example.

Stronghold to be demolished: spending too much time shopping—acquiring possessions or envisioning ways I can acquire them—and not enough time studying God's Word

What I need to do to demolish it: shop only for essentials; spend time developing my spiritual life

" Do not store up for yourselves treasures on earth, where moth and rust destroy, and where thieves break in and steal. But store up for yourselves treasures in heaven, where moth and rust do not destroy, and where thieves do not break in and steal. For where your treasure is, there your heart will be also. No one can serve two masters. Either he will hate the one and love the other, or he will be devoted to the one and despise the other. You cannot serve both God and Money. Therefore I tell you, do not worry about your life, what you will eat or drink; or about your body, what you will wear. Is not life more important than food, and the body more important than clothes? Look at the birds of the air; they do not sow or reap or store away in barns, and yet your heavenly Father feeds them. Are you not much more valuable than they? But seek first his kingdom and his righteousness, and all these things will be given to you as well' " (Matt. 6:19-21,24-26,33).

Spiritual weapons to be used: Sword of the Spirit—to remind me of the need for heavenly, and not earthly, treasures; Breastplate of Righteousness—to claim God's protection to help me live rightly and to put my priorities in the right place; Shield of Faith—to help me believe that God will provide for my needs

Now you try it.

Stronghold to be demolished: _____

_____

What I need to do to demolish it: _____

_____

Spiritual weapon(s) to be used: _____

_____

 Begin preparing for the Prayer Workshop that will follow week 6 by developing a personal prayer journal. The following material will tell you how.

HOW TO DEVELOP YOUR PERSONAL PRAYER JOURNAL

Make your journal person. Because this article suggests that you copy items in this book and in books 1 and 2, you may wish to use an 8½-by-11-inch loose-leaf binder so that you can punch holes in the pages as you copy and file them under the categories listed. Even if you copy material from this book or from books 1 and 2, plan to bring your *MasterLife* books to the Prayer Workshop so that you can refer to your Daily Master Communication Guides.

Purposes of Your Personal Prayer Journal
1. To help you organize your personal life and your prayer life
2. To equip you to minister to your world through prayer
3. To remind you of what to pray about
4. To enable you to monitor your spiritual growth and walk

The Meaning of Your Personal Prayer Journal
1. *Personal* means that you should design and use a prayer journal that fits your particular needs and personality.
2. *Prayer* means that the focus should be on regularly meeting God in prayer, not on praying from habit.
3. *Journal* means that it is a guide and a record of your communication with God.

Design and use a prayer journal that fits your particular needs and personality.

Organizing Your Personal Prayer Journal

1. Prepare tabs in your notebook for three main divisions:
   a. Prayer Resources
   b. Prayer Lists
   c. Personal Guidance

2. *Prayer Resources.* Behind this tab insert copies of or notes about the locations of prayer resources you have studied in *MasterLife.* Later you may place additional resources behind this tab.
   a. The Disciple's Cross, book 1
   b. Prayer-Covenant List (to date), books 1, 2, and 3
   c. The Disciple's Personality, book 2
   d. "Principles of Conversational Prayer," book 2
   e. Weeks 2 and 4, book 3
   f. Relational-Witnessing Chart, book 3
   g. The Spiritual Armor, book 3
   h. "Guide to Thanksgiving," book 3
   i. "Guide to Praise," book 3
   j. "Guide to Confession and Forgiveness," book 3
   k. "Guide to Praying in Faith," book 3
   l. "Guide to Intercession," book 3
   m. "Guide to Extended Prayer," book 3

3. *Prayer Lists.* Behind this tab place tabs for two subdivisions: Categories and Calendar.
   a. *Categories.* Prepare separate pages for each of the following categories and place them behind the Categories tab. You may want to add other categories to meet your needs. Secure additional blank copies of the Prayer-Covenant List. Include your current Prayer-Covenant List, and your Relational-Witnessing Chart as a basis for determining the objects you will list under each category. Examples of categories:
      - family members
      - relatives
      - close friends
      - business associates
      - persons in authority
      - missionaries
      - church leaders
      - disciples
      - countries
   b. *Calendar.* You may wish to organize further the categories you have listed according to the frequency with which you will pray about different concerns. If so, move some of the preceding category pages or prepare separate pages as follows and place them behind the Calendar tab.
      - *Daily prayer list.* Include persons or items for which you pray every day, such as personal and family needs and missionaries.
      - *Weekly prayer list.* Arrange lists under the Categories tab so that you pray for a different category each day.
      - *Monthly prayer list.* Spend a half day or a day in prayer each month and review your prayer lists and answers.

You may wish to organize further the categories you have listed according to the frequency with which you will pray about different concerns.

• *Annual prayer list.* List your life purpose; your annual goals; and items for which you pray only annually, such as events on your church or denominational calendars and specific countries.

4. *Personal Guidance.* Behind this tab place the following lists, which you will learn to prepare in this week's study.

a. *Life purpose.*

b. *Life goals.*

c. *Monthly goals.* Compile this list during your half or full day in prayer each month. Monthly goals should be specific and should contribute to life goals.

d. *Weekly goals.* Develop this list during your weekly planning session. This is a sample list of weekly goals:

• Read and mark my Bible 10 minutes a day.

• Memorize a new verse each week.

• Do physical exercise three times each week.

• Have individual Bible study one hour each week.

• Witness to one person each week.

• Take notes on one sermon each week.

• Have a half day of prayer each month.

List your weekly goals on a chart like the one on page 143. You may record the time you spend in each activity or simply check the items when completed. Write the date for each day on a separate line. At the end of the day or at the beginning of the next day, fill in the items you have done, completing only the blanks that apply to that day. For example, the half day of prayer a month would be filled in only on the day you completed that activity.

Using Your Personal Prayer Journal

1. Begin where you are and develop your journal as you go.

2. Use your personal prayer journal each day.

   a. Pray for persons on your daily prayer list.

   b. Pray for the particular prayer-list category you have designated for that day.

   c. Mark your personal-guidance list each day.

3. Plan to spend a half day in prayer once a month.

4. Plan an annual evaluation time.

5. Keep developing your personal prayer journal to fit you.

 Read Psalm 119:121-128 during your quiet time today. Let God speak to you through this passage. Then complete the Daily Master Communication Guide in the margin.

DAILY MASTER COMMUNICATION GUIDE

PSALM 119:121-128

What God said to me:

_____

_____

_____

_____

_____

_____

_____

What I said to God:

_____

_____

_____

_____

_____

_____

_____

_____

DAY 2

In Line with God's Will

I had to wait for 15 years until God prepared me.

On our third furlough from missionary service in Indonesia God revealed to me through prayer and Scripture that He wanted me to join the staff of my denomination's discipleship ministry. In that position I would develop *MasterLife* and LIFE courses, which would equip God's people to serve Him and go on mission with Him to all peoples of the world. As I was preparing to talk with the staff of my denomination's publishing house in detail, God impressed me with Exodus 18:14-27, in which Moses received helpful counsel from his father-in-law, Jethro. When I read his words to Moses in verses 19-21, I felt that God was speaking to me, and I began to consider how.

The first thing He showed me was in verse 19: " 'Listen now to me and I will give you some advice, and may God be with you. You must be the people's representative before God and bring their disputes to him.' " I sensed God telling me that I should be an intercessor for His people and that I should bring their causes, or issues, before Him.

The second teaching was easy to understand, because it related to what I anticipated doing in *MasterLife*. Verse 20 says, " 'Teach them the decrees and laws, and show them the way to live and the duties they are to perform.' " "Teach them" and "show them" are discipleship. "The way to live and the duties they are to perform" are the content of discipleship and ministry.

The third point confused me. Moses was told to choose people to lead who would be rulers of thousands, hundreds, fifties, and tens (see v. 21). Although I would be supervising a few persons in this new task, that in no way compared to what this Scripture seemed to indicate. Over the next 15 years I wondered if this referred to the numerous *MasterLife* leaders and trainers. Yet I often wondered if God had more for me to do that related to this third part of the Bible promise.

If we remain faithful to Him, He shows us how He wants to fulfill His purpose in us.

The result of this soul-searching about my life was that I had to wait for 15 years until God prepared me and led me to my present position at our denomination's International Mission Board. My main responsibility is to direct the work of more than 4,000 missionaries and 15,000 volunteers each year around the world by working with 14 regional leaders. Each regional leader works with approximately 300 missionaries in up to 25 missions in each region. They are organized on the local-station or unit level, which is similar to the small unit in Moses' time.

We often do not understand what God has in mind when He begins to share with us what He wants to do with our lives. If we remain faithful to Him, He shows us how He wants to fulfill His purpose in us. Many times He opens our vision to what He is planning through a Scripture He places on our hearts.

SETTING LIFE GOALS

Many people talk about discovering God's will for their lives. God says that His will is bringing the world to Himself. That includes salvation and sanctification for all who accept Him.

Read 2 Peter 3:9, 1 Timothy 2:3-4, and 1 Thessalonians 4:3 in the margin. Underline the statement in each verse that reveals God's will to us.

You do not have to discover the overarching aspects of God's will. He has revealed them. Your life purpose should relate to the salvation of the world and the sanctification of God's people. After you settle your life purpose, then you may concentrate on life goals by asking how you can best carry out God's will in your decisions about marriage, occupation, and other areas of your life.

> A life purpose is an overarching goal for you to accomplish in your lifetime. It provides direction for everyday activities and determines your priorities. A life goal is a specific objective for an important area of your life. Achieving all of your life goals should equal achieving your life purpose.

Read the following decisions and write *purpose* beside those that relate to life purpose and *goal* beside steps to achieve life goals.

_____ 1. Choosing a good vocation
_____ 2. Marrying a Christian
_____ 3. Living for God's glory
_____ 4. Serving persons in need
_____ 5. Using my home as a base for ministry
_____ 6. Accepting myself as God accepts me

A purpose is something that is clearly in line with God's revealed will; goals represent ways to carry out God's will. Statements 3 and 4 relate to life purpose and statements 1, 2, 5, and 6 to life goals.

Mark 12:29-31, with which you became familiar in day 1, illustrates a believer's life purpose. If you love God, you want to be like Him. You want to achieve His purposes. If you love those around you, you want them to have all God intended for them, including eternal life.

Can you recall from day 1 the two broad purposes for a believer's life that are listed in Mark 12:29-31? Look back at the verses on page 85 if you need to refresh your memory.

_____

_____

"The Lord is not slow in keeping his promise, as some understand slowness. He is patient with you, not wanting anyone to perish, but everyone to come to repentance" (2 Pet. 3:9).

"This is good, and pleases God our Savior, who wants all men to be saved and to come to a knowledge of the truth" (1 Tim. 2:3-4).

"It is God's will that you should be sanctified" (1 Thess. 4:3).

If you love God, you want to be like Him. You want to achieve His purposes.

You need life goals and convictions about what God wants you to do as you move in faith with Him to achieve His purposes.

These purposes are overarching objectives on which you can bank your life. To achieve God's purposes, it is necessary to have intermediate life goals that lead to the ultimate objective. You need life goals and convictions about what God wants you to do as you move in faith with Him to achieve His purposes.

Jesus' life purposes were to glorify the Father and to accomplish God's plan for the redemption of humankind. To achieve those purposes, He set life goals, described in John 17, that included—
- revealing the Father;
- reconciling the world to Himself;
- discipling those the Father gave Him to carry out His work.

Explain your understanding of the relationship between life purpose and life goals.

_____

Personal life goals lead to the accomplishment of your life purpose.

 Ephesians 6:18, this week's Scripture-memory verse, says to pray about "all kinds of prayers and requests." Do you believe that verse of Scripture applies to requests for revealing life goals to you? ❏ Yes ❏ No Say the verse aloud from one to three times to remind yourself of this promise.

Mark 12:29-31 mentions loving your neighbor. Show God's love to someone every day this week.

One of Jesus' life goals was to accomplish His Father's purpose for the redemption of humanity. Is this your purpose? If so, the next piece of the Spiritual Armor will help you accomplish this purpose.

PUTTING ON THE SPIRITUAL ARMOR

This week's study focuses on the Gospel Shoes part of the Spiritual Armor presentation—feet fitted with the readiness that comes from the gospel of peace. Turn to pages 129–31 and review the Spiritual Armor presentation, with special emphasis on the soldier's fitted feet. By the end of this study you will be able to explain the entire presentation in your own words.

Get ready before the battle begins.

Picture the soldier's studded sandals on your feet. The preparation of the gospel of peace means that you are ready for battle. It reminds you to do three things:
1. Be prepared. Get ready before the battle begins. Pray that God will prepare you for any possibility.
2. Share the gospel. The readiness that comes from the gospel of peace means to be ready to proclaim the gospel. Ask God to prepare you to witness for Him.

...

3. Intercede for the lost. You are prepared to attack the enemy through prayer or witness. Paul was effective in witness because he prayed for the lost (see Rom. 10:1). Pray for lost friends on your prayer lists. Visualize the countries of the world, with their millions of lost people, and pray for their salvation.

 Focus on the first of the three reminders. Stop and ask God to prepare you for whatever battles come your way today.

GOD'S WORD IN YOUR HEART AND HAND

In the two previous weeks you have learned to imagine yourself grasping God's Word in your hand as you hold the Sword of the Spirit, God's Word. The Bible uses several illustrations for the Word that suggest why a firm grasp of the Word is necessary for effective application.

Read the section "Level 3: Illustration" (p. 134) in the God's Word in Your Heart and Hand presentation. Then record the symbols that the presentation mentions. As you write each, explain how it relates to the grasp you have on the Word.

1. _____

   _____

2. _____

   _____

3. _____

   _____

4. _____

   _____

 Select one level of the God's Word in Your Heart and Hand presentation and share it with your family or a Christian friend.

 Read Psalm 119:129-136 during your quiet time today. Then complete the Daily Master Communication Guide in the margin.

DAILY MASTER COMMUNICATION GUIDE

PSALM 119:129-136

What God said to me:

_____

_____

_____

_____

_____

_____

_____

What I said to God:

_____

_____

_____

_____

_____

_____

_____

_____

"Now the men of Judah approached Joshua at Gilgal, and Caleb son of Jephunneh the Kenizzite said to him, 'You know what the Lord said to Moses the man of God at Kadesh Barnea about you and me. I was forty years old when Moses the servant of the Lord sent me from Kadesh Barnea to explore the land. And I brought him back a report according to my convictions, but my brothers who went up with me made the hearts of the people melt with fear. I, however, followed the Lord my God wholeheartedly. So on that day Moses swore to me, "The land on which your feet have walked will be your inheritance and that of your children forever, because you have followed the Lord my God wholeheartedly." Now then, just as the Lord promised, he has kept me alive for forty-five years since the time he said this to Moses, while Israel moved about in the desert. So here I am today, eighty-five years old! I am still as strong today as the day Moses sent me out; I'm just as vigorous to go out to battle now as I was then. Now give me this hill country that the Lord promised me that day. You yourself heard then that the Anakites were there and their cities were large and fortified, but the Lord helping me, I will drive them out just as he said.' Then Joshua blessed Caleb son of Jephunneh and gave him Hebron as his inheritance. So Hebron has belonged to Caleb son of Jephunneh the Kenizzite ever since, because he followed

DAY 3

Achieving God's Purposes

An Old Testament account illustrates the importance of having a life purpose and life goals. Read Joshua 14:6-14 in the margin. Joshua and Caleb were the 2 spies who gave a positive report in Numbers 13, while the other 10 spies did not believe that God would defeat the people in the promised land.

Although Caleb had to wander through the wilderness for 45 years after Israel refused to conquer Canaan, he had a purpose that kept him going. He had a mountain God wanted him to claim. As they entered the promised land, Caleb said: "This is my job. I want the mountain God promised me."

Match the following questions and answers.

1. What was Caleb's life purpose?

2. What was Caleb's specific life goal?

3. How do you know that his goal was ordained by God?

4. What was the basis of Caleb's faith?

5. How did his goal fit with his life purpose?

a. The large, fortified enemy cities were unconquerable without God.

b. A promise from God about his life goal

c. The achieving of his life goal fulfilled his life purpose.

d. To follow the Lord fully

e. To take the land as his inheritance

Caleb was committed to following the Lord fully. That was his life purpose. His life goal was to take the land as his inheritance, which God had ordained and promised him through Moses. The goal was impossible without the Lord's help because the enemy cities were large, fortified, and unconquerable without God. His acquisition of Hebron as an inheritance glorified God and signified that Caleb had followed the Lord wholeheartedly. The correct answers are 1. d, 2. e, 3. a, 4. b, 5. c.

CHARACTERISTICS OF LIFE GOALS
Caleb's goals have three important characteristics that should also characterize your goals:
1. Life goals are God-revealed rather than conceived by you.
2. Life goals are too big to achieve without God's power.
3. Life goals arrange your life so that you can achieve your life purpose.

Consider the first characteristic: Life goals are God-revealed rather

than conceived by you. Read Matthew 16:21-23 in the margin. Write *G* beside the God-revealed goal and *H* beside the goal conceived by human beings.

___G___ Jesus would suffer, die, and rise again.
___H___ Jesus would remain with them as an earthly king.

Obviously, Jesus' followers conceived their own ideas about what direction His life should take. They wanted to set a goal for Him that He would remain with them and reign on earth. But Jesus operated by a God-revealed goal—that he must be killed and rise from the dead. You have also seen that Caleb's life goal came from God.

Now look at the second characteristic: Life goals are too big to achieve without God's power. Only God's power working in you can propel you to achieve your goals. At 85 years of age Caleb could not conquer the giants in his country by human strength. In Colossians 1:28 Paul stated that his goal was to present everyone perfect in Christ. In the next verse he explained how he would accomplish this: "To this end I labor, struggling with all his energy, which so powerfully works in me" (Col. 1:29).

Why do you think God wants to be the power source for achieving His purposes?

God wants you to depend on Him. He receives the glory of working through you. Because of your sinfulness and humanity, you are limited in what you can do. You cannot do God's work without His help. He wants His energy to work powerfully in you. John 15:5 says that apart from Him, you can do nothing.

Recall the third characteristic: Life goals arrange your life so that you can achieve your life purpose. What do you think kept Caleb going those 45 years as he wandered with the disobedient Israelites? He could have said: "God, why do I have to stay in the wilderness with these turkeys? I believe that You could have led us into the promised land long ago." However, because he stayed focused on his life goals and held on to God's promise to him, he was ready to take the promised land in God's time.

Remembering your life goals helps you order your priorities. Many times your choices are not between good and evil but between good and best. Satan often wants you to settle for merely good things if that keeps you from waiting for God's best gifts.

See if you can list the three characteristics of life goals.

1. _____

the Lord, the God of Israel, wholeheartedly" (Josh. 14:6-14).

"From that time on Jesus began to explain to his disciples that he must go to Jerusalem and suffer many things at the hands of the elders, chief priests and teachers of the law, and that he must be killed and on the third day be raised to life. Peter took him aside and began to rebuke him. 'Never, Lord!' he said. 'This shall never happen to you.' Jesus turned and said to Peter, 'Get behind me, Satan! You are a stumbling block to me; you do not have in mind the things of God, but the things of men' " (Matt. 16:21-23).

Remembering your life goals helps you order your priorities.

DAILY MASTER COMMUNICATION GUIDE

PSALM 119:137-144

What God said to me:

_____

_____

_____

_____

_____

_____

_____

What I said to God:

_____

_____

_____

_____

_____

_____

_____

2. _____

3. _____

When you make important choices in life, such as your vocation or marriage partner, ask yourself, _Will this choice help me achieve God's purpose for my life?_ If so, it is worthy of your efforts to attain it. If you set life goals without first determining your life purpose, you often substitute your goals for God's purposes.

When you set worthy goals, it is as though you put on a new set of glasses to view your future. In the long run, a worthy goal will bring you peace, will help you look at things in a long-term way, will keep you focused, and will help you measure all things in light of God's purposes.

Caleb followed God fully in taking possession of Hebron. Jesus followed God fully in revealing the Father, in reconciling the world to Himself, and in discipling those who would carry out His work.

What evidence do you have that the goals you presently work toward will accomplish your life purpose?

_____

PUTTING ON THE SPIRITUAL ARMOR
In day 2 you learned the importance of putting on the Gospel Shoes as you continued learning the Spiritual Armor presentation. You learned three steps for having your feet fitted with the readiness that comes from the gospel of peace. Review the reminders on pages 92–93.

 Focus on the second reminder. Stop and ask God to make you ready to witness for Him.

One way you can be prepared for a witnessing situation is to have God's Word at instant recall. You have been memorizing Scriptures throughout your study of _MasterLife_. If you studied book 1, you learned suggestions for memorizing Scripture. You may want to refer to that guide as you continue your Scripture-memory work.

 Work on this week's Scripture-memory verse, Ephesians 6:18, and review your memory verses from previous weeks.

 Read Psalm 119:137-144 during your quiet time today. Let God speak to you through this passage. Then complete the Daily Master Communication Guide in the margin.

DAY 4

Learning to Set Priorities

After you have determined your life purpose and have totally committed yourself to Christ in carrying out those purposes, you can move with clarity to set priorities. Loving God and loving your neighbor are the overarching objectives toward which you always move in your life purpose. Every time you make a decision, involve yourself in a relationship, or invest time or money, check it against your life purpose. If you question whether a particular action truly moves you toward accomplishing your life purpose, you may need to reconsider the action.

TOWARD MATURITY
The Phillips version of the Scriptures translates Romans 12:2 as follows: "Don't let the world around you squeeze you into its own mold, but let God remold your minds from within, so that you may prove in practice that the plan of God for you is good, meets all His demands, and moves toward the goal of true maturity." God's plan is that you move toward maturity.

In the Scripture above, underline the three things God is doing to remold your mind as His purpose for your life.

The verse says that as God remolds you, you can prove in practice that God's plan for you is good, meets all of His demands, and moves toward the goal of true maturity.

What do the verses in the margin say that a growing disciple does? Match each reference with the corresponding statement.

___ 1. Philippians 2:5   a. Knows his or her responsibility and acts on it
___ 2. Colossians 3:1-2   b. Is equipped with the mind of Christ
___ 3 Ephesians 5:15   c. Has high priorities

Knowing where you are going in life is exciting when you have the mind of Christ and engage it, know what your responsibility is and do it, and have high priorities. The answers are 1. b, 2. c, 3. a.

Your next concern is to develop a plan for moving toward accomplishing your life purpose.

HOW TO SET PRIORITIES
The following diagram shows what your priorities should be. Ask yourself: *What is God most concerned about in my life? What is His priority for*

Every time you make a decision, involve yourself in a relationship, or invest time or money, check it against your life purpose.

"Your attitude should be the same as that of Christ Jesus" (Phil. 2:5).

"Since, then, you have been raised with Christ, set your hearts on things above, where Christ is seated at the right hand of God. Set your minds on things above, not on earthly things" (Col. 3:1-2).

"Live life, then, with a due sense of responsibility, not as men who do not know the meaning of life but as those who do" (Eph. 5:15, Phillips).

me? The diagram depicts basic life goals—the major items that form the framework for building a life under God's plan. A definite order exists for developing these goals.

Most people make the mistake of starting at the top with mate and career before they set the previous four goals in the sequence shown in the diagram. Note how the priorities progress. First is the foundation.

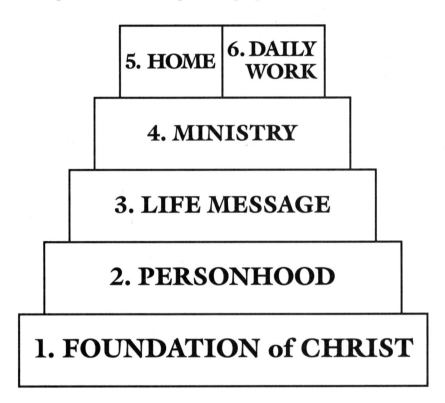

"Just as you received Christ Jesus as Lord, continue to live in him, rooted and built up in him, strengthened in the faith as you were taught, and overflowing with thankfulness" (Col. 2:6-7).

"No one can lay any foundation other than the one already laid, which is Jesus Christ. If any man builds on this foundation using gold, silver, costly stones, wood, hay or straw, his work will be shown for what it is, because the Day will bring it to light. It will be revealed with fire, and the fire will test the quality of each man's work" (1 Cor. 3:11-13).

Read Colossians 2:6-7 in the margin. In whom are you to live and build your life after you receive Christ as your Savior and Lord?

_____

THE FOUNDATION OF CHRIST

Build and root your life in Jesus Christ. He is the foundation of your life. First Corinthians 3:11-13, in the margin, presents an analogy Paul used to illustrate the concept of building a life on Jesus Christ. You first begin with the foundation and then select the building materials. You, as the builder, are responsible for the building itself and the permanence of the materials selected. When it is completed, the Building Inspector will examine it.

Be certain that you build every aspect of your life on Jesus Christ. The life goal that relates to this building block answers the question, *Are Christ and His kingdom my first priority?*

In the blank pyramid on the following page write *foundation of Christ* and *Matthew 6:33* on the lower building block.

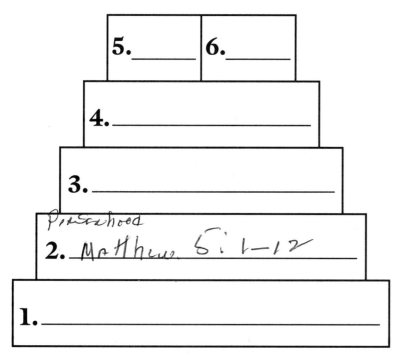

5. ____ 6. ____

4. _____

3. _____

Personhood
2. Matthew 5:1-12 _____

1. _____

PERSONHOOD
The first building block to be placed on the foundation of Christ is you. God is primarily concerned about you.

Write *personhood* **and** *Matthew 5:1-12* **on the second block of the pyramid.**

God wants to guide you to become all He intended. He is more concerned about the kind of person you become than about what career you choose. He is more concerned about inner qualities than about how you look. This second building block deals with life goals that answer the question, *What kind of person am I becoming?*

God begins with the task of producing in you the character of Jesus Christ. Until this begins to happen, Christ cannot use you effectively.

If you are not clear about the kind of person God wants you to be, read the following passages of Scripture.
- **Psalm 139:13-16**
- **Matthew 6:33**
- **Luke 2:52**
- **Acts 24:16**
- **Romans 12:1-2**
- **1 Corinthians 12:7** √
- **2 Corinthians 5:17** √
- **Galatians 5:22-23** √
- **Ephesians 5:18** √
- **Colossians 3:5-27**
- **1 Thessalonians 4:1-8** √
- **1 Peter 3:3-4** √
- **1 John 5:11-13**

Say aloud this week's Scripture-memory verse, Ephesians 6:18. Do you believe that helping you set life goals is included in "all kinds of prayers and requests"? ❑ Yes ❑ No If so, stop and ask God to help you in this process of determining goals.

What God said to me:

_____
_____
_____
_____
_____
_____
_____

What I said to God:

_____
_____
_____
_____
_____
_____
_____

PUTTING ON THE SPIRITUAL ARMOR

This week you have learned the importance of putting on the Gospel Shoes as you have continued learning the Spiritual Armor presentation. Review on pages 92–93 the three steps you learned for having your feet fitted with the readiness that comes from the gospel of peace.

✝ **Focus on the third reminder. Stop and pray that lost friends will have Christ as the foundation for their lives. Then visualize the countries of the world, with their millions of lost people, and pray for their salvation.**

✝ **Share with your family, a Christian friend, or a group the Gospel Shoes part of the Spiritual Armor.**

✝ **As you pray, use "Guide to Intercession," which follows.**

"I urge, then, first of all, that requests, prayers, intercession and thanksgiving be made for everyone" (1 Tim. 2:1).

"... for kings and all those in authority, that we may live peaceful and quiet lives in all godliness and holiness. This is good, and pleases God our Savior, who wants all men to be saved and to come to a knowledge of the truth" (1 Tim. 2:2-4).

"There is one God and one mediator between God and men, the man Christ Jesus, who gave himself as a ransom for all men—the testimony given in its proper time. And for this purpose I was appointed a herald and an apostle—I am telling the truth, I am not lying—and a teacher of the true faith to the Gentiles" (1 Tim. 2:5-7).

"I want men everywhere to lift up holy hands in prayer, without anger or disputing" (1 Tim. 2:8).

GUIDE TO INTERCESSION

Intercession is the ministry of a disciple and the community of faith to bring to God the needs of the church and the world. It can result in changed lives, changed churches, and a changed world.

Begin a ministry of intercession by following these suggestions.

1. Make intercession your first priority (see 1 Tim. 2:1 in the margin). Spend much of your prayer time in intercession.
2. Use all types of prayers in your intercession, combining praise, thanksgiving, requests, and intercession.
3. Intercede for all people (see 1 Tim. 2:2-4 in the margin).
4. Intercede with an all-embracing purpose. Intercession is not limited to specific life needs and crises. Intercession should seek salvation, peace, godliness, quietness, and holiness for all people (see 1 Tim. 2:5-7 in the margin).
5. Pray in unity with other disciples (see 1 Tim. 2:8 in the margin).
6. Pray on the basis of God's character.
7. Stand before God in place of the person in need, ready to sacrifice yourself to have the need met, as Moses, Paul, and Jesus did.
8. Persevere until you prevail.
9. Remember that the Lord Himself is your partner in intercession (see John 17; Rom. 8:26-27).
10. Remain confident, for the promise of intercession is sure (see Matt. 7:7; Jas. 5:16).

✝ **Read Psalm 119:145-152 during your quiet time today. Let God speak to you through this passage. Then complete the Daily Master Communication Guide in the margin on page 99.**

Matt 6: 19-34, 7, 24-27
5: 13-16, 40-48
7 P.tw 4. 10 ; Acts 1: 8
Hob 10: 21-25
Col 1: 28-29   Psalms 119; 153-160
                        Lord
Romans 12: 12-13
Eph 5: 21

DAY 5

Building a Life for God

Yesterday you learned the foundation block for determining your life goals, and you studied the first block for building a life according to God's plan. Today you will study the remaining four blocks.

LIFE MESSAGE

The next building block you place on the foundation of Christ is your life message.

Write *life message* **and** *Matthew 5:13-16* **in the third block in the pyramid on page 99.**

The life goals you write at this level answer the questions: *What do others see in my life? What does my life say to others?* Your life message grows from your personhood. If you are truly becoming a Christlike person, those who know you and observe your life see it. Your life message is the signpost that reveals to others who you really are. They recognize your realness and sincerity. You are your life message. Your life message is the total of your experiences from which you can speak with authority because you have done what you said. It characterizes how others perceive you.

In my first pastorate I hoped that people would remember the messages I preached. Then I noticed what the members said about previous pastors. They never mentioned their messages but made comments like "Brother Jones really loved people," "Brother Smith was a great prayer," and "Brother Tom was a walking Bible." Each was a life message!

Read Matthew 5:16 in the margin. Who gets the credit when you live as a shining light (a Christlike example) before others?

_____

Even though people may see good qualities in you, the source of all good in you is your Father in heaven. Your life message should reflect Him and honor Him. You develop this message when you make Christ the center of your life, when you internalize God's Word, and when you develop your spiritual gifts.

MINISTRY

Ministry flows from your personhood and your life message. It is a natural overflow, not a forced effort. As you drink the water Jesus gives, an overflow will naturally occur. Read Matthew 5:40-48 in the margin.

" 'Let your light shine before men, that they may see your good deeds and praise your Father in heaven' " (Matt. 5:16).

" 'If someone wants to sue you and take your tunic, let him have your cloak as well. If someone forces you to go one mile, go with him two miles. Give to the one who asks you, and do not turn away from the one who wants to borrow from you. You have heard that it was said, "Love your neighbor and hate your enemy." But I tell you: Love your enemies and pray for those who persecute you, that you may be sons of your Father in heaven. He causes his sun to rise on the evil and the good, and sends rain on the righteous and the unrighteous. If you love those who love you, what reward will you get? Are not even the tax collectors doing that? And if you greet only your brothers, what are you doing more than others? Do not even pagans do that? Be perfect, therefore, as your heavenly Father is perfect' " (Matt. 5: 40-48).

Write *ministry* and *Matthew 5:40-48* on the fourth block in the pyramid on page 99.

Ministry answers the question, *How can I share my life with others?* The verses in the margin give ideas about life goals involving ministry.

Read the verses in the margin and match their references with the ideas they convey.

_e_ 1. Matthew 5:13   a. Using the gifts God gave you
_a_ 2. 1 Peter 4:10   b. Sharing Christ
_b_ 3. Acts 1:8   c. Making disciples
_d_ 4. Hebrews 10:24-25   d. Serving through the church
_c_ 5. Colossians 1:28-29   e. Penetrating your part of the secular world
_f_ 6. Romans 12:12-13   f. Meeting human needs

God has called you to a life of ministry. No disciple is exempt from this call. Concentrate on walking with Christ and on becoming like Him. Learn to see people through His eyes, and He will give you a ministry. The correct answers are 1. e, 2. a, 3. b, 4. d, 5. c, 6. f.

HOME
Your home is a vital part of your ministry.

Read the verses in the margin on page 103. On what should both a marital union and a home be based?

_____

Write *home*, *Ephesians 5:21*, and *Matthew 7:24-27* on the top left block in the pyramid on page 99.

Christ is the foundation of a wise person's home and the center of our home relationships. Your home is the most natural place to demonstrate what Christ is doing in your life and will do in others' lives. The home may speak to the world more quickly than the church does. The question is, *How can I make my home a platform for my ministry?*

Both married and single persons should consider how their special circumstances can best contribute to their life goals. A growing disciple who is planning marriage should never consider marrying a person who does not have a similar concept of building a life and a relationship on Christ. For those who seek a life partner, the home building block answers the question, *Who is the best person I can marry in order to have the most effective ministry together?*

For Christians, marriage is a partnership, a spiritual union of two persons whose chief desire in life is to glorify God and to become like Jesus Christ. First Peter 3:7 calls husband and wife the "joint heirs of the

margin verses: Matt. 5:13; 1 Pet. 4:10; Acts 1:8; Heb. 10:24-25; Col. 1:28-29; Rom. 12:12-13.

grace of life" (RSV). Priscilla and Aquila (see Rom. 16:3-5) understood their marriage in this light and used their home as a gathering place for the church. If you are married, determine to build your marriage into a relationship that becomes a penetrating witness in the world and that shows Christ's power in true love and purpose. For a married couple, the question is, *How does God intend to use our relationship in ministry together?*

You do not have to be married to be Christ's follower or to minister. If you are single, the question is, *How can I use my singleness to increase my ministry?* Your home is still a focal point for ministry.

DAILY WORK
You can gain a new vision for the way God can use you as an influence in your career or job by studying Matthew 6:19-34.

Write *daily work* and *Matthew 6:19-34* on the top right block in the pyramid on page 99.

The daily-work building block answers the question, *How can I allow Christ to use my career to minister?* Or if you are deciding on a career or employment, it answers the question, *What career would best enable me to have an effective ministry in the world?* Look at your daily work as one of the focal points of your ministry.

If believers followed this concept, it would literally revolutionize the secular work world. Whatever your job, work at it with all your heart, as serving the Lord and not the paycheck. Instead of goofing off or complaining, exhibit the spirit of Christ in attitudes, relationships, work habits, and decision making. The salt can penetrate the day-by-day work world, enabling you to touch people's lives significantly by the way you work. When they see your message, they will be open to ministry.

Read the following prayer. Then pray it either by reading it aloud or by saying a similar prayer in your own words.

Lord, as I go to work, give me a vision of what You want me to be and do to influence my coworkers for Jesus Christ. Help me live in such a way that my message will be clear yet gentle and not overbearing. Help me demonstrate genuine love and be aware of opportunities You give for ministry and verbal witness. Help me make my job a penetrating point of my ministry for You in the world.

As you consider your present or prospective career, be sure that you are willing to change your career direction or to consider a call to a church-related ministry if God leads.

In *MasterLife 4: The Disciple's Mission* you will spend more time considering what God wants to accomplish in the world through you.

"Submit to one another out of reverence for Christ" (Eph. 5:21).

" 'Everyone who hears these words of mine and puts them into practice is like a wise man who built his house on the rock' " (Matt. 7:24).

Whatever your job, work at it with all your heart, as serving the Lord.

KEY QUESTIONS
- **What kind of person am I becoming?**
- **What do others see in my life? What does my life say to others?**
- **How can I share my life with others?**
- **How can I make my home a platform for my ministry? Who is the best person I can marry in order to have the most effective ministry together? How does God intend to use our relationship in ministry together? or How can I use my singleness to increase my ministry?**
- **How can I allow Christ to use my career to minister? or What career would best enable me to have an effective ministry in the world?**

You have probably become more aware of your need to witness.

Apply what you have learned this week by writing one major life goal related to each of the following building blocks. Refer to the questions in the margin as you write your goals. Then number your goals in the order of increasing priority.

Personhood: _____

_____

Message: _____

_____

Ministry: _____

_____

Home: _____

_____

Daily work: _____

_____

DEMOLISHING PERSONAL SPIRITUAL STRONGHOLDS
In day 1 you identified a stronghold you wanted to demolish in the area of greed. Today give a progress report on how you have used the spiritual weapon(s) you listed to demolish this stronghold.

How I have used a spiritual weapon(s) to demolish the stronghold of greed:

_____

_____

Some people cannot build their life goals on a foundation of Christ because they have never heard the gospel message. As you have listed the names of lost persons on your Relational-Witnessing Chart, you have probably become more aware of your need to witness to those with whom you come in contact.

After reading "Expanding Your Witness Circle" on the following pages, continue adding names to the Relational-Witnessing Chart (p. 135) and to the Prayer-Covenant List (p. 143).

EXPANDING YOUR WITNESS CIRCLE

Begin expanding your witness circle by witnessing to the persons with whom you have close relationships, but do not stop there. Enlarge your circles of influence to include Person X. Person X is any person or any group of persons outside your circles of friends and associates with whom you could form a relationship. Minister to this person's needs and cultivate the friendship.

Jesus demonstrated the principles of lifestyle witnessing when He met the Samaritan woman (see John 4).[1] Follow His pattern as you design your personal strategy for lifestyle witnessing.

Relate to Lost Persons and Cultivate Witnessing Relationships

1. *Geographically.* Examine your traffic patterns. Are you going out of your way to cultivate witnessing relationships?
2. *Socially.* Examine your social relationships. The longer people have been church members, the fewer friends they have outside the church. Plan your calendar to ensure that you spend sufficient time cultivating relationships. Use your home to increase your witnessing opportunities by—
   - inviting persons to dinner;
   - having small-group fellowships in which a brief testimony is shared and individual conversations follow;
   - holding Bible-study fellowships;
   - offering special classes such as sewing, cooking, piano, nutrition, money management, arts, crafts, or drama;
   - forming special clubs such as reading clubs;
   - inviting newcomers in the community;
   - being available for counseling;
   - tutoring.

Relate to Felt Needs

As you talk with others, you often hear them express basic needs like love, self-esteem, meaning, a sense of security, and assurance of an afterlife. These can be avenues for ministry as well as for the verbal communication of the gospel.

Help Them Understand Their Real Need

Help people see their need for a personal relationship with Christ. Otherwise, they may never associate their loneliness or heartache with their need for Christ. As you deepen your relationships, share the way Christ has satisfied the deepest longings of your soul.

Maintain a Spirit of Acceptance

Although you do not approve of the lifestyle, maintain a spirit of love and compassion. Your concept of sanctification is faulty if you think that Christians should be isolated from the world (see John 17:15). Jesus was the friend of sinners.

Enlarge your circles of influence to include Person X.

Help people see their need for a personal relationship with Christ.

DAILY MASTER COMMUNICATION GUIDE

PSALM 119:153-160

What God said to me:

_____

_____

_____

_____

_____

_____

What I said to God:

_____

_____

_____

_____

_____

_____

Guide Them to Understand the Implications of the Gospel
Do not communicate that salvation is a matter of having the right religion. As you witness, always focus on the need of a personal relationship with Christ. Avoid discussing the merits of one religion over another.

Maintain a sense of urgency about leading persons to Christ. However, if they do not understand the implications of the gospel when it is first presented to them, continue to share patiently as the Holy Spirit works in their hearts. One woman said of another, "She built a bridge from her heart to mine, and Jesus Christ walked across." That is what witnessing is all about.

Are you building relationships? Check the statements that apply.
❑ **I refrain from being judgmental about another person's lifestyle.**
❑ **I enlist prayer partners to pray for my witnessing opportunities.**
❑ **I look for opportunities to share what Christ has done for me.**
❑ **I try to be patient while Christ works in others' hearts if they do not respond at first.**

Here are more suggestions for using a witnessing booklet.
• As you read the booklet, be sure to allow time and provide an opportunity for the person to pray to receive Christ.
• Be sure that you have left the individual with enough information, whether or not the person has accepted Christ. Phrase this part of your conversation this way: "Here are some things you will need to know when you are ready to receive Christ."

 Read Psalm 119:153-160 during your quiet time today. Let God speak to you through this passage. Then complete the Daily Master Communication Guide in the margin.

HAS THIS WEEK MADE A DIFFERENCE?
Review "My Walk with the Master This Week" at the beginning of this week's material. Mark the activities you have finished by drawing vertical lines in the diamonds beside them. Finish any incomplete activities. Think about what you will say during your group session about your work on these activities.

As you conclude your study of "Look to Jesus," I hope you realize that by determining your life purpose and life goals, you have an additional arsenal of weapons to use in Satan's relentless attack. By following Jesus' purpose for your life, you can stay on course in your walk as His disciple.

[1]These categories are adapted from *Continuing Witness Training* (Alpharetta, Ga.: The North American Mission Board of the Southern Baptist Convention). Used by permission.

WEEK 6

Stand Victorious

This Week's Goal
You will be able to stand victorious in spiritual warfare.

My Walk with the Master This Week
You will complete the following activities to develop the six biblical disciplines. When you have completed each activity, draw a vertical line in the diamond beside it.

SPEND TIME WITH THE MASTER
◇ Have a quiet time each day. Check each day you have a quiet time: ❑ Sunday ❑ Monday ❑ Tuesday ❑ Wednesday ❑ Thursday ❑ Friday ❑ Saturday

LIVE IN THE WORD
◇ Read your Bible every day. Write what God says to you and what you say to God.
◇ Memorize Ephesians 3:20-21.
◇ Review 1 John 4:4, 2 Timothy 3:16-17, Psalm 1:2-3, 1 John 5:14-15, and Ephesians 6:18.

PRAY IN FAITH
◇ Read "Guide to Extended Prayer."
◇ List what you should pray about during the Prayer Workshop.
◇ Pray with your prayer partner about sharing your testimony with a lost person.

FELLOWSHIP WITH BELIEVERS
◇ Show God's love to someone every day this week.

WITNESS TO THE WORLD
◇ Share with someone your personal testimony or a witness presentation.

MINISTER TO OTHERS
◇ Be a servant to someone who needs your help.
◇ Learn the Belt of Truth part of the Spiritual Armor.
◇ Explain the entire Spiritual Armor presentation to someone.

This Week's Scripture-Memory Verses
"Now to him who is able to do immeasurably more than all we ask or imagine, according to his power that is at work within us, to him be glory in the church and in Christ Jesus throughout all generations, forever and ever! Amen" (Eph. 3:20-21).

DAY 1
Seeking God

When you realize that you are at war, seek God.

Although you fight an unceasing battle against the enemy, you can conclude this study feeling confident that you have the ultimate weapons in prayer and in the Word to deliver you. The battle against Satan and against the forces of evil is fought first on your knees.

God has used many of my experiences as a pastor, an evangelist, a missionary, and a denominational leader to teach me this truth. One Scripture passage that has been particularly helpful in spiritual warfare is 2 Chronicles 20. This passage tells the story of Jehoshaphat, king of Judah, who was informed that a vast army of Moabites, Ammonites, and Meunites was on its way to make war against him. Read 2 Chronicles 20:1-4 in the margin.

This passage sets the stage for the five principles of spiritual warfare you will study this week. Today you will focus on the first principle.

FIVE PRINCIPLES OF SPIRITUAL WARFARE
1. **The seeking-God principle**
2. The knowing-God principle
3. The depending-on-God principle
4. The believing-God principle
5. The worshiping-God principle

To whom did Jehoshaphat and the people of Judah turn for help when they realized that they were at war?

_____

SEEK GOD
When you realize that you are at war, seek God, just as the people of Judah did when they realized that the three armies were coming their way. The seeking-God principle states that you always first seek God in a problem. He knows the enemy you are fighting, just as He knew the three kings who came against Jehoshaphat.

What one word in 2 Chronicles 20:1-4 describes Jehoshaphat's reaction when he heard the news that he was under siege?

_____

Who joined Jehoshaphat in calling on God for help?

_____

When he realized that he was at war, Jehoshaphat was alarmed. The people of Judah joined their king in sincere pursuit of God's leadership. The seeking-God principle includes the mandate to seek Him not just individually but corporately. If you have a personal problem or a problem that involves others, such as your family or church, pray as a group for an extended time.

A HEART FOR THE LORD

Jehoshaphat's heart was devoted to the ways of the Lord, as 2 Chronicles 17:3-6, in the margin, illustrates. Turning to God was not something he did only in an emergency. He had sought God earlier when he began his reign. When you fight spiritual battles, make sure that your heart is wholeheartedly for the Lord.

Not only had Jehoshaphat sought the Lord, but he had also sought to bring others closer to God. Read 2 Chronicles 17:7,9 in the margin.

Scripture also reports that Jehoshaphat had made a mistake early. Second Chronicles 18:3, in the margin, says that Jehoshaphat had aligned himself with the wrong people. By aligning himself with Ahab by marriage, he had tried to fight the battle with someone who was not of the same heart. You cannot solve a problem by consulting someone who does not have the same commitment to Christ you do.

As you studied in 2 Chronicles 20, Jehoshaphat later learned to call on the right person first. The same seeking-God principle appears throughout Scripture. You see the small boy David fighting Goliath and winning. You see the people of Israel, though weak and enslaved in Egypt, delivered by God. You see a little boy's lunch being used to feed five thousand people. Dependence on God is the crucial element.

This week's Scripture-memory verses, Ephesians 3:20-21, **describe what happens when you depend on God: more than you can ever imagine. Turn to page 107 and read the verses aloud from one to three times to begin memorizing them.**

TRUST GOD

I had seen God at work in scriptural examples, but I had never understood the principle of how to fight in spiritual warfare until I discovered it in Deuteronomy 20. How do you go to war when you are surrounded by the enemy? The answer lies in Deuteronomy 20, Moses' message to the children of Israel before they entered the promised land.

Read Deuteronomy 20:1-4, which begins in the margin and continues on the next page. When the Israelites stood in formation to enter a battle with a more strongly fortified enemy, what were they to do?

"The Lord was with Jehoshaphat because in his early years he walked in the ways his father David had followed. He did not consult the Baals but sought the God of his father and followed his commands rather than the practices of Israel. The Lord established the kingdom under his control; and all Judah brought gifts to Jehoshaphat, so that he had great wealth and honor. His heart was devoted to the ways of the Lord" (2 Chron. 17:3-6).

"In the third year of his reign he sent his officials Ben-Hail, Obadiah, Zechariah, Nethanel and Micaiah to teach in the towns of Judah. They taught throughout Judah, taking with them the Book of the Law of the Lord; they went around to all the towns of Judah and taught the people" (2 Chron. 17:7,9).

"Ahab king of Israel asked Jehoshaphat king of Judah, 'Will you go with me against Ramoth Gildead?' Jehoshaphat replied, 'I am as you are; and my people as your people; we will join you at war' " (2 Chron. 18:3).

" 'When you go to war against your enemies and see horses and chariots and an army greater than yours, do not be afraid of them, because the Lord your God, who brought you up out of Egypt, will be with you. When you are about to go into battle, the priest shall come forward and address the army. He shall say: "Hear, O Israel, today you

are going into battle against your enemies. Do not be fainthearted or afraid; do not be terrified or give way to panic before them. For the Lord your God is the one who goes with you to fight for you against your enemies to give you victory" ' " (Deut. 20:1-4).

" 'Do not judge, or you too will be judged. For in the same way you judge others, you will be judged, and with the measure you use, it will be measured to you. Why do you look at the speck of sawdust in your brother's eye and pay no attention to the plank in your own eye? How can you say to your brother, "Let me take the speck out of your eye," when all the time there is a plank in your own eye? You hypocrite, first take the plank out of your own eye, and then you will see clearly to remove the speck from your brother's eye' " (Matt. 7:1-5).

"By the grace given me I say to every one of you: do not think of yourself more highly than you ought, but rather think of yourself with sober judgment, in accordance with the measure of faith God has given you" (Rom. 12:3).

"Do nothing out of selfish ambition or vain conceit, but in humility consider others better than yourselves" (Phil. 2:3).

The people were to call the priest, who would encourage them to trust in God. When you go into battle against the enemy, make sure that you are not afraid but trust God. Fear is faith in the enemy. If you believe that the enemy is stronger than you and your God, you will not win the battle.

No doubt you have found yourself in a spiritual battle during this study as you have attempted to demolish the spiritual strongholds Satan has established in you. Today you will examine another area of your life in which you will let the Holy Spirit build Christlike character.

DEMOLISHING PERSONAL SPIRITUAL STRONGHOLDS
In previous weeks you examined the strongholds of bitterness, speech, lust, religious ritual, and greed. Today look at the area of pride in your life and prayerfully consider how the Lord might be directing you to demolish this stronghold.

Read the verses in the margin that address the stronghold of pride. If we have true humility, we work on our own faults first instead of judging someone else. We keep our opinions of ourselves in check, and we put others first instead of ourselves.

After you have read the Scripture verses, describe the area of pride in your life that needs to be demolished, what you need to do to demolish it, and the spiritual weapon(s) to be used in demolishing it. Later this week you will record your progress. Here is an example.

Stronghold to be demolished: the idea that befriending someone in need is beneath me; fearing what my friends would think if they saw me associating with someone who has fewer advantages than I

What I need to do to demolish it: set aside my pride and concern about what others think of me; do what God leads me to do.

Spiritual weapon to be used: Belt of Truth—to remind me of what the Bible says about the pitfalls of pride and to see myself as I really am in God's sight instead of comparing myself to others

Now you try it.

Stronghold to be demolished:

_____

What I need to do to demolish it:

_____

Spiritual weapon(s) to be used: _____

_____

DAILY MASTER COMMUNICATION GUIDE

PSALM 119:161-168

→ Show God's love to someone every day this week.

↕ Continue to prepare your personal prayer journal, which you will use in the Prayer Workshop that follows this study. Refer to pages 87–89 for items you need to include in your journal.

↑ Read Psalm 119:161-168 during your quiet time today. Let God speak to you through this passage. Then complete the Daily Master Communication Guide in the margin.

DAY 2

Knowing God

Today you will continue studying principles of spiritual warfare. Read the second way to win spiritual battles, which appears below in bold type. Write the first principle, which you learned yesterday.

What God said to me:

_____

_____

_____

_____

_____

_____

_____

_____

FIVE PRINCIPLES OF SPIRITUAL WARFARE
1. _SEEKING God_
2. **The knowing-God principle**
3. The depending-on-God principle
4. The believing-God principle
5. The worshiping-God principle

You will begin your study today by examining the knowing-God principle. Because you know God, you can base your prayers on—
- His person;
- His promises;
- His purposes;
- His previous acts.

What I said to God:

_____

_____

_____

_____

_____

_____

_____

GOD'S PERSON
In the margin on page 112 read in 2 Chronicles 20:6 the way Jehoshaphat faced the threat of attack from the three mighty armies. Underline words Jehoshaphat used to depict God's power.

How great is this God to whom you pray? It will take all of eternity for you to know Him, but you can partially understand who He is as

" 'O Lord, God of our fathers, are you not the God who is in heaven? You rule over all the kingdoms of the nations. Power and might are in your hand, and no one can withstand you' " (2 Chron. 20:6).

[handwritten: God Power]

[handwritten: faith in God is the chief weapon(s)]

" 'O our God, did you not drive out the inhabitants of this land before your people Israel and give it forever to the descendants of Abraham your friend?' " (2 Chron. 20:7).

"They have lived in [the land] and have built in it a sanctuary for your Name, saying 'If calamity comes upon us, whether the sword of judgment, or plague or famine, we will stand in your presence before this temple that bears your Name and will cry out to you in our distress, and you will hear us and save us' " (2 Chron. 20:8-9).

you read God's Word or look at the heavens He spoke into being.

The Hubble Spacecraft mapped the universe and determined that this world is much bigger than scientists originally thought. They claim that we have just seen light that started 15 billion light years ago. They once thought that the largest structure in all the universe was something called the Great Wall. It was 200 million light years across. But with this exploration they discovered that the largest structure is 10 billion light years across. That is 60 billion trillion miles.[1]

Do you know how God looks at the universe? Isaiah 40:12 says that He has—

measured the waters in the hollow of his hand,
or with the breadth of his hand marked off the heavens.

Somewhere in that universe is what scientists would call a third-rate solar system with a small star we call the sun, around which revolve some planets. We call one of these the world God so loved that He gave His only begotten Son to redeem (see John 3:16).

How do you feel when you realize that the God who created a universe of this magnitude cares about you when you pray in the midst of spiritual warfare?
❑ I can't believe that He would care for me that much.
❑ I want to call on His power to defeat Satan in my battles.
❑ I have difficulty believing it. I feel unworthy.
❑ Other: _____

GOD'S PROMISES
Because you know God, you can pray on the basis of His promises.

Read 2 Chronicles 20:7 in the margin. On the basis of what promise does Jehoshaphat pray?

[handwritten: Pray for what Promise Jesus(?) our for father Abraham, lessing(?) God]

Jehoshaphat based his prayer on God's promise to Abraham in Genesis 12:3 to give the Israelites the land: " 'I will bless those who bless you, and whoever curses you I will curse; and all peoples on earth will be blessed through you' " and on the basis of God's promise in Joshua 1:3: " 'I will give you every place where you set your foot, as I promised Moses.' " Jehoshaphat was saying, "We're in the land You promised us, and now these armies are trying to take it away from us."

In 2 Chronicles 20:8-9 Jehoshaphat cited a second promise.

Read 2 Chronicles 20:8-9 in the margin. What did Jehoshaphat believe that God had promised He would do?

_____

When you are praying in spiritual warfare, base your prayer not only on who God is and what He does but also on what He has promised. Jehoshaphat believed that God had promised to save the Israelites. In many experiences I would have stepped back and not moved ahead except for the fact that God had directed me to act.

List the first two qualities of God on which you can base your prayers.
1. His _PReVIOUS Acts_
2. His _PAST Action_   *Red Sea* ↓
3. His purposes
4. His previous acts

GOD'S PURPOSES

Because you know God, you can pray according to His purposes. Discover from the past what He wanted to happen. In 2 Chronicles 20:8-9 Jehoshaphat looked back at God's intention for the Israelites.

Read 2 Chronicles 20:8-9 in the margin. What was God's purpose for the people of Israel?

_____

Jehoshaphat reminded God that His purpose was to establish them in the land. He identified God's overall, long-range purpose, saying: "We're in the midst of Your purpose, O God. One reason we ask You to answer our prayer is that we're doing what You wanted us to do."

GOD'S PREVIOUS ACTS

Because you know God, you can base your prayer on His previous acts. Jehoshaphat did this in 2 Chronicles 20:10-11: " 'Here are men from Ammon, Moab and Mount Seir, whose territory you would not allow Israel to invade when they came from Egypt; so they turned away from them and did not destroy them. See how they are repaying us by coming to drive us out of the possession you gave us as an inheritance.' "

Jehoshaphat petitioned God on the basis of His past actions, saying: "They're coming up to destroy the land You promised us. If that was Your will then, how does this relate to Your will now?" This is what Henry Blackaby in *Experiencing God* calls a spiritual marker—a time when you knew that God spoke to you or led you.[2] When you are dealing with a problem in spiritual warfare, recall that time and ask, "God, how does this present situation relate to times when I know that You spoke to me or led me?" What God does is consistent. What He tells you to do now will be consistent with what He has told you to do at other key times in your life. His answer will continue the good work He has begun in you (see Phil. 1:6).

They were Afraid for their Life Lost their Faith

"They have lived in [the land] and have built in it a sanctuary for your Name, saying 'If calamity comes upon us, whether the sword of judgment, or plague or famine, we will stand in your presence before this temple that bears your Name and will cry out to you in our distress, and you will hear us and save us' " (2 Chron. 20:8-9).

(11)

What God tells you to do now will be consistent with what He has told you to do at other key times in your life.

DAILY MASTER COMMUNICATION GUIDE

PSALM 119:169-176

What God said to me:

_____

_____

_____

_____

_____

_____

_____

_____

What I said to God:

_____

_____

_____

_____

_____

_____

_____

_____

Describe a spiritual marker that pointed to God's previous acts and helped you make a decision.

_____

Review the knowing-God principle by writing the four qualities of God on which you can base your prayers:
1. His p_____
2. His p_____
3. His p_____
4. His p_____

Prayer is the cutting edge, the contact with God that makes everything happen. You pray on the basis of His person, His promises, His purposes, and His previous acts in applying the knowing-God principle.

Say aloud this week's Scripture-memory verses, Ephesians 3:20-21. Do you believe that promise? ❑ Yes ❑ No Repeat the verses several times to remind yourself of this promise. Review your previous Scripture-memory verses.

The ministry you provide someone might fulfill that person's prayer promise. Be a servant to someone who needs your help. You could help someone who is sick, homebound, lonely, or hungry. You can visit, write a card, or call—whatever you think would minister to this person.

PUTTING ON THE SPIRITUAL ARMOR
This week's study emphasizes the Belt of Truth, the last item in the Spiritual Armor. Turn to pages 129–31 and review the Spiritual Armor presentation, with special emphasis on the Belt of Truth. By the end of this study you will be able to explain the entire presentation in your own words.

Picture the Belt of Truth, which holds the rest of the armor in place. _Truth_ means _integrity and moral uprightness._ Let it remind you to do the following.
1. Be true to yourself and to God when you pray or fight a spiritual battle.
2. Hold to the truth. Satan, the father of lies, would like to deceive you.
3. Master your emotions. Your emotions should be guided by truth rather than by the flesh or by Satan. The Bible speaks of the area of the body covered by the Belt of Truth as "bowels" (KJV), or inward parts, referring to the place where feelings reside or to the feelings themselves. The Belt of Truth helps you control your emotions and not compromise because of your feelings. If the Belt of Truth is not in place, you cannot expect your prayers to be answered.

Have you noticed that the Spiritual Armor covers the parts of your personality you studied in *MasterLife 2: The Disciple's Personality?* The Helmet of Salvation protects your mind. The Breastplate of Righteousness protects your heart, or will. The Belt of Truth protects your emotions.

✝ **Focus on the first of the three reminders. Stop and ask God to be true to you when you pray or fight a spiritual battle. Ask for strength not to compromise the truth because of your feelings when you are engaged in spiritual warfare.**

✝ **Read Psalm 119:169-176 during your quiet time today. Then complete the Daily Master Communication Guide in the margin on page 114.**

115
119

DAY 3
Depending on God

After you have sought God's help and have acknowledged His ability to deal with your problem, depend on Him to show you the way. Depending on God, in bold type below, is the third of five principles of spiritual warfare you are studying. Write the first two you have learned.

Depend on God to show you the way.

> **FIVE PRINCIPLES OF SPIRITUAL WARFARE**
> 1. The ___SEEKing___ principle
> 2. The ___Ahem you___ principle
> 3. **The depending-on-God principle**
> 4. The believing-God principle
> 5. The worshiping-God principle

WINNING THE BATTLE ON YOUR KNEES
As Jehoshaphat anticipated the siege from the three kings, the prophet Jahaziel arrived and gave him a word from the Lord.

Read 2 Chronicles 20:14-15 in the margin. Underline key words or phrases that gave Jehoshaphat courage in battle. Describe ways to apply these reminders when you are in spiritual warfare.

___Do Not be Afraid and discoud___
___The battle is God___

As the prophet reminded Jehoshaphat, God is in charge even in a des-

"The Spirit of the Lord came upon Jahaziel son of Zechariah, the son of Benaiah, the son of Jeiel, the son of Mattaniah, a Levite and a descendant of Asaph, as he stood in the assembly. He said, 'Listen, King Jehoshaphat and all who live in Judah and Jerusalem! This is what the Lord says to you: "Do not be afraid or discouraged because of this vast army. For the battle is not yours but God's"'" (2 Chron. 20:14-15).

427

perate situation when you base your prayers on Him and His revealed will. Although despairing at such times comes naturally, God can win the victory against all human odds. Remember that it is God's battle and that He goes to war through you. Therefore, you can turn over the battle to Him and let Him be the mighty warrior rather than rely on your own strength.

The prophet then advised Jehoshaphat about the next day's events. Read 2 Chronicles 20:16-17 in the margin. The prophet told Jehoshaphat that he would not have to fight this battle. In the midst of your battle seek a Word from the Lord to show you what to do. Prayer leads you to God's Word and helps you apply it to your situation in faith. If God tells you to go, you go with dependence on Him. You must first win the battle on your knees. Once you know that it is His battle, you can go in confidence.

ARMED FOR BATTLE

John Piper notes that "the word for *fight* in 1 Timothy (*agonizethai*, from which we get the word *agonize*) is used repeatedly in describing the Christian life."[3] Jesus said, " 'Make every effort to enter through the narrow door; because many, I tell you, will try to enter and will not be able' " (Luke 13:24). Paul compared the Christian life to a race: "Every athlete strives and uses self-control in all things. They do it to obtain a perishable crown, but we do it to obtain an imperishable one" (1 Cor. 9:25). Paul described running a race, fighting a boxing match, and striving against the forces of his own body. In 1 Corinthians 9:26-27 he wrote: "I do not run like a man running aimlessly; I do not fight like a man beating the air. No, I beat my body and make it my slave so that after I have preached to others, I myself will not be disqualified for the prize." He strove with all the energy God gave him, and he kept his body under subjection.

Check the words or traits that most characterize you, fitting you to win in spiritual warfare.

❑ generous ❑ dependable
❑ good listener ❑ realistic
❑ tenacious ❑ optimistic
❑ loyal ❑ level-headed
❑ affectionate ❑ creative

 Recall this week's Scripture-memory verses, Ephesians 3:20-21. Why are you to give glory to the Father?

_____

The Father is due glory because He is able to do immeasurably more than all we ask or imagine. Even fighting the most insurmountable battles is no problem for Him because of His power.

" ' "*Tomorrow march down against them. They will be climbing up by the Pass of Ziz, and you will find them at the end of the gorge in the Desert of Jeruel. You will not have to fight this battle. Take up your positions; stand firm and see the deliverance the Lord will give you, O Judah and Jerusalem. Do not be afraid; do not be discouraged. Go out to face them tomorrow, and the Lord will be with you" ' " (2 Chron. 20:16-17).*

struggling

PUTTING ON THE SPIRITUAL ARMOR
In day 2 you studied the importance of putting on the Belt of Truth as you continued to learn the Spiritual Armor presentation. You learned three steps for putting on the belt. Review them on page 114.

✝ **Focus on the second reminder. Stop and ask God to help you hold to the truth of His Word and not fall prey to the lies Satan wants you to believe.**

✝ **Read 2 Chronicles 20:1-29, the passage you are studying about Jehoshaphat's response to the three attacking kings, during your quiet time today. Let God speak to you** through this passage. Then complete the Daily Master Communication Guide in the margin.

DAY 4

Believing God

God wants us to live by faith, based on God's Word. After Jehoshaphat claimed the promise the prophet Jahaziel delivered, he bowed and worshiped the Lord. Read 2 Chronicles 20:18 in the margin on page 118.

When God gives you a Word, claim His promise and believe. Accept the promise that God will take care of you, even when the odds against you seem overwhelming. The believing-God principle, in bold type below, is the fourth of five principles for winning spiritual battles. Write the first three principles you have studied.

FIVE PRINCIPLES OF SPIRITUAL WARFARE
1. The ___Seeking___ principle
2. The ___Knowing___ principle
3. The ___defending___ principle
4. **The believing-God principle**
5. The worshiping-God principle

SIGNS THAT YOU BELIEVE
One way to know that a person has believed God is when he or she begins praising God for what He has promised. Because he was aware of God's promise, Jehoshaphat praised God. He had reverence for God because of His mighty acts. Jehoshaphat knew who had spoken, and he believed. Before he took any other action, he bowed before God, who was worthy of his praise.

Jehoshaphat demonstrated his faith not only when he praised God

Next tuesday

"Jehoshaphat bowed with his face to the ground, and all the people of Judah and Jerusalem fell down in worship before the Lord" (2 Chron. 20:18).

"Some Levites from the Kohathites and Korahites stood up and praised the Lord, the God of Israel, with very loud voice" (2 Chron. 20:19).

"Early in the morning they left for the Desert of Tekoa. As they set out, Jehoshaphat stood and said, 'Listen to me, Judah and people of Jerusalem! Have faith in the Lord your God and you will be upheld; have faith in his prophets and you will be successful'" (2 Chron. 20:20).

"An angel of the Lord said to Philip, 'Go south to the road—the desert road—that goes down from Jerusalem to Gaza.' So he started out, and on his way he met an Ethiopian eunuch, an important official in charge of all the treasury of Candace, queen of the Ethiopians. This man had gone to Jerusalem to worship, and on his way home was sitting in his chariot reading the book of Isaiah the prophet. The Spirit told Philip, 'Go to that chariot and stay near it.' Then Philip began with that very passage of Scripture and told him the good news about Jesus. As they traveled along the road, they came to some water and the eunuch said, 'Look, here is water. Why shouldn't I be baptized?'" (Acts 8:26-29,35-37).

but also when he led others to praise. Read verse 19 in the margin.

The response of Jehoshaphat and the people is an important one for you to model. They immediately responded to the Lord's presence and work in their lives, based on what God had told them.

Follow Jehoshaphat's example by praying. If God has given you a scriptural promise for a problem, praise Him for who He is and for the way you believe that He will act.

The second way you know that Jehoshaphat believed God is that he obeyed Him. What you do after you believe God shows how much you believe Him. After Jehoshaphat and the people praised God, he acted on what God had told him. He believed and obeyed. Read 2 Chronicles 20:20 in the margin. Not only did Jehoshaphat believe, but he also encouraged the faith of others.

Early the next morning Jehoshaphat encouraged the troops and called on them to have faith. Even though he knew that the three kings' mighty armies were ready to overwhelm them, Jehoshaphat told the troops that they must march on. He believed, he obeyed, and he called the others to obedience. When you are in spiritual warfare, win the battle on your knees and obey the direction God gives you.

The same principle of believing and obeying applied when Philip was told to go down to the desert and minister to the eunuch. God's directive probably made little sense to Philip. He had been proclaiming Christ in Samaria, where a great revival had occurred. Few people lived in the desert. But God knew that the eunuch was there, that he needed the gospel, and that he would then take the gospel to Ethiopia. This was all part of God's plan. Read in the margin the verses from Acts.

Describe a time when you obeyed God even though what He told you to do did not make sense.

_____

_____

God gives you the direction by which He plans to bring victory, but you must obey God to experience it. At times God calls you from the crowds—the big things—to one person, a seemingly small thing.

 Continue memorizing this week's Scripture-memory verses. See if you can write them from memory on a sheet of paper.

PUTTING ON THE SPIRITUAL ARMOR
This week you have learned the importance of putting on the Belt of Truth as you continued learning the Spiritual Armor presentation. Review on page 114 the three steps for putting on the Belt of Truth.

Focus on the third reminder. Stop and ask God to help you master your emotions and to allow your spirit to be guided by truth rather than by the flesh or Satan. Ask Him to help you not to compromise the truth because of your feelings.

 Explain the entire Spiritual Armor presentation to someone.

PRAYER WORKSHOP

As you approach the end of this study, you are preparing for the upcoming Prayer Workshop, when you will pray for a half day. Perhaps you wonder how you can pray for an extended period of time. Most people testify that after they get started, a half day is not long enough. In addition, most find the workshop to be life-changing.

 To help you prepare for your Prayer Workshop and for future prayer times, read "Guide to Extended Prayer."

GUIDE TO EXTENDED PRAYER

Jesus Is Our Model

Jesus' entire life and ministry were bathed in prayer. Jesus prayed on the following occasions.
1. When He was busy (see Mark 1:35)
2. When He was tired (see Matt. 14:23)
3. When He needed to make a decision (see Luke 6:12)
4. When He prepared to launch His ministry (see Luke 4:1-2)
5. When He faced the cross (see Matt. 26:39-44). When you face cross bearing or redemptive service, an extended time of prayer can prepare you for the trials you face.
6. When He felt the need—
   • for fellowship with the Father (see John 17);
   • for strength to perform His ministry (see Matt. 26:39-44);
   • to know the Father's will (see Matt. 26:39-44);
   • to intercede for others (see Luke 6:12; John 17).

When Should You Pray?

1. When you want to glorify God and express your love to Him
2. When you need fellowship with the Master
3. When you need guidance
4. When you need strength
5. When you face a critical or new phase of ministry
6. When you need spiritual awakening
7. When others need your prayers
8. When the Lord's will is not being done on earth
9. When laborers are needed for the harvest

DAILY MASTER COMMUNICATION GUIDE

ACTS 8

What God said to me:

_____

_____

_____

_____

_____

_____

What I said to God:

_____

_____

_____

_____

_____

_____

(handwritten: EPHESIANS 3: 26,21)

Ask God to show you what you should pray about during the upcoming Prayer Workshop.

Read Acts 8, the complete story of Philip and the eunuch, during your quiet time today. Let God speak to you through this passage. Then complete the Daily Master Communication Guide in the margin on page 119.

DAY 5

Worshiping God

As the people praised God in 2 Chronicles 20:18-19, which you read yesterday, they had a great victory time before the battle. When you really believe God, you praise Him. And although they had not been to battle, Jehoshaphat was worshiping God. That brings you to the fifth principle of spiritual warfare, which appears in bold type below. Write the principles you have already studied.

> FIVE PRINCIPLES OF SPIRITUAL WARFARE
> 1. *Seeking*
> 2. *Knowing*
> 3. *defending*
> 4. *believing*
> 5. The worshiping-God principle

Jehoshaphat did something strange. Read 2 Chronicles 20:21, in the margin, to learn what it was. Why do you think he did that?

_____

Jehoshaphat put the choir at the front of the army because he believed that his people would not have to fight this battle. He believed the promises he had received from God: " 'You will not have to fight this battle. Take up your positions; stand firm and see the deliverance the Lord will give you, O Judah and Jerusalem. Do not be afraid; do not be discouraged. Go out to face them tomorrow, and the Lord will be with you' " (v. 17). God had told him that it was His battle, and Jehoshaphat believed.

GOD DELIVERS THE VICTORY
What happened next? Read 2 Chronicles 20:22-24 in the margin. At the very moment the people began to praise God, the enemy began killing one another. When Jehoshaphat and his people arrived, they expected

"After consulting the people, Jehoshaphat appointed men to sing to the Lord and to praise him for the splendor of his holiness as they went out at the head of the army, saying,
'Give thanks to the Lord,
for his love endures forever' " (2 Chron. 20:21).

"As they began to sing and praise, the Lord set ambushes against the men of Ammon and Moab and Mount Seir who were invading Judah, and they were defeated. The men of Ammon and Moab rose up against the men from Mount Seir to destroy and annihilate them. After they finished slaughtering the men from Seir, they helped to destroy one another. When the men of Judah came to the place that overlooks the desert and looked toward the vast army, they saw only dead bodies lying on the ground; no one had escaped" (2 Chron. 20:22-24).

to see a vast army but saw only dead bodies. God had been true to His word. They did not have to fight the battle after all.

This account from Jehoshaphat's life does not mean that you never have to fight battles. The secret is that the battle is won on your knees. The Lord fights for you. That is why David could kill Goliath, Gideon could defeat a host, and Samson could kill two thousand people by himself. Our problem is that we fight the battle on our own, with our own understanding and ability, instead of learning to hear and believe God. We must learn to obey, whether or not it seems to makes sense.

Describe a time when you tried to fight a battle on your own instead of leaning on God.

_____

_____

When Jehoshaphat and his men arrived, it took three days to collect the plunder. Read 2 Chronicles 20:25-28 in the margin.

In 2 Chronicles 20:25-28 underline words or phrases that illustrate the fifth principle of spiritual warfare: worshiping God.

The battle of King Jehoshaphat against the mighty armies began and ended with the worship of God. You may have underlined "praised the Lord" and "went to the temple of the Lord with harps and lutes and trumpets." When you petition God, worshiping Him with thanksgiving in your heart is an important follow-up to that petition.

Stop and praise God for who He is. Thank Him for answering a recent petition.

Are you using the Praying in Faith form to pray about a problem, as you learned to do in week 4? Has God given you a Scripture that applies to your problem? I suggest that you apply the last three steps to pray in faith that He will answer. At the upcoming Prayer Workshop you will also review the six steps for praying in faith.

DEMOLISHING PERSONAL SPIRITUAL STRONGHOLDS
In day 1 you identified a stronghold you wanted to demolish in the area of pride. Today give a progress report on how you have used the spiritual weapon(s) you listed to demolish this stronghold.

How I am using a spiritual weapon(s) to help demolish the stronghold of pride:

_____

The secret is that the battle is won on your knees.

"Jehoshaphat and his men went to carry off their plunder, and they found among them a great amount of equipment and clothing and also articles of value—more than they could take away. There was so much plunder that it took three days to collect it. On the fourth day they assembled in the Valley of Beracah, where they praised the Lord. This is why it is called the Valley of Beracah to this day. Then, led by Jehoshaphat, all the men of Judah and Jerusalem returned joyfully to Jerusalem, for the Lord had given them cause to rejoice over their enemies. They entered Jerusalem and went to the temple of the Lord with harps and lutes and trumpets" (2 Chron. 20:25-28).

DAILY MASTER COMMUNICATION GUIDE

1 SAMUEL 15

What God said to me:

_____

_____

_____

_____

_____

_____

_____

What I said to God:

_____

_____

_____

_____

_____

_____

_____

_____

_____

RELATIONAL WITNESSING

Throughout this study you have recorded the names of lost persons on your Relational-Witnessing Chart and have focused on expanding your witness circle. You have learned how to use a witnessing booklet with a lost person. You learned in book 2 how to share your testimony with a lost person. Here is a witnessing opportunity I once had.

Having returned a rental car to a site about 10 minutes from the Albuquerque airport, I began talking to the driver who was taking me to catch my plane. He was a college student who was working during the summer to earn extra money for college. I asked him his major, and he told me. I asked him what he wanted to do in life, and he told me. I then asked, "After that, what?" He said, "I guess I want to get married, have children, make a lot of money, and enjoy myself." I kept asking, "After that, what?" until he realized that he had run out of time in this world. He said, "I guess I haven't thought about that." I told him: "It's really important for you to think about it, because only when you have answered that question do you know how to live. Only when you're ready to die are you ready to live. In fact, I was like you one time. I had an experience that changed my life. May I tell you about that?" He agreed, and I gave my testimony.

After I finished and we had arrived at the airport, I asked: "Are you willing to turn from your sins and confess your faith in Christ right now? We can bow our heads in prayer, and you can ask Christ to come into your life." He immediately did so.

 Pray with your prayer partner, in person or by telephone, about sharing your testimony with a lost person.

 Share with someone this week your personal testimony or a witness presentation.

 Read 1 Samuel 15, the full passage about Saul's disobedience to God, during your quiet time today. Let God speak to you through this passage. Then complete the Daily Master Communication Guide in the margin.

 On a sheet of paper write from memory the six Scripture-memory passages you have memorized during this study.

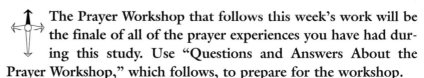 **The Prayer Workshop that follows this week's work will be the finale of all of the prayer experiences you have had during this study.** Use "Questions and Answers About the Prayer Workshop," which follows, to prepare for the workshop.

QUESTIONS AND ANSWERS ABOUT THE PRAYER WORKSHOP

Why Have It?
1. To have extended, uninterrupted fellowship with God
2. To evaluate what God has been doing and saying in your life
3. To solidify Christ's lordship in all aspects of your life
4. To receive guidance for future plans and ministries
5. To concentrate prayer on your major concerns
6. To intercede for others

Why a Half Day of Prayer?
1. It prepares you for a larger ministry. Jesus spent much time in prayer before He began another phase of ministry.
2. It is a basic building block in your continuing life as a disciple. You should have an extended time of prayer each month.

Extended prayer is a basic building block in your continuing life as a disciple.

What Should I Bring?
1. Bible (several versions and translations if desired)
2. The *MasterLife* books you have completed
3. Your personal prayer journal you began preparing in week 5
4. Paper or a notebook and a pencil or a pen
5. Life goals to date
6. Sack lunch, if your group leader asks you to bring one
7. Scripture-memory verses from books 1, 2, and 3

What Is the Schedule?
1. Announcements: 5 minutes
2. Individual prayer time: 3 hours
3. Share-and-prayer time for each member: 20 minutes
4. MasterBuilder presentation: 30 minutes
5. Wrap-up: 5 minutes

How Can I Pray for That Long?
1. Prayer is conversing with God. Listen to Him at least as much as you talk to Him.
2. Use as many or as few of the prayer resources in your personal prayer journal as you wish in any order. Include all of the elements of prayer, using "Guide to Thanksgiving" (p. 13), "Guide to Praise" (pp. 36–37), "Guide to Confession and Forgiveness" (pp. 54–55), "Guide to Praying in Faith" (pp. 67–80), "Guide to Intercession" (p. 100), and "Guide to Extended Prayer" (p. 119). You may also pray through the Disciple's Personality (pp. 127–28) and the Spiritual Armor (pp. 129–31).
3. Use your Prayer-Covenant List to pray for your needs and others' needs.

Listen to Him at least as much as you talk to Him.

Detect any patterns in what God has said to you and/or in what you have said to Him.

4. Use the Personal Guidance section of your prayer journal.
   - Read through your Daily Master Communication Guides to detect any patterns in what God has said to you and/or in what you have said to Him. Note the answers to your prayers, evidences of spiritual growth, helpful insights, and commitments or concerns you need to pray about.
   - Review your life purpose, life goals, and planning sheets. Ask God to help you write, refine, or complete these items today.
   - Focus your prayers on making progress toward your goals.
5. Read your Bible. Listen to God speak to you. Meditate on your Scripture-memory verses. Review your daily work in your *MasterLife* books and the applications you have made.
6. Do not become too introspective. Ask God to forgive your shortcomings; then move on to pray for other persons and concerns.
7. Think of your resources as a smorgasbord. Start with anything you want and return for more as many times as you like.

What Can I Do If I Think of Other Things?
1. Pray for whatever occurs to you. Perhaps God placed that thought in your mind so that you will deal with a certain issue.
2. Write down things you need to do later so that you can forget them now.
3. List things that continue to come to mind. Ask God why. You are not preparing a speech to give to God. You are communicating with Him mind to mind, heart to heart, and spirit to Spirit. You are dialoguing with Him even as you think.

How Can I Stay Alert and Awake?
1. Pray aloud.
2. Vary what you are doing, such as praising, reading God's Word, meditating, evaluating, praying for vision, and interceding.
3. Change your position often: sit, walk, stand, and kneel.
4. Get adequate sleep the night before.

Consult your notes in preparation for your next extended prayer time to ensure balance in your prayers.

How Can I Make My Prayer Time Meaningful?
1. Keep notes on what you do. Write down the time you begin and complete each activity.
2. Consult your notes in preparation for your next extended prayer time to ensure balance in your prayers. For example, if you spent most of this time praying about your needs, next time pray more for the needs of others.
3. During the share-and-prayer time tell the group what you did and how the experience affected you.

Write lists in your personal prayer journal of what you should pray about during the Prayer Workshop. Use "Questions and Answers About the Prayer Workshop" to prepare your lists.

HAS THIS WEEK MADE A DIFFERENCE?
Review "My Walk with the Master This Week" at the beginning of this week's material. Mark the activities you have finished by drawing vertical lines in the diamonds beside them. Finish any incomplete activities.

Congratulations on completing your study of *MasterLife 3: The Disciple's Victory.* I hope that you have learned how you can win the battle against the world, the flesh, and the devil by praying in faith and by claiming promises from God's Word.

Be sure to prepare for and attend the Prayer Workshop that follows this study. This time of fellowship with God may be unlike anything you have experienced before and will be an important step in your deepening relationship with Him. In addition, you will receive a preview of *MasterLife 4: The Disciple's Mission,* which I hope you are planning to study next. May God bless you as you grow in Christ.

The Prayer Workshop will be an important step in your deepening relationship with God.

[1]Paul Hoversten, *USA Today,* 24 April 1992.
[2]Henry T. Blackaby and Claude V. King, *Experiencing God: Knowing and Doing the Will of God* (Nashville: LifeWay Press, 1990), 103.
[3]John Piper, *Let the Nations Be Glad! The Supremacy of God in Missions* (Grand Rapids, Mich.: Baker Books, 1993), 42.

The Disciple's Cross

The Disciple's Cross provides an instrument for visualizing and understanding your opportunities and responsibilities as a disciple of Christ. It depicts the six biblical disciplines of a balanced Christian life. *MasterLife 1: The Disciple's Cross* interprets the biblical meanings of the disciplines and illustrates in detail how to draw and present the Disciple's Cross.

Because *MasterLife 3: The Disciple's Victory* refers to elements of the Disciple's Cross and your weekly work includes assignments related to the six disciplines, a brief summary of the Disciple's Cross is provided here.

As a disciple of Jesus Christ, you have—

1 Lord as the first priority of your life;

2 relationships: a vertical relationship with God and horizontal relationships with others;

3 commitments: deny self, take up your cross daily, and follow Christ;

4 resources to center your life in Christ: the Word, prayer, fellowship, and witness;

5 ministries that grow from the four resources: teaching/preaching, worship/intercession, nurture, evangelism, and service;

6 disciplines of a disciple: spend time with the Master, live in the Word, pray in faith, fellowship with believers, witness to the world, and minister to others.

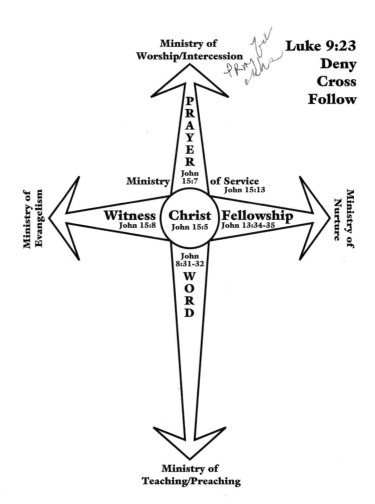

The Disciple's Personality

The Disciple's Personality provides an instrument for understanding why you think, feel, and act as you do and explains how to become more Christlike in character and behavior. *MasterLife 2: The Disciple's Personality* explains the biblical teachings about your personality and illustrates in detail how to draw and present the Disciple's Personality. Because *MasterLife 3: The Disciple's Victory* refers to elements of the Disciple's Personality, a brief summary of the presentation is provided here.

THE NATURAL PERSON

The circle in the center of this drawing represents you—your total personality. The Bible describes you as a unity. When you understand each element of your personality and how it functions, you will discover how to integrate your personality under the lordship of Christ. The Bible pictures you as a body, which makes it possible for you to participate in and communicate with creation and to be identified as a unique personality. The Bible pictures you as a soul, or total self, with the ability to think, will, and feel. The Bible pictures you as spirit, which gives you the capacity to fellowship

and work with God. However, the flesh, or lower nature, entered our personalities at the fall of humanity. The flesh is the human capacity to sin and to follow Satan instead of God. The top door in the drawing—the door of the spirit—allows you to relate to God, while the bottom door—the door of the flesh—allows you to relate to Satan. Humanity's free will stands between these two doors. The big *I*—the ego—took over when the first human beings chose to turn from God and to follow Satan. At that point humanity closed the door of the spirit and shut God out. Consequently, people inherit a nature inclined toward sin and make deliberate choices to do things their own way instead of following Christ.

THE WORLDLY CHRISTIAN

The circle at the center of this drawing represents the worldly Christian. This person has opened the door of the spirit but has left open the door of the flesh. At some point this person was born again by the power of the Holy Spirit but failed to grow as he or she should (see 2 Pet. 1:3-11). The letter *s* in *spirit* has a capital *S* traced over it to show that the Holy Spirit is a part of

The Natural Person
1 Cor. 2:14
GOD

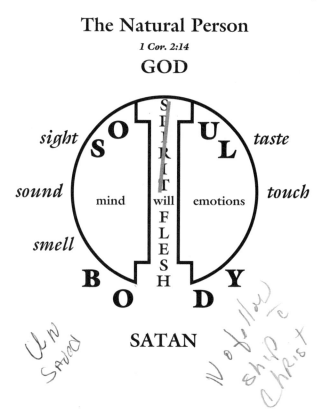

SATAN

The Worldly Christian
1 Cor. 3:1-3
GOD

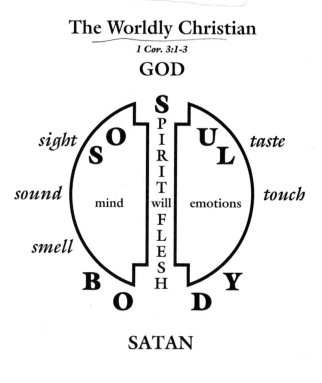

SATAN

this person's spirit eternally. However, since the worldly Christian has the door of the flesh open in addition to the door of the Spirit, Satan still has access to this person. The world, the flesh, and the devil seek to dominate this person's thoughts, will, and emotions. This person experiences conflict and finds it is difficult to have victory in his or her Christian life.

THE SPIRITUAL CHRISTIAN

The circle in this drawing represents the spiritual Christian. When you open the door of the spirit, the Spirit of God enters your personality. As Christ's disciple, you are promised victory over the world, the flesh, and the devil. Your will is located between the door of the spirit and the door of the flesh. When you let Christ master your life, His death on the cross (notice the cross in the center of the circle) gives you a life of victory (see Gal. 2:20). Because considering your flesh crucified is an act of your will, Christ within you helps you keep the door of the spirit open and the door of the flesh closed. Because you are filled with the Spirit of God, God takes control of your mind, your will, your emotions, and therefore your soul and body.

HOW TO HAVE VICTORY

Here is how to make Christ the Master of your total personality:

1. Ask God to help you to will to do the right thing (see Phil. 2:13).
2. Open the door of the spirit to the Spirit of God by asking Him to fill you (see Eph. 5:18).
3. Close the door of the flesh to Satan by confessing your sins and by claiming Christ's crucifixion of the flesh (see Gal. 5:24).
4. Renew your mind by saturating it in the Word of God (see Rom. 12:2).
5. Allow the Holy Spirit to master your emotions by producing the fruit of the Spirit in you (see Gal. 5:22-23).
6. Present your body to Christ as an instrument of righteousness (see Rom. 6:12-13).
7. Love the Lord your God with all your heart, with all your soul, with all your mind, and with all your strength (see Mark 12:30).

Spiritual ARmoR ouR Goal is to be Victious in christ

The Spiritual Christian
Gal. 2:20
1 Thess. 5:23-24
GOD
Eph. 5:18

sight · taste

sound · touch

smell

SOUL — SPIRIT — mind (Rom. 12:2) · will (Phil. 2:13) · emotions (Gal. 5:22-23) — FLESH — CRUCIFIED

Rom. 6:12-13

1 Cor. 6:19-20 **BODY** Rom. 12:1

SATAN

PAUL Romans 12. 1-~

Review TRombone change Living sacrifice for the Lord Sanctity

Renew by The Holy spirit

The Spiritual Armor

Use the following presentation to explain to another person how God equips Christians to wage spiritual warfare. The material below is the presentation you make to the other person. Learn to present it in your own words in a natural way. Directions to you are in parentheses. You are not expected to quote all of the Scripture references. They are provided for optional study.

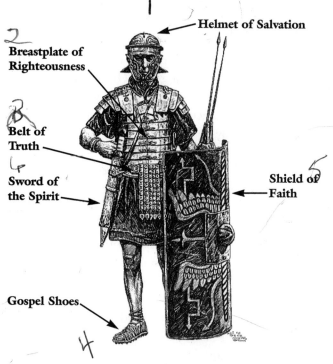

Helmet of Salvation

Breastplate of Righteousness

Belt of Truth

Sword of the Spirit

Shield of Faith

Gospel Shoes

As a disciple you know that you are at war. You have experienced spiritual conflict in your personality between the forces of good and the forces of evil. You have discovered that no matter how many battles you win, Satan always returns to fight another day. Remember that you are not fighting only a private war. You are a part of God's army, called to defeat Satan and his evil forces. You live behind enemy lines, and spiritual warfare continually takes place around you in the world.

God equips Christians to win the battle (read Eph. 6:10-20). He wants every believer to stand against Satan and all of his schemes in spiritual warfare (refer to v. 11). He wants you to stand your ground in the

day of evil and then finally to conquer and to be standing when the battle is over (refer to v. 13). He warns that you are fighting not against flesh and blood but against rulers, authorities, and powers of this dark world and against the spiritual forces of evil in the heavenly realms (refer to v. 12). The way to gain victory over evil spiritual forces is to use the Spiritual Armor mentioned in this passage: truth, righteousness, the gospel of peace, faith, salvation, and the Word of God. Paul compared each of these spiritual resources to a part of a Roman soldier's armor. He knew each piece well because he was possibly chained to a Roman soldier.

It is significant that Paul concluded the list of Spiritual Armor with an exhortation to prayer: "praying in the Spirit on all occasions with all kinds of prayers and requests." A spiritual warrior begins on his or her knees. Through prayer this warrior clothes himself or herself with the other articles of Spiritual Armor before going out to meet the foe.

Verse 18 focuses on prayer as a specific arena of warfare, placing emphasis on—

• praying on all occasions;
• all kinds of prayer but specifically supplication;
• alertness;
• perseverance;
• all of the saints.

Spiritual battles begin with or should quickly move to prayer. It is one means God uses to strengthen you in the power of His might. When you have armed yourself with the Spiritual Armor, you can claim victories through prayer. Then you can move out to see these prayers answered in the battlefield of the world.

Winning the victory first in prayer is illustrated by an Old Testament account. Jehoshaphat was threatened with an attack by three kings (refer to 2 Chron. 20: 1-15). He called the whole nation to prayer. After the nation had observed a period of fasting and prayer, God assured the people in verses 15-17: " 'The battle is not yours, but God's. ... You will not have to fight this battle. Take up your positions; stand firm and see the deliverance the Lord will give you.' " The next morning Jehoshaphat encouraged his people to believe God. He placed the choir in front of the army as it marched into battle. What an unusual attack force! What faith in God! By the time they reached the battlefield, God had caused the three enemy armies to annihilate one another. Israel walked out on the battlefield and simply gathered the spoils.

The secret of victory is this: first win the battle in prayer; then you can attack the enemy and claim the victory God has already won. Sometimes you must do more than march into battle, but you can be assured that God has already guaranteed you the victory.

You are clothed with protective Spiritual Armor. Your mind is protected by the Helmet of Salvation, your heart or will by the Breastplate of Righteousness, and your emotions by the Belt of Truth. As you march, you wear Gospel Shoes—the readiness that comes from the gospel of peace. In one hand you hold the Sword of the Spirit, which is the Word of God. In the other hand you hold the Shield of Faith. This armor may be used in at least three ways:

1. When you seek release from Satan's dominion in an area of your life
2. When Satan attacks you
3. When you attack Satan. You attack Satan when you enter his realm to claim, through intercession or witness, persons he has captured. First John 5:19 says, "We know that we are children of God, and that the whole world is under the control of the evil one." The lost and backslidden are under Satan's control, and he fights to keep them.

Let me explain how symbolically to put on each part of the Spiritual Armor through prayer.

THE HELMET OF SALVATION
Picture the Helmet of Salvation you received when Christ saved you. Let this symbol remind you to do the following.

1. Thank God that you are His child. First John 4:4 says, "The one who is in you is greater than the one who is in the world." Thank Him for your salvation.
2. Praise God for eternal life. The helmet protects you at all times in any battle. Praise Him for it.
3. Claim the mind of Christ. First Corinthians 2:16 says that we have the mind of Christ. It was given to you when you were saved.

Second Corinthians 10:3-5 says: "Though we live in the world, we do not wage war as the world does. The weapons we fight with are not the weapons of the world. On the contrary, they have divine power to demolish strongholds. We demolish arguments and every pretension that sets itself up against the knowledge of God, and we take captive every thought to make it obedient to Christ."

THE BREASTPLATE OF RIGHTEOUSNESS
Picture the Breastplate of Righteousness that Christ gave you and that has produced righteous living in you. Think of it as symbolically protecting your heart or your will. Let it remind you to do the following.

1. Ask God to search your heart to reveal any wicked ways in it (refer to Ps. 139:23-24).
2. Confess any sin (refer to 1 John 1:9).
3. Claim Christ's righteousness to cover your sins and to give you right standing with Him (refer to 2 Cor. 5:21). Keep the breastplate firmly fastened in place with upright character and righteous living.

Psalm 66:18 says,

If I had cherished sin in my heart,
the Lord would not have listened.

THE BELT OF TRUTH
Picture the Belt of Truth, which holds the rest of the armor in place. *Truth* means *integrity* and *moral uprightness*. Let the Belt of Truth remind you to do the following.

1. Be true to yourself and to God when you pray or fight a spiritual battle.
2. Hold to the truth. Satan, the father of lies, would like to deceive you.
3. Master your emotions. Your emotions should be guided by truth rather than by the flesh or by Satan. The Bible speaks of the area of the body covered by the Belt of Truth as "bowels" (KJV), or inward parts, referring to the place where feelings reside or to the feelings themselves. The Belt of Truth helps you control your emotions and not compromise because of your feelings. If the Belt of Truth is not in place, you cannot expect your prayers to be answered.

James 4:3 says, "When you ask, you do not receive, because you ask with wrong motives, that you may spend what you get on your pleasures."

THE GOSPEL SHOES

Picture on your feet a soldier's studded sandals. The Gospel Shoes—the readiness that comes from the gospel of peace—means that you are prepared for battle. Let this gospel of peace remind you to do the following.

1. Be prepared. Get ready before the battle begins. Pray that God will prepare you for any possibility.
2. Share the gospel. The readiness that comes from the gospel of peace is being ready to proclaim the gospel. Ask God to prepare you to witness for Him.
3. Intercede for the lost. You are prepared to attack the enemy through prayer or through witness. Paul was effective in witness because he prayed for the lost (refer to Rom. 10:1). Pray for lost friends on your prayer lists. Visualize the countries of the world, with their millions of lost people, and pray for their salvation.

First Timothy 2:1,3-4 says: "I urge, then, first of all, that requests, prayers, intercession and thanksgiving be made for everyone. This is good, and pleases God our Savior, who wants all men to be saved and to come to a knowledge of the truth."

THE SHIELD OF FAITH

Above all, picture yourself holding the Shield of Faith in your left hand. The Roman shield was a long, oblong piece of wood. When the enemy's fiery arrows hit it, they buried themselves in the wood and were extinguished. So as the arrows of evil are aimed at you, advance with the Shield of Faith and quench the fiery darts of the wicked. Let the Shield of Faith remind you to do the following.

1. Claim the victory. Faith is the victory that overcomes the world (refer to 1 John 5:4).
2. Advance in faith. Faith without works is dead (refer to Jas. 2:20). Put feet to your prayers.
3. Quench all of the fiery darts of the wicked.

Mark 11:24 says, " 'I tell you, whatever you ask for in prayer, believe that you have received it, and it will be yours.' "

THE SWORD OF THE SPIRIT

Picture the Sword of the Spirit, the Word of God, in your right hand. *Word* here means *God's utterance,* referring to God's speaking to you about specific situations. Let the sword in your hand remind you to do the following.

1. Grasp the Word. According to Hebrews 4:12, God's Word is an offensive weapon and "is living and active. Sharper than any double-edge sword, it penetrates even to dividing soul and spirit, joints and marrow; it judges the thoughts and attitudes of the heart." Use it whether or not the enemy acknowledges that it is God's Word.
2. Let the Holy Spirit use the Word. It is His sword.
3. Pray on the basis of the Word. The Spirit will use the Word to reveal God's will to you and to help you know what to pray for (refer to John 16:13-15) and do.

Matthew 4:1-10 says that Jesus prayed and fasted for 40 days, but when Jesus was tempted, God's Word put Satan to flight.

PRAYER BATTLES

The Spiritual Armor prepares you to intercede for others. Now you are in a position to pray for others and to expect an answer. Ephesians 6:18 says: "Pray in the Spirit on all occasions with all kinds of prayers and requests. With this in mind, be alert and always keep on praying for all the saints." The battle is on! Advance dressed in the armor of God. Persevere in intercession until the victory is won and you stand victorious with your trophies of grace. Pray that God's plan will be executed and that His gospel will be proclaimed boldly (refer to Eph. 6:19-20).

This kind of prayer requires more than five minutes. It may take an hour, a day, a week, or longer. Every advance of the Kingdom depends on the prayers of the saints. God has made you a partner in establishing the Kingdom and commands you to put on the Spiritual Armor in prayer and then to enter spiritual warfare.

Set aside special times for prayer warfare in addition to regular times of prayer. Begin with an hour a week and expand the time to a day of fasting and prayer. God intends that every believer pray always "with all kinds of prayers and requests." When God wants to do something in the world, He moves people to pray for it. Our greatest privilege is to fight in His army on behalf of others.

The battle in prayer prepares you for the battle in the world. Without prayer you go into battle without the whole armor of God. Use the spiritual weapons as you move behind enemy lines.

God's Word in Your Heart and Hand

Use the following presentation to explain to others how to get God's Word into their hearts and lives. The material below is the presentation you make to others. Learn to present it in your own words in a natural way. Directions to you are in parentheses.

As you pray through the Spiritual Armor, imagine yourself grasping the Word of God in your hand as you hold the Sword of the Spirit. The following illustration will show you how to grasp God's Word in your hand so that no one can take it away. The illustration is divided into three levels so that you can choose the levels appropriate for a specific situation.

LEVEL 1: DEMONSTRATION

Hear the Word. You can use your hand to illustrate how to live in the Word and to get the Word into your heart. Your little finger illustrates the first way you receive the Word. (Point to your little finger.)

Can you tell me the simplest way to receive the Word—a way almost anyone can receive it? (Allow time for the person to respond. Affirm responses that convey the idea of hearing.)

Hearing the Word is the first way you receive it. Even a child or a person who cannot read can hear the Word.

Think about the Word. The second way you live in the Word and the Word lives in you is to think about it

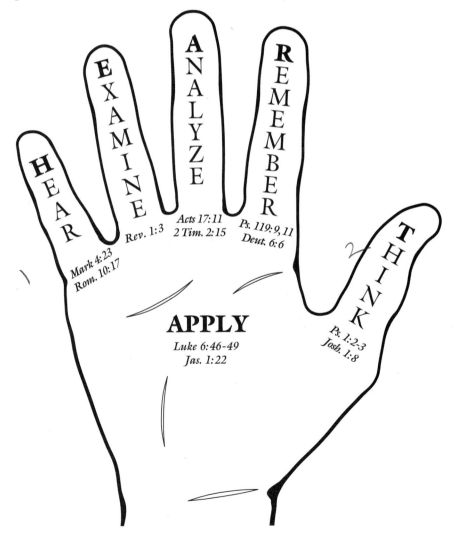

HEAR
Mark 4:23
Rom. 10:17

EXAMINE
Rev. 1:3

ANALYZE
Acts 17:11
2 Tim. 2:15

REMEMBER
Ps. 119:9, 11
Deut. 6:6

THINK
Ps. 1:2-3
Josh. 1:8

APPLY
Luke 6:46-49
Jas. 1:22

or meditate on it. The thumb represents this function. (Point to your thumb.)

When I grip a Bible with my little finger—which is "hear"—and my thumb—which is "think about what I hear" (for example, the pastor's sermon)—then I have a grasp of God's Word. But I do not have a firm enough grasp to hold it if someone else tries to take it from me.

(Tell the person to take the Bible from you while you grip it with your finger and thumb.) See, I can't grasp it firmly.

Examine the Word. Therefore, the ring finger becomes important. (Point to your ring finger.) This finger represents the next way you understand God's Word. What is that? (Allow time for the person to respond. Affirm responses that convey the idea of examining.)

Yes, examining, or reading, the Word is an additional way to abide in the Word; it helps you go deeper. But even with this level added, someone can still take the Bible out of my hand if he or she wants to.

(Tell the person to pull the Bible from your grasp while you hold it with the two fingers and the thumb.)

Analyze the Word. What is a way to live more deeply in the Word and to get it into your heart? (Allow time for the person to respond. Affirm responses that convey the idea of analyzing.)

When you analyze, or study, the Word, you go deeper into it. The middle finger represents analyzing the Word. (Point to your middle finger.)

When I hear, think about, examine, and analyze the Word, someone has more difficulty taking it from my grasp. Can you still take it from me? (Holding the Bible with the three fingers and the thumb, allow the person to pull it from your grasp after a struggle.)

Remember the Word. The most effective way to get the Word into your heart is illustrated by the index finger. (Point to your index finger.) Which way is that? (Allow time for the person to respond. Affirm responses that convey the idea of remembering.)

When you remember, or memorize, the Word, it really lives in you, you live in it, and God's promises become your possessions. If I hear, think about, examine, analyze, and remember the Word, I have a firm grasp of it, and no one can take it from me. (Grasping the Bible by the spine, tell the person to try to take it from your grasp, but pull it out of his or her grasp.)

Apply the Word. Another way to get a firm grasp on God's Word is to apply it. Notice that I held the Bible so that it fit firmly in the palm of my hand. Getting the Word into your heart is essential, but the only way to abide fully in the Word is to apply it to your life.

LEVEL 2: EXPLANATION

Now I will add Scripture references to the points in the hand presentation. (Place your right hand palm up or left hand palm down on a sheet of paper and draw an outline around it like the one shown on p. 132.)

(Write *Hear* on the little finger with a capital *H* at the tip of the finger. As you quote or read the verse, write the reference *Mark 4:23*.) " 'If anyone has ears to hear, let him hear.' " (As you quote or read the verse, write the reference *Romans 10:17*.) "Faith comes from hearing the message, and the message is heard through the word of Christ."

(Write *Think* on the thumb with a capital *T* at the tip of the thumb. As you quote or read the verses, write the reference *Psalm 1:2-3*.)

His delight is in the law of the Lord,
and on his law he meditates day and night.

(As you quote or read the verse, write the reference *Joshua 1:8*.) " 'Do not let this Book of the Law depart from your mouth; meditate on it day and night, so that you may be careful to do everything written in it. Then you will be prosperous and successful.' "

(Write *Examine* on the ring finger with a capital *E* at the tip of the finger. As you quote or read the verse, write the reference *Revelation 1:3*.) "Blessed is the one who reads the words of this prophecy, and blessed are those who hear it and take to heart what is written in it, because the time is near."

(Write *Analyze* on the middle finger with a capital *A* at the tip of the finger. As you quote or read the verse, write the reference *Acts 17:11*.) "The Bereans were of more noble character than the Thessalonians, for they received the message with great eagerness and examined the Scriptures every day to see if what Paul said was true." (As you quote or read the verse, write the reference *2 Timothy 2:15*.) "Do your best to present yourself to God as one approved, a workman who does not need to be ashamed and who correctly handles the word of truth."

(Write *Remember* on the index finger with a capital *R* at the tip of the finger. As you quote or read the verses, write the reference *Psalm 119:9,11.*)

How can a young man keep his way pure?
By living according to your word.
I have hidden your word in my heart
that I might not sin against you.

(As you quote or read the verse, write the reference *Deuteronomy 6:6.*) "These commandments that I give you today are to be upon your hearts."

(In the center of the hand write *Apply.* As you quote or read the verses, write the reference *Luke 6:46-49.*) " 'Why do you call me, "Lord, Lord," and do not do what I say? I will show you what he is like who comes to me and hears my words and puts them into practice. He is like a man building a house, who dug down deep and laid the foundation on rock. When a flood came, the torrent struck that house but could not shake it, because it was well built. But the one who hears my words and does not put them into practice is like a man who built a house on the ground without a foundation. The moment the torrent struck that house, it collapsed and its destruction was complete." What was the difference between the two men who built the house? Both of them heard, but only one acted. (As you quote or read the verse, write a second reference, *James 1:22.*) "Do not merely listen to the word, and so deceive yourselves. Do what it says."

Look at the letters written at the tips of the three middle fingers. What do you see? (*ear*) Now add the little finger, and you have what Jesus said to do with your ears. (*hear*)

Now read the letters at the tips of all five fingers. What word do they spell? (*heart*) That is the way to get God's Word into your heart. And the word *apply* in the center of the hand is the way to get His Word into your life.

LEVEL 3: ILLUSTRATION
Let me explain why having a good grasp of the Word is so important. The Bible uses several illustrations for itself. As I mention each symbol and its Scripture reference, tell me why a firm grasp of the Word is necessary for effective application.

One symbol for the Word is found in Jeremiah 15:16—

When your words came, I ate them;
they were my joy and my heart's delight,
for I bear your name,
O Lord God Almighty

—and in Matthew 4:4: "Jesus answered, 'It is written: "Man does not live on bread alone, but on every word that comes from the mouth of God.' ' " In these passages the Word is pictured as food. How would a good grasp of the Word allow you to use it as food? (The person's response should convey the idea of drawing nourishment from it and nourishing others, satisfying your own spiritual hunger and the spiritual hunger of others.)

Another symbol is light, found in Psalm 119:105:

Your word is a lamp to my feet
and a light for my path.

How would a grasp of the lamp of the Word help you apply it? (The person's response should convey the idea of being able to hold the lamp so that you could see, being able to take it with you, being able to light another lamp, and so on.)

Other symbols in the Bible include fire and a hammer in Jeremiah 23:29: " 'Is not my word like fire,' " declares the Lord, " 'and like a hammer that breaks a rock in pieces?' " Imagine trying to use either a hammer or fire if you did not have a good grasp of it.

Perhaps the most important symbol for the Word is the sword. Ephesians 6:17 says, "Take the helmet of salvation and the sword of the Spirit, which is the word of God." Imagine how dangerous it would be to wield such a sharp and powerful weapon without having a good grasp of it.

The more you get God's Word into your heart, the better you can use it and apply it. This simple illustration shows you how you can abide in the Word.

Relational-Witnessing Chart

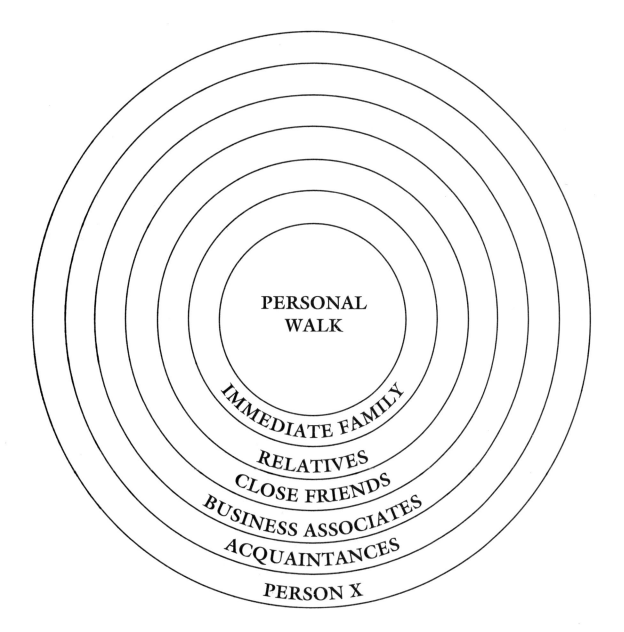

PERSONAL
WALK

IMMEDIATE FAMILY

RELATIVES

CLOSE FRIENDS

BUSINESS ASSOCIATES

ACQUAINTANCES

PERSON X

Guide to Meditation

Date _____

Verse reference _____

Pray for wisdom and surrender to the Holy Spirit so that He will make the Word come alive in your heart.

Perimeter of the Verse
Read the verses before and after the verse to establish the theme and the setting, which will aid you in interpretation. Then write a summary of the passage.

_____

_____

_____

_____

_____

Paraphrase the Verse
Write the verse in your own words. Say your paraphrase aloud.

_____

_____

_____

_____

Pulverize the Verse
1. Emphasize a different word in the verse as you read or repeat it.
2. Write at least two important words from those you have emphasized in the verse.

_____   _____

3. Ask these questions about the two words to relate the Scripture to your needs:

What? _____

Why? _____

When? _____

Where? _____

Who? _____

How? _____

Personalize the Verse

Let the Holy Spirit apply the verse to a need, a challenge, an opportunity, or a failure in your life. What will you *do* about this verse as it relates to your life? Be specific.

_____

_____

_____

_____

_____

_____

Pray the Verse Back to God

Pray the verse back to God, making it personal. Vocalize or write the verse as you pray it back to God.

_____

_____

_____

_____

_____

_____

_____

_____

Parallel Passages
Refer to other passages that emphasize the truth of the verse.

Reference   Summary Thought

_____   _____

_____   _____

_____   _____

Problems in the Verse
List thoughts or ideas you might not understand or might have difficulty applying in your life. Discuss them with a Sunday School teacher or with a Christian friend.

_____

_____

_____

_____

Possibilities for Helping Others Through the Verse
Write a way you can use the verse to help another person.

_____

_____

Protracted Study
Record plans for further study of this verse. List notes, ideas, and outlines.

_____

_____

_____

_____

Praying in Faith

GOD COMMUNICATES TRUTH TO ME

Step 1: Abide in Christ
What is the problem?

_____

_____

How could God possibly use my problem?
❑ A platform for God to demonstrate His power
❑ A blessing from God for which I have not asked
❑ An opportunity for God to develop in me faith, love, patience, or another Christlike character trait
❑ An opportunity for me to develop a more effective prayer life

Rewrite the problem in the form of a question to God.

_____

_____

Am I abiding in Christ and committed to His will for my life? ❑ Yes ❑ No

Step 2: Abide in the Word
Ask yourself:
• Have I brought my problem to God first? ❑ Yes ❑ No
• Am I systematically abiding in His Word? ❑ Yes ❑ No
• Am I willing to wait for His solution? ❑ Yes ❑ No

Step 3: Allow the Holy Spirit to Lead You in Truth
Am I allowing the Holy Spirit to fill me, to lead me to a Scripture, and to apply it to my problem? ❑ Yes ❑ No What is the Scripture? _____
How do I think this Scripture applies to my problem?

_____

_____

_____

_____

I COMMUNICATE FAITH TO GOD

Step 4: Ask According to God's Will
What is my specific request?

_____

_____

Step 5: Accept God's Will in Faith
What do I believe that God will do about my problem?

_____

_____

Do I accept God's promise as a God-revealed certainty? ❑ Yes ❑ No

Step 6: Act on the Basis of God's Word to You
What actions(s) will I take, based on this Word from God?

_____

_____

_____

What action(s) did God take in answer to my prayer of faith?

_____

_____

What else do I need to do?

_____

_____

Date submitted to God _____

Date answered _____

Hearing the Word

Date _____ **Place** _____

Speaker _____ **Text** _____

Title _____

Message
Points, explanation, illustrations, application:

_____

_____

_____

_____

_____

_____

_____

_____

_____

_____

_____

_____

_____

_____

Summary
The main thing the speaker wants me to do, be, and/or feel as a result of this message:

_____

_____

_____

Application to My Life
What did God say to me through this message?

_____

_____

_____

How does my life measure up to this word?

_____

_____

_____

What action(s) will I take to bring my life in line with this word?

_____

_____

_____

_____

What truth do I need to study further?

_____

_____

Weekly-Goals Chart

Date	Take Notes on One Sermon	Read Word 10 Minutes a Day	Study Word One Time a Week	Memorize One or Two Verses a Week	Review 12 Verses a Day	Pray 10 Minutes a Day	Witness One Time a Week	Exercise Three Times a Week

Prayer-Covenant List

Request	Date	Bible Promise	Answer	Date

CHRISTIAN GROWTH STUDY PLAN
Preparing Christians to Serve

In the **Christian Growth Study Plan (formerly the Church Study Course)** *MasterLife 3: The Disciple's Victory* is a resource for course credit in the subject area Personal Life in the Christian Growth category of diploma plans. To receive credit, read the book; complete the learning activities; attend group sessions; show your work to your pastor, a staff member, or a church leader; and complete the following information. This page may be duplicated. Send the completed page to:

Christian Growth Study Plan
127 Ninth Avenue, North, MSN 117
Nashville, TN 37234-0117
FAX: (615) 251-5067

For information about the Christian Growth Study Plan, refer to the current *Christian Growth Study Plan Catalog.* Your church office may have a copy. If not, request a free copy from the Christian Growth Study Plan office, (615) 251-2525.

MasterLife 3: The Disciple's Victory
COURSE NUMBER: CG-0170
PARTICIPANT INFORMATION

Social Security Number   Personal CGSP Number*   Date of Birth

| | | | | - | | | - | | | | | | | | | | - | | | | - | | | | | | | - | | - | | |

Name (First, MI, Last)   Home Phone
☐Mr.   ☐Miss
☐Mrs.   ☐

Address (Street, Route, or P.O. Box)   City, State   ZIP

CHURCH INFORMATION

Church Name

Address (Street, Route, or P.O. Box)   City, State   ZIP

CHANGE REQUEST ONLY

☐Former Name

☐Former Address   City, State   ZIP

☐Former Church   City, State   ZIP

Signature of Pastor, Conference Leader, or Other Church Leader   Date

*New participants are requested but not required to give SS# and date of birth. Existing participants, please give CGSP# when using SS# for the first time. Thereafter, only one ID# is required. *Mail to:* Christian Growth Study Plan, 127 Ninth Ave., North, MSN 117, Nashville, TN 37234-0117. Fax: (615) 251-5067.

THE DISCIPLE'S MISSION

MasterLife

BOOK 4

Avery T. Willis, Jr.
Kay Moore

Dorothy Echols
9.2) 352-8048

LifeWay Press
Nashville, Tennessee

ISBN 0-7673-2582-6
Dewey Decimal Classification: 248.4
Subject Heading: DISCIPLESHIP

This book is text for course CG-0171 in the subject area Personal Life in the Christian Growth Study Plan.

Unless otherwise noted, Scripture quotations are from the Holy Bible,
New International Version,
copyright © 1973, 1978, 1984 by International Bible Society.

Printed in the United States of America

Design: Edward Crawford
Cover illustration: Mick Wiggins

LifeWay Press
127 Ninth Avenue, North
Nashville, Tennessee 37234

Contents

The Authors

AVERY T. WILLIS, JR., the author and developer of *MasterLife,* is the senior vice-president of overseas operations at the International Mission Board of the Southern Baptist Convention. The original *MasterLife: Discipleship Training for Leaders,* published in 1980, has been used by more than 250,000 people in the United States and has been translated into more than 50 different languages for use by untold thousands. Willis is also the author of *Indonesian Revival: Why Two Million Came to Christ, The Biblical Basis of Missions, MasterBuilder: Multiplying Leaders, BibleGuide to Discipleship and Doctrine,* and several books in Indonesian.

Willis served for 10 years as a pastor in Oklahoma and Texas and for 14 years as a missionary to Indonesia, during which he served for 6 years as the president of the Indonesian Baptist Theological Seminary. Before assuming his present position, he served as the director of the Adult Department of the Discipleship and Family Development Division, the Sunday School Board of the Southern Baptist Convention, where he introduced the Lay Institute for Equipping (LIFE), a series of in-depth discipleship courses.

KAY MOORE served as the coauthor of this updated edition of *MasterLife.* Formerly a design editor in the Adult Department of the Discipleship and Family Development Division, the Sunday School Board of the Southern Baptist Convention, she led the editorial team that produced the LIFE Support Series, biblically based courses that help people deal with critical issues in their lives. A writer, editor, and conference leader, Moore has authored or coauthored numerous books on family life, relationships, and inspirational topics. She is the author of *Gathering the Missing Pieces in an Adopted Life* and is a frequent contributor to religious magazines and devotional guides.

Introduction

MasterLife is a developmental, small-group discipleship process that will help you develop a lifelong, obedient relationship with Christ. This book, *MasterLife 4: The Disciple's Mission,* is the last of four books in that discipleship process. The other three books are *MasterLife 1: The Disciple's Cross, MasterLife 2: The Disciple's Personality,* and *MasterLife 3: The Disciple's Victory.* These studies will enable you to acknowledge Christ as your Master and to master life in Him.

WHAT'S IN IT FOR YOU

The goal of *MasterLife* is your discipleship—for you to become like Christ. To do that, you must follow Jesus, learn to do the things He instructed His followers to do, and help others become His disciples. In these ways *MasterLife* will enable you to discover the satisfaction of following Christ as His disciple and the joy of that relationship with Him. *MasterLife* was designed to help you make the following definition of *discipleship* a way of life:

> Christian discipleship is developing a personal, lifelong, obedient relationship with Jesus Christ in which He transforms your character into Christlikeness; changes your values into Kingdom values; and involves you in His mission in the home, the church, and the world.

In *MasterLife 1: The Disciple's Cross* you explored your personal relationship with Jesus Christ. You learned how to draw the Disciple's Cross to illustrate the balanced life Christ wants His disciples to have. You learned that Christ wants to be at the center of your life so that everything you do is an outgrowth of your relationship with Him.

In *MasterLife 2: The Disciple's Personality* you focused on Christ's transforming your character into Christlikeness through the work of the Holy Spirit. You learned how to live a life of victory by building Christlike character. You were introduced to your personal counselor, the Holy Spirit, who lives in you and teaches, guides, directs, prays for, and empowers you to do God's will and work.

In *MasterLife 3: The Disciple's Victory* you focused on victory in spiritual warfare. You learned how to advance against the enemy with the defensive weapons of the Spiritual Armor, which protect you, and the offensive weapons, which lead you to confront the world, the flesh, and the devil. As you began demolishing your personal spiritual strongholds to "take captive every thought to make it obedient to Christ" (2 Cor. 10:5), you learned to believe God for all He wants to do through you.

MasterLife 4: The Disciple's Mission will take you to the next stage in your discipleship journey by teaching you what it means to " 'go and make disciples of all nations' " (Matt. 28:19). As you examine MasterBuilder, an illustration of lifelong spiritual growth, you will make plans for your continued spiritual growth, witness to lost persons, and begin discipling other believers. You will discover your spiritual gifts and will determine a ministry to which God is leading you. This study will equip you with many skills you need to make disciples and to minister to others. In addition, you will continue to practice the six disciplines you learned in *MasterLife 1: The Disciple's Cross:*

- Spend time with the Master
- Live in the Word
- Pray in faith
- Fellowship with believers
- Witness to the world
- Minister to others

THE *MASTERLIFE* PROCESS

MasterLife 4: The Disciple's Mission is part of a 24-week discipleship process. Completing all four courses in *MasterLife* will provide you information and experiences you need to be Christ's disciple.

The *MasterLife* process involves six elements. Each element is essential to your study of *MasterLife*.

1. The *daily activities* in this book lead you into a closer walk with Christ.

2. The *weekly assignments* in "My Walk with the Master This Week" will change your life.
3. The *leader* is a major element. Discipleship is a relationship. It is not something you do by yourself. You need human models, instruction, and accountability to become what Christ intends for you to be.
4. The weekly *group sessions* help you reflect on the concepts and experiences in *MasterLife* and help you apply the ideas to your life. Each session also provides training for the next stage of spiritual growth.
5. *Christ* is the Discipler, and you become His disciple. As you fully depend on Him, He works through each of the previous elements to support you.
6. The body of Christ—the *church*—is vital for complete discipling to take place. You depend on Christian friends for fellowship, strength, ministry opportunities, and support.

HOW TO STUDY THIS BOOK
Each day for five days a week you will be expected to study a segment of the material in this workbook and to complete the related activities. You may need from 20 to 30 minutes of study time each day. Even if you find that you can study the material in less time, spreading the study over five days will give you time to apply the truths to your life.

You will notice that discipline logos appear before various assignments. These logos look like this:

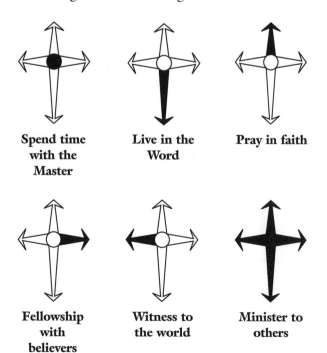

Spend time with the Master **Live in the Word** **Pray in faith**

Fellowship with believers **Witness to the world** **Minister to others**

These logos link certain activities to the six disciplines you are learning to incorporate into your life as a disciple. These activities are part of your weekly assignments, which are outlined in "My Walk with the Master This Week" at the beginning of each week's material. The discipline logos differentiate your weekly assignments from the activities related to your study for that particular day.

Set a definite time and select a quiet place to study with little or no interruption. Keep a Bible handy to find Scriptures as directed in the material. Memorizing Scripture is an important part of your work. Set aside a portion of your study period for memory work. Unless I have deliberately chosen another version for a specific emphasis, all Scriptures in *MasterLife* are quoted from the *New International Version* of the Bible. However, feel free to memorize Scripture from any version of the Bible you prefer. I suggest that you write each memory verse on a card that you can review often during the week.

After completing each day's assignments, turn to the beginning of the week's material. If you completed an activity that corresponds to one listed under "My Walk with the Master This Week," place a vertical line in the diamond beside the activity. During the following group session a member of the group will verify your work and will add a horizontal line in the diamond, forming a cross in each diamond. This process will confirm that you have completed each weekly assignment before you continue. You may do the assignments at your own pace, but be sure to complete all of them before the next group session.

MASTERBUILDER
On pages 123–27 you will find the MasterBuilder presentation. MasterBuilder, which illustrates the path of spiritual growth, will be the focal point for all you learn in this book. Each week you will focus on a different stage of MasterBuilder. By the end of the study you will be able to draw the MasterBuilder diagram and to explain it in your own words. As a disciple of Christ, you can learn to identify your stage and others' stages on the pathway of spiritual growth and to help yourself and others grow.

7 $\frac{30}{8^{30}}$ 7⁸ — 8⁰⁰

Good word

Dimensions of Discipleship

Read from 2 Timothy 2 the verses indicated, complete the statements, and be prepared to share your answers with your group.

1. Read verse 1. One aim of discipleship: that you be _STRONG in GRACE_
CalossiAN 2:6 God's LOVE Ephesian 2:8 about
2. Read verse 2. Part of the mission of discipleship: _TEAching others about_
God The WAy God wantsus to do. witNess to other
_____

3. Read verse 3. Part of the commitment of discipleship: _do not let Nothing turn you_ _Sharing being a Good Soldier_
Thing will bE hard, but keep on in Jesus Name around
4. Read verse 4. The focus of discipleship: _is to Please God And not be_
Plusing The World or man we most be follower of Christ
5. Read verse 5. The discipline of discipleship: _TRAiN, Jul Study daily_
chRist Rule
6. Read verse 7. The teacher in discipleship: _SPeak The TRuth (Do not LIE)_ what
A teach in faith ful God will give you understan Think back ESay
7. Read verse 8. The foundation of discipleship: _PRay all time in & out of Seen_
lifting up Holy Hands
8. Read verse 9. The potency of discipleship: _I'm sopping but God's Word donot_
Change. God's word not bonds Acts 20:31
9. Read verse 10. The fruit and ultimate reason for discipleship: _When we do Everything for Jesus Sake_
be faithful To The ENd
Salvation by grace, teach all People og Jesus so they will follow Jesus Christ
God The word 12
10. Read verse 15. The challenge of discipleship: _Study God's word, daily to_ 120
be able to stand. shun All Eu, lis Possible) do Not be ashame 300et
StRaight is the way I give People the Right word
11. Read verses 20-21. The secret of individual usefulness in discipleship: _wood, clay, Gold, silm_ Roman 9:21
wood & clay, u believe God of silm believe 1 Tin 3:5
Give God our best
be the kind of Person Also
12. Read verse 21. The finished product of discipleship: _M of The master's use_
Can use his highest Pera 'Cor 6:18
13. Read verses 24-25a. The essential nature of discipleship: _Servant Must be gentle unto Patinjt_
meekness
14. Read verses 25b-26. Part of the ministry of discipleship: _Study_

BiblE
Basce instructin before Leaving EARth

Discipleship Covenant

To participate in *MasterLife*, you are asked to dedicate yourself to God and to your *MasterLife* group by making the following commitments. You may not currently be able to do everything listed, but by signing this covenant, you pledge to adopt these practices as you progress through the study.

As a disciple of Jesus Christ, I commit myself to—
- acknowledge Jesus Christ as Lord of my life each day;
- attend all group sessions unless providentially hindered;
- spend from 20 to 30 minutes a day as needed to complete all assignments;
- have a daily quiet time; ~~to Minster Understand~~
- keep a Daily Master Communication Guide about the way God speaks to me and I speak to Him;
- be faithful to my church in attendance and stewardship; Service
- love and encourage each group member;
- share my faith with others; All man kind
- keep in confidence anything that others share in the group sessions; Worldly Christian
- submit myself to others willingly in accountability; Liberty To God
- become a discipler of others as God gives opportunities;
- support my church financially by practicing biblical giving; Give Tithe
- pray daily for group members. Pray for me

Write things down   Worldly Christian

Faithful Attendance, Service   Willingness Spiritual

(Experience No Name)   Giving 1/10 To the Lord

talk to other About Christ   1 Cor 10: 26

Serve them if you are able   Pray for each other

Signed _Dorothy D. Eshell_   Date _9-19-2___

(margin notes: Encourage PAUL) (Credit Resource Fund) Thursday by 17th Remember

WEEK 1

Righting Wrong Relationships

This Week's Goal

You will evaluate your relationships with others and will seek reconciliation when needed.

My Walk with the Master This Week

You will complete the following activities to develop the six biblical disciplines. When you have completed each activity, draw a vertical line in the diamond beside it.

 SPEND TIME WITH THE MASTER
◈ Have a quiet time each day. Check each day you have a quiet time: ❑ Sunday
❑ Monday ❑ Tuesday ❑ Wednesday ❑ Thursday ❑ Friday ❑ Saturday

 LIVE IN THE WORD
◇ Read your Bible every day. Write what God says to you and what you say to God.
◇ Memorize Matthew 5:23-24.

 PRAY IN FAITH
◇ Pray with your prayer partner.

 FELLOWSHIP WITH BELIEVERS
◇ Read "How to Use the Relationship Quotient Form."
◇ Complete the Relationship Quotient form with your spouse, a family member, or a close friend.

 WITNESS TO THE WORLD
◇ Write the names of lost persons on your Prayer-Covenant List.
◇ Visit at least one neighbor this week.

 MINISTER TO OTHERS
◇ Complete the Personal-Assessment Worksheet.
◇ Read the MasterBuilder presentation.

This Week's Scripture-Memory Verses

" 'If you are offering your gift at the altar and there remember that your brother has something against you, leave your gift there in front of the altar. First go and be reconciled to your brother; then come and offer your gift' " (Matt. 5:23-24).

DAY 1

The Importance of Relationships

Establishing relationships is essential to advancing the gospel and to making disciples of all nations.

Worldly Christmas

Fellowship among Christians is at the heart of your Christian experience.

At your first group session your leader introduced you to MasterBuilder, which depicts the path of discipleship and spiritual growth. MasterBuilder illustrates that relationships are vitally important in spreading the gospel and in carrying out Christ's mission. What is our mission as Christ's disciples?

> A disciple's mission is to—
> • glorify God by being a lifelong, obedient disciple of the Lord Jesus Christ;
> • glorify God by making disciples of all nations;
> • join God's mission to—
> —glorify His name;
> —exalt Christ as Lord;
> —reconcile the world to Himself;
> —establish His kingdom.

Establishing relationships is essential to advancing the gospel and to making disciples of all nations. Poor relationships erect barriers to witnessing, to establishing a spiritual child, to training and discipling another person, to equipping a disciple maker, or to serving as a colaborer. Before we study each stage of spiritual growth in MasterBuilder, we will focus on the importance of maintaining healthy relationships.

Christians function as a loving family, but they experience misunderstandings and hurt, just as families do. This week's study is designed to help you know what to do when a problem arises in a relationship. At the end of this week you should be able to—
• list three reasons relationships should be restored immediately;
• explain what action to take if you are the offender;
• identify six steps to take if you are offended;
• describe the role of a peacemaker.

THE HEART OF YOUR EXPERIENCE
Fellowship among Christians is at the heart of your Christian experience. Your relationship with God through Christ binds you together with other Christians as the body of Christ.

Jesus' death on the cross paid the penalty for your sin and restored the broken relationship with God (see Rom. 5:1). It also made possible right relationships among God's children. John tells you that your love for God is reflected by your love for one another (see 1 John 4:21).

Read 1 John 3:14 in the margin. How do we know that we have passed from death to life?

bECAuSE we Love OuR bRoTHeRs

"We know that we have passed from death to life, because we love our brothers. Anyone who does not love remains in death" (1 John 3:14).

Love for one another is the way we see evidence that we have been delivered from spiritual death to eternal life in Christ. Someone who demonstrates Christlike love for others testifies that he or she has eternal life.

We are to love others in word and deed, as 1 John 3:18, in the margin, says. However, sin still interrupts fellowship among us.

"Dear children, let us not love with words or tongue but with actions and in truth" (1 John 3:18).

Underline causes of problems between you and others.

jealousy	covetousness	bitterness
pride	insensitivity	impatience
anger	gossip	tactlessness
misunderstanding	boasting	greed

Differences of opinions, personality clashes, and power struggles also damage the love relationship among individuals. Jesus' disciples struggled with loving one another in spite of human sinfulness.

Read Matthew 20:20-24 in the margin.

With whom were the disciples angry? James + John

Why were they angry? PRom not place in the Kigh

"Then the mother of Zebedee's sons came to Jesus with her sons and, kneeling down, asked a favor of him. 'What is it you want?' he asked. She said, 'Grant that one of these two sons of mine may sit at your right and the other at your left in your kingdom.' 'You don't know what you are asking,' Jesus said to them. 'Can you drink the cup I am going to drink?' 'We can,' they answered. Jesus said to them, 'You will indeed drink from my cup, but to sit at my right or left is not for me to grant. These places belong to those for whom they have been prepared by my Father.' When the ten heard about this, they were indignant with the two brothers" (Matt. 20:20-24).

The disciples were angry with James and John and became jealous of them because they wanted prominent places in the Kingdom.

Our relationship with Christ makes restored relationships possible. By asking forgiveness, we can be reconciled with God and one another.

Read 1 John 1:7 in the margin.

What is the source of Christian fellowship? out of fellowship with one another

What cleanses (restores) that fellowship? b/ God of Jesus

Our relationship with God through Christ is the source of Christian fellowship. The blood of Jesus restores fellowship.

"If we walk in the light, as he is in the light, we have fellowship with one another, and the blood of Jesus, his Son, purifies us from all sin" (1 John 1:7).

⬆✝⬇ This week's Scripture-memory verses, Matthew 5:23-24, describe the seriousness of estranged, bitter relationships. To begin memorizing these verses, go back to page 9 and read them aloud from one to three times.

Recall the vertical and horizontal bars of the Disciple's Cross (see p. 122). The vertical crossbar, depicting the Word and prayer, represents your relationship with God. If you live in the Word and pray in faith, that vertical relationship affects your horizontal relationships of fellowshipping with believers and witnessing to the world.

ON MISSION WITH THE MASTER

 Read the MasterBuilder presentation on pages 123–27. You do not need to memorize it but should learn its principles. Beginning in week 2, you will focus on a different stage of spiritual growth each week. By the end of this study you will be able to draw the MasterBuilder diagram and to explain it in your own words.

The place to begin understanding the role of relationships in your life as a disciple is your daily quiet time, when you truly communicate with God—both hearing His message to you and communicating with Him.

 During your quiet time today read 1 John 3:11-24, which teaches how to relate to others. Then complete the Daily Master Communication Guide in the margin.

DAY 2

What Christ Commands

As you learned in day 1, Christians are not immune to relationship problems. People attack you, ignore you, gossip about you, and avoid you even if you try to live a Christ-honoring life. You are also susceptible to the same sins in the way you treat others. However, when you become aware of a relationship problem, immediately take steps to correct it. Such action is necessary for three reasons:

- Wrong relationships affect your relationship with God.
- You are commanded to restore relationships.
- You are to restore right relationships as a witness to the unsaved world.

YOUR RELATIONSHIP WITH GOD

First we will consider how wrong relationships affect your relationship with God.

Read the first two Scriptures in the margin on the following page and summarize them.

Matthew 6:14-15: _Sin distroy MAN fellowshp_
You must forgive yourself As well As other
followship is restored when we forgive others
1 John 4:20-21: _Proper fellowship is when we_
are able to Love & forgive our brother
then truly we Can say we Love God

Sin destroys human fellowship, according to Matthew 6:14-15. If you do not forgive others when they wrong you, how can you expect God to forgive you? Fellowship on the human level is restored through forgiveness. First John 4:20-21 reiterates the seriousness of proper fellowship with others. If you do not love your brother, it makes little sense to say that you love God.

CHRIST'S COMMAND
The second reason to restore relationships is that Christ commands it.

See if you can write from memory Matthew 5:23-24, this week's Scripture-memory verses, in the margin below the reference. Then read Matthew 18:21-22 and John 13:34-35 and write _true_ or _false_ beside each statement below.

False You are commanded to restore relationships only if the other person has wronged you, according to Matthew 5:23-24.

True According to Matthew 18:21-22, you are required to forgive 77 times.

False According to John 13:34-35, you are not expected to love one another as Christ loved you.

The three Scriptures command you to restore relationships, no matter who is at fault. You are to forgive again and again. Christ showed you how to love others, and you are expected to love in the same way He loved you. The second statement is true; the others are false.

A WITNESS TO THE WORLD
Third, you are to restore relationships because of your witness to the unsaved world. Jesus told His disciples that they could be easily identified.

You just read John 13:34-35. Check what this passage says is the mark of a true disciple.
❏ A Galilean accent   ☒ Love for one another
❏ The sign of the fish

Jesus said that love for one another identifies His true disciples. How can you tell others about God's love if you are unloving toward fellow

" 'If you forgive men when they sin against you, your heavenly Father will also forgive you. But if you do not forgive men their sins, your Father will not forgive your sins' " (Matt. 6: 14-15).

"If anyone says, 'I love God,' yet hates his brother, he is a liar. For anyone who does not love his brother, whom he has seen, cannot love God, whom he has not seen. And he has given us this command: Whoever loves God must also love his brother" (1 John 4:20-21).

Matthew 5:23-24:
if we are mad
at some one + Come
to bring our Gift
to God we Most Leave
our gift go And
Ask our Thing for
give + Thy Love
And give our Gift
to christ

"Then Peter came to Jesus and asked, 'Lord, how many times shall I forgive my brother when he sins against me? Up to seven times?' Jesus answered, 'I tell you, not seven times, but seventy-seven times' " (Matt. 18:21-22).

" 'A new command I give you: Love one another. As I have loved you, so you must love one another. By this all men will know that you are my disciples, if you love one another' " (John 13:34-35).

"All this is from God, who reconciled us to himself through Christ and gave us the ministry of reconciliation" (2 Cor. 5:18).

believers? Just as God reconciled the world to Himself through Christ, you have been given the ministry of reconciliation. Read 2 Corinthians 5:18 in the margin.

Your relationship with Christ shows in how you treat people. Others watch you model how to live the Christian life. If they hear you say that you are a Christian but see you harboring bitterness, unforgiveness, or a critical spirit, your words do not count.

 List on your Prayer-Covenant List (p. 131) the names of unsaved friends and family members. Pray with your prayer partner that they will be open to the gospel. Ask your prayer partner to pray for you as you seek God's will for your life, mission, and ministry. Also ask him or her to pray that you will be a role model in your relationships.

WITNESSING FOR THE MASTER

As you have studied this material about relationships, you may have felt a desire to improve relationships with persons in your life and to take measures to prevent relational problems. You can use the Relationship Quotient form on page 132 with family members and with close friends to discuss your relationships, to understand your relationships better, and to improve your relationships.

Read "How to Use the Relationship Quotient Form," which follows.

Use the Relationship Quotient form to understand your relationships better.

HOW TO USE THE RELATIONSHIP QUOTIENT FORM

Use the Relationship Quotient form on page 132 with only one person at a time. Make copies to use with others. Each person will need a separate form.

1. Examine the Relationship Quotient form. Notice that it features seven relationship quotients that you will evaluate. Each quotient has two extremes, such as "closed, open" in your sharing relationship and "does not listen, listens" in your listening relationship. Between these extremes is a line with seven marks to indicate the degree to which each person demonstrates that characteristic. The words *she/he* above the line and *I* below the line indicate that you are to place your evaluation of the other person's relationship quotient above the line and your evaluation of your own relationship quotient below the line.

2. Make sure each of you understands the meaning of each relationship quotient.
   a. *Sharing relationship quotient.* Do you share your inner feelings and thoughts, or do you keep them to yourself? Do you usually have to guess how the other feels?
   b. *Listening relationship quotient.* Do you listen attentively and with understanding to the other person, or do you turn him

or her off? Do you respond from habit, or do you give your full attention to what your partner says?

c. *Nurturing relationship quotient.* Do you support, encourage, aid, and cherish? Are you loyal, or do you tear down, neglect, hinder, or leave the other alone? Do you know that the other person is actively seeking your best interest at all times?

d. *Affirmation relationship quotient.* Do you verbally affirm each other by praising or speaking well of him or her to the person and/or to others, or do you habitually criticize, belittle, blame, reprimand, or condemn the other person?

e. *Spiritual relationship quotient.* Do you talk intimately with each other about your spiritual journey? Do you openly share what is happening in your relationship with God, struggles, victories, and dreams? Or do you remain distant, closed, or uncommunicative about your spiritual state?

f. *Developmental relationship quotient.* Do you help the other person feel free to grow and become all God intended, or do you manipulate or restrict the other person to make him or her do or be what you want?

g. *Physical relationship quotient.* Are you affectionate? Do you relate properly to the other person physically, or are you unresponsive, uninterested, or cold toward the other person?

3. Each family member or friend should complete a separate Relationship Quotient form without seeing what the other person has done. Each person should follow these instructions.

a. Above each line on the form, place a mark that indicates the way the other person relates to you.

b. Below each line on the form, place a mark that indicates the way you relate to the other person.

4. After you and the other person have completed your forms, compare your evaluations. Discuss why you ranked each other as you did, paying particular attention to the reasons you ranked each other differently. The reasons for these different perceptions of your relationship are as important as the differences themselves.

5. Discuss what you can do to improve your relationship in each area. The most important thing you can do is listen. Try to understand what the other person says. Do not try to defend yourself. Do not be defensive or argue about how the person rated you. These are honest evaluations, whether or not you like them. Do not condemn or blame. If you disagree with the person, you may cut off an avenue of communication that is beginning to open. If you rated the person higher than he or she did, you may encourage the person by explaining why.

6. Notice the areas in which you rated yourself poorly. Decide on a course of action to improve. Discuss what you can do together to improve your relationship.

Do you help the other person feel free to grow and become all God intended?

Discuss what you can do together to improve your relationship.

What God said to me:

_____

_____

_____

_____

_____

_____

What I said to God:

_____

_____

_____

_____

_____

_____

7. Identify the relationship quotient in which you need the most help and begin to design a project to improve in this area. Any mark to the left of the center crossbar on your form or on the other person's form shows that you need to work on that particular relationship quotient. Ask the other person to help you. Your attitude may be the reason the other person gave himself or herself a poor score. For example, perhaps the other person marked himself or herself "closed" on sharing because he or she was uneasy about what your reaction would be if he or she were more open.

8. The purpose of the Relationship Quotient form is not a professional, clinical evaluation of your relationships with others. Rather, it is a vehicle to begin dialogue about your relationship. You may need to ask for help in resolving difficulties. Pray about your relationship. Covenant to help each other develop a better relationship.

 Complete the Relationship Quotient form with your spouse, a family member, or a close friend before the next group session.

 During your quiet time today read Matthew 5:21-48, which elaborates on how you are to treat people. Then complete the Daily Master Communication Guide in the margin.

DAY 3

~

Taking the First Steps

My former pastor, Tom Elliff, once experienced a deep hurt that caused him to become very bitter. When Tom sought from God a message on how to forgive, he learned several lessons based on Matthew 18:

- Forgiveness is a deliberate decision of the will. Even if the other person never asks for forgiveness, you can still say in advance, "I choose to consider you no longer in debt to me."
- Satan tempts you to retry that person's case in your emotions and reminds you of how much you hurt. You can respond, "No, on July 12 I made a deliberate, volitional decision to release that person."
- Forgiveness removes you from torment. Unforgiveness can even have physical symptoms that can harm you.
- When you forgive someone, you place that person's case in God's court, saying, "I trust You in Your sovereign mercy to deal with

this person in a better way than I can."
- Forgiveness causes you to rely on God's resources. When you do not forgive, it is as though you are saying: "God, You don't hold the ultimate key to my joy. That person does." When you forgive, you rely on God's forgiveness, which is available to you.

THE DANGER OF BITTERNESS

Seeking a person to right a wrong relationship requires a great deal of personal initiative and courage. But doing this is necessary to begin the process. You may be tempted to postpone doing anything about the estranged relationship, rationalizing that things should cool off or that you need to wait until the mood is right.

The writer of Hebrews explained the danger of not immediately resolving a situation.

Read Hebrews 12:15 in the margin and underline the danger it specifies.
- **The person may forget about it.**
- **You may decide not to forgive the person.**
- **Bitterness may grow up and defile many.**

"See to it that no one misses the grace of God and that no bitter root grows up to cause trouble and defile many" (Heb. 12:15).

If you put off taking action to right a bruised relationship, a root of bitterness will spring up. Have you ever met a bitter person? You can be sure that it began with unforgiveness and resentment, which grew until they consumed his or her personality and then began to spill over on everyone. Bitterness may begin to consume you and to sap your energy. If you act quickly, the energy wasted on fretting about the broken friendship can be channeled into other areas. A spirit of reconciliation should be a distinguishing mark of Christians.

In this week's Scripture-memory verses, Matthew 5:23-24, Jesus described a disciple who realized the need to mend a broken relationship. First see how much of this passage you can say from memory. Then answer this question: Where was the disciple when the realization came?

_____

According to the passage, the disciple was at the altar when he realized that something was amiss in a relationship. In God's presence you can become aware of needs and problems in relationships. As you open yourself to His Spirit, He examines your heart and convicts you of sin. He makes known His will for your attitudes and actions.

Matthew 5:23-24 also describes the process for mending broken relationships. It does not specify whether the person at the altar was the offender or the one offended. But it says that if you remember that your brother has something against you, then you are to seek reconciliation.

A spirit of reconciliation should be a distinguishing mark of Christians.

"If we confess our sins, he is faithful and just and will forgive us our sins and purify us from all unrighteousness" (1 John 1:9).

If you have caused the offense, what does 1 John 1:9, in the margin, tell you to do?

_____

Without exception every person sins, but God promises that He will be faithful in forgiving our sins when we confess them. We do not have to wonder whether God will forgive us.

You must also confess to the wronged person by verbalizing your specific offense and by asking forgiveness.

Which of the following approaches is best?
❏ "I was wrong, but if you had not ..."
❏ "If I have been wrong, forgive me."
❏ "I am sorry that you are angry at me."
☑ "I was wrong to _____. Will you forgive me?"

Your confession is not conditional. It does not occur with an attitude of ifs or maybe's. Approach the matter with an awareness of your sin. The act that provoked or prompted your anger is immaterial. Your responsibilities are to confess your wrong and to ask for forgiveness.

TRAINING IN MINISTRY
The following section will teach you skills for approaching another person face-to-face to work out a difficulty.

The Bible gives clear commands and instructions for being reconciled.

HOW TO SEEK RECONCILIATION
Perhaps the single most damaging obstacle to God's work and to revival among His children is an unforgiving spirit. This attitude prevents reconciliation. If you have carried this burden for years, now is the time to be free of it. The Bible gives clear commands and instructions for being reconciled.

Your Responsibilities
1. Seek peace: "Make every effort to live in peace with all men" (Heb. 12:14).
   a. Seek reconciliation with anyone you dislike, have offended, or have not forgiven.
   b. Try to reconcile with anyone who has something against you, whether or not you are wrong.
   c. Try to reconcile with anyone who has wronged you.
   d. Seek to be a peacemaker (see Matt. 5:9).
2. Be pure and holy (see Heb. 12:14-15).
   a. Seek personal cleansing from the Lord before you attempt to be reconciled with anyone.
   b. Seek to have pure relationships with others so that they can experience God's grace and can be forgiven (see Heb. 12:15).

c. Diligently look for opportunities to make peace rather than spread gossip or talk about others.

3. Prevent bitterness and resentment (see Heb. 12:15).

   a. Unforgiven sin plants roots of bitterness that yield evil fruit and cause many people to be defiled (contaminated) (see Heb. 12:15).

   b. Unreconciled relationships develop roots of bitterness that make a relationship continually grow worse.

Your Resources

1. You have God's forgiveness (see Matt. 18:21-35).

   a. God has forgiven you of a greater sin than anyone has ever committed against you. Your sin sent His Son to the cross.

   b. You can afford to forgive others because you have been forgiven. They may not be able to forgive if they do not experience the grace, love, and joy you experience (see Matt. 18: 23-35).

2. You have fellowship with God (see 1 John 1)

   a. Walk openly and honestly with God in the light, as Jesus did. Do not try to hide anything from God.

   b. Walk openly and honestly with others in the light. Confess your sins to other believers as well as to God (see Jas. 5:16).

   c. God wants you to experience full fellowship with Him and with others. Confessing your sins to God and others opens your relationships with them.

3. If the Holy Spirit has impressed you with a need, you can be sure that He is also at work in the other person or that He wants to use you to help the other person become aware of conviction by the Holy Spirit.

Your Reconciliation

1. Attempt reconciliation privately. Find a place where you can talk together uninterrupted.

2. Confess your shortcomings. (If the Holy Spirit has not convicted you of any sin, omit step 2 and move to step 3.)

   a. The right way to confess:

   • Say, "I've been thinking a lot about our relationship, and the Lord has convicted me of my [state wrong attitude] toward you and my actions when I [state wrong actions]. Possible wrong attitudes are an unforgiving spirit, bitterness, resentment, pride, and a judgmental attitude. Possible wrong actions are ignoring you; avoiding you; talking about you; criticizing you; arguing with you; trying to tear you down; embarrassing you; teasing, annoying, or provoking you; and tempting you. Do not qualify your request at this point by saying, "Perhaps I have ..." or "If I have. ..." You are confessing a sin of which the Holy Spirit has convicted you. Do

God has forgiven you of a greater sin than anyone has ever committed against you.

Confess your shortcomings.

not try to lessen the conviction by persuading the other person to minimize your sin or to dismiss it. The other person may have wronged you, but if you reacted wrongly in attitude or action, confess your sin and let the Holy Spirit convict the other person of his or her sin.

- Continue by saying: "I have asked God to forgive me, and I believe that He has. Now I would like to ask you to forgive me." Use the word *forgive* and urge the other person to say that he or she forgives you if he or she does. The other person will usually try to minimize your wrong instead of taking the responsibility to forgive you, for example: "Oh, it's nothing," "I've done the same thing," or "Never mind." Say something like this: "I don't know how it looks to you, but it is important for me to know that you forgive me. If you can forgive me, please say so." If the person does not forgive you, say, "I'm sorry for what I've done, and I hope that someday you can forgive me."

b. The wrong way to confess is to blame the other person or to minimize your sin, such as "I just can't seem to relate to you" or "I acted wrongly, but you had done [state action], and I …" These statements suggest that the other person is really at fault.

Ask if you have offended the person in any way.

3. Ask if you have offended the person in any way.
   a. If the person says yes, ask him or her to tell you how. Listen and try to see the situation from the other person's point of view.
   - If the assessment of the situation is accurate, ask the person to forgive you.
   - If it is not true, state the truth as objectively as you can.
   - If the facts are stated accurately but the motive the other person interpreted in your action is not accurate, tell him or her that you did not intend to leave that impression or had never viewed the situation like that. Promise to be more careful about your actions in the future. Assure the person that you are acting from right motives.
   b. If the person says no, ask why he or she thinks that your relationship has not been good.
   - Discuss underlying problems that are revealed.
   - The person may feel that no problem exists. If so, accept that opinion and pledge to love and help each other.

If another person has sinned against you, express your feelings to the person in a spirit of love.

4. If another person has sinned against you, express your feelings to the person in a spirit of love (see Matt. 18:15-17; Gal. 6:1).
   a. Do not ignore the problem. The tendency is to let it go. If you ignore the problem, you are not ensuring that "no one misses the grace of God" (Heb. 12:15). By facing the problem, you may help the other person seek God's forgiveness. That person may not even be aware of the problem or may

not know that anyone else is aware of it.

   b. Use language that expresses your feelings about the action against you rather than language that accuses. For example, begin your statement with "I felt hurt when I learned that you had not invited me to serve on the committee again this year" or "I felt embarrassed when I learned that you made these remarks about me." Beginning a conversation with "You did [state action] to me" automatically puts the other person on the defensive and dilutes the possibility that the other person will hear the depth of your feelings. However, the other person has difficulty arguing with you about the fact that you feel hurt, embarrassed, or afraid.

   c. If your private appeal does not effect reconciliation, ask other mature, compassionate Christians to help you seek reconciliation.

   d. If the matter still cannot be resolved, the possibility exists that the congregation should be involved in the attempt to bring about reconciliation. Even this final effort may fail, and alienation may still be a reality. By the person's attitude and refusal to be reconciled, this person may choose to isolate himself or herself from you and the congregation. However, the Scripture is clear that your attitude should continue to be one of deep concern, love, and desire for reconciliation.

   e. Bear in mind that you seek reconciliation, not justification or vindication. The process outlined is valid only when you follow it because of a sincere, loving desire to restore fellowship between you and a brother or sister.

5. Pray together that God will help both of you walk in His light and have a pure, honest relationship in the future.

6. Prayerfully examine all of your relationships.

   a. List the persons with whom you need to seek reconciliation.

   b. Use this guide in reconciliation, beginning with the most difficult situation.

   c. Continue to seek reconciliation until you fulfill God's command: "If it is possible, as far as it depends on you, live at peace with everyone" (Rom. 12:18).

Ask for the Holy Spirit to impress on you any relationship needing reconciliation. You may want to write the person's initials in the margin. Referring to "How to Seek Reconciliation," think about the steps you need to take to make this relationship right. You will learn additional steps to take in tomorrow's work.

 Read Matthew 18:21-35, a passage about forgiveness, during your quiet time today. Then complete the Daily Master Communication Guide in the margin.

DAILY MASTER COMMUNICATION GUIDE

MATTHEW 18:21-35

What God said to me:

_____

_____

_____

_____

_____

_____

_____

What I said to God:

_____

_____

_____

_____

_____

_____

_____

DAY 4

Making Restitution

*Y*esterday you learned the importance of confessing and asking forgiveness. But you may need to go even farther. After you have asked for forgiveness, you may need to make restitution. Zacchaeus followed his confession with a promise to restore fourfold what he had taken unjustly. Read Luke 19:8 in the margin.

"Zacchaeus stood up and said to the Lord, 'Look, Lord! Here and now I give half of my possessions to the poor, and if I have cheated anybody out of anything, I will pay back four times the amount' " (Luke 19:8).

Which of the following represent proper restitution?
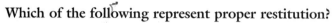
❑ **1. Tell others involved that you were wrong.**
❑ **2. Publicly retract statements that were gossip, slander, or lies.**
❑ **3. Return stolen property.**
❑ **4. Replace or repair damaged property.**
☑ **5. Offer to help with a project or a chore.**

Making restitution goes beyond saying, "I'm sorry." It puts feet to your apologies. Making restitution involves doing as much as you can to reverse the damage of your words or actions. All of the statements represent restitution except 5. Offering to help with a project or a chore would make restitution only if it were related to the wrong you did. Doing an unrelated chore or project is more penance than restitution.

In the following case study underline phrases that show ways Sam made restitution.

Sam did not trust Jack, so he spread lies about Jack at work in an effort to make trouble for him. Coworkers began snubbing Jack because they believed the gossip Sam spread. Later, Sam learned that his view of Jack was inaccurate. He learned that Jack was a decent, honorable person. He got to know Jack better and realized that he could be trusted.

Feeling badly that he had said and done things to hurt Jack, Sam asked Jack to forgive him. Sam also went to each person to whom he had gossiped and admitted that he had lied about Jack. Then he used his influence at work to have Jack appointed to a committee on which his reliability would be evident.

You may have underlined most of the last two sentences. Sam tried to correct the gossip and to improve Jack's situation at work. Sam's restitution went beyond words; he put feet to his words and went out of his way to try to restore Jack's good name.

TAKE THE INITIATIVE

If a Christian has offended you, you may be tempted to wait for that person to take the initiative in resolving your problem. However, in Matthew 18:15-17 Jesus instructed the wounded party to take action.

Read Matthew 18:15-17 in the margin and number these events in the proper order.

_5_ If the presence of witnesses does not accomplish reconciliation, take the matter to the church.

_2_ Go to the one who offends you and seek reconciliation.

_3_ If the two of you can agree, the relationship is restored.

_1_ A fellow Christian offends you.

_4_ If the offender refuses to be reconciled, take two or more Christian friends with you and seek reconciliation.

_6_ If the offender fails to heed the church's advice, treat this person as a sinner.

To continue good fellowship in the body, Christians must settle disputes. If a Christian offends another Christian, efforts must be made for the two to resolve matters; ideally, the rift is mended. If that does not work, friends can be asked to encourage reconciliation. If these efforts do not resolve the matter, then the body itself can be enlisted for help. If this last effort fails, the person has proved to be unconcerned for the fellowship and in effect disassociates himself or herself from the church. The correct order of the statements is 5, 2, 3, 1, 4, 6.

If all attempts fail and a fellow Christian refuses to reconcile differences, the Scripture says that you should relate to him or her as you would relate to a sinner. The Scripture does not say that the person has ceased to be your brother or sister in Christ, nor does it say that the offended person or the church is entitled to engage in acts of bitterness, vindictiveness, revenge, or alienation. We are all sinners. The attitude of the offended toward the offender should continue to be one of love and deep concern. The relationship changes, not the Christian attitude.

Continue memorizing this week's Scripture-memory verses, Matthew 5:23-24. Describe how you intend to apply the verses to your life and to use them to resolve relationship difficulties.

> " 'If your brother sins against you, go and show him his fault, just between the two of you. If he listens to you, you have won your brother over. But if he will not listen, take one or two others along, so that "every matter may be established by the testimony of two or three witnesses." If he refuses to listen to them, tell it to the church; and if he refuses to listen even to the church, treat him as you would a pagan or a tax collector' " (Matt. 18:15-17).

The attitude of the offended toward the offender should continue to be one of love and deep concern.

WITNESSING FOR THE MASTER

Perhaps the work you did in _MasterLife 3: The Disciple's Victory_ on your Relational-Witnessing Chart comes to mind when you think about reconciliation. If relationships are not right with persons in your circles of influence, sharing the gospel will be impossible.

The late seminary professor Oscar Thompson summarized this truth

DAILY MASTER COMMUNICATION GUIDE

1 JOHN 4:7-21

What God said to me:

_____

_____

_____

_____

_____

_____

_____

What I said to God:

_____

_____

_____

_____

_____

_____

_____

_____

in his book *Concentric Circles of Concern.* Thompson said that God holds us responsible for everyone he brings into our spheres of influence. "When we have ruptured relationships horizontally, we also have a ruptured relationship vertically, with God," he wrote. Thompson said that because of ruptured relationships among relatives and close friends, we often want to skip those closest to us and reach out to persons we barely know in order to salve our consciences. When this happens, Thompson said, "It is not that we do not know the Lord. It is just that he is not really Lord of our lives. We are not willing to let him be Lord of everything and accept people in his conditions. ... If we are genuine, we will want to share with those closest to us."

As Thompson explained this concept in class one day, a student named Jim stated that he had problems with this way of looking at witnessing. "My father abandoned my mother and me 26½ years ago," the student cried. "I am 27 years old. I have never seen him. I do not want to see him." Thompson responded: "If I cannot forgive another on the grounds of God's infinite grace, then God is going to have great difficulty forgiving me. Your father does not deserve forgiveness, but neither do you and neither do I."

Jim replied that he did not know his father's whereabouts or whether he was even alive. Thompson responded: "It does not matter. Your problem is one of attitude. You take it to God, let him tell you what to do, and leave it there. If God helps you find your father, you will know what to do.

"Weeks passed. One day Jim burst into class to tell me that through a series of events stemming from a death in the family, his father had called him, out of the blue. His father said he had learned that Jim was studying for the ministry. He wanted Jim to know that he had become a Christian. The father asked for Jim's forgiveness and asked if he could attend Jim's graduation.

"In May of that year, we were marching in the processional of the graduation exercise," Thompson wrote. Someone grabbed me out of the line. It was Jim. He took me over to a little man who looked up through his trifocals. In tears, Jim said, 'Dr. Thompson, this is my father.' "[1]

List on your Prayer-Covenant List (p. 131) the names of persons in your circles of influence who do not know Christ. Then ask God to remove bitterness and unforgiveness from your life as you relate to those persons.

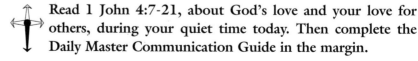

Read 1 John 4:7-21, about God's love and your love for others, during your quiet time today. Then complete the Daily Master Communication Guide in the margin.

DAY 5

Living at Peace

In day 4 you began to explore the scriptural approach to resolving difficulties with others. You will continue studying this topic today.

HOW TO SEEK RECONCILIATION

In Matthew 18:15-17, in the margin, Jesus instructed us to seek reconciliation from the one who offends. In a face-to-face confrontation, give the benefit of the doubt. Be willing to admit your part in the problem or ask if you have done something that has caused the situation. Relationship problems cause spiritual problems. Prayer is a spiritual vehicle that brings spiritual solutions.

How does prayer help resolve conflict?

Yes

You may have responded that prayer enables you to see your sin and to grant forgiveness. Prayer also prepares your heart to deal with the other person's response. The Holy Spirit prepares the way in conversations that are necessary to resolve interpersonal difficulties.

Matthew 18:15-17 suggests that witnesses might be needed to verify your attempt at reconciliation. The other person who accompanies you does not necessarily need to do or say anything in the interchange. This person's role is to be an observer or a witness to the fact that you have done everything possible to bring reconciliation. His or her presence is an encouragement and a support to you as you seek to honor Christ in the way you resolve the difficulty.

A witness, or a peacemaker, should be a mature Christian who is objective and Spirit-led. In Galatians 6:1, in the margin, Paul gave advice to peacemakers.

Summarize Paul's advice in your own words.

_____

_____

Paul said that persons who are spiritual should help a wrongdoer see his or her fault but should do so in a gentle way. Love for one another involves discipline offered gently but firmly, being careful that the peacemaker does not fall into the same sin as the offender.

Once the relationship has been restored—or once you have exhaust-

" 'If your brother sins against you, go and show him his fault, just between the two of you. If he listens to you, you have won your brother over. But if he will not listen, take one or two others along, so that every matter may be established by the testimony of two or three witnesses. If he refuses to listen to them, tell it to the church; and if he refuses to listen even to the church, treat him as you would a pagan or a tax collector' " (Matt. 18: 15-17).

"Brothers, if someone is caught in a sin, you who are spiritual should restore him gently. But watch yourself, or you also may be tempted" (Gal. 6:1).

If you, before God, have prayerfully and scripturally entered the reconciliation, you are not at fault if the other person does not respond in a Christlike manner.

ed all of the means at your disposal—you are cleansed and free from guilt. If you, before God, have prayerfully and scripturally entered the reconciliation, you are not at fault if the other person does not respond in a Christlike manner. Before God you are cleansed. God's forgiveness is complete, and yours is also. Forgive the other person without reservation and forgive yourself.

 In this week's Scripture-memory verses, Matthew 5:23-24, where does a Christian end the process of reconciliation? See if you can recite the verses from memory before answering.

_____

You end the process where you began: before God in worship.

Ask God to reveal anyone whom you may have offended or who has offended you to the point that you are unable to worship in peace. Write the action you will take to restore the relationship.

_____

_____

PREPARING TO MINISTER
In this section each week you will prepare for the ministry God has in store for you.

 Complete the Personal-Assessment Worksheet that follows, based on what you know about MasterBuilder and a disciple's stages of development.

PERSONAL-ASSESSMENT WORKSHEET

Spiritually Dead	Spiritual Child	Spiritual Disciple	Disciple Maker	Colaborer in Ministry
_____	_____	_____	_____	_____

1. Circle the highest stage you have reached in your spiritual development.
2. Write on the line below each stage the name of a person you are helping develop through that stage toward the next stage.
3. Draw a plus sign (+) above any stage you need to model better.

4. Rank in order the following tasks by writing *1* through *5* on the lines above the tasks, with *1* designating the task you spend the most time doing.

_____   _____   _____   _____   _____

Witness   **Establish**   **Train**   **Equip**   **Commission**

_____   _____   _____   _____   _____

5. Given your spiritual gifts, job, and the needs of a person you are discipling, rank the tasks in order according to the emphasis you feel you should be giving to each one. Write *1* through *5* on the lines below each task.
6. You may not yet be doing one or more of the tasks of a MasterBuilder. Circle the tasks for which you need additional training.

Based on what you have learned about relationships, complete the Relationship Quotient form (p. 132) with your spouse, a family member, or a close friend if you have not already done so. Discuss what you learn.

Visit at least one neighbor this week. Tell the neighbor that you would like to pray for each family member by name. Ask if the neighbor wants to share anything for you to pray about. List names and requests on your Prayer-Covenant List (p. 131). Your prayers and continued interest may lead to an opportunity to share the gospel later.

During your quiet time today read Ephesians 4:25-32, which instructs Christians in how to treat one another. Then complete the Daily Master Communication Guide in the margin.

HAS THIS WEEK MADE A DIFFERENCE?
Review "My Walk with the Master This Week" at the beginning of this week's material. Mark the activities you have finished by drawing vertical lines in the diamonds beside them. Finish any incomplete activities. Think about what you will say during your group session about your work on these activities.

I hope that this study of "Righting Wrong Relationships" has provided practical help for a challenging area of your Christian life. You can master God-given skills to deal with others in a way that honors Christ and paves the way for you to be on mission for Him in the world.

---

[1]W. Oscar Thompson, Jr., *Concentric Circles of Concern* (Nashville: Broadman Press, 1981), 22–27.

DAILY MASTER COMMUNICATION GUIDE
EPHESIANS 4:25-32

What God said to me:

_____

_____

_____

_____

_____

_____

_____

What I said to God:

_____

_____

_____

_____

_____

_____

_____

WEEK 2

Witnessing and Discipling Through Relationships

This Week's Goal

You will be able to share your faith, to assume your task of discipling others, and to use prayer as a resource for ministry to others.

My Walk with the Master This Week

You will complete the following activities to develop the six biblical disciplines. When you have completed each activity, draw a vertical line in the diamond beside it.

SPEND TIME WITH THE MASTER
◇ Have a quiet time each day. Check each day you have a quiet time: ❏ Sunday ❏ Monday ❏ Tuesday ❏ Wednesday ❏ Thursday ❏ Friday ❏ Saturday

LIVE IN THE WORD
◇ Read your Bible every day. Write what God says to you and what you say to God.
◇ Memorize Romans 6:23.
◇ Review Matthew 5:23-24.

PRAY IN FAITH
◇ Pray for persons in ministries of evangelism.
◇ Pray with your spouse or prayer partner for your neighbors.

FELLOWSHIP WITH BELIEVERS
◇ Use the Relationship Quotient form with a family member.

WITNESS TO THE WORLD
◇ List the names of lost persons on your Prayer-Covenant List.
◇ Begin learning the Gospel in Hand presentation.
◇ Visit your neighbors and ask for prayer requests.
◇ Study "An Approach to Witnessing."

MINISTER TO OTHERS
◇ Learn the traits of a spiritually dead person, as presented in MasterBuilder.

This Week's Scripture-Memory Verse

"The wages of sin is death, but the gift of God is eternal life in Christ Jesus our Lord" (Rom. 6:23).

DAY 1

Relationships Are Everything

As I was leaving *MasterLife* training in Spartanburg, South Carolina, I prayed: "Lord, help me be friendly with the persons who sit around me on the plane. I tend to sleep or read a book, but if I am friendly, I will share my faith. Help me find where you are at work and join you."

On the plane from Spartanburg to Atlanta no one sat within 15 rows of me. But when I got on the plane from Atlanta to Dallas, two men sat beside me. One was a light-heavyweight boxer, and the other was his trainer. I thought of different questions I could ask to begin to witness, but the Lord did not tell me to use any of them. So I talked with the men about other subjects for a while.

The boxer finally turned to me and said, "What do you do?" I said, "I wrote a course and conduct a seminar called *MasterLife*. It helps people know how to master life." Both of the men turned toward me and asked, almost in unison, "How?" I shared that we can know the Master and that He lives in us. The boxer said, "You know, my dad did something like that not long ago, and man, is he different!" I replied: "God is at work all around us. God is at work in your life, then, isn't He?" He said, "Yeah, I guess so." He then told me that his best buddy had recently prayed and had been changed. "He won't go drinking with me on Saturday night," the boxer said. "He's really different."

I said: "Do you know what I prayed before I got on this plane? I prayed, 'Lord, let me sit by somebody whose life You are working in.' " The boxer replied, "Hey, man, that's heavy!"

Before we landed in Dallas, both of these men prayed and asked Christ to become their Savior and Lord. Did I win them to Christ? No. That was the work of the Holy Spirit. But I reaped where somebody else had sown because I took the time to cultivate relationships.

As you studied in week 1, relationships are everything. No witnessing or discipling can occur when relationships are estranged. You must cultivate relationships so that you will have opportunities to witness and make disciples. At the end of this week you will be able to—

- cite Scriptures that describe the condition of spiritually dead persons;
- explain the importance of reaching spiritually dead persons;
- explain how to approach individuals when you want to share your faith;
- list four degrees of receptivity commonly encountered in witnessing;
- list ways Jesus discipled others.

I reaped where somebody else had sown because I took the time to cultivate relationships.

Cultivate relationships so that you will have opportunities to witness and make disciples.

THE MODEL RELATIONSHIP

John 17 depicts the model relationship in the Bible—the relationship between the Father and His Son—and the relationship between Christ and His disciples. Whether you are trying to win persons to the Lord or to make disciples of Christians, it occurs in the context of relationships. Christ provided our model, first in His relationship with God and then in His relationships with those God gave Him. Jesus spoke about these relationships in His last prayer to the Father among His disciples the night before He was to die on the cross. These tender passages reveal His heart's innermost feelings and purposes.

"After Jesus said this, he looked toward heaven and prayed: 'Father, the time has come. Glorify your Son, that your Son may glorify you' " (John 17:1).

Read John 17:1 in the margin. What was Jesus' purpose?

Glorify God

Jesus' purpose was to glorify the Father. Glorifying the Father involves revealing something about God's person or nature and acknowledging the priority He has in your life. In His close relationship with the Father, Jesus showed who was number one with Him.

In week 1 you learned that your mission as a disciple is to glorify God by being a disciple, by making disciples of all nations, and by joining God on mission.

How can you glorify the Father? Check the answers that apply or add others.

☑ Set aside time each day to spend with the Master.
☑ Reflect your priorities in the way you spend money.
☑ Choose leisure activities that honor Christ and do not cause others to stumble.
☑ Utilize opportunities to tell about the Father's goodness to you.
❑ Other: _____

As you share the gospel and make disciples, you seek to glorify God the same way Jesus did. You accomplish that in all of the ways listed.

GOD-GIVEN WORK

" 'I have brought you glory on earth by completing the work you gave me to do' " (John 17:4).

Read John 17:4 in the margin. When Jesus spoke of "the work you gave me to do," what was that work?

Life To those who believed

Jesus' work was to give life to those who believed and to equip His disciples for the task ahead. Jesus provides a model for you. The work the Father has sent you to do should be that of making disciples of all nations. Recall the definition of *discipleship* you read in the introduction to this book:

Christian discipleship is developing a personal, lifelong, obedient relationship with Jesus Christ in which He transforms your character into Christlikeness; changes your values into Kingdom values; and involves you in His mission in the home, the church, and the world.

Jesus spoke of this work again in John 17:6. Read that verse in the margin.

Who gave Jesus the disciples to teach? *The Father*

Even though the New Testament describes Jesus' calling the disciples, the Father gave them to Him. Follow this model as you make disciples. God provides persons for you to witness to, teach and train, and serve as a role model. They are not your disciples; they are given by God. When you accept the assignment of a Sunday School class to teach, a discipleship study to lead, or someone to disciple one-to-one, make sure that this is God's will for you, not merely your notion of persons who need your guidance. If you set out to glorify yourself, God will not use you and will not bless your time investment.

In John 17:6 who gave Jesus the work? *The Father*

The Father was doing the work (read John 5:17 in the margin) and gave Jesus a part of that work. As amazing as it may seem, Jesus did not do it all. He did what the Father gave Him to do: to be God's Son, to teach the disciples, and to reconcile the world to Himself. He said, in effect, "I have revealed You to those You gave me."

Whom has God given you to disciple?

My children, Derek.

Are you earnestly praying that God will send you individuals to disciple? ☑ Yes ❏ No

Are you giving Him credit for anything He reveals to you that you can use to disciple another person? ☑ Yes ❏ No

Is everything you do and say turning those individuals to Jesus? ❏ Yes ❏ No *Not all the time*

Stop and ask God to help you with the questions you just answered. Ask Him to help you look to Jesus and His relationship with the Father as a model. Ask Him to direct you to other persons you can disciple.

" 'I have revealed you to those whom you gave me out of the world. They were yours; you gave them to me and they have obeyed your word' " (John 17:6).

"Jesus said to them, 'My father is always at his work to this very day, and I, too, am working' " (John 5:17).

"There is no one who understands, no one who seeks God" (Rom. 3:11).

"The man without the Spirit does not accept the things that come from the Spirit of God, for they are foolishness to him, and he cannot understand them because they are spiritually discerned" (1 Cor. 2:14).

"As for you, you were dead in your transgressions and sins, in which you used to live when you followed the ways of this world and of the ruler of the kingdom of the air, the spirit who is now at work in those who are disobedient. All of us also lived among them at one time, gratifying the cravings of our sinful nature and following its desires and thoughts" (Eph. 2:1).

DAILY MASTER COMMUNICATION GUIDE

JOHN 17

What God said to me:

_____

_____

_____

_____

_____

_____

_____

What I said to God:

_____

_____

_____

_____

_____

_____

_____

_____

Make sure that you select persons to disciple soon if you have not already done so. Your assignments for the remainder of this study will assume that you are actively discipling others.

This week's Scripture-memory verse, Romans 6:23, summarizes the theme Jesus came to teach and preach. What is that message? After answering, turn to page 28 and read the verse aloud from one to three times to begin memorizing it.

The message is that the wages of sin is death, but the gift of God is eternal life. Before a person hears the good news of Jesus, he or she is spiritually dead. This person lives in sin. Because he or she does not have the gift of God, which is eternal life, this person is destined to die.

ON MISSION WITH THE MASTER

Reread the MasterBuilder presentation on pages 123–27, with particular emphasis on the teachings about a spiritually dead person. By the end of this study you will be able to draw the MasterBuilder diagram and to explain it in your own words.

Read Romans 3:11, 1 Corinthians 2:14, and Ephesians 2:1 in the margin on the previous page. Underline words or phrases that describe a spiritually dead person.

These verses point out that a spiritually dead person does not understand, does not seek God, and does not accept the things of the Spirit, instead following the ways of the world. This person follows Satan and gratifies the cravings of the sinful nature. Later this week you will learn more about this person and what you can do to help.

 Ask God to remind you of spiritually dead individuals. List their names on your Prayer-Covenant List (p. 131). Ask God to move your heart with compassion for these persons.

 List on your Prayer-Covenant List (p. 131) the names of persons in ministries of evangelism, such as church, television, personal, and group. Pray for these persons.

 During your quiet time today read John 17, on which you are focusing this week. Then complete the Daily Master Communication Guide in the margin.

DAY 2

Teaching Obedience

Obedience is another area mentioned in John 17:6-7 that can be a model for how you disciple others. Read these verses in the margin. They not only underscore that the disciples were given to Jesus by God but also point out three truths to emulate in your discipling:
- Jesus revealed the Father to the disciples.
- Jesus taught the disciples that the Father was the source of all they learned.
- Jesus taught the disciples to be obedient.

JESUS REVEALED THE FATHER
Jesus revealed to His disciples all that God wanted to have known about Himself. Every time Jesus functioned, He revealed the Father, as when He raised Lazarus, when He fed the multitudes, and when He taught God's Word.

How can you reveal God to those you disciple?

_____

_____

_____

You can demonstrate God's trustworthiness by keeping commitments and confidences. You can teach others God's Word. You can make sure they know that your teaching comes from God. You can show concern for the challenges they face in spiritual growth. You can demonstrate patience and forgiveness when they disappoint you.

THE FATHER IS THE SOURCE
Jesus taught the disciples that God was the source of all they learned. Jesus said, in effect: "I am not reporting on anything of my own conjecture. I am taking what the Father has given me, and I am giving it to them." He did not just give them information; He let them know who the Source was. You can pray, "Lord, I'd like to say only what you say—no more, no less."

Jesus did not take credit for anything He said. Scripture records Him as saying, " 'I gave them the words you gave me' " (John 17:8). When you are making disciples, give God credit for all you teach and model. Teach them that everything comes from God and not from you or others.

" 'I have revealed you to those whom you gave me out of the world. They were yours; you gave them to me and they have obeyed your word. Now they know that everything you have given me comes from you' " *(John 17:6-7).*

When you are making disciples, give God credit for all you teach and model.

**DAILY MASTER
COMMUNICATION
GUIDE**

LUKE 19:28-35

What God said to me:

_____

_____

_____

_____

_____

_____

_____

What I said to God:

_____

_____

_____

_____

_____

_____

_____

_____

JESUS TAUGHT OBEDIENCE

Jesus taught the disciples to obey His Word. On the occasions when they did not respond to Him in obedience, He continued to teach them His Word in all kinds of situations until they learned to obey. The disciples were superficial and impulsive at times, but they did what Jesus said to do. Even when He asked them to do something that did not make sense, they obeyed. A disciple obeys. To teach a relationship of obedience, Jesus used an obedience-based curriculum.

Are you discipling others to be obedient? If they are to be on mission with God, they must learn to walk in obedient relationships with Him, regardless of the consequences.

According to John 17:6, how does obedience help you identify those the Father has given you to disciple?

_____

Those who truly belong to the Father are obedient. Obedience is the identifying mark of a disciple. If someone is consistently disobedient, it is questionable whether this person is truly a follower of Christ.

Jesus did not look for leaders when He chose His disciples. In fact, the word *leader* is used only three times in the entire *King James Version* of the Bible. Jesus looked for servants who were obedient so that He could be the leader. Why did He choose the 12 disciples? They were not leaders, but they could be servants who would allow Him to lead. When you help others establish relationships of obedient servanthood to God, He equips them to be His leaders.

 List the names of neighbors on your Prayer-Covenant List (p. 131). Pray with your spouse or prayer partner for them.

WITNESSING FOR THE MASTER

As you have thought about spiritually dead persons, you may have wanted to learn a way to present the gospel to a lost person. The Gospel in Hand presentation on pages 128–31 is a simple way to explain the good news of Christ. Read the presentation. You do not need to draw the hand today. You will be asked to draw it next week.

Review Matthew 5:22-24, which you memorized last week.

During your quiet time today read Luke 19:28-35, which describes a time when the disciples were obedient even though they probably did not understand what Jesus asked them to do. Then complete the Daily Master Communication Guide in the margin.

DAY 3

Salvation: The Key Relationship

Jesus wants to establish us in an eternal relationship with the Father. Salvation must occur before people can be discipled in lifelong, obedient relationships with Christ. John 17 records Jesus' innermost thoughts about that relationship.

Read John 17:2-4 in the margin. Why did God give Jesus authority over all people?
❏ **To demand that they follow God's set of rules**
❏ **To establish an earthly kingdom**
❏ **To provide eternal life**

In John 17:2-4 underline the words that show what Jesus defines as eternal life.

God gave Jesus authority not so that He could throw His weight around or mandate that the disciples legalistically follow a set of rules. God did not send Jesus to earth to establish an earthly kingdom. He gave Jesus authority on earth so that He could give His followers eternal life. Jesus defined *eternal life* as *knowing the only true God and Jesus Christ.*

A RELATIONSHIP WITH GOD
Eternal life is a relationship—an intimate, personal relationship with the Father and the Son. The relationship of which Jesus spoke in John 17:2-4 was the reason for creation. When we sin, we rebel against this relationship with God in an act that attempts to put us, instead of Him, in control. We fall short of His standard because we have gone our own way, as Isaiah 53:6, in the margin, says.

Eternal life is knowing God and being kept by Him in a relationship that lasts forever. Your purpose is to bring people into relationships with Christ, as Jesus brought the disciples into relationships with the Father. Henry Blackaby, the author of *Experiencing God,* depicts our relationship with God as a partnership: "He's given us the partnership with Him of revealing Him to a watching world in order to bring people into relationships with Him." How can you do this? First, learn more about the condition of the spiritually dead—those who do not have intimate, personal relationships with God. Then you will learn specific guidelines for witnessing.

ON MISSION WITH THE MASTER
In day 1 you began learning traits of a spiritually dead person, as illus-

" 'You granted him authority over all people that he might give eternal life to all those you have given him. Now this is eternal life: that they may know you, the only true God, and Jesus Christ, whom you have sent. I have brought you glory on earth by completing the work you gave me to do' " (John 17:2-4).

We all, like sheep, have gone astray,
*   each of us has turned to his own way;*
and the Lord has laid on him
*   the iniquity of us all (Isa. 53:6).*

trated in MasterBuilder. Today you will learn more about spiritually dead persons so that you will know how to relate to them. By the end of this study you will be able to draw the MasterBuilder diagram and to explain it in your own words.

 Read the verses in the margin and underline words or phrases that describe a spiritually dead person.

"Remember at that time you were separate from Christ, excluded from citizenship in Israel and foreigners to the covenants of the promise, without hope, and without God in the world" (Eph. 2:12).

The verses you read state that a spiritually dead person is separated from Christ and is without God. He or she is separated from the life of God, is ignorant in heart, is given over to sensuality, and has a continual lust for things of the world.

"They are darkened in their understanding and separated from the life of God because of the ignorance that is in them due to the hardening of their hearts" (Eph. 4:18).

Stop and ask God to make you more aware of the darkness that envelops the lives of those who do not have loving, intimate, personal relationships with Him. Ask Him to use you to introduce others to Christ.

"Having lost all sensitivity, they have given themselves over to sensuality so as to indulge in every kind of impurity, with a continual lust for more" (Eph. 4:19).

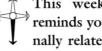 **This week's Scripture-memory verse, Romans 6:23, reminds you of the wages of sin for those who are not eternally related to God. See how much of the verse you can write from memory in the margin.**

TRAINING IN MINISTRY

 Read "An Approach to Witnessing," which follows, to learn how to approach individuals when you want to share your faith.

AN APPROACH TO WITNESSING
This section provides practical suggestions for beginning to witness.

Cultivating Friends for Christ
Use the acrostic CULTIVATING to explore ways to cultivate witnessing relationships:
Create opportunities by making new friends.
Use crises as stepping-stones toward a witness.
Listen to what others want to talk about.
Take time to pray for your lost friends.
Invite lost friends to your home or church for a meal, a Bible study, or a fellowship.
Visit lost neighbors, newcomers, and prospects.
Arouse interest by asking who, what, where, why, when, and how.
Think about witnessing so that you will be ready.
Introduce spiritual matters naturally.
Nurture relationships by being interested in lost friends' concerns.
Go out of your way to include your lost friends in your interests.

Approaching a Home to Witness

Besides witnessing through relationships, you need to witness to persons who do not have relationships with Christians. One way is to visit homes. If you have never done this, ask someone who is experienced to go with you. Follow these instructions.

1. Memorize the name of the prospect and other information from the prospect card. Do not take the card to the door with you.
2. Park on the street. Do not block the driveway.
3. Note clues to the family interests and size, such as toys in the yard, a well-manicured lawn, a boat trailer, and so on.
4. Ring the doorbell and step back one or two steps. Do not appear too anxious to get inside as if you had something to sell.
5. Smile, identify yourself, and immediately state the purpose of your visit. For safety reasons people need to know immediately who you are and why you have come. Add other information you may have.

Initiating a Witnessing Conversation

The following instructions apply to anyone, whether you have met the person casually, have gone to the person's home to visit, or have known the person for some time.

1. Be friendly and pleasant.
2. Give honest, sincere compliments.
3. Accept any apologies and move to another subject.
4. Ask questions that move smoothly from natural conversation to spiritual matters. Earn the right to be heard by listening to and showing interest in all of the person's answers. Use the acrostic FIRE to keep the conversation moving toward spiritual matters:

Family. Ask about the person's spouse, children, hometown, and so on. Draw parallels with your experience.

Interests. Ask, What do you do in your spare time? Show interest in any hobbies, sports, community activities, and so on that are mentioned. Draw parallels with your experience.

Religion. Ask, When you attend church, where do you go? Ask other questions about the person's religious background. Relate that background to your experience or to that of friends or relatives. You may give your personal testimony at this point if appropriate.

Exploratory questions.
   a. Ask the first exploratory question: Do you know for certain that you have eternal life and will go to heaven when you die?
   • If the answer is yes, ask, Would you mind sharing when you accepted Christ? If the person gives an appropriate answer, follow up with questions about his or her level of commitment, asking about baptism, church attendance, and discipleship.
   • If the answer is negative (and it usually is), continue the presentation. Note that your emphasis is on discerning whether

Use the acrostic FIRE to keep the conversation moving toward spiritual matters:
- **Family**
- **Interests**
- **Religion**
- **Exploratory questions**

DAILY MASTER COMMUNICATION GUIDE

ROMANS 6

What God said to me:

_____

_____

_____

_____

_____

_____

_____

What I said to God:

_____

_____

_____

_____

_____

_____

_____

_____

the person trusts Christ as personal Savior. If you did not give your testimony earlier, this may be an appropriate time.

b. Ask the second exploratory question: Suppose you were standing before God right now and He asked you, "Why should I let you into My heaven?" What do you think you would say?

• If the person answers appropriately that Jesus Christ is his or her Savior and Lord, ask the person about his or her personal experience and assurance of salvation.

• If the person answers by referring to his or her good works, you can be relatively certain that this person does not understand the gospel. Continue by asking, "Is there anything else?" to allow the person to reveal all of his or her substitutes for Christ.

c. Make a transition to the gospel presentation: "I have good news for you. May I share it with you?"

• If the person gives you permission, share the gospel presentation. Getting permission in advance prevents the person's cutting the conversation short later.

• If the person declines to allow you to share the presentation, graciously say: "I'd like to share it with you sometime. It will take about 10 minutes [if the person seems in a hurry]. Maybe sometime we can get together at your convenience." Sometimes the person will say, "If it's that short, go ahead and tell me now." Keep your presentation to 10 minutes except for questions the person might ask.

Conclusion

The preceding approach allows you to answer many objections before the person can raise them. It also reveals the other person's spiritual condition. Do not try to force someone to listen if the person does not give you permission to share.[1]

As you have studied today about salvation, maybe you realized that you have never established this eternal relationship with the Father. The Bible says "Everyone who calls on the name of the Lord will be saved" (Rom. 10:13). Use this prayer to make this important commitment.

Lord Jesus, I need You. I am a sinner. I want You to be my Savior and my Lord. I accept Your death on the cross as the payment for my sins, and I now entrust my life to Your care. Thank You for forgiving me and for giving me a new life. Please help me grow in my understanding of Your love and power so that my life will bring glory and honor to You. Amen.

Signed _____ Date_____

I hope that you do not feel awkward if you began this study thinking that you were a Christian, only to realize that you had never fully given your heart and life to Christ. Often, as people learn through *MasterLife* what it means to commit their lives to Christ, they become aware that they have not taken this crucial first step.

During your quiet time today read Romans 6, on which the Gospel in Hand presentation, which you learned yesterday, is based. Then complete the Daily Master Communication Guide in the margin on the previous page.

DAY 4

Praying for Disciples

Another way you can learn from the way Jesus related to His disciples is to study Jesus' prayer for them in John 17.

In the passage in the margin, for whom did Jesus pray?
❑ **The disciples**　　❑ **The world**　　❑ **The Pharisees**

Jesus made a point to say that He was not praying for the world but specifically for the disciples. He distinguished them from the world because they had a knowledge of God, while the world did not. He was ready to send them into the world to carry on His ministry.

This prayer shows not only Jesus' heart for the disciples but also what your heart should be for other persons. Do not minimize the role of prayer for those you disciple.

Have you ever felt that praying for someone within your sphere of influence was not enough? ❑ **Yes** ❑ **No Does it make you feel better to realize that Jesus considered prayer for His followers the most—not the least—He could do for them?** ❑ **Yes** ❑ **No**

PRAY FOR PROTECTION
First, Jesus prayed for the Father to protect His followers. The importance of this role in discipleship cannot be overstated. The disciples needed the Father's watchcare and guidance as they went into the world so that they could be effective witnesses for Him. Jesus knew that the Father's power could preserve the disciples on their mission with Him.

What are ways you as a disciple maker can protect those you lead from the evil one? Respond on the following page.

" 'I pray for them. I am not praying for the world, but for those you have given me, for they are yours. All I have is yours, and all you have is mine. And glory has come to me through them. I will remain in the world no longer, but they are still in the world, and I am coming to you. Holy Father, protect them by the power of your name—the name you gave me—so that they may be one as we are one. While I was with them, I protected them and kept them safe by that name you gave me. None has been lost except the one doomed to destruction so that Scripture would be fulfilled. My prayer is not that you take them out of the world but that you protect them from the evil one' " (John 17:9-12,15).

_____

_____

Besides praying for those you are discipling, you can teach them about the evil one and about the reality of spiritual warfare, which you studied in *MasterLife 3: The Disciple's Victory*. You can teach them to obey, as Jesus taught His disciples. You can take them with you on witnessing visits, church visitation, and hospital visitation. In John 16:33 Jesus told the disciples: " 'I have told you these things, so that in me you may have peace. In this world you will have trouble. But take heart! I have overcome the world.' " You can describe how He has delivered you in times of temptation.

PRAY FOR SANCTIFICATION

Jesus also prayed that the disciples would be sanctified. Read John 17:17-23 in the margin.

Sanctified **means** *set apart.* **How did Jesus ask that the disciples be sanctified?**

_____

By holding to God's Word, the disciples would be set apart so that they would know they were different and not of the world. Jesus said that He sanctified Himself so that they too could be truly sanctified (see v. 18). If you live and proclaim God's Word, you are different from those around you. Those you disciple see you living differently from the world. The persons you lead will respond to what you do. Make sure that those you lead know they are different from the world and know the implications of being different.

Describe a time when you emulated someone who lived differently from the world's standards.

_____

_____

PRAY FOR UNITY

Jesus also prayed for the disciples' unity. The unity of the Father, Son, and Spirit are so close that you cannot completely separate their roles. The Lord wants His followers to have that same kind of unity. You must help believers see that they are a part of one family—past, present, and future. God desires total unity for believers.

How can you model unity for those you lead?

" 'Sanctify them by the truth; your word is truth. As you sent me into the world, I have sent them into the world. For them I sanctify myself, that they too may be truly sanctified. My prayer is not for them alone. I pray also for those who will believe in me through their message, that all of them may be one, Father, just as you are in me and I am in you. May they also be in us so that the world may believe that you have sent me. I have given them the glory that you gave me, that they may be one as we are one; I in them and you in me. May they be brought to complete unity to let the world know that you sent me and have loved them even as you have loved me' " (John 17:17-23).

Five Theo
bRing them in
Grow them up
Send them out 1-30-2001

☐ **Verbally support members of the church staff and avoid criticism and gossip.**
☐ **Regularly attend worship and church activities.**
☐ **Resolve differences with other church members by acting in love.**

If you promote unity among the body, you are an encourager, a participator, and a peacemaker. Those you disciple will watch how you relate to others in the body of Christ.

Continue to work on this week's Scripture-memory verse, Romans 6:23. Describe how you intend to apply this passage in your efforts to lead others to salvation.

Matt 13: 3-9-18-23

WITNESSING FOR THE MASTER

Leading someone to Christ is difficult without first developing a relationship with the person. Last week you learned how to use the Relationship Quotient form (p. 132) to gain fresh insights into your relationships with others. You began using the form with your spouse, a family member, or a close friend. Continue to use the Relationship Quotient form with family members until you have talked with each one by the end of this study.

PREPARING TO MINISTER

As you prepare to witness, you can learn to detect the person's degree of receptivity. Then you can tailor your witnessing to the person's specific need. The following categories give you a biblical way to evaluate attitudes that create barriers to the gospel. Read Matthew 13:3-9,18-23 in the margin.

This parable shows you what to expect when you approach lost persons with the gospel. When the gospel seed is sown, lost persons will respond in different ways. The degrees of receptivity may be described in the following ways.

- *Good soil.* Very receptive.
- *Rocky soil.* Gives the gospel only a shallow hearing and has accepted only a part. Depends on good works to attempt to earn salvation.
- *Thorny soil.* Either does not understand or does not accept the lordship of Jesus. Rates his or her spiritual need by health, wealth, success, and peer acceptance.
- *Hard soil.* Thinks that a person cannot know for certain that God exists. Feels no need for God or religion.

Testing the soil means that you determine the person's readiness to receive the gospel. As you test the soil, you can learn to detect four atti-

" 'A farmer went out to sow his seed. As he was scattering the seed, some fell along the path, and the birds came and ate it up. Some fell on rocky places, where it did not have much soil. It sprang up quickly, because the soil was shallow. But when the sun came up, the plants were scorched, and they withered because they had no root. Other seed fell among thorns, which grew up and choked the plants. Still other seed fell on good soil, where it produced a crop—a hundred, sixty or thirty times what was sown. He who has ears, let him hear. Listen then to what the parable of the sower means: When anyone hears the message about the kingdom and does not understand it, the evil one comes and snatches away what was sown in his heart. This is the seed sown along the path. The one who received the seed that fell on rocky places is the man who hears the word and at once receives it with joy. But since he has no root, he lasts only a short time. When trouble or persecution comes because of the word, he quickly falls away. The one who received the seed that fell among the thorns is the man who hears the word, but the worries of this life and the deceitfulness of wealth choke it, making it unfruitful. But the one who received the seed that fell on good soil is the man who hears the word and understands it. He produces a crop, yielding a hundred, sixty or thirty times what was sown' " (Matt. 13: 3-9,18-23).

DAILY MASTER COMMUNICATION GUIDE

✍

JOHN 16

What God said to me:

_____

_____

_____

_____

_____

_____

_____

_____

What I said to God:

_____

_____

_____

_____

_____

_____

_____

_____

_____

tudes that determine a person's receptivity to the gospel:

- *Attitude toward spiritual need.* This refers to the person's realization of his or her need for God and openness to spiritual counsel.
- *Attitude toward church and religion.* This reflects the person's degree of willingness to attend church and the perceived credibility of church leaders.
- *Attitude toward the witness.* This attitude is based on trust in the messenger and determines in whom the lost person will confide.
- *Attitude toward testing the soil.* This describes the person's response to the witnessing approach and determines how far you were able to progress.

Yesterday you learned the acrostic FIRE (family, interests, religious background, and exploratory questions) as a way to introduce a witnessing conversation. It can also be used to test the soil.

Draw lines connecting each topic in the FIRE acrostic with the attitude it is most likely to reveal. Some topics may match more than one attitude.

Family	**Attitude toward spiritual need**
Interests	**Attitude toward church and religion**
Religious background	**Attitude toward the witness**
Exploratory questions	**Attitude toward testing the soil**

You probably matched the columns this way: *Family:* attitude toward the witness. *Interests:* attitude toward the witness. *Religious background:* attitude toward church and religion and attitude toward testing the soil. *Exploratory questions:* attitude toward spiritual need and attitude toward testing the soil.

Use the FIRE acrostic to learn the person's receptivity. Then you will know whether you can proceed with a witness or whether you must take time to cultivate the relationship.

The course *Witnessing Through Your Relationships* teaches ways to cultivate positive, friendly relationships with persons in your circles of influence. Pray and ask for the Spirit to make the persons receptive. When they face needs or crises or ask questions, test the soil again to determine when to witness.[2]

 Read John 16 during your quiet time today. Then complete the Daily Master Communication Guide in the margin.

DAY 5

Commanded to Witness

Earlier this week you learned that Jesus, in John 17, told the Father that He had completed His work by training the disciples. Jesus sought fruitful disciples who would carry on His work after He was no longer physically on earth.

Read John 17:20: " 'My prayer is not for them alone. I pray also for those who will believe in me through their message.' " What was Jesus' purpose for the disciples?

_____

Jesus prayed not only for those closest to Him, whom he had discipled, but also for those who would come to a saving knowledge of Him because of the disciples' witness. That was His second purpose for the disciples: to witness to others so that they would believe.

Read John 17:24: " 'Father, I want those you have given me to be with me where I am, and to see my glory, the glory you have given me because you loved me before the creation of the world.' " What did Jesus want the disciples to do?

_____

He wanted His disciples to see His glory—not just these 12 but all who believe. Jesus' concern was not limited to that moment. He wanted all future generations of believers who would spring from these disciples' witness to see His glory. Revelation 7:9-10, in the margin, describes the completion of that task.

Read Revelation 7:9-10 in the margin. Underline the words identifying those who will glorify Christ in heaven.

Part of the task He has left you is to do what He was doing on earth: to bring people into the saving knowledge of the Father and the Son, Jesus Christ, who gives eternal life.

FIELDS RIPE FOR HARVEST
In John 4, just after Jesus' experience with the woman at the well, His disciples returned from the town with food and urged Him to eat. Read John 4:31-38 in the margin.

"I looked and there before me was a great multitude that no one could count, from every nation, tribe, people and language, standing before the throne and in front of the Lamb. They were wearing white robes and were holding palm branches in their hands. And they cried out in a loud voice:
'Salvation belongs to our God,
who sits on the throne,
and to the Lamb' " (Rev. 7:9-10).

"His disciples urged him, 'Rabbi, eat something.' But he said to them, 'I have food to eat that you know nothing about.' Then his disciples said to each other, 'Could someone have brought him food?' 'My food,' said Jesus, 'is to do the will of him who sent me and to finish his work. Do you not say, 'Four months more and then the harvest? I tell you, open your eyes and look at the fields! They are ripe for harvest. Even now the reaper draws his wages, even now he harvests the crop for eternal life, so that the sower and the reaper may be glad together. Thus the saying, "One sows and another reaps" is true. I sent you to reap what you have not worked for. Others have done the hard work, and you have reaped the benefits of their labor' " (John 4:31-38).

This passage tells us that Jesus came to do the Father's will and to finish His work. He described this as His food, or that for which He hungered. He went on to state that the fields were ripe for harvest. He wanted the disciples to be part of the work God had sent Him to do. Jesus alerted them that souls were waiting to be harvested immediately.

"The Lord is not slow in keeping his promise, as some understand slowness. He is patient with you, not wanting anyone to perish, but everyone to come to repentance" (2 Pet. 3:9).

" 'God so loved the world that he gave his one and only Son, that whoever believes in him shall not perish but have eternal life' " (John 3:16).

"This is good, and pleases God our Savior, who wants all men to be saved and to come to a knowledge of the truth" (1 Tim. 2:3-4).

" 'In the past God overlooked such ignorance, but now he commands all people everywhere to repent' " (Acts 17:30).

Read the four verses in the margin and write in your own words what the Father's will is.

_____

_____

_____

The Father wants no one to perish. He wants all to repent and to come to a saving knowledge of Him. This is the Father's will that Jesus came to do: to set the process in motion so that others would tell of the Father's saving power even when He was no longer physically on earth.

Using an analogy of harvesting wheat, Jesus told His disciples that much more work needed to be done. Jesus' work was not only developing these individuals to be disciples but also making them understand that they needed to reap the harvest. The disciples did not recognize the Samaritans, the woman at the well, or the town where they bought food as being lost. They were concentrating on getting food. Jesus focused them on the harvest of lost souls that waited.

REAPING THE HARVEST

We often see a mission field in our neighborhoods as people from every nationality immigrate. As Christians we should see them as people with whom we should share the good news. In addition, people in many other nations have never heard of Jesus Christ. We need to take the gospel to them.

Jesus wants you to cooperate with others in reaping the harvest. While some sow, others reap. When people do not respond, trust that others will reap that harvest if and when it ripens. When you witness, you are not witnessing alone. God continues to work in these persons' lives until they are ready to respond to Him.

No matter whether you sow or reap, Jesus said in John 4:36 that the goal is for the sower and the reaper to rejoice together.

Jesus said in John 17:24 that He really wanted His followers to see His glory. Finish what God wants you to do: by sharing the gospel with those for whom Jesus died, you reveal God's ultimate purpose for us, which is to glorify God. Review on the following page the mission statement you read in week 1.

A disciple's mission is to—
• glorify God by being a lifelong, obedient disciple of the Lord Jesus Christ;
• glorify God by making disciples of all nations;
• join God's mission to—
—glorify His name;
—exalt Christ as Lord;
—reconcile the world to Himself;
—establish His kingdom.

Read John 15:16 in the margin. What is Jesus' purpose for you?

_____

" 'You did not choose me, but I chose you and appointed you to go and bear fruit—fruit that will last' " (John 15:16).

Jesus' purpose is that you bear fruit and that your fruit last. He desires that you bring people to a saving knowledge of Him and that, like the disciples, you enable that fruit to last by discipling others.

ON MISSION WITH THE MASTER
Earlier this week you learned traits of a spiritual dead person, as illustrated in MasterBuilder. For the spiritually dead person to be born to new life in Christ, two things must occur. Each person—you and the spiritually dead person—has a task.

List the tasks of a witness and a spiritually dead person in the Spiritually Dead stage of MasterBuilder. If you cannot recall them, review the MasterBuilder presentation on pages 123–27.

Witness: _____

Spiritually dead person: _____

The MasterBuilder's task with the spiritually dead person is to witness to what Christ has done and is doing in our lives. The spiritually dead person's task is to respond.

List the names of persons to whom you have witnessed and their responses.

Persons to Whom I Have Witnessed   **Responses**

_____   _____

_____   _____

_____   _____

DAILY MASTER COMMUNICATION GUIDE

＊

JOHN 4:31-38

What God said to me:

_____

_____

_____

_____

_____

_____

What I said to God:

_____

_____

_____

_____

_____

_____

_____

We are to witness regardless of the response. Stop and pray for the spiritually dead persons to whom you have witnessed but who did not accept Christ. Ask God to help you be faithful in your witness regardless of the response.

 Review the Gospel in Hand presentation on pages 128–31.

 Continue to visit your neighbors and to ask for prayer requests. List their names and requests on your Prayer-Covenant List (p. 131). Ask the neighbor you visited last week for an update on the areas for which he or she requested prayer. Assure the neighbor that you will continue to pray. When the request is answered, be ready to witness.

During your quiet time today read John 4:31-38, which records Jesus' teaching about the harvest. Then complete the Daily Master Communication Guide in the margin.

HAS THIS WEEK MADE A DIFFERENCE?
Review "My Walk with the Master This Week" at the beginning of this week's material. Mark the activities you have finished by drawing vertical lines in the diamonds beside them. Finish any incomplete activities. Think about what you will say during your group session about your work on these activities.

I hope that this study of "Witnessing and Discipling Through Relationships" has given you a new vision of Jesus' purpose for His followers and of the importance of the discipling process during His earthly ministry. Look to Jesus' example as you seek to disciple those God has given you. Your tasks start with salvation and continue as you make fruit that lasts. I hope that you are also developing greater compassion for spiritually dead persons and a greater urgency about reaping this harvest.

---

[1]Adapted from *Continuing Witness Training* (Alpharetta, Ga.: The North American Mission Board of the Southern Baptist Convention). Used by permission.
[2]Adapted from Jack R. Smith and Jennifer Kennedy Dean, *Witnessing Through Your Relationships* (Nashville: LifeWay Press, 1994), 58–62. Available from the Customer Service Center; 127 Ninth Avenue, North; Nashville, TN 37234; 1-800-458-2772; and from Baptist Book Stores and Lifeway Christian Stores.

WEEK 3

Establishing Spiritual Children

This Week's Goal

You will be able to disciple new Christians.

My Walk with the Master This Week

You will complete the following activities to develop the six biblical disciplines. When you have completed each activity, draw a vertical line in the diamond beside it.

SPEND TIME WITH THE MASTER

◇ Have a quiet time each day. Check each day you have a quiet time: ❑ Sunday ❑ Monday ❑ Tuesday ❑ Wednesday ❑ Thursday ❑ Friday ❑ Saturday

LIVE IN THE WORD

◇ Read your Bible every day. Write what God says to you and what you say to God.
◇ Memorize 1 Peter 2:2-3.
◇ Review Matthew 5:23-24 and Romans 6:23.

PRAY IN FAITH

◇ Pray with your prayer partner in person or by telephone.
◇ Pray for your neighbors' prayer requests.

FELLOWSHIP WITH BELIEVERS

◇ Try to reconcile with the person with whom reconciliation will be the most difficult. Use the Spiritual Armor to pray beforehand.
◇ Encourage a new Christian or talk with a spiritual child.

WITNESS TO THE WORLD

◇ Practice the Gospel in Hand presentation.
◇ Visit a non-Christian for whom you have been praying.

MINISTER TO OTHERS

◇ Learn the traits of a spiritual child, as presented in MasterBuilder.
◇ Learn how to use the booklet *Welcome to God's Family* to follow up a new Christian.

This Week's Scripture-Memory Verses

"Like newborn babies, crave pure spiritual milk, so that by it you may grow up in your salvation, now that you have tasted that the Lord is good" (1 Pet. 2:2-3).

DAY 1

Following Up

I began to talk with Joe about what becoming a Christian would mean to him.

When I lived in Nashville, I tried to exercise at the YMCA three times a week. I often talked with the trainer, Joe Case, about how to use the equipment. One day I saw Joe reading the Bible and immediately knew that God was at work there. I asked Joe about his reading. He responded: "When I was in college, we used to discuss a lot of different things in the dorm. One day we were arguing about the Bible, and one of the fellows asked me, 'Have you ever read the Bible?' I said, 'No.' He said, 'Then shut up until you do.' That's been a while, but I began to think that I really ought to read it. Several months ago I started reading Genesis, and I'm about two-thirds of the way through."

I began to talk with Joe about what becoming a Christian would mean to him. He did not respond immediately but showed interest. I shared with him as opportunities came and gave him books to read. Over time we developed a friendship. One day when I went to work out, no one but Joe was in the workout room. The Lord seemed to say that this was my opportunity to lead Joe to Christ. I began to talk with him. Then we stepped into an empty racquetball court, and Joe asked Christ to come into his life.

The next week when I went into the workout room, Joe had already been baptized. Every day Joe followed me around, talking to me about the Christian life. He reported: "The other day I was in a restaurant, and a man pushed in front of me. I let him do it. That's not like me because I'm a boxer, and I don't usually let people push me around. I thought: *What in the world is happening to me? I don't let people do things like that.* Then I realized that it's Jesus in me."

Another time Joe said: "I really missed a good opportunity to witness, and I'm so sorry about it. I was sitting in a restaurant, and some guys were saying things they shouldn't say. A waitress spoke up against what they were saying. I kept quiet, and now I'm sorry. I should have spoken up with her." I responded: "Don't worry. The Lord will give you another chance. Just be ready when it comes." When the next opportunity came, Joe was prepared to give a witness.

I felt privileged to watch Joe in his pilgrimage from being spiritually dead to being a joyful new believer.

I felt privileged to watch Joe in his pilgrimage from being spiritually dead to being a joyful new believer. The follow-up with this new Christian was easy because I had a time and a place to do it. As he grew, he had many questions I could help answer.

How would you follow up a new Christian? That is what you will learn in this week's study—how to establish a spiritual child in the faith. At the end of this week you will be able to—

- explain the importance of follow-up with new Christians;
- cite Scriptures that describe the condition of spiritual children;

- list New Testament methods of follow-up;
- use five practical guidelines to follow up new Christians.

NURTURING A NEW BELIEVER

Follow-up is nurturing a new Christian from the time of his or her spiritual birth until this person can begin to care for himself or herself spiritually. Three reasons people do not follow up new Christians are:

- They do not care.
- They do not know how to follow up.
- They presume that someone else will follow up.

The Great Commission suggests the importance of follow-up. Read Matthew 28:19-20 in the margin. Carefully examining this command will help you grasp more fully the meaning of follow-up.

The word *go* in the Great Commission is a participle. Literally, it means *As you go, make disciples of all nations. Make disciples* comes from a word that means *to make learners* or *to turn into disciples*. This suggests a process rather than an instant occurrence.

Baptizing speaks of an open commitment in the name of the Father, Son, and Holy Spirit—the one God who revealed Himself in three personal aspects. Finally, *teaching to observe* can be translated *teaching to obey, guard, and keep inviolate*. It communicates that discipling is not finished until the disciples are actually doing Christ's commands.

" 'Go and make disciples of all nations, baptizing them in the name of the Father and of the Son and of the Holy Spirit, and teaching them to obey everything I have commanded you' " (Matt. 28:19-20).

Check the following statements that are true.
❑ **Making disciples of all nations is optional.**
❑ **A person becomes a mature disciple instantly after conversion.**
❑ **A discipler can feel a sense of accomplishment only when a disciple is obeying what Christ taught.**

Follow-up is written between the lines throughout the Great Commission. Helping new converts become obedient is what Christ had in mind when He gave this great command. The last statement is the only true one.

Jesus surely intended that the new convert immediately move from conversion into the process of discipleship. A church's task is not complete until the convert is baptized, taught, and trained to do the work of winning, teaching, and training others. Herschel Hobbs wrote about the Great Commission: "Evangelism is more than winning a person to Christ. It does not end with conversion any more than a full life ends with birth. It is only the beginning."[1]

Why should you follow up new converts?

- It is implicit in Christ's command (see Matt. 28:19-20).
- Christ Himself is our model (see Mark 3:14).
- We love Christ (see John 21:15-17).
- Christ desires mature Christians who grow in God's kingdom.
- A new Christian needs the help, support, and nurture that only other Christians can give.

A church's task is not complete until the convert is baptized, taught, and trained to do the work of winning, teaching, and training others.

"The Lord said to Ananias, 'Go! This man is my chosen instrument to carry my name before the Gentiles and their kings and before the people of Israel. I will show him how much he must suffer for my name.' Then Ananias went to the house and entered it. Placing his hand on Saul, he said, 'Brother Saul, the Lord—Jesus, who appeared to you on the road as you were coming here—has sent me so that you may see again and be filled with the Holy Spirit.' Immediately, something like scales fell from Saul's eyes, and he could see again. He got up and was baptized, and after taking some food, he regained his strength" (Acts 9:15-19).

"When he came to Jerusalem, he tried to join the disciples, but they were all afraid of him, not believing that he really was a disciple. But Barnabas took him and brought him to the apostles. He told them how Saul on his journey had seen the Lord and that the Lord had spoken to him, and how in Damascus he had preached fearlessly in the name of Jesus. So Saul stayed with them and moved about freely in Jerusalem, speaking boldly in the name of the Lord" (Acts 9:26-28).

In the previous list of reasons to follow up new converts, rank the reasons in order of importance to you. Use a scale of 1 to 5, with 1 being the most important. Explain why you ranked them as you did.

_____

OFFER IMMEDIATE GUIDANCE

Immediate follow-up is essential for a new believer. God used Ananias to follow up Paul after he was converted on the Damascus road.

Read Acts 9:15-19 in the margin. What did Ananias do to follow up Paul?

_____

At the Lord's direction Ananias visited Paul, told him that he came in Jesus' name, and indicated that he knew about Paul's conversion on the road to Damascus. Under Ananias's ministry performed in the name of the Lord, Paul recovered his sight, received the Holy Spirit, and was baptized.

Although Ananias was the first person to help Paul, Barnabas, an experienced discipler, came along later for more in-depth discipling. Read in Acts 9:26-28, in the margin, about the initial step Barnabas took in dealing with Paul as a new Christian.

In Acts 9:26-28 what did Barnabas do to help establish Paul, then still known as Saul, as a new Christian?

_____

_____

Barnabas arrived at a crucial time in Paul's efforts to establish himself and to gain credibility with the core members of the early church. Even though the disciples were skeptical of him, Barnabas provided a character reference for Paul, who had persecuted the church before his conversion. He commended Paul to the apostles by relating Paul's conversion experience and introduced him as one whose faith was sincere. This word from Barnabas appears to be exactly what the disciples needed to receive Paul into their fold as a Christian brother. Soon the disciples accepted Paul to the extent that they rescued him from physical harm (see Acts 9:29-30).

What ways do these verses teach that you can help nurture a spiritual child? On the following page, check the statements that apply.

❑ Introduce a new believer to mature Christians who can serve as role models.

❑ Help find a small group in which the new Christian can have fellowship and can learn.

❑ Tell others and help the new Christian tell how and when he or she trusted Christ as Savior.

❑ Protect the person from those who oppose his or her decision.

❑ Buy the new Christian a sweatshirt bearing the sign of the fish.

Helping establish a new Christian among new friends and supporters and vouching for that person's sincerity are important ways to plant this person in the faith. All except the last answer are ways you can help.

INTRODUCE CHRISTIAN ROLE MODELS

In Acts 11:25-26, in the margin, Barnabas again served as a discipler for Paul, still known as Saul. Barnabas sought Saul and brought him with him. They stayed together for a year, during which Saul learned from Barnabas. You too can make special efforts to ensure that new Christians associate with Christian role models. Work alongside them and meet with them frequently as they become familiar with the Word and begin living the Christian life.

 This week's Scripture-memory verses, 1 Peter 2:2-3, say that spiritual children "grow up in your salvation." What do you think that means?

_____

Turn to page 47 and read the verses aloud from one to three times to begin memorizing them.

ON MISSION WITH THE MASTER

Reread the MasterBuilder presentation on pages 123–27, with particular emphasis on the teachings about a spiritual child. By the end of this study you will be able to draw the MasterBuilder diagram and to explain it in your own words.

Spiritual children are not necessarily new Christians but may be worldly Christians who have never been established as disciples of Christ. The challenge of working with new Christians is to help them apply Christian principles in daily living. The challenge with those who have been in the Spiritual Child stage for some time is to rekindle their original enthusiasm and the belief that they can have victorious lives.

Read 1 Corinthians 3:1 and Ephesians 4:14 in the margin. Then check the statements on the following page that describe a spiritual child.

"Then Barnabas went to Tarsus to look for Saul, and when he found him, he brought him to Antioch. So for a whole year Barnabas and Saul met with the church and taught great numbers of people. The disciples were called Christians first at Antioch" (Acts 11:25-26).

"Brothers, I could not address you as spiritual but as worldly—mere infants in Christ. I gave you milk, not solid food, for you were not yet ready for it. Indeed, you are still not ready. You are still worldly. For since there is jealousy and quarreling among you, are you not worldly? Are you not acting like mere men?" (1 Cor. 3:1).

"Then we will no longer be infants, tossed back and forth by the waves, and blown here and there by every wind of teaching and by the cunning and craftiness of men in their deceitful scheming" (Eph. 4:14).

DAILY MASTER COMMUNICATION GUIDE

ACTS 9:19-31

What God said to me:

_____

_____

_____

_____

_____

_____

_____

What I said to God:

_____

_____

_____

_____

_____

_____

_____

❑ 1. Takes his or her orientation from the world and is not ready for the solid food of instruction
❑ 2. Is prone to jealousy and quarreling
❑ 3. Is well grounded in the faith
❑ 4. Is prone to temptation
❑ 5. Is prone to believe false teaching
❑ 6. Is not discerning about persons who are harmful influences

When I became a pastor, I discovered that many people who had been Christians for years were still spiritual children. It is tragic that a large percentage of those who profess Christ do not demonstrate His lordship by their behavior. All of the statements except number 3 describe spiritual children. This week you will learn more about spiritual children and what you can do to help them.

Ask God to bring to mind new Christians you need to nurture.

 Pray with your prayer partner in person or by telephone.

 During your quiet time today read Acts 9:19-31. Then complete the Daily Master Communication Guide in the margin.

DAY 2

Encouraging Others

The very name of Barnabas, about whom you studied in day 1, indicates something about his role in the spread of Christianity. Read Acts 4:36-37 in the margin on the next page.

That generous act of selling a field and giving the proceeds to the apostles' ministry was undoubtedly an encouraging act. This provided the apostles resources to distribute to those who had need and demonstrated that someone believed in their message enough to give to them generously. It also encouraged other Christians to sell their possessions and to give them to meet the needs of the whole body.

ENCOURAGE AS YOU DISCIPLE

Encouraging new Christians is an important way you can nurture new believers. Barnabas was known as the great encourager, as the verses from Acts 11, in the margin on the next page, describe.

In Acts 11:22-24 underline what Barnabas did when he saw that God was at work in the church at Antioch.

Barnabas was apparently moved by what he saw in the early church at Antioch. After he saw what was going on, he encouraged the members to remain true to the Lord and to be steadfast in the faith. You can encourage new Christians by reminding them of God's truth and by urging them to remain true to it, regardless of oppression.

Who encouraged you as a new Christian? Write their names and describe what they did.

_____

_____

Later, Barnabas encouraged Paul as he accompanied him on his missionary journey.

Read Acts 13:1-3 in the margin. What do you think might have happened if Paul had gone on his missionary journey without an experienced Christian to work alongside him and encourage him?

_____

We do not know for sure, but we can imagine that Paul needed someone experienced in the faith to provide spiritual leadership at this crucial time in the church's history. We can imagine that Barnabas, a mature Christian, was an important role model for Paul as he learned skills that would serve him later when he was on his own. Notice that these passages usually refer to the duo as Barnabas and Saul, with Barnabas's name occurring first. (Later the order changes to Paul and Barnabas.) At this point Barnabas is still exercising the leadership role while Paul grows in the faith.

ENCOURAGE NEW BELIEVERS
As Paul and Barnabas made their missionary journey to Antioch of Pisidia (different from Antioch in Syria), we see them encouraging others again. Read Acts 13:43 in the margin.

In Acts 13:43 underline phrases that show roles a discipler has with new Christians.

You may have underlined "talked with them" and "urged them to continue in the grace of God." Sometimes just a reminder from an experienced Christian about God's grace and provision is the encouraging nudge a new Christian needs. Merely spending time with a new Christian and talking about his or her Christian pilgrimage can encourage that person.

"Joseph, a Levite from Cyprus, whom the apostles called Barnabas (which means Son of Encouragement), sold a field he owned and brought the money and put it at the apostles' feet" (Acts 4:36-37).

"News of this reached the ears of the church at Jerusalem, and they sent Barnabas to Antioch. When he arrived and saw the evidence of the grace of God, he was glad and encouraged them all to remain true to the Lord with all their hearts. He was a good man, full of the Holy Spirit and faith, and a great number of people were brought to the Lord" (Acts 11:22-24).

"In the church at Antioch there were prophets and teachers: Barnabas, Simeon called Niger, Lucius of Cyrene, Manean (who had been brought up with Herod the tetrarch) and Saul. While they were worshiping the Lord and fasting, the Holy Spirit said, 'Set apart for me Barnabas and Saul for the work to which I have called them.' So after they had fasted and prayed, they placed their hands on them and sent them off" (Acts 13:1-3).

"When the congregation was dismissed, many of the Jews and devout converts to Judaism followed Paul and Barnabas, who talked with them and urged them to continue in the grace of God" (Acts 13:43).

Perhaps some of the persons you are discipling are new believers. What are ways you could encourage them?

_____

_____

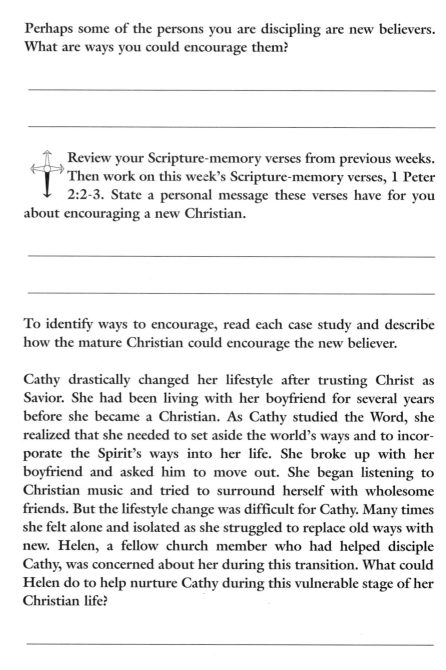 Review your Scripture-memory verses from previous weeks. Then work on this week's Scripture-memory verses, 1 Peter 2:2-3. State a personal message these verses have for you about encouraging a new Christian.

_____

_____

To identify ways to encourage, read each case study and describe how the mature Christian could encourage the new believer.

Cathy drastically changed her lifestyle after trusting Christ as Savior. She had been living with her boyfriend for several years before she became a Christian. As Cathy studied the Word, she realized that she needed to set aside the world's ways and to incorporate the Spirit's ways into her life. She broke up with her boyfriend and asked him to move out. She began listening to Christian music and tried to surround herself with wholesome friends. But the lifestyle change was difficult for Cathy. Many times she felt alone and isolated as she struggled to replace old ways with new. Helen, a fellow church member who had helped disciple Cathy, was concerned about her during this transition. What could Helen do to help nurture Cathy during this vulnerable stage of her Christian life?

_____

_____

Before George became a Christian, he had been addicted to pornography. After he trusted Christ, George realized that sexually explicit literature should have no place in his life. Although George could set aside his addiction when he was at home, temptation was great when he was traveling. Walter, a member of George's Sunday School class, knew about George's struggles with temptation and wanted to help him overcome them. What could Walter do to help establish George in his Christian walk?

DAILY MASTER COMMUNICATION GUIDE

ACTS 13

What God said to me:

_____

_____

_____

_____

_____

_____

_____

What I said to God:

_____

_____

_____

_____

_____

_____

_____

_____

_____

_____

_____

Phil knew that having a daily quiet time is an important part of the Christian life. But Phil had never prayed before he became a Christian and had never owned a Bible when he was growing up. He was uncertain how to approach the Father in prayer and how to begin a systematic pattern of daily Bible reading. He also had difficulty understanding Bible language and concepts. Steve, Phil's Sunday School teacher, sensed that Phil felt uncomfortable in class because he was new to the Christian life, while other members were experienced Christians. How could Steve help Phil?

_____

_____

Helen could help Cathy by contacting her frequently or by sending notes of encouragement. She could help Cathy find a Christian room-mate and meet more Christian friends. Walter could offer to be George's accountability partner when he traveled. He could pray with George before his trips and could encourage George to call him anytime he was tempted while on the road. He could teach George to memorize Scriptures such as 1 Peter 2:1, 1 Corinthians 10:13, and Philippians 4:13. Steve could privately teach Phil the basic elements of prayer (thanksgiving, praise, confession, asking). He could introduce him to devotional guides as patterns for Bible reading. He could be available to answer Phil's questions and could be sensitive to his needs during Sunday School discussions.

 You have already been praying for your neighbors, some of whom may have shared needs or concerns that you wrote on your Prayer-Covenant List (p. 131). Pray for your neighbors' requests.

During your quiet time today read Acts 13. Then complete the Daily Master Communication Guide in the margin.

DAY 3

Establishing Young Christians

" 'Come, follow me,' Jesus said, 'and I will make you fishers of men.' At once they left their nets and followed him" (Matt. 4:19-20).

" 'I tell you that you are Peter, and on this rock I will build my church, and the gates of Hades will not overcome it' " (Matt. 16:18).

"Peter took him aside and began to rebuke him. 'Never, Lord!' he said. 'This shall never happen to you!' Jesus turned and said to Peter, 'Get behind me, Satan! You are a stumbling block to me; you do not have in mind the things of God, but the things of men' " (Matt. 16:22-23).

" 'Simon, Simon, Satan has asked to sift you as wheat. But I have prayed for you, Simon, that your faith may not fail. And when you have turned back, strengthen your brothers' " (Luke 22:31-32).

"When they had finished eating, Jesus said to Simon Peter, 'Simon son of John, do you truly love me more than these?' 'Yes, Lord,' he said, 'you know that I love you.' Jesus said, 'Feed my lambs.' Again Jesus said, 'Simon son of John, do you truly love me?' He answered, 'Yes, Lord, you know that I love you.' Jesus said, 'Take care of my sheep' " (John 21:15-16).

Jesus and Paul are our best models for establishing spiritual children. Today you will learn ways they encouraged new believers to grow.

ENCOURAGE GROWTH

Jesus used the quality of faith to encourage His new believers. His expectations of them actually influenced what they became.

Jesus' first encounter with Peter was after John the Baptist pointed Andrew, Peter's brother, to Christ. Andrew then brought Peter to Jesus (see John 1:40-42). Later, Jesus healed Peter's mother-in-law (see Mark 1:29-31) and then used Peter's boat (see Luke 5:3). In all of these instances Jesus was building a relationship with Peter and was allowing him to observe Him in various situations. This set the stage for the discipling that was to come.

Jesus called Peter when He saw him and his brother, Andrew, fishing. He immediately stated His expectations for Peter. Read Matthew 4:19-20 in the margin.

Read Matthew 16:18 in the margin. What impact do you think it had on Simon when Jesus said that His new name would be Peter, the rock?

_____

Even though Simon might not have thoroughly understood what Jesus meant when He spoke to him in Matthew 16:18, the confidence Jesus expressed about him no doubt made him aware that Jesus saw potential in him and made him want to improve.

Jesus used means other than encouragement to disciple Peter. In Matthew 16:22-23, in the margin, Jesus rebuked Peter for thinking like a human and for rebuking Jesus when He talked about the cross.

In Luke 22:31-32, in the margin, Jesus told Peter He knew that he would ultimately succeed even though his faith would be weak at first.

Finally, Jesus commissioned Peter and gave him a task in John 21:15-16, in the margin, when He asked Peter to feed His lambs and sheep. His assignment to Peter indicated that Jesus believed in him and entrusted to him His important work on earth.

Based on what you have read about Jesus' discipling Peter, list ways you can nurture a new believer.

_____

TAKE RESPONSIBILITY
Just as God intends for children to be reared in homes, He expects His spiritual children to be reared in personal, supportive, shepherding environments. Too often we depend on written materials and programs to disciple new believers, but programs do not make disciples. Someone must feel responsible for spiritual children. Only concerned disciples make worthy spiritual parents.

Paul did not merely make converts and leave them to their own maturity process. One of the best examples of his follow-up occurs in 1 Thessalonians 2—3. Paul illustrated his concern by referring to three family relationships.

Read the passages in the margin. Match each reference below with the family relationship described in the passage.
____ 1. 1 Thessalonians 2:1-5   a. mother
____ 2. 1 Thessalonians 2:6-7   b. father
____ 3. 1 Thessalonians 2:11-12   c. brother

Paul indicated that, like a mother, the apostles ministered with care and sacrificial love. Like a father, the apostles encouraged, comforted, and reminded them how to live. Like a brother, Paul addressed them as equals, showing how close and concerned a brother should be for other Christians. He used these terms to establish new Christians in relationships in God's family. The correct answers are 1. c, 2. a, 3. b.

You have seen that Paul compares follow-up to a parent's caring for a child (see Gal. 4:19; 1 Thess. 2:7-12). A spiritual parent should—
1. protect (see 1 Pet. 5:8; 1 Cor. 10:13);
2. teach (see Col. 2:6-7);
3. be a model (see Phil. 4:9);
4. work with the new convert until he or she can present himself or herself to Christ as a mature person (see Col. 1:28-29).

ON MISSION WITH THE MASTER
In day 1 you began learning the traits of a spiritual child, as illustrated in MasterBuilder. Today you will learn more traits of spiritual children so that you can encourage them to grow spiritually. By the end of this study you will be able to draw the MasterBuilder diagram and to explain it in your own words.

 Read the following Scriptures and underline words that describe a spiritual child.

We have much to say about this, but it is hard to explain because you are slow to learn. In fact, though by this time you ought to be teachers, you need someone to teach you the elementary truths of God's word all over again. You need milk, not solid food! Anyone who lives on milk, being still

"You know, brothers, that our visit to you was not a failure. We had previously suffered and been insulted in Philippi, as you know, but with the help of our God we dared to tell you his gospel in spite of strong opposition. For the appeal we make does not spring from error or impure motives, nor are we trying to trick you. On the contrary, we speak as men approved by God to be entrusted with the gospel. We are not trying to please men but God, who tests our hearts. You know we never used flattery, nor did we put on a mask to cover up greed—God is our witness" (1 Thess. 2:1-5).

"As apostles of Christ we could have been a burden to you, but we were gentle among you, like a mother caring for her little children" (1 Thess. 2:6-7).

"You know that we dealt with each of you as a father deals with his own children, encouraging, comforting and urging you to live lives worthy of God, who calls you into his kingdom and glory" (1 Thess. 2:11-12).

DAILY MASTER COMMUNICATION GUIDE

1 THESSALONIANS 2—3

What God said to me:

_____

_____

_____

_____

_____

_____

_____

What I said to God:

_____

_____

_____

_____

_____

_____

_____

_____

an infant, is not acquainted with the teaching about righteousness. but solid food is for the mature, who by constant use have trained themselves to distinguish good from evil (Heb. 5:11-14).

You want something but don't get it. You kill and covet, but you cannot have what you want. You quarrel and fight. You do not have, because you do not ask God. When you ask, you do not receive, because you ask with wrong motives, that you may spend what you get on your pleasures. You adulterous people, don't you know that friendship with the world is hatred toward God? Anyone who chooses to be a friend of the world becomes an enemy of God (Jas. 4:2-4).

These verses say that a spiritual child needs to grow. Hebrews 5:11-14 says that this person is slow to learn, needs someone to teach him or her, and has not trained himself or herself to distinguish good from evil. James 4:2-4 says that this person is prone to quarrel and fight, does not pray, asks with wrong motives, and is a friend of the world.

Many older Christians who still match the profile of the spiritual child would like to grow but do not know how. They may have rededicated their lives several times and made new resolutions, only to return to bad habits. They represent one of the most fruitful fields for disciple making. Many have given up on the possibility of living the life of a disciple that you experience. You can give them hope.

 Encourage a new Christian or talk with a spiritual child.

This week's Scripture-memory verses, 1 Peter 2:2-3, emphasize the importance of nurturing new Christians. See how much of these verses you can write from memory on a sheet of paper.

WITNESSING FOR THE MASTER

Last week you learned a simple presentation of the gospel that you can use with a lost person. Turn to pages 128–31 and review the Gospel in Hand presentation. Then learn how to draw the hand as the presentation shows. Practice the presentation with a friend or a family member.

 During your quiet time today read 1 Thessalonians 2—3. Then complete the Daily Master Communication Guide in the margin.

DAY 4

Examples of Follow-Up

You can learn more about establishing spiritual children by studying ways the early church followed up its converts.

Read Acts 2:42-47 in the margin and underline words or phrases that indicate what the first church did to follow up new Christians.

You may have underlined "devoted themselves to the apostles' teaching," "fellowship," "breaking of bread," "prayer," "believers were together," "gave to anyone as he had need," "continued to meet together," "ate together," and "praising God." These common ways the early church nurtured new Christians led to church growth.

Read Acts 11:19-23 in the margin. Describe how the Jerusalem church followed up new converts in distant cities.

_____

_____

The Jerusalem church did not forget or abandon converts in distant cities. They remembered the new Christians in Antioch and sent persons to encourage them. One of those was Barnabas. It is important not to forget about new Christians, leaving them to find their own ways, especially those who are far away.

 Continue to work on this week's Scripture-memory verses, 1 Peter 2:2-3. Describe how you intend to apply these verses to your need to disciple others as they mature in Christ.

_____

_____

TRAINING IN MINISTRY

Immediate follow-up with a new Christian involves using the booklet *Welcome to God's Family*, a copy of which your leader probably gave you at your previous group session. Learn the basic ideas in the booklet so that you can explain the concepts to a new believer in your own words without having to read from the booklet. Give a copy of the booklet to the person immediately after he or she accepts Christ.

"They devoted themselves to the apostles' teaching, and to the fellowship, to the breaking of bread and to prayer. Everyone was filled with awe, and many wonders and miraculous signs were done by the apostles. All the believers were together and had everything in common. Selling their possessions and goods, they gave to anyone as he had need. Every day they continued to meet together in the temple courts. They broke bread in their homes and ate together with glad and sincere hearts, praising God and enjoying the favor of all the people. And the Lord added to their number daily those who were being saved" (Acts 2: 42-47).

"Those who had been scattered by the persecution in connection with Stephen traveled as far as Phoenicia, Cyprus and Antioch, telling the message only to Jews. Some of them, however, men from Cyprus and Cyrene, went to Antioch and began to speak to Greeks also, telling them the good news about the Lord Jesus. The Lord's hand was with them, and a great number of people believed and turned to the Lord. News of this reached the ears of the church at Jerusalem, and they sent Barnabas to Antioch. When he arrived and saw the evidence of the grace of God, he was glad and encouraged them all to remain true to the Lord with all their hearts" (Acts 11:19-23).

DAILY MASTER COMMUNICATION GUIDE

ACTS 11

What God said to me:

_____

_____

_____

_____

_____

_____

What I said to God:

_____

_____

_____

_____

_____

_____

_____

PREPARING TO MINISTER

Sometimes you may need to nurture a new Christian but do not have available a copy of _Welcome to God's Family_. Write how you could use the following disciplines of the Disciple's Cross to teach the points in _Welcome to God's Family_.

Live in the Word: _____

_____

Pray in faith: _____

_____

Fellowship with believers: _____

_____

Witness to the world: _____

_____

You might have written ideas similar to the following.
- The discipline of living in the Word equates with feeding on God's Word daily.
- The discipline of praying in faith equates with breathing a prayer regularly.
- The discipline of fellowshipping with believers equates with joining your new church family immediately.
- The discipline of witnessing to the world equates with communicating your faith soon.

WITNESSING FOR THE MASTER

 In previous weeks you listed the names of lost persons on your Prayer-Covenant List (p. 131). Visit one of the non-Christians you have listed. Serve the person, share a word of truth with him or her, give your testimony, or share the gospel. Ask someone you are establishing in the faith to join you.

Read Acts 11 during your quiet time today. Then complete the Daily Master Communication Guide in the margin.

DAY 5

*How to Follow Up
a New Christian*

This week you have examined the models of Barnabas, Paul, Jesus, and the early church in discipling spiritual children. You have studied the biblical basis of following up new converts and the pitfalls of not doing so. Today you will learn how to nurture new believers.

Just as a newborn baby needs nurture, a new Christian needs day-to-day counsel and guidance. Today you will learn practical guidelines for follow-up. You can use them as you lead a new Christian through the booklet *Welcome to God's Family,* which you learned about in day 4, or *Survival Kit,* a six-week study designed to give a new Christian the best start in the Christian life.[2] Your leader should have given you a copy of *Survival Kit* during your previous group session.

You will explore these guidelines for following up a new believer:

1. Tell the person why.
2. Show the person how.
3. Get the person started.
4. Keep the person going.
5. Help the person reproduce his or her faith.

TELL THE PERSON WHY

Read 2 Timothy 2:2 in the margin. Telling a person why you are giving training in discipleship is important, whether the training is in the form of *Welcome to God's Family; Survival Kit;* or instruction in how to read the Bible, pray, or witness. First, the person must understand the significance of what is being taught—the reason you are taking time to explain it and the reason it is important to the Christian life. If the spiritual child you are establishing does not know the why, often he or she will think of it as a how—just another activity. Telling new Christians why the training is essential to a relationship with Christ will help them grow, will protect them from temptation and Satan, and will help them be more mature in Christ.

For example, if you were showing a new Christian how to use *Survival Kit,* you would explain that the study is important because nearly all new Christians go through predictable stages in replacing the old nature with the new nature. If you were explaining to a new Christian why he or she needs to be baptized, you would state that we need to obey Christ's commands.

Just as a newborn baby needs nurture, a new Christian needs day-to-day counsel and guidance.

"The things you have heard me say in the presence of many witnesses entrust to reliable men who will also be qualified to teach others" (2 Tim. 2:2).

"Whatever you have learned or received or heard from me, or seen in me—put it into practice. And the God of peace will be with you" (Phil. 4:9).

"Now I commit you to God and to the word of his grace, which can build you up and give you an inheritance among all those who are sanctified" (Acts 20:32).

"So I will always remind you of these things, even though you know them and are firmly established in the truth you now have. I think it is right to refresh your memory as long as I live in the tent of this body, because I know that I will soon put it aside, as our Lord Jesus Christ has made clear to me. And I will make every effort to see that after my departure you will always be able to remember these things" (2 Pet. 1:12-15).

SHOW THE PERSON HOW

Read Philippians 4:9 in the margin. Many people want to grow in the Christian life but do not know how. They have been inspired, challenged, and made to feel guilty for not doing certain things, but no one has made the effort to tell them how. You can use much of your *MasterLife* to disciple a new Christian. For example, you can explain how to find Scriptures in the Bible, how to pray, how to overcome temptation, how to win in spiritual warfare, and how to keep a Prayer-Covenant List. You can explain the major types of prayer—thanksgiving, praise, confession, and asking. Give the person specific assignments and teach him or her how to do them.

GET THE PERSON STARTED

Read Acts 20:32 in the margin. Getting the person started moves the person from the information stage to the action stage. You need not only to tell the person how but also to help the individual begin doing what you are teaching. This helps move the person from the theoretical to the practical. Application is the step that changes the person's life.

For example, begin *Survival Kit* with the person by helping him or her fill out the first day's activities. Work through two or three activities with the person until he or she gets the idea. Then let the person continue the day's work, answering any questions that arise.

KEEP THE PERSON GOING

Read 2 Peter 1:12-15 in the margin. Hold the person accountable by checking what he or she does. Do what is necessary to help the person become a successful, obedient disciple.

It is easier to get people started than to keep them going. Most are not disciplined. Think of the discipline required in *MasterLife*.

What has kept you going in the *MasterLife* process?

_____

Perhaps you were disciplined by the fact that someone would be checking you at your group session. Perhaps it was checking each activity in "My Walk with the Master" after you completed each week's work. Perhaps you had a prayer partner who prayed for your progress.

Ask the person studying *Survival Kit* to meet with you so that you can check his or her work. It is best to do this in person, but if not possible, telephone the person and ask what he or she has learned that week. Ask whether the person has encountered any problems. Maintain weekly contact for the six weeks the person is studying *Survival Kit*.

Share with the person your personal struggle to stay disciplined. Help the person become motivated to do the work on his or her own; avoid shaming the person because he or she did not complete an assignment. Remember that new Christians fight a variety of problems: unfamiliar territory, a lack of discipline, Satan's attacks, and the effort required to change from one lifestyle to another. Invite the person to participate in church activities with you. Perhaps you could lead the individual through *MasterLife 1: The Disciple's Cross* to learn the disciplines of the Christian life.

HELP THE PERSON REPRODUCE HIS OR HER FAITH
Read John 15:16 in the margin. Teach the person how to share with someone else what you have shared with him or her. All your discipling should be "pass-on-able." God made us to reproduce our faith. It is normal and natural for a Christian to want to reproduce. A new Christian has an innate desire to share with someone else. You can teach the person how to do this.

Often, a brand-new Christian's witness can immediately win someone else. Encourage the new Christian to share whatever you have taught the individual. When you give out the booklet *Welcome to God's Family*, tell the person that he or she might want to share this with someone else. After the person has completed *Survival Kit*, ask the spiritual child to lead someone else through the course.

" 'You did not choose me, but I chose you and appointed you to go and bear fruit—fruit that will last. Then the Father will give you whatever you ask in my name' " (John 15:16).

List the five guidelines for following up a spiritual child.

1. _____

2. _____

3. _____

4. _____

5. _____

ON MISSION WITH THE MASTER
This week you have learned the traits of a spiritual child, as illustrated in MasterBuilder.

Write your task for helping a spiritual child move along the path of spiritual growth in the Spiritual Child stage of MasterBuilder. If you cannot recall it, review the MasterBuilder presentation on pages 123–27.

The MasterBuilder's task with the spiritual child is to establish him or her. This week you have read examples of how Barnabas, Paul, Jesus, and the early church established new Christians. You can follow their models. As you have learned, you develop others by praying for them,

DAILY MASTER
COMMUNICATION
GUIDE

2 PETER 1:5-9

What God said to me:

_____

_____

_____

_____

_____

_____

What I said to God:

_____

_____

_____

_____

_____

_____

_____

spending time with them, encouraging them, introducing them to other Christians, worshiping corporately with them, and pointing them to God's Word as their Guidebook for life. Your task is to establish that person in the faith.

List the names of new Christians you are helping develop and ways you see them becoming more established in the faith.

_____

_____

_____

Stop and pray for the new Christians you are developing. Ask the Father to help you be a patient, consistent role model for them.

 Say aloud this week's Scripture-memory verses, 1 Peter 2: 2-3, to your prayer partner or to a family member.

In weeks 1 and 2 you learned that it is difficult to present the gospel to someone with whom you do not have a good relationship. It is also difficult to disciple a new Christian with whom you have a poor relationship.

 Try to reconcile with the person with whom reconciliation will be the most difficult. Use the Spiritual Armor to pray beforehand. If you do not remember the Spiritual Armor presentation, refer to pages 129–31 in book 3.

Today during your quiet time read 2 Peter 1:5-9, which describes qualities of a productive Christian. Then complete the Daily Master Communication Guide in the margin.

HAS THIS WEEK MADE A DIFFERENCE?
Review "My Walk with the Master This Week" at the beginning of this week's material. Mark the activities you have finished by drawing vertical lines in the diamonds beside them. Finish any incomplete activities. Think about what you will say during your group session about your work on these activities.

[1]Herschel H. Hobbs, _The Gospel of Matthew_ (Grand Rapids: Baker Book House, 1961), 134.
[2] _Welcome to God's Family_ and _Survival Kit_ are available from the Customer Service Center; 127 Ninth Avenue, North; Nashville, TN 37234; 1-800-458-2772; and from Baptist Book Stores and Lifeway Christian Stores.

WEEK 4

Maturing as a Disciple

This Week's Goal

You will be able to outline a personal process of spiritual growth and to begin helping another believer grow toward spiritual maturity.

My Walk with the Master This Week

You will complete the following activities to develop the six biblical disciplines. When you have completed each activity, draw a vertical line in the diamond beside it.

SPEND TIME WITH THE MASTER
◇ Have a quiet time each day. Check each day you have a quiet time: ❑ Sunday ❑ Monday ❑ Tuesday ❑ Wednesday ❑ Thursday ❑ Friday ❑ Saturday
◇ Describe ways you have been blessed during your quiet times.

LIVE IN THE WORD
◇ Read your Bible every day. Write what God says to you and what you say to God.
◇ Memorize Luke 6:40.
◇ Review Matthew 5:23-24, Romans 6:23, and 1 Peter 2:2-3.

PRAY IN FAITH
◇ Pray to have a servant heart.

FELLOWSHIP WITH BELIEVERS
◇ Spend meaningful time with a family member or a friend.

WITNESS TO THE WORLD
◇ Read "How to Lead to Commitment." Explain it to someone in your own words.
◇ Explain the Gospel in Hand presentation to a lost person.

MINISTER TO OTHERS
◇ Learn the traits of a spiritual disciple, as presented in MasterBuilder.
◇ Use the money your leader gave you to minister to someone.
◇ Study "Guide to Financial Partnership with God."
◇ Help someone you are discipling formulate a plan for spiritual growth.

This Week's Scripture-Memory Verse

" 'A student is not above his teacher, but everyone who is fully trained will be like his teacher' " (Luke 6:40).

DAY 1

Growing Toward Maturity

"He has rescued us from the dominion of darkness and brought us into the kingdom of the Son he loves, in whom we have redemption, the forgiveness of sins" (Col. 1:13-14).

"Once you were alienated from God and were enemies in your minds because of your evil behavior. But now he has reconciled you by Christ's physical body through death to present you holy in his sight, without blemish and free from accusation" (Col. 1:21-22).

"He has reconciled you by Christ's physical body through death to present you holy in his sight, without blemish and free from accusation" (Col. 1:22).

"He has rescued us from the dominion of darkness and brought us into the kingdom of the Son he loves" (Col. 1:13).

"Since the day we heard about you, we have not stopped praying for you and asking God to fill you with the knowledge of his will through all spiritual wisdom and understanding" (Col. 1:9).

"We pray this in order that you may live a life worthy of the Lord and may please him in every way: bearing fruit in every good work, growing in the knowledge of God" (Col. 1:10).

When Shirley and I were dating, she worked in an architect's office. One day a man came in and asked to purchase a sheet of drawing paper 45 feet long. He said that he wanted to draw a picture of his spiritual life and needed that much paper to do so.

How do you measure your spiritual maturity? God's purpose is for every person to be spiritually mature, and He has provided the way for you to continually grow. This week you will explore what it means to be a spiritual disciple, determine your stage in the growth process, and make plans to improve. At the end of this week you will be able to—

- list three ways you can grow toward Christian maturity;
- commit to giving financially to God's work;
- list five principles Jesus used to develop disciples;
- explain ways to apply the five principles to your discipleship and to the growth of other believers;
- describe the characteristics of a spiritual disciple.

In Colossians 1:21—2:8 Paul revealed God's purpose for every believer to be perfectly complete in Christ and described the roles Christ, a disciple, and a discipler have in the process of spiritual growth. As you study that passage today, you will learn about—

- God's provision for you;
- God's plan for you;
- God's purpose for you.

GOD'S PROVISION FOR YOU

First, consider God's provision for you to grow toward maturity in Christ. Read Colossians 1:13-14,21-22 in the margin.

Underline phrases in these two passages that specify what God has provided for you.

Perhaps you underlined "rescued us from the dominion of darkness," "brought us into the kingdom of the Son," "redemption," "forgiveness," "reconciled you," and "present you holy."

Stop and thank God for His provision you read about.

GOD'S PLAN FOR YOU

God's Word gives His expectations for your spiritual growth.

Read the remaining verses in the margin. Match their references with the statements of what God wants you to accomplish.

_____ 1. Colossians 1:22   a. Be brought into Christ's king-
                               dom.

_____ 2. Colossians 1:13   b. Be filled with the knowledge of
                               His will.

_____ 3. Colossians 1:9   c. Be presented holy without blem-
                               ish or accusation.

_____ 4. Colossians 1:10   d. Live a life worthy of the Lord and
                               please Him.

As you strive toward completion, God wants you please Him, to be filled with the knowledge of His will, to be holy without blemish, and to be part of His kingdom. The answers are 1. c, 2. a, 3. b, 4. d.

Read Colossians 1:10-12 in the margin. Underline the results if you take the steps listed in the previous activity as you strive toward completion.

This verse tells you that you will bear fruit in every good work, grow in the knowledge of God, be strengthened with all power, have great endurance and patience, and joyfully give thanks.

GOD'S PURPOSE FOR YOU
God has high expectations for you, but He also instructs you in how to grow toward maturity. God reveals His purpose for your spiritual growth. Read Colossians 2:6 in the margin.

This verse contains three illustrations of growth. The first illustration is human growth, which is reflected in the MasterBuilder stages of spiritual development: the spiritual child, the spiritual disciple (adult), the disciple maker (parent), and the spiritual colaborer (grandparent.)

Read Ephesians 4:14-15 in the margin and underline words that indicate the growth of a body.

Did you underline _grow up_?
The second illustration of a disciple's growth is the growth of a plant.

Read Ephesians 3:17 in the margin. What picture comes to mind when you think about being rooted and established?

_____

You might have described a tree with a root system that withstands high winds. If you are rooted and established, you can withstand life's temptations and difficulties.

The third illustration of a disciple's growth is the construction of a building. What does it mean to be built up in Him? Read 1 Corinthians 3:11 in the margin.

"Bearing fruit in every good work, growing in the knowledge of God, being strengthened with all power according to his glorious might so that you may have great endurance and patience, and joyfully giving thanks to the Father, who has qualified you to share in the inheritance of the saints in the kingdom of light" (Col. 1: 10-12).

"Just as you received Christ Jesus as Lord, continue to live [walk, KJV] in him, rooted and built up in him, strengthened in the faith as you were taught, and overflowing with thankfulness" (Col. 2:6).

"We will no longer be infants, tossed back and forth by the waves, and blown here and there by every wind of teaching and by the cunning and craftiness of men in their deceitful scheming. Instead, speaking the truth in love, we will in all things grow up into him who is the Head, that is, Christ" (Eph. 4:14-15).

"I pray that you, being rooted and established in love, may have power, together with all the saints, to grasp how wide and long and high and deep is the love of Christ" (Eph. 3:17).

"No one can lay any foundation other than the one already laid, which is Jesus Christ" (1 Cor. 3:11).

DAILY MASTER COMMUNICATION GUIDE

COLOSSIANS 2

What God said to me:

_____

_____

_____

_____

_____

_____

_____

What I said to God:

_____

_____

_____

_____

_____

_____

_____

_____

Being built up in Him is a significant mark of a mature spiritual disciple. If the foundation of your life is not in Christ, you have no chance for spiritual growth because your life is built on the wrong foundation. How do you build this foundation? The disciplines of the Disciple's Cross can help you build a solid foundation for spiritual growth.

Tomorrow you will examine additional characteristics of a mature disciple. In days 3 through 5, you will learn ways to help others grow toward spiritual maturity.

ON MISSION WITH THE MASTER

Reread the MasterBuilder presentation on pages 123–27, with particular emphasis on the teachings about a spiritual disciple. By the end of this study you will be able to draw the MasterBuilder diagram and to explain it in your own words.

Read the following Scriptures and underline words or phrases that describe a spiritual disciple.

I write to you, fathers, because you have known him who is from the beginning. I write to you, young men, because you are strong, and the word of God lives in you, and you have overcome the evil one (1 John 2:14).

To the Jews who had believed him, Jesus said, "If you hold to my teaching, you are really my disciples" (John 8:31).

The verses state that a spiritual disciple is strong, that God's Word lives in this person, and that the person overcomes the evil one. He or she also holds to Christ's teachings.

Circle the level to which you feel you have matured in each area, with 5 being the highest level of maturity:

I am strong.	1	2	3	4	5
God's Word lives in me.	1	2	3	4	5
I overcome the evil one.	1	2	3	4	5
I hold to Christ's teachings.	1	2	3	4	5

Stop and ask God to help you become a mature spiritual disciple in these areas.

Ask God to begin placing in your heart the names of spiritual children whom you need to help become spiritual disciples. Ask Him to help you understand their needs and to be open to providing the training they need.

 This week's Scripture-memory verse, Luke 6:40, refers to the importance of being fully trained and to the teacher's role. To begin memorizing this verse, write it in the margin from one to three times.

 Read Colossians 2 during your quiet time today. Then complete the Daily Master Communication Guide in the margin on page 68.

 Describe ways you have been blessed during your quiet times since beginning *MasterLife*.

_____

_____

DAY 2

The Grace of Giving

Becoming a more spiritually mature Christian involves learning the role of giving in your life as a disciple. I have met tithers who were not spiritual disciples, but I have never met a spiritual disciple who did not give to God's work at least 10 percent of his or her income.

Today we will examine 2 Corinthians 4—9 to learn the answers to these key questions about giving:
• Why should you give?
• How much should you give?
• What are the benefits of giving?

WHY SHOULD YOU GIVE?
You may wonder why you should give to others when you and your family have many needs. Read 2 Corinthians 4:4-7 in the margin.

The first reason you should give is that the god of this world, Satan, has blinded unbelievers' minds. Three-fourths of the people of this world are not Christians, and about 1.68 billion people have never heard about Jesus.[1] Your giving provides the means for people to hear the gospel.

The second reason you should give is that you have experienced God's grace in salvation. The Creator shone the light of salvation in your heart by sending Jesus. Now you may see God's glory. You give from gratitude for God's gift to you.

Read 2 Corinthians 5:11,14,19-20 in the margin. These verses make additional statements about giving:
1. You give because you have the responsibility to share God's grace

"The god of this age has blinded the minds of unbelievers, so that they cannot see the light of the gospel of the glory of Christ, who is the image of God. For we do not preach ourselves, but Jesus Christ as Lord, and ourselves as your servants for Jesus' sake. For God, who said, 'Let light shine out of darkness,' made his light shine in our hearts to give us the light of the knowledge of the glory of God in the face of Christ. But we have this treasure in jars of clay to show that this all-surpassing power is from God and not from us" (2 Cor. 4:4-7).

"Since, then, we know what it is to fear the Lord, we try to persuade men" (2 Cor. 5:11).

"Christ's love compels us, because we are convinced that one died for all, and therefore all died" (2 Cor. 5:14).

"He has committed to us the message of reconciliation. We are therefore Christ's ambassadors as though God were making his appeal through us" (2 Cor. 5:19-20).

with the lost. When you give, you join other Christians in taking the gospel to the lost around the world.

2. You give because of God's impending judgment. Millions in the large cities of the world do not know Christ—3 million in Singapore, 4 million in Canton, 6 million in Hong Kong, 9 million in Jakarta, 9 million in Manila, and 25 million in Tokyo.[2] You know that they will go to hell without Christ.

3. You give because God's love compels you. You are motivated to give not by what you see in others but by what you see in Him. You want to share Christ because He has committed to you the ministry of reconciliation and has made you His ambassador.

How can you be Christ's ambassador and instrument?
❑ **Tell others about Christ.**
❑ **Minister to persons who have needs.**
❑ **Pray for the unsaved.**
❑ **Sacrificially give your resources.**

All of the statements are ways to be Christ's ambassador.

HOW MUCH SHOULD YOU GIVE?
You can measure your giving by the standards in 2 Corinthians 8.

Read 2 Corinthians 8:8-9 in the margin. How much did Christ give?

_____

Christ gave from His riches. He gave up the glories of heaven to experience the poverty of earth. He gave His life on the cross so that you can experience salvation.

Paul also used the Macedonian churches as examples of giving from poverty.

Read 2 Corinthians 8:1-5 in the margin. Underline the statement that tells what the Macedonian churches gave.

The Macedonian churches gave of themselves, as well as giving their material wealth to the Lord. They gave as they were able and even beyond their ability to give.

Read 2 Corinthians 8:13-15 in the margin. These verses say that giving is not designed to make you suffer but to provide for others in their need. You should give according to your means. Often, people who give are then given to in equal portion when they are in need.

What is the equality that 2 Corinthians 8:13-15 talks about?

_____

"I am not commanding you, but I want to test the sincerity of your love by comparing it with the earnestness of others. For you know the grace of our Lord Jesus Christ, that though he was rich, yet for your sakes he became poor, so that you through his poverty might become rich" (2 Cor. 8:8-9).

"Now, brothers, we want you to know about the grace that God has given the Macedonian churches. Out of the most severe trial, their overflowing joy and their extreme poverty welled up in rich generosity. For I testify that they gave as much as they were able, and even beyond their ability. Entirely on their own, they urgently pleaded with us for the privilege of sharing in this service to the saints. And they did not do as we expected, but they gave themselves first to the Lord and then to us in keeping with God's will" (2 Cor. 8:1-5).

"Our desire is not that others might be relieved while you are hard pressed, but that there might be equality. At the present time your plenty will supply what they need, so that in turn their plenty will supply what you need. Then there will be equality" (2 Cor. 8:13-15).

When you think about equality, remember that each day between 35,000 and 41,000 children die of hunger and related diseases.³ You can try to equalize the plenty you have. Giving should result in equally meeting the needs of all of God's family.

Look at the measurements of giving in the verses you have studied. Compare what you give to these examples. Stop and ask God whether your giving pleases Him.

WHAT ARE THE BENEFITS OF GIVING?

One benefit of your giving appears in 2 Corinthians 9:6-7, which appears in the margin. This passage speaks of giving what you have decided in your heart to give. How do you decide what that is? People have various ways to determine this. When I was a college student, I began putting an extra 10 percent beyond my tithe into a special bank account each week. At the end of the year it was a joy to give this extra 10 percent for missions. But more importantly, I learned that I could not outgive God. He graciously gave me far more than the extra amount I gave.

This passage also admonishes you not to give grudgingly or because you feel that you must. Stewardship involves willing, cheerful generosity, not grudging gifts. The original language says that God loves a hilarious giver! You are not to give until it hurts but until you feel good!

Read 2 Corinthians 9:8-15 in the margin. What will happen to you when you give? Check the statements that apply.
❑ 1. Giving brings God's blessings to meet your needs.
❑ 2. Giving keeps bad things from happening to you.
❑ 3. Giving brings gratitude to God.
❑ 4. Giving brings an enhanced ability to keep giving.
❑ 5. Giving supplies the needs of persons God loves.
❑ 6. Giving causes persons to whom you give to pray for you.

Giving does not keep bad things from happening to you. You live in a fallen world, and generously giving does not protect you from hurt, heartache, and physical injury. However, God pours out His blessings on those who are good stewards of His resources. His grace abounds at all times so that you have all you need to meet life's challenges. All of the statements except number 2 are promises expressed in the passage you read.

GIVE WITH THANKS

Paul had one final word about giving: "Thanks be to God for his indescribable gift!" (2 Cor. 9:15). God's indescribable gift was His Son, who gave the ultimate gift for you. He is the greatest Giver anyone has ever known. He is responsible for all you have, especially your salvation in Christ.

"Remember this: Whoever sows sparingly will also reap sparingly, and whoever sows generously will also reap generously. Each man should give what he has decided in his heart to give, not reluctantly or under compulsion, for God loves a cheerful giver" (2 Cor. 9:6-7).

"God is able to make all grace abound to you, so that in all things at all times, having all that you need, you will abound in every good work. ... Now he who supplies seed to the sower and bread for food will also supply and increase your store of seed and will enlarge the harvest of your righteousness. You will be made rich in every way so you can be generous on every occasion, and through us your generosity will result in thanksgiving to God. This service that you perform is not only supplying the needs of God's people but is also overflowing in many expressions of thanks to God. Because of the service by which you have proved yourselves, men will praise God for the obedience that accompanies your confession of the gospel of Christ, and for your generosity in sharing with them and with everyone else. And in their prayers for you their hearts will go out to you, because of the surpassing grace God has given you" (2 Cor. 9: 8-15).

✝ In your previous group session your leader gave you an amount of money with which to minister to someone in need. Use the money for that purpose before the next group session. Summarize how you used the money to help someone, how the person reacted, and how you felt.

_____

_____

✝ Read "Guide to Financial Partnership with God," which follows. Read the Scriptures and pray that God will guide you to become a financial partner with Him. Pray about signing the guide to make a covenant between you and God or to renew your partnership.

"The earth is the Lord's, and everything in it,
   the world, and all who live in it" (Ps. 24:1).

"You made him ruler over the works of your hands;
   you put everything under his feet" (Ps. 8:6).

"My God will meet all your needs according to his glorious riches in Christ Jesus" (Phil. 4:19).

"If the willingness is there, the gift is acceptable according to what one has, not according to what he does not have" (2 Cor. 8:12).

> ## GUIDE TO FINANCIAL PARTNERSHIP WITH GOD
> God established a partnership with humanity when He created the world and gave people dominion over it (see Gen. 1:26). The people He created failed to follow basic principles of stewardship. The result was a chaotic economic situation that still prevails.
>
> The Bible restates God's principles and promises in one sentence: " 'Seek first his kingdom and his righteousness, and all these things will be given to you as well' " (Matt. 6:33). "These things" means your physical needs (see Matt. 6:19-34). If you put God's kingdom first, He puts your needs first. God wants to supply all of your needs (see Phil. 4:19). Have you withdrawn from your economic partnership with Him by not living by His principles? Financial problems may signal that one or more of God's economic principles have been violated.
>
> This guide will help you establish or renew a partnership with God. Initial each principle by which you are currently living.
>
> ### Step 1: Accept the Principles for Recognizing God's Ownership
> Initial the principles you presently accept.
> _____ God is the sovereign Creator, owner, and ruler of everything (see Ps. 24:1 in the margin).
> _____ God has made people the stewards, or overseers, of all creation (see Ps. 8:6 in the margin).
> _____ God meets all needs of the steward who faithfully manages all God has entrusted to him or her (see Phil. 4:19 in the margin).
> _____ God will judge the steward on the basis of what this person has rather than what he or she does not have (see 2 Cor. 8:12 in the margin).

Step 2: Practice the Principles of Responsibility

Initial the principles you presently practice.

_____ I glorify God by the way I manage the possessions He has given me to oversee (see 1 Cor. 10:31 in the margin; also see Matt. 6:33).

_____ I properly manage my finances (see 1 Tim. 5:8 in the margin).

_____ I manage my finances in order to tithe through my church (see Mal. 3:8-11).

_____ I give more than the tithe (see 1 Cor. 16:1-2 in the margin; also see Prov. 11:24-25; Acts 4:32-37).

_____ I give to the government by paying taxes (see Luke 20:25; Rom. 13:1-7).

_____ I properly administer the funds I have so that I can take care of my family, give to my church, and pay taxes without defrauding any of these groups.

Knowing the preceding principles heightens your sense of responsibility, but practicing them brings victory. The following steps will help you practice God's principles and become a full partner with the Master.

Step 3: Respond to the Principles of Reliance by Believing in God's Ability

Initial the following principles to which you are willing to respond to in faith.

_____ I trust God to bless the righteous (see Ps. 37:3-4; Prov. 22:4).

_____ I trust God to bless the person who prays (see Matt. 7:7-8; John 15:7; Jas. 5:16).

_____ I trust God to bless the diligent worker (see Ps. 1:3; Prov. 10:16; 11:25; 12:11; 13:4).

_____ I believe that I should limit my desires to what God provides (see Phil. 4:11-12 and 1 Tim. 6:6 in the margin; also see Prov. 15:16).

Step 4: Invest According to the Principles of Reward

Initial the principles to which you are willing to commit your resources.

_____ I will invest my possessions in God's economy because it will bring no sorrow (see Prov. 10:22; this verse means that because God blesses, you will have no regrets about investing in His kingdom).

_____ I will invest my material resources as a demonstration of my faith (see Heb. 11:6 in the margin).

_____ I will rely on God to bless according to His promises (see Mal. 3:10; Luke 6:38).

"Whether you eat or drink or whatever you do, do it all for the glory of God" (1 Cor. 10:31).

"If anyone does not provide for his relatives, and especially for his immediate family, he has denied the faith and is worse than an unbeliever" (1 Tim. 5:8).

"About the collection for God's people: Do what I told the Galatian churches to do. On the first day of every week, each one of you should set aside a sum of money in keeping with his income, saving it up, so that when I come no collections will have to be made" (1 Cor. 16:1-2).

"I have learned to be content whatever the circumstances. I know what it is to be in need, and I know what it is to have plenty. I have learned the secret of being content in any and every situation, whether well fed or hungry, whether living in plenty or in want" (Phil. 4: 11-12).

"Godliness with contentment is a great gain. For we brought nothing into the world, and we can take nothing out of it" (1 Tim. 6:6).

"Without faith it is impossible to please God, because anyone who comes to him must believe that he exists and that he rewards those who earnestly seek him" (Heb. 11:6).

DAILY MASTER COMMUNICATION GUIDE

2 CORINTHIANS 9

What God said to me:

_____

_____

_____

_____

_____

_____

_____

What I said to God:

_____

_____

_____

_____

_____

_____

_____

_____

_____

_____ I will depend on God to take care of an inheritance for my children and grandchildren (see Prov. 13:22).

Step 5: Change Your Lifestyle According to the Principles of Restoration

If your lifestyle prevents your being a full partner with the Master, initial the following steps you will take to restore your relationship as a full partner.

_____ I repent of failing to follow God's principles and ask for restoration (see Ps. 32:1-7; Prov. 28:13).

_____ I will immediately begin practicing biblical stewardship by tithing and giving gifts through my church, paying taxes, and managing financial matters according to Scripture.

_____ I will eliminate nonessentials until I can pay all of my payments to creditors (see Prov. 22:1).

_____ I will arrange to repay my creditors by the fairest means possible as soon as I can (see Prov. 11:3; 20:18).

_____ I will patiently continue to get my financial matters in order until I can live a Christian lifestyle that pleases God (see Prov. 21:5; 28:6). I will remember that it may take as long to get out of financial difficulty as it did to get into it.

God has stated His principles and has committed Himself to them. I commit myself to full financial partnership with God. I will be a good steward of all He entrusts to me and will depend on Him to supply my needs.

Signed _____ Date _____

 This week's Scripture-memory verse, Luke 6:40, mentions a student's emulating the teacher. I hope that on page 68 you identified qualities in yourself that you feel are worthy for another disciple to emulate. See if you can write the verse from memory in the margin.

Read 2 Corinthians 9 during your quiet time today. Then complete the Daily Master Communication Guide in the margin.

DAY 3

Discipling Others

As you have studied this week's work, you have no doubt been think-ing about your progress as a disciple. By retaking the Discipleship Inventory you completed in *MasterLife 1: The Disciple's Cross*, you can measure the progress you have made in *MasterLife*.

The ultimate model is Jesus, who shows us the Father.

PREPARING TO MINISTER
Complete the Discipleship Inventory on pages 133–37. Score your inventory, using the instructions your leader gave you. Compare your score with that of the inventory you took at the end of book 1 (pp. 139–43).

Now identify an area in which you need to grow. You may choose one of the five categories in the inventory—attitudes, behavior, relationships, ministry, or doctrine—or you may choose a specific behavior or characteristic you want to work on in today's lesson. List it here.

HOW JESUS HELPED HIS DISCIPLES GROW
Today you will examine the way Jesus helped His disciples grow. You can use the same process to grow as a spiritual disciple. Try it with the behavior or characteristic you have identified.

During the next three days we will study five principles Jesus used to develop disciples and the disciples' responses to these principles.

PRINCIPLES OF DISCIPLING
1. A discipler **models**; the disciple **imitates**.
2. A discipler **explains**; the disciple **experiments**.
3. A discipler **coaches**; the disciple **applies**.
4. A discipler **supports**; the disciple **demonstrates**.
5. A discipler **commissions**; the disciple **represents**.

MODELING
The ultimate model is Jesus, who shows us the Father. Jesus' disciples had the advantage of being able to observe Jesus' actions, which they could recall and apply to their situations.

In Matthew 4:19-20, in the margin, Jesus invited Peter to follow Him. Peter was content to follow Jesus and to do what He did. In Matthew 8:23 the disciples were content to do what Jesus did after a long day of teaching and healing. He modeled; they followed.

" 'Come, follow me,' Jesus said, 'and I will make you fishers of men.' At once they left their nets and followed him" (Matt. 4:19-20).

"He got into the boat and his disciples followed him" (Matt. 8:23).

Unlike the disciples, we must depend on secondary sources to reconstruct Jesus' modeling. Essentially, you get this information through the Word and through the direct illumination of the Holy Spirit. His model is shown in the Scripture, and the Holy Spirit interprets and illuminates how Christ's model applies to you.

Write instances you can recall from Jesus' life that demonstrate the area you want to improve.

_____

_____

Modeling is particularly helpful in skill training. The discipler models the way something is done, and the disciple imitates the model. Imitation is the first step in learning to develop a skill. It is difficult to believe what you cannot conceive, and it is difficult to conceive what you have never seen. A discipler does not just teach information, skills, and attitudes. He or she imparts a lifestyle.

Another source of discipling is Christ living through others. As others follow Christ, they become models you can follow.

A discipler does not just teach information, skills, and attitudes. He or she imparts a lifestyle.

Write the names of two or three persons who have the behavior or characteristic you desire for your life. Think of ways you can learn to imitate how they consistently demonstrate this trait.

_____

When the Word, the Spirit, and a model give a consistent message, you have strong impetus to grow.

This week's Scripture-memory verse, Luke 6:40, emphasizes the role of modeling in your discipling. To practice your memory work, say the verse aloud to a family member or a close friend.

Now review your memory verses from previous weeks.

EXPLAINING

A model does not stand alone; it needs explanation. For example, you may live a good Christian life, but if you do not explain that you are living this life by God's grace and power, an observer may think you can do it because of your upbringing or heredity. Jesus explained the things He modeled so that His disciples would not misunderstand. He wanted them to know that all He taught them came from God and the reason He was teaching it to them. Read John 17:7 in the margin.

" 'Now they know that everything you have given me comes from you' " (John 17:7).

Ask the person who models your chosen behavior or characteristic to explain how he or she practices it.

The response to explaining is to experiment. Experimentation allows you to apply the discipler's explanation to your life.

Write one or more ways you can experiment with the behavior or characteristic you wish to develop.

_____

ON MISSION WITH THE MASTER
Earlier this week you studied the traits of a spiritual disciple. How do you keep moving along the path of spiritual growth, as the MasterBuilder illustration shows? To nurture a disciple, both the disciple and the discipler have responsibilities.

 What tasks do a spiritual disciple and a discipler have in the Spiritual Disciple stage of MasterBuilder? If you cannot recall them, review the MasterBuilder presentation on pages 123–27.

Disciple: _____

Discipler: _____

As a discipler you should be able to train spiritual disciples, your ultimate goal being to give them resources so that they become responsible for their own growth. You want them to be able to feed themselves spiritually and to bear much fruit. You cannot cause the growth, but you can create opportunities for the persons to grow.

A spiritual disciple's goal is to grow more spiritually mature. By the end of this stage you should be bearing fruit and living a holy life. During this stage character is developed, and the spiritual life is built from the right materials (see 1 Cor. 3:16). In the Spiritual Disciple stage the disciple and the discipler each has about 50 percent of the responsibility for the disciple's growth.

 Pray to have a servant heart.

Read 1 Corinthians 3:1-15 during your quiet time today. Then complete the Daily Master Communication Guide in the margin.

DAY 4

Coaching and Supporting

A coach helps disciples live a truth or a lifestyle after they have mastered it.

Today you will continue learning five principles Jesus used to develop disciples:

> **PRINCIPLES OF DISCIPLING**
> 1. A discipler **models;** the disciple **imitates.**
> 2. A discipler **explains;** the disciple **experiments.**
> 3. A discipler **coaches;** the disciple **applies.**
> 4. A discipler **supports;** the disciple **demonstrates.**
> 5. A discipler **commissions;** the disciple **represents.**

COACHING

Coaching is the third principle Jesus used to develop disciples. Through coaching, a discipler guides disciples to do something more skillfully until the person becomes comfortable with the new way of doing things. The coach helps disciples find their own way to an appropriate style of behavior. A wise coach knows when to let persons learn on their own and when to intervene.

A coach helps disciples live a truth or a lifestyle after they have mastered it. Consider the apprentice model people used in the past to learn trades such as blacksmithing or carpentry. Once the apprentice had learned all he could from a master, he was ready to work on his own. The modern business world has adopted this model, which is usually called a mentor-protégé relationship.

The disciple's response to coaching is application. The person actually does the skill being coached so that the coach can observe. Then the coach gives positive encouragement or tells the disciple how to improve. The disciples learned because Jesus' teachings were a part of life. Jesus taught truths again and again by various means that involved all of the senses. A disciple has learned a truth when it has become a part of the person's lifestyle.

A disciple has learned a truth when it has become a part of the person's lifestyle.

When I wanted to train my friend Bud to witness, I invited him to go with me and watch as I modeled witnessing. After watching me several times, he began to imitate what he saw me do. He did not imitate everything all at once but gradually learned various elements.

Modeling is important because motivation to witness is more caught than taught. Before we went to see a lost person, I explained what I was doing and told Bud what I expected the person to do and what I would do. Afterward, I explained what I did and why I changed what I had planned because the person did not respond as I had expected. Bud began to experiment on his own. I asked him to give his personal testimony at the point when I usually gave mine. I coached him, and he applied what he learned to different situations.

Think of a person who might coach you in the behavior or characteristic you are trying to incorporate into your life. Write this person's initials in the margin. Ask that person to coach you in that area of growth.

SUPPORTING

Support the person you are discipling as he or she demonstrates the desired behavior or characteristic. Barnabas supported Paul by accompanying him and teaching alongside him until Paul was fully mature in the faith. Likewise, Jesus supported His disciples by praying for them, teaching them, rebuking them when necessary, and allowing them to observe Him minister in various situations.

Support the person you are discipling as he or she demonstrates the desired behavior or characteristic.

WITNESSING FOR THE MASTER

You have been learning the Gospel in Hand presentation to use with lost persons. "How to Lead to Commitment," which follows, teaches you how to bring your witnessing to a conclusion.

HOW TO LEAD TO COMMITMENT

A presentation of the gospel is not complete unless hearers are challenged to accept Christ as Savior. Make a deliberate effort to lead the lost person to make that commitment.

Why Lead to Commitment?

1. *It is biblical.* Jesus gave this kind of invitation to individuals (see Matt. 4:19; 9:9; John 1:43-49).
2. *It is logical.* The good news of Jesus is an offer of salvation; forgiveness of sin; and eternal fellowship with God through the saving work of His Son, Jesus. This offer necessitates a decision by everyone who hears the message. If the witness does not encourage acceptance of Christ, the message is incomplete.
3. *It is practical.*
   a. The gospel and an invitation should not be confined to a church building. God intends for Christians to carry the gospel and an invitation to the world, not to wait for the world to come to a church building.
   b. Sharing the gospel without providing an opportunity for commitment frustrates those who hear the gospel. It can reinforce their habit of delaying this important decision and can further harden their hearts.
   c. By nature, people are slow to move spiritually. They need encouragement to respond to the offer of the gospel (see 2 Cor. 5:11 in the margin).

Leading to Commitment

Offering a person-to-person invitation should be considered care-

"Since, then, we know what it is to fear the Lord, we try to persuade men. What we are is plain to God, and I hope it is also plain to your conscience" (2 Cor. 5:11).

The witness must clearly explain exactly what the lost person must do to accept Christ as Savior.

fully. The witness should know exactly what he or she is going to say when asking for a commitment. The witness should even memorize the exact words to use. This may sound strict, but the moment in which a witness asks a person to accept Christ is often tense. Often, the witness is nervous, and the lost person knows that he or she is faced with a decision of eternal significance. The witness must clearly explain exactly what the lost person must do to accept Christ as Savior. Immediately after your gospel presentation, move into the appeal through these questions:

1. *Does this make sense to you?* This question tests the lost person's grasp of the gospel. It is also a transitional question that moves the discussion to the listener's response.
   a. If the response is yes, move to the next question.
   b. If the answer is no, quickly review the main points of the gospel presentation. As you proceed, ask, "Do you understand this point?" Negative responses like "I'm not sure" or "That is very complicated; I will have to think about it" could indicate a lack of interest, conviction, or understanding. Deal honestly with the question.

2. *Do you know any reason you would not be willing to receive God's free gift?* This negative commitment question addresses the lost person's willingness to receive God's offer of salvation. The question speaks to a person's will. In your gospel presentation you discuss accepting God's free gift, turning from sin, and placing faith in Jesus, so this question is not the first encounter the lost person has had with these phrases. Again, if the lost person has any questions or excuses at this point, deal with them honestly, openly, and positively.

Deal with questions or excuses honestly, openly, and positively.

3. *Are you willing to turn from your sin and to place your faith in Christ now?* This is a positive commitment question. If the lost person says yes, say: "Here is how to do it: We will pray. I'll pray first; then you pray when I've finished. Tell God in your own words what we've been talking about. Remember the three things you need to do to receive eternal life. Tell them to God like this:
   a. God, I am a sinner, and I've done wrong against You. I'm sorry, and I repent of my sin.
   b. I confess Your Son, Jesus Christ, as my Savior and Lord. I trust His sacrifice on the cross as payment for my sin.
   c. I receive Jesus Christ and Your gift of eternal life right now. Thank You for saving me. Amen.
   If you have trouble remembering these three things, I'll lead you in the prayer, and you can pray them after me."

Dealing with a Negative Response

The human decision-making process is often complex. The human mind often rationalizes to the point that a person does not understand all that is going on in his or her own mind. Sometimes a person says no to Christ, but the no actually covers a desire to say yes. In a situation like this, the witness must be extremely sensitive to the Holy Spirit's leadership. Often, the witness can help the lost person with the reasoning process. Perhaps you need to withdraw and use a different approach a few minutes later. For example, remind parents that their decision affects not only their lives but also their children's lives. Other appeals may be that Jesus gives a sense of purpose, that Jesus gives peace for deep inner conflict, or that Jesus helps resolve domestic conflicts.

Determine the extent of such second efforts according to the Holy Spirit's leadership. Never be insulting and never place your desire to have the person accept Christ above the lost person's integrity. But do not fail to ask for a decision. That extra urging may be what the lost person needs.

When you are convinced that the lost person's mind is determined not to accept Christ, the following steps may be helpful.

1. Have in your Bible a list of persons for whom you are praying. Turn to the list and say: "I believe that the time will soon come when you will want to accept Christ. I want you to know that I really care. Would you sign my prayer list? I promise that each time I review the names, I will pray that God will help you make this important decision."

2. Leave a gospel tract with the person and encourage him or her to read it carefully that night. Remind the person that he or she can accept Christ at any time in any place. Say: "If you accept Christ, please call me as soon as possible. My name, address, and phone number are recorded on this tract."

3. Close the visit with prayer. Thank God for the opportunity you have had. Express appreciation for the time the lost person has given you. Leave with a pleasant demeanor.[4]

 Explain "How to Lead to Commitment" to someone in your own words.

 Spend meaningful time with a family member doing something that person is interested in. If you do not have a family member nearby, choose a friend for this activity.

 Read Acts 26:1-23 during your quiet time today. Then complete the Daily Master Communication Guide in the margin.

DAILY MASTER COMMUNICATION GUIDE

ACTS 26:1-23

What God said to me:

_____

_____

_____

_____

_____

_____

_____

What I said to God:

_____

_____

_____

_____

_____

_____

_____

DAY 5

Someone to Cheer You On

Today you will study the last of five principles Jesus used to develop disciples.

> **PRINCIPLES OF DISCIPLING**
> 1. A discipler **models**; the disciple **imitates**.
> 2. A discipler **explains**; the disciple **experiments**.
> 3. A discipler **coaches**; the disciple **applies**.
> 4. A discipler **supports**; the disciple **demonstrates**.
> 5. A discipler **commissions**; the disciple **represents**.

The final principle is critical. The persons you disciple must believe that they have specific responsibilities as Christ's disciples, as well as someone to affirm and believe in them.

COMMISSIONING

One reason Christians do not perform the ministries God has given them is that they have not been commissioned. Persons who have been trained need an individual or a group to validate their ministries.

At this stage the person has mastered the skill or behavior to the degree that he or she represents that truth. This person is an example for others. At this stage the person models behaviors and characteristics for other disciples to imitate, beginning another cycle of discipling.

Read the Scriptures in the margin. In Acts 13:1-3 how did the church commission Barnabas and Saul?

_____

_____

In John 21:16-17 and Acts 1:8 how did Jesus commission Peter?

_____

The church commissioned Barnabas and Saul by affirming them, by pledging its support for the particular ministry to which they had been called, by fasting, and by praying. Jesus commissioned Peter by giving Him a particular task to do and by empowering him.

When you validate others' ministries, you make them aware that someone is standing on the sidelines serving as their cheering section and prayer warrior. You also become accountability partners with them—someone to whom they feel they need to answer for the quality and consistency of their ministries.

"In the church at Antioch there were prophets and teachers: Barnabas, Simon called Niger, Lucius of Cyrene, Manaen (who had been brought up with Herod the tetrarch) and Saul. While they were worshiping the Lord and fasting, the Holy Spirit said, 'Set apart for me Barnabas and Saul for the work to which I have called them.' So after they had fasted and prayed, they placed their hands on them and sent them off" (Acts 13:1-3).

"Jesus said, 'Simon son of John, do you truly love me?' He answered, 'Yes, Lord, you know that I love you.' Jesus said, 'Take care of my sheep.' The third time he said to him, 'Simon son of John, do you love me?' Peter was hurt because Jesus asked him the third time, 'Do you love me?' He said, 'Lord, you know all things; you know that I love you.' Jesus said, 'Feed my sheep' " (John 21:16-17).

" 'You will receive power when the Holy Spirit comes on you; and you will be my witnesses in Jerusalem, and in all Judea and Samaria, and to the ends of the earth' " (Acts 1:8).

To review, list the five principles Jesus used to develop disciples and a disciple's response to each.

1. _____

2. _____

3. _____

4. _____

5. _____

✝ Help someone you are discipling formulate a plan for spiritual growth. Review with this person the principles of discipling you have studied this week. Offer to serve as a mentor.

✝ This week's Scripture-memory verse, Luke 6:40, reminds you of the importance of training well. See if you can say the verse from memory. Write how this verse speaks to you personally in your role as a disciple maker.

_____

TRAINING IN MINISTRY

✝ You have learned the Gospel in Hand presentation. Try explaining the presentation to a lost person. You may want to invite someone who has modeled it to accompany you.

✝ Read Acts 13:1-12 during your quiet time today. Then complete the Daily Master Communication Guide in the margin.

HAS THIS WEEK MADE A DIFFERENCE?
Review "My Walk with the Master This Week" at the beginning of this week's material. Mark the activities you have finished by drawing vertical lines in the diamonds beside them. Finish any incomplete activities. Think about what you will say during your group session about your work on these activities.

---

[1]International Mission Board statistics.
[2]Ibid.
[3]Ibid.
[4]Adapted from *Continuing Witness Training* (Alpharetta, Ga.: The North American Mission Board of the Southern Baptist Convention). Used by permission.

DAILY MASTER COMMUNICATION GUIDE
ACTS 13:1-12

What God said to me:

_____

_____

_____

_____

_____

_____

_____

What I said to God:

_____

_____

_____

_____

_____

_____

_____

WEEK 5
Training Disciples

This Week's Goal
You will be able to help others develop as disciples of Christ.

My Walk with the Master This Week
You will complete the following activities to develop the six biblical disciplines. When you have completed each activity, draw a vertical line in the diamond beside it.

SPEND TIME WITH THE MASTER
◇ Have a quiet time each day. Check each day you have a quiet time: ❑ Sunday
❑ Monday ❑ Tuesday ❑ Wednesday ❑ Thursday ❑ Friday ❑ Saturday

LIVE IN THE WORD
◇ Read your Bible every day. Write what God says to you and what you say to God.
◇ Memorize 2 Chronicles 16:9.
◇ Review Luke 6:40, Matthew 5:23-24, Romans 6:23, and 1 Peter 2:2-3.

PRAY IN FAITH
◇ Pray each day for persons in different ministries.
◇ Pray for the persons you are discipling.
◇ Begin praying about the upcoming Spiritual-Gifts Workshop.

FELLOWSHIP WITH BELIEVERS
◇ Read "How to Conduct Family Worship."
◇ Conduct family worship with the members of your family who are willing. If you are single, have a quiet time with another person every day for one week.
◇ Pledge to support someone in your church.

WITNESS TO THE WORLD
◇ Share your faith with someone who is not a Christian.

MINISTER TO OTHERS
◇ Read "How to Model."
◇ Learn the traits of a disciple maker, as presented in MasterBuilder.
◇ Use "How to Prepare a Message from a Bible Study" to prepare a message outline based on a Sunday School lesson, a devotional, or a sermon.

This Week's Scripture-Memory Verse
"The eyes of the Lord range throughout the earth to strengthen those whose hearts are fully committed to him" (2 Chron. 16:9).

DAY 1

Model Dependence on Christ

One day I asked my grandmother, who was 89 at the time, how many descendants she had. "62," she answered quickly. In jest I asked, "My, how did you raise them all?" She answered: "I didn't raise them all, thank goodness. I just raised 6 of them." "What about the rest?" I asked. "Well, I helped some on the 19 grandchildren; I helped some on you. But I didn't do much on the 35 great-grandchildren or the 2 great-great-grandchildren. Their parents took care of them."

In these past few years her great-great-grandchildren have multiplied and are even producing great-great-great-grandchildren! It all started when my grandparents did a good job of rearing their children by passing on God's truths to them. This was also true of Timothy. Read about his heritage in 2 Timothy 1:5 in the margin.

Last week you learned how to develop as a spiritual disciple. Your next step on the path of spiritual growth is to become a disciple maker. In this week's study you will learn how to disciple others. At the end of this week you will be able to—

- state three principles for multiplying disciples;
- name your source of power for making disciples;
- list the tasks of a disciple maker;
- cite five resources for discipling others;
- explain two ways a disciple maker passes on truths to others;
- explain three ways a multiplying discipler can serve in difficult times and places.

THE NECESSITY OF DISCIPLING OTHERS

The heart of the Great Commission focuses on multiplying disciples. The only command in Matthew 28:19 is "make disciples." Going, baptizing, and teaching are parts of that command. You may be faithful to go, baptize, and teach, but if you do not make disciples who will teach others, your effectiveness will end with one generation.

You have studied principles Jesus used to train disciples so that you can do the same thing. You also need to know why it is important for you to disciple others.

The Scriptures in the margin give important reasons to train others as disciples. Match their references below with the reasons for discipleship that the verses mention.

_D_ 1. Matthew 5:1-2   a. Jesus commanded you to do so.

_B_ 2. 2 Timothy 2:2   b. Paul taught others by example and words.

_C_ 3. Acts 2:37-38   c. The disciples trained others.

_A_ 4. Matthew 28:19-20   d. Jesus taught His disciples.

"I have been reminded of your sincere faith, which first lived in your grandmother Lois and in your mother Eunice and, I am persuaded, now lives in you also" (2 Tim. 1:5).

"When he saw the crowds, he went up on a mountainside and sat down. His disciples came to him, and he began to teach them" (Matt. 5:1-2).

"The things you have heard me say in the presence of many witnesses entrust to reliable men who will also be qualified to teach others" (2 Tim. 2:2).

"When the people heard this, they were cut to the heart and said to Peter and the other apostles, 'Brothers, what shall we do?' Peter replied, 'Repent and be baptized, every one of you, in the name of Jesus Christ for the forgiveness of your sins. And you will receive the gift of the Holy Spirit' " (Acts 2:37-38).

" 'Go and make disciples of all nations, baptizing them in the name of the Father and of the Son and of the Holy Spirit, and teaching them to obey everything I have commanded you. And surely I am with you always, to the very end of the age' " (Matt. 28:19-20).

You need to train others to be disciples because Jesus made disciples and then commanded the disciples to do likewise. The disciples He made went on to become bold and to teach others. The New Testament is full of Paul's examples and teachings. The correct answer are 1. d, 2. b, 3. c, 4. a. In addition to these reasons, you become a better disciple when you try to teach others. As you prepare, explain, model, and encourage, your own faith is strengthened. Often you learn as much as or more than your student does.

You may believe that you are not ready to make disciples. If you have progressed this far in *MasterLife,* people are noticing the changes in your life. Some would like to have what you have.

BECOMING A MULTIPLIER

The principles of discipling you will study this week, based on 2 Timothy 2:1-3, in the margin, will provide you a way to multiply disciples instead of just adding members to your church who never grow in their faith:

> **PRINCIPLES FOR MULTIPLYING DISCIPLES**
> 1. **Be a good model of Jesus Christ.**
> 2. Entrust truths to reliable disciples.
> 3. Minister for Christ even in difficult times and places.

The secret that lies in these principles is one strategic way Christ plans for the gospel to be preached in the whole world before the end of the world. That secret is multiplication. If a disciple trains a disciple to train another disciple, and so on, the equation is changed from addition to multiplication. Instead of 1 plus 1 plus 1, 2 become 4, then 8, then 16, and so forth. If each number is doubled only 33 times, the total is more than 8,159,000,000! That is more than the world's present population.

If I witness faithfully but do not teach those I win to witness, I am in the 1-plus-1 mode. But if I teach each person to witness, to be a disciple, and to make disciples, I become a multiplier.

You will begin today with the first principle of multiplication, listed in bold type in the box above.

BE A GOOD MODEL OF JESUS CHRIST

Paul's first words in 2 Timothy 2 are "You then, my son." The word *then* refers to chapter 1, in which Paul gave examples of two ineffective disciples and one good one.

In 2 Timothy 1:13-16, in the margin, draw one line under the name of the effective disciple and two lines under the names of the ineffective ones.

In this passage Paul reminded Timothy that he himself was a model for the younger man, as was Onesiphorus, while Phygelus and

"You then, my son, be strong in the grace that is in Christ Jesus. And the things you have heard me say in the presence of many witnesses entrust to reliable men who will also be qualified to teach others. Endure hardship with us like a good soldier of Christ Jesus" (2 Tim. 2:1-3).

"What you heard from me, keep as the pattern of sound teaching with faith and love in Christ Jesus. Guard the good deposit that was entrusted to you—guard it with the help of the Holy Spirit who lives in us. You know that everyone in the province of Asia has deserted me, including Phygelus and Hermogenes. May the Lord show mercy to the household of Onesiphorus, because he often refreshed me and was not ashamed of my chains" (2 Tim. 1:13-16).

Hermogenes had deserted the cause. Few of us can live beyond our models. Paul pointed beyond himself to Christ, but he clearly stated that he had been a faithful model for Timothy to follow. Seeing a truth in action is necessary before you can imitate it. Being a good model is the single most important factor in multiplying disciples.

Who have been Christlike models in discipling you? List their names or initials here.

_____

_____

✝ **Some of the models you listed may serve the Lord in various ministries. Each day this week pray for persons in different ministries. Also pray for those who have been role models for you.**

Paul's first command to Timothy in chapter 2 was "be strong in the grace that is in Christ Jesus" (2 Tim. 2:1). "Be strong" is in the imperative mood; it is a command. It is in the passive voice; the strength does not originate with you but with Jesus Christ. It is in the present tense; it is a continuing reality. A good translation is "Keep on being made strong by the grace of Christ." Jesus said, " 'If a man remains in me and I in him, he will bear much fruit; apart from me you can do nothing' " (John 15:5).

What is the secret of being strong as a disciple?

_____

You can be a disciple only because of Christ's grace. The secret of a disciple's life is living in Christ and letting Him live through you to accomplish His will.

Read 2 Timothy 1:6-7 in the margin. How had God equipped Timothy?

_____

The gift of God is the Holy Spirit that lived in Timothy. Paul told Timothy to stir up the gift of God, which had been given to him when Paul had laid hands on him. In verse 7 he added that God did not give us a spirit of fear but of power, love, and self-control. Spirit-filled disciples can show more to the persons they are training than they can tell them.

Being a good model is the single most important factor in multiplying disciples.

"For this reason I remind you to fan into flame the gift of God, which is in you through the laying on of my hands. For God did not give us a spirit of timidity, but a spirit of power, of love and of self-discipline" (2 Tim. 1:6-7).

ON MISSION WITH THE MASTER

✝ Reread the MasterBuilder presentation on pages 123–27, with particular emphasis on the teachings about a disciple maker. By the end of this study you will be able to draw the MasterBuilder diagram and to explain it in your own words.

The Bible tells you several tasks a disciple maker does.

" 'I gave them the words you gave me and they accepted them. They knew with certainty that I came from you, and they believed that you sent me' " (John 17:8).

" 'I pray for them. I am not praying for the world, but for those you have given me, for they are yours' " (John 17:9).

" 'While I was with them, I protected them and kept them safe by that name you gave me. None has been lost except the one doomed to destruction so that Scripture would be fulfilled' " (John 17:12).

" 'My prayer is not for them alone. I pray also for those who will believe in me through their message' " (John 17:20).

"Jesus said, 'Simon son of John, do you truly love me?' 'Yes, Lord, you know that I love you.' Jesus said, 'Take care of my sheep' " (John 21:16).

Read the verses in the margin. Then match their references below with the statements that describe what a disciple maker does.

_D_ 1. John 17:8   a. Prays for them
_A_ 2. John 17:9   b. Takes care of them
_C_ 3. John 17:12   c. Protects them
_E_ 4. John 17:20   d. Gives God's words to them
_B_ 5. John 21:16   e. Prays for their disciples

These passages give numerous examples of how Christ equipped His disciples to be disciple makers. He was concerned not only with training these but also with equipping them to produce other disciples so that the gospel would continue to be proclaimed. The correct answers to the activity are 1. d, 2. a, 3. c, 4. e, 5. b.

✝ As you disciple other believers, are you fulfilling the five tasks you just studied? Pray and ask God to reveal ways you need to improve. Then pray for the persons you are discipling, as well as for those they will disciple.

✝ Read on page 84 this week's Scripture-memory verse, 2 Chronicles 16:9, which addresses the importance of having a heart that completely belongs to Christ. Why do you think this is important for a person who wants to be a disciple maker?

✝ Throughout your study of *MasterLife* you have been encouraged to maintain a daily quiet time by completing the Daily Master Communication Guide in each day's material. After this study you will want to continue practicing the discipline of spending time with the Master. I encourage you to keep a journal in which you record each day what God says to you and what you say to God. An excellent journal is *Day by Day in God's Kingdom: A Discipleship Journal*, which suggests Scriptures and memory verses and allows room for you to record what you experience in your quiet time.[1] For the remaining two weeks of your study, Daily Master Communication Guides will not be provided. Begin using a journal instead. Read 2 Timothy 1 during your quiet time today. Then record notes in your journal.

DAY 2

Resources for Discipling

Yesterday you learned the importance of modeling Jesus Christ and of depending on His power as you multiply disciples. Today you will learn five important resources to use in discipling others.

PRAYER

An essential resource for a disciple maker is prayer. In 2 Timothy 1:3, in the margin, Paul set the example by praying for Timothy night and day. The prayers of others join your prayers, giving your disciples strength.

Name those who are praying for you as you disciple others.

_____

"I thank God, whom I serve, as my forefathers did, with a clear conscience, as night and day I constantly remember you in my prayers" (2 Tim. 1:3).

WITNESSING

Live and give your testimony as you seek to multiply disciples. In 2 Timothy 1:8 Paul wrote of his own example of bearing witness to Christ. He entreated Timothy to follow that lead and not to be ashamed to testify of our Lord. The only way to produce soul-winners is to show them by example how to bear testimony in everyday life.

In 2 Timothy 1:8, in the margin, underline the source of your ability to bear witness.

 Share your faith with someone who is not a Christian. Take a friend with you who does not witness often and can benefit from hearing you share your testimony.

"Do not be ashamed to testify about our Lord, or ashamed of me his prisoner. But join with me in suffering for the gospel, by the power of God" (2 Tim. 1:8).

FELLOWSHIP

Be sure to make disciples in the context of the fellowship of believers. No disciple should have only one mentor. Besides Paul Timothy's mother and grandmother were his teachers and supporters, as well. When you neglect accountability to the body of Christ, you can easily become self-centered instead of following the way of the Spirit.

Check ways the fellowship of believers supports you.
❑ **Prays for me**
❑ **Encourages me to witness**
❑ **Helps equip me as I minister**
❑ **Holds me accountable for my spiritual growth**
❑ **Offers identity and support when the world buffets me**
❑ **Other:** _____

No disciple should have only one mentor.

Pledge to support someone in your church in one of the ways listed. Whom will you support? _____

How will you support this person or these persons?

_____

THE WORD

"What you heard from me, keep as the pattern of sound teaching, with faith and love in Christ Jesus. Guard the good deposit that was entrusted to you—guard it with the help of the Holy Spirit who lives in us" (2 Tim. 1:13-14).

In 2 Timothy 1:13-14, in the margin, Paul told Timothy to depend on the truths entrusted to him by the Holy Spirit. Everything a disciple does should be based on God's Word. Jesus said, " 'If you hold to my teaching, you are really my disciples' " (John 8:31). A disciple must spend time daily reading, studying, memorizing, meditating on, and applying God's Word.

In the last sentence in the previous paragraph, draw a star above the aspect of living in God's Word that you most need to work on.

MINISTRY

An effective disciple maker ministers to others. Put feet to your faith and serve those around you in need. Paul described Onesiphorus as such a servant. Read 2 Timothy 1:16-18 in the margin.

"May the Lord show mercy to the household of Onesiphorus, because he often refreshed me and was not ashamed of my chains. On the contrary, when he was in Rome, he searched hard for me until he found me. May the Lord grant that he will find mercy from the Lord on that day! You know very well in how many ways he helped me in Ephesus" (2 Tim. 1:16-18).

To be centered in Christ, a disciple must keep all of these disciplines in balance. You cannot teach what you do not practice. You probably recognized that the five resources you have studied from 2 Timothy correspond to five disciplines of the Disciple's Cross (see p. 122).

ON MISSION WITH THE MASTER

In day 1 you began learning tasks of a disciple maker, as illustrated in MasterBuilder. Today you will continue to learn how to make disciples. By the end of this study you will be able to draw the MasterBuilder diagram and to explain it in your own words.

Find and read the following verses. This time the verses are not printed in the margin so that you can practice using your Bible to find Scriptures. Match the references with the statements that present tasks of a disciple maker.

___ 1. Luke 6:40
___ 2. Colossians 1:28
___ 3. 1 Thessalonians 2:7
___ 4. 1 Thessalonians 2:8
___ 5. 1 Thessalonians 2:19
___ 6. 1 Thessalonians 3:1-3

a. Considers those discipled as hope, joy, and crown
b. Sends others to help
c. Trains them
d. Cares for them like a mother
e. Shares life with them
f. Seeks to present them perfect in Christ by proclaiming, admonishing, and teaching them

You can see from these verses that a disciple maker is intimately related to the one being discipled. When you share your life with someone and consider that person your hope, joy, and crown, you have a deep, abiding relationship with this person. Caring for someone like a mother hardly represents a casual acquaintance. Yet despite this deep affection, the disciple maker is willing to admonish when necessary. The answers are 1. c, 2. f, 3. d, 4. e, 5. a, 6. b.

Think about your involvement in discipling others. In the previous exercise check the reference of the Scripture that best describes you as a disciple maker. Draw a star beside one you need to work on.

 Read aloud this week's Scripture-memory verse, 2 Chronicles 16:9, on page 84 to begin memorizing it. Then review your memory verses from previous weeks.

 Read Luke 10:1-16 during your quiet time today. Then record notes in your journal.

DAY 3

Multiply Reproducing Disciples

John and Jerry Hilbun were middle-aged when they participated in their first *MasterLife* group. Over the next five years they discipled more than 30 persons in their small-town church. These persons discipled more than 100 others, who then multiplied to more than 200 by the time John and Jerry were appointed as missionaries to Barbados, where the chain reaction continues.

This week you are studying three principles for multiplying disciples. Today you will examine the second principle, which appears in bold type in the box below.

PRINCIPLES FOR MULTIPLYING DISCIPLES
1. Be a good model of Jesus Christ.
2. **Entrust truths to reliable disciples.**
3. Minister for Christ even in difficult times and places.

ENTRUST TRUTHS TO RELIABLE DISCIPLES
In 2 Timothy 2:2, in the margin, Paul told Timothy to pass on to others what he had heard Paul teach. Every truth you receive adds to your responsibility to pass on truth to others. In Matthew 25:26 Jesus called the servant who hid his talents wicked and lazy. What have you received

A disciple maker is intimately related to the one being discipled.

Every truth you receive adds to your responsibility to pass on truth to others.

"The things you have heard me say in the presence of many witnesses entrust to reliable men who will also be qualified to teach others" (2 Tim. 2:2).

from preachers, teachers, and nurturers? Pass it on. God holds you in debt to succeeding generations.

When I was first taught 2 Timothy 2:2, the person teaching me emphasized one-to-one discipleship. After studying the verse, I found that the opposite is true.

"The things you have heard me say in the presence of many witnesses entrust to reliable men who will also be qualified to teach others" (2 Tim. 2:2).

In 2 Timothy 2:2, in the margin, underline the words that refer to making disciples in a group.

Did you underline "in the presence of many witnesses," "men," and "others"?

Many years of experience have taught me that the best disciples are made in a group, as Jesus and Paul made disciples. That does not mean that they or you are not to spend time in one-to-one training but that they need more than one example to become balanced disciples.

Circle where the following did most of their discipling.

Jesus:	one-to-one	⟨group⟩
Peter:	one-to-one	⟨group⟩
Paul:	one-to-one	⟨group⟩

Jesus, Peter, and Paul did most of their discipling in groups.

Today you will study two ways to choose disciples:
1. Select faithful disciples.
2. Invest in able disciples.

SELECT FAITHFUL DISCIPLES

Paul chose well those he invited to follow him in his ministry. He refused to take John Mark a second time because this follower had deserted the missionary party earlier. Paul also witnessed the unfaithfulness of Phygellus and Hermogenes. He was concerned about faithfulness because he wanted every effort to count.

You may think that you have an unlimited amount of time to disciple those God has given you. However, you can make only so many disciples in a lifetime. Your effectiveness in discipling them will determine how much they multiply.

You can make only so many disciples in a lifetime.

Jesus said that disciples who are faithful in a few things would be given more responsibility but that if they were not faithful, they would lose what they had. The word *faithful* means *personal trust and reliance* or *trustworthy and reliable.* When you choose persons in whom to invest your life, do not be tempted to select those with the best personalities or with the most obvious gifts. Instead, choose those who are faithful.

 This week's Scripture-memory verse, 2 Chronicles 16:9, states that the Lord seeks people who are faithful. See if you can say this verse from memory.

Jesus did not select the disciples on a whim. God revealed them to Him. John 17:6, in the margin, says, " 'They were yours; you gave them to me.' " This verse also says that the disciples were faithful: " 'They have obeyed your word.' " Just as God gave the disciples to Jesus, He will entrust persons to you to disciple for Him. When God entrusts someone to you, He expects you to guard that trust and not to treat it casually.

INVEST IN ABLE DISCIPLES
Faithfulness is not the only characteristic to look for when you choose persons to disciple. Invest in able disciples. Paul says in 2 Timothy 2:2, "The things you have heard me say in the presence of many witnesses entrust to reliable men who will also be qualified to teach others." The word *entrust* means *to commit, deposit, or invest*. The best place to invest your resources is in persons—reliable, able persons. The word *able* means *competent* or *worthy*. Ability appears in unexpected persons, so earnestly pray for God's leadership. Jesus' original disciples did not look promising to anyone else. Be sure God leads you to the ones He gives you to disciple. Investing in persons who will be able to teach others is the only way to keep the chain of multiplication going.

If disciples are not faithful to pass on what has been committed to them, each generation will reproduce itself with more difficulty. Halfhearted disciples tend to pass on their halfheartedness, which produces diminishing returns. Invest your life in making disciples of faithful persons who will be able to teach others also.

ON MISSION WITH THE MASTER
In days 1 and 2 you learned tasks of a disciple maker. How do you keep a disciple moving along the path of spiritual growth as the MasterBuilder illustration shows? To nurture a disciple, both the disciple maker and the disciple have responsibilities.

List the tasks of a disciple maker and a disciple in the Disciple Maker stage of MasterBuilder. If you cannot recall them, review the MasterBuilder presentation on pages 123–27.

Disciple maker: _____

Disciple: _____

A disciple maker's task is to equip the disciple. This is an apprenticeship relationship in which the discipler is a spiritual mentor. The spiritual mentor trains the apprentice and equips this person to multiply disciples. You are moving toward a partnership with this person, as Barnabas and Paul as mentor and apprentice but later became colaborers. At the end of this stage the person is ready to help others become

" 'I have revealed you to those whom you gave me out of the world. They were yours; you gave them to me and they have obeyed your word' " (John 17:6).

Just as God gave the disciples to Jesus, He will entrust persons to you to disciple for Him.

The spiritual disciple moves from being concerned only about his or her own growth to being concerned about others' growth.

spiritual disciples. The spiritual disciple moves from being concerned only about his or her own growth to being concerned about others' growth.

The disciple's task, in response to being equipped, is to reproduce. The disciple establishes a mentoring relationship that equips another apprentice as a disciple maker.

MasterLife has equipped you to lead others as they become spiritual disciples. Are you willing to lead your own *MasterLife* group? ❏ Yes ❏ No Do you need a coleader to help you? ❏ Yes ❏ No

As you pray about whether to lead a *MasterLife* group, consider reading the introduction to *MasterLife Leader Guide* and viewing the videotaped presentation on how to be an effective group leader.

Write the names of persons God might want you to disciple, using *MasterLife*.

_____

Ask yourself about each: *Is this person faithful and able?*

 Pray for the disciples you are discipling and for those you could lead in a *MasterLife* group. Ask the Father to prepare you to mentor these persons so that they can reproduce.

 Read 2 Timothy 2 during your quiet time today. Then record notes in your journal.

DAY 4

Minister in Spite of Hardship

Wayne and Frances Fuller made Christ their first priority. As missionaries to Lebanon, Frances directed the publishing house, and Wayne managed the facilities. They were hurrying to translate and print *MasterLife* in time for joint training of Arabs and Jews who were to meet in Cyprus. In the middle of the process, fighting broke out. As the Fullers and others assembled notebooks, shells fell next to their building. Everyone ran to the basement, but Frances did not see Wayne. She went back upstairs and found him assembling notebooks. The Fullers served in hard times in hard places to multiply disciples.

Today you will study the final principle in 2 Timothy 2 for multiplying disciples. It appears in bold type in the box on the following page.

PRINCIPLES FOR MULTIPLYING DISCIPLES
1. Be a good model of Jesus Christ.
2. Entrust truths to reliable disciples.
3. **Minister for Christ even in difficult times and places.**

MINISTER FOR CHRIST EVEN IN DIFFICULT TIMES AND PLACES

Second Timothy 2:3 says, "Thou therefore endure hardness, as a good soldier of Jesus Christ" (KJV). By using the word *therefore*, Paul linked two key ideas: multiplying faithful, reproducing disciples and ministering in difficult times and places. With three illustrations Paul described three components of ministering in hardship:
1. Place first the priority of pleasing Christ.
2. Pay the price of purity to win the prize.
3. Persevere with patience until the harvest.
   You will study these three points today and tomorrow.

PLACE FIRST THE PRIORITY OF PLEASING CHRIST

Paul urged Timothy to "endure hardship with us like a good soldier of Christ Jesus" (2 Tim. 2:3). The word *hardship* originates from a word that means *a joint suffering*. From its root we get the word *pathos*. Since you fight evil, you are fighting a spiritual war and should expect to suffer. Paul told Timothy that he was in a battle against the world, the flesh, and the devil. You too are behind enemy lines.

In Paul's day a commander enlisted his own soldiers. The soldier, then, had one responsibility: to please his commander. A soldier in battle cannot question the chain of command, or everything will become chaos. The same is true if you question your Lord in times of hardship. Jesus must be the first priority. Family, possessions, or other purposes are secondary. Read Luke 14:26-27,33 in the margin.

Have you given up everything for Christ? Check the following areas that still have priority over Christ.
❑ **My job**
❑ **Obtaining material possessions**
❑ **Leisuretime interests**
❑ **Gaining the approval of family members**
❑ **Achieving an important role at church**
❑ **Other:** _____

Paul continued in 2 Timothy 2:4, "No man that warreth entangleth himself with the affairs of this life; that he may please him who hath chosen him to be a soldier" (KJV). The words translated "entangleth himself" means *to inweave oneself* or *to be involved in*. It is a picture of getting your feet entangled in a net just as the bugle sounds for battle. The soldier cannot afford to be involved in civilian matters on the day of bat-

" 'If anyone comes to me and does not hate his father and mother, his wife and children, his brothers and sisters—yes, even his own life—he cannot be my disciple. And anyone who does not carry his cross and follow me cannot be my disciple. In the same way, any of you who does not give up everything he has cannot be my disciple' " (Luke 14:26-27,33).

tle, or he cannot please his enlisting commander. The word *enlisted* is the same word translated "appointed" in John 15:16, in which Jesus said, " 'You did not choose me, but I chose you and appointed you to go and bear fruit—fruit that will last.' "

Examine your life and answer the following questions. Check the statements that apply to you.
❑ **I am entangled in the things of the world.**
❑ **Things of the world prevent me from making Christ my first priority.**
❑ **Things of the world keep me from making disciples.**

Examine the statements you checked. What would be necessary for you to get your priorities straight?

_____

_____

What would be necessary for you to get your priorities straight?

 What does this week's Scripture-memory verse, 2 Chronicles 16:9, say about keeping your priorities straight? Try to say the verse aloud from memory.

TRAINING IN MINISTRY

Much of what you do to equip disciples involves modeling. Read "How to Model," which follows, to learn how to model in a Christlike way.

HOW TO MODEL
Modeling follows a specific five-stage sequence.
1. *I do it whether or not anybody knows it.* If it is in my life and I do it because it is right, it makes no difference whether anyone else knows or sees.
2. *I do it, and you observe.* This is basically what Jesus did with the disciples at first. Initially, they were with Him to observe. Part of discipling involves merely letting persons into your life and taking them with you.
3. *You do it, and I observe you.* I give you an assignment, such as "This time when we're sharing Christ, why don't you give your testimony or quote this verse?" Then evaluate afterward.
4. *You do it and report.* I do not accompany you. I give you an assignment. You complete it and tell me what happened.
5. *You begin doing it whether or not anybody knows it.* It has now become a character trait as you are transformed into Christlikeness.

A SERVANT HEART

Part of modeling is having a servant heart. Read Matthew 23:8-11 in the margin.

The Kingdom way is the opposite of the world's way. You need to be a servant like Christ. Even though He had all of the titles and riches of heaven, He left them to become a servant.

 Spend time in prayer for the persons you are discipling. Ask the Lord to show you what you need to do to develop a servant heart as you model.

 Read Matthew 23:1-15 during your quiet time today. Then record notes in your journal.

" 'You are not to be called "Rabbi," for you have only one Master and you are all brothers. And do not call anyone on earth "father," for you have one Father, and he is in heaven. Nor are you to be called "teacher," for you have one Teacher, the Christ. The greatest among you will be your servant' " (Matt. 23:8-11).

PREPARING TO MINISTER

Ministering to your family is first and foremost before you prepare to minister to others. If having family worship is not a part of your family's life at this point, prayerfully consider establishing this practice as you read the following material.

 Read "How to Conduct Family Worship," which follows. Complete the activities as you read.

HOW TO CONDUCT FAMILY WORSHIP

Why should your family worship God in the home? Because the Lord commands it. Read Deuteronomy 6:6-9 in the margin.

Families who have faithfully honored God through worship in their homes have found that this practice has strengthened and enriched their home lives more than anything else.

A Leader

Successful family worship needs a leader or a sponsor who recognizes the value of this practice and is committed to faithfully maintaining it in spite of obstacles. If one member of the family makes the firm resolve "With God's help and the leadership of the Holy Spirit, I will lead my family to honor God through worship in my home," the battle is almost won.

Who should take the lead in family worship? Usually, the husband and father should accept this responsibility, since he is the natural spiritual leader of the home. Read Ephesians 6:4 in the margin.

However, worship in the home should not be neglected if the father is unwilling to accept this responsibility or is absent temporarily. The family member to whom God has revealed the need for worship should seek the other family members' commitment to the practice. Best results are obtained when every family member is enlisted to participate. The family member who is committed to

"These commandments that I give you today are to be upon your hearts. Impress them on your children. Talk about them when you sit at home and when you walk along the road, when you lie down and when you get up. Tie them as symbols on your hands and bind them on your foreheads. Write them on the doorframes of your houses and on your gates" (Deut. 6:6-9).

"Fathers, do not exasperate your children; instead, bring them up in the training and instruction of the Lord" (Eph. 6:4).

The family needs the discipline of an appointed time to meet God for worship in the home.

The Bible should be central in worship in the home.

family worship should serve as a sponsor, an encourager, or a facilitator and may not lead each family devotion. All family members from the youngest to the oldest should be encouraged to take turns leading the worship experience.

The person in my home who would likely initiate family worship:

_____

A Time
An established time for worship is as important for a family as for a congregation. The family needs the discipline of an appointed time to meet God for worship in the home.

The best time for worship varies with different families. Some families begin each day with worship. For other families early morning may be the worst time. Many families worship before or after a mealtime. Each family should find a time for worship that fits its routine. Once this time is agreed on, the family should be committed to reserving this time to meet God in worship.

The time I am considering for family worship: _____

A Place
Just as most congregations build a church as a place for worship, a family needs a place to worship in the home. Select a place where the family is least likely to be interrupted by the telephone, television, visitors, and other distractions. Once this place is selected, place resources for worship there for ready use.

The place I am considering for family worship: _____

Worship Resources
The Bible should be central in worship in the home. Many families find a modern-language translation of the Bible helpful, particularly with children. Bible-study aids, such as a concordance, a commentary, a dictionary, and an atlas, are also useful but are not essential. Many families choose to use a devotional book or magazine in family worship.[2]

Resources my family can use in family worship:

_____

A Method
Begin with the Word. Someone reads aloud a selected passage from the Bible. Then the passage may be discussed, with one or more

members saying what the passage means. If a devotional book or magazine is used, the passage suggested for each day and the accompanying comment on the passage may be read aloud.

Follow the Bible discussion with a time of sharing. This may be a testimony by a family member about an experience with God or the sharing of a helpful Bible passage. The family may wish to sing together or to listen to religious music.

Close with prayer. Special prayer requests may be mentioned. One member may lead in prayer, or each member may pray briefly.

A method I am considering for family worship:

_____

_____

Follow the Bible discussion with a time of sharing.

 Conduct family worship with the members of your family who are willing. If you are single, have a quiet time with another person every day for one week.

DAY 5

Purity and Perseverance

When I visited Kenya once, missionary Allan Stigney said to me: "Tell me about the persons you are discipling. Then I will know more about you than you can tell me about yourself." Allan's words, which carry significant implications for reproducing disciples, have rung in my ears ever since. The proof is not only that your disciples last but also that they have Christ's character and that they multiply other disciples. If your disciples are standing still and doing nothing with the truth you impart to them, either your discipling was inadequate or your life did not model your teaching.

Yesterday you began studying the necessity of multiplying disciples in difficult times and places. You have already studied the first point below:
1. Place first the priority of pleasing Christ.
2. Pay the price of purity to win the prize.
3. Persevere with patience until the harvest.

Today you will focus on the second and third points Paul made about this subject in 2 Timothy.

PAY THE PRICE OF PURITY TO WIN THE PRIZE
Playing by the Lord's rules is necessary for a person who is called to

"Tell me about the persons you are discipling. Then I will know more about you than you can tell me about yourself."

"If anyone competes as an athlete, he does not receive the victor's crown unless he competes according to the rules" (2 Tim. 2:5).

multiply disciples. Read in the margin what 2 Timothy 2:5 says about this. This verse refers to a specific contest, not just to an event. A nation's athletic team does not go to the Olympics in general; it competes in specific events. Most of your failures are not in general but in specific contests. It is in the particular event that you must be careful not to cut corners or break rules. Paul admonished His readers to serve the Lord with their whole hearts rather than pursue secondary goals.

Can you recall a time when a misstep negatively affected your witness for Christ? Check any of these you have done:
❑ **I spoke in anger in front of impressionable children.**
❑ **I made remarks that were not Christlike.**
❑ **I spent too much time at work instead of with my family.**
❑ **I failed to keep the sabbath day holy.**
❑ **I laughed at an off-color joke in the presence of others who were looking to me as an example.**
❑ **Other:** _____

People pay more attention to what you do than to what you say. Serving Christ during difficult times and places requires conducting yourself in a way that is above reproach so that others will know your heart is completely His.

This week's Scripture-memory verse, 2 Chronicles 16:9, says that the Lord recognizes those who are pure in heart. Say the verse from memory to your prayer partner or to a family member.

PERSEVERE WITH PATIENCE UNTIL THE HARVEST
In 2 Timothy 2:6 Paul used the analogy of a farmer: "The hard-working farmer should be the first to receive a share of the crops." Being a farmer requires perseverance. Not only must you wait for the crop to grow, but you must also keep fertilizing it, cultivating it, and removing weeds. But if you continue, you will reap the harvest.

When I planted things as a child, I dug them up the next day to see if they were growing! Do not expect a disciple you nurture to mature too quickly. You cannot evaluate how much progress is being made in discipleship while the crop is still young.

Do not expect a disciple you nurture to mature too quickly.

Giving up too quickly and becoming frustrated because your efforts do not seem to bear fruit are dangers disciple makers must avoid. Even Jesus did not see instant results; He persevered and saw eternal results. If you model the life of a disciple by being strong in the grace of Jesus Christ and by persevering, you can multiply disciples.

Check the following commitments you are willing to make.
❑ **I will invest my life in faithful disciples who are able to teach others.**

❑ I will endure hardship and will make multiplying disciples my first priority to please my Commander.
❑ I will compete according to the rules.
❑ I will persevere until the crop matures.

If you checked any of the statements, you will be the first one to enjoy the rewards. You can multiply disciples and rejoice in the harvest.

TRAINING IN MINISTRY
One discipling skill you can develop for God's use is bringing a devotional or delivering a message. The following instructions will help you communicate what God shows you through His Word.

✝ Select a Bible study or a Scripture passage and develop the outline for a message. As you follow the instructions below, write your plans on a separate sheet of paper.

One discipling skill you can develop for God's use is bringing a devotional or delivering a message.

HOW TO PREPARE A MESSAGE BASED ON A BIBLE STUDY

Have you ever noticed how difficult it is to communicate to others what you have felt or discovered in a personal Bible study? The reason is that if others are studying with you, they are involved and are communicating on the same wavelength. But when you are trying to convey the same ideas in a devotional, speech, sermon, or lecture, others pay less attention, usually because they are not involved or because the study is not presented in terms of their needs and interests. Therefore, when you present a message based on a Bible study, it is important to follow a different procedure for presenting it than you did for studying it.

Key Idea
1. Select one main idea from the Scripture passage or summarize the passage in one sentence that focuses on the main idea.
2. Write the idea as simply and as concisely as possible.

Objective
1. State your objective in terms of what listeners will be able to understand, do, or feel at the conclusion of your message.
2. Write this objective in a precise and personal form. Example: I want my listeners to seek reconciliation with a person with whom they have a problem.

Title
1. Choose a title that describes what you will talk about. Avoid catchy titles that do not describe your content.
2. Use a title that will interest listeners—something they would like to know more about.

State your objective in terms of what listeners will be able to understand, do, or feel at the conclusion of your message.

The outline usually grows from the Scripture passage.

3. Most titles should be limited to from three to five key words.
4. Although a title is not mandatory, it helps focus the message for listeners and helps you relate the outline to the key idea.

Outline

1. The outline usually grows from the Scripture passage. Write the way the biblical writer divided or developed what he said.
2. The outline should consist of parts of the key idea, explanations of it, or questions about it.
3. You may use as many or as few points as you need. You usually do not need many subpoints if you take this functional approach:
   a. Explain what the Bible says about the point.
   b. Illustrate it.
   c. Apply it.

Presentation

1. **Introduction**
   a. *Ho-hum* is listeners' attitude until you get their attention. You can catch their interest in one of several ways:
      • A startling statement
      • An interesting illustration
      • A striking question
      • Something the person is already interested in
   b. *Why bring that up?* is the question on the mind of the person whose interest you have caught. Present the need or ask the question your message is to answer. Make the case for the need as strong as possible. Convince the listener that you are going to say something worth listening to.

2. **Body of the message**
   a. *How does it work?* is the question in listeners' minds after you have told them that you have an answer to the need. Your explanation should show God's answer. You may present your outline with explanations, illustrations, and applications. Or you could eliminate the outline and make the answer one point that you explain, illustrate, and apply.
   b. *For example?* is the question in listeners' minds each time you explain a point or a principle. Illustrations are the windows that let light into listeners' minds. Even though you have several other illustrations, you should have one that helps listeners visualize what will happen if your message is applied in real life.

3. **Conclusion**
   a. *So what?* is listeners' response after you have presented your message. What do you want them to do about it?
   b. Spell out the action steps that need to be taken, based on the Scripture passage.

Present the need or ask the question your message is to answer.

c. Challenge listeners to apply the key idea of your message to their lives. Speak directly to their wills by asking, "Will you do this?" instead of appealing to guilt by asking, "Shouldn't you do this?" Encourage them to do it. Describe others who have done so and the results they had. Ask for personal commitments.

Evaluation

When you have prepared your message, evaluate how listeners will respond to it by considering their projected thoughts, listed in the margin.

As you speak, listeners think:
1. **Ho-hum**
2. **Why bring that up?**
3. **How does it work?**
4. **For example?**
5. **So what?**

At the end of this study you will attend a Spiritual-Gifts Workshop, which will help you identify your gifts and focus on areas in which you can minister. Begin praying for your experience at this workshop. Pray that God will show you the ministry He wants you to be involved in.

 Read 2 Timothy 4 during your quiet time today. Then record notes in your journal.

HAS THIS WEEK MADE A DIFFERENCE?

Review "My Walk with the Master This Week" at the beginning of this week's material. Mark the activities you have finished by drawing vertical lines in the diamonds beside them. Finish any incomplete activities. Think about what you will say during your group session about your work on these activities.

I hope that this week's study of "Training Disciples" has caused you to think about the persons you are discipling and to ask yourself if you are truly reproducing multiplying disciples.

Evaluate your discipling by asking yourself these questions:
❑ **Am I modeling dependence on Christ?**
❑ **Am I multiplying faithful and able disciples?**
❑ **Am I ministering in difficult times and places?**

---

[1] *Day by Day in God's Kingdom: A Discipleship Journal* (item 0-7673-2577-X) is available from the Customer Service Center; 127 Ninth Avenue, North; Nashville, TN 37234; 1-800-458-2772; and from Baptist Book Stores and Lifeway Christian Stores.
[2] *Open Windows* is a daily-devotional magazine available from the Customer Service Center; 127 Ninth Avenue, North; Nashville, TN 37234; 1-800-458-2772.

WEEK 6

Ministering as Colaborers

This Week's Goal

You will be able to work with colaborers as a disciple-making team on mission with God.

My Walk with the Master This Week

You will complete the following activities to develop the six biblical disciplines. When you have completed each activity, draw a vertical line in the diamond beside it.

SPEND TIME WITH THE MASTER
◇ Have a quiet time each day. Check each day you have a quiet time: ❑ Sunday ❑ Monday ❑ Tuesday ❑ Wednesday ❑ Thursday ❑ Friday ❑ Saturday

LIVE IN THE WORD
◇ Read your Bible every day. Write what God says to you and what you say to God.
◇ Memorize Matthew 28:19-20.
◇ Review Luke 6:40, Matthew 5:23-24, Romans 6:23, 1 Peter 2:2-3, and 2 Chronicles 16:9.

PRAY IN FAITH
◇ Pray that God will help you find the area of ministry He wants for you.
◇ Pray about leading a *MasterLife* group.
◇ Plan a half-day prayer retreat.

FELLOWSHIP WITH BELIEVERS
◇ Enlist one or more accountability partners.

WITNESS TO THE WORLD
◇ Read "How Shall They Hear?"
◇ Examine a world map and pray for the world.
◇ Witness to someone, using the Gospel in Hand presentation.

MINISTER TO OTHERS
◇ Learn the traits of a colaborer, as presented in MasterBuilder.
◇ Read "An Adventure in Ministry."
◇ Complete the Spiritual-Gifts Inventory.
◇ Meet with your *MasterLife* leader to discuss your plans for further discipleship.

This Week's Scripture-Memory Verses

" 'Go and make disciples of all nations, baptizing them in the name of the Father and of the Son and of the Holy Spirit, and teaching them to obey everything I have commanded you. And surely I am with you always, to the very end of the age' " (Matt. 28:19-20).

DAY 1

Gifts of God's Grace

When I was a missionary in Indonesia, I began to disciple a seminary student named Youtie. Youtie started pastoring a small house church, teaching the members everything I taught him. Many of them were former Communists who had been Christians for only six months or less, but they soon wore out their Bibles because Youtie diligently discipled them. Soon the members added a room to the church to accommodate more members and started Bible studies in the 10 areas around the house church. When Youtie's group had grown numerically and spiritually, it built a fine brick church in Semarang.

Later Youtie became a missionary to Kalimantan (Borneo). He and the five families who went with him started 25 churches and baptized more than two thousand people in two years.

Youtie is not my disciple. He is the Lord's disciple. I discipled him to deepen his relationship with the living Lord. Youtie went beyond being a disciple and a disciple maker. He became a colaborer in ministry, leading teams of disciple makers to go on mission with God.

The last stage on the path of spiritual growth is becoming a colaborer in ministry. In addition to making disciples, as you learned to do last week, you must learn to work with others in ministry as a disciple-making team. This week's study explains how believers are equipped to serve God. At the end of this week you will be able to—
- define *spiritual gifts;*
- explain how spiritual gifts are used in ministry;
- recognize the differences among spiritual gifts, the fruit of the Spirit, and talents;
- name your spiritual gifts;
- identify a ministry to which you are being called;
- make plans for further discipleship.

WHAT ARE SPIRITUAL GIFTS?
Read 1 Corinthians 12:4-14 in your Bible. Again, the passage is not printed in the margin so that you can practice finding and reading Scriptures on your own.

In verse 4 the word *gifts* is a translation of the Greek word *charismata,* which means *gifts of grace.* It refers to gifts based on the love of the giver, not on the merit of the ones who receive them.

Read Romans 12:6 in the margin. What did Paul say is the basis for receiving spiritual gifts?
❑ God's needs   ❑ God's requirements   ☒ God's grace

Youtie became a colaborer in ministry, leading teams of disciple makers to go on mission with God.

"We have different gifts, according to the grace given us" (Rom. 12:6).

"If a man's gift is prophesying, let him use it in proportion to his faith. If it is serving, let him serve; if it is teaching, let him teach; if it is encouraging, let him encourage; if it is contributing to the needs of others, let him give generously; if it is leadership, let him govern diligently; if it is showing mercy, let him do it cheerfully" (Rom. 12:6-8).

"To one there is given through the Spirit the message of wisdom, to another the message of knowledge by means of the same Spirit, to another faith by the same Spirit, to another gifts of healing by that one Spirit, to another miraculous powers, to another prophecy, to another distinguishing between spirits, to another speaking in different kinds of tongues, and to still another the interpretation of tongues" (1 Cor. 12:8-10).

"In the church God has appointed first of all apostles, second prophets, third teachers, then workers of miracles, also those having gifts of healing, those able to help others, those with gifts of administration, and those speaking in different kinds of tongues" (1 Cor. 12: 28-30).

"It was he who gave some to be apostles, some to be prophets, some to be evangelists, and some to be pastors and teachers" (Eph. 4:11).

You can see from this verse that spiritual gifts are rooted in God's grace. Grace is what God has done for you in Christ that you do not deserve. Just as you are saved by God's grace, you are also given spiritual gifts by God's grace. He gives you spiritual gifts because He wants you to be equipped for His service.

> Spiritual gifts are spiritual abilities given to believers by the Holy Spirit to equip them to carry out God's work in the world.

Read the verses in the margin and 1 Peter 4:11 in the margin on page 107. Beside each reference below write the number of spiritual gifts the passage mentions.

____ 1. Romans 12:6-8
____ 2. 1 Corinthians 12:8-10
____ 3. 1 Corinthians 12:28-30
____ 4. Ephesians 4:11
____ 5. 1 Peter 4:11

The number and names of spiritual gifts vary in each list. You probably answered 1. 7, 2. 9, 3. 8, 4. 5, 5. 2.

Define *spiritual gifts* by using the following key words: *abilities, believers, equip, God's work, world.*

_____

_____

Check your definition against the one in the box on this page.

GIFTS AND FRUIT
Spiritual gifts differ from spiritual fruit. The fruit of the Spirit, which you studied in *MasterLife 2: The Disciple's Personality*, is listed in Galatians 5:22-23.

Write *gifts* over the column describing spiritual gifts and *fruit* over the column describing the fruit of the Spirit.

_____	_____
Relate to service	Relates to character
Are the means to an end	Is an end
What a person has	What a person is
Given from without	Is produced from within
All are not possessed by every believer.	Every variety should be in every believer.

I hope you answered that the column on the left lists characteristics of spiritual gifts and that the column on the right lists traits of the fruit of the Spirit. Possessing spiritual gifts does not indicate the goodness of a person's life or character. Although the Corinthians excelled in gifts, the church was riddled with problems like envy, carnality, and discord.

Read 1 Corinthians 12:29-30 in the margin. Check the implied answer to Paul's question: ❑ Yes ❑ No

Although no Christian is expected to possess all spiritual gifts, every Christian should seek to develop and exhibit all of the fruit of the Spirit. These Christlike qualities are to characterize your life, while spiritual gifts enable you to serve God with your life. Spiritual fruit represents the kind of person you are to be, while spiritual gifts emphasize what you are equipped to do.

Circle the fruit of the Spirit and underline the spiritual gifts.
To love / To preach ²To be kind ³To have peace
To heal ⁴To have joy To help ⁵To be faithful

You should have circled *to love, to be kind, to have peace, to have joy, to be faithful* and underlined *to preach, to heal, to help.*

 The areas of ministry mentioned in Matthew 28:19-20, this week's Scripture-memory verses, are witnessing to others and making disciples—tasks expected of everyone. Read these verses aloud from your Bible several times to begin memorizing them.

Every day this week, review all of the verses you have memorized during this study.

ON MISSION WITH THE MASTER

Reread MasterBuilder on pages 123–27, with particular emphasis on the teachings about a colaborer in ministry. By the end of this study you will be able to draw the MasterBuilder diagram and to explain it in your own words.

First Corinthians 3:8-9 recognizes the work of a colaborer. Read those verses in the margin.
This passage indicates that we are all fellow workers with God. It describes a shared ministry. For God's kingdom to grow, all believers must witness and serve—lay members as well as ministerial staff.
Jesus taught His disciples the concept of a shared ministry. Read Mark 3:13-15 in the margin.
Paul also described working alongside colaborers and his gratitude for them. Read Romans 16:1-4 in the margin on the following page.

"If anyone speaks, he should do it as one speaking the very words of God. If anyone serves, he should do it with the strength God provides, so that in all things God may be praised through Jesus Christ" (1 Pet. 4:11).

"Are all apostles? Are all prophets? Are all teachers? Do all work miracles? Do all have gifts of healing? Do all speak in tongues? Do all interpret?" (1 Cor. 12:29-30).

"The man who plants and the man who waters have one purpose, and each will be rewarded according to his own labor. For we are God's fellow workers; you are God's field, God's building" (1 Cor. 3:8-9).

"Jesus went up on a mountainside and called to him those he wanted, and they came to him. He appointed twelve—designating them apostles—that they might be with him and that he might send them out to preach and to have authority to drive out demons" (Mark 3:13-15).

"I commend to you our sister Phoebe, a servant of the church in Cenchrea. I ask you to receive her in the Lord in a way worthy of the saints and to give her any help she may need from you, for she has been a great help to many people, including me. Greet Priscilla and Aquila, my fellow workers in Christ Jesus. They have risked their lives for me. Not only I but all the churches of the Gentiles are grateful to them" (Rom. 16: 1-4).

Based on the verses you read, check the statements that are true about colaborers.
❏ **A discipler feels superior to colaborers.**
❏ **Colaborers exercise authority over team members.**
❏ **Jesus utilized the disciples only to keep Him company.**
❏ **A colaborer may have to suffer for the cause of Christ.**

A feeling of equality characterizes the relationship among colaborers. Even if the relationship is that of disciple and discipler, no feeling of superiority exists. Colaborers are capable of performing the same tasks and have full authority to minister. No colaborer autocratically leads the team. Although the disciples were with Jesus as He ministered, He also sent them out to preach and heal. However, a colaborer may endure persecution. The only true statement in the activity is the last one.

Ask God to begin putting on your heart the names of persons you could commission to be colaborers. Maybe some of the persons you are discipling are ready to be colaborers in ministry.

 Read 1 Corinthians 12 during your quiet time today. Then record notes in your journal.

DAY 2

One Body, Many Members

You receive your talents when you are born physically. You receive your spiritual gifts when you are born again spiritually.

Yesterday you learned that spiritual gifts differ from the fruit of the Spirit. Spiritual gifts also differ from talents. You receive your talents when you are born physically. You receive your spiritual gifts when you are born again spiritually. Christians and non-Christians possess talents. A gift is a spiritual ability that only Christians possess. For example, faith is a gift; the ability to sing is a talent. Talents are natural abilities; gifts are spiritual abilities. Talents depend on natural instincts; gifts, on spiritual endowment. Talents inspire or entertain; gifts are used to build up the church.

Although talents and spiritual gifts are not the same, both are God-given. Recognizing this fact, Christians should develop their talents fully and should use them in God's service. You may be able to use a talent with a gift. For example, the gift of encouragement or evangelism may be exercised through the medium of music.

Write *G*, *F*, or *T* beside each statement on the following page to indicate whether it describes a spiritual gift, a fruit, or a talent, respectively.

_____ 1. Spiritual abilities
_____ 2. Natural abilities
_____ 3. Spiritual qualities
_____ 4. Given to believers to equip them for service
_____ 5. Can all be attained by yielding to the Spirit

Check your work to see if you answered 1. G, 2. T, 3. F, 4. G, 5. F.

HOW SPIRITUAL GIFTS ARE GIVEN

Every believer has been given at least one spiritual gift. Read 1 Peter 4:10 and 1 Corinthians 12:7 in the margin. In God's family of grace everyone is important. If you look down on yourself as being unable to do anything significant for the Lord, you are not being humble. You are undiscerning and perhaps ungrateful. Therefore, a Christian should never say, "I'm a nobody." Instead, say: "I am a child of God. I have received spiritual gifts. Therefore, I will exercise my gifts in ministry."

"Each one should use whatever gift he has received to serve others, faithfully administering God's grace in its various forms" (1 Pet. 4:10).

"To each one the manifestation of the Spirit is given for the common good" (1 Cor. 12:7).

Read 1 Corinthians 12:11 in the margin. Explain how spiritual gifts are distributed.

_____

"All these are the work of one and the same Spirit, and he gives them to each one, just as he determines" (1 Cor. 12:11).

You cannot choose the spiritual gifts you prefer. God distributes them as He thinks best. The gifts of the Spirit are just that—gifts. Because you do not earn them or work for them, you have no grounds for bragging about your gifts.

Read 1 Corinthians 12:17-20 in the margin. What conclusion did Paul draw?

_____

Paul concluded that there are many members but one body and that all members need one another. Each part of the body exists to serve the whole, and God knows how each part can be used best. He gives you spiritual gifts that enable you to help the body of Christ operate effectively and efficiently.

"If the whole body were an eye, where would the sense of hearing be? If the whole body were an ear, where would the sense of smell be? But in fact God has arranged the parts in the body, every one of them, just as he wanted them to be. If they were all one part, where would the body be? As it is, there are many parts, but one body" (1 Cor. 12:17-20).

Reread Romans 12:6-8; 1 Corinthians 12:8-10,28-30; Ephesians 4:11; and 1 Peter 4:11, which you read in the margins on pages 106–7. Then list what you think your gifts are.

_____

At the Spiritual-Gifts Workshop that follows this study, you and your group members will help one another discover and confirm your gifts.

Plan a half-day prayer retreat to follow this study. You need to plan a retreat each month to pray about God's plan for your life. Record the date you select: _____.

ON MISSION WITH THE MASTER

In day 1 you began learning traits of a colaborer in ministry, as illustrated in MasterBuilder. Today you will continue to learn how to be a colaborer. By the end of this study you will be able to draw the MasterBuilder diagram and to explain it in your own words.

 Read Acts 6:2-4 in the margin, which describes traits of a colaborer in ministry. Then check the statements below that describe what colaborers do.

❑ Colaborers consult together.
❑ Colaborers pray together.
❑ Colaborers minister in the Word together.
❑ Colaborers serve together.
❑ Colaborers compete to see who is most important.

"The Twelve gathered all the disciples together and said, 'It would not be right for us to neglect the ministry of the word of God in order to wait on tables. Brothers, choose seven men from among you who are known to be full of the Spirit and wisdom. We will turn this responsibility over to them and will give our attention to prayer and the ministry of the word' " (Acts 6:2-4).

Colaborers work together in harmony. Only the last statement is not a trait of a spiritual colaborer.

 Continue to memorize this week's Scripture-memory verses, Matthew 28:19-20. See if you can write them in the margin from memory.

Read Acts 15 during your quiet time today. Then record notes in your journal.

DAY 3

Building Up the Body of Christ

Every believer should know his or her gifts and should allow the Holy Spirit to develop them. But what is the purpose of spiritual gifts?

"Since you are eager to have spiritual gifts, try to excel in gifts that build up the church" (1 Cor. 14:12).

First Corinthians 14:12 states how to use your spiritual gifts. Read the verse in the margin and check the correct answer.
❑ To rule over others ❑ To build up the church ❑ To gain prestige

Spiritual gifts are to enhance the body of Christ or to make it stronger. God says that you are to use your spiritual gifts in ministry, not to earn others' admiration or to gain status. Using spiritual gifts improperly displeases God and shows ingratitude for the gifts He has given you.

PREPARING GOD'S PEOPLE
The concept of building up the body of Christ appears again in Ephesians 4:11-13.

Read Ephesians 4:11-13 in the margin. Who is to do the work of ministry and to build up the body of Christ?

_____

God's people are to build up the body of Christ. The equippers in this verse, who are to prepare God's people, are apostles, prophets, evangelists, pastors, and teachers. They are to equip all believers to do the work of ministry.

What is the standard for maturity in Ephesians 4:11-13?

_____

We are to attain to the whole measure the fullness of Christ. He wants His gifts to be used to help His body grow internally and in out-reach to others.

HOW ARE YOU USING YOUR GIFTS?
The parable of the talents in Matthew 25:14-30 uses financial invest-ments to teach that you will be held responsible for the way you use your gifts. In the day of judgment you will not be praised for your wealth, your possessions, or your fame. You will be praised if you can properly respond to the question "Did you faithfully use the gifts I gave you?"

How would you respond if God asked you at this moment the question you just read? Explain your answer.

_____

First Peter 4:10 says, "Each one should use whatever gift he has received to serve others, faithfully administering God's grace in its vari-ous forms." Use your gifts to serve others.

This week's Scripture-memory verses, Matthew 28:19-20, name special ways you are commanded to use your spiritu-al gifts. Say the verses from memory to your prayer partner or a friend. Share with that person what you believe the verses command you to do.

"It was he who gave some to be apostles, some to be prophets, some to be evangelists, and some to be pastors and teachers, to prepare God's people for works of service, so that the body of Christ may be built up until we all reach unity in the faith and in the knowledge of the Son of God and become mature, attaining to the whole measure of the fullness of Christ" (Eph. 4:11-13).

Use your gifts to serve others.

" 'God so loved the world that he gave his one and only Son, that whoever believes in him shall not perish but have eternal life' " (John 3:16).

"He is the atoning sacrifice for our sins, and not only for ours but also for the sins of the whole world" (1 John 2:2).

"You then, my son, be strong in the grace that is in Christ Jesus. And the things you have heard me say in the presence of many witnesses entrust to reliable men who will also be qualified to teach others. Endure hardship with us like a good soldier of Christ Jesus" (2 Tim. 2:1-3).

"How great is the love the Father has lavished on us, that we should be called children of God! And that is what we are! The reason the world does not know us is that it did not know him" (1 John 3:1).

" 'Go and make disciples of all nations, baptizing them in the name of the Father and of the Son and of the Holy Spirit, and teaching them to obey everything I have commanded you. And surely I am with you always, to the very end of the age' " (Matt. 28:19-20).

" 'You will receive power when the Holy Spirit comes on you; and you will be my witnesses in Jerusalem, and in all Judea and Samaria, and to the ends of the earth' " (Acts 1:8).

ON MISSION WITH THE MASTER

In days 1 and 2 you learned traits of a colaborer. How do you keep a disciple moving along the path of spiritual growth as the MasterBuilder illustration shows? To encourage a disciple to be a colaborer, both the discipler and the disciple have responsibilities.

 List the tasks of a discipler and a disciple in the Colaborer in Ministry stage of MasterBuilder. If you cannot recall them, review the MasterBuilder presentation on pages 123–27.

Discipler: _____   Disciple: _____

The discipler's task with the disciple is to commission for ministry, with the goal being Kingdom growth. The relationship is a partnership with others who are involved in Kingdom growth. After the disciple has identified a ministry in which he or she wants to work, commission the disciple to perform that ministry.

The disciple's task is to multiply, using the gifts God has given. The discipler encourages, helps, and strengthens. The discipler's responsibility has decreased, while the disciple's has increased.

Stop and pray that you will become an effective colaborer. Ask the Father to help you find the area of ministry He wants for you and that He will bless others through you.

WITNESSING FOR THE MASTER

Read "How Shall They Hear?" which follows.

HOW SHALL THEY HEAR?

There are approximately 4 billion non-Christians in the world, 1.68 billion of whom have never heard of Christ, do not have the Bible in their languages, and have never known a Christian. Why are we Christians not reaching these people?

- It is not because God does not love every person (see John 3:16 in the margin).
- It is not because Christ did not die for every person (see 1 John 2:2 in the margin).
- It is not because God does not want every person to be saved (see 2 Tim. 2:1-3 in the margin).
- It is not because God did not save us (see 1 John 3:1 in the margin).
- It is not because Jesus did not command us to make disciples of all nations (see Matt. 28:19-20 in the margin).
- It is not because God did not empower us (see Acts 1:8 in the margin).

Christ commanded His disciples to make disciples of all nations. If each of us does our part, we can reach them. How?

1. Each of us must center his or her *life purpose* in God's purpose (see 2 Pet. 3:9 in the margin). What is on God's heart—the world—should also be at the center of your life purpose (see John 3:16). God wants His people to fulfill His purpose to be obedient, servant priests to the nations (see Ex. 19:5-6 and 1 Pet. 2:9-10 in the margin).

2. Each of us must set *life goals* in line with God's goal (see Matt. 28:19-20). God's goal for you is to "make disciples of all nations." Your life goals should involve being all God wants you to be and doing all God wants you to do. You may want to join thousands of Christians who are involved in short-term, long-term, or career-missionary efforts. However, your life goal has more to do with being a missionary at heart than with your geographical location.

3. We must adjust our *lifestyles* to use all of our possessions in the best way for the greatest good of the largest number of people. The average American makes more money in one week than the average person in many countries makes in one year. God has not blessed us with riches so that we can hoard them or use them all for ourselves.

4. Each of us must use the *lifeline of prayer* to intercede for the world (see Luke 10:2 in the margin). We need to present the world's needs to God and to bring God's message to the world. Through prayer we can reach millions who live in countries where traditional missionaries are not allowed to serve. God's plan for reaching the world depends on His power. What is impossible with human beings is possible with God.

If you make God's purpose your life purpose, God's goal your life goal, God's lifestyle of giving your lifestyle, and God's lifeline of prayer your daily link to Him and the world, you will have done your part to ensure that the lost hear the good news of Jesus.

Evaluate your role in reaching the world for Christ. Underline the number that represents your present position in each area, with 5 being highest. Then circle the number of the level to which you are willing for God to lead you.

Life purpose:	1	2	3	4	5
Life goals:	1	2	3	4	5
Lifestyle:	1	2	3	4	5
Lifeline of prayer:	1	2	3	4	5

"The Lord is not slow in keeping his promise, as some understand slowness. He is patient with you, not wanting anyone to perish, but everyone to come to repentance" (2 Pet. 3:9).

" ' "If you obey me fully and keep my covenant, then out of all nations you will be my treasured possession. Although the whole earth is mine, you will be for me a kingdom of priests and a holy nation" ' " (Ex. 19:5-6).

"You are a chosen people, a royal priesthood, a holy nation, a people belonging to God, that you may declare the praises of him who called you out of darkness into his wonderful light. Once you were not a people, but now you are the people of God; once you had not received mercy, but now you have received mercy" (1 Pet. 2:9-10).

" 'The harvest is plentiful, but the workers are few. Ask the Lord of the harvest, therefore, to send out workers into his harvest field' " (Luke 10:2).

 Examine a world map and pray for the world. Use the one on page 137 in *MasterLife 1: The Disciple's Cross* if you wish.

Witness to someone this week, using the Gospel in Hand presentation. If you wish, take a *MasterLife* group member with you for support or assistance.

 Read Matthew 25:14-30, the parable of the talents, during your quiet time today. Then record notes in your journal.

DAY 4

Ministering with Others

Believers should function as a unit, aware of other members of the body and concerned about their well-being. God's purpose in giving different gifts to believers is to bind all Christians into one interdependent body. In this way everybody can minister to someone.

DEVELOPING YOUR GIFT
Read 2 Timothy 1:6 in the margin. What did Paul tell Timothy to do about developing his gift?

_____

"For this reason I remind you to fan into flame the gift of God, which is in you through the laying on of my hands" (2 Tim. 1:6).

Paul told Timothy to stir up and use his gift as a pastor and teacher.

Unfortunately, spiritual gifts can be misused and even counterfeited. Read 1 John 4:1 and 1 Corinthians 12:1-4 in the margin. You are warned to test the spirits and not to be ignorant about Satan's influences. Satan does not act by himself. Evil spirits carry out his work. They deceive God's people by leading them to believe that the Holy Spirit is inspiring a teacher or a preacher when the message comes from the devil. But you are not to ignore the Holy Spirit and His gifts just because some persons abuse or misuse their gifts.

"Dear friends, do not believe every spirit, but test the spirits to see whether they are from God, because many false prophets have gone out into the world" (1 John 4:1).

"About spiritual gifts, brothers, I do not want you to be ignorant. You know that when you were pagans, somehow or other you were influenced and led astray to mute idols. Therefore I tell you that no one who is speaking by the Spirit of God says, 'Jesus be cursed,' and no one can say, 'Jesus is Lord,' except by the Holy Spirit" (1 Cor. 12:1-4).

According to 1 Corinthians 14:1, in the margin, what should be present in the life of a person who uses his or her spiritual gifts wisely? Circle the correct answer.
     power   fame   love   intelligence

Paul positioned his teachings about love, 1 Corinthians 13, in the middle of his long discourse on spiritual gifts (1 Cor. 12—14). Without love the gifts of the Spirit are a sounding gong, a clanging cymbal, and nothing (see 1 Cor. 13:1-3). Believers are to be filled with love and the other fruit of the Spirit. Paul wrote 1 Corinthians to a church that was arguing about which gifts are best. He called love "the most excellent way," superior to the exercise of any gift (see 1 Cor. 12:31).

"Follow the way of love and eagerly desire spiritual gifts" (1 Cor. 14:1).

Underline the proper test of a Spirit-filled life:
Ability to preach   **Speaking in tongues**   **Fruit of the Spirit**

A church filled with believers who exercise their spiritual gifts in a loving way will be characterized by unity. Read Ephesians 4:16 and 1 Corinthians 12:24-26 in the margin.

Describe in your own words how you can help bring about this unity in the body of Christ.

_____

PREPARING TO MINISTER

✝ **Read "An Adventure in Ministry," which follows, to learn how to make plans for ministering to others.**

"From him the whole body, joined and held together by every supporting ligament, grows and builds itself up in love, as each part does its work" (Eph. 4:16).

"God has combined the members of the body and has given greater honor to the parts that lacked it, so that there should be no division in the body, but that its parts should have equal concern for each other. If one part suffers, every part suffers with it; if one part is honored, every part rejoices with it" (1 Cor. 12:24-26).

AN ADVENTURE IN MINISTRY

The Biblical Basis of Your Ministry

1. *Every believer is a minister and has a ministry to perform.* The New Testament word translated *minister* comes from the Greek word *diakonos*. The root word, *diakonia*, means *the office and work of a servant*. It referred to domestic duties or religious functions. The person who performed these duties was called a minister or a servant. All Christians are to be servant ministers. The priesthood of believers is a biblical teaching that we are all equal before God, we all have direct access to the Father, and we all have a responsibility to minister to others in Christ's name (see Ex. 19:5-6; Isa. 61:4-6; 1 Pet. 2:9; Rev. 1:6).

2. *Every believer was called to ministry when he or she was called to follow Christ* (see Matt. 4:19; Luke 14:26-27; 1 Cor. 1:26-29; Eph. 1:18; 2 Thess. 1:11; 2 Tim. 1:9). We are to be chosen people who are priests to the nations and who show forth the praises of His glory (see 1 Pet. 2:9).

3. *Every believer has one or more spiritual gifts that enable him or her to minister* (see Rom. 12:4-6; 1 Cor. 12:7; Eph. 4:7; 1 Pet. 4:10-11). One way to discover your ministry is to discover the spiritual gifts God has given to you for ministry. Spiritual gifts are discovered as you study the Bible, as you serve or minister, and as the church confirms your gifts.

4. *Every believer should be equipped to do the work of ministry.* Ephesians 4:11-12 says that Christ has endowed the church with apostles, prophets, evangelists, pastors, and teachers to equip believers for their ministries. Although all believers are ministers, God has given some of them the responsibility of equipping the others. The word translated *to perfect* or *to equip* means *to put a*

Every believer was called to ministry when he or she was called to follow Christ.

Equippers are to prepare all believers to minister.

person in a right place or condition, to restore, to educate, to train, to guide, or *to prepare a person to do a task.* Equippers are to prepare all believers to minister.

The Process of Personal Development in Ministry
Because believers have been called to minister, they need to—
1. discover their spiritual gifts;
2. discover avenues of ministry;
3. train to perform their ministries for Christ in His power;
4. be commissioned as colaborers in ministry.

You can explore the ministries of serving, teaching/preaching, evangelism, nurture, and worship/intercession by using the procedure described below. The Spiritual-Gifts Workshop that follows this study will help you discover your spiritual gifts and focus on an area of ministry for which you have been gifted.

The Procedure for Exploring a Ministry
After choosing an area of ministry you want to be involved in, follow these instructions to explore the ministry.
1. *Ministry.* Write the name of the ministry you want to examine. Study it for a week.
2. *Biblical basis.* Make notes as you complete a Bible study of the ministry. Write what the passage teaches about the ministry and add insights from parallel passages and other persons' comments. Bible studies of the ministry areas on the Disciple's Cross are included in the Life Helps section of *Disciple's Study Bible.*[1]
3. *Practical application.* Write several applications of the biblical insights in a modern setting. Listing examples of how the ministry is being done today will give you choices of ways to get involved in that ministry.
4. *Personal application.* Explore the ministry area to discover whether God wants you to specialize in it. Choose to take one or more of the following actions.
   a. Observe someone who is doing the ministry. Write what you have learned or how you feel about it.
   b. Do something in the ministry area. Help someone who needs that ministry. Assist someone who is doing that ministry. Choose a partner and perform the ministry action together.
   c. Research the ministry. Talk to persons who are involved in it. Read an article or a book about it. View a movie or a videotape or listen to an audiotape about it. Write what you have learned and/or report it to someone.
5. *Verification.* Write a way you and/or someone else could know that you have completed the ministry action. You may also write the results of the ministry action in your life or in others' lives. A statement of verification helps you be more specific in writing your plans for ministry.

Explore the ministry area to discover whether God wants you to specialize in it.

As you consider how you will use your spiritual gifts, pray about leading a *MasterLife* group.

Read Ephesians 4:1-16, describing the use of spiritual gifts in the body of Christ, during your quiet time today. Then record notes in your journal.

DAY 5

Using Your Gifts

Now that you have examined what spiritual gifts are and are not, learn how you can discover and use your gifts for God's glory. Today you will learn six ways to gain awareness of your gifts:

1. Believe that you are gifted.
2. Pray.
3. Discover your gifts.
4. Accept responsibility for using your gifts.
5. Consider your desires.
6. Accept the confirmation of others.

God desires to reveal your spiritual gifts to you.

BELIEVE THAT YOU ARE GIFTED
Spiritual gifts are not special rewards for the spiritual elite. Spiritual gifts are given to every believer.

Do you have difficulty believing that you are gifted? ❑ Yes ❑ No If so, review the teachings about spiritual gifts in this week's material and read in the margins the Scriptures you have studied about spiritual gifts. Ask for the Holy Spirit to reveal the truth about your giftedness through this review.

PRAY
God desires to reveal your spiritual gifts to you.

In James 4:2, in the margin, underline two words that indicate what you need to do for God to make you aware of your gifts.

"You do not have, because you do not ask God" (Jas. 4:2).

If you want to be aware of your spiritual gifts, *ask God* to show you what spiritual gifts He has given you. God delights in answering prayers that are prayed according to His purposes.

DISCOVER YOUR GIFTS
It is important for a ministering colaborer to know the gifts he or she has received from the Holy Spirit.

"If a man's gift is prophesying, let him use it in proportion to his faith. If it is serving, let him serve; if it is teaching, let him teach; if it is encouraging, let him encourage; if it is contributing to the needs of others, let him give generously; if it is leadership, let him govern diligently; if it is showing mercy, let him do it cheerfully" (Rom. 12:6-8).

"To one there is given through the Spirit the message of wisdom, to another the message of knowledge by means of the same Spirit, to another faith by the same Spirit, to another gifts of healing by that one Spirit, to another miraculous powers, to another prophecy, to another distinguishing between spirits, to another speaking in different kinds of tongues, and to still another the interpretation of tongues" (1 Cor. 12:8-10).

"In the church God has appointed first of all apostles, second prophets, third teachers, then workers of miracles, also those having gifts of healing, those able to help others, those with gifts of administration, and those speaking in different kinds of tongues. Are all apostles? Are all prophets? Are all teachers? Do all work miracles? Do all have gifts of healing? Do all speak in tongues? Do all interpret? But early desire the greater gifts" (1 Cor. 12:28-30).

Complete the Spiritual-Gifts Inventory on pages 138–41 in preparation for the Spiritual-Gifts Workshop that will follow this study. Score your inventory and read the definitions of spiritual gifts on page 142 to understand the gifts you possess. After attending the workshop, you should know your primary spiritual gifts and should be ready to exercise them in ministry.

Study the Bible passages in the margin, which list spiritual gifts. If you discovered any of these gifts when you completed the Spiritual-Gifts Inventory, underline them and be sensitive to evidence of them in your life.

ACCEPT RESPONSIBILITY FOR USING YOUR GIFTS

Many commands in the New Testament operate in the area of spiritual gifts. In addition, everyone is commanded to evangelize, show mercy, encourage, give, and help, whether or not you possess those gifts. As you obey in these areas, the Holy Spirit may unveil certain gifts you were not aware of.

This week's Scripture-memory verses, Matthew 28:19-20, command us to go and make disciples, regardless of the gifts we have. Check your memorization of the verses by saying them aloud from one to three times.

CONSIDER YOUR DESIRES

What do you enjoy doing? To what are you drawn? What seems to come naturally to you? Your enjoyment of or desire for a gift may be God's way of showing you that you possess that gift.

Apply these questions to yourself:

What do you enjoy doing? _____

_____

To what are you drawn? _____

_____

What comes naturally to you? _____

_____

ACCEPT THE CONFIRMATION OF OTHERS

Others may see a gift in you long before you are aware of it.

In what areas do people ask for your help? _____

_____

What have you done in the past for which you were genuinely complimented?

_____

Many Christians live in spiritual poverty, unaware of their spiritual gifts. When gifts lie unused and neglected, potential for Christian ministry is wasted. Unwrap your gifts and dedicate them to the ministries God has given you. When you discern a gift in a fellow believer, encourage that person to develop the gift.

> Read 2 Corinthians 4 during your quiet time today. Then record notes in your journal.

TRAINING IN MINISTRY

Even though your study of *MasterLife* is drawing to a close, you will want to continue growing as a disciple of Jesus Christ. Ask a church-staff member or your *MasterLife* group leader about additional discipleship-training opportunities in your church.[2]

The following areas of discipleship are listed under the disciplines of the Disciple's Cross. Check the subjects in which you feel that you need to grow. Feel free to list other areas in the margin.

Spend Time with the Master
❑ Knowing God's will
❑ The mind of Christ
❑ Living in the Spirit

Pray in Faith
❑ How to develop a prayer life
❑ How to conduct a prayer ministry

Witness to the World
❑ Witnessing through relationships
❑ Counseling new believers

Live in the Word
❑ Survey of the Old Testament
❑ Survey of the New Testament
❑ Foundational Christian doctrines

Fellowship with Believers
❑ Parenting skills
❑ Strengthening marriage

Minister to Others
❑ Counseling persons with problems
❑ Making peace with a painful past
❑ Grief recovery
❑ Divorce recovery

When gifts lie unused and neglected, potential for Christian ministry is wasted.

Discuss your plans for further discipleship.

✝ Arrange a meeting with your *MasterLife* leader to discuss your experience in *MasterLife* and your plans for further discipleship. Be prepared to share your responses to the following.

1. In what ways have you grown spiritually during *MasterLife?*
2. In which stage of development are you in MasterBuilder?
3. On what areas of growth do you want to work in the future? Refer to the Discipleship Inventory on pages 133–37.
4. What ministry do you feel that God wants you to do?
   • What are your spiritual gifts? Refer to the Spiritual-Gifts Inventory on pages 138–41.
   • What ministries have you performed in the past through which God has blessed others?
   • What do you feel that God is calling you to do?
   • What subjects of study would equip you to perform this ministry better? See the list in the previous activity.
   • What actions should you take now to gain more experience in that ministry?
5. How do you plan to disciple others?

Enlist one or more accountability partners.

Throughout *MasterLife* you have had a group of fellow disciples to hold you accountable for growth and ministry. Enlist one or more accountability partners who will help you remain disciplined after this study has ended. Decide the extent to which you want these persons to keep track of your progress in discipleship growth and establish a process of accountability with them.

HAS THIS WEEK MADE A DIFFERENCE?
Review "My Walk with the Master This Week" at the beginning of this week's material. Mark the activities you have finished by drawing vertical lines in the diamonds beside them. Finish any incomplete activities. Think about what you will say during your group session about your work on these activities.

I hope that through this study of "Ministering as Colaborers" you have learned how disciples are equipped and commissioned to do the work of the Kingdom. Be sure to complete your experience with *MasterLife 4: The Disciple's Mission* by attending the Spiritual-Gifts Workshop that will follow this study. You will gain a fuller understanding of your spiritual gifts and of the ministry God has for you.

To conclude *MasterLife,* read this stirring statement of what it means to be a disciple. It was written by a young African pastor.

I'm part of the fellowship of the unashamed. I have Holy Spirit power. The die has been cast. I have stepped over the line. The decision has been made. I'm a disciple of His. I won't look back, let up, slow down, back away, or be still.

My past is redeemed, my present makes sense, my future is secure. I'm finished and done with low living, sight walking, small planning, smooth knees, colorless dreams, tamed visions, mundane talking, cheap living, and dwarfed goals.

I no longer need preeminence, prosperity, position, promotions, plaudits, or popularity. I don't have to be right, first, tops, recognized, praised, regarded, or rewarded. I now live by faith, lean on His presence, walk by patience, lift by prayer, and labor by power.

My face is set, my gait is fast, my goal is heaven, my road is narrow, my way is rough, my companions are few, my Guide is reliable, my mission is clear. I cannot be bought, compromised, detoured, lured away, turned back, deluded, or delayed. I will not flinch in the face of sacrifice, hesitate in the presence of the adversary, negotiate at the table of the enemy, ponder at the pool of popularity, or meander in the maze of mediocrity.

I won't give up, shut up, let up, until I have stayed up, stored up, prayed up, paid up, and preached up for the cause of Christ. I am a disciple of Jesus. I must go till He comes, give till I drop, preach till all know, and work till He stops me. And when He comes for His own, He will have no problem recognizing me—my banner will be clear.

"I now live by faith, lean on His presence, walk by patience, lift by prayer, and labor by power."

Are you totally committed to Jesus, as this pastor described? When He comes for His own, will He recognize you as His disciple because your banner will be clear?

Are you totally committed to Jesus?

If you can answer yes to the two previous questions, stop and tell Jesus the way you feel about your discipleship and what you pray He will accomplish through you.

Congratulations on completing *MasterLife*. May God bless you as you continue to pursue a lifelong, obedient relationship with your Master.

---

[1]*Disciple's Study Bible* is available from the Customer Service Center; 127 Ninth Avenue, North; Nashville, TN 37234; 1-800-458-2772; and from Baptist Book Stores and Lifeway Christian Stores.
[2]For a brochure of available discipleship courses, write to the Adult Discipleship and Family Department, MSN 151; 127 Ninth Avenue, North; Nashville, TN 37234-0151.

The Disciple's Cross

The Disciple's Cross provides an instrument for visualizing and understanding your opportunities and responsibilities as a disciple of Christ. It depicts the six biblical disciplines of a balanced Christian life. *MasterLife 1: The Disciple's Cross* interprets the biblical meanings of the disciplines and illustrates in detail how to draw and present the Disciple's Cross.

Because *MasterLife 4: The Disciple's Mission* refers to elements of the Disciple's Cross and your weekly work includes assignments related to the six disciplines, a brief overview of the Disciple's Cross is provided here.

As a disciple of Jesus Christ, you have—

1 Lord as the first priority of your life;

2 relationships: a vertical relationship with God and horizontal relationships with others;

3 commitments: deny self, take up your cross daily, and follow Christ;

4 resources to center your life in Christ: the Word, prayer, fellowship, and witness;

5 ministries that grow from the four resources: teaching/preaching, worship/intercession, nurture, evangelism, and service;

6 disciplines of a disciple: spend time with the Master, live in the Word, pray in faith, fellowship with believers, witness to the world, and minister to others. By practicing these biblical principles, you can abide in Christ and can be useful in the Master's service.

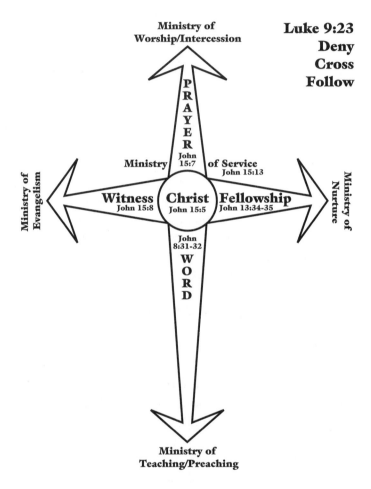

Luke 9:23
Deny
Cross
Follow

Ministry of
Worship/Intercession

PRAYER
John 15:7

Ministry of Service
John 15:13

Ministry of Evangelism

Witness
John 15:8

Christ
John 15:5

Fellowship
John 13:34-35

Ministry of Nurture

John 8:31-32
WORD

Ministry of
Teaching/Preaching

MasterBuilder

Anyone can see the number of apples on a tree, but not many people can see the number of trees in an apple. You can be one of the few who can look beyond persons' outer appearance to discern their ultimate potential for becoming disciple makers and colaborers in ministry. Jesus saw beyond the shifting sands of Simon and called him Peter, the rock. Barnabas saw beyond the quitter, John Mark, and dedicated his ministry to developing the future writer of the Gospel of Mark. You too can become a MasterBuilder who helps disciples make disciples who can minister together as colaborers.

A disciple's mission is to glorify God just as Jesus glorified Him (see John 17:1-4). You can glorify God by becoming a disciple of Jesus Christ and by making disciples who are like Him. In Mark 3:14-15 Jesus said that he appointed the twelve so that they would be with Him. They spent the next three years learning to be His disciples. The verses go on to say that Jesus' purpose was then to send them forth to preach and to cast out demons—that is, to do His mission. When He calls you, He knows not only what you will become but also how you will be able to help others become His disciples. What God has done in your life, He can do in others' lives through you. Therefore, Jesus said that His Great Commission is for us to make disciples of all nations (see Matt. 28:19-20).

I will explain a picture of the discipling process called MasterBuilder. This presentation overviews the stages of development in a disciple's life, describes what happens in each stage, and outlines ways a discipler enables disciples to become what Christ wants them to be.

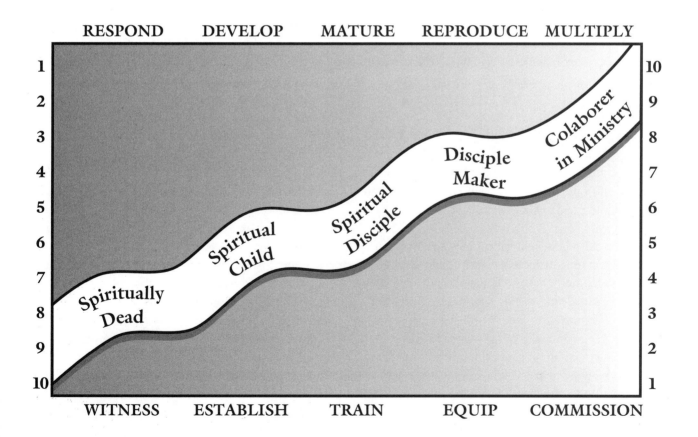

THE PATH OF SPIRITUAL GROWTH

The path shown in the diagram represents your life-long spiritual growth. Notice that the path goes up and down because spiritual growth is not a consistently upward process. In some periods you grow fast, and in others you seem to plateau. However, a disciple should have a distinctively upward growth trend. The words at the bottom of the diagram name the tasks of a discipler. The words at the top name the tasks of a disciple in response to a discipler's actions.

We can identify five stages of spiritual growth. First, people are **spiritually dead** in their sins and do not know Christ. Spiritually dead persons cannot respond to Christ except as the Holy Spirit draws them. When the Spirit of God convicts persons and they repent, call on Jesus, and are saved, they become **spiritual children.** Spiritual children have many of the same traits as physical children. As they grow, they become **spiritual disciples.** As spiritual disciples mature, they become **disciple makers,** helping others in the same growth process. As disciple makers continue to develop, they finally become **colaborers in ministry** with other spiritual disciples, who continue to reach the lost and make disciples. The mission, then, is to develop disciples as Jesus did, who will make disciples of all nations.

As you consider this process, determine your stage of spiritual development. Also decide how you can help others develop at each stage of spiritual growth.

JESUS' EXAMPLE

Paul wrote: "By the grace God has given me, I laid a foundation as an expert builder, and someone else is building on it. But each one should be careful how he builds. For no one can lay any foundation other than the one already laid, which is Jesus Christ" (1 Cor. 3:10-11).

Jesus' model of discipling illustrates the work of a MasterBuilder. Jesus helped his disciples grow at each stage of development. When He first called them, they were **spiritually dead,** so His task was to witness to them. Jesus witnessed to what the Father was saying and doing. He continually bore witness to the Father in everything He taught and did. He said in John 14:10: " 'The words I say to you are not just my own. Rather, it is the Father, living in me, who is doing his work.' "

You are to do what Jesus did: witness to what Christ has done and to what God is doing in your life. Take every opportunity to glorify God and to emphasize that He is always working and that you are joining Him in His work.

Notice in the disciple's tasks at the top of the diagram that a spiritually dead person must respond to the discipler's task of witnessing. The Bible teaches that the response depends on the condition of the heart. The one who witnesses does not determine the response. The more often people hear others witness of Christ, the more likely they are to respond.

When spiritually dead persons respond to Christ, turning from their sins and asking Him to come into their lives, they are born again and become His **spiritual children.** After the disciples started following Jesus, He began to establish them in the faith and in relationship to the Father and to one another. However, as spiritual children, the disciples often showed childlike characteristics. They argued about who would be first in the kingdom of God. They showed their anger at a Samaritan village that did not receive Jesus, threatening to call down fire from heaven. They acted impulsively and made many mistakes. However, Jesus continued to nurture them so that He could present them to the Father. Jesus prayed in John 17:6: " 'I have revealed you to those whom you gave me out of the world. They were yours: you gave them to me and they have obeyed your word.' " Jesus helped these spiritual children grow.

Jesus wants you to establish spiritual children in the disciplines of the Christian life until they become **spiritual disciples.** Use the disciplines of the Disciple's Cross to help spiritual children begin to develop. When you train persons, you usually have to do something more than once. Jesus continually had to teach the disciples and to correct them until they finally understood.

The next stage is that of **disciple maker.** Jesus expects His disciples to bear fruit in the form of other disciples. A MasterBuilder's task is to equip disciples to make disciples. Equipping goes beyond training. When you equip persons, they understand concepts and skills so well that they can adjust to any situation and can complete a task. This is what Jesus did with His disciples. After He had ascended to heaven, the Holy Spirit worked in the disciples' lives to help them remember His teachings, with which they could train others.

A disciple maker should be equipped to reproduce. God manifested Himself in Jesus not just to reveal Himself to the world but so that Jesus might be the first of many sons (see Rom. 8:29). Jesus spent three years with the twelve not only for their benefit but also so that they would make disciples of all nations. Jesus equips you through discipleship not only for your sake but also so that He can produce disciples through you.

In the next stage the MasterBuilder commissions disciples as **colaborers in ministry.** When Jesus called the disciples to follow Him, He said that He wanted them to be with Him. When He had finished discipling them, He told them to go make disciples of all nations and that He would be with them. The disciples then became colaborers in ministry with Him. God intended for all nations of the world to be blessed through the disciples. As colaborers in ministry, they became a team, continuing to multiply disciples throughout the Book of Acts.

THE DISCIPLES' EXAMPLE

The disciples also followed the MasterBuilder process in the Book of Acts. First, they bore witness to **spiritually dead** persons who had killed the Lord Jesus (see Acts 2:23). They said they must witness in Jesus' name even if it meant going to prison. They testified that they had seen Him, had known Him, and had experienced Him. In response more than three thousand people came to Christ at Pentecost.

The disciples immediately began to establish **spiritual children**. They did the same things Jesus had done with them:

> *They devoted themselves to the apostles' teaching and to the fellowship, to the breaking of bread and to prayer. Everyone was filled with awe. … Every day they continued to meet together in the temple courts. They broke bread in their homes and ate together with glad and sincere hearts, praising God and enjoying the favor of all the people. And the Lord added to their number those who were being saved (Acts 2:42-47).*

The thousands of people who responded began to develop into **spiritual disciples** as the disciples continued to train them. In Acts 6:3 seven believers who were "known to be full of the Spirit and wisdom" were selected for ministry. The disciples continued to equip the believers until they became **disciple makers.** In Acts 8 Philip, one of the seven, went to Samaria and proclaimed the gospel to the Samaritans. Then the Holy Spirit took him to the desert to witness to the Ethiopian eunuch. When persecution came, Acts 8:4 says that "those who had been scattered preached the word wherever they went." The disciples who were scattered abroad felt commissioned as **colaborers in ministry** and began to multiply throughout the known world.

PAUL'S EXAMPLE

Paul persecuted the church until his life-changing experience on the road to Damascus, when this **spiritually dead** person responded to Christ. God sent Ananias to help Paul understand what had happened and to begin establishing him as a **spiritual child.** Paul developed quickly and began witnessing and preaching. He went to Jerusalem, where Barnabas began to establish him more fully in the faith. Then Paul went to Arabia for three years, where the Lord trained and equipped him. After he matured in the faith and became a **spiritual disciple,** he went back to Tarsus and began to make disciples.

About 10 years later, Barnabas was called to go to Antioch to help many Gentile Christians who had come to faith in Christ. Remembering Paul, Barnabas traveled the 120 miles to Tarsus to find him. He brought Paul back to Antioch, and he and Paul taught the new Christians there for one year. Barnabas was training and equipping Paul to be a **disciple maker.** As they reproduced disciples, God blessed their ministry and called them to take the gospel to the nations. The church at Antioch commissioned them to take the gospel to those who had not heard. They went as **colaborers in ministry** to multiply disciples.

Paul continued to follow this same process of developing spiritual disciple makers and colaborers in ministry. One person who came to Christ was a young man named Timothy, who began to develop, mature, and reproduce as Paul established, trained, and equipped him. Later, Paul wrote to Timothy: "The things you have heard me say in the presence of many witnesses entrust to reliable men who will also be qualified to teach others" (2 Tim. 2:2). Five generations of disciples are represented: Barnabas discipled Paul. Paul discipled Timothy. Timothy was to disciple faithful men. The faithful men were to teach others also. Paul not only lived this process but also taught it and commanded Timothy to follow it.

God works this way in our day. Someone witnessed to you, and you responded. After you responded and became a spiritual child, others established and trained you. Through *MasterLife* you are being trained as a disciple, equipped to make disciples, and commissioned to be a colaborer in ministry in order to multiply disciples to the ends of the earth.

Paul gave three illustrations of how to work as a MasterBuilder. These analogies reveal the process of growing spiritually and of helping others grow.

A child. Paul wrote: "I gave you milk, not solid food, for you were not yet ready for it. Indeed, you are still not ready" (1 Cor. 3:2). The way you can tell what stage persons are in is by the way they partake of spiritual food. Spiritually dead persons do not eat and assimilate God's Word. Spiritual children cannot feed themselves. Others, such as a Sunday School teacher, the pastor, and books, must feed them the Word by making it simpler so that they can understand it. However, spiritual disciples can feed themselves. Although they continue to benefit from others, they learn to study the Bible for themselves so that they grow and mature. When persons become disciple makers, their interests lie in feeding others. They want to help others grow as they have grown. Colaborers in ministry concentrate on multiplying the food so that multitudes can feed on the gospel.

A field. Paul wrote, "I planted the seed, Apollos watered it, but God made it grow" (1 Cor. 3:6). Someone must plant the seed by witnessing. Jesus' parable in Matthew 13:1-9 shows that the seed's growth depends on the response of the soil. God draws people to Himself so that they can respond. If they receive the seed of the Word in their hearts, they have eternal life. Then you water it so that they begin to develop. As they develop, you continue to work the ground by training them until they become mature. They grow and bear fruit. When this fruit has matured, it falls on the ground and dies, but in doing so, it multiplies. Jesus said: " 'Unless a kernel of wheat falls to the ground and dies, it remains only a single seed. But if it dies, it produces many

seeds' " (John 12:24). The seed begins to reproduce and multiply, and God receives glory.

A builder. Paul said that he was a wise MasterBuilder but that someone else had laid the foundation. In 1 Corinthians 3:12-16 he wrote:

If any man builds on this foundation using gold, silver, costly stones, wood, hay or straw, his work will be shown for what it is, because the Day will bring it to light. It will be revealed with fire, and the fire will test the quality of each man's work. If what he has built survives, he will receive his reward. If it is burned up, he will suffer loss; he himself will be saved, but only as one escaping through the flames. Don't you know that you yourselves are God's temple and that God's Spirit lives in you?

After you have laid the foundation by witnessing, you begin to establish the spiritual child in Christ. When this person begins to develop, you train and build him or her into a spiritual disciple. The spiritual temple continues to grow until other spiritual temples (congregations) are established. As they continue to multiply, Christ's church is planted among all people.

APPLYING MASTERBUILDER
Here are several guidelines you can learn from the MasterBuilder presentation.

1. As you develop, help someone through the stages you have already experienced. For example, even a spiritual child can witness to a spiritually dead person. A spiritual disciple can establish a spiritual child. A disciple maker can train a spiritual disciple. A colaborer in ministry can equip a disciple maker. As you train another person in the stage you have passed through, you learn more about it and make it more a part of your life.

2. Simultaneously help persons at different stages, although your ministry may focus on persons at one stage. If you are a disciple maker, you may spend most of your time training spiritual disciples, but never stop witnessing to the spiritually dead or establishing spiritual children. You are the model for the persons you train. If you do not continue to wit-

ness regularly, those you train will tend not to witness. As you help disciples develop spiritually, encourage them to disciple persons at each stage they have already experienced.

3. God uses you as only one component of the discipling process. He is the great MasterBuilder. He also uses the church, the environment, discipleship groups, and other colaborers to help others grow. You are not completely responsible for failures or successes. You do not work alone. You work with other colaborers to help persons become all God intends for them to be.

4. Maintain a vision of what God wants to accomplish through you and through those you train. Keep looking for the needs of persons at every stage and keep looking beyond those needs to God's purpose. At each stage ask a different question:
   • What would make this spiritually dead person open to the gospel?
   • What would make this spiritual child spiritually hungry?
   • What would make this spiritual disciple want to grow to maturity?
   • What would make this disciple maker concerned about other disciples' spiritual growth and multiplication?
   • What would keep this colaborer in ministry focused on Kingdom growth and on a world vision of God's mission?

   As disciples show more interest, give them more time and help. The natural tendencies are to neglect the growing person and to help those who are not growing. Continue focusing on those who are growing in order to produce multipliers and colaborers who can help with the spiritually dead and spiritual children.

5. Shift the responsibility from yourself to the person you disciple as you see that person develop. Notice the numbers 1 through 10 on the sides of the MasterBuilder diagram. The numbers on the left reflect the discipler's responsibility, while the numbers on the right reflect the disciple's responsibility. The discipler's and disciple's responsibilities gradually shift as the disciple grows:
   • For the spiritually dead the discipler has a responsibility of 9 or 10, while the spiritually dead person has a responsibility of only 1 or 2.

• For a spiritual child the discipler has a responsibility of 7 or 8, and the spiritual child has a responsibility of 3 or 4.
• For a spiritual disciple both the discipler and the disciple have responsibilities of 5 or 6.
• For a disciple maker the discipler has a responsibility of 3 or 4, and the disciple maker has a responsibility of 7 or 8.
• For a colaborer in ministry the discipler has a responsibility of only 1 or 2, while the colaborer has a responsibility of 9 or 10. By this point the person works on his or her own, with only occasional contact with and encouragement from the discipler.

6. Do not try to omit steps in this development process of spiritual growth. Some people want to become leaders before they become followers, resulting in colaborers in ministry who still show characteristics of a spiritual child.

Keep making disciples until all people of the world have an opportunity to hear the gospel of Christ and to become His disciples. One day we will join people from every tribe, language, people, and nation to glorify God. James 5:7-8 says: "Be patient, then, brothers, until the Lord's coming. See how the farmer waits for the land to yield its valuable crop and how patient he is for the autumn and spring rains. You too, be patient and stand firm, because the Lord's coming is near." At that time Christ's mission will be accomplished.

The Gospel in Hand

This simple presentation of the gospel uses one verse of Scripture to share the gospel with a lost person. It consists of a series of questions and answers about each word in Romans 6:23. If you can involve the person in thinking about the meaning of each word or concept in the verse, his or her feelings about it, and its relationship to other ideas, the Holy Spirit can use the questions to bring conviction. Wait for an answer. It will reveal the person's spiritual state and will enable you to respond appropriately. Affirm what you can and restate the meaning of the word.

The following is the presentation you make to the lost person. Directions to you are in parentheses for drawing the hand diagram one step at a time.

"The wages of sin is death, but the gift of God is eternal life in Christ Jesus our Lord" (Rom. 6:23).

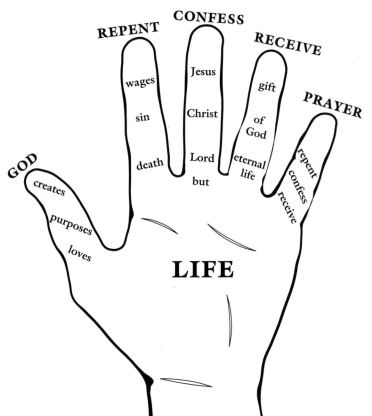

I will draw a hand that illustrates what we will talk about. (Put your left hand palm up or your right hand palm down on a sheet of paper and draw an outline around it.) This is a picture of life—life as God planned it, life as it actually turns out, and life as God re-creates it. I will use one verse of Scripture to make clear God's plan for our lives. Would you read Romans 6:23 while I write it? (Open your Bible to Romans 6:23 and give it to the person to read aloud while you write the verse at the top center of the page.)

(Write *God* above the thumb; *creates, purposes,* and *loves* on the thumb; and *life* in the palm.) God has the whole world, including you and me, in His hand. The thumb represents you. He created the world, and He made you. God loves you and has a purpose for your life. (Point to the word *life* on the palm.) He wants you to have a full and meaningful life. He wants to give you eternal life—life that lasts forever. God wants you to have life and to live it under His protection and guidance.

However, God does not always give the thumbs-up sign when He looks at your life. I can understand that. As I look back on my life, I see that I have never measured up to my own expectations, so I know that I don't measure up to God's expectations. Have you ever felt that way about yourself? (Wait for an answer.)

WAGES

This verse explains what is wrong: "The wages of sin is death." (Underline the word *wages* in the verse. Write the word *wages* on the top of the index finger.) How would you define *wages*? (Wait for an answer.) Wages are earnings for work done. How would you feel if, when payday arrived, your boss refused to pay you the wages that you were due? (Wait for an answer.) We all know that it is right for a person to get what he or she deserves. We all earn wages for how we have lived our lives.

SIN

(Underline *sin* in the verse and write it in the middle of the index finger.) The index finger represents sin. What do you think when you hear the word *sin*? (Wait for an answer. Agree when possible and add enough information to be sure that the person is aware of his or her sin.) Sin is many things. It is breaking God's law or disobeying what He tells you to do. It is doing what is wrong. It can also be an attitude.

Sin is falling short of the glory of God. The glory of God is most clearly seen in Jesus. If Jesus were standing here in the flesh, could you say that you are as good as Jesus? (Wait for an answer.) Certainly not. None of us are. We all fall short of His glory. However, each of us is responsible for his or her own sin. We are born with a tendency to sin. Unfortunately, each of us would rather do things our own way than God's way, and that is the heart of sin.

At any point in life has God seemed far away? (Wait for an answer.) Sin separates you from God. Imagine that a family member broke something of yours that was very expensive and precious to you. Would that create a problem or a distance in your relationship? (Wait for an answer.) Regardless of how you might react, your sin creates separation between you and the holy God.

DEATH

(Underline *death* in the verse and write it on the bottom of the index finger.) What do you think when the word *death* is mentioned? (Wait for an answer.) Death is separation—separation from God. If you choose to reject God while you are alive, that separation will extend into eternity. The separation will ultimately result in eternal torment in hell. You will experience separation from God not only today but also forever in hell.

The index finger is used for pointing. Think how many times you have used that finger to point at someone or something in an accusing way. I feel that God points His finger at me and says, "You have sinned, and you deserve to die."

BUT

(Underline *but* in the verse and write it on the palm below the middle finger.) What we have talked about so far has been bad news. But God has good news for you. The next word in the verse is *but*. That is a very important word in the verse because it indicates that hope exists for you even though you have sinned and

deserve death and hell. Now you are going to see what God does to make up for what you have done. God comes into the picture to fulfill His purpose and to give you eternal life. I want to show you God's full purpose for you.

GIFT

(Underline *gift* in the verse and write it on the top of the ring finger. Point to what is written on the index finger and the ring finger to contrast what we have done and what God does.) What is the difference between a gift and wages? (Wait for an answer.) A gift is not earned by the person who receives it, but someone else pays for it. Some people try to earn God's favor and eternal life by doing good deeds, living moral lives, or taking part in religious and charitable activities.

Suppose you bought a special gift for a close friend to show how much the person means to you. How would you feel if the friend refused to accept the gift without first paying you for it? (Wait for an answer.) God feels the same way about your trying to earn eternal life. Eternal life is a gift from God, and you can do nothing to earn it. (Hold out your pen.) Suppose I wanted to give you this pen and said: "I'll give this to you if you pay the taxes I paid on it." Is that a gift? No, it may be a bargain but not a gift.

OF GOD

(Underline *of God* in the verse and write it in the middle of the ring finger. Point to the contrast between *sin* on the left part of the hand and *of God* on the right.) All of us have sinned, but God is perfect and has not. God wants to give you a gift. I can't give it to you. A church can't give it to you. You can't earn it. No one can give you this gift but God. The gift of God is eternal life. Why do you think God wants to give you a gift? Think about why anyone wants to give someone a precious gift. (Wait for an answer.) God wants to give you the gift of eternal life because He loves you.

ETERNAL LIFE

(Underline *eternal life* in the verse and write it on the bottom of the ring finger. Point to the contrast between *death* on the left side of the hand and *eternal life* on the right.) What do you think eternal life is? (Wait for an answer.) Eternal life is a relationship with God forever. Just as separation from God, or death, starts in this life and extends into eternity, eternal life starts now and continues forever. Nothing can separate you from Him forever after you have accepted the eternal life He offers you.

JESUS

The middle finger represents the Lord Jesus Christ. Notice that it stands taller than the other fingers and in the center of all of them. Likewise, Jesus is Lord of all and at the center of God's purpose. Notice that the middle finger stands between the index and the ring fingers. You must go through Jesus, God's only, one-of-a-kind Son, to receive eternal life as a gift from God. The only way to bring God and sinful people together was for God to give His only Son to die for your sin on the cross. Only the One who purchased the gift for you with His life can give eternal life to you.

Each name of Jesus has a special meaning to those who want eternal life. (Underline *Jesus* in the verse and write it on the top of the middle finger.) *Jesus* is the earthly name of God's one and only Son. Jesus had to leave the Father's side in heaven to become a human being like you in order to save you. He suffered temptations and learned obedience as you do, although He never sinned.

CHRIST

(Underline *Christ* in the verse and write it in the middle of the middle finger.) *Christ* is Jesus' heavenly name. It means *Messiah, King, the anointed One.* Heaven's King allowed Himself to be crucified on the cross for your sins. You should have died for your sins, but He died in your place.

LORD

(Underline *Lord* in the verse and write it on the bottom of the middle finger.) *Lord* signifies that Jesus rose from the dead, defeating death, hell, and Satan. The Bible says that Jesus is Lord over everything and that one day everyone will bow to Him and confess that He is Lord.

Christ's life on earth, death on the cross, and resurrection from the dead made eternal life possible for us. How do you get this eternal life that the Lord Jesus Christ offers you? For Jesus to be your Savior and Lord, you must trust your whole life to Him.

PRAYER

(Write *prayer* above the little finger.) You enter this new relationship with God through prayer. The little finger stands for you in prayer. You may feel small, thinking that you are not worthy to ask Christ to save you. None of us are. But He is willing and waiting for you to ask. He says that whoever calls on Him will be saved. In your prayer tell God that you repent of your sin, confess Jesus Christ as your Savior and Lord, and receive His gift of eternal life. (Write *repent, confess, receive* on the little finger.)

REPENT

(Write *repent* above the index finger.) Recall that the index finger represents sin. First you must repent of your sin. What do you think the word *repent* means? (Wait for an answer.) *Repent* means that you turn around and go to Christ. In the past you have gone your own way and have moved away from God. *Repent* means to turn from the direction in which you are going. It is like driving down the road and realizing that you are driving in the wrong direction. You then turn around and travel the other way. *Repent* means recognizing that you have sinned and are headed toward death and hell. Then you stop, turn toward Christ, and go God's way. You make a commitment to Christ as your Savior and Lord and ask Him to change the pattern of your life. You tell God that you are sorry for doing things your own way and that you want to turn back to Him.

CONFESS

(Write *confess* above the middle finger.) Recall that the middle finger represents Christ. You confess Christ as your Savior and Lord and believe in your heart that He died for your sins and that God raised Him from the dead.

RECEIVE

(Write *receive* above the ring finger.) Recall that the ring finger represents eternal life. When you receive Christ as your Savior and Lord, you receive eternal life. You begin a new relationship with God and start to experience new, eternal life. When a man proposes to a woman, he usually gives her a ring as a promise of His love. What does she have to do to make the ring hers? (Wait for an answer.) The ring becomes hers only when she receives it and commits herself to be faithful to him. The gift of eternal life becomes yours when you receive Jesus as your Savior and Lord and commit yourself to follow Him all your life.

(Point to *life* on the palm.) The moment you pray a prayer in which you tell God that you repent of your sin, confess Jesus Christ as Savior and Lord, and receive Him, He immediately gives you new life, and you are born again spiritually.

CONCLUSION

Does what we have discussed make sense to you? (Wait for an answer.) On the basis of what I have explained, what must a person do to have a new relationship with God and to receive His gift of eternal life? (Wait for an answer.) Have you ever done that? (Wait for an answer.) Are you willing to turn from your sin and to place your faith in Jesus right now? (Wait for an answer. If it is positive, proceed. If negative, follow the instructions in "How to Lead to Commitment," p. 79.)

All you have to do is ask Jesus to forgive you of your sins and to come into your life as your Savior and Lord. You can do it right now. You can pray in your own words. If that is a problem, I will help you. Would you like to bow your head with me and ask Him now? I will pray first, and then you talk to Him in your own words. God knows your heart and will understand what you mean.

Prayer-Covenant List 400 9/15

Request	Date	Bible Promise	Answer	Date
Family	2/16/2001			

Relationship Quotient

My relationship quotient with _____

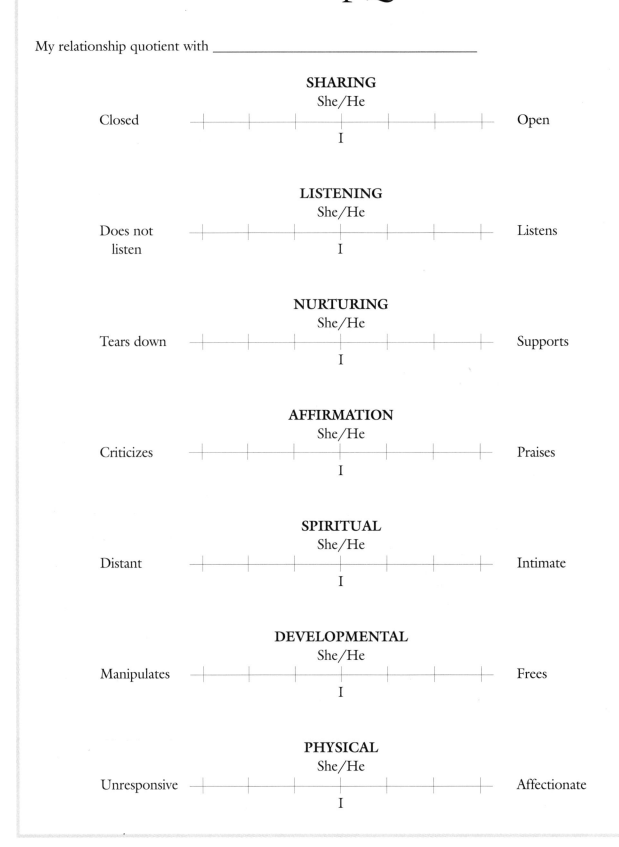

SHARING
She/He

Closed ————————————— Open
I

LISTENING
She/He

Does not ————————————— Listens
listen
I

NURTURING
She/He

Tears down ————————————— Supports
I

AFFIRMATION
She/He

Criticizes ————————————— Praises
I

SPIRITUAL
She/He

Distant ————————————— Intimate
I

DEVELOPMENTAL
She/He

Manipulates ————————————— Frees
I

PHYSICAL
She/He

Unresponsive ————————————— Affectionate
I

Discipleship Inventory

This Discipleship Inventory[1] measures the functional discipleship level of individuals, groups, and churches. By using the inventory, believers can assess their development by considering 30 characteristics of a New Testament disciple in the categories of attitudes, behavior, relationships, ministry, and doctrine.

Follow these directions to complete the inventory:

- Respond to each statement as honestly as possible. Select an answer that most clearly reflects your life as it is, not as you would like it to be.
- Choose one answer for each statement.
- Note changes in the types of answers from section to section.
- Do not spend too much time on any one question.

How true is each of the following statements of you? Choose from these responses:

    1 = never true   4 = often true
    2 = rarely true   5 = almost always true
    3 = sometimes true

1. I strive to live by the Bible's moral and ethical teachings. **1 2 3 4 5**
2. Reading and studying the Bible has made significant changes in the way I live my life. **1 2 3 4 5**
3. My faith shapes how I think and act each day. **1 2 3 4 5**
4. I talk with other persons about my beliefs in Christ as Savior and Lord. **1 2 3 4 5**
5. I take time for periods of prayer or meditation. **1 2 3 4 5**
6. Because God has forgiven me, I respond with a forgiving attitude when others wrong me. **1 2 3 4 5**
7. While interacting with others in everyday contacts, I seek opportunities to speak out about Jesus Christ. **1 2 3 4 5**
8. My neighbors and the persons I work with know that I am a Christian. **1 2 3 4 5**
9. I go out of my way to show love to persons I meet. **1 2 3 4 5**
10. When I realize that I have disobeyed a specific teaching of the Bible, I correct the wrongdoing. **1 2 3 4 5**
11. I pray for God's help when I have needs or problems. **1 2 3 4 5**
12. I share personal feelings and needs with Christian friends. **1 2 3 4 5**
13. I hold a grudge when treated unfairly. **1 2 3 4 5**
14. I devote time to reading and studying the Bible. **1 2 3 4 5**
15. I like to worship and pray with others. **1 2 3 4 5**
16. I use my gifts and talents to serve others. **1 2 3 4 5**
17. When I become aware that I have offended someone, I go to him or her to admit and correct my wrongdoing. **1 2 3 4 5**
18. I pray for the salvation of friends and acquaintances who are not professing Christians. **1 2 3 4 5**
19. I work to remove barriers or problems that develop between me and my friends. **1 2 3 4 5**
20. I feel too inadequate to help others. **1 2 3 4 5**

How often, if ever, do you do each of the following? Choose from these responses:

1 = seldom or never   4 = several times a week
2 = about once a month 5 = once a day or more
3 = about once a week

21. Pray with other Christians, other than during church **1 2 3 4 5**
22. Participate in a small-group Bible study, other than Sunday School **1 2 3 4 5**
23. Pray or meditate, other than at church or before meals **1 2 3 4 5**
24. Memorize verses or passages of the Bible **1 2 3 4 5**
25. Study the Bible on my own **1 2 3 4 5**
26. Pray specifically for missions and missionaries **1 2 3 4 5**

Indicate how much you agree or disagree with each of the following statements. Choose from these responses:

1 = definitely disagree   4 = tend to agree
2 = tend to disagree   5 = definitely agree
3 = not sure

27. It is my personal responsibility to share the gospel message with non-Christians in my life. **1 2 3 4 5**

28. Once a person is saved, he cannot lose his salvation. **1 2 3 4 5**

29. I often accept other Christians' constructive criticism and correction. **1 2 3 4 5**

30. I believe that the Holy Spirit is active in my life. **1 2 3 4 5**

31. If a person sincerely seeks God, she can obtain eternal life through religions other than Christianity. **1 2 3 4 5**

32. I know how to explain the gospel clearly to another person without relying on an evangelistic tract. **1 2 3 4 5**

33. A Christian should consider himself accountable to other Christians. **1 2 3 4 5**

34. A Christian should regularly find ways to tell others about Jesus. **1 2 3 4 5**

35. Salvation is available only through receiving Jesus Christ. **1 2 3 4 5**

36. The way I live my Christian life is not others' business. **1 2 3 4 5**

37. The Holy Spirit comes into a person the moment she accepts Jesus as Savior. **1 2 3 4 5**

38. A literal place called hell exists. **1 2 3 4 5**

39. I believe that I have a personal responsibility to help the poor and hungry. **1 2 3 4 5**

40. The complete indwelling of the Holy Spirit occurs through an experience that is usually separate and distinct from the conversion experience. **1 2 3 4 5**

How many hours during the past month have you done each of the following through church, other organizations, or on your own? Do not count time spent in a paid job. Choose from these responses:

    1 = 0 hours   4 = 6–9 hours
    2 = 1–2 hours   5 = 10 hours or more
    3 = 3–5 hours

41. Donated time helping persons who are poor, hungry, sick, or unable to care for themselves (don't count family members) **1 2 3 4 5**

42. Visited those who have visited my church **1 2 3 4 5**

43. Helped friends or neighbors with problems **1 2 3 4 5**

44. Been involved in a missions-related ministry or cause (for example, teaching about missions, raising money for missions, missions volunteer work) **1 2 3 4 5**

45. Visited persons in the hospital **1 2 3 4 5**

46. Given volunteer time at my church to teach, lead, serve on a committee, or help with a program or event **1 2 3 4 5**

47. Visited in the homes of Christian friends **1 2 3 4 5**

48. Visited the elderly or the homebound **1 2 3 4 5**

How true is each of the following statements for you? Choose from these responses:

    1 = absolutely false   4 = mostly true
    2 = somewhat false   5 = absolutely true
    3 = not sure

49. I am open and responsive to Bible teachers in my church. **1 2 3 4 5**

50. I readily receive and forgive those who offend me. **1 2 3 4 5**

51. I see myself as loved and valued by God. **1 2 3 4 5**

52. I express genuine praise and gratitude to God even in the midst of difficult circumstances. **1 2 3 4 5**

53. I avoid close relationships with others who hinder the expression of my Christian values and principles. **1 2 3 4 5**

54. I am consciously aware that God placed me on earth to contribute to the fulfillment of His plans and purposes. **1 2 3 4 5**

55. I recognize that everything I have belongs to God. **1 2 3 4 5**

56. My life is filled with stress and anxiety. **1 2 3 4 5**

57. I believe that God will always provide my basic needs in life. **1 2 3 4 5**

58. I am somewhat hesitant to let others know that I am a Christian. **1 2 3 4 5**

59. I avoid situations in which I might be tempted by sexual immorality. **1 2 3 4 5**

60. I am presently struggling with an unforgiving attitude toward another person. **1 2 3 4 5**

61. I feel very inferior to others in my church.
1 2 3 4 5
62. I seek God first in expressing my values and setting my priorities. 1 2 3 4 5
63. I am able to remain confident of God's love and provision even during very difficult circumstances.
1 2 3 4 5
64. I forgive those who offend me even if they do not apologize. 1 2 3 4 5
65. Being a Christian is a private matter and does not need to be discussed with others. 1 2 3 4 5

Last year what percentage of your income did you contribute to each of the following? Choose from these responses:

1 = 0%	4 = 6–9%
2 = 1–2%	5 = 10% and above
3 = 3–5%	

66. To my church 1 2 3 4 5
67. To other religious groups or religious organizations 1 2 3 4 5
68. To charities or social-service organizations
1 2 3 4 5
69. To foreign missions (through my church and denomination) 1 2 3 4 5

For the following question choose from these responses:

1 = none	4 = the majority
2 = a few	5 = all
3 = several	

70. How many of your closest friends do you consider to be unbelievers? 1 2 3 4 5

How often have you done each of the following during the past year? Choose from these responses:

1 = never	4 = 6–9 times
2 = once	5 = 10 times or more
3 = 2–5 times	

71. Clearly felt God's presence in my life 1 2 3 4 5
72. Shared with someone how to become a Christian
1 2 3 4 5
73. Invited an unchurched person to attend church, Bible study, or another evangelistic event
1 2 3 4 5
74. Experienced the Holy Spirit's providing understanding, guidance, or conviction of sin
1 2 3 4 5
75. Met with a new Christian to help him grow spiritually 1 2 3 4 5
76. Told others about God's work in my life
1 2 3 4 5
77. Helped someone pray to receive Christ
1 2 3 4 5
78. Gave a gospel tract or similar literature to an unbeliever 1 2 3 4 5

Indicate how much you agree or disagree with each of the following. Choose from these responses:

1 = strongly disagree	4 = agree
2 = disagree	5 = strongly agree
3 = not sure	

79. It is very important for every Christian to serve others. 1 2 3 4 5
80. One day God will hold me accountable for how I used my time, money, and talents. 1 2 3 4 5
81. All Christians are to follow Bible teachings.
1 2 3 4 5
82. The Bible is the authoritative source of wisdom for daily living. 1 2 3 4 5
83. A Christian must learn to deny herself to serve Christ effectively. 1 2 3 4 5
84. I have a hard time accepting myself. 1 2 3 4 5
85. I have identified my primary spiritual gift.
1 2 3 4 5
86. Following death, an unbeliever goes to a place called hell. 1 2 3 4 5
87. All of the Bible's moral and ethical teachings are binding for the modern Christian. 1 2 3 4 5
88. Giving time to a specific ministry in the church is necessary for a Christian's spiritual welfare.
1 2 3 4 5
89. Regardless of my circumstances, I believe God always keeps His promises. 1 2 3 4 5
90. Without the death of Jesus, salvation would not be possible. 1 2 3 4 5
91. The Bible is a completely reliable revelation from God. 1 2 3 4 5

Indicate how well-trained and prepared you believe you are in the following areas. Choose from these responses:

1 = not trained at all   4 = adequately
2 = somewhat trained   trained
3 = average   5 = well-trained

92. Presenting the plan of salvation 1 2 3 4 5
93. Individually following up or helping a new Christian grow and develop spiritually 1 2 3 4 5
94. Leading someone to pray to receive Christ 1 2 3 4 5
95. Visiting a prospect for my church 1 2 3 4 5
96. Leading a small-group Bible study 1 2 3 4 5
97. Sharing my personal testimony about how I became a Christian 1 2 3 4 5

How often during the past two or three years have you done each of the following? Choose from these responses:

1 = never   4 = weekly
2 = a few times   5 = daily
3 = monthly

98. Read the Bible by myself 1 2 3 4 5
99. Consciously put into practice the teachings of the Bible 1 2 3 4 5
100. Prayed by myself 1 2 3 4 5
101. Provided help to needy persons in my town or city 1 2 3 4 5
102. Read and studied about the Christian faith 1 2 3 4 5
103. Participated in Bible studies, religious programs, or groups outside my church 1 2 3 4 5
104. Made the necessary changes when I realized, as a result of exposure to the Bible, that an aspect of my life was not right 1 2 3 4 5
105. Shared an insight, idea, principle, or guideline from the Bible with others 1 2 3 4 5
106. Experienced the care, love, and support of other persons in a church 1 2 3 4 5
107. Directly tried to encourage someone to believe in Jesus Christ 1 2 3 4 5
108. Intentionally spent time building friendships with non-Christians 1 2 3 4 5

How true is each of these statements for you? Choose from these responses:

1 = never true   4 = often true
2 = rarely true   5 = almost always true
3 = sometimes true

109. I feel God's presence in my relationships with other persons. 1 2 3 4 5
110. I treat persons of the other gender in a pure and holy manner. 1 2 3 4 5
111. When convicted of sin in my life, I readily confess it to God as sin. 1 2 3 4 5
112. Through prayer I seek to discern God's will for my life. 1 2 3 4 5
113. I readily forgive others because of my understanding that God has forgiven me. 1 2 3 4 5
114. I help others with their religious questions and struggles. 1 2 3 4 5
115. I have learned through my faith and the Scriptures how to sacrifice for the good of others. 1 2 3 4 5
116. I share my faults and weaknesses with others whom I consider to be close to me. 1 2 3 4 5
117. I am generally the same person in private that I am in public. 1 2 3 4 5
118. When God makes me aware of His specific will for me in an area of my life, I follow His leading. 1 2 3 4 5
119. I regularly find myself choosing God's way over my way in specific instances. 1 2 3 4 5
120. I am honest in my dealings with others. 1 2 3 4 5
121. I regularly pray for my church's ministry. 1 2 3 4 5

How often do you attend the following activities? Choose from these responses:

1 = never   4 = weekly
2 = a few times   5 = more than once a week
3 = monthly

122. Worship services at my church 1 2 3 4 5
123. Sunday School class 1 2 3 4 5
124. Bible studies other than Sunday School 1 2 3 4 5
125. Prayer groups or prayer meetings 1 2 3 4 5

Indicate how much you agree or disagree with each of the following statements. Choose from these responses:

1 = definitely disagree   4 = tend to agree
2 = tend to disagree   5 = definitely agree
3 = not sure

126. God fulfills His plan primarily through believers within a local-church context. 1 2 3 4 5

127. Christ designated local churches as His means and environment for nurturing believers in the faith. **1 2 3 4 5**

128. A new believer should experience believer's baptism by immersion prior to acceptance by a local church as a member. **1 2 3 4 5**

129. Baptism and the Lord's Supper are local church ordinances and should not be practiced outside the gathered church. **1 2 3 4 5**

130. Each person born into the world inherited a sinful nature as a result of Adam's fall and is thereby separated from God and is in need of a Savior. **1 2 3 4 5**

131. Each local church is autonomous, with Jesus Christ as the Head, and should work together with other churches to spread the gospel to all people. **1 2 3 4 5**

132. There is only one true and personal God, who reveals Himself to humanity as God the Father, God the Son, and God the Holy Spirit. **1 2 3 4 5**

133. Christ will return a second time to receive His believers, living and dead, unto Himself and to bring the world to an appropriate end. **1 2 3 4 5**

134. Jesus Christ is God's Son, who died on the cross for the sins of the world and was resurrected from the dead. **1 2 3 4 5**

135. Jesus Christ, during His incarnate life on earth, was fully God and fully man. **1 2 3 4 5**

136. How religious or spiritual would you say your 3 or 4 best friends are? **1 2 3**
    1 = not very religious
    2 = somewhat religious
    3 = very religious

137. How many of your closest friends are professing Christians? **1 2 3 4 5**
    1 = none   4 = the majority
    2 = a few   5 = all
    3 = several

138. Are you male or female? **Male   Female**

139. Indicate your age group: **1 2 3 4 5**
    1 = 18–22   4 = 41–50
    2 = 23–30   5 = 51–60
    3 = 31–40   6 = 61 and over

140. I have been an active member of a local church.
    1 2 3 4 5

1 = never   4 = a large part of my life
2 = a short time   5 = most of my life
    in my life
3 = about half of
    my life

141. How long have you been a Christian?
    1 2 3 4 5 6
    1 = less than 1 year   4 = 6–10 years
    2 = 1–3 years   5 = 11–20 years
    3 = 4–5 years   6 = More than 20 years

142. Identifying as a member of a local church wherever I live is—**1 2 3 4 5**
    1 = unnecessary   4 = of great value
    2 = of little value   5 = imperative
    3 = of some value

143. Have you ever been involved in discipleship training (an organized, weekly discipleship group)?   **Yes   No**
    If so, which discipleship-training program were you involved in?

144. *MasterLife*   **Yes   No**
145. Navigators   **Yes   No**
146. *Survival Kit*   **Yes   No**
147. Evangelism Explosion   **Yes   No**
148. *Continuing Witness Training*   **Yes   No**
    If other, please provide the name:

    _____

149. How many weeks were you involved in this discipleship training? **1 2 3 4 5**
    1 = 0–5 weeks   4 = 16–25 weeks
    2 = 6–10 weeks   5 = More than 25 weeks
    3 = 11–15 weeks

150. When were you involved in this training?
    From _____ to _____

151. Was this discipleship training sponsored by your local church?   **Yes   No**
    If not, what group or organization sponsored the training?_____

152. Have you ever been discipled one-to-one by another Christian?   **Yes   No**

---

[1]James Slack and Brad Waggoner, "The Discipleship Inventory" (Richmond: The International Mission Board of the Southern Baptist Convention). Used by permission.

Spiritual-Gifts Inventory

This Spiritual-Gifts Inventory[1] consists of 86 items. Some items reflect concrete actions, other items are descriptive traits, and still others are statements of beliefs. As you read each item in the inventory, choose one of the following responses.

> 5 Highly characteristic of me or definitely true for me
>
> 4 Most of the time would describe me or be true for me
>
> 3 Frequently characteristic of me or true for me—about 50 percent of the time
>
> 2 Occasionally characteristic of me or true for me—about 25 percent of the time
>
> 1 Not at all characteristic of me or definitely untrue for me

In the blank beside each item place the number corresponding to the response that most accurately describes you.

Do not spend too much time on any one item. This is not a test, so there are no wrong answers. Usually, your immediate response is best. Give an answer for each item. Do not skip any items.

___ 1. I have the ability to organize ideas, resources, time, and persons effectively.

___ 2. I am willing to study and prepare for the task of teaching.

___ 3. I am able to relate God's truths to specific situations.

___ 4. I inspire persons to right actions by pointing out the blessings of this path.

___ 5. I have a God-given ability to help others grow in their faith.

___ 6. I possess a special ability to communicate the truth of salvation.

___ 7. I am sensitive to persons' hurts.

___ 8. I experience joy in meeting needs through sharing possessions.

___ 9. I enjoy study.

___ 10. I have delivered God's messages of warning and judgment.

___ 11. I am able to sense the true motivation of persons and movements.

___ 12. I trust God in difficult situations.

___ 13. I have a strong desire to contribute to the establishment of new churches.

___ 14. I feel that God has used me as the agent in a supernatural event.

___ 15. I enjoy doing things for persons in need.

___ 16. I am sensitive to persons who suffer physical, mental, or emotional sickness.

___ 17. I can delegate and assign meaningful work.

___ 18. I have an ability and a desire to teach.

___ 19. I am usually able to analyze a situation correctly.

___ 20. I have a tendency to encourage and reward others.

___ 21. I am willing to take the initiative in helping other Christians grow in their faith.

___ 22. I am unafraid to share with lost persons.

___ 23. I am acutely aware of such emotions as loneliness, pain, fear, and anger in others.

___ 24. I am a cheerful giver.

___ 25. I spend time researching facts.

___ 26. I feel that I have a message from God to deliver to others.

___ 27. I can recognize when a person is genuine/honest.

___ 28. I am willing to yield to God's will rather than to question and waver.

___ 29. I would like to be more active in taking the gospel to persons in other lands.

___ 30. Doing things for persons in need makes me happy.

___ 31. I am willing to be an instrument in healing others' physical, emotional, and mental hurts.

___ 32. I am successful in getting a group to do its work joyfully.

___ 33. I have the ability to plan learning approaches.

___ 34. I have been able to offer solutions to spiritual problems others face.

___ 35. I can identify persons who need encouragement.

___ 36. I have trained Christians to be more obedient disciples of Christ.

___ 37. I am willing to do whatever is necessary for others to come to Christ.

___ 38. I am drawn to persons who are hurting.

___ 39. I am a generous giver.

___ 40. I am able to discover new truths.

___ 41. I have spiritual insights from Scripture about issues and persons that compel me to speak out.

___ 42. I can sense when a person is acting in accordance with God's will.

___ 43. I can trust in God even when conditions look dark.

___ 44. I have a strong desire to take the gospel to places where it has never been heard.

___ 45. Others have testified of God's working in miraculous ways in the lives of persons to whom I have ministered.

___ 46. I enjoy helping persons.

___ 47. I understand scriptural teachings about healing.

___ 48. I have been able to make effective and efficient plans for accomplishing a group's goals.

___ 49. I understand the variety of ways persons learn.

___ 50. Fellow Christians often consult me when they are struggling to make difficult decisions.

___ 51. I think about ways I can comfort and encourage others in my congregation.

___ 52. I am able to give spiritual direction to others.

___ 53. I am able to present the gospel to lost persons in such a way that they accept the Lord and His salvation.

___ 54. I possess an unusual capacity to understand the feelings of persons in distress.

___ 55. I have a strong sense of stewardship based on the recognition of God's ownership of all things.

___ 56. I know where to get information.

___ 57. I have delivered to other persons messages that have come directly from God.

___ 58. I can sense when a person is acting under God's leadership.

___ 59. I try to be in God's will continually.

___ 60. I feel that I should take the gospel to persons who have beliefs different from mine.

___ 61. I have faith that God can do the impossible in a needy situation.

___ 62. I love to do things for others.

___ 63. I am skilled in setting forth positive and precise steps of action.

___ 64. I explain Scripture in such a way that others understand it.

___ 65. I can usually see spiritual solutions to problems.

___ 66. I am glad when persons who need comfort, consolation, encouragement, and counsel seek my help.

___ 67. I am able to nurture others.

___ 68. I feel at ease in sharing Christ with nonbelievers.

___ 69. I recognize the signs of stress and distress in others.

___ 70. I desire to give generously and unpretentiously to worthwhile projects and ministries.

___ 71. I can organize facts into meaningful relationships.

___ 72. God gives me messages to deliver to His people.

___ 73. I am able to sense whether persons are being honest when they describe their religious experiences.

___ 74. I try to be available for God to use.

___ 75. I enjoy presenting the gospel to persons of other cultures or backgrounds.

___ 76. God has used me in miraculous answers to prayer.

___ 77. I enjoy doing little things that help others.

___ 78. I can plan a strategy and "bring others aboard."

___ 79. I can give a clear, uncomplicated presentation.

___ 80. I have been able to apply biblical truths to the specific needs of my church.

___ 81. God has used me to encourage others to live Christlike lives.

___ 82. I have sensed the need to help others become more effective in their ministries.

___ 83. I like to talk about Jesus with persons who do not know Him.

___ 84. I have a wide range of study resources.

___ 85. I feel assured that a situation will change for God's glory even when the situation seems impossible.

___ 86. I am aware that God still heals persons as He did in biblical times.

SCORING YOUR INVENTORY

1. For each gift listed, place in the box the number of the response that you gave to each item indicated.
2. For each gift add the numbers in the boxes and put the total in the box labeled "Total."
3. For each gift divide the total by the number indicated and place the result in the box labeled "Score." (Round each number to one decimal place, such as 3.7.) This is your score for the gift.

LEADERSHIP

☐ ☐ ☐ ☐ ☐ ☐ ☐ ☐

Item 1 + Item 17 + Item 32 + Item 48 + Item 63 + Item 78 = Total ÷ 6 = Score

TEACHING

☐ ☐ ☐ ☐ ☐ ☐ ☐ ☐

Item 2 + Item 18 + Item 33 + Item 49 + Item 64 + Item 79 = Total ÷ 6 = Score

KNOWLEDGE

☐ ☐ ☐ ☐ ☐ ☐ ☐ ☐

Item 9 + Item 25 + Item 40 + Item 56 + Item 71 + Item 84 = Total ÷ 6 = Score

WISDOM

☐ ☐ ☐ ☐ ☐ ☐ ☐ ☐

Item 3 + Item 19 + Item 34 + Item 50 + Item 65 + Item 80 = Total ÷ 6 = Score

PROPHECY

☐ ☐ ☐ ☐ ☐ ☐ ☐

Item 10 + Item 26 +Item 41 + Item 57 + Item 72 = Total ÷ 5 = Score

SPIRITUAL DISCERNMENT

☐ ☐ ☐ ☐ ☐ ☐ ☐

Item 11 + Item 27 + Item 42 +Item 58 + Item 73 = Total ÷ 5 = Score

EXHORTATION

☐ ☐ ☐ ☐ ☐ ☐ ☐ ☐

Item 4 + Item 20 + Item 35 + Item 51 + Item 66 + Item 81 = Total ÷ 6 = Score

SHEPHERDING

☐ ☐ ☐ ☐ ☐ ☐ ☐ ☐

Item 5 + Item 21 + Item 36 + Item 52 + Item 67 +Item 82 = Total ÷ 6 = Score

FAITH

☐ ☐ ☐ ☐ ☐ ☐ ☐ ☐

Item 12 + Item 28 + Item 43 + Item 59 + Item 74 + Item 85 = Total ÷ 6 = Score

EVANGELISM

☐ ☐ ☐ ☐ ☐ ☐ ☐ ☐

Item 6 + Item 22 + Item 37 + Item 53 + Item 68 + Item 83 = Total ÷ 6 = Score

APOSTLESHIP

☐ ☐ ☐ ☐ ☐ ☐ ☐

Item 13 + Item 29 + Item 44 + Item 60 + Item 75 = Total ÷ 5 = Score

MIRACLES

☐ ☐ ☐ ☐ ☐ ☐

Item 14 + Item 45 + Item 61 + Item 76 = Total ÷ 4 = Score

HELPS

☐ ☐ ☐ ☐ ☐ ☐ ☐

Item 15 + Item 30 +Item 46 + Item 62 + Item 77 = Total ÷ 5 = Score

MERCY

☐ ☐ ☐ ☐ ☐ ☐ ☐

Item 7 + Item 23 + Item 38 + Item 54 + Item 69 = Total ÷ 5 = Score

GIVING

☐ ☐ ☐ ☐ ☐ ☐ ☐

Item 8 + Item 24 + Item 39 + Item 55 + Item 70 = Total ÷ 5 = Score

HEALING

☐ ☐ ☐ ☐ ☐ ☐

Item 16 + Item 31 + Item 47 + Item 86 = Total ÷ 4 = Score

Definitions of Spiritual Gifts

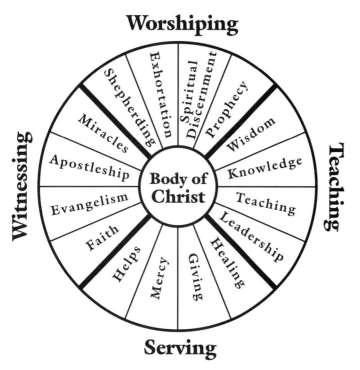

to communicate spiritual truths in such a way that they are relevant to the church's health and ministry and in such a way that others will learn
- *Leadership:* the special ability to set goals in accordance with God's will, to communicate those goals to others, and to motivate others to work together to achieve those goals

Worshiping
- *Prophecy:* the special ability to receive a message from God and then to communicate that message to others through a divinely anointed utterance
- *Spiritual discernment:* the ability to know which actions and teachings that are claimed to be of God are actually of God rather than human or satanic
- *Exhortation:* the special ability to comfort and encourage others as well as to motivate others to right actions
- *Shepherding:* the ability to build up, equip, and guide Christians in spiritual growth and maturity

Witnessing
- *Faith:* the special ability to affirm God's power to intervene in the world today and to be a part of this intervention through prayer and the Holy Spirit's power
- *Evangelism:* the ability to comprehend the lost condition of people in the world and to present Christ effectively so that persons will accept salvation in Jesus
- *Apostleship:* the ability to share God's message of reconciliation; to start new Bible-study groups and churches; or to cross cultural, language, or racial barriers to present the gospel
- *Miracles:* the special ability to serve as a human intermediary through whom God works to bring about events that cannot be explained by natural law

Serving
- *Helps (ministry):* the desire and ability to recognize the day-to-day needs of others and to meet those needs personally
- *Mercy:* the ability to feel sympathy and compassion for and to meet the needs of persons who suffer distress and crisis from physical, mental, or emotional problems
- *Giving:* the special ability and desire to contribute material resources to others and the Lord's work with liberality and cheerfulness
- *Healing:* the God-given ability to help others regain physical, mental, or spiritual health through the direct action of God

Teaching
- *Wisdom:* the ability to gain insight into the practical application of God's truths to specific situations
- *Knowledge:* the ability to discover, understand, clarify, and communicate information that relates to the life, growth, and well-being of the church
- *Teaching:* the special ability to study God's Word and

Index

CHRISTIAN GROWTH STUDY PLAN

Preparing Christians to Serve

In the **Christian Growth Study Plan (formerly the Church Study Course)** *MasterLife 4: The Disciple's Mission* is a resource for course credit in the subject area Personal Life in the Christian Growth category of diploma plans. To receive credit, read the book; complete the learning activities; attend group sessions; show your work to your pastor, a staff member, or a church leader; and complete the following information. This page may be duplicated. Send the completed page to:

**Christian Growth Study Plan
127 Ninth Avenue, North, MSN 117
Nashville, TN 37234-0117
FAX: (615) 251-5067**

For information about the Christian Growth Study Plan, refer to the current *Christian Growth Study Plan Catalog*. Your church office may have a copy. If not, request a free copy from the Christian Growth Study Plan office, (615) 251-2525.

MasterLife 4: The Disciple's Mission
COURSE NUMBER: CG-0171
PARTICIPANT INFORMATION

Social Security Number	Personal CGSP Number*	Date of Birth
| | |–| | |–| | | |	| | | |–| | |–| | |	| |–| |–| |

Name (First, MI, Last)		Home Phone
☐Mr. ☐Miss		
☐Mrs. ☐		| | |–| | |–| | |

Address (Street, Route, or P.O. Box)	City, State	ZIP

CHURCH INFORMATION

Church Name

Address (Street, Route, or P.O. Box)	City, State	ZIP

CHANGE REQUEST ONLY

☐Former Name

☐Former Address	City, State	ZIP

☐Former Church	City, State	ZIP

Signature of Pastor, Conference Leader, or Other Church Leader	Date

*New participants are requested but not required to give SS# and date of birth. Existing participants, please give CGSP# when using SS# for the first time.
Thereafter, only one ID# is required. *Mail to:* Christian Growth Study Plan, 127 Ninth Ave., North, MSN 117, Nashville, TN 37234-0117. Fax: (615) 251-5067.